D1625972

W. H. AUDEN

A biography

Also by Humphrey Carpenter

J. R. R. Tolkien: a biography
The Inklings: C. S. Lewis, J. R. R. Tolkien, Charles Williams,
  and their friends
Jesus (Past Masters series*)*

For children:
The Joshers
The Captain Hook Affair

With Mari Prichard:
A Thames Companion

W. H. AUDEN
A biography

by
Humphrey Carpenter

London
GEORGE ALLEN & UNWIN
Boston   Sydney

First published in 1981

GEORGE ALLEN & UNWIN LTD
40 Museum Street, London WC1A 1LU

© George Allen & Unwin (Publishers) Ltd, 1981
Quotations from previously unpublished writings by
W. H. Auden © the Estate of W. H. Auden, 1981

British Library Cataloguing in Publication Data

Carpenter, Humphrey.
   W. H. Auden.
   1. Auden, W H – Biography
   2. Poets, English – 20th century – Biography
   821'.912   PR6001.U4Z   80-41985

ISBN 0-04-928044-9

Typeset in 10 on 12 point Bembo by Alan Sutton Publishing Ltd, Gloucester
and printed and bound in Great Britain by
William Clowes (Beccles) Limited, Beccles and London.

CONTENTS

ILLUSTRATIONS

AUTHOR'S NOTE

This is the first account of Auden's life to make use of the large number of his letters and other manuscripts which are now accessible, and, though the book is not an 'authorised' biography and was undertaken on my own initiative and not at the request of Auden's executors, I am very grateful to his Estate for permission to quote from these previously unpublished writings.

It is not a book of literary criticism. I have not usually engaged in a critical discussion of Auden's writings. But I have tried to show how they often arose from the circumstances of his life, and I have also attempted to identify the themes and ideas that concerned him. I hope I have also managed to convey my own huge enthusiasm for his poetry.

H. C.
Oxford, 1980

PREFACE: AUDEN AND BIOGRAPHY

'Biographies of writers,' declared W. H. Auden, 'are always superfluous and usually in bad taste. A writer is a maker, not a man of action. To be sure, some, in a sense all, of his works are transmutations of his personal experiences, but no knowledge of the raw ingredients will explain the peculiar flavour of the verbal dishes he invites the public to taste: his private life is, or should be, of no concern to anybody except himself, his family and his friends.'

Auden wrote this towards the end of his life, but it was an opinion that he had held for many years. He even suggested that most writers would prefer their work to be published anonymously, so that the reader would have to concentrate on the writing itself and not at all on the writer. He was also (he said) opposed in principle to the publication of, or quotation from, a writer's letters after his death, which he declared was just as dishonourable as reading someone's private correspondence while he was out of the room. As to literary biographers, he branded them as, in the mass, 'gossip-writers and voyeurs calling themselves scholars'.

So it scarcely came as a surprise when, after his death in September 1973, his executors published his request that his friends should burn any of his letters that they might have kept, when they had 'done with them', and should on no account show them to anyone else. Auden himself had explained, in a conversation with one of his executors not long before his death, that this was in order 'to make a biography impossible'.

In the months that followed Auden's death, a very few of his friends did burn one or two of his letters. But most preserved what they had, and several people gave or sold letters to public collections. Meanwhile many of his friends, far from doing anything to hinder the writing of a life, published (in various books and journals) their own memoirs of him, which provided valuable material upon which a biographer could work.

At first sight it may seem as if they were riding roughshod over Auden's last wishes. But it is not as simple as that. Here, as so often in his life, Auden adopted a dogmatic attitude which did not reflect the full range of his opinions, and which he sometimes flatly contradicted.

Certainly he often attacked the principle of literary biography, but in practice he made a lot of exceptions. When reviewing actual examples of the genre he was almost always enthusiastic, finding a whole variety of reasons for waiving his rule. We need a biography of Pope, he said, because so many of Pope's poems grew from specific events which need explaining; we want a life of Trollope because his autobiography leaves out a great deal; of Wagner because he was a monster; of Gerard Manley Hopkins because he had a romantically difficult relationship with his art. Auden's 'no biography' rule was in other words (as his literary executor Edward Mendelson has put it) 'flexible enough to be bent backwards'.

The same is true of his attitude to writers' letters. He usually reviewed published collections of them in friendly terms, and was only censorious when he thought that something private had been included which was merely personal and threw no light on the writer's work. He himself made a selection of Van Gogh's letters for publication, and he would have published an edition of the letters of Sydney Smith if someone else had not done it first. As to his own letters, he gave permission for a large number of quotations from them to be published, in academic books and the like, during his lifetime.

He also left a great deal of autobiographical writing. He once declared: 'No poet should *ever* write an autobiography'; yet he did a great deal towards preserving a record of his own life. Not only does his poetry contain innumerable autobiographical passages, but several poems (including two of his longest, 'Letter to Lord Byron' and 'New Year Letter') are largely autobiographical in character. Among his prose writings, too, there are all kinds of remarks about events in his life. And in his later years he allowed journalists to visit him in his New York apartment and at his summer house in Austria, letting them publish interviews with him which often recorded highly personal details of his life.

So there is a great deal of information for a biographer to draw upon. But would Auden, in the end, have approved of a biography being written?

It is possible that he might on the grounds that he was something of a 'man of action', who lived a life so full of interest that it deserves to be recorded for its own sake. This was a justification of biography that he accepted – with one proviso. 'The biography of an artist, if his life as a man was sufficiently interesting, is permissible,' he wrote, 'provided that the biographer and his readers realise that such an account throws no light whatsoever upon the artist's work.'

This last point, of course, brings us back to Auden's fundamental objection to a writer's biography. 'I do believe, however,' he once added, 'that, more often than most people realise, his works may throw light upon his life.'

I

England

I

Childhood

Wystan Hugh Auden was born on the twenty-first of February 1907, in the city of York in the north of England, the third and last child of George Augustus Auden and Constance Rosalie Bicknell.

He was the youngest of three boys. Later in his life he liked to point out that in fairy-tales it is the youngest of the three brothers who succeeds in the quest and wins the prize. 'I, after all, am the Fortunate One,' he wrote in a poem, 'The Happy-Go-Lucky, the spoilt Third Son'.

He had hazel eyes, and hair and eyebrows so fair that they looked bleached. His skin, too, was very pale, almost white. His face was marked by one small peculiarity, a brown mole on the right cheek. He had big chubby hands, and soon developed flat feet. He was physically clumsy, and took to biting his nails.

The fairness of hair and skin were inherited from his father, but in features he looked more like his mother. From the time of his birth he was very close to her, partly because being the youngest child he was never displaced by another; partly, too, because there was a gap of several years between himself and his elder brothers, so that they tended to go off by themselves and leave him with their mother. (This large gap was the consequence of a miscarriage between the second and third births.) But his closeness to his mother was, he himself came to believe, chiefly the result of her wanting it to be that way. He felt that she had sought to achieve with him, from the beginning, 'a conscious spiritual, in a sense, adult relationship'.

Besides being the youngest child he was also the youngest grandchild in the family; and later at school, being a bright boy, he was very often the youngest in the class. All this gave him, he said, 'the lifelong conviction that in any company I am the youngest person present'. Certainly to the end of his life he behaved like a precocious and highly praised youngest child.

His elder brothers were called Bernard and John. By contrast his own first name, Wystan, was exotic; but it reflected one of his father's great interests in life. George Auden was a doctor of medicine by profession, but he was also widely read in many other fields, among them Saxon and Norse antiquities. This was partly the result of his having been educated at Repton School in Derbyshire, for the parish church there has a particularly fine Saxon crypt which attracted his attention when he was young. The church is dedicated to St Wystan, a Mercian prince who was murdered in the year 849 after he had objected to the uncanonical marriage of his widowed mother to his uncle – 'a rather Hamlet-like story', remarked Wystan Auden.

The story of St Wystan is recorded in a *Little Guide to Shropshire,* under the entry for Wistanstow, the place in that county where he was martyred. The author of the *Little Guide* was Wystan Auden's uncle, the Rev. J. E. Auden, and Wystan carefully preserved his own copy of it. He was very possessive about his first name; he said he would be 'furious' if he ever met another Wystan.

His second Christian name, Hugh, was chosen in honour of his mother's brother-in-law Hugh Culley, headmaster of Monmouth Grammar School. In adult life Wystan Hugh Auden became addicted to crosswords and liked to work out anagrams from his own name. One of his favourites was 'Why shun a nude tag?' Another was 'Hug a shady wet nun'. He remarked that all you can get from 'T. S. Eliot' is 'litotes'.

His father had a medical practice as a general physician in York, and by the time of his third son's birth he was doing very well. Dr Auden had begun work in York eight years earlier, in 1899, just after his marriage, when (at the age of twenty-seven) he had set up home and surgery at 76 Bootham, a big and rather ugly brick house in a smart street just outside the old city wall, within sight of York Minster. By the time that Wystan was born in 1907 he had moved his family to a larger and more attractive house just down the road. This was 54 Bootham, built in the Georgian style, with a portico around the front door. Things were going well enough for Dr Auden to employ a coachman to drive him round to his patients, and for him and his wife to have two maids and a cook to run the house.

It is true that prosperity did not in itself secure the Auden family's social position. The status of doctors in Edwardian society was ambiguous to say the least. In the York street-directory Dr Auden, like other medical men, was listed not under *Private Residents*, but under *Commercial* – which amounted to saying that doctors were no better than tradesmen. When Wystan Auden's mother had announced to one of her aunts that she was going to marry a doctor, she was told: 'Marry him if you must, but no one will call on you!' On the other hand Dr Auden was the son of a clergyman, and this made him rather more acceptable socially. Moreover he was making something of a mark in York because of his intellectual accomplishments. When the British Association for the Advancement of Science held a meeting in the city in the year before Wystan's birth, Dr Auden was chosen to edit the *Historical and Scientific Survey of York and District* which was published to mark the occasion, and himself wrote the chapter on the region's prehistory and archaeology.

So there would probably have been a secure future for the Audens if they had remained in York. Wystan's childhood would have been spent in the shadow of York Minster, one of the finest medieval cathedrals in England, and he would have lived, during those years in which his imagination was developing, in a city that still looked much as it had done before the Industrial Revolution. But that was not what happened. When he was one and a half, in 1908, his family left York and moved south to Birmingham.

His father had been appointed Birmingham's first School Medical Officer, a pioneer job which would chiefly mean inspecting and where necessary improving the sanitary arrangements in the schools controlled by the city's Education Committee. It would not be easy work, for Birmingham and the surrounding suburbs had grown during the nine-teenth century into one of the biggest industrial sprawls in the Midlands. Its schools were often poorly built, and many of the children were being brought up in grim conditions. The job also meant a drop in salary for Dr Auden, for the Birmingham Education Committee could not afford to pay him as much as he had earned in his lucrative practice in York. This did not really matter very much, for he had a small private income, and the family could still afford to keep servants after the move to Birmingham. Nevertheless Wystan, looking back, was certain that the decrease in salary had cost a real moral effort to his father, who he said was 'one of those persons who cannot disburse even the smallest sums without mental anguish'.

Though Dr Auden's work was in Birmingham itself, the house he acquired for his family stood some miles outside the city, in Solihull, which is nowadays a suburb of Birmingham but was then a large village a little detached from the south-eastern edge of the city. It was here, at 'Apsley House' in Lode Lane, that Wystan began to be aware of his surroundings.

These were not at first sight very interesting. Solihull was an undis-tinguished settlement of houses and small shops, most of them recently built. Down the road, however, was something that the small boy did find exciting: the local gasworks. He was often taken there on walks because, though sturdy and generally healthy, he did have slight bron-chial trouble, and the fumes from the gasworks were thought to be good for his chest. He loved it there. 'Those at the gasworks were my favourite men,' he wrote of his early childhood, remembering the smells and pipes and huge gasometers which rose and fell. The gasworks was the first place that seemed to him (he said) 'numinous', arousing a feeling of wonder and awe.

Beyond home and Solihull lay, to the north, industrial Birmingham.

Nothing was more exciting to Wystan than a train ride from Solihull into the city with its smoking chimneys and huge warehouses, and then (if he was lucky) onwards by another train, further north, where the line ran to Wolverhampton – past the canal, and between mile after mile of blackened factories with furnaces flaring up as the train passed. He never forgot this sight:

> Clearer than Scafell Pike, my heart has stamped on
> The view from Birmingham to Wolverhampton.

At home, his first memories were largely of the minor crises of family life: his father lancing an abscess in the terrier's foot, and the occasion when he himself nearly poisoned his mother by stuffing tobacco into the coffee pot. But the abiding impression was of a childhood 'full of love and good things to eat'.

Not that everything was exactly idyllic. The food, produced by Ada the cook, was just the usual stuff of Edwardian households, though it was no less welcome to the Auden boys for that. 'There are certain tastes which those who have never experienced them as children can neither understand nor cure,' wrote Wystan towards the end of his life. 'Who but an Englishman, for example, can know the delights of stone cold leathery toast for breakfast, or the wonders of "Dead Man's Leg"?' – a nickname for suet pudding. Nor were things entirely perfect where love was concerned. His parents were in some ways oddly matched. His mother was strong-willed and rather neurotic; his father, three years younger, was mild-mannered and gentle. 'No gentler father ever lived,' said Wystan, but added: 'Too gentle, I used sometimes to think, for as a husband he was often henpecked.' When Wystan grew up he liked to play a game of devising more suitable mates for his parents. For instance: 'Ma should have married a robust Italian who was very sexy, and cheated on her. She would have hated it, but it would have kept her on her toes. Pa should have married someone weaker than he and utterly devoted to him. But of course, if they had, I shouldn't be here'. And what he chiefly remembered of his parents, despite their differences and difficulties, was that they 'loved us and treated us gently'.

He learnt a good deal from each of them. His mother taught him to enjoy churchgoing. Both his parents were themselves the children of Church of England vicars, but while his father now had a rather detached and intellectual attitude towards religion, his mother was a deeply believing Christian. She saw to it that family prayers were held daily, and she took the children to morning and evening services at Solihull parish church every Sunday. Her inclinations were High Church, and later she and the children began to go further afield on Sundays, to Anglo-Catholic churches with High Mass, candles and incense. At the age of six, Wystan acted as a 'boat boy' at these services. Dressed in a red cassock and white linen cotta, he learnt to serve at the altar, carrying the boat-shaped container that held the incense-grains. Looking back on this, he felt it had been a thoroughly good thing that his first encounter with religion was aesthetic rather than intellectual. 'My first religious memories are of exciting magical rites,' he recalled, 'rather than of listening to sermons.'

From his father he acquired an interest in legends and stories, and in ideas. Before Wystan could read, Dr Auden, who had a sound knowledge of classical literature, entertained him with tales of the Trojan War and of quarrels among the gods of Olympus. He also told Wystan about other mythological figures – Thor, Loki, and the rest of the deities of Icelandic legend. Dr Auden was particularly keen that his son should learn these tales, for not only was he deeply fond of Norse antiquities but he also believed that his own family name, Auden, showed that he himself was of Icelandic descent.

He believed this because 'Auden' resembles the Icelandic name Auðun or Auðunn (pronounced 'Authunn' with a hard *th* as in 'there'), which is often found in early Norse literature and has survived as a modern Icelandic surname. George Auden apparently believed that his family was descended from or related to, a certain Auðun Skökull,[1] who is recorded as one of the first Norse settlers in Iceland in the ninth century; and he told Wystan that before the settlement the Audens' remote ancestors had lived on the coast of the Vík, the bay to the north of modern Denmark from which the Vikings had sailed.

It is possible that this account of the family's early history is true. The Auden ancestors might have been migrants from Iceland to Britain, possibly as a result of the fishing trade in waters between the two countries – though if this did happen it must have been well before the early eighteenth century, by which time Wystan's great-great-grandfather William Auden (the earliest member of the family who can be traced) was a landed gentleman living at Rowley Regis, not far from Birmingham, with an income (it is said) deriving largely from the discovery of coal under family lands.

More probable, however, is the explanation that the Audens of England and the Auðuns of Iceland had only a remote connection, more than a thousand years ago, in a common Scandinavian origin, before the settlement of Iceland or the Viking invasions of Britain. And even this does not seem very likely. Experts on English surnames do not believe 'Auden' to be related to 'Auðun' at all, but suspect it to be just a variant of 'Alden' or 'Aldwyn', or perhaps 'Edwin'. (The Lancashire place-name Audenshaw was formerly spelt 'Aldwyneshaw'.) If this is true, then 'Auden' is probably ultimately derived from Anglo-Saxon *Healfdene*,

[1]The name 'Skökull' means 'carriage-pole', and seems also to have been used as slang for 'penis'. Auden refers to 'Auden Skökull' in the first canto of 'Letter to Lord Byron'.

'half Dane', or from *Ealdwine*, 'old friend', or possibly from *Eadwine*, 'rich friend'.[1]

Whatever the truth about his ancestry, Wystan Auden enjoyed believing that he was Norse by descent – not just on his father's side but his mother's as well. His mother's family, the Bicknells, had real proof of this, for they could trace their line back to the Norman (and so ultimately Norse) family of Paveley or de Pavelly, who, in the thirteenth century, acquired by marriage the ancient manor of Bykenhulle – now spelt Bickenhall and corrupted gradually into the family name of Bicknell – which is a few miles north-west of Ilminster in Somerset. So it was that Wystan Auden could describe himself whimsically as 'pure Nordic'; and he added: 'In my childhood dreams Iceland was holy ground.'

If Dr Auden allowed his fancy to run away when he was talking about ancestry, in other respects he was a factually-minded man, and widely read; and his attitude to knowledge greatly influenced Wystan. At Cambridge in the 1890s he had read Natural Science, in which he took a First, and he won gold medals there and later at St Bartholomew's Hospital, London, where he went to train as a doctor. He knew a lot about the history of medicine from classical times onwards, and besides being fluent in Latin and Greek (he was elected Secretary of the local Classical Association in Birmingham) he was sufficiently accomplished in modern languages to be able to translate works on archaeology and antiquities from German and Danish into English. Moreover he ignored the conventional distinctions between the humanities and the sciences. 'In my father's library,' recalled Wystan, 'scientific books stood side by side with works of poetry and fiction, and it never occurred to me to think of one as being less or more "humane" than the other.' He added: 'My father's library not only taught me to read, but dictated my choice of reading. It was not the library of a literary man nor of a narrow specialist, but was a heterogeneous collection of books on many subjects, and included very few novels. In consequence my reading has always been wide and casual rather than scholarly, and in the main non-literary.'

Certainly many of the books that fascinated Wystan in childhood were not 'literature' in the usual sense of the word. Favourites which he remembered from early days included *The Edinburgh School of Surgery*, *Mrs Beeton's Book of Household Management*, and *Dangers to Health*, a

---

[1]Another theory traces the name, via the Latin form *Audoenus*, which is found in Domesday Book, to the French *Ouen*, the name of the saint who is also known as St Owen or St Audoenus, after whom Rouen is named. This seems quite plausible in view of the fact that some members of the Auden family believe that their ancestors were Huguenots. A number of place-names in France and Belgium have the stem *Aud-*.

It is sometimes stated that 'Auden' may derive from Anglo-Saxon *Ælfwine*, 'elf-friend', but this is a misreading of P. H. Reaney, *A Dictionary of British Surnames*, where *Ælfwine* is given as the *first* name of one Ælfwine Aldine, whose *surname* may be an early form of 'Auden'.

Victorian treatise on plumbing, illustrated with coloured plates. On the other hand there were plenty of the classics of Victorian and Edwardian children's books on the nursery shelves. Wystan never lost his early adoration of Edward Lear, Lewis Carroll and Beatrix Potter, who remained sacred names to him throughout his life. He was also brought up on Hans Andersen, Farrar's *Eric, or, Little by Little,* and George MacDonald, whose *The Princess and the Goblin* he thought 'the only English children's book in the same class as the Alice books'. Jules Verne, Rider Haggard and the Sherlock Holmes stories came a little later. It was, in fact, the typical literary fare of a child of his generation, and poetry did not play an especially big part in it. The first 'serious' poetry he remembered enjoying was *In Memoriam,* which his father used to read aloud, and Poe's 'The Raven' and 'The Bells'. From an early age Wystan learnt to think of poetry as something to be read aloud or recited – an attitude which remained with him for the rest of his life. He himself soon developed a fondness for the poems of Christina Rossetti and R. H. Barham, which he recited to his schoolfellows; he also chanted American ballads and verses by Belloc and Lewis Carroll. Poetry seemed to him on the whole something that was fun, a joke; he loved the horrific-comic verses in Hoffman's *Struwwelpeter*, Belloc's *Cautionary Tales*, and Harry Graham's *Ruthless Rhymes for Heartless Homes*. This, for example, was one of his favourite verses from the Graham book:

> In the drinking well
> Which the plumber built her,
> Aunt Maria fell;
> We must buy a filter.

He said of it: 'When I was a child, this was the kind of poetry I most enjoyed.'

He learnt something else from his father. George Auden's work as a doctor had made him consider not just the practice and history of medicine but also its philosophy. He liked to quote an aphorism that a doctor should 'care more for the individual patient than for the special features of his disease', and he would tell Wystan: 'Healing is not a science, but the intuitive art of wooing Nature.' Wystan was impressed, and for the rest of his life remained interested in the philosophy of medicine. Perhaps, too, his vision of himself as a surgeon or healer, which haunts much of his early poetry, reflects his father's influence.

Certainly it was during his childhood that he first became aware of psychology. His father was greatly interested in this new and contro-versial subject, and bought books by pioneer psychologists as soon as they were published. In Birmingham, besides his work as School Medical Officer, Dr Auden acted as 'Honorary Psychologist' to the children's hospital, and he also became medical adviser to a local institution for the mentally handicapped. As Wystan grew older, he learnt something about his father's work in the field. Indeed from an early age he applied something of the psychologist's detached and clinical analysis to members of his own family, especially his aunts and uncles.

There were a good many of these relatives in his life. His only surviving grandparent was his father's mother, who lived at Horninglow, near Repton, where her husband had been Vicar until his death at a comparatively early age. When Wystan was four, he was excited by his first visit to her, by train; for the railway line passed through a coal-field, whose pit-heads and coal tips were important additions to his growing private landscape of industrial scenery – which already included gas-works, railways, factories and canals. Trips to his grandmother were, however, rare, for she and his mother were not on easy terms. He saw rather more of his other Auden relatives, but they did not earn much admiration from him. Most of them were clergymen or solicitors or the like, and only Uncle Harry, his father's younger bachelor brother, seemed interesting. He was an industrial chemist by profession, and owned a motor car. (More privately, his inclinations were homosexual, and he collected photographs of naked choirboys.) Wystan liked Uncle Harry, but otherwise his father's family struck him as 'phlegmatic, earnest, rather slow, inclined to be miserly, and endowed with excellent health'.

He spent quite a lot of time with his maternal aunts and uncles, the Bicknells, especially with two aunts and an uncle who had houses in Monmouth and apartments in Brooke Street, off Holborn in London – the uncle was headmaster of the Mercer's School, nearby. There was not much to choose between the Audens and the Bicknells socially; the Bicknell grandfather, like his Auden counterpart, had been a clergyman – the Vicar of Wroxham near Norwich – and he too had died in early middle age. Here too there was the same large number of uncles and aunts, eight in all,[1] who were, like the Audens, employed in or married to members of respectable but dull professions. And just as in his father's family there was one member who was 'simple' – Uncle Lewis Auden, who was cared for by a housekeeper – so the Bicknells numbered among them Aunt Daisy, 'not all there', who lived with Anglican nuns. But the character of his mother's family struck Wystan as being psycho-logically quite different from that of the Audens. At an early age he began to realise that they were, as he put it, 'quick, short-tempered, generous, and liable to physical ill-health, hysteria, and neuroticism'; he himself thought he took after them in all these respects except for the ill-health. He had already decided by the age of six that 'most of the adults I

---

[1] Auden several times stated that his parents were each one of seven children, but this was an error. His mother's family consisted of six daughters and two sons and his father's of seven sons and one daughter.

knew were stupid', and in particular the Bicknell aunts with their favourite illnesses earned his amused contempt. Though the actual word was not yet in current use, he knew from watching them that 'illness could be psychosomatic'.

He did not hesitate to criticise his Bicknell aunts if they said something ignorant or silly, and as a result they thought him (as he later realised) 'a precocious, insolent little monster'. Nor did his scornful attitude please his brother John, who was devoted to the aunts, not least because he felt that they gave him more love and attention than he received at home, where Wystan now seemed to absorb all the parental affection – particularly from their mother.

Constance Auden was in many ways an unusual mother. As a girl she had learnt to be largely independent; both her parents had died when she was young, and she had been brought up largely by a bachelor uncle, with whose own sudden death she had had to cope when travelling abroad with him at the age of eighteen. Later she went to London University and studied French, at a time when very few women were receiving a university education. She then remained in London and took up nursing, with the idea of becoming an Anglican medical missionary. It was while she was working at St Bartholomew's Hospital that she met George Auden, who was three years her junior – she was born in 1869, he in 1872. But though she was independent-minded and well educated she was not especially 'progressive' in her ideas. She had not, for example, liked the idea of her husband undertaking gynaecological work as part of his medical practice in York, and she was glad when his change of job meant he could give it up.

She was musical, and she encouraged Wystan to learn the piano. He proved to be competent at it if not specially talented. He also had quite a good treble voice, and sometimes sang duets with her. When he was eight she taught him the words and music of the love-potion scene from Wagner's *Tristan and Isolde*, and together they sang this intensely erotic duet, Wystan taking the part of Isolde. She was, Wystan said as he looked back at this, sometimes 'very odd indeed'.

He loved her deeply, but he felt that their close relationship had set up a great tension in himself. He once wrote a few lines of verse about this, which he did not publish:

> Tommy did as mother told him
>   Till his soul had split;
> One half thought of angels
>   And the other half of shit.

Looking back to his childhood, he felt that he could ascribe almost everything in his adult character to the relationship with his mother: his physical clumsiness (the result, he believed, of being encouraged to be mentally precocious); his sexual make-up (he thought the feminine streak in him grew from identifying with his mother); and even his intelligence. 'I think we shall find', he once said, 'that all intelligent people are the product of psychological conflict in childhood.' He suspected that intellectual achievement – especially artistic achievement – grows from the child's attempt to 'understand the mechanism of the trap' in which it finds itself. As he put it in 'Letter to Lord Byron': 'No one thinks unless a complex makes him.'

No doubt this is largely true; certainly he never got away from his mother. As an adult he loved to invoke her imaginary judgement on his own or other people's behaviour: his usual phrase of criticism of any conduct that earned his disapproval was 'Mother wouldn't like it.'

But the chief characteristic of his childhood was security, a security that gave him the immense unshakeable self-confidence that was his overriding attribute. He was himself, indeed, remarkably un-neurotic in manner, largely because he was in the habit of assuming that things would turn out as he wanted them to – which, perhaps as a result, they usually did.

Moreover, as he himself once suggested, a neurosis may not be so much the *cause* of intellectual and artistic achievement as the *means* by which it is achieved. 'The so-called traumatic experience', he wrote, 'is not an accident, but the opportunity for which the child has been patiently waiting – had it not occurred, it would have found another, equally trivial – in order to find a necessity and direction for its existence, in order that its life may become a serious matter.'

*

In 1913, when Wystan was six, the Auden family moved to another house in Solihull, 13 Homer Road, near the station of the Great Western Railway. That summer, they spent a month's holiday at Rhayader in mid-Wales. John Auden, then aged nine, kept a diary of the holiday, illustrated by photographs, and this provides a close glimpse of the Audens. On fine days there are walks and bicycle-rides, Wystan travelling pillion on his father's machine. One day Dr Auden teaches his sons to climb rocks – the boys, especially John, are beginning to take an interest in geology. On Sundays they are taken to the Catechism Service, and sometimes they return to church in the evenings. An Auden uncle and two cousins visit them, and they are given a ride in a motor car. It is, as Wystan himself remarked of family life during these years, 'a world still largely Victorian'. The only oddity is the family's habit, especially on rainy days, of investigating local factories and other places with machinery. Here are some of John Auden's diary entries:

Sat 9th Aug. Rained in the morning. We went to the Tannery. Mr

Batten was the head. He showed us round the works.
Wed 13th Aug. Rained a little in the morning but we went to the
wolen mill where we saw the Carding machine.
Thursday 14th Aug. We visited the Water Works. Mr Swan took us
over and took us in a tunnel. He showed us the Filterbeds and the
Power Station. Wystan went in a hopper.

There is a photograph of Wystan staring over a rail at the machinery in
the power station. Some lines that he wrote many years later recall his
feelings at such moments:

> Those beautiful machines that never talked
> But let the small boy worship them and learn
> All their long names whose hardness made him proud.

It was not so much that he wanted to understand machinery and to know
how it worked; rather that he wanted to love it and make it part of his
private imaginative world, of which the gasworks had been the beginning.
And when the next year, at Easter 1914, the family went back to Wales
for their holiday and this time stayed further north, and he saw the tiny
Festiniog Railway that ran from the slate quarries to the sea at Portmadoc,
he added narrow-gauge railways to his map of special numinous places
and objects.

Then in August 1914 war broke out, and George Auden immediately
joined the Royal Army Medical Corps. During the next four years he
served in Gallipoli, Egypt and France, and his family saw almost nothing
of him.[1]

Everything changed. The Solihull house was only kept on for a few
months until Wystan went away to school – his brothers had been at
boarding school for some time. Then his mother packed up the furniture,
disposed of the lease of the house, and lived with relatives during term
time, reuniting herself with the boys in the school holidays, usually in
furnished rooms in different parts of the country. So it was that from
1915 until 1918 Wystan had no settled home.

He loved this nomadic life. Each holidays, in a different 'home', he
could discover new things to add to his private map. It was now that it
acquired two very important features: limestone and lead mines.

Finding themselves in a whole series of new places, the Auden boys

---

[1] In an interview in the *Observer* Colour Magazine, 7 November 1971, Auden recalled that
one of the last times he saw his father before Dr Auden joined the R.A.M.C. was when his
parents put on fancy dress for a party: 'She had on his clothes and a false moustache, and he
was wearing hers. . . . I suppose they thought it would amuse me. I was terrified.' John
Auden says that this incident in fact happened in 1912, when Wystan was five.

explored their surroundings energetically, collecting fossils, rubbing church brasses, going on long walks, investigating prehistoric hill forts and caves, looking at stone circles and Norman churches and Saxon crosses. Soon after the beginning of the war they spent a holiday at Bradwell in Derbyshire, on the edge of the Pennine limestone. From this base they visited the nearby Blue John Caves (named after the mineral found there), and were guided down long steep passages to caverns hollowed out by underground rivers, whose roofs, hung with stalactites, echoed to the perpetual trickle of water. Wystan was greatly impressed, but what struck him as still more dramatic were the disused lead mines whose remains could be seen here and there on the moors. He began to be fascinated by lead mining, and from now on, in his imagination, 'thought myself a mining engineer'.

This is how he described his private passion: 'I spent a great many of my waking hours in the construction and elaboration of a private sacred world, the basic elements of which were a landscape, northern and limestone, and an industry, lead mining.' In his imagination he was, he said, the 'sole autocrat' of this dream country – whose features also included narrow-gauge tramways and overshot waterwheels.

He took his landscape seriously, and asked his mother and other adults to procure for him textbooks with titles such as *Machinery for Metalliferous Mines*, maps, guidebooks, and photographs; and he persuaded them to take him down a real mine if ever there was a chance. He especially relished the technical vocabulary of mining, the names of mines and of the veins found in them, and the geological terms relating to mining. 'A word like *pyrites*', he said, 'was for me not simply an indicative sign; it was the Proper Name of a Sacred Being, so that, when I heard an aunt pronounce it *pirrits* I was shocked . . . Ignorance was impiety.' He studied diagrams of water turbines, winding engines, roller crushers, and the other equipment of mining. He also made his fantasy landscape submit to rules; in selecting what objects were to be included in it, he allowed himself to choose between (for instance) various types of real water turbine which could be found in a manufacturer's catalogue, but not to invent any non-existent machinery nor to use magical means in operating his imaginary mines.

Those adults who knew anything about his interest in mining assumed, not surprisingly, that he was genuinely scientific in temperament, and was probably gifted to become what he himself declared (and believed) he would be, a mining engineer. But the truth was that he had no practical mechanical ability whatsoever. However genuinely technical and scientific his interest in mines might appear to be, it was actually (as he later realised) a romantic and quite unpractical love-affair which had nothing to do with real mining. The machinery, the tunnels, the geological information, all attracted him because of their names and because they were symbols of something else, though he could not say of what. It was, in fact, an obsession which marked him out for something very far removed from engineering. 'I doubt,' he said, 'if a person with both these passions, for the word and for the symbol, could become anything but a poet.'

2

School

In the autumn of 1915, when Wystan was eight, he was sent as a boarder to St Edmund's School at Hindhead in Surrey, a preparatory establishment of some fifty boys which his brother John was already attending – Bernard had been sent to another school.

He was not especially miserable during his first few weeks there. 'I am certain that if a boy is to be sent away to school at all,' he said, looking back, 'it is kinder to send him at an early age. A boy of seven or eight seems to get over his homesickness very quickly.' On the other hand he summed up his school as 'a primitive tribe ruled by benevolent or malignant demons'.

It certainly was a primitive way of life: cold baths were taken every morning, the headmaster not infrequently caned his pupils, and the boys themselves meted out punishment to their victims by throwing them into gorse bushes. But it was no worse than most preparatory schools at that time, and better than many. The building, a late nineteenth-century house, was set in open country and surrounded by large hilly grounds in which the boys could play. Music was taken seriously, and Wystan was able to sing in the school choir, as well as continuing to learn the piano. The teaching was on the whole good.

The timetable consisted chiefly of Latin and Greek, mathematics, French, and divinity. There was also a little history and geography, but English was not taught, except for 'spelling, derivations and synonyms'. The classical teaching was chiefly in the hands of the headmaster, Cyril Morgan-Brown, son of the school's founder and nicknamed 'Ciddy' by the boys. Adults often found him an unimpressive figure with his dazed, tired expression; to the boys he was unpredictable and sometimes brutal. If he happened to be in a bad temper he might beat a pupil for a trivial error. At his best he was not encouraging. Once when John Auden spelt the Latin word *misit* as *missit*, Ciddy snapped: 'A boy who does *that* will never make anything of his life.' But Wystan Auden said that, despite all this, 'Ciddy' was an excellent teacher to whom he owed a great deal. He felt, in fact, that the intensive study of Latin and Greek from an early age had helped him to make better use of the English language: 'Anybody who has spent many hours of his youth translating into and out of two languages so syntactically and rhetorically different from his own, learns something about his mother tongue which I do not think can be learned as well in any other way. For instance, it inculcates the habit, whenever one uses a word, of automatically asking: "What is its exact meaning?" '

The teaching of mathematics was, on the other hand, nothing like as good. It was mostly done by rote, without an explanation of basic principles, and by using mnemonics like this, which Wystan had to learn:

> Minus times Minus equals Plus;
> The reason for this we need not discuss.

If he was nervous of Ciddy in particular, Wystan found the teaching staff in general at St Edmund's to be alarming. It was the first time that he had come seriously into contact with adults outside his own family, and he discovered them to be 'hairy monsters with terrifying voices and eccentric habits'. When he read, in a history book, the story of King John gnawing the rush-mat in a rage, it did not surprise him in the least; this was just how his schoolmasters behaved.

During his time at St Edmund's the staff were in fact more odd than they would usually have been; for the war was gradually using up all the able-bodied younger men, so that the regular teachers at the school had long ago vanished and been replaced by a series of temporary masters of steadily increasing strangeness. 'Assistant masters, young and old,' Wystan remembered, 'came and went, becoming more peculiar each year. The oddest had a name to match – Captain Reginald Oscar Gartside-Bagnall. He had written a play, *The Waves* – a barefaced crib, I later discovered, from *The Bells* – which he used to real aloud in a Henry Irving voice to his awed and astonished favourites.' These favourites, of whom Wystan was apparently one, were also given beer and biscuits, and may perhaps have had sexual advances made to them, for Wystan recorded cryptically that 'Reggy's' moral character was 'all at sea'. But his feelings towards this outlandish man were chiefly of gratitude for being given his 'earliest visions of the great wide world'. And there were, of course, saner people at St Edmund's, most notably 'Ciddy's' daughter Rosamira (known as 'Miss Rosa'), of whom Wystan was especially fond, and who behaved to him with almost maternal kindness.

Apart from causing a regular turnover in the teaching staff, the war had comparatively little effect on school life. The food was not notably worse than in peace-time, though the shortages did mean that the boys were not supposed to overeat. Once when Wystan took a second slice of bread and margarine (something that was actually permitted) a master remarked: 'Auden, I see, wants the Huns to win.' The school's chief contribution to the war effort was to run its own miniature Officers' Training Corps, the boys (the oldest of whom was thirteen) marching up and down with wooden rifles. The Corps held regular 'field days', when the boys conducted military operations in the Surrey countryside, using wooden rattles to make the noise of machine-gun fire. Here is a report of one of these occasions, in June 1917, when John Auden was still at St Edmund's with his younger brother:

> No. 1 machine-gun, under Corpl. Auden (junior), was posted on the left ahead of his elder brother, and his patrol was connected with the centre by connecting files. . . O. C. Red Force did a rather unwise thing. Being afraid of being cut off from the ridge to which he wished to retreat, he managed to get a message through to No. 1 gun to cover his retreat, and retired instantly by short rushes, some covering while others rushed (machine-gun fire did not seem to be forthcoming, but, as he learnt afterwards, Corpl. Auden (junior) was engaged on his own.). . . Corpl. Auden (senior) then turned up and asked for advice. Corpl. Auden (junior) replied that the machine-gun was going to retire, and could he hold out a bit longer until he had reached the top and could cover his retreat. This was done, and then both turned their attention to the enemy's advance, and during the charge the Corporal gave them a good deal of lead, but was unable to stop them.

Fun as this was, the boys did realise that the war was more than just an excuse for playing at soldiers. Many of them had already lost fathers or elder brothers, and those who had been bereaved wore black arm-bands at school for a few weeks and were treated respectfully. On the other hand most of them were too young to feel serious grief, and they had a certain gruesome interest in bereavement. If a boy was taken out of class to be told of a death in the family, his friends would crowd round him afterwards and ask him eagerly: 'Did you blub much?' And if a boy grew tired of mourning, all he had to do was take off his black arm-band and join in the games again. As Wystan said, the real war was for them not the hostilities against Germany but the perpetual struggles of school life:

> The Great War had begun: but masters' scrutiny
>   And fists of big boys were the war to us;
> It was as harmless as the Indian Mutiny,
>   A beating from the Head was dangerous.

Wystan himself was on the whole winning this private war. From the first, he impressed everyone at St Edmund's with his self-assurance and his rather clinical detachment. He later recalled that he had tried to shake the poise of the matron on his first day at school by remarking, with the air of a psychologist: 'I like to see the various types of boys.' His contemporaries at school were impressed by his air of authority and his wide general knowledge, culled from his father's library and now shown off to them. One of them, Harold Llewellyn Smith, noted that the young Auden liked 'talking for effect', and remembered the occasion when, after two classes who usually shared one room were split for disciplinary reasons, Auden dubbed the event 'The Great Schism', and treated his schoolfellows to a short lecture on the late fourteenth century. He was then aged ten.

He was doing quite well academically, though he was untidy, lazy, and inclined to be cheeky to the masters. The other boys liked him well enough; at first they called him 'Witny' or 'Witty', a version of 'Wystan' that was used by his mother; later he acquired the title 'Dodo Minor', but this had no significance, being merely a junior version of the nickname given to his brother John, who wore spectacles and looked a little dodo-like. Outside classroom work, Wystan enjoyed his music, and though he was (in his own words) 'a rabbit at all games' nobody minded this very much. He was allowed to pursue more intellectual hobbies, such as collecting shells and insects, which he exhibited in school competitions. He, in return, did not regard himself as superior to those of his schoolfellows who liked sport. 'I think', he wrote, 'I can honestly say I never thought that my minority concerns were superior to the concerns of the majority. At school, my total lack of interest in and aptitude for games of any kind did not make me despise athletes; on the contrary, I greatly admired them, as I have always admired anybody who does something well, but I did not envy them, because I knew that their skill could never be mine . . . I have never, I think, wanted to "belong" to a group whose interests were not mine, nor have I resented exclusion. Why should they accept me? All I have ever asked is that others should go their way and let me go mine.'

At St Edmund's they did let him go his way, more than might have been the case at some schools. But he was not really happy there. To his schoolfellows he may have seemed self-assured, but in his own eyes he was largely a failure. Compared to those of his schoolfriends who were popular and successful at games, he felt himself (he said) to be 'grubby and inferior and dull'. Moreover he thought that this was deserved, that his position as an outsider was all part of the eternal scheme of things, and that he was (as he put it) 'doomed to a life of failure and envy'.

He reacted this way largely because the 'very intense group life' (as he called it) of boarding school was exactly the kind of life that suited him least. He believed that, while there is a certain type of person for whom such a life is ideal, and a majority for whom it is at least tolerable, there are always a few like himself for whom it is awful, largely because they are condemned to spending all their time at school at close quarters to other people, when by nature they really require solitude. And he noticed that the effect on himself of being made to lead such a life against his will was to create in him the habit of being contemptuous towards his fellow men, and especially towards the class of people with whom he was at school – the middle class. Boarding school was therefore, he concluded, 'a not unimportant factor in my adoption of left political views'.

★

One of Wystan's earliest pieces of writing to have survived is the series of entries he made at the age of ten in the diary kept by the Auden family during the Easter holidays of 1917, which they spent at Totland Bay in the Isle of Wight, staying as usual in furnished rooms. Here is Wystan's account of the journey down to the Isle from school in Surrey:

> Left Haslemere by the 10.40 train got don to Portsmouth at 12.0. clock. A portly Archdeacon was in our carriage (initials E. S. I. Paper stamped St Jude's Vicarage Southsea). He was writing his sermon biusily. We had a very nice time on Portsmouth quay, watching steam ferrys running about . . . Unfortunately a short heavy snowstorm came one which did not stop before we got on board. There were glorious paddle engines on board with huge cranks . . . Then we came on to Freshwater, travelling with some nice New Zealand nurses, who told us, that a little while ago, They were in a hospital ship coming from Havre with 600 wounded on board and they ran strait into culver cliff at 4 a.m. The captain had been on the bridge till 10 minutes before when the chief officer took his place and was told to look out for culver light. He mistook the cliff for a cloud and ran strait into it. They were got off in a few hours and managed to get into Southampton under an escort. She was put into dry dock and it was found that she was torn from the bows to beyond the middle of the ship, but the sand ballast acted as a sort of cement and so the ship kept afloat. The chief officer shot himself. We arrived at Freshwater to find only an old growler which was engaged, but the man who engaged it said we could come too.

The other entries in the diary show that family life on holiday was not outwardly very different from what it had been before the war. The boys go off on long walks collecting fossils; their mother takes them frequently to church, or if the weather is bad organises a makeshift service at home; and one evening Wystan gives a 'Grand Concert' of piano solos and duets with his mother. Yet, looking back over this period of his life, Wystan was sure that the absence of his father had affected him. 'To some degree I lost him psychologically,' he said, adding that this had happened when he was seven, the age (he said) when 'a son begins to take serious notice of his father and needs him most'. He felt that, in consequence, he and his father 'never really came to know each other'.

He had the companionship of his elder brothers, and he and John got on well, and had a certain amount in common. But he was never close to Bernard, who was now away at school at Shrewsbury, and was not proving to be of an academic turn of mind. Wystan was, in fact, often left alone with his mother. He remembered one incident in particular from these years:

> Father at the wars,
> Mother, tongue-tied with shyness,
> struggling to tell him
> the Facts of Life he dared not
> tell her he knew already.

He was, for some reason, circumcised when he was seven, an age so late that the operation made a great psychological impression on him. He once told a friend that it had been 'really something'.

His understanding of sex was more thorough than that of most boys of his age, largely because he had managed to look through the manuals of anatomy in his father's library. At school he passed on what he knew to his contemporaries, illustrating his lectures with crude drawings on the blackboard. They were impressed by his arcane knowledge, as they were also by the jumble of information about geology and lead mining (complete with technical terms) that he recited to them.

'To several of us, including myself,' recalled one of his listeners at St Edmund's, 'he confided the first naughty stupendous breath-taking hints about the facts of sex. I remember him chiefly for his naughtiness, his insolence, his smirking tantalizing air of knowing disreputable and exciting secrets. With his hinted forbidden knowledge and stock of mispronounced scientific words, portentously uttered, he enjoyed among us, his semi-savage credulous schoolfellows, the status of a kind of witch-doctor.'

The person who wrote this reminiscence was, in 1917, a boy of thirteen at St Edmund's named Christopher William Bradshaw-Isherwood, the son of a professional soldier who had been killed at Ypres. This year, Wystan reached the top form of the school and began to get to know Bradshaw-Isherwood, who was already a member of it. Isherwood (as he preferred to be called) was amused by young Auden, with his stubby ink-stained fingers and the frown which seemed to be his permanent expression. 'I see him frowning', wrote Isherwood, 'as he sings opposite me in the choir, surpliced, in an enormous Eton collar, above which his great red flaps of ears stand out on either side of his narrow scowling pudding-white face.' Auden in his turn vividly remembered his first sight of Isherwood, 'a small boy with enormous head and large eyes, carefully copying down the work of the boy at the desk next to his'.

Auden soon decided that he approved of Isherwood. They went for a walk together one Sunday, through the unremarkable Surrey countryside, and Isherwood said: 'I think God must have been tired when He made this country.' Auden later said that this was the first time he heard a remark which he decided was witty.

Once or twice he and Isherwood had a religious argument. Auden, loyal to his Anglo-Catholic home, railed against evangelical churches where the cross was merely painted on the wall behind the altar. He said: 'They ought to be burnt down and their vicars put in prison'. Isherwood, who came from a more Low Church family, defended the other view, though without any real heat. On another occasion he and Auden, together with Harold Llewellyn Smith, worked out, surreptitiously during a game of cricket, the plot of a historical novel they intended to write together (but never did). In fact Auden and Isherwood did not, as yet, get to know each other very closely. There were, after all, two and a half years between them; and in December 1918 Isherwood left St Edmund's to go to Repton. Auden remained there for a further eighteen months; and though his father was an Old Reptonian it was not to that school that he was eventually sent, but to Gresham's School at Holt in Norfolk.

By this time the war was over. Dr Auden had returned to his family, and they were living once again in a permanent home. They had not gone back to Solihull, but instead had acquired a house at 42 Lordswood Road in the centre of Harborne, another nondescript village-suburb of Birmingham, to the west of the city. Dr Auden's books and the family furniture had come out of store, and life went on much as it had before the war; though there were a few changes. Bernard left school and sailed for Canada, where he was to take up farming. John was now at Marlborough, from where in due course he went to Cambridge to read Natural Science, with the intention of becoming a geologist. And though Dr Auden himself had resumed his work as School Medical Officer for Birmingham, he also took up a part-time appointment as Professor of Public Health at Birmingham University, where he proved a much-liked lecturer, with a reputation for lacing his instruction on hygiene and sanitation with tags of Latin verse.

Wystan himself paid little attention to the surroundings of his new home, much preferring whenever possible to spend his holidays in the limestone landscape of the Pennines. At some time during his schooldays, probably when staying with friends, he began to visit a stretch of country in the north-western part of the Pennine range, around Alston and Nenthead. This area fascinated him, for it had once been a major centre for the lead mining industry. He acquired a technical manual, *Lead and Zinc Ores of Northumberland and Alston Moor*, and also a book that gave an account of a journey down one of the Alston mines, written by a Victorian traveller, Thomas Sopwith. Meanwhile he himself explored the area whenever he could, climbing the hill near the village of Rook-hope that is known as Bolt's Law, where a chimney (part of the ruins of a lead mine) pointed at the sky, and mine machinery lay abandoned and rusting in the grass near the open shaft.

> In Rookhope I was first aware
> Of Self and Not-self, Death and Dread:
> Adits were entrances which led
> Down to the Outlawed, to the Others,
> The Terrible, the Merciful, the Mothers;
> Alone in the hot day I knelt
> Upon the edge of shafts and felt
> The deep *Urmutterfurcht* [primeval anxiety] that drives
> Us into knowledge all our lives,
> The far interior of our fate
> To civilize and to create. . .

He was now more deeply attracted by the derelict workings, which seemed to him full of symbolism, than by those mines that were still operating. Yet to his parents his interest in mining still appeared to be genuinely scientific. It was perhaps because they expected him to take an interest in science that they sent him to Gresham's School, which specialised in the teaching of scientific subjects.

★

Wystan was encouraged to try for a scholarship to Gresham's. He had done fairly well at St Edmund's; in his last term he won the Form Prize for the top form, and also the First Prize for Mathematics.[1] He also helped to form a school Literary Society, of which he became the first President; its main function was to hold readings from Shakespeare, though the minutes of one meeting also record 'the defenestration of the President'. In fact he just missed a scholarship, and when he went to Gresham's in September 1920 it was without any award to help his parents pay the fees.

Gresham's seemed at first sight a civilised school that made good use of its pleasant surroundings. It was set on the edge of the small north

---

[1]Though he did well in mathematics at school, he seems to have lost touch with it in later years, to his regret. He remarked (in an unpublished interview commissioned for *Time* magazine): 'I was cut off from mathematics. And that is a tragedy. That means half the world lost. Scientists have no difficulty understanding all the humanities, but if you don't have mathematics you can't understand what they're up to.'

Norfolk town of Holt, within five miles of the sea and of salt marshes populated by rare sea-birds. The boys were allowed to go wherever they wanted in the countryside, provided that they were back in time for meals and classes. At school they were permitted a reasonable amount of privacy, both at night-time (each boy's bed was in a cubicle) and in the day, when they could spend their spare time in a study. 'We all have studies,' Wystan wrote soon after he arrived at Gresham's. 'Your first few terms you share with about three others, then less; finally you get a single study.' He summed up his new school favourably: 'The buildings are excellent and also the teaching.'

Certainly the buildings, if not outstanding, compared well with the architecture of many public schools. They were mostly very recent in date, and had been erected as part of a major expansion of Gresham's by G. W. S. Howson, who became headmaster in 1900. When Howson took over Gresham's it was merely a small local school (Sir John Gresham's Free Grammar School) with forty boys and four masters. Nineteen years later, at Howson's death, it was six times as large, and new buildings were still going up. A year after Auden arrived, a biology laboratory was opened. As for the teaching, the special emphasis on science, which was comparatively unusual for a public school of this time, absorbed a lot of the school's energies, and the arts did not get a lot of attention. Only a little Latin was taught and no Greek, while English received scant notice. Nevertheless it was to the Latin and English teachers at Gresham's that Auden felt he owed most. The Latin master, a clergyman named Field who was nicknamed 'Beaky' because of his hawklike nose, never tired, Auden remembered, 'of showing us the shallowness of those who despised the classics'. English teaching, such as there was, lay in the hands of a master known as 'Tock' Tyler, who had a magnificent bass reading voice. 'From listening to him reading the Bible or Shakespeare,' said Auden, 'I learnt more about poetry and the humanities than from any course of University lectures'.

In many ways Gresham's was a liberal school. Howson, who had taught at Uppingham, another 'progressive' public school, had been (in his time as headmaster at Gresham's) firmly opposed to the hero-worship of athletes. For this reason Gresham's was not allowed to play games against other schools, and the boys were even forbidden to cheer at their own football matches. The intellect was rated highly, and great honour was paid to boys who won scholarships. Politically, too, the tone (as shown in school debates) was liberal, and though there was an Officers' Training Corps it was regarded by most boys with some distaste. Corporal punishment and bullying were practically unknown, and there was no snobbery about social class. The boys generally behaved to each other in a civilised fashion.

On the other hand the moral outlook was anything but liberal. Howson had come to Gresham's with the belief that a boy was capable of obeying a higher ethical code than schoolboy conventions commonly allowed, and he decided that it was his duty above everything else to mould the characters of his pupils according to this higher code. He himself interviewed all new boys soon after they arrived, and spoke to them about the moral ideals of the school. He asked them to make a promise to him that they would not themselves indulge in, and would try to prevent other boys indulging in, three things: smoking, swearing, and 'indecency'. Once the boys had made this promise to him, they were asked to repeat it to their housemaster, who gave them a further lecture on morals. There were two sanctions: if a boy broke any of his promises he was expected to 'own up'; if he discovered another boy breaking one, he should first try to persuade the culprit to confess, and then, if this failed, should report him to the authorities.

By the time that Auden arrived at the school, Howson's 'Honour System' (as it was called) was in the hands of his successor as headmaster, J. R. Eccles, who lacked Howson's powerful personality. He was a fussy, precise, bustling bachelor with the manner of an over-energetic scout leader. Eccles reinforced the Honour System with sermons in the school chapel in which he warned the boys about the dangers of mastur-bation – which, of course, was an activity the Honour System was especially designed to suppress. The result of these sermons, and of lectures on the same subject by the housemasters, was to cause anxiety among the boys. Yet on the whole the Honour System worked, at least superficially. Boys did go to their housemasters and confess minor infringements, and though no doubt major crimes against the code were sometimes committed in secret, swearing, smoking and 'smut' were virtually unknown.

Auden, on the other hand, looking back at his time at Gresham's, judged the Honour System to have been totally disastrous from the point of view of the boys. He wrote of it: 'I believe no more potent engine for turning them into neurotic innocents, for perpetuating those very faults of character which it was intended to cure, was ever devised.' Of course (he said) the Honour System 'worked', for it operated by appealing to the boys' feeling of loyalty and honour, the only emotion that was as yet fully developed in them. As a result it was effective in suppressing their other, less developed, emotions, including their sexual feelings. 'But', he wrote, 'if you deny these other emotions their expression and develop-ment, however silly or shocking they may seem to you, they will not only never grow up, but they will go backward, for human nature cannot stand still; they will, like all things that are shut up, go bad on you.'

Even more strongly, he was opposed to the Honour System's demand that boys should if necessary act as informers on each other. 'It meant', he wrote ten years after leaving Gresham's, 'that the whole of our moral life was based on fear, on fear of the community, not to mention the temptation it offered to the natural informer, and fear is not a healthy basis. It makes one furtive and dishonest and unadventurous. The best reason I have for opposing Fascism is that at school I lived in a Fascist state.'

He did not enjoy his first year at Gresham's, finding it difficult to get on with the other junior boys in his house, Farfield, and disliking his housemaster, a bachelor named Robertson. He had been put in too low a class for his ability, and he found the work absurdly easy. There was, however, the school library, where he could go and read, and which he found to be magnificently stocked with books. Also he soon came to admire the senior boy, T. O. Garland, who was house-prefect of Farfield. 'A really good prefect is as rare as a comet,' he wrote of Garland, 'but he was a born leader and the only person, boy or master, who ever made the conventional house and school loyalties have any meaning for me.' Garland, who took care to explain to the junior boys that the headmaster's warnings against masturbation were unnecessarily alarmist, was in his turn impressed by Auden, or at least by his stubbornness. An incident occurred when Auden and the two boys with whom he shared a study were accused of damaging another boy's straw hat by using it as a target for a home-made gun. Garland recalled of this: 'I third-degreed those boys separately. The two older boys quite quickly agreed that they had been responsible. But Auden stuck out for a long time. He would have nothing to do with any admission. I remember this impressed me. It took a lot of persuading him that the others had made confessions, and it was really rather a waste of time him sticking to his lies. I quite admired him for it. It seemed to me that he was behaving with a much more staunch sense of loyalty to his two pals than they were taking to each other.'

By Auden's third term at Gresham's his life there began to improve. He started to take part in the Debating Society, acted a small part in a house play, and was given the role of Ursula in the school production of *Much Ado About Nothing*. In the autumn he was allowed to try again for the scholarship he had missed. This time he won the first of two open awards, and was promptly moved up two forms as a result. From now on he progressed fairly effortlessly up the school in academic work. His English essays were much admired, and were often read out to the class. At least one of his schoolfellows, Michael Fordham, thought him 'brilliant in all subjects'; though he took no more trouble than was necessary, and was regarded by some people as lazy. Games did not appeal to him any more than they had done at St Edmund's – athletically he was pathetic,' commented Fordham – but he sang in the choir, took lessons on the organ as well as the piano, and became friends with Walter Greatorex, the music master.

Greatorex, a good organist, was something of an outsider at Gresham's, having come there reputedly after some small scandal at another school caused by his homosexuality. He was, recalled Auden, 'the first schoolmaster to treat me as an equal human being'. Elsewhere he wrote of Greatorex: 'He was what the ideal schoolmaster should be, ready to be a friend and not a beak, to give the adolescent all the comfort and stimulus of a personal relation, without at the same time making any demands for himself in return, a temptation which must assail all those who are capable of attracting and influencing their juniors. He was in the best sense of the word indifferent, and if the whole of the rest of my schooldays had been hateful, which they weren't, his existence alone would make me recall them with pleasure.'

It was at about this time that Auden began to lose his religious beliefs. He was confirmed during 1920, when he was thirteen, and in his last term at St Edmund's he went through what he called a 'period of ecclesiastical *Schwärmerei* [enthusiasm]', enjoying making his confession, a practice encouraged by the school chaplain, who had High Church leanings. But religion at Gresham's was, Auden soon found, religion without real dogma, and therefore (as he put it) 'nothing but vague uplift, as flat as an old bottle of soda water'. He began to suspect that the devout phase he had been going through was really a case of pseudo-devotion, behind which lay 'quite straightforward and unredeemed eroticism'. Also, at home in the school holidays, attending one of the local Anglo-Catholic churches with his mother, he began to notice that many of the most devoted worshippers were unfortunate in one way or another: they suffered from physical or mental ill-health, or were unhappily married, or were too unattractive to get married. He began to suspect that 'people only love God when no one else will love them'. He also began to feel that, now he was old enough for some kind of real personal belief, the language and imagery of the Church were something that he could not seriously use himself; for instance the phrase 'Lamb of God' was, for him, 'liable to evoke ridiculous images'. A little later he noticed that many of the writers whose books excited him were not Christians. As a result, he gradually ceased to take any active interest in Christianity or to accept its doctrines. On the other hand he did continue to go to church with some enthusiasm, thanks to the fact that he enjoyed singing in the school choir at Gresham's both before and after his voice broke. He also retained a vague conviction that 'life is ruled by mysterious forces'.

His lapse from religion was a gradual process, concurrent with his growing awareness of sexual feelings. By 1922, when he was fifteen, he had begun to be sexually attracted to at least one of his schoolfellows. In many public schools, where mild homosexual intrigues and scandals were part of daily life, such feelings would probably not have seemed very serious. But the Gresham's Honour System was designed to suppress exactly this sort of thing, and to make the boys feel profoundly uncomfortable about sex. As a result, Auden probably felt guilty about what he was experiencing. Certainly he did nothing – at least at first – to make his feelings known to the boy to whom he felt the attraction.

This was Robert Medley, a year older than him, who had been absent from school for most of 1921 recovering from a road accident (his bicycle had skidded and thrown him under a steam-wagon). Medley returned to Gresham's early in 1922 and joined the school's new Sociological Society, which had been formed ostensibly to study contemporary social, political and economic issues, but was really (as Auden said) an excuse to have 'a grand time visiting factories in a charabanc'. It was on one of these trips, on 22 March 1922, that Auden managed to get to know Medley (a slim, dark-haired boy), contriving to sit next to him in the bus.

Medley had returned to Gresham's disillusioned with school, feeling that he did not belong, and intending to get through it as quickly as possible. In this mood, he was impressed by Auden, who, though younger than himself, already had a clinical detachment from school life. Medley, who was interested in painting, had a number of artistic friends, but he found that Auden was also more articulate than any of them.

He and Auden had plenty to talk about. Medley's attitudes were largely a mixture of William Morris socialism and Blake–Shelley romanticism. He rejected religion and refused to be confirmed. It was this last topic that they discussed on the Sunday following the charabanc trip, going for a walk together across fields near the school. Medley made an attack on the Church; Auden's drift away from religion had scarcely yet begun, and he surprised Medley by declaring himself to be a believer. 'An argument followed,' Medley remembered, 'and to soften what I feared might become a serious breach, after a pause, I asked him if he wrote poetry, confessing by way of exchange that I did. I was a little surprised that he had not tried and suggested he might do so.'

Auden's vision of himself and his future was at this time a little muddled. He was still toying with the idea of a career as a mining engineer, but he entertained other fancies – crazes for such things as motor-cycles and photography. Medley's casual question suddenly provided quite a different answer to the puzzle of what he ought to do with his life:

> Kicking a little stone, he turned to me
> And said, 'Tell me, do you write poetry?'
> I never had, and said so, but I knew
> That very moment what I wished to do .

3
Poetry

According to Auden, the first poem that he wrote was a sonnet on Blea Tarn, a pool high in the Lake District, in the heart of Wordsworth country – he, his father and his brother John stayed in the Lakes during the summer of 1922. Auden later lost the manuscript of the sonnet, though he could remember that it ended

> and in the quiet
> Oblivion of thy water let them stay.

He said: 'Who or what *They* were, I cannot, for the life of me, recall.'

His mother, on the other hand, maintained that his earliest poem was one called 'California', named after a small village near his Birmingham home. A manuscript of this is among a large collection of his early work that she preserved, and eventually gave to a family friend (Auden said he wished she hadn't, and alleged that the preservation of a poet's juvenilia was just a form of idle curiosity rather than real scholarship):

> The twinkling lamps stream up the hill
> Past the farm and past the mill
> Right at the top of the road one sees
> A round moon like a Stilton cheese.
>
> A man could walk along that track
> Fetch the moon and bring it back
> Or gather stars up in his hand
> Like strawberries on English land.
>
> 'But how should I, a poor man, dare
> To meet so close the full-moon's stare?'
> For this I stopped, and stood quite still
> Then turned with quick steps down that hill.

This was simple stuff. But Auden soon became more ambitious. By December 1922, nine months after Robert Medley had suggested he try writing poetry, some verses of his were published, unsigned, in the school magazine, *The Gresham*, under the title 'Dawn':

> Far into the vast the mists grow dim,
> A deep and holy silence broods around,
> Fire burns beyond the vaporous rim,
> And crystal-like the dew bestrews the ground.
>
> The last laggard star has fled the glowing sky,
> Comes a quiet stirring and a gentle light,
> A vast pulsating music, throbbing harmony,
> Behold the sun delivered from the gloom of night!

This sort of thing was, as Auden later realised, an imitation of what he thought poetry was like, not a copy of any particular poet so much as a pastiche of 'poetry-in-general'. At the time, of course, it seemed quite brilliant to him. 'Never again', he wrote many years later, 'will a poet feel so inspired, so certain of genius, as he feels in those first days as his pencil flies across the page.' Even now he was beginning to learn a few things about technique – for example, that words could sometimes change their metrical quantities when they were put alongside other words. He had also started, for the first time in his life, to read serious poetry for pleasure, beginning to search through books of poetry in the hope of finding something that would give him suggestions as to what he could write.

For many months he browsed about in the school library, taking up some poet for a few weeks and then dropping him for another. Probably Wordsworth was among his earliest models (there are lines in his first few poems which suggest this), and he was certainly impressed for a time by W. H. Davies, and by 'A. E.' (the Irishman G. W. Russell). He was also delighted by Walter de la Mare, and tried writing a poem rather in de la Mare's style, about two children who push stones through a wall which are caught by a little green man on the other side. Meanwhile he went on searching through the school library 'without finding what I really wanted'.

*

In the summer term of 1922 he took the leading role of Katherina in a school production of *The Taming of the Shrew*. It was a hard part for a schoolboy, and was made more difficult by a bad wig and a dreadful costume. The part of Petruchio was taken by Sebastian Shaw, who later became a professional actor; he remembered Auden with 'red wrists projecting from frilly sleeves and never knowing what to do with his hands. His voice however was clear and his diction excellent.' The reviewer in *The Gresham* wrote of Auden's performance: 'It reflected the greatest credit on him that he contrived to infuse considerable dignity into his passionate outbursts and, moreover, by his spirited performance, showed that determination can overcome almost insurmountable difficulties.'

That summer holiday he went, voluntarily, to the annual camp of the school's Officer Training Corps, which Robert Medley thought an extremely odd thing to do, given Auden's cynical view of such things, besides the fact that he was (as Medley put it) 'the most unlikely of soldiers'. But the O. T. C. did appeal to Auden's sense of the absurd, and the summer camp also gave him the chance to witness some of the Gresham's contingent abandoning their virtuous ways when they came into contact with boys from less inhibited schools. On the whole, however, Auden was not sociable at school and kept out of corporate activities as much as possible. He continued to have a profound dislike of Gresham's ethos and (on a personal level) of his housemaster Robertson. One evening during 'prep', Robertson caught him writing a poem when he should have been working, and remarked: 'You shouldn't waste your sweetness on the desert air like this, Auden.' Ten years later, Auden was still unable to think of this incident without wishing Robertson evil.

His sense of being an outsider at Gresham's was reinforced by his sexual feelings for Robert Medley. On his side Medley, though himself attracted to another boy, had no idea of Auden's emotions; but there was an occasion when Auden managed to contrive a few seconds' close physical contact. This was at the school swimming pool during the summer term of 1922. Medley, an excellent swimmer, was fooling around with other boys and doing double-dives with them from the top diving board, a feat which required that one of them ride pick-a-back on the other's shoulders. Auden was watching, and after a while he asked Medley to do the same with him. Medley agreed, and showed Auden how to grip with his legs; and together they dived. Auden emerged from the water with a badly bleeding nose. 'Feeling responsible,' said Medley, 'I was very upset, but it was the first time I had encountered his innate physical clumsiness. Also I suppose it was as near as we, or most of us, ever got to an embrace at Gresham's.'

Auden took to wandering off by himself away from the school in the early hours of the morning, although this was against the rules. One of the other boys (a naturalist who had special permission to be out at this hour) spotted him very early one day several miles from school, standing alone on the shore at Weybourne, looking at the sea. Auden himself, recalling his schooldays some years later, remembered watching a snow storm come up from the sea at Salthouse, and walking in a June dawn at Hempstead Mill, a couple of miles from Gresham's. He called these 'only the two most vivid of a hundred such experiences'. He tried to get something of them into his poetry:

> On the cold waterfall the flush of dawn gleams bright
> As the wind shouts by his nightly laughter voicing
> The sun rolls back the gorgeous fabric of the night
> And the stars go down behind the hills rejoicing.

He also attempted some close observation of nature:

> Autumn is come, dear kindly dame
> With love that puts us men to shame
> We cannot stir outside the house
> Some hare will cross our path or mouse
> Apples like ruby gems are set
> Deep in long grass thats green and wet
> And when along the lanes we go
> Red berries wink on each hedgerow
> Burdock keeps clinging to our coats
> And 'Old Man's Beard' drapes all the roads.

(He scarcely bothered to punctuate his poems, professing not to understand the art, and, both in poems and letters, often omitted apostrophes from words that needed them. These omissions and other idiosyncrasies have been reproduced in transcriptions in this book.)

Auden had not written many poems like this before he realised he had no real aptitude for noticing the details of nature. He put this down largely to defective sight, damaged in some way (he said) during early adolescence, with the result that he was myopic. He had glasses, but for some reason rarely wore them – he did not need them for reading – though without them he could not see his surroundings very clearly. He did not mind this very much; indeed he once admitted that his short sight was 'probably a retreat from reality, a desire to shut the real world out'. In fact none of his senses seemed to be highly developed; everything had to be scanned by his intellect before he could become really aware of it. During a period of his adult life when he was impressed by the ideas of Jung, he described himself as a Thinking-Intuitive (like his mother), rather than someone who is characterised by Feeling and Sensation.

He eventually made his lack of sense-perception into a virtue, declaring that humanity is naturally anthropocentric and interested only in itself, so that Art should be concerned chiefly with human life and should use landscape just as a background. 'To me Art's subject is the human clay,' he wrote in a 1936 poem, 'And landscape but a background to a torso.'

His own chief concern during much of his schooldays was his unhappy love for Robert Medley, a love which he did not have the courage to declare or do anything about. Several of his poems written at this time have the theme of beauty or sensual attraction being unwillingly rejected because of cowardice, as in this one, 'To a Toadstool':

> O Scarlet Beauty with thy milk white eyes
> See! I have plucked thee up thou lovely thing.
> For he, I know, who eats thee shall be wise
> And see the fairies dancing in a ring
> Shall learn to read the willows sighs
> And share the passion of the nightingale.
> But I have heard too oft mens' tales and lies
> So now with hand pressed close to lip I quail.

At the end of 1922, Robert Medley left Gresham's to go to art school in London. Auden visited him there, and together they went to the theatre to see such things as Capek's *Insect Play* and *R. U. R.* Auden also stayed with Medley's family during several holidays that they were spending in the Yorkshire dales, at Appletreewick in Wharfedale and (on another occasion) at Askrigg in Wensleydale. The village of Appletreewick delighted him – he wrote a poem about it – and he was also greatly taken with Swaledale, a little to the north of Askrigg. He added both these places to his private numinous map.

Medley also came to stay with the Auden family in Harborne. One day while he was there, Dr Auden found a poem among his son's manuscripts (Wystan was in the habit of showing his poetry to his parents) which described Medley at the school swimming pool. Thinking that he detected an erotic element in it, Auden's father confronted the two boys with the matter, though in his usual mild manner. He explained (recalled Medley) 'that he himself as a young man had also enjoyed a close friendship, but that it was not desirable, nor had it ever gone "that" far – had we in fact gone "that" far? It was with relief that we were truthfully able to assure him that our relationship was purely platonic.' Dr Auden was satisfied, and there was no further interference in the friendship.

The poem about Medley at the swimming pool does not survive, but there is another from this period which seems to reflect Auden's feelings for him. It probably refers to one of the holidays they spent together in Yorkshire, for the setting is a moorland landscape, where 'we two' spent a week that was 'happiness-lit':

> Who deafened our ears during those days,
> Who dulled our eyes,
> That life's great doxology we failed
> To recognize?
>
> No whisper fell when we watched the wheel
> Toss at the mill:
> 'You never knew days richer than these,
> Nor ever will.'

> Then standing at sundown on the cliff,
> It fired your hair;
> No voice said to me: 'You will not find
> Two souls as rare.'

The diction in his poems was becoming more sure now. This was largely because he had found a whole new range of stylistic models in Walter de la Mare's verse anthology *Come Hither*, which he was given soon after its publication in 1923. He was excited by this book, not just because it introduced him to poets he had never heard of, but also because de la Mare (who had organised the anthology by subject–matter rather than by the poets themselves) juxtaposed serious poetry with nursery rhymes, ballads, and broadly comic verse. Auden later said that from *Come Hither* he learnt 'that poetry does not have to be great or even serious to be good'.

As a result he began to write poems on all kinds of subjects. A selection of titles from this period gives some idea of the range of topics: 'The Circus', 'On Seeing Some Dutch Pictures', 'Inn Song', 'Joy', 'The Miner's Wife', 'On a Greek Tomb Relief'. His output was now very large; Medley received 'sheaves of poems' from him, and many of Auden's letters home to his parents had a poem (or even two or three) tucked in with them, scrawled in his uneven and not always legible handwriting on a piece of paper torn from an exercise book. 'I wonder what you will think of this,' he wrote at the bottom of a piece of free verse. 'It is an experiment.' And on another poem: 'So sorry I forgot to send this last Sunday. Here it is.'

Come Hither introduced him to the work of Robert Frost (as yet scarcely known in England), who was represented in the anthology by three poems. Auden was soon copying Frost's tone of voice in a poem called 'The Robin':

> Yes, always now
> He follows me
> About the lawn
> From tree to tree.
>
> And if I go
> Raspberry-picking
> He'll perch among
> The canes to sing. . .
>
> If he but knew
> What we men be
> He would not thus
> Hop after me.

The Georgian poets were scarcely represented in *Come Hither*, and the moderns not at all, which Auden (looking back) thought had been a good thing. 'The dangers of too early a sophistication and contact with "modern" writers are so great,' he wrote, 'and I have seen sterility result too often not to be sceptical about the value of any academic courses in the contemporary arts. I was fortunate indeed in finding the only poet who wrote of my world.'

This was Thomas Hardy, many of whose poems he found in the de la Mare anthology, and to whom he felt an immediate affinity. 'For more than a year I read no one else,' he recalled of the period 1923-4, when he was getting to know all Hardy's books in the Wessex edition, novels as well as poetry. 'I smuggled them into class, carried them about on Sunday walks, and took them up to the dormitory to read in the early morning, though they were far too unwieldy to read in bed with comfort.'

He had no difficulty in later years in explaining Hardy's appeal to him, for it seemed natural to him that an introverted adolescent, unhappy in a boarding-school society in which he did not shine, should want to take refuge in the work of a writer who was largely pessimistic and regarded the universe as hostile. He also liked Hardy because he wrote poems about unhappy love, which Auden could apply to his own situation; because the world about which Hardy wrote was recognisably the world of his own childhood; and (rather oddly) because Hardy looked like his own father, with 'that broad unpampered moustache, bald forehead and deeply lined sympathetic face'.

Hardy's pessimistic philosophy soon started to appear in Auden's poems:

> What are we men whose mind to life brings
>   Unpatterned gauges,
> Whom suns may stir to imaginings,
>   Who hold a mere chance
>   Of significance,
> And call the scratch on the surface of things
>   Wisdom of ages?

He chose several Hardy-like subjects and titles, such as 'He Revisits the Spot' and 'The Carter's Funeral'. More important, he began to apply Hardy's tone of voice to a subject that was already dear to his own imagination: industrial machinery and landscape, especially in a derelict state. Poems with titles such as 'The Old Colliery' started to appear in the notebook in which he was now writing his verse:

> The iron wheel hangs
> Above the shaft
> Rusted and broken
> Where once men laughed. . .

Another subject he chose for this approach was a rusting traction-engine, while a third and more ambitious poem in his Hardy voice described Allendale, a town in the lead-mining district near Alston:

> The smelting-mill stack is crumbling, no smoke is alive there,
> Down in the valley the furnace no lead-ore of worth burns;
> Now tombs of decaying industries, not to strive there
>   Many more earth-turns.

All these poems ended forlornly or pessimistically, often with un-answered questions about the meaning of life. In fact such pessimism was, despite Auden's present discontent, not really natural to him, and after a time it disappeared from his poetry. He did, however, learn something else from Hardy which remained in his imagination for the rest of his life: 'What I valued most in Hardy, then, as I still do,' he wrote in the 1940s, 'was his hawk's vision, his way of looking at life from a very great height.' Auden was here thinking of the opening chapter of *The Return of the Native,* with its description of Egdon Heath seen from far above, and of the stage directions in *The Dynasts* – in other words of Hardy's prose and drama rather than his verse. But for Auden himself the 'hawk's vision' was to become an important part of poetry.

★

The fact that he was now writing poetry did not alter his parents' expectation that he would take up some kind of scientific career, and when he was sixteen and had to make a decision about what subject to choose for university entrance, it was agreed that he should specialise in science. Probably his family medical background and the fact that Gresham's had a new and flourishing biology department played a part in the decision that biology rather than physics should be his principal subject. At all events he began, in September 1923, to spend most of his time studying zoology and botany, with some chemistry.

'In Zoology I have been doing the Crayfish all the last week', he wrote to his parents in October 1923, 'and have got to compare the nervous and excretory systems in the Protozoa, Coelentera and Worms, quite an interesting subject.' He did well at his work. The process of dissecting organisms and examining them through a microscope suited his habit of mind. To some extent his view, in his poetry of the 1930s, of the poet as a surgeon owes something to this training as a biologist. 'Section these dwellings,' he wrote in *The Dog Beneath the Skin,* 'expose the life of a people.'

Meanwhile his poetry had received a new stimulus. In the same letter in which he described his early work in zoology, he told his parents: 'I have a little surprise for you; I have had some things accepted for the

1924 volume of Public School Verse; so shall make my first appearance in print so to speak next year. Don't tell anybody this will you; not even any of the family.'

This was the result of a friendship that he had begun with a man of twenty-six named Michael Davidson, who was working on the staff of a Norwich newspaper, and who, many years later, was to begin his autobiography: 'This is the life-history of a lover of boys.' Davidson, an ex-public schoolboy, had been wounded on the Somme; after the war he became a regular soldier, but stayed in the army for only one night; he then went to South Africa and set up a pig farm with a sixteen-year-old Welsh boy for partner; and now he had come back to England and was working in East Anglia as a journalist. His sister was married to the violin teacher at Gresham's; hence he knew Greatorex, the music master, in whose house he was introduced to Auden.

'Auden, as I remember him then,' he wrote, 'was tall and gangling, with fair limp hair across a pale forehead and clumsy limbs apt to go adrift; and an odd, cogitative face that was frighteningly unboyish. He seemed too engrossed in *thought* to be boyish; it was the face of a mind far older than its age and already had that look of puritan sternness which signifies contempt for all intellectual time-wasting.'

At their first meeting, Davidson was 'bewitched' by Auden, not because of physical attractiveness (he found none), but because he believed that this boy of sixteen – an age which held a special fascination for him – had something of genius. 'The maturity of even his smallest remarks,' he wrote of Auden, 'a kind of inspired wisdom which, in his company, one couldn't help being aware of, was alarming; and I knew instantly that, though ten years older, I was shamefully his inferior in intellect and learning.' Davidson decided that 'I had found my boy Keats or Chatterton, on whom I would lavish all I could muster of literary maternalism. I was in love.'

Davidson made sexual advances to Auden, which were rejected, 'not on moral grounds', said Auden, 'but because I thought him unattractive'. Davidson, undeterred, pursued the friendship, taking great pains to encourage and help Auden with his poetry.

Auden regarded Davidson's feelings for him quite dispassionately, looking on him almost as a clinical specimen. 'He once told me, as if stating an interesting scientific fact,' recalled Davidson, 'that I was the first adult homosexual he had met.' But he was also tactful, and when Davidson sent him some verses addressed to him 'he was kind enough', recalled Davidson, 'to ignore their poetic dreadfulness and stern enough to keep silent on the sentiment they conveyed'. Meanwhile Auden greatly valued the encouragement Davidson was giving to his experiments in poetry. 'I owe him a great deal,' he said many years later.

He sent Davidson every poem he wrote, and Davidson replied with criticisms, or rather with discussion and suggestions. Davidson also

scoured the literary journals for anything that might interest Auden, and
ordered for him (at his own expense) copies of new books of poetry and
criticism. Letters between the two of them were full of excited discoveries
of writers who were fresh to them.

Among these discoveries was Edward Thomas. Auden remembered
that in the autumn of 1924 there was a 'palace revolution', after which his
admired Thomas Hardy had to share the kingdom with Edward Thomas.
He wrote a poem in the style of Thomas, called 'The Rookery', about a
row of elms suddenly and unexpectedly deserted by rooks:

> When we were half asleep we thought it seemed
> Stiller than usual; but no one dreamed
> That aught was wrong until we came downstairs
> And looked, as we had done these many years,
> At the huge wall of elms that flanked the lawn. . .

He also wrote a poem addressed to Thomas ('here and there your music
and your words are read / And someone learns what elms and badgers
said / To you who loved them and are dead'), and another to Richard
Jefferies, whose adventure story *Bevis* was, he declared, the only tolerable
book about boyhood. Then there were months when he was under the
influence of A. E. Housman, of whom he later said: 'To my generation
no other English poet seemed so perfectly to express the sensibility of a
male adolescent.' Housman's aggressiveness towards God appealed to
him, and he wrote verses like this:

> Wake and be merry, you are strong;
>   You may have it as you please
> A little while, though God ere long
>   Break your back across his knees.

But Auden was getting to the stage where he no longer needed to
borrow a style or a philosophy. He had begun to use a tone of voice that
was not quite like anybody else's:

> It was quiet in there after the crushing
> Mill; the only sounds were the clacking belt
> And the steady throb of waters rushing
> That told of the wild joy those waters felt
> In falling; the quiet gave us room to talk.
> 'How many horsepower is the huge turbine?'
> 'Seventy; the beck is dammed at Greenearth Fork,
> Three hundred feet of head; the new pipe line
> Will give another hundred though at least;
> The mill wants power badly.' He turned a wheel
> The flapping of the driving belt increased
> And the hum grew shriller. . .

Lead mines and their machinery, pumping engines, and 'the long slow curving of the Fells' (as he described them) now dominated many of his poems, and were pictured in a very individual manner; so it was a pity that his 'first appearance in print so to speak' in the 1924 *Public School Verse* failed to demonstrate any of this.

According to Michael Davidson's later recollections, he sent the publishers of *Public School Verse* some of Auden's poems, without consulting Auden himself – though if this is true, Auden does not seem to have been at all cross about it; his letter to his parents suggests he was pleased at getting into print. In fact when the 1924 volume appeared, only one poem by Auden was included, an unadventurous little piece called 'Woods in Rain' ('It is a lovely sight and good / To see rain falling in a wood. . .'). Perhaps it was fortunate that the poet's name was misprinted as 'W. H. Arden'.

Michael Davidson soon abandoned his newspaper job in Norwich and drifted to London. He and Auden continued to correspond, and early in 1925 Auden sent him an elegy on a schoolboy who died as the result of a fall from a tree:

> The wagtails splutter in the stream
> And sparrows quarrel round the door,
> We have not woken from the dream
> Its wonder stirs us as before;
> But one of us will never bring
> His music to a latter spring.
>
> He found the earliest thrushes' nest
> Before us all; his was a grace
> Like poplars with their leaves at rest
> Or pony in the wind; his face
> Was keen with solitude, to fears
> And griefs unknown in sixteen years.
>
> That spring was early and the time
> Was swift with us from day to day
> Far into April, till his climb
> To look into a squirrel's drey.
> The rotten branches bore him well
> For he had reached it when he fell.
>
> Three weeks he lay and watched a rook
> Or lilac hanging in the rain,
> A pair of wrynecks came and took
> The nesting box outside the pane
> And hatched their brood; the first one cried
> Upon the morning that he died.

No dog barked in the street below
The churchyard where they dug his grave,
The day wore nothing strange to show
That earth took back the dust she gave,
And cuckoos they were calling still
When we had left him in the hill.

This was written in the spring term of 1925, during Auden's last year
at Gresham's. As this year progressed he 'went for long solitary walks,
played the organ, hardly spoke to anyone unless I had to, and was
extremely happy'. He also managed to win an Exhibition (a minor
scholarship) in Natural Science to Christ Church, Oxford. This was after
an interview at Oxford conducted by Julian Huxley, then a young
university lecturer in zoology, who showed him a bone and asked what
it was. Auden answered: 'The pelvis of a bird' – which was correct;
Huxley remarked that some candidates had said it was the skull of an
extinct reptile.

He was not totally solitary during his last year at school. In his final term
he spent time with a boy two years younger than himself, named John
Pudney. 'He fell in love with me,' Pudney remembered, 'and said so
very decorously – we still addressed each other by our surnames.' Auden
had now ceased to pay any serious attention to the Gresham's rules,
somewhat to Pudney's astonishment. 'He would climb up a pipe into my
study in the early hours of the morning before anyone was awake,'
Pudney remembered, 'to leave a message and to make a few corrections
to the prep which was left out on my desk. He would defy half a dozen
school rules by ordering a massive tea of eggs and strawberries and
cream at a local farmhouse – for we were never allowed to mix with the
locals. When we walked, we followed paths carefully chosen because
they were out of bounds.' Auden did not, however, make any sexual
advances to Pudney, though later he regretted this. Instead, remembered
Pudney, he 'lectured me about homosexuality and self-abuse', and talked
about psychology, in which he was now interested – he had got to
know some of the writings of Freud, to which his father was paying a lot
of attention, and had acquired his own copies of Freud's writings, which
he sometimes lent to friends at school. 'Wystan did not talk like a boy,'
said Pudney. 'He spoke a language which was mature, worldly, intellectually challenging.'

Auden showed Pudney the manuscripts of his poems, or sometimes
read them aloud. He also looked at Pudney's own efforts at verse, and
was very critical of them. Pudney in his turn was too shy and too
admiring to criticise what Auden wrote. He was therefore surprised
when, one morning in the summer term, 'Wystan declared that his
poems were worse than mine because they were more pretentious. His
work made some claim upon the intellect, whereas mine was just the

harmless jingle of a schoolboy who had thumbed through the *Oxford Book of English Verse*. He led me into the dripping green twilight of the school woods as he developed this theme of self-deprecation. It was a Wagnerian scene, with East Anglian winds sounding gusty chords of doom. The climax was dreadful. As we approached the larger of the school ponds, I was commanded to stand back while the poet, tossing back his pale straight hair, drew his manuscripts from his pockets and went on alone, to commit literary suicide by casting them into the depths.' The deed done, Auden declared that 'he had got poetry out of his system once and for all and that the human race would be saved by science'.

This was not entirely tomfoolery, for Auden was at least half inclined to devote himself entirely to science – Michael Davidson recalled that at this time he 'had made up his mind to become a psychologist'. But his commitment to poetry was now too strong to be abandoned at a whim, and that same evening Pudney and another boy were summoned to keep watch while Auden waded back into the pool to retrieve the manuscripts, which fortunately were still afloat.

At the end of his final term, Auden took part in a production at Gresham's of *The Tempest*. He played the role of Caliban. This was his own choice – he had made a special effort to be selected for it – and he gave a remarkable performance. Robert Medley, who heard about the production from Auden, realised that Auden was encapsulating in his interpretation of the role his feelings towards Gresham's. 'Wystan perceived', wrote Medley, 'that, implicated in Caliban, was a protest against the Honour System, under which he had suffered so much; the occasion for making a witty, personal and deeply felt "send-up" of the system was not to be missed.' Some years later he chose to write one of his most remarkable poems in the voice of Caliban.

He left school, in his own words, 'a confirmed anarchist individualist'. At home in Birmingham he spent part of his summer holiday learning to drive; he was already riding a motor-cycle. 'The Motor Bike went beautifully,' he wrote to Michael Davidson. 'I only had one collision and that at about 6 m.p.h.' During the summer he also went with his father for his first trip abroad, to Austria, where they attended the Salzburg Festival and stayed at Kitzbühel in the Tyrol, in the house of one Frau Hedwig Petzold, partly so that Wystan should learn German – which on this occasion he scarcely did. At the end of the summer he went up to Oxford as an undergraduate; not with any great enthusiasm, but valuing it as at least an escape from the family circle. He was still extremely close to his mother – he gave her his first manuscript notebook of poems together with a dedicatory verse – but things were not easy between them. Oxford would at least be a refuge from this. He went there, as one of his new undergraduate friends observed, regarding it rather as 'a convenient hotel'.

4

Oxford

His college, Christ Church, was in fact rather like a hotel. It was very large by Oxford standards, big enough for a single undergraduate to be almost anonymous in it. Auden's first-year rooms were in an out-of-the-way corner, in the attic of Staircase 1, Meadow Building. The rooms looked out over Christ Church Meadow, but the building itself, a mid-nineteenth-century pile, did not match up to the splendour of the rest of the college.

In the various rooms beneath him were a third-year scholar named Emlyn Williams, whose mind was more on acting and writing plays than academic work; a don, F. A. Lindemann the physicist (later Lord Cherwell), who became Churchill's scientific adviser during the Second World War; and a second-year undergraduate (also a scholar) named Stanley Fisher. Emlyn Williams and Auden never got to know each other except by sight, while Lindemann was rarely seen at all by the other people on his staircase. But Fisher and Auden soon became friends.

On the evening before term began, Fisher was waiting in a neighbouring room for the arrival of its occupant, Sidney Newman the college organ scholar, when (Fisher remembered) 'hard upon a peremptory knock, the door burst open in an explosion of legs and, with an upward jerk of the head and a flourish of pipe in hand, the visitor said, "I want to join the Musical Union." When I explained that I was not its college secretary, he turned to leave but I called him back and told him I would give Newman his name and see that his application went through. "Auden, W. H. Auden," he said.'

Fisher introduced himself and, gathering that Auden was interested in music, mentioned that, though he could not play the piano himself, he kept one in his rooms for friends who could. He did not know, as he said this, that Auden could never resist a piano. From now on, Auden was in Fisher's rooms at least once a day, strumming out hymn tunes or Anglican chants or grinding through Bach's forty-eight Preludes and

Fugues in a manner that another undergraduate described as 'loud, confident, but wonderfully inaccurate'.

Fisher, Sidney Newman and other undergraduates who began to get to know Auden were greatly struck by this odd-looking freshman. One of them described him as having 'a more than ordinary boyishness, a fresh unwrinkled pink face and an amazing intellectual ebullience', and added that Auden's rapid voluble conversation 'had always a kind of positive character which distinguished him from most of us'. Another described him as 'loosely put together, flat-footed, with big chubby hands and well-bitten nails, fumbling with a cigarette, and a big mobile face good at expressing contrived notions'. He was, this friend observed, 'conventionally dressed and tidy, but wore his clothes as if they did not fit'. The cigarette habit came a little later; when he first arrived at Oxford, Auden preferred a big pipe which somebody called 'volcano-like', and which he smoked insatiably, explaining: 'Insufficient weaning. I must have something to suck.' He would smoke while playing Fisher's piano, scattering ash all over the keyboard.

On his first visit to play the piano he asked if Fisher ever wrote poetry. Fisher said he did, and showed Auden his collection. Auden said he liked one of them, about a Yorkshire fossil, but made no further comment, and never spoke about them again. Fisher gathered that Auden himself was a poet, and asked to see his work. Auden, instead of fetching his manuscripts from his room (remembered Fisher), 'took his pipe out of his mouth, lifted his chin, and recited poems for nearly half an hour'. Fisher was excited, not only by the poems themselves but by Auden's way of reciting them in a flat, unemotional, quite 'unpoetic' manner that (as another undergraduate friend observed) 'submerged the intellectual meaning under the level horizontal line of the words'. Auden had by now come to believe in the importance of reading poetry aloud (he was later to define poetry as 'memorable speech' and to say that 'no poetry. . . which when mastered is not better heard than read is good poetry'), and he often introduced his friends to his own poems for the first time by reciting them. He had a good memory, and towards the end of his life claimed to be able to recognise any line of verse – though not every word of prose – that he had ever written. He could also quote huge chunks of other writers' work by heart, though Louis MacNeice remarked that 'he nearly always gets it wrong'.

Fisher made efforts to write down the poems that Auden recited to him. He and Auden soon discovered that they had several things in common. Fisher, the son of an Anglican clergyman and a scholar from Leeds Grammar School, had come up to Christ Church, like Auden, to study biology, though he had now changed subjects and was reading English. He knew Auden's lead-mining district of Alston Moor, and also Appletreewick, the Yorkshire village where Auden had stayed with the Medleys, and which, Auden said, was the place he most desired to live in. Fisher had the distinct impression that Auden resented his knowing these places; he felt he was trespassing on private territory. Nevertheless he and Auden got on well enough to go for a walk together at least once a fortnight during Auden's first two terms at Christ Church.

'We will go for a walk this afternoon,' Auden would announce (Fisher observed that the 'we' had a royal overtone). Auden walked fast, taking no notice of his surroundings and talking all the time, waving his pipe. 'I was not clever enough', said Fisher, 'to be an adequate anvil for the hammers of his mind, but I was a good listener.'

Auden's conversation on these walks – or rather, his monologues – was largely on four topics. The first was the impossibility of becoming a really good poet if he stayed at Oxford. He was sure, he said, that the undergraduate way of life was far too conducive to idleness, and he had already dismissed the University as an artificial institution quite out of touch with the real world. On the other hand, when Fisher suggested that he might take an interest in the college's Mission to the dockland area of London, Auden dismissed this as the kind of do-gooding that his mother would recommend. Auden also said – and this was his second topic – that it was quite impossible for him to live at home in Harborne because he was always having terrible rows with his mother. He was dreading going home for the Christmas vacation, and he asked if he might come and stay for part of it at Fisher's home – which Fisher gladly arranged. The third topic was the impossibility of believing in a personal God. Fisher, who held such a belief (he later became a priest in the Church of England), was challenged by Auden to produce philosophical or scientific proof of the existence of God, Auden of course dismissing any that Fisher did offer. Some months later, Auden gave Fisher a copy of a poem he had written on this subject:

> . . . We draw our squares about the Universe
> To make the habit of it suit our purse. . .
> Expound our neat cigar-philosophies,
> With God above, as harmless as you please,
> The keeper of a Paradise for fools,
> A dear Arch-Monad in horn spectacles.

Auden told Fisher that Christian beliefs were all of a piece with what he called Fisher's 'abysmal romanticism'; and this was the fourth topic on their walks – the necessity of being a classical poet rather than a romantic.

Auden told Fisher that he had now entirely abjured romanticism and regarded himself as a classic. But this did not mean he had ceased to admire romantic poets; rather, that he now admired their 'classical' qualities. Thomas Hardy (he said) was classical in that he was a realist. Housman was a classic because he was 'austere' – a favourite word of Auden's at that time. Walter de la Mare, though extremely romantic, passed the test because he had perfect technique. Fisher found all this rather confusing. Meanwhile Auden took to reciting long passages of Samuel Johnson, and removed from his sitting-room wall a watercolour of an Apennine shepherd-boy which Fisher had pointed out was indubitably romantic. He handed it to Fisher, wrote on the back 'To my Romantic friend Stanley', signed this inscription 'W', and added beneath his initial: 'An incurable classic'.

★

Ten days before Christmas 1925, shortly after the end of his first term at Oxford, Auden travelled to Norbury in South London, where Stanley Fisher's family lived. He stayed with them for a week. They found him rather an exhausting guest.

He rose virtually at dawn, a time of day he found good for working, and once up he talked so loudly that he could not be ignored. At meals he shovelled enormous quantities of food into his mouth with no regard for his neighbours' needs. He usually paid no attention to what he was eating – he claimed to have 'the digestion of a horse' – but he could sometimes have unexpected fads. When he was staying (some time later) with Stephen Spender's family and the dish-cover was lifted at lunch, he exclaimed in tones of severe condemnation, like those of a judge passing sentence: '*Boiled ham!*'

He demanded and drank an endless succession of cups of tea. It was as if (remarked another friend) 'his large, white, apparently bloodless body needed continual reinforcements of warmth'. A cloudy day was enough to make him demand that a fire be lit, and when occupying the sitting room he would soon scatter tobacco ash over it or burn the furniture with cigarettes. Any apology for this that could be got from him was to say the least perfunctory. He was not entirely untamed: to ladies he was punctiliously polite, opening doors for them, carrying bags and parcels, and, when walking in the street with them, insisting on going on the outside of the pavement. These were the social rules his mother had taught him. But he could quell a meal into silence by his taciturnity and by the frown which was his usual expression. He was sometimes discovered in the middle of the night raiding the larder for cold potatoes or other left-overs ('I just wanted to see if that beef was still there,' he explained on one such occasion). He invariably piled a huge weight of bedclothes on his bed: blankets, eiderdowns, bedspreads, anything that would make it heavy. If there were not enough of these he would appropriate anything else he could find. At the Fishers' he put the bedroom carpet on his bed. Staying with another family, he took down the bedroom curtains and used these as extra blankets. Another time it was the stair-carpet. Once he was discovered in the morning sleeping beneath (among other things) a large framed picture.

A couple of days after Auden had arrived, Stanley Fisher was telephoned by Christopher Isherwood, who had been at school at Repton with his brother. Isherwood lived not very far away, in Kensington, and said he would be glad if Fisher would come and have tea with him. Fisher answered that he had a friend named Auden staying with him. The name brought an instant response: could this, asked Isherwood, be the same Auden with whom he had been at prep school? A few questions confirmed that it was. The invitation was immediately extended to them both.

Isherwood was twenty-one, and had left Cambridge the previous summer after deliberately ruining his final examination papers. He was now at home in London, making some sort of living as secretary to a musical family, the Mangeots, and quarrelling with his mother. At Cambridge he had written a novel which he then rejected as worthless. He had now begun another.

When Isherwood saw Auden he thought his old school friend had changed very little: 'True, he had grown enormously; but his small pale yellow eyes were still screwed painfully together in the same short-sighted scowl and his stumpy immature fingers were still nail-bitten and stained – nicotine was now mixed with the ink. He was expensively but untidily dressed in a chocolate-brown suit which needed pressing, complete with one of the new fashionable double-breasted waistcoats. His coarse woollen socks were tumbled, all anyhow, around his babyishly shapeless naked ankles.' While Isherwood and Fisher talked, Auden sat silently smoking his pipe and frowning, occasionally pulling a book from the shelves, glancing at it casually, and then dropping it carelessly on the floor, unconscious of Isherwood's irritation at this. It was not until Fisher, who had another engagement, left him alone with Isherwood that he began to behave less aggressively. The two of them started to joke about their time at St Edmund's and to do impersonations of the staff and their oddities – 'Reggy' reading from his absurd drama *The Waves*, and 'Ciddy' preaching in chapel (this was one of Auden's favourite turns). They were soon laughing helplessly; as Isherwood put it, the 'prep school atmosphere' had reasserted itself.

Just as he was saying goodbye to Isherwood, Auden mentioned that he now wrote poetry. 'He was deliberately a little over-casual in making this announcement,' Isherwood noticed. Isherwood thought this revelation was very surprising, almost improper. He regarded Auden as someone who knew about machinery, and who would have no real literary taste. But he asked, a little patronisingly, to see some of the poems. Auden gruffly agreed, and a few days later Isherwood received a bundle of manuscript through the post. The handwriting was ungainly and sometimes illegible, but the poems themselves impressed Isherwood, not because of brilliance – 'they were neither startlingly good nor startlingly bad', he said – but because they were, as he put it, 'efficient, imitative and extremely competent'. This surprised him because, at St Edmund's, Auden had always struck him as 'an essentially slap-dash person'.

*

Back at Oxford for the spring term, Auden got to know another occupant of his staircase in Meadow Building, a history scholar named David Ayerst; they were both members of the college Essay Club – the only club (apart from the Musical Union) that Auden ever joined at Oxford. Ayerst, who nicknamed Auden 'The Child' because he looked juvenile for somebody of such erudition, was senior to Auden by two years, but was greatly impressed by what he called 'the sharpness and power of his ice-cold imagination'. But he and Stanley Fisher were also struck by the fact that there was now quite another side to Auden: a regular indulgence in homosexual activity.

Looking back over his schooldays at Gresham's, where any suggestion of sex had been repressed by the Honour System, Auden remarked that when pupils educated under such a code leave school they find themselves defenceless: 'Either the print has taken so deep that they remain frozen and undeveloped, or else, their infantalised instinct suddenly released, they plunge into foolish and damaging dissipation.' There is no question to which category he regarded himself as belonging. Just as when he left school he resolved never to take a cold bath again, so he also decided to abandon any restraint on his sexuality.

Given this decision, the almost inevitable result in his present circumstances was homosexuality. Certainly there were female undergraduates at Oxford, and a few of the bolder ones did manage to waive the conventions of chaperonage. But they were, as Auden remarked, the exception: 'There were three or four girls in my day who had somehow managed to get out and, like token Jews in a Wasp community, were accepted by us. Not every lunch party was stag, but at a mixed one the female faces were almost always the same.' For the most part the male undergraduates kept their own company. Also at this time homosexuality was fashionable, or at least had been fashionable among the generation at Oxford that had immediately preceded Auden's – 'that debauched eccentric generation', Auden called it, 'That. . . made new glosses on the noun Amor'. Some of them were still up at the University, moving in Oxford's intellectual circles and setting themselves in deliberate opposition to the college athletes, who by tradition had normal sexual tastes. Louis MacNeice, who came up to Oxford not long after Auden, observed this: 'I discovered that in Oxford homosexuality and "intelligence", heterosexuality and brawn, were almost inexorably paired.' (MacNeice added: 'This left me out in the cold and I took to drink.')

Auden did not indulge in the manners of an 'aesthete', nor join the effete circle that was still gathering in the George Restaurant at Oxford – 'the master decadents', MacNeice called them – even though the principal members of that circle were at Christ Church, and Auden was later to become friends with one of them, Brian Howard. But he did take advantage of, or was affected by, the fact that Oxford's climate was still strongly homosexual.

He was, his friends soon learned, devoting certain evenings to sexual adventures, returning at a late hour to give them a clinical account of his pursuits and captures, and of experiments in *fellatio*, this being his preferred form of sex.[1] He told them these things no doubt partly to shock, partly to inform them (especially Fisher) about the ways of the world, and partly perhaps in order to demonstrate to them how free he was from guilt. Ayerst was not entirely convinced about this; privately he suspected that Auden did in truth experience guilty feelings about what he was doing, but was ashamed of these feelings and determined to be liberated from them. Certainly a poem Auden wrote at about this time suggests that he valued the peace that followed after lust was satisfied:

> . . . As surely as the wind
> Will bring a lark song from the cloud, not rain,
> Shall I know the meaning of lust again;
> Nor sunshine on the weir's unconscious roar
> Can change whatever I might be before.
> I know it, yet for this brief hour or so
> I am content, unthinking and aglow. . .

Most of his friends, however, thought he was as completely free from guilt as he was from inhibition, and that all this was part of his plan for himself as an artist. Stephen Spender (who came to know Auden a little later at Oxford) observed of this: 'Self-knowledge, complete lack of inhibition and sense of guilt, were essential to the fulfilment of his aims.'

Self-knowledge he certainly possessed, or believed that he possessed. He was well versed in Freud, and, far from boasting of his sexual prowess, ascribed his promiscuity to a wish to compensate for the

---

[1] I have recorded this detail because Auden himself argued that it was necessary to be explicit about sexual practices when recording the lives of homosexuals. In his review of J. R. Ackerley's autobiography *My Father and Myself,* written in 1969, he says: 'Frank as he is, Mr Ackerley is never quite explicit about what he *really* preferred to do in bed. The omission is important because all "abnormal" sex-acts are rites of symbolic magic, and one can only properly understand the actual personal relation if one knows the symbolic role each expects the other to play. . . I conclude that [Ackerley] did not belong to either of the two commonest classes of homosexuals, neither to the "orals" who play Son-and/or-Mother, nor to the "anals" who play Wife-and/or-Husband. My guess is that. . . the acts he really preferred were the most "brotherly", Plain-Sewing and Princeton-First-Year' (*Forewords and Afterwords*, p. 453). 'Princeton-First-Year' is apparently a variation of 'Princeton Rub', a term for *coitus contra ventrem;* 'Plain-Sewing' is naval slang for mutual masturbation. Auden was proud of being the first person to use these terms in print.

smallness of his penis, about which he believed he had a complex. On the other hand if he did not boast he certainly loved to gossip about his own and his friends' affairs – though later he became much more discreet about his own.

During these early months of promiscuity at Oxford he claimed to abjure love. Lust, he told Stanley Fisher, was an appetite and needed to be satisfied, but love was to be avoided as a snare. This, however, was wishful thinking rather than a rule he managed to obey. David Ayerst noted that he was always falling in love with some young man or other, usually one who was quite unattainable and obviously heterosexual – they were frequently athletes. Conversely, those who were prepared to have sex with him were usually undergraduate acquaintances or friends whom he liked but for whom he had little or no romantic feeling. His technique with them was to arrive in their rooms, lock the door, and say bluntly: 'You know what I've come for.' On other occasions he would have sex with some stranger on a train – 'Wystan could always, on the brief train journey to London, make a contact,' wrote his Christ Church contemporary A. L. Rowse. Or he would invite a friend to his own rooms in college so that they could experiment sexually. One morning the 'scout' who looked after his staircase discovered him in bed with an undergraduate from Magdalen. Auden had to buy the man's silence with a five-pound note, a large sum which he could ill afford.[1]

Auden himself was only too aware of the conflicting sides of his sexuality, the satisfied lust and unsatisfiable love. He was contemptuous of himself for feeling what he called 'the pathetic thrill of devotion. . . for the loved heterosexual', and maintained that a nobler and preferable sentiment was the deep devotion of one comrade for another: 'That is the right way, yes, and lechery in the dark room.' But as yet he found no relationship which could satisfy both needs. Nor was he sure that this was what he wanted. In 1927 he wrote to an undergraduate friend: 'There still lingers in my mind the idea of something indecent in a mutual homosexual relation.'[2]

★

[1] Another version of this story has it that Auden bribed the scout in advance – rather than being discovered *in flagrante* – and afterwards remarked that the experience 'hadn't been worth five pounds'.

[2] The story is sometimes told – for example, by A. J. Ayer, in *Part of My Life* (Collins, 1977, p. 81) – that Auden made a malicious complaint to the Christ Church authorities about the behaviour of one of the dons in the college, R. H. Dundas, who was well known for his habit of asking undergraduates about their sex-lives and instructing them in the 'facts of life'. It is said that when Auden complained about this, Dundas was so upset that he took a year's sabbatical leave to go round the world. In fact Dundas took his sabbatical in 1931, three years after Auden left the college, so there seems to be no truth in the story. But Auden did nickname Dundas 'the third baboon', a reference to the story of two baboons copulating in a clearing while a third baboon watched from the trees, chattering enviously and masturbating.

During the Easter vacation he wrote to Stanley Fisher, from his home in Harborne: 'Look here. Can you come and stay for two or three days the week after Easter week. Family relations have been tres difficile and you are the only man who can put things right, because you understand my little failings and peculiarities so well.' In a postscript Auden added: 'Vacation chastity is very trying.'

Fisher agreed to pay a visit, and when he arrived at Harborne he was struck by the character of Auden's mother. He found her mind 'inflexible, not visionary like my mother's, and she was censorious, not encouraging'. Fisher learnt that she now disapproved of almost anything that Wystan said or did. She was upset by his loss of religious belief, and she disliked the poetry he was now writing, much preferring his earlier schoolboy verse – which he himself now disowned. She also told Fisher that she disapproved of the bad friends he chose – 'from which category she excluded me, after an alarming pause'. Fisher also noticed that Auden was deeply upset by the frequent quarrels with his mother; after a particularly stormy breakfast one day, Auden went upstairs and burst into tears. Mrs Auden gave Fisher no chance to defend Wystan; so, when he got home to South London and wrote to thank her for the visit, Fisher took the chance to explain that he himself admired Wystan and felt it a privilege to be a friend of his:

> Genius [he wrote] is always a little difficult to manage and there is no doubt that he has a very large share of it. The fact that he is naturally more self-sufficient than most people explains why he finds so little need for a personal God – or for a mother – but that does not make things easier for you!

This was Mrs Auden's reply:

> You gauge Wystan wonderfully well for so short an acquaintance, but we mothers know more of the actual tendencies for good and evil in our sons' characters than anyone else can possible know. For one thing, we have known them from babyhood when acting a part was impossible and it is true that 'the child is father to the man'. So when one has known the childish weaknesses or strength one cannot help realizing how things are going and how much danger lies ahead.
>
> Do not think that I do not realize all the good points – of course I do – but I also know the weak ones – and I cannot help feeling that self-sacrifice, self-discipline, (self-control even) are looked upon with scorn – instead of as the highest ideals possible. You say that he realizes that intemperance in any form chokes the channels – but for all that he is not temperate in anything. (A trifling example is his

way of eating food whenever he sees it – a small matter in itself –
but indicative of much.)

As regards our relationship to each other, he depended on me
more than any of the others until lately, and twice in later years at
school I was able to come to his help in crises.[1] (I do not know if he
has ever mentioned things of this kind to you.) He probably did *not*
tell you that that morning when he burst into tears he very soon
took the opportunity I gave him of saying how sorry he was for
being so unutterably 'rude'. As a matter of fact he is as much his old
self as possible when we are alone together. Nothing could have
been happier than this last week, but when his friends are there he
likes to assert his independence of me! As an inmate of a household
he *is* trying – so untidy and thoughtless of others.[2]

Mrs Auden was about to leave England and pay a visit to her eldest son,
Bernard, in Canada; and she concluded her letter by asking Fisher to
write to her there now and then 'to tell me how things are going'. She
would (she said) be homesick for letters, and Wystan 'scarcely ever
writes'. Fisher recognised this as in effect a request that he should spy on
Wystan. He discontinued the correspondence.

★

Early in May 1926, at the beginning of Auden's first summer term at
Oxford, the General Strike was proclaimed, and contingents of undergraduates immediately set off for London, a few – perhaps fifty or so – to
help the strikers, but by far the majority to assist the Government by
acting as volunteer police or by driving public transport. Few of them
took the Strike very seriously; for most, it was simply a piece of fun.

[1]One of these crises may have been an incident described by Auden's schoolfellow
Michael Fordham, in a letter to the present writer: 'When on a school expedition – I think it
was in Devon or Cornwall but what it was about I can't remember – Auden caused
consternation by meeting or going with a prostitute. This became a subject of much
cogitation amongst the staff and eventually he was ceremonially given six strokes of the
cane before the school prefects by the headmaster! As beating was not a method of
punishment in the school it was unusual – the only occasion that it was used when I was
there.'

[2]A view of Mrs Auden as she appeared to someone outside the family is provided by
Mary Sandbach in a letter to *Adam International Review,* Nos 385–90 (1974-5). p. 104: 'The
Audens were our neighbours in Harborne. . . We were all fond of Dr Auden, but could not
stand his wife, who was an unattractive, domineering kind of woman.' In a letter to the
present writer, Mary Sandbach adds: 'I think that my opinion of Mrs Auden is probably
coloured by what my parents said about her. They accused her of manipulating her sons'
lives.'

Auden himself did not follow the lead of the majority, but decided to support the strikers, not because of any serious appreciation of the issues but simply, as he said himself, 'out of sheer contrariness'. His Christ Church friend David Ayerst was Chairman of the University Labour Club, and was helping to organise support for the strikers. Auden's choice of sides in the Strike was undoubtedly influenced by his friendship with Ayerst, but he did not join the Labour Club or take any part in political activities at Oxford; he had at most a vaguely liberal or socialist outlook, tending to side with 'the people', whoever they might be, against the entrenched and parent-like authority of conservatism. Even now that he had taken sides in the Strike he did not really appreciate what he was doing. He went to London and, for a few days, drove a car for the Trades Union Congress.[1] One morning he delivered R. H. Tawney to his house in Mecklenburgh Square. 'It happened', Auden recalled, 'that a first cousin of mine, married to a stockbroker, lived a few doors away, so I paid a call. The three of us were just sitting down to lunch when her husband asked me if I had come up to London to be a Special Constable [i.e. to work for the Government]. "No," I said, "I am driving a car for the T. U. C." Whereupon, to my utter astonishment, he ordered me to leave the house. It had never occurred to me that anybody took the General Strike seriously.'

The Strike was soon called off, and Auden and his fellow under-graduates returned to Oxford without having had their interest in politics really aroused. 'Inflation in Germany and Austria,' he afterwards wrote of this period, 'Fascism in Italy, whatever fears or hopes they may have aroused in our elders, went unnoticed by us. Before 1930, I never opened a newspaper.'

By this time – the beginning of the summer term of 1926 – Auden had changed subjects in his academic work. He soon came to realise that he would not achieve anything by continuing to study biology – that, as he put it, 'I was not cut out to be a scientist'. He was obliged to work at scientific subjects throughout his first year, so as to pass the Preliminary Examination in Natural Science; by Christmas 1925 he had successfully taken the papers in Zoology and Botany, but not until the summer of 1926 did he obtain a pass in Chemistry. By then, he had obtained Christ Church's permission to abandon scientific studies and read another subject for the Final Honour Examination which would gain him his degree. Despite this, he did not give up all interest in science. For the rest of his life he regularly read scientific books for enjoyment and interest, and often drew on them for ideas and images in his poetry, to a degree

[1]The car was apparently Auden's own. As V. M. Allom remembers it, the vehicle was a French three-wheeler, a D'Yrsan, which Auden shared with another undergraduate whose name Allom does not recall. No reference to this car appears elsewhere in records of Auden's life at this time.

that showed an understanding of science that was remarkable for a poet. But he no longer made any claim to be a real scientist. 'When I am in the company of scientists,' he once said, 'I feel like a curate who has strayed into a drawing-room full of dukes.'

His first thought on a new choice of subject was that he should read Philosophy, Politics and Economics, the course of study known as 'Modern Greats' or 'P. P. E.' During his second term, while he was still officially studying science, he borrowed a number of philosophical books from Christ Church library, and attended tutorials with Roy Harrod, who taught economics at Christ Church, and with the philosopher Gilbert Ryle. But while philosophy no doubt interested Auden, his ignorance of world affairs cannot have helped him to get to grips with politics and economics, and Harrod found him a timid and uncertain pupil. By the beginning of the summer term Auden decided that P. P. E. was not for him, and had made up his mind that instead he would change to English Language and Literature. 'I had no intention of studying English literature academically,' he wrote of this decision, 'but I wanted to read it, and the English School would give me official licence to do so.'

Christ Church did not at this time employ anybody to teach English, being (said Auden) 'far too snooty' to do so. English was a comparatively new Honour School in the University, and was disparaged in some quarters as a soft option. Auden had therefore to look elsewhere for a tutor. Stanley Fisher, who was reading English, was being taught by H. F. B. Brett-Smith of Corpus Christi; but Fisher warned Auden that 'the Bretter' was a dull, discouraging tutor. They formed the idea that they might both get taken on by David Nichol Smith of Merton, and they called on him to ask if they could be his pupils. 'This was not a success,' recalled Fisher. 'He was already overburdened with pupils, he said, and Wystan wore his fiercest frown and fixed him in an unfocused stare, so that the consequent note of polite refusal was only to be expected.' Eventually an arrangement was made that Auden should be sent for tutorials to Exeter College, where English literature was taught by a newly-appointed don of twenty-seven, an Anglo-Irishman named Nevill Coghill.

'One morning he stood before me scowling,' remembered Coghill of his first meeting with Auden. 'I can still see him as clearly as I did that morning – the forbidding scowl, the uncombed flop of blond, revolutionary hair, the large expressive mouth, the big bones of the face and the sandy complexion that had a certain roughness of surface, not unlike an Epstein maquette. He had a slight slouch and grey flannel bags as baggy as my own. I liked the look of him and inwardly hoped he felt the same about me.'

They began tutorials together, and Auden found he did indeed like Coghill. 'He was not a guru,' he said of him. 'I never took a deep breath before knocking on his door. On the contrary, he put me so at ease that I felt I could say anything to him, however silly, whether about literature or my personal life, without fear of being laughed at or rebuked.' Coghill was certainly tolerant. One day he arrived in his rooms to find Auden already there, reading one of Coghill's letters ('waiting in his room for a friend / We start so soon to turn over his letters', Auden once wrote in a poem). Auden looked up, quite unabashed at being discovered, and complained that a page was missing. Nor did Coghill ever forget a conversation they had after it was agreed that he would become Auden's tutor: 'Wanting to plan his work with some relevance to his needs and interests, I asked him what he proposed in later life. "I am going to be a poet." "Ah yes!" I said in my lordly way – one is capable of every blunder at twenty-seven – "that's the right way to start reading English. It will give you insight into the technical side of your subject, if you try to write poetry; there's more in it than just an *O Altitudo!* Besides, writing your poems will improve your prose." I felt rather pleased with that. But the scowl had returned. "You don't understand at all," he said. "I mean a great poet." '

Coghill soon got used to this kind of remark. He found the tutorial hour with Auden the liveliest of his week. Auden would arrive bursting with the urgency of communicating some discovery. Had Coghill read Dasent's translation of *Njal's Saga*? Did he know the Mozart Horn Quintet in E flat? Or he would talk about some joke or scandal of the week. Coghill accepted all this just as enthusiastically as he listened to Auden's essay on whatever poet or novelist he had been reading since their last tutorial.

Auden's interest was, predictably, in poetry more than in fiction. He enjoyed Trollope and Dickens (he could quote whole pages of Dickens by heart), he was fond of Jane Austen, and he liked nineteenth-century Russian novelists, but he had little taste for modern novels – though he did eventually come to like the outlandishly 'camp' stories of Ronald Firbank, and became an addict of detective stories. As to his undergraduate reading in poetry, he soon decided that Wordsworth was 'a most bleak old bore'. Indeed the Romantics in general did not appeal to him, and he said he had 'no use' for Keats or Shelley. The metaphysical poets were at that time very fashionable among undergraduates, and he did not dissent from this enthusiasm, though he preferred Herbert to Donne. Among sixteenth-century poets he was excited to discover Skelton. But, unfashionably, he was also delighted by Pope and Dryden. Of Pope he said: 'At his best there are few poets who can rival his fusion of vision and language.' Dryden he judged to be 'pre-eminent in English literature as the poet of Common Sense. . . the ideal poet to read when one is weary, as I often am, of Poetry with a capital P'. Even more unfashionable was the enthusiasm he quickly developed for a part of the English syllabus that was often unpopular with undergraduates at Oxford, Anglo-Saxon.

A fellow undergraduate was astonished to discover that Auden 'really admired the boring Anglo-Saxon poets'. Auden himself said of Anglo-Saxon that 'it was my first introduction to the "barbaric" poetry of the North, and I was immediately fascinated both by its metric and its rhetorical devices, so different from the post-Chaucerian poetry with which I was familiar'. This is not to say that he became expert in Anglo-Saxon. He was taught it not by Coghill but by a lecturer in Anglo-Saxon, Charles Wrenn, who instructed him also in philology and the history of the English language. Wrenn concentrated on the mechanics of Anglo-Saxon rather than its imaginative appeal; Auden said of him: 'Wrenn was so much a philologist that he couldn't read anything beyond the words.' Auden's interest in Anglo-Saxon arose, in fact, not out of tutorials with Wrenn but largely from lectures by the thirty-four-year-old Professor of Anglo-Saxon, J. R. R. Tolkien. He said of Tolkien's lectures: 'I do not remember a single word he said but at a certain point he recited, and magnificently, a long passage of *Beowulf*. I was spellbound. This poetry, I knew, was going to be my dish.'

He took enough trouble with Anglo-Saxon to be able to appreciate *The Dream of the Rood, The Wanderer* and *The Seafarer,* as well as some of the *Exeter Book* riddles and at least part of *Beowulf*. Among Middle English poetry he was particularly attracted by *Piers Plowman*, preferring it to Chaucer. Elements from all of these were to appear in his own poetry. He himself said of this: 'Anglo-Saxon and Middle English poetry have been one of my strongest, most lasting influences.' He was also attracted, no doubt partly because of childhood memories of his father's stories, by the Icelandic sagas, which he read in translation, and by early Irish poetry. 'In general the further away from you in time or feeling that poets are,' he said, 'the more you can get out of them for your own use. Often some piece of technique thus learnt really unchains one's own Daimon quite suddenly.'

Much of his work in the English School at Oxford was supposed to consist of reading literary criticism and mastering the accepted critical attitudes. This did not attract him. He described his own critical writing as 'more intuitive than analytic', and almost the only critic he admired was W. P. Ker, whose essays delighted him largely because of what they had to say about prosody – he was already familiar with Saintsbury's *History of English Prosody*. He also approved of I. A. Richards's essay *Science and Poetry*, and his *Principles of Literary Criticism* – he told Stephen Spender that it was a scandal that the *Times Literary Supplement* had only given the latter a short notice – but most modern critics did not interest him. In fact the English School as a whole gradually came to seem to him to be mistakenly organised, at least for someone with his interests and talents.

'My own recommendation', he wrote some years later, 'would be to forbid any student to read English Literature or Sociology who did not

intend to become a teacher of those subjects.' Elsewhere he said: 'If it is
probably unwise for a poet to read English, this is not because he will
learn nothing thereby which will be of profit to him as a poet. He may
very well learn a great deal. It is because the only ways of earning his
living for which it will qualify him are teaching or literary journalism.' It
seemed to him that, should there ever be established that most unlikely
thing, a curriculum specifically intended for the professional training of
poets, it ought to take an entirely different line from the usual English
literature course. This is what he once proposed for the course of study at
his imaginary 'Bardic College':

1. In addition to English, at least one ancient language, probably
    Greek or Hebrew, and two modern languages.
2. Thousands of lines of poetry in these languages to be learnt by
    heart.
3. Instruction in prosody, rhetoric and comparative philology.
4. The only critical exercise would be the writing of pastiche and
    parody. All critical writing, other than historical or textual,
    would be banned from the college library.
5. Courses in mathematics, natural history, geology, meteorology,
    archaeology, mythology, liturgies and cooking.
6. Every student would be expected to take personal charge of a
    domestic animal and a garden plot.

Beneath the element of facetiousness in this, there lies a perfectly serious
demand for a training in technique, and for a general education in such
non-literary subjects as are likely to be useful to a poet. Auden was
probably not consciously aware of the lack of such a training and
education while he was studying at Oxford; but there is no doubt that,
despite Coghill's teaching, he found that the English syllabus was not
satisfying his needs.

As a result, he was not working hard at it. He spent a lot of time
reading books, but not necessarily the books he ought to have been
attending to. Psychology continued to attract him, and he was also
interested in the work of the anthropologist W. H. R. Rivers. A friend
described his conversation this year (1926) as peppered with 'curious and
suggestive phrases from Jung, Rivers, Kretschmer and Freud'. Meanwhile as far as his work for the English School was concerned he felt
'guilty at being so idle'. He even said, looking back over this period, that
he had anticipated disaster: 'I knew very well what sort of degree I was
going to get and what a bitter disappointment this was going to be to my
parents.' This may or may not be true; his friends at Oxford observed no
such forebodings on his part, and thought he was perfectly self-confident
in his academic work. But he was undoubtedly unhappy in one respect: 'At nineteen, I was self-critical enough to know that the poems

I was writing were still merely derivative, that I had not yet found my own voice.'

*

During the summer term of 1926, Auden became friends with a Christ Church undergraduate named Tom Driberg, who like himself had worked for the T.U.C. in the General Strike. Driberg was homosexually promiscuous, but though the two now became good friends their relationship (said Driberg) was 'chaste'. Driberg introduced Auden to the poetry of T. S. Eliot.

During this term he showed Auden a back number of the *Criterion* dating from 1922, which contained *The Waste Land*. The two of them read the poem together – 'read it, at first,' recalled Driberg, 'with incredulous hilarity (the Mrs Porter bit, for instance); read it, again and again, with growing awe.'

Auden realised that Eliot was describing the true nature of the society in which he was living. 'Whatever its character,' he said, 'the provincial England of 1907, when I was born, was Tennysonian in outlook; whatever its outlook the England of 1925 when I went up to Oxford was *The Waste Land* in character.'

He bought Eliot's *Poems 1909-1925*. Shortly afterwards he went for a tutorial to Coghill and told him: 'I have torn up all my poems.' Coghill asked why. 'Because they were no good. . . You ought to read Eliot. I've been reading Eliot. I now see the way I want to write.'

He was soon producing Eliotic poems:

> Under such pines
> I gave a penny for his thoughts. He sent
> A photograph signed, but spiders crawled across it
> Obscuring the face.
>
> What does it mean?
> After the hymn we sat, wiped sticky fingers,
> Thinking of home, What does it mean
> To us, here, now?

'Eliot was now the master,' observed Christopher Isherwood of the poems that Auden was now writing, which were indeed like parodies of Eliot. Unexplained allusions, obscure scientific terms, startling and apparently unrelated images were all jumbled together to cook up the Eliotic mixture:

> Love mutual has reached its first eutectic,
> And we must separate. The train runs, pushing
> The spirit into undiscovered lands,

Far from the sirens calling in the Park
For Ulysses, dressed up like a sore finger,
To roll like Nebuchadnezzar in the grass;
From wattled parsons gabbling over graves;
From sunken acreage of basement kitchens. . .
We are embraced by lichenous desires,
Change Wanderlüst to Weltschmerz in the Underground.
The poodle has returned to her old vomit,
We to our cottages like crouched Ophelias,
Where Job squats awkwardly upon his ashpit,
Scraping himself with blunted occam razors
He sharpened once to shave the Absolute.

He adopted not just Eliot's style but his whole attitude to poetry. In Eliot's essay 'Tradition and the Individual Talent' (published in 1919) Auden found the statement that 'poetry is not a turning loose of emotion, but an escape from emotion' – which, of course, harmonised with his current concern to be 'classical' and 'austere'. In this essay, Eliot argued that the poet should undergo a 'process of depersonalisation', a surrender of his own personality in order that he may become a receptacle for seizing and storing up material from which poetry can be made. Auden decided to take this literally.

He began to cultivate impersonality. 'The poet must look like a stockbroker,' he told his friends; in other words, there must be nothing 'poetic' about a poet's manner. And he declared that the most beautiful walk in Oxford was not 'poetic' scenery but the dingiest part of the river towpath, which ran past the city's gasworks, a scene that corresponded closely to Eliot's 'dull canal. . . round behind the gashouse' in *The Waste Land*.

'Wystan's favourite walk was past the gas-works,' recalled Cecil Day-Lewis,[1] who got to know Auden just when Eliot's influence on him was at its height. But if Auden's intention in this choice of walk was to convince his friends of the ordinariness of poets, he entirely failed. 'As likely as not,' Day-Lewis remembered of Auden on these gasworks walks, 'he was carrying a starting-pistol and wearing an extraordinary black, lay-reader's type of frock-coat which came half way down to his knees and had been rescued by him from one of his mother's jumble sales. How he came by the starting-pistol, I do not clearly remember.'

Auden was shrewd enough to observe, very quickly, that he should not continue to use Eliot as a stylistic influence. 'Like Tennyson, he was a hugely idiosyncratic poet,' he wrote of Eliot many years later, 'and one sensed that if one took him as a poetic model, one could only write Eliot-and-water.' Traces of Eliot continued to appear in his poetry up to the

---

[1] I have spelt Day-Lewis's surname with a hyphen, as Sean Day-Lewis, in his biography of his father (1980) states this to be correct.

end of his life, but the period in which he was writing pastiche-Eliot was very short indeed, a mere matter of months. Even at the time when he was copying Eliot, he was discovering and showing enthusiasm for other, very different poets. Stanley Fisher introduced him to the verse of Emily Dickinson; and Auden subsequently wrote a short poem in her style, called 'Amor Vincit Omnia':

> Six feet from One to One.
> Yet what change would have been
> Were you upon the sun
> Or epochs in between? . . .

He also admired Wilfred Owen, partly for his technique and also for the detachment of his war poems, which (he told Stephen Spender) he thought far preferable to the sentimentality of Sassoon. Robert Graves's work pleased him too; he said later in his life that Graves was 'one of the very few poets whose volumes I have always bought the moment they appeared'. He was impressed also by Gerard Manley Hopkins, and occasionally copied him, though he soon realised that Hopkins too was a dangerous influence; he once said: 'Hopkins ought to be kept on a special shelf like a dirty book, and only allowed to readers who won't be ruined by him.'

Eliot's importance for Auden was, then, limited. When towards the end of his life Auden made a list of those elder modern poets from whom he believed he had learnt most, he did not include Eliot's name.[1] Elsewhere he said that Hardy's colloquial diction had influenced him more than Eliot's, 'which one could steal but never make one's own'. And he eventually awarded the title of 'the greatest long poem written in English in this century' not to *The Waste Land* but to David Jones's *Anathemata*.

By the time he had passed through his Eliot phase, Auden was arguably the best undergraduate poet at Oxford. Admittedly the competition was not very great: the 1925 volume of *Oxford Poetry* (a book published annually by Blackwell's) contained work – by, among others, Graham Greene, Cecil Day-Lewis and A. L. Rowse – most of which was mediocre and dull, the few exceptions being some ornately 'decadent' verse by the arch-aesthete of Christ Church, Harold Acton (a typical line was 'We groin with lappered morphews of the mind'). Against such a background, Auden's verse seemed adventurous and fresh. He began to get it published in undergraduate periodicals during his third term at the University, when *Oxford Outlook* printed (in May 1926) sixty-four lines of blank verse that he had written during the previous vacation. This poem, 'Lead's the Best', was a celebration of the abandoned lead mines of the Pennines and the men who had once worked them; it concluded with

[1]The list is in *A Certain World*, p. 372.

the wry observation that the ruined workings were no more than 'Themes for a poet's pretty sunset thoughts'. Also during that summer term, the *Oxford University Review* published 'Cinders', the poem Auden had given to Stanley Fisher, which attacked the notion of a personal God; and *Cherwell* printed two of his short pieces about love, 'At Parting' and 'Portrait', in the latter of which the sex of the beloved was slightly ambiguous:

> The lips so apt for deeds of passion
> The hair to stifle a man's breath
> The symmetry of form beneath
> An Irish mackintosh. . .

This was much more successful than his poem 'The Sunken Lane', published in June in the *Oxford Magazine,* where the lover is identified as female and the sentiment, perhaps in consequence, is hollow:

> Fine evenings always bring their thoughts of her,
> But beech woods chiefly – their silence astir
> So like her movements. . .

Certainly the quality of his poems was still uneven. But by the end of the summer term his reputation was high enough for him to be asked to be joint editor of the 1926 volume of *Oxford Poetry,* together with Charles Plumb, an undergraduate who had co-edited the 1925 issue. Plumb and Auden had different tastes, and the preface to the book, which is probably the work of Plumb, has an air of compromise:

> We have endeavoured to pacify, if not to content, both the pro-
> gressive and the reactionary. . . If it is a natural preference to inhabit
> a room with casements opening upon Fairyland, one of them at
> least should open upon the Waste Land. At the same time the
> progressive would be unreasonable to expect confidence until he has
> proved that his destination justifies his speed.

Despite this, Auden was able to include in the book one of his most Eliot-like pieces, 'Thomas Epilogises'.[1] When he left Oxford to begin the summer vacation of 1926, he could be confident that, in undergraduate circles at least, he had made a reputation as a poet.

★

[1] This poem contains the lines 'Isobel, who with her leaping breasts / Pursued me through a Summer', of which Auden said many years later that they were the worst he had ever written, and would have made an ideal caption for a Thurber cartoon.

He intended to invite David Ayerst to stay with him at Harborne during the summer, but Mrs Auden returned from her visit to Bernard in Canada, and the plan had to be abandoned. 'My mother is here who is insane,' he wrote to Ayerst, 'and guests are an impossibility. . . This place is bloody dull. Only one decent affair.'

To relieve the tedium he went to stay with Christopher Isherwood, who was on holiday at Freshwater Bay in the Isle of Wight. For the occasion, Auden acquired a broad-brimmed black felt hat, which he chose to wear above grey flannels and a black evening bow tie. Isherwood thought that the hat was a sham, a piece of Oxford exhibitionism; and the young men and girls at Freshwater sniggered at it. But Auden was undismayed. 'Laughter', he declared, 'is the first sign of sexual attraction.' He embarrassed Isherwood in public places by holding forth, at the top of his voice, on whatever happened to be occupying his mind: 'Of course, intellect's the only thing that matters at *all*. . . I've absolutely no use for colour. Only form. . . Poetry's got to be made up of images of form. I hate sunsets and flowers. And I loathe the *sea*. The sea is formless. . .' Isherwood, despite his embarrassment, observed that, unlike the hat, the loud dogmatic statements were not sham. He realised that Auden was, as he put it, 'merely experimenting aloud; saying over the latest things he had read in books, to hear how they sounded'. He also saw that they were intended to be something like small talk; for Auden was trying in his own odd way to be the model guest. As Isherwood put it, 'He really wanted every minute of his visit to be a success – on the highest intellectual plane.' And there was, too, an element of caricature in these performances. Auden was no mimic, but he liked acting roles, a favourite one being that of a lunatic clergyman preaching to his flock. It was sometimes difficult to say exactly where this performance ended and the real Auden began.

During the Isle of Wight holiday, Isherwood gradually realised that Auden not only admired him but looked up to him as a sort of literary elder brother. Auden showed him poems that he was writing, and responded readily to any criticisms that Isherwood made. This is how Isherwood described it, writing some years later:

[Wystan], who was as lazy as he was prolific, agreed without hesitation to any suggestion I cared to make; never stopping to ask himself whether my judgement was right or wrong. If I wanted an adjective altered, it was altered then and there. But if I suggested that a passage should be rewritten, [Wystan] would say: 'Much better scrap the whole thing,' and throw the poem, without a murmur, into the waste-paper basket. If, on the other hand, I had praised a line in a poem otherwise condemned, then that line would reappear in a new poem. And if I didn't like this poem, either, but admired a second line, then both the lines would appear in a third poem, and so on – until a poem had been evolved which was a little anthology of my favourite lines, strung together without even an attempt to make connected sense. For this reason, most of [Wystan's] work at that period was extraordinarily obscure.

This account needs to be treated with caution. For a start, it comes from Isherwood's *Lions and Shadows,* which, though autobiographical in form, contains – as Isherwood himself emphasises in the preface – caricatures of his friends rather than accurate portraits. The figure of 'Hugh Weston', Isherwood's name in the book for Auden (all his friends are given pseudonyms), is not offered to the reader as a totally true picture of Auden. No doubt there is some exaggeration in the account of poems being reconstructed from Isherwood's favourite lines, without consideration for sense. Certainly by no means all of Auden's poetry written at this period is 'extraordinarily obscure'. On the other hand it must be said that there are quite a lot of instances in Auden's early poetry where phrases and lines are rescued from a rejected poem and put into a new one, not always with the strictest regard for sense.[1]

Isherwood, then, probably exaggerated, but not very much. He did not, however, claim ever to have taken part in the actual creation of Auden's poems. He said of them that they were like rabbits Auden produced from a hat – 'they couldn't be talked about before they appeared'.

If Auden looked up to Isherwood in literary matters, he did not hesitate to lecture him on other topics. He encouraged Isherwood to read the sagas – he had brought *Grettir* and *Burnt Njal* with him – and the two of them talked about how the Norse warriors with their feuds, practical jokes and dark threats were just like the inmates of English boarding schools. More alarmingly for Isherwood, Auden also harangued him about sex.

Isherwood had been 'yearningly romantic' about boys at his public school, and at Cambridge had gone to bed with one male undergraduate;

---

[1]Examples of the same phrase used twice include: 'breasts / The Hill "Thalassa!" on the tongue' (unpublished poem, circa 1926-7, in an undated letter to W. L. McElwee (British Library)) and 'To breast the final hill, / Thalassa on the tongue' (*English Auden,* p. 24); 'There was no food in the assaulted city' (ibid., p. 411) and 'Yet there's no peace in this assaulted city' (ibid., p. 32); 'To focus stars more sharply in the sky' (ibid., p. 437) and 'Focussing stars more sharply in the sky' (ibid., p. 39); 'Like Solomon and Sheba, wrong for years' (ibid., p. 438) and 'Holders of one position, wrong for years' (ibid., p. 45); 'Love, is this love, that notable forked-one / Riding away from the farm' (ibid., p. 441 and – with slight changes – p. 68); and 'The frozen buzzard / Flipped down the weir and carried out to sea' (ibid., pp. 437, 40). Stephen Spender records, in *World Within World,* seeing Auden altering an early version of these last lines at Isherwood's suggestion.

but he was now in a state of considerable confusion about his sexuality. Auden, when he discovered this, made it his task to sort Isherwood out. 'He intruded everywhere,' said Isherwood, 'upon my old-maidish tidiness, my intimate little fads, my private ailments, my most secret sexual fears.'

Auden's own attitude to sex, said Isherwood, 'fairly took my breath away'. Isherwood discovered that Auden was no Don Juan in that he did not hunt for sexual adventures, but simply took what came his way with a matter-of-fact hearty appetite – the same attitude that he showed to food. He described his sexual experiences to Isherwood, who 'found his shameless prosaic anecdotes only too hard to forget, as I lay restlessly awake at night listening to the waves, alone in my single bed'. Isherwood was in fact greatly unsettled. After the Isle of Wight holiday he went to France with another friend, Edward Upward, whom he then suddenly abandoned, going off in pursuit of a boy he had met on the train. Later, he bought a revolver and threatened suicide. Altogether, Auden had given him (as Isherwood put it) 'a badly-needed shaking up'.

For some weeks after this, he avoided Auden's company, but he soon began seeing him again; and after a few months he and Auden started to have sex together, 'unromantically', said Isherwood, 'but with much pleasure'.

Certainly they were very fond of each other. Isherwood once spread an old overcoat of Auden's on his bed when he went to sleep because it made him feel close to Auden. No doubt Auden felt much the same about Isherwood; indeed he may conceivably have had stronger feelings of attachment – though, if so, Isherwood was not aware of it. But they took care never to express their affection in serious terms, and they frequently made fun – both privately and in print – of each other's physical appearance. Isherwood wrote of Auden's 'stumpy immature fingers' and 'small pale yellow eyes', while Auden mocked Isherwood's 'squat spruce body and enormous head', and called him 'a cross between a cavalry major and a rather prim landlady'.

There was, then, no romantic love in their relationship. Nor was there any very great sexual excitement (at least for Isherwood) when they went to bed together – which they did, said Isherwood, 'whenever an opportunity offered itself'. Isherwood found Auden too much like himself in physique and character to experience the *frisson* which only an opposite in type could give him. The clue to understanding their sexual relationship is that it was schoolboy in character.

'Their friendship', wrote Isherwood, looking back impersonally many years later, 'was rooted in schoolboy memories and the mood of its sexuality was adolescent. . . They couldn't think of themselves as lovers, yet sex had given their friendship an extra dimension. They were conscious of this and it embarrassed them slightly – that is to say, the sophisticated adult friends were embarrassed by the schoolboy sex partners.' Isherwood suspected that it was because of this embarrassment that they made fun of each other's appearance, as if to dispel any suggestion that the relationship was serious. Elsewhere he said: 'The value of the sex making was that it kept an adolescent quality in our relationship alive – almost as if we could go back together into the past whenever we were so inclined.' In other words, they could become schoolboys again by getting into bed together.

*

Back at Oxford in the autumn of 1926 for the start of his second year at the University, Auden changed his rooms at Christ Church, moving into a handsome oak-panelled set, 'Peck V.5,' high in a corner of the eighteenth-century Peckwater quadrangle. He paid little attention to the view from his windows, keeping the curtains closed for most of the time because he claimed he could only work by artificial light. These rooms – which, beside bedroom and sitting room, included a closet where he installed a piano – soon became something of a legend among other undergraduates. The rumour got around that he kept on his mantelpiece a decaying orange, thoroughly mildewed on the side that faced the wall, to remind himself of the fate of the West; and that in his desk was a loaded revolver, always ready for despatching its owner should he decide that life was a failure. (This was in fact probably the starting-pistol Day-Lewis had seen.) Such legends were encouraged by Auden's manner of dress. At various times he was seen with a cane and a monocle, or in a clergyman's panama hat, or an old medical jacket of his father's or, if he had suddenly decided to look fashionable (which sometimes happened), his double-breasted brown suit. But despite this exhibitionism he never had anything remotely of the dandy about him. He did not take clothes seriously, and seemed incapable of wearing them tidily.

With his change of rooms at Christ Church he largely changed his friends. He no longer needed Stanley Fisher as an intimate, and he now saw little of David Ayerst, who had taken his degree. Among new acquaintances was a Magdalen undergraduate named John Betjeman, whom Auden first met in the summer term of 1926. He was amused by Betjeman's taste for High Anglicanism and Victorian Gothic, all of which (said Auden) exactly harmonised with his own childhood memories of provincial gaslit towns, seaside lodgings, harmoniums, and High Mass. Their enthusiasm for these things was so similar that Auden once suggested facetiously that he had actually created Betjeman himself, out of his own substance. 'I can never make up my mind', he said, 'whether Mr Betjeman was born after the flesh or whether he was magically conceived by myself in a punt on the Cherwell one summer evening in 1926. I have no memory of company on the outward journey on that occasion; I only know that *two* of us returned. Since that day, Mr Betjeman has indubitably existed, – but I *wonder*.'

Betjeman, for his part, was disturbed to find that the obscure Victorian and Edwardian poets whom he regarded as his particular province were already well known to Auden, who considered them to be of no special value. He was also taken aback to hear Auden dismiss the fashionable Sitwells in a sentence, yet praise Anglo-Saxon verse that he, Betjeman, thought so boring. But he found Auden compelling. 'He was always healthily intolerant of the pretentious,' Betjeman said. 'I remember his coming into my rooms at Oxford and looking at my bookshelves and seeing there all the books that were fashionable at the time, but among them were several volumes of Edmund Blunden's poems. "These are what you really like" he said, and he was quite right.'

Betjeman was proud of his friendships with the smart 'aesthetic' set at Christ Church (which included Brian Howard and Harold Acton) and with Maurice Bowra, the Wadham College don around whom many of this circle gathered. He believed that Auden was not in the least interested in these grand friends of his – but here he was wrong. Auden later wrote of Maurice Bowra's set: 'I was not "in", but dearly wished I could be.' He said that its members impressed him because 'at an age when most young men are floundering about, they were already formed characters'.

Auden did not become involved with Betjeman's friends, no doubt partly for financial reasons. They were most of them rich, or at least comfortably off, while he could not afford extravagances, especially where drink was concerned – 'If at Oxford and for many years afterwards I drank little,' he said, 'this was a matter of chance (none of my friends drank heavily) and of money (I could not afford to drink much or often).' But it was also because he was independent and did not need to join existing circles or sets of undergraduates.[1] He preferred to find his own friends.

Among those whose company he now sought was Cecil Day-Lewis, an undergraduate in his fourth and final year reading Greats (Ancient History and Classical Philosophy) at Wadham College. Day-Lewis, who had already published his first book of poems at his own expense, was one of those whose work Auden and his fellow editor had chosen for the 1926 *Oxford Poetry*. So was Rex Warner, another fourth-year Wadham undergraduate who shared digs in St Giles with Day-Lewis, and who was unusual among Oxford poets in being a University rugger blue.

[1] The nearest that Auden seems to have got to the Brian Howard–Harold Acton 'set' at Christ Church was an occasion in his first term when he was a guest at a party at the Hypocrites' Club, in which the Howard-Acton circle took a prominent part, and which had rooms in St Aldate's, near Christ Church. At this party he met for the first time, and made sexual advances to, V. M. ('Peter') Allom, an undergraduate at Exeter College. Allom did not respond sexually, but became friends with Auden for the rest of their undergraduate years.

Auden was keen to get to know Warner because he had combined his athletic achievement with getting a First Class in Honour Moderations in Latin and Greek literature. Warner and Auden became friends; Auden described Warner in a poem as 'Rex who looked at much and much saw through'. But the friendship between them was not as close as between Auden and Day-Lewis.

An 'exceptional intelligence' was Day-Lewis's first impression of Auden. It was not the first time he had encountered such a thing at Oxford, but Auden was (he said) unusual in that he had dedicated such an intelligence to poetry: 'It was his vitality, though, rather than his intellectual power, which most impressed me at the start – a vitality so abundant that, overflowing into certain poses and follies and wildly unrealistic notions, it gave these an air of authority, an illusion of rightness, which enticed some contemporaries into taking them over-seriously.'

Most of Auden's undergraduate friends were indeed daunted by the opinions, pronouncements and judgements that he threw at them. Gertrude Stein, he said, was marvellous. Sophie Tucker was 'absolutely the *only* woman comedian'. The cinema was doomed, as was the whole of modern realistic drama. Only music-hall was any good. Ballet ought to be forbidden. People should amuse themselves by going to dog races or dirt tracks – the dirt track was 'the saga world translated into terms of the machine age'. As to poetry, a poet must have no opinions, no decided views. Poetry must certainly have nothing whatever to do with politics.

Auden's friends found all this hard enough to keep up with, not least because he had read very widely in subjects about which he pronounced. He was extraordinarily good, they noted, at extracting what was import-ant in a book in just a few minutes: he could turn the pages fast, and find the crucial passages immediately. He also had a remarkable, almost photographic, memory for what he had read, so that soon he had a large fund of knowledge at his disposal on which to base his pronouncements. This was disarming, as was his fondness for obscure words. In his conversation as in his poetry, he used a vocabulary drawn from scientific, psychological and philosophical terminology, and from his discoveries among the pages of the *Oxford English Dictionary*. Words like 'glabrous', 'sordes', 'callipygous', 'peptonised' (which all appeared in his poetry during this period) delighted him but disconcerted his listeners. 'I did not understand much of what Wystan said,' recorded one undergraduate contemporary, who nevertheless 'felt it was important because of the portentous manner in which he said it'.

Equally disconcerting – indeed more so – was his habit of entirely changing his mind. He praised Gertrude Stein to Isherwood in the autumn of 1926, but a few months later told Stephen Spender that he thought she was 'tripe'. Such sudden shifts were not uncommon. Spender, indeed, remarked that the opinions Auden held at Oxford 'impressed themselves on me the more because he reversed most of them shortly after he left'. Nor did he like to admit he had changed his opinion; his previous pronouncement seemed simply to have been wiped from his memory. This was characteristic of his behaviour in other ways. A friend noted: 'When he did make a blunder, the following week it had "never happened".' Auden once described himself as someone

> who bans from recall any painful image:
> foul behaviour, whether by Myself or Others,
> days of dejection, breakages, poor cooking,
>   are suppressed promptly.

One reason why he changed his mind was simply that he had expressed himself too strongly on the first occasion and needed to modify his original opinion. But he could never hold any view half-heartedly. Spender noted that 'one of Auden's characteristics is to make a cult of whatever he happens to be doing, which becomes to him what the poet must do'. Auden himself warned that his opinions – and those of any writer – should be treated cautiously because they were for the most part 'manifestations of his debate with himself as to what he should do next and what he should avoid'. Looking back on his time at Oxford he wrote: 'If an undergraduate announces to his tutor one morning that Gertrude Stein is the greatest writer who ever lived or that Shakespeare is no good, he is really only saying something like this: "I don't know what to write yet or how, but yesterday while reading Gertrude Stein, I thought I saw a clue" or "Reading Shakespeare yesterday, I realized that one of the faults in what I write is a tendency to rhetorical bombast."' He was in fact fully aware of his dogmatism: 'By nature I am all too prone to be a doctrinaire tyrant and schoolmaster, with an itch to mind other people's business and to burn at the stake those who disagree with me.' Nor did he wish people to take his pronouncements too seriously. 'Always remember, please,' he once wrote to a friend, 'my phantasy of myself as the Mad Clergyman. Of course I believe that I preach sense, but it is always meant to be taken cum grano. The trouble with most congregations is that either they refuse to listen to a word, or else they swallow everything quite literally.'

Though he did not always take himself too seriously, he certainly recognised, by now, that he was remarkably gifted. He accepted this fact quite calmly, but did not for a moment dispute it. On the other hand he believed that, while he could acquire knowledge quickly and easily on a superficial level, he was a slow learner of more profound things. 'I am really someone who has to grow very slowly,' he once wrote in a letter. 'I develop slower than most people.'

Those who got to know him well discovered that the intellectual brilliance and the dogmatism were balanced by a kind of humility, even simplicity; one of his friends at Oxford disconcerted those who only knew Auden's more public face by calling him 'really very kind and quite simple'. Another friend noticed that he 'had what madmen lack, a saving sense of the ridiculous'. But certainly at first acquaintance during his undergraduate years he could be overwhelming. Cecil Day-Lewis said he was 'perhaps best taken in smallish doses'.

Day-Lewis was impressed by Auden's poetry. He found it difficult to understand and sometimes unsympathetic, but always vigorous and novel – it was, he said, a poetry which 'knew its own mind'. Meanwhile Auden introduced Day-Lewis to the poetry of Hardy and Robert Frost; and Day-Lewis in turn made Auden acquainted with the later poems of Yeats. This had a great effect on Auden, who later said he had 'learned a good deal' from Yeats. But he was now mature enough not to adopt Yeats's style wholesale in the way that he had, for a time, adopted Eliot's. Day-Lewis, by contrast, though several years Auden's senior, was so struck by his fellow undergraduate that, as he said himself, 'my own verse became for a time pastiche-Auden'.

During the autumn term of 1926, when Day-Lewis and Auden were getting to know each other, an undergraduate named Louis MacNeice was spending his first term at Merton College, reading classics. Auden soon got to know 'this tall dark languid undergraduate. . . rather foppishly dressed', who, said Auden, gave the initial impression of 'a lazy over-gregarious man who spent more time than he should pub-crawling'. Auden soon discovered the sharpness of MacNeice's mind, and came to admire him; but for the time being the two of them did not get to know each other very well. MacNeice visited Auden at Christ Church – 'You came away from his presence always encouraged,' he said; 'here at least was someone to whom ideas were friendly' – and he retained a vivid impression of Auden busily 'getting on with the job'. But as undergraduates they led largely separate lives.

More important to Auden was a friendship of a different kind, in effect a love-affair. During this autumn he became very attached to a freshman at Christ Church, a history scholar named W. L. (Bill) McElwee, who had just come up from Sedbergh School. Auden made his feelings clear to McElwee; an unpublished poem, entitled 'Quique amavit' and bearing the dedication 'To the onlie begetter Mr W. L.', is in part a declaration of love, though it goes on to consider in obscure terms the complexities of the process of loving:

> You here? Which You? As lids unclose, the You
> Crushing a cigarette-end in a saucer,
> You in a kitchen, drinking, wet with snow,
> Confound the Present You. . .

It is impossible to be certain what sort of relationship Auden had with McElwee. Most of Auden's friends had the impression that McElwee was not prepared to respond to Auden's love, and would not go to bed with him, though he was flattered by the attention. According to one undergraduate contemporary, however, Auden reported that he and McElwee had made an arrangement to go to bed regularly once a week. If this was true, Auden mentioned it to no one else, and most people had the impression that his feelings for McElwee left him unhappy and unsatisfied.

Auden and McElwee agreed to spend part of the Christmas vacation of 1926 visiting Austria. After this trip, Auden wrote to David Ayerst: 'I had a very good three weeks in Austria with McElwee and no complications thank God!' By this he presumably meant that there were no homosexual complications. On the other hand it appears that during this holiday he did have a heterosexual entanglement. He and McElwee visited Kitzbühel, staying in the house of Frau Hedwig Petzold, where Auden and his father had been guests during their Austrian trip in the summer of 1925. Auden later told his brother John and one or two close friends that his first sexual experience with a woman was when he went to bed with Frau Petzold, and it seems almost certain that it was during this 1926 visit that it happened. It appears that it was she rather than he who made the initial advances. She was some years older than him. He did not say whether he had enjoyed the experience. After this he saw her again in 1934, when he was passing through the Tyrol on a motoring holiday; and after the Second World War he often visited her at Kitzbühel. But there was apparently no further sexual involvement, and in the later period of the friendship he seems to have regarded her as a mother- or aunt-figure, for many of his letters to her at that time address her as 'Dearest Tante Hedwig'.

Early in 1927 Auden visited McElwee's family, staying for part of the Easter vacation at their home in the country near Wellington in Somerset. Here he was greatly charmed by McElwee's dashingly handsome brother Pat, who began to supplant Bill McElwee in his affections. This upset Bill, who began to refer to himself as 'the discarded mistress'. (Soon afterwards he became engaged to be married.) After his visit, Auden wrote to Bill: 'Of my stay with you I cannot speak decently. Anyway you know what I feel dont you? Please give my love to Patrick and extract his impressions for me. I must know if I was successful. All my love, Wystan.'

In June, he submitted a selection of his recent poetry to the London publishers Faber & Gwyer (later Faber & Faber) at the suggestion of Sacheverell Sitwell. As Sitwell remembers it, he was asked to meet Auden by Francis Birrell, whom he recalls as being a distant cousin of Auden (a relationship that Auden's family can neither confirm nor deny). At Birrell's suggestion, he gave Auden a meal in a London restaurant. In an undated letter to Isherwood, almost certainly written in June 1927, Auden wrote: 'I had dinner with Sacheverell Sitwell the other day. . . He has made me send my things to Eliot which I did to-day. What he will say God knows.'[1]

T. S. Eliot read all the poetry that was submitted to Faber's. He took three months to reply to Auden. 'I am very slow to make up my mind,' he eventually wrote to him on 9 September. 'I do not feel that any of the enclosed is quite right, but I should be interested to follow your work.'

Auden was not too depressed. He told Isherwood: 'On the whole coming from Eliot's reserve I think it is really quite complimentary.' Meanwhile he arranged that he and Cecil Day-Lewis should jointly edit the 1927 *Oxford Poetry*; and in the summer vacation, after McElwee had stayed with him at Harborne, he and Day-Lewis set off to his favourite village of Appletreewick in Yorkshire where they were to work together on the book. 'Here all is rain and stone walls stuck on the hills like strips of liquorice', he wrote to McElwee from the New Inn at Appletreewick. 'The chauffeur at our pub is an Adonis, and there is a girl like a nut-thatcher.' He and Day-Lewis sifted through the poems they had been offered, selecting among other things several pieces by Louis MacNeice and Rex Warner, some Sitwellian word-music by Tom Driberg, and, as a private joke, an Eliotic parody, or rather a parody of Auden's own recent Eliot phase. They printed this anonymously under the title 'Souvenir des Vacances'; it was in fact by Christopher Isherwood: 'That day the steak was bad, he came. We found / The cormorant shot last year for a spy. . .' Another anonymous piece was 'An Ornithological View of Existence', a poem written by V. M. Allom, an undergraduate friend of Auden, who would not allow Auden to identify him as its author. Allom was devoted to Auden, and had addressed the poem to him on his birthday.

Auden and Day-Lewis also wrote a preface to the volume. This preface, with its definition of poetry as 'the formation of private spheres out of a public chaos', was taken in later years by several literary critics to be an early manifesto of a new movement in poetry. In actual fact it was – as Day-Lewis admitted – largely a piece of self-mockery. It did, however contain one particularly revealing statement about poetry, almost certainly the work of Auden: 'Emotion is no longer necessarily to be analysed by "recollection in tranquillity":[2] it is to be prehended emotionally and

---

[1] According to Sir Sacheverell Sitwell, the meal was held in order to introduce Auden to Eliot, and Eliot was present at it. But if this is so, it seems strange that Auden should not have mentioned meeting Eliot when he told Isherwood about the meal.

[2] This phrase is, of course, Wordsworth's. In August 1927, shortly after returning from his holiday with Day-Lewis, Auden wrote to V. M. Allom: 'The preface to Oxford Poetry is as important as the preface to the lyrical ballads.'

intellectually at once.' This is a key to the kind of poetry Auden now
began to write.

★

It was probably during this Yorkshire holiday, though with memories of
the Alston Moor lead-mining area in mind, that Auden produced a poem
which marked a turning point in his search for his own poetic voice.
Here it is in full:

> I chose this lean country
> For seven day content,
> To satisfy the want
> Of eye and ear, to see
> The slow fastidious line
> That disciplines the fell,
> A curlew's creaking call
> From angles unforeseen,
> The drumming of a snipe,
> Surprise where driven sleet
> Had scalded to the bone
> And streams were acrid yet
> To an unaccustomed lip.
>
> So stepping yesterday
> To climb a crooked valley,
> I scrambled in a hurry
> To twist the bend and see
> Sheds crumbling stone by stone,
> The awkward waterwheel
> Of a deserted mine;
> And sitting by the fall
> Spoke with a poet there
> Of Margaret the brazen leech,
> And that severe Christopher,
> Of such and such and such
> Till talk tripped over love,
> And both dropped silent in
> The contemplation of
> A singular vision
> And sceptical beholder,
> While a defiant bird
> Fell down and scolding stood
> Upon a sun-white boulder.

Last night, sucked giddy down
The funnel of my dream,
I saw myself within
A buried engine-room.
Dynamos, boilers, lay
In tickling silence, I
Gripping an oily rail,
Talked feverishly to one
Professional listener
Who puckered mouth and brow
In ecstasy of pain,
'I know, I know, I know'
And reached his hand for mine.

Now in a brown study
At the water-logged quarry,
I think how everyman
Shall strain and be undone,
Sit, querulous and sallow
Under the abject willow,
Turning a stoic shoulder
On a Saint Martin's summer,
Till death shall sponge away
The idiotic sun,
And lead this people to
A mildewed dormitory.
But as I see them go,
A blackbird's sudden scurry
Lets broken treetwigs fall
To shake the torpid pool;
And, breaking from the copse,
I climb the hill, my corpse
Already wept, and pass
Alive into the house.

There are, of course, private references in the poem. The 'poet' in the second stanza may be Day-Lewis; 'Margaret the brazen leech' was Day-Lewis's friend Margaret Marshall, a psychiatrist, who later became Auden's brother John's first wife ('leech' is here used in the sense of 'doctor'); and 'that severe Christopher' is of course Isherwood. But these references are not put in to amuse the coterie of Auden's friends; they are meant to be as obscure as is the unexplained 'professional listener' of the dream in the third stanza. The poem is a self-contained private world, a 'private sphere' as the *Oxford Poetry* preface put it. Built up of fragments from Auden's memory – the landscape of the Cumbrian fells round Alston, a deserted lead mine, an underground engine-room such as the one he saw during his childhood holiday at Rhayader, a waterlogged quarry perhaps seen in North Wales, even public school (the 'mildewed dormitory') – it creates a 'lean country' which is a country of the mind, a piece of private incommunicable feeling, a setting for some experience of pain (probably frustrated love) which is itself obscure and unexplained. The obscurity itself is the whole point of the poem, and of others that Auden was shortly to write.

In July 1927, after returning from his holiday with Day-Lewis, Auden set off with his father to visit Yugoslavia. The trip was apparently not a success. 'I once went to Yugoslavia with father and wished I was dead,' Auden wrote some years later, though he told Stephen Spender that some of the Yugoslav boys were the most beautiful he had ever seen. The journey gave rise to another poem, as obscure and strange as 'I chose this lean country', with an opening that seems to reflect Auden's experiences travelling across Europe:

> On the frontier at dawn getting down,
> Hot eyes were soothed with swallows: ploughs began
> Upon the stunted ridge behind the town,
> And bridles flashed. . .

He and his father visited Dubrovnik and Split, and after a few weeks returned to England, where, back home in Harborne, Auden wrote a poem which was the first that he was to preserve later in life in collections of his poems; in other words it was the first piece that, looking back, he judged to be mature and competent. It was entitled, appropriately, given its significance in his life, 'The Watershed'. Or rather, when he first printed it, it had no title at all. He was going through a period of believing that a poem should not need a title to explain it but, as he told John Betjeman, 'should be its own title'.

The new poem, which began 'Who stands, the crux left of the watershed', superficially resembled his earlier celebration of lead mines, 'Lead's the Best'; it also borrowed from a short piece he had written in schooldays, 'The Pumping Engine, Cashwell'. But while these had simply revelled in the old mine workings and the decaying machinery, the new poem made such things into sombre and sinister images: 'dismantled washing-floors', a 'ramshackle engine', and a solitary man whose coffin is laid in 'long abandoned levels'. These became symbols of something more than just 'an industry already comatose', which is the ostensible subject of the poem. And 'The Watershed' ends with the poet, a young middle-class intellectual, turning away baffled and frustrated, feeling that this 'lean country' is hostile to him and will not communicate with him.

Towards the end of the summer vacation of 1927, Auden travelled to the north of Scotland, where, at Carr Bridge near Inverness, he joined a reading party of undergraduates organised by Ernest Jacob, tutor in medieval history at Christ Church. They stayed in lodgings, working at their own studies in the morning and going for walks in the afternoon. Auden wrote a poem beginning 'Suppose they met, the inevitable procedure / Of hand to nape would drown the staling cry / Of cuckoos'. It expressed regret at the failure to consummate love because of the pressure of old outdated morality; the lovers in the poem 'slept apart though doors were never locked' because they still feared 'that doddering Jehovah whom they mocked'. The last line, 'Down they fell; sorrow they had after that', was an echo of Anglo-Saxon or early Middle English poetry. After he had returned to Harborne, Auden wrote another poem ('Nor was that final, for about that time') which contained a direct borrowing from *The Dream of the Rood* (line 13): 'Wonderful was that cross and I full of sin'. But despite his fascination with Anglo-Saxon, his academic work was not going well. During this year he wrote to Bill McElwee: 'I am depressed about work. . . My mind works abominably slowly, in a vague mush of tepid ideas. . . and I am lazy, impatient and feeble.'

★

He returned to Oxford to begin his final year there. His tutor Nevill Coghill noticed that Auden now had great intellectual prestige among his fellow undergraduates. 'His sayings were widely misquoted,' wrote Coghill, 'and would appear in their garbled form, in the essays of my other pupils. These being cross-examined, and their nonsense laid bare, still held the trump, which they would play when nothing else would save them: "*Well, anyhow, that's what Wystan says.*"' David Ayerst, looking back many years later, observed that Auden's influence over his contemporaries at Oxford was immense – while, in return, Auden himself was scarcely influenced by any of them.

Auden was fully aware of his prestige in undergraduate circles. Indeed he cultivated it by the manner in which he behaved. 'Calling on Auden was a serious business,' one of them recalled. 'On the occasion of my fulfilling my first appointment, he was seated in a darkened room with the curtains drawn, and a lamp on a table at his elbow, so that he could see me clearly and I could only see the light reflected on his pale face. . . He jerked his head up and asked me to sit down. There followed a rather terse cross-examination. . . "What poets do you like?" he asked. "Blunden," I said. "Not bad. Who else?" I mentioned another name. "Up the wrong pole." Another. "Written ravishing lines, but has the mind of a ninny.". . . He asked me how often I wrote poetry. Without reflecting, I replied that I wrote about four poems a day. He was astonished and exclaimed: "What energy!" I asked him how often he wrote a poem. He replied: "I write about one in three weeks." After this I started writing only one poem in three weeks.'

This account was written by Stephen Spender, who arrived at Oxford as an undergraduate this term, the autumn of 1927. Spender, an immensely tall young man with wild curly hair (Louis MacNeice called him a 'towering angel not quite sure if he was fallen'), came from a London family where Liberal politics and writing were the chief occupations. He had been fascinated ever since arriving at the University by the legend that surrounded Auden. When a mutual friend, A. H. Campbell, eventually gave a luncheon party at which Spender and Auden were introduced to each other, Spender found the reality just as remarkable as that legend.

Auden, he discovered, now seemed to regard himself as the leader of a new movement. As Spender put it, 'a group of emergent artists existed in his mind, like a cabinet in the mind of a party leader'. Each member was to have his own function when, so to speak, they came to power. Isherwood was to be the Novelist; Auden's school-friend Robert Medley would be the Painter; Cecil Day-Lewis, who had now taken his degree and was teaching at a preparatory school in North Oxford, was to be in it too. Stephen Spender was surprised to find that, after a few weeks, Auden considered him to be a member as well.

Spender showed Auden his own poems and did not receive much encouragement. 'After I had known him six weeks', he said, 'he must have approved of as many of my lines. Therefore it was rather surprising to discover that he considered me a member of "the Gang". Once I told him I wondered whether I ought to write prose, and he answered: "You must write nothing but poetry, we do not want to lose you for poetry." This remark produced in me a choking moment of hope mingled with despair, in which I cried: "But do you really think I am any good?" "Of course," he replied frigidly. "But why?" "Because you are so infinitely capable of being humiliated. Art is born of humiliation," he added in his icy voice – and left me wondering when *he* could feel humiliated.'

Though 'the Gang' may have existed in Auden's mind, he made no attempt to gather its members together for any kind of meeting, or to issue orders to them. Spender noted that, however group-conscious he might be, Auden preferred to see his friends one at a time, rather in the manner of an inquisitor or analyst – though it is true that Auden eventually introduced Spender to Isherwood; they met in Auden's rooms one bright sunny day when the curtains were drawn as usual and Auden wore a green shade over his eyes: 'like an amateur chemist', said Spender. Spender also found that Auden took a delight in running his friends' lives, especially their sex-lives; Spender's private problems were soon being exposed and analysed just as Isherwood's had been. Meanwhile Spender, like Day-Lewis, began to write poems containing Auden-like references to factories and gasometers.

Auden's own emotional life was no more satisfactory than it had been. In the autumn of 1927 Bill McElwee introduced him to a Christ Church freshman named Gabriel Carritt, who like McElwee had come to Oxford from Sedbergh. Carritt, who had captained the Sedbergh rugby

team, was strikingly attractive, and Auden soon fell in love with him and
told him so. The two of them then had what Spender described as a
'mildly tormenting and tormented relationship', which was painful to
Auden because Carritt would not respond to his sexual advances. This
pain seems to lie behind a poem Auden wrote in November 1927, a few
weeks after he had met and fallen in love with Carritt. Though it is as
mysterious and difficult to interpret as are most of his poems from this
period, the subject seems to be the failure of nerve when the lover is faced
with the challenge of actual sexual action. The imagery is an extraordinary
mixture of public schools, Icelandic sagas, and surgical operations:

> Because sap fell away
> Before cold night's attack, we see
> A harried vegetation.
> Upon our failure come
> Down to the lower changing-room,
> Honours on pegs, cast humours, we sit lax,
> In close ungenerous intimacy,
> Remember
> Falling in slush, shaking hands
> With a snub-nosed winner;
> Open a random locker, sniff with distaste
> At a mouldy passion.
>
> Love, is this love, that notable forked-one,
> Riding away from the farm, the ill word said,
> Fought at the frozen dam? Who prophesied
> Such lethal factors, understood
> The indolent ulcer? Brought in now,
> Love lies at surgical extremity;
> Gauze pressed over the mouth, a breathed surrender.

The original manuscript bears the note 'For G. C.', and the poem
certainly refers to Carritt; in a later, unpublished, poem addressed to
him, Auden wrote: 'The snub-nosed winner I called you. . .'[1]

He said that he regarded Carritt as a 'winner' because of Carritt's
spiritual peace. He wrote to him, a few years later: 'Your peculiar virtue
– and of course you know this – is as a comforter. You will always be
surrounded by people with superior talents and less peace of spirit who

---

[1] It has often been said, with justification, that Auden's love-poetry transcends the love-
affairs which prompted it, and that it is a mistake to search too closely for the particular
circumstances behind each poem. Nevertheless Auden wrote, into Chester Kallman's copy
of *Poems* (the 1934 American edition), in about 1939, the initials of some of the lovers or
loved-ones who had prompted particular poems. Among these, the poem 'From the very
first coming down' (written in December 1927) is marked 'W. M.' (McElwee). Later
poems are, in several cases, identified as having been inspired by Auden's various Berlin
boyfriends during 1928-9.

will be devoted to you.' The remark about 'superior talents' shows that he did not think of Carritt as being his equal intellectually, and when Carritt showed him some poems that he had written, Auden was merciless. 'Re the poem,' he wrote to Carritt, 'I find it exceedingly difficult to say much. It is very carefully written, there are admirable lines; it whiffs beautifully of you – but – what shall I say – it is the poetry of the perfect patron; the sort of thing King James of Scotland would have delighted Dunbar with. I don't mean that it was not worth writing – you enjoyed doing it and it will always please your friends – but I do not feel it is the work of a creative mind.'

He continued to love Carritt despite the difficulties of their relationship. Three years after they had first met he wrote to him: 'I realise that though I seldom see you and do not think of you very often, whenever I do I know that there is no one I love so much, no one with whom I feel so complete a trust, a blood-brotherhood in the Lawrence sense.'

During December 1927 and January 1928, at Oxford and at home in Harborne, Auden wrote three poems whose subject was the difficulties of love: 'From the very first coming down', 'The four sat on in the bare room', and 'Control of the passes was, he saw, the key' – the latter being the poem to which he later gave the title 'The Secret Agent', and in which the figure of the Spy seems to represent the sexual urges of the individual which are destroyed (shot for treachery) by the conscious will. But if Auden's unsatisfied love for Carritt was the immediate cause of some of these poems, it was no more than a pretext for them. The poems themselves, with their dream-like imagery, entirely transcend the personal circumstances behind them.[1] The charge could even be levelled against Auden that he entered into such relationships as his entanglement with Carritt in order to stimulate his art. Spender may have suspected something of the sort when he wrote: 'Auden, despite his perceptiveness, lacked something in human relationships. He forced issues too much, made everyone too conscious of himself and therefore was in the position of an observer who is a disturbing force in the behaviour he observes. Sometimes he gave the impression of playing an intellectual game with himself and with others and this meant that in the long run he was rather isolated.'

★

Carritt's father was an Oxford don who taught philosophy at University College, and the family lived just outside Oxford, on Boar's Hill. Auden

---

[1]This dream element was a piece of conscious craft by Auden, and was not usually the product either of real dreams or of stream-of-consciousness writing. Auden said: 'Only once in my life have I had a dream which, on conscious consideration, seemed interesting enough to write down' (*A Certain World*, p. 126). This dream appears in *Letters from Iceland* (2nd edition), pp. 146-7. The poem 'Dear, though the night is gone' was also based on a real dream.

visited them often, and after initially shocking them by his bluntness ('Mrs Carritt,' he remarked one day, 'my tea tastes like tepid piss') he was accepted as an entertaining addition to the household, striking up with Mrs Carritt an almost mother–son relationship. He also went on long walks with Gabriel Carritt in the neighbourhood of Oxford. It was during one of these that Carritt noticed an odd characteristic – 'Auden's belief in fate', as he put it. They were walking on the downs near Wantage when Auden discovered he had lost three pounds from his trouser pocket. 'Never mind,' he said, 'we will pick them up on the way back.' Four hours later, in the dusk, as they returned along the ridgeway, they saw three notes fluttering in the grass. Auden picked them up and put them back in his pocket without a word. He retained this attitude of mind to the end of his life; he was, he said himself, someone who, when he reached a cross-roads, assumed that the traffic-lights would turn green for him.

At the Carritts', Auden met another undergraduate, Richard Crossman, who was already interested in politics but also played rugby and wrote poems. Auden admired, indeed rather envied, the handsome and ambitious Crossman; he referred to him in an unpublished poem as 'Dick. . . whose mind is muscular, whose body strong'. It seems that he and Crossman (who was going through a homosexual phase) went to bed together on at least one occasion. Carritt was not aware of this side to his friends' relationship, but Auden himself claimed in later years that it had happened.

Auden persuaded Crossman to come on an expedition to Sedbergh, Carritt's and McElwee's old school in the north of England, to watch Carritt play rugby there in an old boys' match. Sedbergh had in fact come to fascinate Auden. It was a peculiarly spartan establishment even by the standard of public schools, and Auden listened with horrified delight as Carritt described the tough boys and masters, their athletic achievements, their feuds and intrigues – especially, of course, sexual. Nor was it only Sedbergh that he found alluring in this respect. He and Isherwood announced that they were planning to compile a three-volume study of preparatory school, public school and university 'confessions'; and for a time Auden's friends at Oxford found their drawers being rifled for any letters suitable for inclusion – such as several written to Gabriel Carritt by an Old Sedberghian now working in South America, who signed himself 'Piggy', and described in them his passion for small boys. Auden copied out these letters, and one day read them aloud to A. L. Rowse, by then a newly-elected Fellow of All Souls, probably with the intention of making Rowse admit his own sexual feelings. Rowse, however, was merely embarrassed, and swiftly brought the proceedings to a close. The 'confessions' book did not proceed beyond this stage.

Sedbergh appears by implication in a poem, as dream-like as those that had preceded it, which Auden wrote in March 1928, beginning 'Taller to-day, we remember similar evenings'; for the 'Captain Ferguson' referred to without explanation in it was an ex-army officer who was on the staff at Sedbergh. There are also shades of the same school in an extended verse and prose composition that Auden began to put together during the first six months of 1928, 'Paid on Both Sides', which he described as 'A Charade'.

Between January and April he wrote a number of short lyrics which, he said later, 'seemed to be part of something', though they were originally intended to be separate poems. This 'something' gradually proved to be a blend of lead-mining country, public schools and Icelandic sagas, with, as a theme, the failure of sexual love through the pressure of social convention and the warped personality of the lover. All this was of course the stuff of the poems he was already composing. What was different was the extended form. Auden decided to attempt dramatic writing, and, since he had been invited by the McElwees to their house in Somerset during the coming August, he selected the form of a charade (a favourite amusement during country-house weekends) in the hope that they might perform it there. It was in fact not strictly a charade in that no guessing of words was involved, but it required no scenery beyond ordinary domestic furniture and objects, and the costumes specified in the stage directions[1] were to be the usual country-house clothes – an evening frock, plus-fours, dinner jackets, a panama hat. The chorus were to wear 'rugger things', with the chorus leader in a scrum cap.

Isherwood believed that 'Paid on Both Sides' grew out of the comparison he and Auden had made between the two worlds of the Icelandic sagas and English boarding schools, which, they maintained, shared a common culture of feuds, practical jokes, and dark threats conveyed in under-statements. This probably was the origin of the 'charade', but even in the first version that Auden wrote – which is considerably shorter than the text he eventually published – the mood is more sombre than this might suggest.

The scene is the territory occupied by two rival families, the Shaws and the Nowers. The harsh-sounding place-names that Auden uses have led some people to suppose he meant to suggest the setting of an Icelandic saga. In fact many of the names are taken from the map of his favourite lead-mining landscape in Cumberland.[2] The play opens with a

[1]Only in the first version of 'Paid', now printed as an appendix to *The English Auden*; no such directions were included in Auden's original published text.

[2]Nattrass, the home of the Shaws, is a farm to the south-east of Alston, and the Nowers' home, Lintzgarth, is near Rookhope, a village to the east of Alston which is itself mentioned in the charade. Brandon Walls and Garrigill are near Rookhope and Alston respectively; and Auden, as if to emphasise the public-school element in 'Paid', also refers in passing to the Hangs, a valley to the north of Gresham's School, and to Cautley, which is near Sedbergh.

choral lament for 'killings in old winter, death of friend's; next, a more specific account of the feud is given – 'A Nower dragged out in the night, a Shaw / Ambushed behind the wall'. The play then shows the feud in action; the motive for each killing is simply revenge: 'He sniped poor Dick last Easter, riding to Flash.' Diction and imagery suggest public schools: 'Keep low and run like hell'; 'Fell on the ball near time, the rushing of forwards stopped.' Aaron Shaw, head of one of the two clans, proposes peace, and the engagement of John Nower and Anne Shaw is announced. Guests arrive for the wedding, anger is put away, and there is dancing and inane chatter. But the mother of Seth Shaw demands that her son kill William Nower, who murdered Seth's brother. Seth gives in, William is shot, and as the play ends there is obviously more killing to come. The concluding chorus refers not just to the feud but to the even deeper conflict between the lovers and the mothers. For, though 'Man thinks to be called the fortunate, / To bring home a wife', he is defeated by the maternal powers – 'His mother and her mother won' – and the result is dryness and sterility: 'His fields are used up where the moles visit, / The contours worn flat. . .'.

Auden probably finished this first version of 'Paid on Both Sides'[1] during June or July 1928. Meanwhile, at the beginning of June, he concluded his undergraduate career at Oxford by taking 'Schools', the examination for his Bachelor of Arts Degree.

During the weeks preceding the examination he was in a bad state of mind about it. At Easter he wrote to Bill McElwee: 'I am just recovering from a week of abject depression which culminated in my getting flu.' And in another letter: 'Schools are becoming a nightmare. I have even less character or intellect than I thought; and I shall start blood-spitting next week.'

When the examination began, at the end of the summer term, Auden's desk was near to that of an undergraduate from Oriel who knew him, J. I. M. Stewart. He noticed that Auden was evidently feeling very distressed during the papers, and thought this strange in 'a figure we all regarded as triumphantly above such petty matters'. After the Anglo-Saxon paper, Bill McElwee found Auden in his rooms, weeping.[2] When the list was posted some weeks later, Auden's name was in the Third Class.

The result puzzled, and has continued to puzzle, Auden's friends. A

---

[1]Laurence Heyworth has discovered that the title was taken by Auden from *Beowulf*, lines 1304-6: 'That was not good bargain, that they should pay on both sides with the lives of friends.'

[2]Stephen Spender comments of this, in a letter to the present writer: 'Auden had very weak and watery eyes (hence the green eye shade). Whilst he was taking his Finals they – not he – wept continuously. He had been overworking before he took Finals and was in an exhausted state.'

First would have caused no surprise; nor for that matter a Fourth or a complete failure, which would have suggested that he held the examination in contempt. But a Third suggests merely poor-quality work, which seems incompatible with his character and abilities.

One explanation may lie in the personality of the examiners, who in the summer of 1928 were J. R. R. Tolkien, Ernest de Selincourt the Wordsworth scholar, Allen Mawer from Liverpool University, and David Nichol Smith, who had refused to take on Auden as a pupil. None of them, not even Auden's admired Tolkien, would have been sympathetic to flights of fancy in the examination answers, least of all Nichol Smith, a severe teacher and critic who in later years, when Auden had become famous, would growl: 'I gave him a Third.' But quite apart from this, Auden had clearly suffered a loss of confidence before the examination, and had either failed to catch up on the work he should have done during the previous two years, or had (conceivably) overworked at the last minute.

He himself was inclined in later years to put the result down to laziness – 'I didn't do a stroke of work,' he once remarked, 'so I got a Third.' He also explained his Third, surely with some truth, as the consequence of having a poet's mind rather than an academic's. 'It is hardly surprising', he wrote, 'if a young poet seldom does well in his examinations. . . There is nothing a would-be poet knows he has to know. He is at the mercy of the immediate moment. . . He makes little distinction between a book, a country walk and a kiss. All are equally experiences to store away in his memory.'

Yet another reason is provided by V. M. Allom, who was a pupil of Nevill Coghill and often attended tutorials with Auden. He writes:

Surprise has often been expressed that at the end of it all Wystan gained only a Third Class, but this does not really surprise me at all. With all his gifts, Nevill was no intellectual disciplinarian, while at the same time he was as yet an inexperienced tutor, apt to overrate the academic chances of interesting pupils. The result was that, so long as he found his pupils intelligent and appreciative, they were left very much to pursue their own ways, and were in consequence apt finally to take Schools ill prepared for the intellectual battle which this entailed. Moreover Wystan, highly intelligent though he was, had nothing of the true scholar in his composition. He was primarily interested in literature as an art, and not as a subject for analytical dissection. Under these circumstances a Third seems to me to be the very natural outcome.

Whatever the reasons for his poor showing in the exam, Auden seems to have been shocked by the result when it was announced in midsummer 1928. He wrote to David Ayerst: 'My dear David: It was nice of you to write. Thank you. "Well now that's done and I'm glad it's over." There is no more to be said except that I probably deserved it, though I dont feel as if I did.'

After going down from Oxford he stayed for some days with Stephen Spender's family at Frognal in north London. Spender had bought a small hand-operated printing press and some type, and was printing a booklet of his own poems. Auden suggested that he might produce a similar pamphlet of his (Auden's) work too. Spender agreed, and Auden put together a sequence of poems he had written in recent months, together with several of the lyrics that were at that moment finding their way into 'Paid on Both Sides'. He arranged the poems roughly in chronological order of composition; they chiefly covered the period May 1927 to August 1928, and included a few fragments from previous years.

Spender had difficulties with the printing. The press, which had only cost him seven pounds, was not really adequate for the job, and would not ink the type evenly. He also made mistakes in the typesetting. After printing slightly more that half of the thirty-seven pages he gave up and, on his return to Oxford for the autumn term, got the Holywell Press to finish it off for him and to bind the small book (which measured only a few inches across) in an orange wrapper. The title-page carried the words: 'W. H. Auden / POEMS / S. H. S. [Spender's initials]: 1928.' The book bore the dedication 'To Christopher Isherwood', on the verso of which was the statement that the edition consisted of 'About 45 copies'.

While Spender was printing the book, Auden was in Belgium. On his return he reported to David Ayerst that he had been 'in Spa for 3 weeks, staying with a psychologist'. Exactly what this means is not clear – David Ayerst himself does not know; possibly the psychologist was a friend of Auden's father, and it is conceivable that during the visit Auden underwent analysis; certainly Isherwood remembers Auden being psycho-analysed at about this time. The letter to Ayerst, which reports that Spa was 'quite an amusing place, full of Lesbians weighing 110 Kilos', seems to imply that, perhaps as the result of analysis, Auden had become bisexual, for it concludes: 'I find I am quite ambidextrous now.' Whatever happened, he was not much impressed by psychiatry. In later years he declared that psychiatrists were 'ruled by an interest in money', and that psychoanalysis was 'doing penance by paying till it hurts'.

On his return from Spa he visited the McElwees in Somerset; but 'Paid on Both Sides' was not performed during his visit as he had intended it to be. 'They refuse to do the play,' he wrote to Isherwood, 'as they say the village won't stand it.'

When the booklet of poems was ready, Auden gave copies to friends,[1]

---

[1]Among those to whom he gave copies were Isherwood, David Ayerst, Gabriel Carritt, Sidney Newman the Christ Church organ scholar, E. R. Dodds, John Layard, and (a little

altering several words in each one before he did so. This was partly to correct Spender's errors, but also to improve one or two poems, for he did not accept the view that a poem was finished the moment it was put into print. He did not, however, make any attempt to improve the punctuation, which was to say the least inadequate in many poems. 'Logical punctuation', he said a few years later, 'is something I don't understand. I can only think of them as breathing indications.'

Among those who received a copy of *Poems* was E. R. Dodds, the Professor of Greek at Birmingham, whom Auden's father had got to know through the local Classical Association. Dodds studied the small booklet carefully, and was struck by the distinctive landscape in the poems – valley and fell, frontier and dam, stream and glacier, ruined mine and flooded quarry – a landscape pregnant with meaning, though precisely what meaning was not clear. Dodds said of the poems: 'I found many of them maddeningly obscure (as I still do); the connections of thought often baffled me; but I recognized the tones of a new, completely individual voice and the presence of some highly compressed message which was trying to force its way into expression.'

To Spender, these poems of Auden's gave the impression of an intellectual game – 'a game to which the name Clinical Detachment might be given'. And he observed that the Auden who had now left Oxford was someone who was beginning to devote his life to 'an intellectual effort to analyse, explain and dominate his circumstances'. As another friend put it, Auden was 'a conceptualizer in quest of intellectual order'. Auden himself agreed with this definition of his mind. 'As you know,' he once wrote to Spender, 'my dominant faculties are intellect and intuition, my weak ones feeling and sensation. This means I have to approach life via the former; I must have knowledge and a great deal of it before I can feel anything.'

★

It seems to have been at about this time, shortly after leaving Oxford, that Auden, quietly and with no explanation to his friends, became engaged to be married. It is not known to whom, though the name 'Sheilah' appears in a journal he began to keep some months later, and may be a reference to his fiancée. Stephen Spender was introduced to her; he remembers that she was a nurse, possibly a psychiatric nurse, and thinks she lived in Birmingham, but he knows nothing more, nor do any

later) Cyril Connolly, to whom he gave Spender's own copy, which he promised to replace but never did. A. L. Rowse also received a copy, but was made to pay for it. Copies are now held by (among other libraries) the Bodleian, the Library of King's College, Cambridge, Durham University Library, Columbia University Library, the New York Public Library (Berg Collection), and the University of Cincinnatti Library.

of Auden's surviving friends or relatives. Auden's first mention of her that has been found is in a letter to Cecil Day-Lewis, written before Christmas 1928, probably during November or early December, where he talks very briefly of 'my fiancée'. It is possible that the engagement was the result of Auden's 'ambidextrous' (bisexual) feelings on his return from Spa. Whatever the truth, his relationship with his fiancée does not seem to have been very important to him, judging by his behaviour in the next few months.

He decided that, before looking for a job, he would spend some time in Berlin. His father had agreed to pay him an allowance until his twenty-third birthday, which would fall in a little over eighteen months' time, and Berlin seemed an attractive place to live for a while. 'I knew no German and no German literature,' he said in explanation of this, 'but I felt out of sympathy with French culture, partly by temperament and partly in revolt against the generation of intellectuals immediately preceding mine, which was strongly Francophile.' Late in August 1928 he wrote to David Ayerst: 'I am going off to Berlin for a year.' And he added: 'Is Berlin very wicked?'

5

Berlin

His first lodgings in Berlin were in a middle-class suburb, Nikolassee, on the east bank of the Wannsee, the city's largest lake. He was a paying guest with the Muthesius family, who lived in the Potsdamer Chaussee. He found that his hosts wanted to practise their English on him, which did not much improve his knowledge of German. But he quickly learnt his way around the city, and managed to get to see an early performance of a new play by the thirty-year-old Bertolt Brecht, with music by Kurt Weill, *Die Dreigroschenoper*.

Auden's appreciation of *The Threepenny Opera* at this first perform-ance was certainly limited by his ignorance of German, and in later years he resisted the suggestion that Brecht was a strong influence on his dra-matic writing. He ascribed the 'Brechtian' use of song in *The Dog Beneath the Skin* to his admiration for what he called the 'wonderful German cabaret' rather than to Brecht himself. He claimed that he was more impressed by Brecht's lyric poetry than by his dramatic work; once he had learnt German, he read and enjoyed some of the songs from *Mahagonny* which were printed in 1927. But the fact that he later collaborated on English translations of several of Brecht's plays suggests that he had more admiration for them than he was sometimes prepared to admit; and when in 1943 a friend gave him a set of *Dreigroschenoper* records for his birthday he said he was 'revelling in nostalgia'.

David Ayerst, knowing that Auden was going to Berlin, had arranged for him to meet a friend of his who was staying in the city for some months, a man named John Layard. Ayerst had met Layard in 1927, and had been struck by him as someone who was mentally sick yet who also had a very powerful personality – someone who was in need of healing, yet who could himself heal others. Soon after Auden's arrival in Berlin, he and Layard began an odd relationship.

The son of a barrister and writer, John Willoughby Layard was a distant cousin of Sir Austen Henry Layard the archaeologist. He was born in 1891, read Medieval and Modern Languages at King's College,

Cambridge, and after graduating visited (in 1914-15) the island of Malekula, which is one of the New Hebrides in the southern Pacific. Layard made this trip initially in company with W. H. R. Rivers, the Cambridge psychologist and anthropologist, in order to conduct field-work among the native population. Returning to England with the intention of publishing an account of his discoveries, Layard suffered a severe nervous breakdown which resulted in physical paralysis. Unable even to walk, he became a patient of the unorthodox American psychologist Homer Lane, who was then living and working in England. Lane managed to cure the paralysis, but Layard was still unable to write his book, and remained mentally sick – he had private means and was not obliged to earn his living. He continued as a patient of Lane, and was utterly distraught when in 1925 Lane was arrested on a technicality under the Aliens Act and insinuations were made about his character – Lane was alleged to have had sexual relations with a woman patient; there were 'indelicate' pictures in his consulting room, and a number of 'French preventatives' were found there. Deportation was threatened, but in any case Lane now left England for France; he caught typhoid in Nice and died there in September 1925. Meanwhile John Layard fled to Vienna in search of psychiatric help, and then went, for the same purpose, to Berlin, where he arrived in 1926. He was still there in 1928 when Auden came over from England.

At David Ayerst's suggestion, Layard telephoned Auden, and was 'horrified at his very pronounced Oxford accent (*I* was always trying to identify myself with whatever place I was living in)'. They arranged that Auden should come round to Layard's Berlin lodgings one afternoon, which he did. He found Layard, with his hawk-like nose and piercing eyes, a man of remarkable personality. He was also greatly interested, during that afternoon, by Layard's exposition of the striking psychological doctrines of Homer Lane.

Lane, who had run reformatories for young offenders in England and America, believed that 'human nature is innately good; the unconscious processes are in no way immoral'. (This has been called 'the Doctrine of Original Virtue'.) Lane argued from this that complete freedom of behaviour – full self-expression – must lead inevitably to goodness, anything unethical quickly being eliminated after initial mistakes. A failure to permit this full self-expression, together with the suppression of desires, especially in childhood, will lead to neurosis. As Auden himself expressed this in a notebook entry not long after he met Layard: '"Be good and you will be happy" is a dangerous inversion. "Be happy and you will be good" is the truth.'

Lane's teachings, of course, bore a certain resemblance to those of Freud, who did not so much influence Lane as work on similar lines; and Auden was already well read in Freud's writings. The originality of Lane was in the view that all instinctive behaviour is not just biologically 'good' but *morally* desirable too – a view that led Lane, in his lectures, into convolutions and inconsistencies which John Layard, in his conversations with Auden, did not attempt to resolve.

Indeed Layard himself went even further, and gave Auden an exposition of human psychology which, while being based on Lane's teachings, also drew on the ideas of others. He went further than Lane in declaring that the term 'God' really means our physical desires, the inner law of our own nature, and that the real 'Devil' is in fact the conscious control of these desires – something that we should avoid at all costs. (This is not at all what Lane believed. He said that conscious control was 'Mother Law', and believed it could be operated sensibly and to good ends.) The only sin, declared Layard, is disobedience to God (our desires) and obedience to the Devil (conscious control). This disobedience results from early 'moral' education, as a result of which we regard God as unreasonable and the Devil as right. We should in fact reject what our educators have told us are the 'right' kinds of feelings – meekness, forbearance, consideration for others, self-sacrifice, even pity – if these have been merely consciously, and thus falsely, induced in us. If we allow our desires to take charge, we will achieve a growth in real spirituality and pureness of heart.

This teaching owes something to D. H. Lawrence, as Auden realised, in particular to Lawrence's *Fantasia of the Unconscious*, published in 1922, which attacks humanity's preference for 'cerebral activity' rather than 'living from the spontaneous centres'. As Lawrence puts it:

It is the impulse we have to live by, not the ideals or the idea. . . The Ideal is *always* evil, no matter what ideal it be. . . 'Be yourself' is the last motto.

Auden was greatly impressed by Lawrence when he first read him, which was either while he was an undergraduate or shortly after. He said of Lawrence: 'It was his message which made the greatest impression on me, so that it was his "think" books like *Fantasia of the Unconscious* rather than his fiction which I read most avidly. As for his poetry, when I first tried to read it, I did not like it; despite my admiration for him, it offended my notions of what poetry should be.'

Another influence on Layard's teaching was, as Auden observed, André Gide, with his insistence that humanity should act without the restraint of accepted morality. Gide, like Layard, called the natural desires 'God', and declared that 'to grow straight you need nothing now but the urge of your sap and the sun's call'.

A third and perhaps even more influential figure behind Layard's ideas was the German psychologist Georg Groddeck, with whom Layard had some slight personal acquaintance. Auden very likely recognised Groddeck's influence when Layard declared to him, in Berlin, that the result of denying the call of 'God' and listening to 'the Devil' was physical illness. Layard had himself, of course, suffered physical disability (paralysis) as a result of mental disturbance, and it was no doubt this that encouraged him to take a psychosomatic view of illness. Layard declared that when disease – any disease – strikes, the body is indicating that the soul is sick; 'purity of heart' has been lost, 'God' has been imprisoned, and 'the Devil' is in charge. Sickness makes the sufferer revert to a helpless and thus childlike state in which a cure of the soul is possible. This idea is not foreign to Homer Lane, who believed that unconscious conflict was the cause of all physical ills, but it owes much more to Groddeck, the remarkable psychologist (he has been called 'the only analyst who influenced Freud') who believed that the deepest element of human personality is the 'It', a mysterious force which rules both body and mind. Auden himself once paraphrased this doctrine of Groddeck's in a poem: 'We are lived by powers we pretend to understand.'

Groddeck held that all diseases are caused by this 'It' for other than purely physical reasons. For example, constipation (he alleged) is an indication that the sufferer is a miser by nature, a hoarder of things. Tonsilitis shows, in the unwillingness to swallow, a desire to guard one-self against outside influences. Hoarseness is 'the It's attempts to prevent something conscious or unconscious from being uttered aloud'. Groddeck continues:

> If the It does not achieve its ends, if its ends are too numerous and too difficult to be achieved by such simple means as hoarseness or constipation, then it will not stop at these, but will grasp at appendicitis, at abscesses, at tumours, at cancer.

Sickness is, in other words, evidence of some self-deception in the sufferer, and can only be eradicated not by medical treatment but by the elimination of this deceit from the personality. Groddeck declared bluntly:

> The way of sickness is no honourable way, and whoever thinks it possible and desirable to be honest would do well to teach the It other ways of action.

Groddeck's teaching on disease was taken over wholesale by John Layard. He believed, for example, that epilepsy was due to 'the suppression of rage', and that septicaemia was caused by 'lack of spirituality quite as much as lack of merely physical hygiene'. And he laughed conventional medical treatment to scorn.

Though Layard's teaching owed its origin to other people, some of whose books Auden may already have read, Layard's own personality gave his doctrines a special force, while Auden for his own part must have been a receptive listener. Layard told him what he wanted to hear.

Certainly he had already practised much of what Layard preached; his own attitude to sex at Oxford had been quite unrestrained by conventional morality. But this attitude had not been shared by all those whom he had loved, and his frustration as a result of this had led him to attack, in his poetry, the 'deceit of instinct' – that is, self-deception practised upon the natural desires – that had dissuaded them from going to bed with him. Moreover he was himself probably now in some confusion about his own psychological make-up. Those of his poems which had been printed by Spender during the summer were chiefly concerned with describing a psychological landscape severely limited by frontiers and watersheds; while the conclusion of 'Paid on Both Sides', in the form in which he had written it shortly before coming to Berlin, emphasised the sterility and psychological failure of the mother-dominated son that Auden believed himself to be. Layard provided a release from all this, a positive doctrine of psychological liberation, helping to free Auden from what he himself once called 'the immense bat-shadow of home'. It was an exhilarating experience for him. 'To those brought up on repression,' he wrote of it, 'the mere release of the unconscious is sufficient to give a sense of value and meaning to life.'

Ironically, Auden seemed to take more readily to Layard's doctrines of liberation than did Layard himself, who was only now, after a long period of mental instability, beginning to come to terms with the fact that, though attracted by women, he was bisexual. Up to now he had done nothing about homosexual feelings that he had experienced, and it was only in Auden's company that he seriously began to act on them. He found Auden very attractive, recording in his memoirs (many years later) that he 'fell for him like a ninepin'. He added: 'He was very beautiful. . . His face was absolutely smooth and angelic – the kind of face that turns out to be really "wicked".'

His first meeting with Auden lasted many hours, so fascinated was Auden with Homer Lane's teachings, and by the time they had finished talking it was too late for Auden to return to his hosts in the suburbs. As Layard afterwards recalled, 'We talked and talked (a lot about Homer Lane – this was the beginning of Wystan's interest in him) late into the night, until I said: "You'd better stop here."' He then suggested to Auden that, as he only had one bed, they had better sleep together in it. 'Although I had had no proper homosexual intercourse in my life,' he wrote, 'I immediately wanted to embrace him. But Wystan said: "No, I've got a boy named Pieps."'

This was how Layard remembered the occasion many years later. Pieps was a youth with whom Auden had an affair early in his stay in Berlin; his name is recorded in a journal Auden began to keep in the spring of 1929. This journal makes it clear that, though Auden rejected Layard's sexual advances at their first meeting, he changed his mind shortly afterwards and agreed to have sex with him. In the journal,

Auden wrote: 'During my first few meetings with John I felt his existence and his exposition of Lane has made a difference to me. . . Going to bed with him at first though was a mistake which lasts. I feel guilty about it. It was so dreary and [illegible] and I didn't get any sleep.'

His friendship with Layard soon became very complicated. In another entry in his journal he wrote: 'The difficulty I think about our relationship is that it began with a certain transference on my side over his psychological ideas. Then being young enough to be his son, he tries to make me into an elder brother and sometimes a mother. I revolt.'

In fact the sexual element between Auden and Layard seems to have disappeared quite quickly from their friendship. Auden probably found it unpleasant because Layard was so much older than himself. Much more to his taste was Pieps, and other adolescent boys who hung about many of the Berlin bars and cafés, and were willing to have sex with English visitors in return for presents or money. Auden had taught himself enough German for such transactions. His affair with Pieps was of this nature; he told Layard: 'I like sex and Pieps likes money; it's a good exchange.' Layard, who had not thought of sex as something for which one should pay, was shocked by this – and then ashamed of being shocked.

Auden patronised one bar in particular, the Cosy Corner, at Zossener-strasse 7, in the working-class district of Hallesches Tor. He took John Layard there one day, and helped him to pick up a boy of his own, called Heine, with whom Layard enjoyed himself for a few weeks. Auden much preferred the company in the Cosy Corner to that of his middle-class hosts in Nikolassee. 'The German proletariat are fine,' he wrote to the girl to whom Bill McElwee was now engaged, 'but I dont like the others very much, so I spend most of my time with Juvenile Delinquents.' He told her that he now had quite a good knowledge of Berlin slang and obscenities, and reported to her: 'Berlin is the buggers daydream. There are 170 male brothels under police control. I could say a lot about my boy, a cross between a rugger hearty and Josephine Baker. We should make D. H. Lawrence look rather blue. I am a mass of bruises.'

This reference to activities with Pieps is explained by John Layard in his memoirs: 'Wystan liked being beaten up a bit. This happened once in my room. It would start with pillow-fights and end with blows; then they would go to bed together. Wystan was rather shy about this being observed.'

Auden mentioned Pieps in letters to a number of friends, telling Cecil Day-Lewis that he 'is the most elemental thing I have yet met: I think my fiancée will have this quality which I feel in need of at present.'

It may seem odd that in view of his engagement Auden should be revelling in 'the buggers' daydream' in Berlin. But it appears that at present he regarded homosexuality as a stage of his development beyond which he would soon progress. A letter from Berlin to Bill McElwee seems to imply this, though it is couched in obscure terms:

I am having the sort of friendships I ought to have had at 16 and didnt. Being late in the day it is expensive. The sort of Homosexuality which should remain when I have done has the same cause as cancer, the wish to have a child. Perhaps there will always be the single-inn-bed variety which is nostalgic – mother told us thats what flowers did.

This last phrase, which also appears in the revised 'Paid on Both Sides', seems to mean, according to an entry in Auden's 1929 journal, that the desire for friendship is often confused with sexual desire, as a result of maternal lectures on 'the facts of life'. 'Single-inn-bed' perhaps refers to the fact that, on walking holidays with friends such as Carritt and McElwee, Auden sometimes shared a bed with them in an inn, but without having sex.

The notion that cancer and homosexuality are both caused by the frustration of the wish to have a child – the 'foiled creative fire' as Auden later called it in a poem – was probably acquired by him from John Layard's Groddeck-inspired teachings, which it certainly recalls; though Auden himself was soon embroidering what Layard had told him, with characteristic exaggeration, and was making it into a psychological doctrine of his own. When he next met Christopher Isherwood, he began to lecture him on the psychosomatic origin of all physical disorders. Rheumatism, he said, was simply a refusal to bend the joints, and therefore an indication of excessive obstinacy. Deformities were visible signs of the struggle between instinct and will. Abnormal tallness such as Stephen Spender's was an attempt to reach heaven. And so the catalogue continued. All these things could be avoided, Auden told Isherwood, by being 'pure-in-heart'. Isherwood was initially irritated by 'this annoying and priggish-sounding phrase', as he called it, but soon began to use it freely himself. 'The pure-in-heart man became our new ideal,' he said. 'He was essentially free and easy, generous with his money and belongings, without worries or inhibitions. . . He was entirely without fear. . . and without sexual guilt. . . Above all, he was profoundly, fundamentally happy.'

Isherwood was not the only friend on whom Auden exercised this new set of ideas. Bill McElwee was suffering from persistent throat trouble, and Auden wrote to his fiancée: 'I am perfectly convinced the disease is psychological, and taking him to throat specialists is a waste of time and money. Perhaps a sanatorium life will be psychologically right but I doubt it. You are much more likely to cure him than anyone else.'

Though Auden later changed his views on human personality, he never entirely abandoned this Groddeckian explanation of illness. In 'New Year Letter' (1940) he ascribed Marx's boils to frustrated love, and in a chart drawn up for his pupils at Swarthmore College in 1943 he implied that cancer and paralysis were the result of certain mistakes of behaviour. Near the end of his life he remarked to a friend that it was odd that Freud died of cancer of the jaw – 'Who'd have thought he was a liar?'

The psychosomatic view of human suffering was in fact full of opportunities for his poetry, as is shown, albeit rather trivially, by verse entries in his journal and in another notebook he was keeping at about the time he was in Berlin:

> He was a housemaster and a bachelor
> But refused to keep dogs
> So he is dying of cancer.

This refers to the fatal illness in 1929 of Robertson, his housemaster at Gresham's.

> Lord have mercy on us
> And take away this pus
>   For iodine
>   Forgives no sin.
>
> Lord, I am six feet tall
> Lord, keep the others small
> Can't I grow seven
> Can't I reach heaven.
>
> Dear o dear
> I've got diarrhea [sic]
> Where can I cast
> My wicked past?

Auden was presumably thinking of these rhymes when he told a friend (early in 1930) that he was 'writing a text book of Psychology in doggerel verses'. Besides these rhymes, the notebook also contains a chart, apparently taken from Homer Lane's teachings, demonstrating how the causes of crime, disease and madness lie in the upsetting of the balance between the conscious and unconscious halves of the mind. Another chart in the notebook attempts to work out a complete scheme of the relationship between disease and psychological illness, and there is a 'Glossary of Christian and Psychological terms' which tries to show that the terminology of Christianity is another form of language for the chief features of psychology; thus, Heaven represents the unconscious and Earth the conscious mind, Hell is the repressed unconscious, the Father the 'ego-instincts', the Son the 'death-instincts', the Holy Ghost the libido, and the Archangels the 'four great ganglia of the body' – 'ganglia' being a favourite term of Lawrence's. The notebook shows the tremendous impression that Layard made on Auden.

That impression can also be seen in the new version of 'Paid on Both Sides' at which Auden worked during his early months in Berlin. This new text retains the original joke, if it can be called a joke, about the similarity between saga heroes and English schoolboys, but it is clearly intended to have a wider significance than the rather local feud of the original play. The Nowers, for example, now have largely German names (Kurt, Zeppel, Walter) which are perhaps intended to be in conflict with the Jewish names of two of the Shaws (Aaron and Seth). More important, this second version of the 'charade' draws out and expands the theme of psychological conflict which was only sketchily present in the first draft. It does this largely in the light of Layard's teachings and of their effect on Auden's personality; he once annotated a copy of the text of 'Paid' with the words: 'A parable of English Middle Class (professional) family life 1907-1929' – the dates are those of his own birth and the year in which he put the finishing touches to 'Paid'.

The new text begins with an account of the death of John Nower's father, who was ambushed by the Shaws while on his way to 'speak with Layard' – that is, presumably, to obtain spiritual healing. His death has brought on the premature birth of John, and John's mother is seen with both the corpse and the baby, appealing for the continuation of the feud. The Chorus then talks of this 'pressure on men' to destroy themselves by respecting social convention. Next, John Nower, now an adult, is seen talking to a member of his clan who is planning to escape from the tragic predicament by emigrating to the Colonies; John himself is sympathetic, but will not follow suit, and thus avoid the real issue. John is then informed that one of the Shaws can easily be besieged and killed during a visit to a woman at a neighbouring farm, and he agrees to this plan. The ambush takes place, and is reported in a terse narrative formula reminiscent of *Beowulf* and *The Battle of Maldon*:

> Day was gone   Night covered sky
> Black over earth   When we came there
> To Brandon Walls   Where Red Shaw lay
> Hateful and sleeping   Unfriendly visit. . .

A Spy from the Shaws is now caught, and is summarily executed, under the orders of John Nower. But John immediately begins to doubt the rightness of this action. He then starts to dream; and it is this dream which especially embodies Auden's new views on human personality.

The dream takes the form of a trial in which the recently shot Spy is the accused, John is the prosecutor, John's mother is the warder, and the rest of the cast are the jury. The meaning of all this is by no means apparent during a casual reading of the play, but what Auden is actually doing is presenting to the audience a divided personality, whose two halves are represented by John and the Spy. John's jingoistic speech at the beginning of the dream ('We have and are making terrific sacrifices but we cannot give in') indicates that he is the repressive conscious mind, while the Spy represents the natural desires which have been repressed. John tries to kill the Spy, but he is stopped with the words: 'This fellow is very ill. But he will get well.'[1] Meanwhile the Spy is 'kept under' by the Mother, who brandishes an enormous feeding bottle with the threat 'Be quiet, or I'll give you a taste of this.'

There now enters an exceedingly enigmatic figure, the Man–Woman, whom Auden seems to have developed from a character in the traditional English mummers' play – from which he took several features of the new version of 'Paid', one of these being the otherwise inexplicable introduction of Father Christmas as the judge in the trial scene. The Man–Woman in the mummers' play was simply a man dressed in women's clothing, without any lines to speak or any obvious significance; but Auden develops this into a symbolical figure who is given the central speech of the play – central, that is, to the psychological predicament of the personality.[2]

This speech tells John (the conscious mind) that he has now lost the chance of real love. He has been educated to think of love as nothing more than scandal ('Traffic in memoirs'), and has indulged freely in masturbation ('You made that an excuse / For playing with yourself') and in cold-blooded attempts at sexual gratification. But he has not really found love. At the end of the speech, John, crying 'I can't bear it', shoots the Spy.

The comic Doctor from the mummers' play now enters, and revives the Spy in traditional fashion; though he is more than a comic figure, for he represents Layard's ideas on psychological disorder. He blames John, the conscious mind, for what has happened, and gives as his diagnosis 'Adamant will, cool brain and laughing spirit'. The Spy is brought back to life by him, and John and the Spy are finally revealed as 'Sharers of the same house' – the two halves of the same personality.

The dream ends; but the play moves to its tragic climax as before. For, though John is now capable of love and is united with his fiancée Anne, and though he now sees the importance of love as a healing power, tragedy is still inevitable because of the maternal possessiveness which ultimately becomes dominant. Auden did not overestimate the healing power of his newly-acquired psychological doctrines, or believe that the whole of society could be conquered through one person's perception of its faults.

The new version of 'Paid on Both Sides' was finished by the end of December 1928. On the last day of the year, Auden wrote to McElwee to

---

[1]These words, and indeed the whole dream, come from an account of an actual dream in W. H. R. Rivers, *Conflict and Dream* (1923), as has been noted in John Fuller's *Reader's Guide to W. H. Auden*.

[2]Soon after writing 'Paid', Auden told Spender: 'I am the Man–Woman.'

say that the manuscript 'goes to Eliot to-day'; for he had decided to submit 'Paid' to the *Criterion*, which T. S. Eliot edited.

Eliot no doubt found the play difficult to understand; its obscurities were even greater than in the first version, and even today much of the detail of its imagery cannot be elucidated by the most patient critics. But its richness of language and sudden surprising shifts of diction are so remarkable as to override the obscurity; and Eliot recognised this. He called the play 'quite a brilliant piece of work', and accepted it for the *Criterion*, where it was eventually published a year later. And he said of Auden: 'This fellow is about the best poet that I have discovered in several years.'

Despite this, Auden himself was by no means happy about his work. In April 1929 he wrote in his journal:

> Damn this laziness. I envy the ease of so many writers. I sit down for an hour or so and think of about two lines. Is this genuine difficulty or just lack of conception. My work is scrappy. I want to do something on a larger scale. Or must I wait till I am fifty. My flabbiness of mind, inability to think, obscure sensibility disgusts me. I know what I write is obscure. Too often this is just being too lazy to think things out properly. When I have an idea I never know whether to finish it off [?] or wait till I have some more. Laziness is [??] impatience.'

★

At Christmas 1928, just as he was finishing the new 'Paid on Both Sides', Auden went back to England for a short visit. He saw Isherwood, and regaled him with stories of the wickedness of Berlin. Presumably he also spent some time with his fiancée. He returned to England again briefly two months later, to celebrate his twenty-second birthday. On this second visit he travelled to Scotland and stayed with Cecil Day-Lewis, who was now married and teaching at Helensburgh.[1] Returning to Berlin, Auden wrote a verse-letter to Day-Lewis which included these lines:

> Should poets marry? You have done, and I
> Engaged, may hope to be so presently.
> What do we offer wives? They can expect
> But disappointments, penury, neglect.

[1]Auden's epithalamium for Day-Lewis's wedding, written late in 1928 in the style of 'Paid on Both Sides', is printed as Appendix I of Sean Day-Lewis's biography of his father (1980).

At the beginning of January 1929 Auden moved his lodgings from Nikolassee to the Hallesches Tor district, not far from the Cosy Corner bar. 'I have moved to a slum,' he told McElwee, as I am tired of german family life.' His new address was Fürbringerstrasse 8 – '50 yrds from my brothel', he said.

He was now writing poems which, like the revised 'Paid on Both Sides', reflected John Layard's teachings and his own sense of liberation as a result of them. These poems were more open and free in manner than the tight, compressed, self-contained pieces printed in the Spender booklet, but they still hid the real subject of most of them – love and the repression of the emotions – under cover of quite a different layer of meaning. For example, in 'From scars where kestrels hover', written in January 1929, the overt subject is heroism. Auden compares the bravado-heroism of those who are 'Fighters for no one's sake' and who indulge in such absurd heroics as night-time journeys to Cape Wrath (a reference to a drunken trip once made by Isherwood) with those whose bravery lies simply in their capacity for endurance; it is love that is really being discussed, and the bravery of the 'host' at the end of the poem is the silent endurance of the rejected lover. Similarly in 'We made all possible preparations', written in December 1928, the subject appears to be political: a representative of a repressive regime justifies action that must be taken in an emergency. But the real subject of the poem is Auden's own emotional condition as perceived through Layard's interpretation, with the conscious mind pictured as a repressive authoritarian government that is eventually overthrown by the previously repressed desires, which have been liberated through a psychological revolution.

In the middle of March 1929, Isherwood came out to Berlin to visit Auden for a few days. Auden immediately took him to the Cosy Corner and introduced him to the boys he knew there. Isherwood met and became infatuated with a boy nicknamed 'Bubi', with whom he had a happy love-affair for the rest of his short stay in Berlin. Auden, amused by this, began on 23 March to write the journal which intermittently recorded events and reflections for the rest of his time in Germany. 'Christophers visit will serve as well as anything else as the introduction to this journal,' he wrote in it; and an early entry describes Isherwood and Bubi playing ping-pong:

> Pimping for someone on whom one has a transference creates the most [*illegible*] feelings. Chiefly I remember Christopher and Bubi playing ping-pong. The sense of bare flesh, the blue sky through the glass and the general sexy atmosphere made me feel like a partici-pant in a fertility rite.

He also wrote a poem, 'Before this loved one / Was that one and that one', which gently mocked Isherwood's claim to have found a genuine love, though the poem was also concerned with Auden's own emotional problems, and may have arisen from one of his own love-affairs.[1] The poem owed much to the style of the American poet Laura Riding, to a degree that her friend Robert Graves later claimed was actually plagiarism. Graves exaggerated, but Auden was certainly influenced by her at this period – he was reading her work in December 1928. He continued to admire her, and some years later described her as 'the only living philosophical poet'.

Isherwood had been spending some months at medical school in London, but by the time he came out to Berlin he had decided, partly as a result of what Auden had told him about John Layard's teachings, that he should give this up and try to make a living from writing – he had now published one novel, *All the Conspirators*, which had been a minor success. Auden now introduced him to Layard. Isherwood was struck by Layard's 'X-ray eyes', but he was at present more interested in the practice of sex with 'Bubi' than with Layard's theorising about it. By the time he left Berlin he was certain that this was the way of life he ought to lead.

Auden himself had become involved with a whole series of boys whom he met in the bars. In his journal, later in the year, he made a list:

Boys had. Germany 1928–29.

Pieps
Cully
Gerhart
Herbert
Unknown from Passage
Unknown from [*semi-illegible name of bar*]
Unknown in Köln
Unknown from [*semi-illegible name of bar*]
Otto.

I regret the [*semi-illegible name of bar, as above*] one. He was not nice and was very dirty; ie Pure lust on my part. All the others were nice people.

'Cully' was possibly a nickname for Kurt Groote, who was the subject of the poem 'Love by ambition' (Auden marked the initials 'K.G.' by this poem), and who is mentioned in 'It was Easter as I walked in the public gardens'.

The length of the list might suggest that Auden was in the habit of 'cruising' – picking up boys for casual sex, through encounters in bars and

[1]In Chester Kallman's copy, Auden wrote the words 'Brian S.' by the poem. This person has not been identified.

other public places. In fact he much preferred to have a steady relationship. 'I have often thought I would go brothel crawling but I can't do it,' he wrote in the journal. 'I become attached to someone, and enter on a relationship at once. Which means of course that I dont want to be free. Complete lechery as Christopher remarked is the end of all pleasure.'

Shortly after beginning to keep the journal, Auden met, in one of the boy-bars, the 'Gerhart' of the list. This youth, whose name is given as 'Gerhart Meyer' in the poem 'It was Easter as I walked in the public gardens', was a sailor. According to Auden's journal, the relationship with Gerhart began on a purely financial basis: '"Give me ten marks and I sleep with you to-night. . . You can pay me on Tuesday."' (Gerhart spoke some English.) Auden seems to have obtained some happiness from the affair, though he recorded their sexual encounters in his journal with coolness and a lack of excitement: 'After dinner we go to bed for three hours.'

It was at about this time, and probably as a result of getting to know the 'Juvenile Delinquents' of the Berlin bars, that he began to write another play, 'The Reformatory', which (judging from the play into which it evolved, 'The Enemies of a Bishop') he probably intended should deal with the subject of young fugitives from the law. He made some preliminary notes for it in the journal:

> Do I want poetry in a play, or is Cocteau right: 'There is a poetry of the theatre, but not in it'? I shall use poetry in *The Reformatory* as interlude . . . I don't want any characters, any ideas in my play, but stage-life, something which is no imitation but a new thing . . . A play is poetry of action. The dialogue should be correspondingly a simplification . . . The Prep School atmosphere: that is what I want.

For the moment, Auden seems to have written only one speech apparently intended as an epilogue.[1] This may have been simply because of lack of time and opportunity, for he now became involved in a series of somewhat dramatic events.

His relationship with John Layard was still complex and by no means easy. 'What I cant understand about J', Auden wrote in his journal, 'is that he appears to be one of those who "have seen the light" once, after which is darkness. To me illumination is a progressive process.' This, and other entries in the journal, suggest that Layard's initially overpowering effect on Auden had now dwindled, and Auden's admiration for Layard had become mixed with a certain amount of contempt. Auden recorded in his journal:

---

[1] Now printed in *The English Auden*, p. 273.

J[ohn:] – 'You know, Wystan, next to Lane and Rivers, I think you are the most intelligent man I have ever met.' Yet he hates my writing. . . When J disagrees with me he says 'You're so young.' But if I suggest to him that he is old, he is hurt.

Layard had in fact met his match in Auden, and the consequence was nearly disastrous.

Layard was mentally very unstable. He felt he had been deserted by Homer Lane, who had died in the middle of giving him psychoanalysis. At Easter 1929 he wrote to a friend in England, Margaret Gardiner, then a young Cambridgeshire schoolteacher, indicating that he was deeply unhappy. She was so disturbed by this that she set out immediately for Berlin. Arriving there, she was met by Auden, whom she did not previously know, and was taken by him to Layard's lodgings, which she found squalid.Layard told her he was going to kill himself, and had only put it off because of the shock it would have given her to arrive and find him dead.

Auden made it perfectly clear to Margaret Gardiner what his attitude was to Layard's suicide threat. 'If he wants to kill himself,' he told her, 'you should let him kill himself. Don't interfere.' She realised that he was following Layard's own doctrine of obedience to one's impulses: if Layard's impulse was to suicide, then he must commit suicide. Nevertheless Auden was perfectly willing to do what he could to help Layard, and he and Margaret Gardiner began to look for rooms for Layard in a pleasant hotel, so that his surroundings would be more cheerful.

They duly found Layard a hotel, and he agreed to move there, though – according to Auden's journal – he remarked to Auden: 'I like the way you satisfy your phantasies of grandeur by getting me in here.' ('This was just,' commented Auden.) Once in the hotel, Layard began to cheer up, though he would not let Margaret Gardiner dispose of his revolver, and insisted on keeping it with him. He had told her that his life was meaningless unless he could be assured of the friendship and support of a young Italian woman, Etta da Viti, who like himself had been a patient of Lane, and who now lived in Paris. Layard was in love with her, but she would have little or nothing to do with him; Layard believed she had been Lane's mistress. Margaret Gardiner decided she must make a rescue attempt: she would go to Paris in the hope of trying to persuade this woman to come and see Layard. At this, Layard became hopeful again, and he and Auden saw her off on the night train to Paris.

Her mission was a failure. Etta da Viti was away from her apartment, and the concierge had no idea when she would return. Margaret Gardiner sent Layard a telegram saying that there was no news, but she would wait in Paris as long as her job allowed. In fact after a few days she had to give up and go back to England for the start of her school term.

Her failure to find Etta da Viti plunged Layard back into despair. The situation was also further complicated by the behaviour of Auden and his new boyfriend Gerhart. According to Auden's journal, Gerhart seems to. have offered to go to bed with Layard: 'Does your friend want a boy? Why doesnt he take me?' Auden seems to have passed on this offer to Layard, and it appears that an encounter between Layard and Gerhart took place – though the journal is far from clear about this:

> *April 2nd.* Rang up John and went to see him late to tell him. I think I knew he would have him, my sex snobbishness wanted him to want him, and my pity to give him some pleasure. When it came to the point I felt miserable or thought I did. Slept badly.

According to Layard, in an account written in his memoirs many years later, he and Gerhart did go to bed together – though the outcome was disastrous: 'Ostensibly Wystan possessed this boy, but the latter was playing with me too. . . I then made up my mind to do the dirty on Wystan: I would take [Gerhart] home. I knew this was a complete betrayal, but I did it. . . He was very beautiful, but I was impotent. That was the last straw. . . I had stolen Wystan's boy, I had gone against every rule, and then been impotent.'

The next day Layard shot himself in the mouth. Astonishingly, he failed to kill himself. The bullet passed through the nasal passages, damaging the nerves, but did no serious damage to the brain, and lodged in the top of the skull. Layard regained consciousness after a few minutes and realised he had bungled the suicide. He decided to take his revolver and go to Auden, in the hope that Auden would finish him off. He managed to get a taxi, and arrived at Auden's lodgings, where he staggered up several flights of steps and was met by a couple of boys who were coming away from Auden's room. Layard's memoirs take up the story:

> I arrived and said: 'Wystan. I've done it.' (I'd never talked to him about it, but I knew he'd know what I meant.) 'But it hasn't killed me. Please finish me off – here's the pistol and ammunition.' I had no doubt he'd do it, out of friendship. But he said: 'I'm terribly sorry, I know you want this, but I can't do it, because I might be hanged if I did. And I don't want to be. Lie down on the divan.' So I lay down; then I passed out.

Auden sent for another taxi, and Layard was taken to hospital, where the bullet was extracted from his head.

Auden's journal adds a further detail to Layard's account of the suicide attempt – that Layard had, contrary to what he says in the memoirs, discussed suicide with Auden, and that Auden had reiterated his remark that if Layard wanted to kill himself then so he should:

April 3rd. John meditating suicide. Kisses me. No more than a plate of cold soup. 'Its not one of the things one forgets.' Temper. I start to leave. 'Must go.' 'I dont think this is very profitable.' 'To whom?' 'To you or to me.' Burst into tears. 'I'm so sorry. You're so decent.' Tried to persuade him to kill himself. Came back home. Heins came [?], then Franz [?]supporting John. He wanted me to finish him off. I wished I could. Retched when he vomited blood. Perhaps this is sympathy. Had to kiss him and disliked it. Appropriate snow storm on the way to hospital. Depressed.

It is impossible to make much of the conversation between Layard and Auden at the beginning of the journal entry, but it seems that they had a quarrel, apparently about their own sexual relations with each other.

After the operation to remove the bullet from Layard's head, Auden sent a telegram to Margaret Gardiner with the news, and in the weeks that followed gave her further bulletins about Layard's progress. Layard was soon reported to be out of danger, though for a time his eyesight was in jeopardy; in the end, however, he made a full recovery. Christopher Isherwood was so fascinated by the story that he put a version of it into his novel *The Memorial,* basing his account on what Layard told him about the experience.

In the weeks that followed the suicide attempt, Auden's coolness towards Layard seems to have faded, and the entries in his journal suggest that he was again strongly taken with Layard's ideas. Layard himself returned to England a few months later, and he and Auden remained on friendly terms and saw quite a lot of each other. It was at about this period that Layard came to admire Jung; eventually, he achieved some distinction as a Jungian analyst, and wrote a book expounding his Jungian ideas about dreams. He also wrote and published his long-planned study of the natives of Malekula, which earned him a doctorate from Oxford University. He married, had one son, and survived into his eighties.

Just as the drama of Layard's would-be suicide was coming to its conclusion, Auden found himself a spectator of another series of equally dramatic events. His affairs and friendships with the 'Juvenile Delinquents' (as he called them) of the Hallesches Tor bars had made him at least vaguely aware of the political unrest in Berlin, and he perhaps got to know several members of the German Communist Party (K.P.D.). Up to this time – Easter 1929 – Auden apparently had a vague and rather sentimental sympathy with the Communist aims; Isherwood noted that he had taken to wearing a German workman's cap – and also to smoking cigars, which were cheap there, with the result, said Isherwood, that he looked like 'an exceedingly dirty millionaire'. Now, the seriousness of the political situation was suddenly made clear to him.

The Weimar Republic of Germany was being governed from the

Berlin Reichstag by a coalition of politically central parties, which had
survived the Munich rising of 1923 led by Hitler, and – more seriously –
the inflationary economic crisis of the same year. The economy was now
nominally stable, and the extremist parties were held in check; both the
Nazis and the Communists had only a modest membership, and the
Nazis were hampered by the fact that Hitler was forbidden to speak
publicly. But both extremist groups were working energetically to gain
power. The Nazis were based in Munich, but their brownshirt street
gangs had already begun to roam Berlin. The Communists had their
headquarters in Berlin itself, where they had won quite a lot of support
among the working classes; hence Auden's probable awareness of their
activities. Like the Nazis, they hoped that the future of Germany might
lie in their hands. But they faced strong opposition, not just from the
Nazis but from the government.

The winter which Auden had been spending in Berlin was one of
marked political unrest. The weather was exceptionally severe, and more
than two and a half million people were unemployed in Germany, with
the result that there was mounting criticism of the Weimar government,
which for its part did its best to suppress the activities of the Communists.
The Communists responded by spreading stories of police atrocities
against their members; and not without justification, for the previous
year the police had shot several Communists during a rally in May.
Auden listened to these stories, and recorded them in a poem:

> Walking home late I listened to a friend
> Talking excitedly of final war
> Of proletariat against police –
> That one shot girl of nineteen through the knees,
> They threw that one down concrete stair . . .

Then, on May Day 1929, came a major clash between the Communists
and the police in Berlin. Public demonstrations had been forbidden, and
it was apparently as a consequence of this that the Communists tried to
take over whole streets, especially in the Neukölln area, not far from
Auden's lodgings. Barricades were erected, using captured tramcars
and building materials, and the street-lamps were smashed. Fighting
continued for five days, leaving 23 killed and 150 injured. 'All this time',
wrote Auden in a poem composed this month, 'was anxiety at night, /
Shooting and barricade in street.' Looking back many years later, he
realised that this was the first time he had become politically aware: 'One
suddenly realised that the whole foundations of life were shaking.'

He did not, however, remain long in Berlin to observe the aftermath
of the riots – the Communists burying their dead with full honours, the
accusations of police brutality, the government orders for the suppression
of the Communist 'Red Fighting Front'. It would be wrong to exaggerate

the degree of political awareness that the riots had awakened in him Margaret Gardiner, who saw quite a lot of him during the later part of 1929, did not observe that he had any lasting interest in politics; she noticed that he, like herself, was concerned with the morals and motives of their friends rather than with politics, though she said that they both 'assumed vaguely that we and our friends were of the left, socialists, without any attempt to define that term'.

Auden left Berlin for a few days in about the third week of May 1929, presumably so that he could see more of Germany. His affair with Gerhart had now come to an end; the boy had played him up badly on a short trip to Hamburg in April, disappearing for a whole night with Auden's money; eventually, back in Berlin, he walked out on Auden without any warning, taking with him John Layard's revolver, which Auden was looking after. Now, in May, travelling with another boy named Herbert, and apparently also with a Dutchman named Dan, Auden made a rapid trip of about a week to Magdeburg, then on through Wernigerode, Kassel, Marburg, Köln and Essen. During this journey they passed through the Harz Mountains, and Auden was struck by the attractions of Rotehütte-Königshof, a village at the foot of the Brocken, the highest peak in the Harz range. He decided to return there later, which he did, spending much of June and July staying in an inn Rotehütte with yet another boyfriend, Otto Küsel. Auden, many years later, put this boy's initials against two poems he wrote in June 1929, 'Upon this line between adventure' and 'Sentries against inner and outer'.

Early in July, Auden and Otto were joined at Rotehütte by Christopher Isherwood, who had come for a holiday. John Layard, by now fully recovered, also came down from Berlin for some days to see them all.

Isherwood saw that Auden had already made himself completely at home at Rotehütte: 'His room was like every other room he had ever lived in, a chaos of books and manuscripts; he was reading and writing with his usual impatient energy.' He welcomed Isherwood 'as one welcomes a guest to one's household', and had the air of owning the whole village. He intrigued the villagers by noisily strumming tunes from the English Hymnal on the piano of the railway station café, and by wrestling naked in a field with Otto.

Otto, however, did not stay with him long. As a result of Isherwood's attempts to contact his own Berlin boyfriend Bubi, with whom he had lost touch, the police arrived at Rotehütte to make inquiries, and discovered that Otto was a fugitive from a reformatory. They took him away. Isherwood now set off for Berlin in search of Bubi, and on Auden's recommendation obtained the help of Francis Turville-Petre, a young archaeologist from an English aristocratic Catholic family (he was the brother of Gabriel Turville-Petre, the Icelandic scholar) who was leading a dissolute life in Berlin; Auden had apparently first met him there some months earlier. Turville-Petre's curious combination of dissipation and inner calm caught Isherwood's imagination, and he and Auden adopted this odd Englishman into their private mythology, nicknaming him 'The Fronny', this being their anglicisation of the Berlin boys' version of his first name, 'Der Franni'.

Isherwood returned empty-handed to Rotehütte, where he received a letter from 'Bubi' saying he was in Amsterdam and was about to embark as a deck-hand to South America. Isherwood and Auden decided to go to Amsterdam to see the boy off. This they did, during July, and after the boy's ship had sailed they toured the city's canals in a tourist launch, amusing themselves with a wild exchange of private jargon and jokes. On disembarking they signed the passenger guest-book, Auden adding a quotation from a poem by Mayakovsky:

> Read about us and marvel!
> You did not live in our time – be sorry!

★

'I loved my time in Germany,' Auden wrote to Bill McElwee, 'and hope to go to Paris next year.' He came back to England in late July, telling John Layard in a letter that he was 'homesick for Germany'. His year there had left him fluent but inexpert in the German language. 'I know so little German,' he said to a friend some years later, and his spoken German remained rather ungrammatical till the end of his life.

He was still engaged to be married, but, at Rotehütte, Isherwood had tried to dissuade him from going on with it. Auden himself was, it seems, already having doubts. 'It is not always realised by half', he wrote in his journal, 'that the attraction of buggery is partly its difficulty and torments. Heterosexual love seems so tame and easy after it. I feel this with Sheilah. There is something in reciprocity that is despair. How one likes to suffer.' On his return to England he decided to follow Isherwood's advice.

'I am probably breaking off my engagement to-day,' he wrote to John Layard from Birmingham on 29 July. 'Bravo Me.' And in his journal he wrote: 'Have broken off my engagement. Never – Never – Never again. She is unhappy. She wants to be pushed [?]. And I should do it. And I wont.' A short time later he told Bill McElwee: 'As you know I was but am no longer engaged. Never, never again. This is a criticism of me not of marriage.'

The engagement had probably not been a complete falsity, a piece of acting. The indications are that up to this time Auden was perfectly willing to be attracted by members of the opposite sex. His schoolboy and undergraduate poems had included a number of rather trite verses about heterosexual love, and a letter to McElwee in 1927 mentioned, if only frivolously, that he 'fell in love' with a bridesmaid at a friend's wedding that year. There was also his sexual experience with Frau Petzold in Austria late in 1926. But it seems that, however willing he may have been to experience sexual desire for a woman, he had not genuinely done so. In about 1931 he wrote to a female friend: 'Many homosexuals, I for example, have only one prejudice against women, a physical one. I am not disgusted but sincerely puzzled at what the attraction is (like watching a game of cricket for the first time).' And he rejected – at least during this part of his life – the notion that he might marry and yet carry on homosexual affairs on the side. 'I don't believe in marriage with separate latch keys,' he wrote of this idea. 'If a pair are really in love the circuit is closed. Its only the brother–sister relationship that permits of affairs. Such a relation for the woman is deathly.'

He was not, at this stage of his life, proud of his homosexuality. In about 1933 he wrote to a friend: 'Homosexuality is on one side a naughty habit like thumb-sucking.' What really concerned him was not his or his friends' particular sexual preferences, but the kind of relationship those preferences led them into. 'The mere fact that A prefers girls and B boys is unimportant,' he wrote in 1932. 'The real cause for alarm lies in the large number of nervous and unhappy people who are incapable of any intimate faithful relationship at all, in whom sensation has remained at or regressed to the infantile level as an end in itself. . . and to whom, therefore, the object is really non–existent. It is true that nearly all homosexual relations are of this kind but so are a large proportion of heterosexual ones and there is nothing to choose between them.'

Homosexual practices were still illegal in Britain, and were punishable by prison sentences. This had the inevitable result of making many of Auden's homosexual friends secretive about their true nature. Some of them even experienced an added *frisson* in their sexual activities because such practices were technically criminal. Auden was not like this; he seems to have been careless about the threat of the law, and made no secret of his homosexuality to most of his heterosexual friends, provided he regarded them as broad-minded. Nor did the illicit nature of his activities seem to excite him; he was coolly indifferent to such consider-ations – though the 'secret society' aspect of homosexuality certainly appealed to him.

After returning from Germany he continued to see Isherwood, who was back in London living with his mother, and the two carried on with their private jargon and jokes, this time on paper. They began to write a play together. It was a continuation of Auden's projected play 'The Reformatory', and they gave it the title 'The Enemies of a Bishop, or Die When I Say When: A Morality in Four Acts'. They dedicated it to Isherwood's Berlin boyfriend Bubi, and to Otto Küsel, who had stayed at Rotehütte with Auden.

'The Prep School atmosphere: that is what I want,' Auden had written in his preliminary notes for 'The Reformatory', and that atmosphere is exactly what he and Isherwood now achieved in their play. The plot and dialogue read like an end-of-term romp. Auden intended that poems should be used in 'The Reformatory' as interludes, and this is precisely what happens in 'The Enemies of a Bishop'. The action simply comes to a halt now and then for a poem to be recited. The result is an odd hotchpotch of fine verse and schoolboy foolery. Most of the poems seem to have come into existence quite independently from the play; though they are themselves excellent, they rarely have any bearing on the action, and their presence does not alter the play's 'Prep School' character.

The plot concerns a young man named Robert Bicknell, whose surname is Auden's mother's maiden name; he is appointed manager of a lead mine in the fells, not far from a Reformatory where his brother Augustus (Auden's father's second Christian name) is governor. Robert is accompanied by a *doppelgänger* named 'the Spectre', who recites Auden's poems at random moments; this character was based, said Isherwood, on a figure in Henrik Galeen's nightmare film *The Student of Prague*, which Auden and Isherwood saw together in Berlin – Auden greatly admired contemporary German cinema. A sub-plot concerns two boys, George and Jimmy, who escape from the Reformatory and arrive at the Nineveh Hotel, one of them disguised as a girl. At the hotel are a pair of villainous brothers, Maximilian and Ceslaus Luder, two figures of the kind with which Isherwood and a friend from Cambridge days, Edward Upward, peopled a private invented world that amused them in undergraduate days and afterwards. This world, 'Mortmere', was a lunatic blend of gothic horror, sexual perversity and sinister happenings, all set in a misleadingly idyllic English rural landscape. Though much of the Mortmere saga existed only in the form of private jokes between Upward and Isherwood, several stories from it were written down by one or other of its inventors, and Auden was very familiar with at least one of these, Upward's 'The Railway Accident'; he wrote to Upward to say how much he had enjoyed it. He and Isherwood obviously both had Mortmere in mind when they were writing 'The Enemies of a Bishop'.

The Luder brothers are pure Mortmere. One is disguised as a parson, the other as a bank manager.

CESLAUS: I must sweat up on this new prayer-book. I bought a copy on the bookstall at Euston.
MAX: By the way, I forgot to tell you. There's one possible I saw yesterday. Mrs Stagg – the wife of the under-manager at Windyacre Mine. We might do worse. Vegery gegoegod bust.
CESLAUS: Tegight cegunt?
MAX: I should think so. Her mouth's small enough, anyway.

Robert Bicknell has fallen in love with Mrs Stagg, and the Spectre encourages him to make love to a dummy representing her. Meanwhile at the hotel, a masculine woman named Ethel Wright, really a police spy, is suspicious of two other guests, Bishop Law and his wife, and she has the Bishop arrested on a charge of 'illicit traffic in women'. It soon appears, however, that the real white-slavers are the Luder brothers; and the Bishop appears 'wearing a police hat and medals' and summons his Flying Squad to pursue and capture them. He then doles out punishments not only to the Luders, who are to be caned, but also to Augustus Bicknell, who has become infatuated with the boy in women's clothes, being under the impression that she is a girl. Augustus is sentenced to a year at Brighton; while Colonel Tearer, a pederast who has been pursuing the other boy, will have to perform 'the Cautley Sport Run every afternoon for two months' – a reference to a custom at Sedbergh School[1] – and must write out five thousand lines every Saturday: 'The motto for this week will be "Mummy's been dead for quite a long time now."' In a final scene, Robert murders the Spectre, but the police arrest him for doing so. As he is led away he recites an epilogue.

As a piece of private amusement in the Mortmere vein the play is mildly entertaining – Auden himself, while writing it, called it 'very funny and very dirty' – but it is hard to believe that its authors meant for one moment that it should be taken seriously. The poems are a different matter, but they are really quite separate from the play. Isherwood admitted, a few years later, that it was 'no more than a charade', and was 'very loosely put together and full of private jokes'. But the fact that he and Auden had copies of the script typed professionally, and were discussing revisions to it around 1931-2, suggests that it was intended for more than purely domestic consumption. Isherwood seemed to imply that at least part of it was meant to be taken seriously when he said: 'The bishop is the hero of the play: he represents sanity, and is an idealized portrait of Homer Lane himself. His enemies are the pseudo-healers, the wilfully ill and the mad. The final curtain goes down on his complete victory.' Isherwood and Auden did not, however, make any attempt to get the play performed.

'The Enemies of a Bishop' was partly the product of the high-spirited mood in which its two authors had returned from Germany. But Auden now had to make some plan for the future, for the allowance his father was paying him would soon come to an end. His family had, in 1924 or 1925, acquired a cottage in the Lake District, 'Wescoe', at Threlkeld, to the north-east of Keswick; and in August 1929 he went there. From Wescoe, he wrote to McElwee: 'I manage to do quite a lot of work up here, having had the adequate amount of copotomy and sodulation for

---

[1]Gabriel Carritt points out that the term is actually 'Cautley Spout', a reference to a waterfall at the end of the ten-mile run.

this year.' But a poem that he wrote during this month suggests he was having difficulty coming to terms with ordinary life again – yet was happy to be home:

> . . . Being alone, the frightened soul
> Returns to this life of sheep and hay
> No longer his: he every hour
> Moves further from this and so must move,
> As child is weaned from his mother and leaves home
> But taking the first steps falters, is vexed,
> Happy only to find home, a place
> Where no tax is levied for being there.

In the early autumn he went to stay for a few days with Margaret Gardiner in Cambridgeshire. Then he returned to his parents' home at Harborne. His brother John was now working abroad as a geologist; Bernard was in Canada, farming; so Wystan was alone with his parents and depending on them for money until he could find a job. He was presumably thinking of his own experience when he wrote, a few years later: 'The unemployed young university graduate is unlikely to starve, but he will have to live at home, ask for his pocket-money, and endure the mutely resentful anxiety of his parents.' And during the summer of 1929 he wrote facetiously to John Layard: 'I have sixpence a week pocket money, two thirds of which is expected to go to Missions.'

The difficulty of living at home was increased by his parents' concern about his homosexuality, of which they were both now well aware. He wrote to McElwee that he was 'compelled from parental suspicion to abandon my one Birmingham romance'. Apparently his mother did not discuss the matter with him, but she was privately distressed; his father accepted that he was homosexual, a notably liberal view for the time, but asked him not to make this a matter of public knowledge in Harborne. Meanwhile his mother remained as irritated as ever by his domestic habits – he sometimes went out to a shop at breakfast time to buy cigarettes in his dressing gown. He in turn often found it preferable to meet his friends by inviting them not to Harborne but to the home near Birmingham University of E. R. Dodds, the Professor of Greek, and his wife, both of whom always made him welcome.

He was now making some attempt to find a job. He asked Margaret Gardiner if she knew of any teaching posts, and she told him that a friend's sister needed a tutor for her son at their London home. Auden accepted the job, which meant living at the house, and at the end of the summer of 1929 he moved to London. His employers were a Colonel Solomon and his wife Flora Benenson, who had kept her maiden name after marriage and gave that surname to their son Peter, then aged eight, who was to be Auden's pupil. (Peter Benenson later helped to found Amnesty International.) Colonel Solomon had been badly wounded in the First World War, and was paralysed from the waist down; he went about in a wheelchair, and was the inspiration for two lines in one of Auden's poems: 'Will you wheel death anywhere / In his invalid chair'. (This appears in 'Will you turn a deaf ear', written in September 1929.) Flora Benenson ran a small semi-private press. Auden learnt that she wanted to commission a translation of Baudelaire's *Journaux Intimes,* and he recommended Isherwood for the job, declaring that Isherwood had a perfect command of French. This was a complete invention, though Isherwood, who was taken on as translator, did just manage the job with the aid of French friends, perpetrating only a few howlers in the published text.[1]

Auden continued to look for more permanent employment. 'Do you by any chance know of a job for me?' he wrote to a friend in London. 'Anything from nursing to burglary. Is it possible to get into a publishing firm in any capacity?' The recipient of this letter was Naomi Mitchison. She had been introduced to Auden by Richard Crossman, who recommended her to ask him for poems for a new magazine with which she was involved. She told Auden she knew of no permanent job for him, but said she would like him to coach her twelve-year-old son Murdoch, who was behind with his Latin after an illness. Auden began to come to the Mitchisons' Hammersmith house several times a week, and proved to be a conscientious tutor, his Latin being adequate for the comparatively simple work required.

He went on looking for a job. During the autumn of 1929 he visited Sedbergh School with Gabriel Carritt, and was vaguely promised a teaching post there in three years' time. But, even supposing he seriously wanted to go to such a place, this was too long to wait. Then, early in 1930, he heard that Cecil Day-Lewis was moving on from his present post at Larchfield Academy, a boys' school not far from Glasgow on the Firth of Clyde. Auden applied for the job, and was accepted.

Before taking up his new post, he had to go into hospital in Birmingham at the end of February 1930 to have an operation for an anal disorder. This was at first diagnosed as an inflamed internal pile; writing to John Layard, Auden called it 'the stigmata of Sodom'. Medical opinion regards it as unlikely that sexual activity could have been the cause, and Auden perhaps meant this as a joke, though he did tell Margaret Gardiner that it had been the result of a sexual encounter of a particularly rough nature with some young man. A few days after the first diagnosis he reported to Layard that 'the thing turned out to be a rectal fissure'. The

[1] It is not clear at what address Auden was living during his months in London. He told Stephen Spender he would be staying at the house of Flora Benenson's sister, Manya Harari, 21 Cambridge Square, W.2., and he certainly spent a lot of time there. But several of his letters were sent from 43 Chester Terrace, S.W.1. The London street-directory for 1929 records this house as being occupied by a Mrs Powys-Wilson. Possibly Auden had digs there.

trouble had been exacerbated by his insistence on bicycling, in defiance of doctor's orders.

Before the operation he asked Layard to visit him, 'to help me get better', adding 'John please come. The pain has been rather bad.' Afterwards, the wound would not heal for many months. But at Easter, he was sufficiently fit to go with Gabriel Carritt on a walking-tour along Hadrian's Wall and through his favourite lead-mining country, where he embarrassed Carritt by ordering champagne in a public bar full of farm workers, and alarmed him by insisting that they take an early morning dip in an icy stream. Then, at the beginning of the summer term of 1930, he arrived in Scotland to take up his first full-time appointment as a teacher. 'I found, to my surprise,' he said, 'that I enjoyed teaching very much, and I continued in that profession for the next five years.'

6

Schoolmaster

Larchfield Academy was a small private school for boys which had seen better days. Its old pupils included John Logie Baird, the inventor of television, and Sir James Frazer, author of *The Golden Bough*. But by 1930 the school was not prospering. Until recently it had taken boys up to the age of eighteen, but it could no longer compete with larger and more celebrated public schools, and now it did not attempt to be more than a preparatory establishment catering for boys between six and thirteen, with just a few older pupils. The forty or so boys were taught in bleak, old-fashioned buildings lit by gas jets, and the headmaster, an elderly dispirited man named Perkins, with a drooping moustache, had largely given up the struggle.

Besides the headmaster himself, who taught classics, there were four members of the staff: Mr Sinkinson, the mathematics master, Miss Ensor, Miss Greenhalge, and Auden himself, whose task was to teach English and French. He also had to take turns of duty supervising the dozen or so boys who were boarders, the rest being day pupils who lived at home, and refereeing games.

He soon settled in. 'Schoolmastering suits me; I thoroughly enjoy it,' he wrote to his brother John, who was working as a geologist in India. 'If you get bored with India, why not try it. I find myself quite enjoying cricket. Perhaps I shall find Rugger the same but I wish I knew the rules.' And in a birthday verse-letter to Gabriel Carritt he wrote: 'Now I'm up here . . . / Paid to teach English to the sons of Scotsmen – / Poor little buggers.'

His predecessor in the job, Day-Lewis, had found his pupils' Glaswegian accents difficult to get used to, and presumably Auden experienced the same problem. But he discovered he had a real liking for the business of teaching. He enjoyed the boys' company ('Twelve year old boys are the best people to talk to,' he remarked to a friend) and he was sympathetic to the rebels in the school, having been rebellious in his own schooldays. Above all he liked influencing his pupils and telling them what they should do with their lives. The job of teacher, in fact, gave a proper outlet to two dominant aspects of his personality: the dogmatic schoolmaster and the would-be healer.

The boys, on the other hand, did not find him the ideal teacher. 'We were rather over-awed by W. H. A. and could not quite get the measure of him,' recalled one of them, Norman Wright. 'Born in Helensburgh of two Scottish parents, this was my first encounter with an "Englishman", and I was not greatly impressed. I could follow only with some difficulty his pronunciation, and, frankly, his reasoning was beyond me. I believe he was the first adult I had met who bit his nails and smoked heavily. I did not admire the habits. He seemed rather aloof and not very companionable. Not a person in whom we would confide. He did accompany us to games but his appearance on the rugby pitch was a bit of a giggle. He wasn't endowed for such sport.'

It was perhaps because he lacked a real rapport with the boys that Auden kept order in class partly by means of clowning. Margaret Gardiner, who visited him at Larchfield, noted this: 'He told me that he believed teachers ought to be clowns; if you stood on your head or played the piano with your feet, the boys would immediately attend, there'd be no difficulty about discipline. You should continuously startle them into interest, he said, keep them alert by letting them catch you out, trip you up.' One of his tricks was teaching the boys to stick stamps on the ceiling by flicking them up on pennies. On another occasion when he had trouble with discipline he told Gabriel Carritt he had threatened 'to cut my prick off' if the boys continued to fool about. He bought a suitable piece of meat from the butcher, and, next time a hullabaloo broke out in class, opened his fly, brought out this meat, and appeared to be actually carrying out the threat with a sharp knife – to horrified cries of 'No, sir! Don't do it!'

The school was situated in the middle of Helensburgh, a modest-sized market town that served largely as a dormitory for Glasgow businessmen, who could be seen every morning hurrying to catch their train. The town itself was rather smugly middle-class – Day-Lewis called it 'this Wimbledon of the North' – but it was surrounded by fine scenery. Loch Lomond and Glen Fruin lay only a few miles away, while across the Clyde the lights of Greenock glimmered alluringly at night (Auden dubbed it 'the wicked city'). Glimpses of these scenes began to appear in Auden's poetry, but he took no particular interest in the area, nor in Scotland on a wider scale. 'I don't think any of the Scottish nationalists are any use,' he wrote to Naomi Mitchison, adding that he thought the Scottish poet Hugh MacDiarmid 'such a fearful intellectual snob and prig', and suggesting that nationalism merely amounted to saying that 'Compton Mackenzie will be king one day'. His attention was caught more by the visible signs of the economic depression from which the whole of Britain was now suffering; for on a train journey into Glasgow he could see the Clydebank shipyards lying idle and silent, as well as the poverty-ridden slums of Glasgow itself. Much the same thing was to be seen in Birmingham, his home town; and on Easter Day 1930, just before travelling to Helensburgh to begin his teaching job, he wrote a poem which must have grown partly out of what he had observed there:

> Get there if you can and see the land you once were proud to own
> Though the roads have almost vanished and the expresses never run:
>
> Smokeless chimneys, damaged bridges, rotting wharves and choked canals,
> Tramlines buckled, smashed trucks lying on their side across the rails;
>
> Power-stations locked, deserted, since they drew the boiler fires;
> Pylons falling or subsiding, trailing dead high-tension wires;
>
> Head-gears gaunt on grass-grown pit-banks, seams abandoned years ago;
> Drop a stone and listen for its splash in flooded dark below. . .

There is, of course, a lot of exaggeration in this – or at least there would be if it were meant to be a picture of Britain in the grip of the Depression. In fact the poem owes a lot to Auden's private landscape of abandoned lead mines, and soon reveals itself as not really concerned with the present state of the country but with the defective emotional condition of the middle-class intellectual, for which the ruined industrial landscape is a symbol. It is yet another reworking of what Auden had learnt from John Layard. But the fact that the psychological theme is now presented in terms of the plight of a nation suggests that Auden was becoming aware, for the first time, of the value of politics for his poetry. It was (he said himself) during this year, 1930, that he began to read newspapers.

At about the time he began teaching at Larchfield, Faber & Faber accepted a volume of his poetry for publication.[1] The book was to include several of the poems that Stephen Spender had printed in 1928, as well as others that Auden had written since then; nothing remained of the selection that Faber's had turned down in 1927. A large number of the poems in the book, perhaps the majority, dealt, under a layer of symbolism, with the emotional plight of the individual, expressed largely according to Layard's ideas; but this would scarcely have been apparent to someone who did not know Auden's private interests. The really striking thing about the book was the range of images and styles – poems in the manner of schoolboy rhymes and cabaret songs were set next to pieces imitating Laura Riding or Anglo-Saxon verse – and the

---

[1]Auden may have submitted a book of his poetry to another London publisher, Victor Gollancz, some time around 1929; this may have been the same collection of poems that was accepted by Faber the next year. Sheila Hodges, in *Gollancz: The Story of a Publishing House* (1978), writes: 'Jon Evans [full-time reader with the firm] tried very hard to persuade Victor to take on Auden, but without success' (p. 73).

almost clinical, Hardy-like detachment with which Auden looked at his subject-matter as if from a great height: 'Consider this and in our time / As the hawk sees it or the helmeted airman. . .'

Auden's book, which was to be called simply *Poems,* was accepted on behalf of Faber's by T. S. Eliot. When Auden was in London he met Eliot, and was as impressed by him as a man as he had been by his poetry. 'So long as one was in Eliot's presence,' he said after Eliot's death in 1965, 'one felt it was impossible to say or do anything base.'[1] Rather late in the day, when Auden's *Poems* were already in proof, Eliot agreed to add 'Paid on Both Sides' to the book – it had already been printed by him in the *Criterion.* He also commissioned Auden to write, for the *Criterion,* his first published book review.

The review was of *Instinct and Intuition: A Study in Mental Duality* by G. H. Dibblee, and it shows that Auden was now tentatively beginning to move away from John Layard's view of personality as a set of unconscious instinctive desires controlled and inhibited by the conscious reasoning mind. Auden, reviewing Dibblee's book, now wrote: 'The reason is an instrument, and cannot of itself control or inhibit anything; what it can do is to cause one desire to modify another.'

Auden began to undertake more book reviews for the *Criterion,* and for other journals, such as F. R. Leavis's *Scrutiny* (Leavis had not yet turned against Auden), *The Listener,* the *New Statesman,* and Geoffrey Grigson's *New Verse.* His aims as a critic were ostensibly simple: to praise the praiseworthy and to give examples from the book under review in the form of quotations as lengthy as the space would permit. He said of this that to arouse interest the critic 'must quote with as little comment as possible'. He implied that he had learnt this from Eliot, whose critical writing did not in itself especially influence him ('I have never understood exactly what the objective correlative is,' he admitted) but whose gift for illustrating his essays with surprising quotations he found instructive.

Auden did not usually write reviews of books he thought were poor. He said that a critic should 'keep silent about works which he believes to be bad, while at the same time vigorously campaigning for those which he believes to be good'. On another occasion he wrote: 'Make it a rule not to review any book which, whatever its faults, you don't basically like.' (He did, however, late in his life, once dismiss a book which he was reviewing as 'an unbook, written, it would seem, by an anal madman'.) He also declared that critics should not tell readers what to think about particular books: 'The one thing I most emphatically do not ask of a critic is that he tells me what I *ought* to approve of or condemn.' Yet he often

---

[1] Auden had the experience, some time in the early 1930s, of being invited to dinner by Eliot and his first wife Vivien, of whose strangeness he was made aware on arrival: 'I told Mrs T. S. E. that I was glad to be there and she said: "Well, Tom's not glad"' (*Tribute,* p. 155).

violated this rule, demanding (for example) that parents should make their children read Grimm's fairly tales, and – in the mid 1950s – declaring that how a reader reacted to Tolkien's *The Lord of the Rings,* which he himself greatly admired, was a test of literary taste. He also often used his reviews as testing-grounds for his own changing opinions, and as a chance to conduct a debate with himself; for example, his 1930 piece about Dibblee's book becomes an argument about D. H. Lawrence. This gave his reviews an intensity and excitement, but it could be disconcerting to the reader, especially as during the 1930s Auden had not found a satisfactory prose style, and was sometimes very obtuse in his way of expressing things.

★

At the end of his first term at Larchfield, Auden spent part of his summer holiday on a short visit to Berlin, where Christopher Isherwood was now living, supported largely by an allowance from an uncle who was homosexual and therefore sympathetic to his nephew's way of life. Auden brought with him to Berlin a proof copy of his *Poems,* which were to be dedicated to Isherwood; besides this public dedication he also composed a personal version for Isherwood in dog-German, full of private jokes. On his return to England he wrote to his brother John: 'I had a wonderful fortnight in Berlin in July. As usual my heart broke up like a treacle tart.' And he told Naomi Mitchison: 'I am much too miser-able at having to leave Berlin to write a decent letter. . . I shall probably exhaust and shock you with Berlin confessions.' During what remained of the summer he attended what he described to his brother as 'Father Parker's scout camp', stayed at his family's Lake District cottage, visited Garrigill in the lead-mining country near Alston, and began to write another play.

It is possible that after writing 'The Enemies of a Bishop' he and Isherwood contemplated another collaboration. A note in Auden's hand, apparently intended for Isherwood and titled 'Some suggestions for the play', refers to there being two actors only, who might be given 'cycloid' and 'schizoid' personalities, and suggests that there be a 'railway motive', a 'Basilisk motive', a 'School scene', 'At least one miracle', and 'A railway book-shop'. But nothing else survives, and Auden's next attempt at dramatic writing was made on his own.

In August 1930 he wrote to his brother John: 'I am writing another play which promises to be quite fun though I don't quite see my way yet.' By late October the play was almost complete; Auden told Naomi Mitchison: 'I have nearly finished a new play which I believe will be the best I can do just now.' When it was done, he sent it to T. S. Eliot for consideration by Faber's. Eliot read it, apparently put it on one side, and did not show it yet to the other directors of the firm. They did, however, read it a year later, and for a time seem to have considered publishing it in one volume with Auden's next work, *The Orators*. But before publication, the play was dropped from the book. Subsequently the manuscript disappeared.

As a result it is, of course, impossible to discover much about the play, but an outline can be reconstructed from a few fragments which survive among Auden's papers. The play was called 'The Fronny'. The title was the nickname Auden and Isherwood used for their Berlin friend Francis Turville-Petre, and the play concerned his disappearance from England and the search made for him by a young man named Alan Norman. It seems that Auden used verse in the play in the same manner as in 'The Enemies of a Bishop' – that is, as detached interludes or choruses rather than as an integral part of the action – and among the poems included in it were those beginning 'Between attention and attention', 'Doom is dark and deeper than any sea-dingle', and 'What's in your mind, my dove, my coney'. The play took Alan Norman through a series of scenes of modern civilisation, including the Nineveh Hotel (from 'The Enemies of a Bishop'), where he became infatuated with a film star. At the end, 'Fronny' made his will and died; the will was full of private jokes about Auden's friends, and the play seems to have been no more suitable for public performance than was 'The Enemies of a Bishop'.

A few days after Auden returned to Larchfield for the autumn term of 1930, his *Poems* were published by Faber's in a slim volume bound in card with a blue paper wrapper. The book roused a little local curiosity at Auden's school and in Helensburgh, where several people bought it, though most who did so were disconcerted by the modernity of the poems and thought the book merely eccentric. Some of the London critics were equally unenthusiastic. The *Times Literary Supplement* declared that Auden's poetry 'is so often peculiar to himself and so eccentric in its terminology that, instead of communicating an experience of value to us, it merely sets our minds a problem in allusions to solve'. *The Listener* put it more bluntly: 'As for Mr Auden, we dare not even hazard a guess what his book is all about.'

Auden took this to heart. 'Am I really so obscure?' he asked Naomi Mitchison. 'Obscurity is a bad fault.' And when his friends Professor and Mrs Dodds at Birmingham taxed him with the incomprehensibility of certain passages he tried to avoid blame by saying that the printer had made a mistake. This was not totally absurd, for his small, unclear handwriting certainly provided printers with a problem, which was exacerbated by his inability to read proofs with any accuracy – 'I find it quite impossible to proof-read my own writings because I automatically read into the text what I meant to write,' he said. Serious mistakes often crept into printed texts of his poems throughout his life, though he once remarked to Margaret Gardiner that these errors sometimes improved the poetry. But of course most of the obscurity in the 1930 *Poems* was not the result of such errors. Nor did it deter some critics from seeing the real merits of the book.

Michael Roberts in the *Adelphi* identified one of Auden's chief character-istics: 'Mr Auden's poetry expresses thought stripped to essentials. After clothing it in commentary and elucidation, the reader realises that, after all, the words themselves gave the exact thought and the strict emotion.' Louis MacNeice echoed this in *The Oxford Outlook*: 'Mr Auden's attempt is to put the soul across in telegrams. But whereas in the everyday telegram the words tend to be, like Morse, mere counters, in the poem-telegram the words stand rather on their own than *for* a meaning behind them.' MacNeice concluded: 'He should certainly be read by those of us who are not old enough to go, or think we go, straight forward.'

MacNeice was of course a friend of Auden's – it was at about this time that he really began to get to know Auden well, for he became a lecturer in classics at Birmingham University and often met Auden at the Dodds' house there. And another friend, Naomi Mitchison, gave Auden (in the *Week-end Review*) the most laudatory notice of all, a notice that was to some extent a 'put-up job', for she was determined to do her best for him. Nevertheless it reflected her very real excitement at what he was writing:

> The poems of the post-war generation are naturally only just appearing. We older ones have to find an attitude towards them. . . Reading Auden's *Poems* I am puzzled and excited. The very young, it seems, admire and imitate him. Dare I spot a winner? He is wantonly obscure sometimes. The 'charade' ['Paid on Both Sides'] is impressive. . . But there are passages in the middle which seem as if they could only be understood by a psycho-analyst . . .
>
> I must. . . advise people to read this book and not to get angry at once with the unintelligibility, but to re-read and accept it as beautiful and a sign of the times, and hope that Auden will go on and keep un-muddled – for I am almost sure his ideas are clear, though he chooses to express them at present in unexplained symbols, perhaps too economically. If this is really only the beginning we have perhaps a master to look forward to.

Her view was shared by others, especially by young poets of Auden's generation. John Pudney, who had been at school with Auden, said that *Poems* 'made a greater impact on me than any work before or since', and explained that the book was valuable to him not just for itself but as 'a symbol of some magic, bright, quick, hard, which illumined the autumn sky in my twenty-first year'. Roy Fuller echoed this when he recalled 'how that pale blue pamphlet dignified / The banalities of my provincial adolescence'. Charles Madge had the same experience: 'There waited for me in the summer morning, / Auden, fiercely, I read, shuddered and knew. . .'. Dylan Thomas, then aged sixteen, bought a copy of *Poems* and kept it carefully, patching it up with adhesive tape when it began to fall apart because of heavy use. John Cornford, a schoolboy poet at Stowe, declared of the book: 'Whatever its ultimate value, it is already of the greatest historical and literary importance.' And Anne Ridler summed up the feelings of many young poets when she said: 'It was Eliot who first made me despair of becoming a poet; Auden. . . who first made me think I saw how to become one.'

Auden's advice began to be sought by some of those who admired *Poems*. John Cornford's English teacher at Stowe sent him one of Cornford's poems, and Auden's comments on it show the importance he was already putting on technique as opposed to 'inspiration'. He wrote to Cornford: 'You might do more with stricter verse forms. . . as the very nature of the form forces the mind to think rather than to recollect'. Yet he added: 'Real poetry originates in the guts and only flowers in the head. But one is always trying to reverse the process and work one's guts from one's head. Just when the Daemon is going to speak, the Prig claps his hand over his mouth and edits it.[1] I can't help feeling you are too afraid of making a fool of yourself. For God's sake never try to be posh.' When John Pudney, too, sent him poems for criticism he wrote in much the same vein: 'Never write from your head, write from your cock. Don't force yourself mentally. Unless the original impulse comes from the guts and gives you a nice warm feeling up the spine, it is cerebral and bogus. . . Much poetry to-day is of this kind, emotional frigging.'

Though *Poems* brought Auden a kind of fame, it was only among a very small circle of readers. Faber's printed one thousand copies of the book, and these stocks lasted for two years. There was a 1933 reprint, with several additions and omissions, but again this was initially of only a thousand copies.

Auden sent a copy to Edward Upward, Isherwood's collaborator in the Mortmere stories, who was teaching at a school in Yorkshire. He told Upward in his accompanying letter: 'I shall never know how much in these poems is filched from you via Christopher.'

Auden was first introduced to Upward in 1927 when the two of them and Isherwood ate together at a Soho restaurant. That evening they argued about religion, in which Upward was mildly interested, and which Auden attacked vehemently. Auden had apparently discovered from Isherwood that Upward would never sit down on lavatory seats, and he therefore gave a noisy oration on people who were nervous of sitting in public lavatories for fear of getting the clap. Upward thought him rather frivolous, but liked his vigour and intellectual excitement. After their meeting, Auden wrote to Upward several times and enclosed poems, which Upward admired. A little later, he acquired a manuscript

[1]Auden is here using the terminology of D. H. Lawrence.

of Upward's Mortmere short story 'The Railway Accident', a bowdlerised version of which was eventually published in 1949. It was then in its unexpurgated form, so that the violent train accident in the first part was paralleled in the second by the equally horrific rape of one of the male characters by three choirboys. Auden liked to read aloud to his friends from this unexpurgated text, though he claimed the rape was the one poorly described episode because of Upward's heterosexual ignorance about such things. As to Upward's influence on *Poems,* it certainly seems likely that certain images and ideas reached Auden via Isherwood from their original source in Upward's Mortmereish imagination.

Auden invited Upward to stay with him at Larchfield during the spring term of 1931, when Upward was having a half-term holiday from his own school. 'When on my first day there', recalled Upward, 'he invited me to lunch at the school's expense his headmaster's welcome to me seemed far from warm. Auden invited me to lunch there again on the second day and this time the headmaster's expression of face was so undisguisedly angry that I would have walked out of the dining room at once but for the fact that this might have seemed unfriendly to Auden.' (When Margaret Gardiner visited him at the school, Auden smuggled her into the staff living-quarters so she could have an illicit bath.) Auden subsequently paid a couple of visits to Upward at his school in Scarborough and at Ottershaw where Upward later taught. 'I was walking along the drive one afternoon to meet him at his lodgings in the village', remembered Upward of the Ottershaw meeting, 'when I heard a deep voice speaking out of the air above me, "Mr Upward, Mr Upward", like the voice of an accusing Jehovah, and I looked up to see Auden who had climbed quite high into a tree and who might have been waiting there for some while before I passed below him.' Upward remembered how, when Auden arrived by train at Scarborough, he 'put on a false red beard just before getting out of the carriage, but owing to a misunderstanding about the time of the train he would be arriving on I was not there waiting for him at the platform barrier and he had to go into one of the station lavatories to take off the beard before he got a taxi to my lodgings'.

During 1930, Auden wrote a short poem which exactly catches this Mortmere mood:

> Having abdicated with comparative ease
> And dismissed the greater part of your friends;
> Escaped in a submarine
> With a false beard, hoping the ports were watched.
> How shall we greet your arrival;
> For it isn't snowing
> And no one will take you for a spy. . .

The mood was one that he exploited very fully, and with remarkable results, in a long work combining prose and poetry which he began to write not long after the publication of *Poems*. This was *The Orators*.

*

During the spring and summer of 1931 he composed four pieces of prose. Each was an oration of one kind or another; hence presumably the title eventually given to the whole work, which is more relevant to these four pieces than to later sections. In the first, 'Address for a Prize-Day', the speaker is an old boy of a public school – though his speech opens with a parody of Auden's old headmasters: 'Commemoration. Commemoration. What does it mean? What does it mean? Not what does it mean to them, there, then. What does it mean to us, here, now? It's a facer, isn't it boys?' After this nonsensical opening, the speech gives an answer to the question 'What do you think about England, this country of ours where nobody is well?' The answer is that we are all of us guilty, like Dante's sinners in Purgatory, of crimes against love. These particular crimes – excessive love, defective love, perverted love – are catalogued, and dire warnings of the consequences are given, largely based on Groddeck's doctrine of psychosomatic illness. Excessive self-lovers are described as 'suffering more and more from cataract or deafness', while the perverted lovers have 'a slight proneness to influenza'. Defective love, itself a Lawrentian as well as a Dantean idea, is also seen in terms of the decay of industrial society – it is compared to 'those ship-cranes along Clydebank, which have done nothing all this year'.

The second piece, 'Argument', draws in its opening section on one of D. H. Lawrence's most characteristic ideas. Lawrence believed that a true unity between instinctive desires and the conscious mind could only be achieved by suppressing all education, except of a few chosen people, and appointing a Leader to direct the people, who were themselves to live entirely naturally on the land. 'Argument' imagines such a Leader in action, operating subversively and planning his revolution. But the speaker in 'Argument', though an initiate of the Leader's group (the four prose pieces are given the sub-title 'The Initiates', and all four speakers are aware of Lawrentian doctrine), is himself a rather absurd figure who hero-worships the Leader and regards 'Him' as quasi-divine. He wants to 'receive the mistaken stab, deliver His message, fall at His feet'. The second part of 'Argument' is a parody of the Church of England litany, petitioning for delivery from neurotic illness and defective forms of love; the prayers are addressed not to God but to celebrated detectives ('O Sexton Blake, deliver us . . . O Poirot, deliver us') and to inn-signs ('O Goat with the Compasses, hear us. . . O Bear with the Ragged Staff, hear us'). The third section of 'Argument' returns to the mood and theme of the first, and the quasi-divinity of the Leader is stressed by a list of 'His' attributes and actions. The whole piece seems in fact to be an imagination of Lawrence's Leader as a Christ-like figure. As to literary style, 'Argument' is largely modelled on the *Anabasis* of St-John Perse, which had been published by Faber's in 1930 in a translation by T. S. Eliot. When *The Orators* had been seen by Eliot, he told Auden that the first book 'seems to me to have lumps of undigested St-John Perse imbedded in it'.

After 'Argument' comes 'Statement'. We have had the Lawrentian view expressed in terms of public school and Anglican religion. Now the mood changes to that of Old English poetry, and Lawrence's ideas are presented in the style of the Anglo-Saxon *Exeter Book*. The first section of 'Statement' suggests some of the crafts which may be practised by the 'uneducated' – Lawrence had written: 'Relieved of [the] hateful incubus of responsibility for general affairs, the populace can again become free and happy and spontaneous. . . The evolving once more of the great spontaneous gestures of life.' Auden's catalogue of these 'spontaneous gestures' is extraordinary:

> One casts metal in black sand; one wipes the eccentrics of a great engine with cotton waste. One jumps out of windows for profit. One makes leather instruments of torture for titled masochists; one makes ink for his son out of oak galls and rusty nails.

Compare the *Exeter Book:* 'One is clever at chess. One is witty at the wine-drinking, a good lord of the beer. One is a builder, good at raising a dwelling.'

The second section of 'Statement' is modelled on the passage in the *Exeter Book* which deals with the various fates of men, and the third section returns to Lawrence, stating very clearly his totalitarian social doctrines: 'The man shall love the work; the woman shall receive him as the divine representative. . . The boy and the girl shall not play together; they shall wait for power.' (Compare Lawrence: 'Keep the girls apart from any familiarity or being "pals" with the boys. . . [or] later on, no deep, magical sex-life is possible.')

The fourth and final piece, 'Letter to a Wound', is based on Auden's own experience with his anal fissure, which failed to heal for many months after his operation in 1930. He uses this experience to suggest how the Lawrentian unity of body and mind, desire and reason, is prevented by psychosomatic illness, or illness caused psychologically and welcomed by the sufferer. The 'wound' (whose precise nature is never specified) is a symbol of some psychological handicap, which becomes deeply loved and absorbs all the sufferer's attention – hence the Wound itself is the recipient of this love-letter: 'For a long time now I have been aware that you are taking up more of my life every day, but I am always being surprised to find how far this has gone. Why, it was only yesterday, I took down all those photographs from my mantelpiece.' The photographs include one of 'Gabriel': even old loved-ones are dismissed, and (the writer tells the Wound) 'nothing will ever part us'.

After writing these four pieces, Auden sent them to Naomi Mitchison for her comments, explaining that they were to form the first part of a work he would call *The Orators*. 'In a sense', he told her, 'the work is my memorial to Lawrence' (who had died eighteen months earlier); 'i.e. the theme is the failure of the romantic conception of personality; that what it inevitably leads to is part 4' (by which he meant 'Letter to a Wound'). His letter to Naomi Mitchison continued:

> Formally I am trying to write abstract drama – all the action implied.
>
> The four parts, corresponding if you like to the four seasons and the four ages of man (Boyhood, Sturm und Drang, Middleage, Oldage), are stages in the development of the Hero (who never appears at all).
>
> Thus Part 1. Introduction to influence.
> Part 2. Personally involved with the hero. Crisis.
> Part 3. Intellectual reconstruction of Hero's teaching. The cerebral life.
> Part 4. The effect of Hero's failure on the emotional life.
> The litany is the chorus to the play.

Auden himself admitted to Naomi Mitchison that these 'marginal notes', as he called them, would not be a great help in elucidating *The Orators*. And when he eventually submitted the work to Eliot at Faber's, he gave a somewhat different account of the four sections of Book One: 'The central theme is a revolutionary hero. The first book describes the effect of him and his failure on those whom he meets.' Neither of these explanations takes account of the large element of parody in the writing, not just parody of literary models (Eliot himself, Gertrude Stein, and the French poet St-John Perse, along with the litany, Anglo-Saxon poetry, and school sermons) but also of Lawrence himself. Time and again Lawrence's doctrines are absurdly juxtaposed with images of an utterly different kind:

> The leader shall be a fear; he shall protect from panic; the people shall reverence the carved stone under the oak-tree. The muscular shall lounge in bars; the puny shall keep diaries in classical Greek. . .
> The censor shall dream of knickers, a nasty beast.

Auden finished Book One of *The Orators* during the summer of 1931. He spent part of his holiday in Germany, staying with Christopher Isherwood on the island of Rügen in the Baltic Sea, where Isherwood had travelled with his current Berlin boyfriend – Auden wrote a birthday poem for Isherwood which mentions Isherwood's struggles to win this boy. Their household on Rügen also included Stephen Spender, who was now living for half of each year in Berlin, and who found Auden still mercilessly analytical of his friends' sexual habits and choices of lovers. Nude sunbathing was *de rigueur* on the island, but Auden would have none of this, and shut himself indoors, writing by artificial light; this was not merely affectation, for his skin blistered easily in the sun. He also continued to encourage Isherwood's work as a writer. Having recently read Isherwood's new novel *The Memorial,* he now declared to friends: 'If it is not at once recognised as a masterpiece, I give up any hope of any taste in the country. By far the best novel outside Lawrence since the war.'

After the Rügen holiday, Auden returned to England, and then took a boat to the Shetlands, in the company of a young man who lived near Larchfield school, and to whom he was attracted. This holiday proved to be the beginning of an affair which brought Auden some happiness. He and the young man stayed in a hotel at Hillswick, and Auden was apparently struck by some of the Shetland place names, for he used some of them – Vadill of Urafirth, Stubba, Smirnadale, Hamar and Sullom – in the second part of *The Orators*, on which he was now beginning work. 'I am now writing the second half,' he told Naomi Mitchison on 12 August. 'I am finding it very difficult but am getting along slowly.'

★

The second section of *The Orators* is even more extraordinary than the first, and is the nearest thing to surrealism that Auden ever wrote. In fact when he was at work on it he had probably not heard of the surrealist movement, and when he did encounter it a few years later he expressed strong reservations about the artistic validity of the uncontrolled release of images and notions from the unconscious mind. Certainly 'Journal of an Airman', the second part of *The Orators* is a piece of verbal anarchy; but its juxtaposition of diary entries, quasi-scientific observations complete with diagrams, plans for absurd military operations, and lists and catalogues of every kind, produces an effect that resembles not so much true surrealism as the more extreme nonsense of Lewis Carroll.

What was Auden trying to achieve in 'Journal of an Airman'? He told Naomi Mitchison that it described 'the situation seen from within the Hero', and added: 'The flying symbolism is I imagine fairly obvious. The chief strands are his Uncle (Heredity-Matrilineal descent and initiations) belief in a universal conspiracy (the secret society mind) kleptomania (the worm in the root).'

The argument of the Journal would seem to be this: a Leader is himself not exempt from psychological disablement, and while the Journal records his plans for the coup which will lead to the birth of the new civilisation, it also observes his own anguished struggle with his particular disability, which is kleptomania – though the Airman refers to this weakness in terms that make it seem more like masturbation. The point is perhaps that the precise nature of the weakness is irrelevant; it is something which seems shameful to the person concerned.

In suggesting that the flying symbolism of the Journal was 'fairly obvious', Auden was not being fully informative about the book's meaning. Dreams of flying are often thought to have a sexual significance, but the flying symbolism in *The Orators* has a more specific origin. In a letter to a reader in August 1932, Auden explained: 'The genesis of the book was a paper written by an anthropologist friend of mine about ritual epilepsy among the Trob[r]iand Islanders, linking it up with the flying power of witches, sexual abnormalities, etc.' The friend was John Layard, and the paper was based on his observations on the island of Malekula in the New Hebrides – not the Trobriand Islands – in 1914–15; he published it in the *Journal of the Royal Anthropological Institute* in 1930. In this paper, Layard gave an account of the behaviour of the island's 'flying tricksters' – a term used by Auden in a poem in the Journal – and argued that their behaviour was modelled on epileptic fits. These 'tricksters', who claimed to have the power of flight, believed that they inherited their magic from their maternal uncles; they used their trickery sometimes to kill their enemies, but often merely for practical jokes. Auden gave his Airman many of the characteristics of these tricksters.

The Journal begins with an analysis of the character of the Leader's 'Enemy' – non-Lawrentian repressive society – here expressed in the catalogue format which Auden often used in *The Orators:*

> Three kinds of enemy walk – the grandiose stunt – the melancholic stagger – the paranoiac sidle.
> Three kinds of enemy bearing – the condor stoop – the toad stupor – the robin's stance.
> Three kinds of enemy face – the fucked hen – the favourite puss – the stone in the rain.

When *The Orators* was being prepared for publication, Eliot asked Auden to delete 'the fucked hen', and suggested 'the June bride' as a substitute, which Auden accepted. According to Auden, the form in which Eliot offered this emendation was 'like a June bride, sore but satisfied'.

Once the identity of 'the Enemy' has been established, the Journal gives an account of the absurd preparations being made by the Airman and his associates for the revolution which is to overthrow this un-Lawrentian society:

> We leave to-morrow. . . After tea Bob and Stan, the boy fishermen, will give an exhibition of Japanese wrestling on the floor of the

lounge. Community singing of wartime songs will lull for a moment all awareness of lost contacts. At dinner an imaginary telegram of regret from a guest who has left the hotel to die may amuse. In the hall a Highland reel will, of course, be attempted, lit up by pocket torches fetched hurriedly from the bedrooms.

The Journal proceeds on its carefully deranged course, drawing largely on the style of Baudelaire's *Journaux Intimes* (which Isherwood had recently translated), and turning sometimes to verse; the forms of Icelandic runic poetry and the ancient Irish triad are used, and there are five stanzas attacking a typical 'Enemy', the Fleet Street newspaper baron, here addressed as 'Beethameer', a name formed by merging Beaverbrook and Rothermere. Fragments from Auden's own life are used: 'Tea to-day at the Cardross Golf Club. A hot-bed. Far too many monks in Sinclair Street.' Sinclair Street is in Helensburgh and Cardross is a few miles away. A passage of free verse which appears to be pure nonsense is in fact an account of part of Auden's 1931 summer holiday:

> There was a family called Do:
> There were Do-a, Do-ee, and other Do-s
> And Uncle Dick and Uncle Wiz had come to stay with them
> (Nobody slept that night).
> Now Do-a loved to bathe before his breakfast
> With Uncle Dick, but Uncle Wiz. . .
>
> Well?
>
> As a matter of fact the farm was in Pembrokeshire.
> The week the Labour Cabinet resigned
> Dick had returned from Germany in love.
> I hate cold water and am very fond of potatoes.

Ramsay MacDonald disbanded his Labour government in August 1931 and formed a coalition to deal with the continuing economic crisis. That month, Auden stayed with Gabriel Carritt's family at a farmhouse in Pembrokshire, where they were joined by Dick Crossman, who had been spending some time in Berlin, a journey he made as a result of Auden's and Isherwood's example. Carritt's father was known as 'Do-a' and his youngest brother as 'Do-ee'. The father liked to bathe in the sea before breakfast, as did Crossman, and he tried to make Wystan Auden, who had acquired the nickname 'Uncle Wiz' from his pupils at Larchfield, join them. But Auden refused to swim, and at night he raided the Carritts' larder for cold potatoes.

Another element is introduced into the Airman's strange jottings with the appearance of his Uncle Henry. This figure was based on Isherwood's homosexual uncle of the same Christian name, who financed his nephew's residence in Berlin. It was probably also founded on Auden's memories of his own uncle Harry, who had similar sexual tastes. But in the Journal it is not the uncle's homosexuality that is so significant as his suicide, which the Airman recalls:

> Fourteenth anniversary of my Uncle's death. Cleaned the air-gun as usual. But what have I done to avenge, to disprove the boy's faked evidence at the inquest?

Auden based this on Edward Upward's cousin, the writer Allen Upward, always known to Edward as 'Uncle Allen', who committed suicide by shooting himself in the heart with an air-gun. In the Journal the point of the Uncle's self-destruction is that it was an admission that the real 'Enemy' is within. Hence *The Orators* really is, as Auden said, about the failure of the Lawrentian concept of personality, for Lawrence did not appreciate that our real enemies are our own weaknesses.

The Airman himself comes to this realisation at the end of the Journal. He gives an account of the 'mobilisation' which is to lead to the long-awaited revolution, an account whose absurdities are drawn partly from the Mortmere stories and partly from a book published in 1931 by General Erich Ludendorff, *The Coming War*. Ludendorff, who had been Chief of Staff in the German army during the 1914-18 war and had since supported Hitler (and quarrelled with him), alleged that 'supernational forces' of Jews, freemasons and Roman Catholics were plotting to bring about another war. In his book he gave a detailed prophecy of what would happen:

> War breaks out!
> There is no declaration of war: the rifles go off themselves.
> Every state in Europe with the exception of Norway, Holland, Spain, Portugal and Turkey and Japan in the Far East, appoints the same day as the first day of mobilisation.
> War in the air and sea begins on the night of that day.

Auden adapted this for his own purposes in *The Orators*:

> *First Day of Mobilisation*·
> At the pre-arranged zero hour the widow bent into a hoop with arthritis gives the signal for attack by unbending on the steps of St Philip's. A preliminary bombardment by obscene telephone messages for not more than two hours destroys the *morale* already weakened by predictions of defeat made by wireless-controlled crows and card-packs. Shock troops equipped with wire-cutters, spanners and stinkbombs, penetrating the houses by infiltration, silence all alarm clocks, screw down the bathroom taps, and remove plugs and paper from the lavatories.

But, as this absurd military operation proceeds, the Airman realises that though he is the Leader, the Hero, he is himself flawed; the true Enemy is within him. 'Do not imagine', he tells himself, 'that you, no more than any other conqueror, escape the mark of grossness.' And the Journal ends with the implication of his death by suicide.[1]

While he was working on 'Journal of an Airman' in August 1931, Auden apparently envisaged it as the concluding part of *The Orators*. But by the time he finished the Journal he had decided to add a third part, to be made up of six poems, several of which were already in existence. (The Journal itself had been composed partly of fragments that already existed in his notebook.) These poems are not merely an afterthought, a group of pieces that Auden happened to have in his drawer and which he attached to the work without their having any real connection with it; they are related to it very closely, and provide a finale to what has gone before.

The first of the 'Six Odes', as they are titled, is a sad record of the non-appearance in present-day society of 'one with power', a true Leader; there is only a troupe of second-rate healers, whom Auden lists, including among them the name 'loony Layard' – which presumably means that he no longer took John Layard very seriously. (Layard, who read the poem, was deeply hurt by being call 'loony'.) The poem also refers to the death of Lawrence himself, and mentions (though only allusively) that this happened, on 2 March 1930, just at the time when Auden was in hospital recovering from the operation on his anal fissure and nursing his 'Wound'. The Ode is full of private references; it opens with a voice saying 'Wystan, Stephen, Christopher, all of you, / Read of your losses.' But this does not mean it was intended solely for Auden's own circle of friends, most of whom, when they read it, could make little more of it or of the rest of *The Orators* than could anybody else. The private jokes, when elucidated, do not reveal any new layer of meaning; it adds nothing to our understanding of the first Ode to know that 'the drunken Scotsman' of the fifth stanza, who is described as saluting 'the moon's hedge-rising', was very likely a man named Snodgrass who indulged in periodic pub crawls with members of the Larchfield school staff (as Cecil Day-Lewis recorded in his autobiography), nor that 'the Mop' of the penultimate stanza was the nickname of his wife, Mrs Snodgrass, she and her husband being known to their children as Mop and Pop. References like this were too private even for Isherwood and Spender to understand. Once again, it is the obscurity itself that is the meaning of the poem.[2]

---

[1] Auden wrote to Henry Bamford Parkes on 6 December 1932: 'The airman's fate can be suicide or Rimbaud's declination.'

[2] Despite this, many of the obscure names and references which Auden threw into his poems at this period can, like 'the Mop', be traced to real sources. Two lines in 'Paid on Both Sides' seem to refer to Sedbergh. 'I hear Chapman did the lake in eight' is probably a reference to Frederick Chapman, who was at school at Sedbergh with Gabriel Carritt and

The second Ode is addressed to Gabriel Carritt, and commemorates his captainship of the Sedbergh School Rugby XV, whose prowess it records, complete with the names and nicknames of the team members, whom Carritt had described to Auden. In Lawrentian terms it proves that body and mind can be united in certain instances, here an athletic victory: 'Never did members conspire till now / In such whole gladness: / Currents of joy incalculable in ohms / Wind from the spine along the moving arms'. The ideas here are pure Lawrence, while the Ode is prosodically a parody or pastiche of Gerard Manley Hopkins.

The third Ode is addressed to Edward Upward, and returns to the despairing mood of the first poem. It describes life under the rule of 'the Enemy', and portrays this in terms of an establishment which is part army camp, part sanatorium, and part public school, where everything is provided but real (Lawrentian) life; the inmates have no need for anything else, but the result for them will be spiritual death. Upward, when he read the poem – which refers implicitly to the fact that he and Auden were both having to earn their living as teachers in boarding schools – guessed that it was influenced by his own short story 'The Colleagues', which Auden had read, and which talks in similar terms about the fate of schoolmasters: 'I shall be here or in places similar to this', says Upward's narrator, 'for the rest of my life.'

Now comes an Ode addressed 'To John Warner, son of Rex and Frances Warner'. After leaving Oxford, Rex Warner (who was later to make a reputation as a novelist and poet) became a schoolmaster, like Auden and Upward. In July 1930, Auden went to stay with him and his wife Frances, at Rex's parents' house at Amberley in Gloucestershire. A son had just been born to them – he was christened Jonathan – and was a fine sturdy boy; Auden pushed him about in his pram, and about eighteen months later sent a manuscript of this poem to the Warners.

The poem announces that here at last is the Leader, in the person of the Warners' infant son, who is to be a messiah to an ailing society: 'Here it is, look! John, son of Warner, / John, son of Warner, shall rescue you.' Under his leadership all Lawrence's ideals will be realised:

---

afterwards made a reputation as an adventurer. 'For where are Basley who won the Ten' alludes to 'The Ten', a celebrated cross-country race at the school, though there was no one by the name of Basley at Sedbergh in Carritt's time. The name 'Mrs Allom' in the poem 'Get there if you can' is an allusion to the mother of Auden's undergraduate friend V. M. Allom, at whose home he stayed for some days in the late 1920s. Mrs Allom's name appears, in the poem, in a list of 'These who have betrayed us nicely' – i.e. enemies of society. V. M. Allom writes of this, in an unpublished memoir of Auden: 'The real trouble between Wystan and my mother was that the latter was a recent convert to the Roman Church and was tactless in her references to religion.' The name 'Dr Frommer' in the same poem is recorded in Auden's 1929 Berlin journal: 'Dr Frommer said, "During the beginning of the war things were wonderful here. Lots of young soldiers, some of them slightly wounded." By choice he made himself immune.' The journal contains no further references to this man, whose identity remains a mystery.

> The few shall be taught who want to understand,
> Most of the rest shall live upon the land;
> Living in one place with a satisfied face
> All of the women and most of the men
> Shall work with their hands and not think again.

In its jaunty progress, this poem mocks various representatives of the Enemy, who in the version in Auden's notebook were identified as actual contemporary English figures: Wyndham Lewis, Robert Graves (described by Auden as 'spooning' with 'Laura' – that is, Laura Riding), and even T. S. Eliot. However, in the text that Auden submitted for publication, the names of Mortmere characters were substituted. The Warner Ode, an extraordinarily vigorous piece of writing, reflects a comment made by Auden to John Pudney in April 1931: 'On the whole I believe that in our time it is only possible to write comic poetry; not the Punch variety, but real slapstick.'

The fifth Ode is headed 'To my pupils'. It describes the war against the Enemy, but as seen from the viewpoint of the Enemy themselves, Auden's pupils in a private boarding school, training in the ranks of the oppressors. Meanwhile the other side are mustering not far away, and defeat seems certain – defeat, that is, of the Enemy:

> All leave is cancelled to-night; we must say good-bye.
> We entrain at once for the North; we shall see in the morning
> The headlands we're doomed to attack; snow down to the tideline:
>   Though the bunting signals
> 'Indoors before it's too late; cut peat for your fires',
>   We shall lie out there.

The sixth and final Ode is a hymn of the Enemy in their defeat, a stylistic parody of the tortuous syntax of the Scottish metrical psalter used at the Larchfield school services, which prays at last for illumination rather than destruction.

Auden composed two short lyrics to serve as prologue and epilogue to *The Orators*. The prologue, 'By landscape reminded once of his mother's figure', shows how the fatal division in the personality originates with the mother, and engenders emotional cowardice and deception; the epilogue, ' " O where are you going?" said reader to rider', suggests that by the end of *The Orators* the Lawrentian view has in a sense won; the Leader, undeterred, renews his resolution to journey off on his quest.

How seriously did Auden himself accept the Lawrentian views put forward in *The Orators*? He told Naomi Mitchison that the theme was the 'failure' of Lawrence's conception of personality. Yet the six Odes and the Journal appear to put forward Lawrence's ideas uncritically, if rather frivolously. After *The Orators* was published, Auden said of it: 'It is meant to be a critique of the fascist outlook [i.e. Lawrence's outlook, which amounted to something like fascism] but from its reception among my contemporaries and on rereading it myself, I see that it can, most of it, be interpreted as a favourable exposition. The whole Journal ought to be completely rewritten.' When he came to look at *The Orators* again thirty-five years later, Auden felt that the work had been largely serious in its support of Lawrence's extreme views. He said he could not recognise himself as the person who wrote it: 'My name on the title-page seems a pseudonym for someone else, someone talented but near the border of sanity, who might well, in a year or two, become a Nazi.' This is surely an exaggeration, and misses the large element of sheer foolery in the work. The fact that much of *The Orators* is parody of one literary model or another suggests that the book is fundamentally largely a joke. On the other hand Auden certainly did admire Lawrence, though not uncritically, at the time when he wrote it. Probably he came closest to the truth when he wrote in 1967:

> My guess to-day is that my unconscious motive in writing [*The Orators*] was therapeutic, to exorcise certain tendencies in myself by allowing them to run riot in phantasy. . . It is precisely the schoolboy atmosphere and diction which act as a moral criticism of the rather ugly emotions and ideas they are employed to express. By making the latter juvenile, they make it impossible to take them seriously. In one of the Odes I express all the sentiments with which his followers hailed the advent of Hitler, but these are rendered, I hope, innocuous by the fact the the Führer so hailed is a new-born baby and the son of a friend.

Work on *The Orators* was finished by the late autumn of 1931. Auden wrote to Gabriel Carritt: 'I have been writing a lot which I suppose you will see some time.' He told Stephen Spender he had written the book 'in sweat and blood'. The manuscript was sent to Faber's, and T. S. Eliot wrote back: 'The second part seems to me quite brilliant though I do not quite get its connexion with the first.' The book was accepted for publication.

*

Larchfield Academy was now in a decline. At the end of October 1931, during his fifth term teaching there, Auden wrote to Gabriel Carritt: 'The school gathers mildew. Numbers down, the headmaster partially blind, his wife growing gradually mad in a canvas shelter in the garden. I spend most of my time adjusting the flow of water to the lavatories.' And to Naomi Mitchison he reported: 'The house with the fives court has been burnt down. The headmaster's wife has taken to climbing trees.'

There was of course a certain amount of fantasy in these accounts of the school's misfortunes. At this time, Auden tended to see things largely in terms of *The Orators*. 'The English countryside', he told a friend after a train journey south from Helensburgh, 'is in a terrible state, full of clergymen disguised as gigolos, and gigolos disguised as clergymen.' Nevertheless things really were in a bad way at Larchfield. After a few months, Perkins the headmaster gave up entirely and retired, and a new man was appointed – who proved even worse. Because of his fondness for drink, Auden gave him the nickname 'the Larchfield boozer'.

Meanwhile Auden was in the middle of an affair with the young man he had taken to the Shetlands. He was, no doubt, also attracted erotically to some of his pupils at Larchfield; a short poem that he wrote in the month after he first began teaching there, 'This lunar beauty', is an appreciation of the beauty of children. It would perhaps have been possible for him to take sexual advantage of his position; he said of his job as schoolmaster: 'It's pleasant as it's easy to secure / The hero worship of the immature'; and many years later he remarked: 'Those [homosexuals] who like "chicken" have relatively few problems: among thirteen- and fourteen-year-old boys there are a great many more Lolitas than the public suspects.' However, at Larchfield he seems to have had no affairs with pupils, but only with the young man, who was in his late teens and lived near the school. Auden referred to him in letters to friends as 'my chum' – he told Gabriel Carritt: 'My Helensburgh chum has taken to sitting on my knee.' The affair prompted a couple of short lyrics that indicate the happiness Auden derived from it; one is 'That night when joy began'; the other, 'For what as easy', includes this stanza:

> Who goes with who
> The bedclothes say
> And I and you
> Go kissed away
> The data given
> The senses even.

Auden, meanwhile, felt the need for friends. 'Please introduce me to some nice people in Scotland,' he wrote to Naomi Mitchison, whose family had a Scottish house. 'I don't know a soul.' In fact he did know the Snodgrass family (alluded to in *The Orators*) who lived opposite the school. 'Pop' Snodgrass, an alcoholic with private means who did no work, could not stand Auden, but 'Mop' liked him – she compared his appearance to that of a newly hatched chicken – and she often gave him supper. He usually had a prodigious appetite; one evening he ate six eggs at a sitting, as well as cold ham and salad. He also became friendly with their daughter Iris, who was engaged to Alan Sinkinson, the mathematics master at Larchfield. Auden wrote an epithalamium for their wedding in the summer of 1932. He got on very well, too, with one of the Snodgrass sons, Arnold, always known as 'Nob', who was an undergraduate at Oxford. When 'Nob' left Oxford with a degree in English he found himself stranded back at Helensburgh quite unable to get a job – the Depression was making it difficult even for graduates to find employment. Auden took trouble to amuse and occupy him. He gave him the freedom of his room at Larchfield, and would deliberately leave books lying open there to intrigue him, works by Wilfred Owen, Housman, and others whom Snodgrass did not know. He also persuaded him to read Groddeck. 'He had a faculty for knowing what spring to touch in me,' recalled Snodgrass. 'I cannot imagine anyone being kinder.'[1]

Snodgrass greatly admired D. H. Lawrence; Auden gave him a copy of *Fantasia of the Unconscious,* but somewhat mocked Snodgrass's 'D. H. Lawrence mysticism' as he called it – an indication that he himself no longer took Lawrence very seriously. When the proofs of his own 'memorial' to Lawrence, *The Orators,* arrived from Faber & Faber, he enlisted Snodgrass's help with correcting them. And, in order to keep Snodgrass's spirits up, he proposed that the two of them should collaborate on an article about public schools. The article, which was apparently on the same lines as Auden's later highly critical piece about Gresham's School in *The Old School* (1934), was duly written and submitted to the journal *Life and Letters,* which apparently accepted it; but it was never published.

By now, Snodgrass had come to know Auden well, but he had no suspicion of his friend's sexual habits. He was flabbergasted when Auden one day said quite casually that he was a homosexual, adding: 'Don't worry, you're not my type.'

Besides having supper at the Snodgrass house, Auden was sometimes invited to meet another Helensburgh resident, Mrs Helen Campbell, widow of the Episcopalian Bishop of Glasgow and the Isles. While dining at her house in the autumn of 1931 he was introduced to her cousin-by-marriage Anne Fremantle, who was aged twenty-one and had just graduated from Oxford. That evening, they discussed religion, and Auden gave no indication that he had rejected his church upbringing. They argued about the Patripassian heresy, the belief that God the Father shared in the physical sufferings of the Son; Anne Fremantle believed it herself, but Auden attacked it because, he said, it was denied by the first of the Thirty-Nine Articles, which declares that God is 'without body, parts, or passions'. And, when the conversation turned to more frivolous things, he quoted the Gilbertian rhyme then in circulation attacking the 1928 version of the Book of Common Prayer as 'A plainly papistical,

[1] 'Nob' Snodgrass was, during his vacations, one of a group of young men who used the Larchfield badminton court in the evenings. Auden used to give them tea after their game, and refers to this briefly in a poem – 'the tea is on the stove; / And up the stair come voices that I love' (*The English Auden,* p. 116).

grossly sophistical, / Most anti-scriptural book'. In other words, he was still very interested in the dogmas and arguments of religion, and he gave no indication to Anne Fremantle that he himself had abandoned belief in a personal God. Yet when next year (1932) he contributed to Naomi Mitchison's *Outline for Boys and Girls and Their Parents,* which had been commissioned by Victor Gollancz as a symposium of informed left-wing views on major topics – Auden's article was on 'Writing' – he told Mrs Mitchison, after the book's publication: 'I agree with the Bishops that Xrist [i.e. Christ] should not have been omitted. Why not attacked.' The *Outline* had been criticised by bishops, headmasters and others for giving no mention of Christ; the implication of Auden's remark seems to be that he thought a book such as this should take an anti-religious line. And in October 1931 he wrote to Christopher Isherwood: 'I've had a most important vision about groups which is going to destroy the Church.' He did not explain what he meant, though it seems that he believed the church would be supplanted by the new community of the group. At all events his attitude to religion was at present far from settled.[1]

It might indeed be said that he had no settled views on anything. His gradual if only partial rejection of Layard's and Lawrence's views left him largely without a dogma. This was evident from a poem of some length he wrote a few months after finishing *The Orators,* in February 1932.

The poem begins with Auden himself leaving Larchfield on foot one morning while his pupils are occupied by exams. He climbs up to the moorland above Helensburgh and, looking around him, sees or dreams that he sees 'The English in all sorts and sizes come / Like an army recruited there'. What he observes, and describes in the poem, is a kind of tapestry or strip-cartoon of contemporary English life. Well-known figures from every walk of society, politics, entertainment, arts, business, the universities, appear one by one and are systematically guyed. At first glance the poem seems to be satirical, but it quickly becomes evident that Auden is being a buffoon rather than a satirist. Certainly he takes no positive political line, but presents all the politicians as equally ridiculous:

> Ramsay MacDonald was rubbing his seat:
> At last he'd been invited to a Leicestershire Meet. . .
> Baldwin was wiping his nose on his pipe;. . .
> Limping but keeping a stiff upper lip
> Churchill was speaking of a battleship:
> It was some little time before I had guessed
> He wasn't describing a woman's breast.

---

[1] Auden's article in the *Outline for Boys and Girls* and his views on the importance of 'groups' at this period of his life are discussed in detail by Edward Mendelson in *Early Auden.*

A passage in the Ode to John Warner in *The Orators* takes a similarly neutral and mocking attitude to politics; among those it attacks are not only Oswald Mosley's extreme right-wingers but also 'the I.L.P.' – the Independent Labour Party, a breakaway group from the main Labour movement. Auden as yet made no distinctions; all politics appeared equally absurd to him.

It was not only politics that he mocked in his 1932 dream-poem, which he entitled 'A Happy New Year'. Among those he guys in it are T. S. Eliot, whom he calls 'Unhappy Eliot choosing his words'; D. H. Lawrence, who is represented by a man declaring 'The colon we know is the seat of the soul', a reference to Lawrence's belief that the personality is partly seated in the 'lower centres' of the body; and even 'My old headmaster in a little pink vest'. The poem ends inconclusively with Auden musing on 'these blurring images / Of the difficult dingy life of our generation'. The point seems to be that although contemporary society is deluged with the dogmas of all kinds of 'healers' it lacks any controlling intelligence. But the poem is too farcical to convey even this comment effectively, and with its host of topical references it was bound to date very quickly. After its initial publication (in *New Country* in 1933) Auden did not reprint it. It is chiefly interesting as an example of his willingness to write schoolboy foolery and doggerel when the occasion seemed to demand it. He once said of this: 'It's awfully important that writers aren't afraid to write badly. . . The moment you're really afraid of writing badly. . . then you'll never write anything any good.'

Strictly speaking, it was the first part of 'A Happy New Year' which Auden did not reprint, for the poem includes a second and much shorter section which he did preserve in collections of his verse. This begins 'Now from my window-sill I watch the night', and is entirely different in tone from what precedes it. In it, Auden prays that his pupils at Larchfield and his other friends at Helensburgh shall be protected from whatever social or political upheaval – perhaps a revolution – may be in store. This prayer is addressed not to God but to two godlike figures who here make the first of several appearances in Auden's poetry, and whom he here describes as 'Lords of Limit. . . / The influential quiet twins / From whom all property begins'; he also compares them to 'erratic examiners', or 'The stocky keepers of a wild estate'. Their precise nature is not made clear, though they are obviously some kind of Fates. Auden very likely took them (as Samuel Hynes suggests) from the 'two witnesses' in the eleventh chapter of the Book of Revelation, who are given authority over the earth; no doubt he was also thinking of D. H. Lawrence's gloss on this passage in his book *Apocalypse,* for Lawrence explained these 'witnesses' as powers that 'put a limit on man' and 'say to him in every earthly or physical activity: thus far and no further. . . They make life possible; but they make life limited.'

Auden had completed the two parts of 'A Happy New Year' by the beginning of March 1932, when he wrote to Naomi Mitchison: 'I have finished a poem of some length.' When it was published a year later he dedicated it to a man he had recently met, whose ideas, during 1932, influenced him strongly, and who for a time occupied the place in his life that had previously been held by 'loony Layard'. This was Gerald Heard.

Heard, who was in his early forties, became well known in the 1930s as a populariser of scientific subjects on the BBC radio series *This Surprising World*. But this was only one of his activities. He had published two substantial books: *The Ascent of Humanity* (1929) and *The Social Substance of Religion* (1931); he also edited a short-lived magazine which advocated 'Scientific Humanism'; and now and then he wrote detective stories. No better description can be given of him than that in P. N. Furbank's life of E. M. Forster: 'Heard. . . was reputed to read two thousand books a year and had an extraordinary flow of information about hygiene, sex, paranormal phenomena and the probable destiny of mankind. He was a dress-fetishist, favouring purple suede shoes and leather jackets with leopard-skin collars, and he had his eyelids painted with what looked like mascara (actually a specific against conjunctivitis). Strangers thought of him, nervously, as a sort of Wellsian supermind or "man of the future". . . Leo Charlton once said: "Have you noticed how Morgan [Forster]'s friends always drop their voices when they talk of him, as if he were Jesus Christ?"'

Heard, who was homosexual, lived with a rich young man named Chris Wood in a modern luxury flat in the West End of London. Auden visited him there on a number of occasions, and Christopher Isherwood recalls the two of them engaging in 'abstruse scientific conversation'. Heard appealed to Auden partly because, like Auden himself, he took an interest in scientific matters from the point of view of the non-scientist; partly because, again like Auden, he sought to make some kind of intellectual order out of the chaos of human history, knowledge and belief; and, perhaps most of all, because he offered an interpretation of human nature which was one step forward from the Lawrentian doctrines which Auden had, in their raw form, almost certainly now rejected.

Heard, like Lawrence, believed that man's nature is divided, and that neurosis arises from the suppression of one half of this nature. But to him the division was not between mind and body or reason and instinct; rather, it was between a subjective, unselfconscious, inner personality – man in his natural state – and an objective, self-regarding, outer mind to which Heard gave the name 'economic man', because it had arisen, he said, as a result of the demands of modern economically-motivated society. He argued that the suppression of the inner personality and the increasing dominance of 'economic man' would lead to neurosis in the individual and to revolution in society at large.

This idea, expressed by Heard in *The Social Substance of Religion,* a book of remarkable unreadability, was taken over wholesale by Auden in his next attempt to write a major poem. Meanwhile he dedicated 'A Happy New Year' to Heard, perhaps because he believed him to be one of the few sane men in a world of mountebanks, a world such as he pictured in the first part of the poem. And in another poem he described Heard as a 'noble amateur', one of those who 'towards the really better world have turned their faces'.

By the time he had finished 'A Happy New Year', Auden was uneasy about *The Orators,* which was about to go to press. He wrote to Eliot at Faber's suggesting that a preface be inserted to apologise for the fact that, as he put it, 'this book is more obscure than it ought to be'. This draft preface also gave an explanation of *The Orators* which differed somewhat from the exegesis Auden had given to Naomi Mitchison:

> The central theme is a revolutionary hero. The first book describes the effect of him and of his failure on those whom he meets; the second book is his own account; and the last some personal reflections on the question of leadership in our time.

Eliot advised Auden against printing this preface, and it was dropped; but Auden remained dissatisfied with the book as it stood, and wrote in reply to a reader's letter a few months later: 'I didn't taken enough trouble over it, and the result is far too obscure and equivocal.' All the same, when Auden had the chance to revise *The Orators* for a second edition in 1934, he did little more than drop some verse passages from the Journal and change the sex of the Airman's lover from female to male.

When *The Orators* was first published in May 1932, many critics commented on the obscurity. Few of them, indeed, were prepared to make more than the vaguest guesses as to what it was all about, though John Hayward in the *Criterion* judged that 'Mr Auden is profoundly dissatisfied with the present state of civilisation in this country', and Graham Greene in the *Oxford Magazine* wrote: 'The subject of the book is political, though it is hard to tell whether the author's sympathies are Communist or Fascist.' Not surprisingly, several reviewers objected to the private jokes, which they thought had been put in for the amusement of a coterie. But there was a remarkable unanimity in the final verdict on *The Orators*. Everyone judged it a tremendous achievement. Hayward, a close friend of Eliot, called it 'the most valuable contribution to English poetry since "The Waste Land" '; Greene described it as 'an astonishing advance on Mr Auden's first book'; and the *Times Literary Supplement* said of Auden: 'He is insolently but exhilaratingly new.'

Many of Auden's contemporaries came to the same conclusion. Like these reviewers, they were not at all sure what *The Orators* meant, but they recognised in its hotchpotch of private allusions, parody, and anti-authoritarianism their own experience of the world. They did not understand it rationally, but they knew very well what Auden was saying. As one of them, the poet and critic Michael Roberts, wrote in the *Adelphi:* 'He experiences the sensibility of a generation.'

Roberts's only reservation about Auden was that 'it still remains to be seen whether he will be able to organise the material with which his technique enables him to deal'; and this comment was echoed by several other reviewers, who hoped that Auden might now proceed towards a more positive and coherent form of expression. A slightly different reservation came from T. S. Eliot, who, while visiting America and lecturing at Harvard, discussed Auden's *Poems* and *The Orators* with Harry Levin, then an undergraduate there. 'Eliot was warm in his commendation and recommendation of both,' recalled Levin, 'while his predictions for Auden's future virtually constituted a laying on of hands. Yet he hinted at one slight caveat against the hazards of facility.' Eliot was also strongly aware of Auden's lack of a settled ideology. Late in 1930 he wrote to Herbert Read: 'I chiefly worry about Auden's ethical principles and convictions, not about his technical ability; or rather, I think that if a man's ethical and religious views and convictions are feeble or limited and incapable of development, then his technical development is restricted.'

★

By the summer term of 1932, Auden had decided to leave Larchfield. The school was in a very poor way – it did not improve until Perkins's successor as headmaster was replaced by yet another man – and Auden's affair with his 'Helensburgh chum' had come to an end in the spring when the young man left the district; a poem that Auden wrote in April refers to their parting: 'O, my magnet, my pomp, my beauty / . . . To-day is parted from me.'

He began to make some attempt to find another job. In the early spring he went with Gerald Heard to visit Dartington, the progressive boarding school in Devon, whose founders were friends of Heard's; and in May he wrote to Dartington asking for a job. The reply (he told Naomi Mitchison) was 'friendly but doubtful'. His letter to her continued 'I really want to go to Ottershaw College, the place started by the man who was sacked from Bryanston. According to Edward Upward, who is there, its the buggers dream: a cross between Mädchen in Uniform and The Castle.' But nothing came of this, and, when the summer term ended early in July, Auden left Larchfield without a job.

He stayed for a few days in London, and had tea with Edith Sitwell, who was well aware of his growing reputation, of which she was jealous and critical. She maintained that he wrote 'uninteresting poetry' and that his work was a 'bore'. But she seems to have been friendly to Auden when they met. He reported to Nob Snodgrass: 'She's just like one of my aunts.' In later years her opinion of Auden's poetry greatly improved.

She met him again often, and they became very friendly; he gave her several of his later books of poetry, and she made marks in her copy of *Another Time* which indicate her approval of several poems in it. She and Auden also delighted to exchange stories of eccentric and tiresome 'fans', from whose attentions they both suffered.

While Auden was in London in the summer of 1932 he stayed with his old schoolfriend, the painter Robert Medley, who was now living with a dancer, choreographer and theatrical director named Rupert Doone. Medley and Doone had suggested that Auden visit them so that they could put a proposal to him about a new theatrical project in which they were involved.

Doone, whose real name was Ernest Reginald Woodfield, was born in 1903, the son of a foreman in a needle factory in Worcestershire. When he was sixteen he ran away to London to go on the stage, and, after training in a ballet school, began to get professional engagements as a dancer, first in London and then in Paris, where at the age of nineteen he was taken up by Cocteau and his circle. Returning to London in 1924, he worked with and understudied Massine in a Cochran revue, and in 1925 produced the dances for an interlude in Nigel Playfair's production of *The Duenna* at the Lyric, Hammersmith, which brought him some recognition. At this time he first met Robert Medley, and in 1926 Medley joined him in Paris. It was there in 1928 that Doone's career as a dancer reached its climax. He was engaged by Ida Rubinstein for her season at the Opéra, where his talent was noticed by Diaghilev. The result was an invitation to join the Ballets Russes as a soloist when they came to Covent Garden in June 1929. This was an exceptional chance for Doone; but his hope of achieving fame in Diaghilev's company was swiftly brought to an end by the impresario's death in August that year. Doone's reaction was to turn aside from a career devoted exclusively to the dance, and to concern himself with other aspects of theatre. In 1930 he began to work at the Festival Theatre, Cambridge, learning acting and the production of plays, largely with Tyrone Guthrie. Here, Doone conceived the idea of forming a group of performers and writers who would create a synthesis of dance, mime and speech, a form of 'total theatre' that would be quite new to the English stage.

Doone said he wanted this group to be 'self-sufficient and independent of purely commercial considerations', to have 'directness and yet fantasy'. A little later, as the project developed, he and the others associated with it also came to believe it should be 'a social force' in the theatre, with vaguely left-wing ideals. The Group Theatre, as it was named, was officially constituted in February 1932. During that spring and summer it mounted a couple of small-scale productions in London and Henley. Now Doone, and Medley, who was working closely with him as the Group Theatre's designer, were keen to persuade Auden to write something for it.

Auden knew Doone a little already – Medley had first introduced them in 1926 – and, like many other people, did not find Doone easy to get on with. Doone's lack of academic education made him insecure in the company of intellectuals, and this insecurity, combined with a determination to get his own way in artistic matters, often made him aggressive or dictatorial. He also had an intuitive rather than a rational mind, and sometimes took a long time to express himself clearly; as Medley puts it, 'Rupert sometimes had to talk a lot of apparently illogical rubbish before he made sense even to himself.' He was, too, very much the ballet-dancer in appearance and manner, and this did not help his relationship with Auden, who early in the proceedings made his own dislike of ballet very clear, calling it, in Doone's hearing, 'an art only fit for adolescents'. ('Rupert blanched slightly at this, but let it pass,' remembers Medley.) There may also, at Auden's first meeting with Doone, have been some degree of jealousy on Auden's side of Doone's relationship with Medley, of whom Auden remained deeply fond. But if this was so, it had disappeared by 1932, and Auden was greatly interested in the proposal which Doone put to him that summer.

As Doone remembered it, 'Auden, Robert Medley and myself were talking about the sort of theatre of ideas we would like to have. I asked Auden if he would write me a ballet to choreograph and perform in, on the theme of Orpheus' descent into the Underworld. At the same time I suggested he might write a play on the theme of *le danse macabre,* the late mediaeval poem, which he had brought me to read.' (Precisely which poem Doone meant is not clear.) Robert Medley, on the other hand, recalled the suggestion as being that Auden should write *either* an Orpheus ballet *or* a 'dance of death' play. At all events, it was the first of the two projects that Auden decided to undertake; he planned to include words in the ballet, for (writing to a friend) he described it as 'a sort of choral ballet affair'. Doone intended, if all went well, to perform it in London.

After staying with Doone and Medley, Auden travelled up to the Lake District and spent some weeks at Wescoe, his family's cottage at Threlkeld, where he began work immediately on the new project. On 20 July he wrote to Doone: 'I'm getting on with the Orpheus stuff. God knows what its like. I'm finding it rather a holiday task, but experience tells me that the pleasure of writing and its value have little connection, so hope for the best.'

Meanwhile he still had to find a new teaching post. On 23 July he wrote to Nob Snodgrass: 'Have you a job. I havent. . . I've just begun entreating Winchester Choirboys to let me teach them French.' And a few days later: 'I have just answered an advertisement in the church times to be an assistant tutor in a country rectory. After supper there will be Harmonium on the lawn and naked bathing will be usual.' Neither of these job-applications came to anything, and Auden began to consider alternatives to teaching. On 28 July he wrote to John Pudney, who was working as a chartered surveyor in London: 'As to jobs. Business would do me perfectly well if I would do them. Let me know anything you may hear of. If its any use, I speak German.'

His mother was with him at the Lake District cottage, and after a few days of her company he invited Nob Snodgrass to pay them a visit: 'Do come if you can, as living alone with Ma is a bit of a strain.' Snodgrass duly came, and found Mrs Auden rather forbidding. In the mornings, Wystan retired to his room to work, emerging for lunch, sometimes to declare triumphantly that he had written 'more than a hundred lines' during the morning, sometimes to say disconsolately that he had been 'constipated' and had produced virtually nothing. In the afternoon he would take Snodgrass on trips in the countryside, visiting not the usual beauty spots of the Lakes but old mine-workings with rusting machinery. On these journeys, Auden usually wore a pair of white shorts which exposed his long pale legs; once, on an expedition with Snodgrass at Helensburgh, he had also worn a red shirt and his old broad-brimmed hat from Oxford days, in which he had now made a bullet hole. Snodgrass was embarrassed to be seen with him.

Snodgrass had now found a job, teaching at a preparatory school in the south of England; and it was at about this time – the beginning of August – that Auden himself was at last successful in finding employment. He was accepted for a post at the Downs School at Colwall in Herefordshire, to start the next month. He spent the latter part of August with the Carritts in Pembrokeshire, and then went again to London for a few days, where he met Christopher Isherwood, who was paying a brief visit from Berlin. He also called on John Pudney.

Pudney was now aged twenty-three, two years younger than Auden, and was continuing to send his own poems to Auden for comment. Auden was severely critical: 'Your subject is too big and important for a series of lyrics. . . You're still a bit tongue-tied. Thats fear. . . Not having seen you I cant say what is the cause of this. Is it sex or lack of a decent group-life? . . . What do you look like now. Send me a photograph.' Pudney, whom Auden had not set eyes on since schooldays at Gresham's, duly sent a photo. He realised that Auden 'wanted to see if I had grown up pretty – and, in the hands of a German photographer, I had'.

When Auden received the picture he wrote back to Pudney: 'I know those Germans. They make everyone look like a sun-bather.' But he concluded his letter: 'At Holt [i.e. Gresham's School] I was a bloody little funk. Had I not been we should have had much fun.' When he was in London early in September he visited Pudney, and had sex with him. Pudney later wrote of this: 'There were no concessions to love. It was just meat he was after.'[1]

[1]Auden seems to have behaved in bed, on at least some occasions, with the manner of a schoolmaster. Describing the seduction of one young man, he told a friend: 'I said to him,

Pudney gave Auden more of his poems to read, and when Auden got back home to Harborne he wrote (on 18 September) to Pudney:

My dear John,

I've read your poems through a number of times. They're no use. They're very much better than what two or three thousand young Englishmen with literary interests are doing; any living writer under forty who is any good has written the same sort of thing, but in themselves they're quite worthless. Dont think I despise you for writing them; your ego has got to shed its droppings just as your intestines have to; but they have exactly the same hygienic value and no more; they're droppings and not babies. Don't ask me what you're to do because I havent the slightest idea. What I feel inclined to say is, chuck all this literary business. Go and do something useful like digging the roads or organising strikes. Forget all about yourself, learn to say 'I'm very ordinary' and one day perhaps it will come back to you. He who loses his life shall find it. The literatteur is as useless to society as a collar stud to a nude woman.

If I can ever help you in any way let me know.

love
Wystan Auden.

After this, Auden set off for his new teaching job.

★

The Downs School at Colwall could scarcely have been more different from Larchfield. It was a flourishing, happy and efficiently-run preparatory school on the edge of a village that lay directly beneath the ridge of the Malvern Hills. A walker who left the school buildings and ascended the steep road behind them would, in less than half an hour, be at the top of the Malverns, gazing out over the plains of the English Midlands and towards Wales in the west. 'Here on the cropped grass of the narrow ridge I stand,' wrote Auden,

> England below me:
> Eastward across the Midland plains
> An express is leaving for a sailors' country;
>   Westward is Wales
> Where on clear evenings the retired and rich
> From the french windows of their sheltered mansions
> See the Sugarloaf standing, an upright sentinel
>   Over Abergavenny.

"You did that bit quite well, not bad for a beginner. Now tomorrow night we'll have a go at such-and-such.'"

The Downs School itself had been founded in 1900 by a Quaker headmaster, and still had strong connections with the Society of Friends. Both the Cadburys and the Rowntrees, wealthy Quaker chocolate-making families, sent boys to it, and the wife of the headmaster, Geoffrey Hoyland, was a Cadbury. 'Our money comes from chocolate,' Auden wrote to Naomi Mitchison. 'Mrs Head is a Cadbury.' There were now over eighty boys in the school, all boarders, and the numbers were still growing. A great emphasis was put on hobbies; music and painting were much encouraged, and there was an outdoor swimming pool and even a model steam railway, big enough for the boys to ride on. The prefects were known as 'leaders'.

Auden's first reactions to the school were mixed. 'This place is an amazing contrast to Larchfield,' he wrote to Nob Snodgrass's sister Iris. 'Wonderful buildings, and food. Open air dormitories etc. 84 boys. The assistant masters who are unmarried (there are 9 staff, 6♂ and 3♀) live in our own house and have dinner there. The headmaster I believe to be a great man, in spite of religion. (We are quakers here.) And yet – apart from the fact that we are very hard worked – I feel homesick for Larchfield. One is so purely a beak here and nothing else, and the atmosphere I find a little intense. I suppose it's what the Communist state will be like; one feels it isnt done not to be enthusiastic about everything. The place is run on scout lines, with packs and leaders. I suppose its very good for their characters, but I cant say I enjoy the spectacle of boys of 13 discussing the characters of boys of 11 round the headmaster's study fire.'

He was indeed hard-worked: besides teaching English and French and helping to supervise games, as at Larchfield, he took lessons in arithmetic and biology. 'It's funny to be doing Fractions,' he remarked in a letter. (Some years later he told a friend he had 'once thought of doing a series of arithmetic textbooks'.) As to biology, he wrote to Doone that he was 'frightfully busy here telling the boys about the balls of Frogs', and added: 'How you would laugh if you saw me taking my gymnastic class.'

He had begun to develop his own theories about the teaching of English. In a review written in the spring of 1933, he said that it was 'fantastic' to make children read literary masterpieces, which were 'the reaction of exceptional adult minds to vast experience', and argued that it was better to link English teaching to the environment – 'e.g. if they are going to read or write about sawing wood, they should saw some themselves first' – and to have movement classes, plenty of acting, and 'very, very little talk'. As to poetry, he wrote: 'By all means set good poetry to be learnt by heart with an eye to the future, but let it be a test of learning, nothing else. Do not enlarge on its beauties, but see that the vocabulary is understood. Devote more time to the technical side; set periodical exercises on concrete subjects, with a list of banned common-place words. They will learn more about the meaning of poetry by writing it, than by any explanation you can give.'

As an encouragement to his pupils to write poetry, Auden persuaded the school to start a magazine in which the boys' compositions could be printed, along with school news and other items of interest. It was called *The Badger* (the Downs School emblem was a badger), and the first issue was published in his second term at the school.[1] A little later he began to organise school plays. Meanwhile the boys themselves tried to puzzle him out.

'To us', wrote one of them, Michael Yates, then aged thirteen and in his last year at the school, 'his arrival was like a glorious firework display. We could hardly believe he had come to *teach*! Completely unconventional, striding about in a large black Flemish hat, waving an umbrella, he entranced us with his eccentricity, tireless energy and sense of fun. We called him Uncle Wiz.'

Some of the boys and one or two of the staff were a little disconcerted by his unpredictability, his heavy smoking, and his nail biting. He carried a box of a hundred cigarettes about with him and littered the outer window-sill of the staff room with stubs. As to his nails, he was never actually seen biting them – perhaps he did it while writing – but the results were clearly visible. A friend wrote: 'Auden's fists are milk-white, pudgy, hairless, but the fingers are stained with nicotine, and the nails are nibbled halfway to the moons.'

Such oddness was made up for by his teaching. 'His classes were in turn traditional, original, or a plain riot of fun,' wrote Michael Yates. 'The requirements of Common Entrance were replaced by a talk on astronomy and the stars. A surfeit of essays gave way to elaborate impromptu plays. To the sixth form he explained the meaning of sex. And he made us read aloud, endlessly, banishing the monotony of the schoolboy's voice. This was not just play; it was a widening of our horizons. But woe betide the boy who misjudged the time for fun and the time for traditional work. Few could be more severe than he. But even his severity could be tempered by the unexpected. On my flipping a paper pellet at my twin brother, he said: "Make me a hundred of these

---

[1]Among compositions by Auden's pupils printed in the first issue of *The Badger* is a poem by R. H. Corson, of which this is the middle of three stanzas:

> Now the snow is falling fast,
> Nurse's flowers will not last;
> But when the sun comes out again
> All her flowers will sprout again.

Three years later, Auden wrote a poem of which this is the first stanza:

> Now the leaves are falling fast,
> Nurse's flowers will not last;
> Nurses to the graves are gone,
> And the prams go rolling on.

and bring them to The Lodge." On handing them to him, I was astonished when he threw them straight into the waste-paper basket without even looking at them. I was asked to sit down whilst he talked about painting, the theatre, and my future!'[1]

Meanwhile Auden continued to be amazed by the school. 'This place is quite incredible,' he wrote to Gabriel Carritt. 'A cross between The Plumed Serpent and the Church Lads Brigade. Lots of gongs and hymns. We have a tribe and four packs. Those who loiter in the lavatories are not thought much of. "Sir," said the tribe leader to me, "I am very interested in reproduction."' After a few weeks of the first term, Auden sought relief. 'Off to Oxford to-morrow for a quiet fuck,' he wrote to Nob Snodgrass one Friday, adding, in a postscript: 'Monday. Returned having had it.'

He now decided to abandon the Orpheus choral-ballet he was writing for the Group Theatre. On 19 October he told Rupert Doone: 'I've written a thing but frankly its no use. I'm afraid you'll think I've let you down but I know its no good. Perhaps one day I shall be able to manage it but not yet. I've got a job here which keeps me hard at it. I can't tell yet what time I shall have to write till I've settled properly in.' Another possible reason for the abandonment of the project may have been that his mind was now being taken up with a long and very ambitious poem which he had begun to write in the summer, a poem which was quite unlike anything he had attempted before.

Back in July he had written to John Hayward, thanking him for his review of *The Orators*, and adding: 'I'm getting to work now on a narrative poem in alliterative verse. God knows how it will turn out.' The manuscript of the first part of the poem is dated 'Sept-Dec 1932', so he seems to have been at work on it throughout his first term at the Downs School. The poem is untitled. This is how it begins:

> In the year of my youth when yoyos came in
> The carriage was sunny and the Clyde was bright
> As I hastened from Helensburgh in the height of summer
> Leaving for home in a lounge suit.
> Sombre were the sixteen skies of Europe,
> The stokers were seasick on the ship of state
> For the decks were dipping though MacDonald was steering.
> Rumours were rife about the Reinmuth object
> And Stiffkey was sued by the See of Norwich
> For poking his parishioners in their private parts.
> Between our vans and the vision the valves were closed.

---

[1] Yates was interested in painting and the theatre, and eventually, largely as a result of Auden's encouragement, became a stage and television designer.

I sat in my still corner while the country ran
Listening to the lulling low of the lines,
And a shadow-train flitted foreshortened through fields
Of the English counties one after another.
Day wore on. I dozed and dreamed. . .

Though the topical references[1] all place the poem's events firmly in 1932, the loosely alliterative metre is meant to recall Middle English poetry in general and *Piers Plowman* in particular. The opening lines are partly modelled on the beginning of Langland's poem:

In a somer seson . when soft was the sonne
I shope me in shroudes . as I a shepe were,
In habite as an heremite . unholy of workes,
Went wyde in this world . wondres to here.

It is on the Malvern Hills that Langland's dreamer lies down to rest and sees his vision, and Auden was of course well aware of this local association of *Piers Plowman* with the district around the Downs School. Naomi Mitchison recalls visiting him at the school and walking with him over the Malverns, while he recited line after line from Langland's poem.

As it progresses, Auden's own poem 'In the year of my youth' (to use the first words as a title) begins to echo not so much Langland as another great poetic dream-vision, the *Divine Comedy*. Auden's dreamer, who from a number of details in the poem is obviously meant to be Auden himself, dreams that his train is entering a station under a 'looming arch of steel' which recalls the entrance to the Inferno. It deposits him on the platform, where a throng of 'Schoolboys in shirts. . . / Daughters of the clergy coming home. . . / Clerks and murderers and commercial travellers' suggests the crowd whose cries Dante hears on his arrival in the underworld. Auden then goes on a tour of the city to which the train has brought him, and this tour (as Lucy McDiarmid has observed) is largely a descent from higher to lower levels of the town, just as Dante and Virgil go downwards through the concentric circles of Hell.

The guide who takes Virgil's role in Auden's poem, who is named 'Sampson', is a sun-tanned, energetic man who meets the dreamer on the station platform. They greet each other as old friends, and take a taxi through the town to a smart hotel where they have dinner. The dreamer

[1]These need some explanation. The yoyo was introduced into England in 1932, and in the same year a planetoid was discovered by the German astronomer Reinmuth. The Vicar of Stiffkey in the diocese of Norwich was deprived of his living on account of immoral conduct.

gathers that Sampson will be taking him next day to join in some kind of sporting event, apparently the meet of a hunt, and he asks for an explanation. Sampson does not give a direct answer, but begins to talk about the decay of human personality, which he declares is the root cause of recent disasters in world history and will lead, in the near future, to revolution and a World War far worse than the one recently fought. He expounds this argument in terms reminiscent of the writings of Gerald Heard – the decay of personality, he says, is the result of the dominance of 'the Economic Man' – and indeed it begins to seem that 'Sampson' is a portrait of Heard himself.

Sampson explains that, as the Depression continues, many of the working-class inhabitants of the town have rebelled against unemployment and misery, and in twos and threes have taken to the hills. He goes on: 'Our companions in the morning would compel them back.' But he gives no further explanation, and he and the dreamer now set out on a night-time tour of the town.

First they pass a gaudy cinema, then a power station, whose turbines Auden lovingly describes; then they walk on into the slum quarter of the town, where the streets are littered with garbage and the poor and unemployed are loitering, 'some slackly standing, / Their faces in the glimmering gaslight grey, / Their eyeballs drugged as a dead rabbit's'. Sampson explains that the unemployment has been largely caused by the closure of the local lead mines because of a government decision to buy foreign lead. He and the dreamer then walk to the Cathedral, which Auden declares to be finer than the great church which dominated his birthplace, York Minster. They encounter an ungainly woman who every evening pays a visit to the graves of her two sons who were killed in the 1914–18 war by a German sniper. Then, descending the slope from the Cathedral, they take a tram to the silent and darkened Cattle Market, where stands a caravan occupied by two old men who have invited them both to tea and biscuits.

The old men are 'Titt and Tool', and the dreamer recognises them as the authors of all the grim textbooks that made his schooldays a misery; Sampson explains that they visit this city each year 'to inspect the choir school'. But they are more than just archetypal pedagogues. They know all about the dreamer and the fact that he is out of work and looking for a job (this is supposedly the summer of 1932, when Auden was trying to find a teaching post), and they say they have 'nearly completed / Our arrangements for you'. They are in fact the Fate-like 'Lords of Limit' of Auden's earlier poem 'A Happy New Year'; and their power over people's lives is demonstrated when Sampson asks them to give special consideration to a friend of his sister's who has lost his job. Titt and Tool tell their secretary to produce the relevant file on the case, but when they see the name of the man's previous employer, who sacked him, they abruptly close the file and change the subject, remarking to Sampson:

'We're simply the servants of a system, you know.' Yet it is made clear that they have great power and influence in the world, as is demonstrated by a song they now sing.

This is the tale of Prince Alpha, a hero universally admired who is nevertheless brought to his knees by Titt and Tool, and is forced to admit that he is not the 'truly strong man'. Titt and Tool then describe their power over human life ('You are the town and we are the clock / We are the guardians of the gate in the rock'), and conclude their song with a hint of what will happen if they are ignored ('The sky is darkening like a stain / Something is going to fall like rain / And it won't be flowers'). Auden later separated Titt and Tool's song from 'In the year of my youth' and printed it as 'The Witnesses', a title which recalls Titt and Tool's origins in the 'two witnesses' of Revelation.

Sampson and the dreamer return to their hotel. The dreamer pledges his loyalty to Sampson in warm terms, and Sampson replies by silently exchanging his wristwatch with his friend's: 'Here let it beat / Touching our flesh your time and mine / Remind our uneven hearts for ever'. They go to the room they are sharing, and the first Canto of 'In the year of my youth' ends with them falling asleep, 'Snug in our warmth and certain we were friends'.

Auden was in the middle of writing this first Canto, which totals more than 900 lines, on 18 October 1932, when he told Naomi Mitchison: 'I am very hard worked but am pegging away at my epic.' He also wrote to Nob Snodgrass: 'I peg away in the few moments I get to myself at my epic. It will [be] alright if it only doesnt become what D.H.L. called "would-be". I enclose a little ditty to go to the tune of Frankie and Johnny.'

This 'little ditty' was a short poem beginning 'I have a handsome profile', and it is noteworthy as being one of the first poems that Auden wrote with an exclusively socio-political content, and which marked the beginning of what has been called his Communist phase.

★

Auden probably read Marx in undergraduate days; apparently in Berlin he had made contact with Communists. But up to 1932 his poetry carried no more than vague left-wing implications, and, when he talked of revolution, the upheaval that he had in mind was predominantly a psychological one. For instance in the poem 'Consider this and in our time' he addresses, in the manner of a revolutionary, various members of the middle classes (financiers, university dons and the like) and tells them grimly 'It is later than you think.' But the poem attacks bourgeois society not on Marxist grounds but because such a society represses the natural instincts; and the crisis prophesied in the closing lines is not social revolution but psychological illness, described in terms taken from

McDougall's *Outline of Abnormal Psychology*: 'Irregular breathing. . . alternate ascendancies. . . the explosion of mania. . . a classic fatigue'. Even the urban poverty and unemployment described in 'In the year of my youth' are presented largely as a consequence of the psychological decay of humanity according to the theories of Gerald Heard.

But other influences were now at work on Auden. Gabriel Carritt had joined the Communist Party, a step that he took while he was studying social problems in America at the time of the Wall Street crash; and Edward Upward, too, was gradually and steadily moving towards Communism. While he was doing so, Upward showed Auden three pieces of writing which described his growing interest in Marxist ideology. The first was an account of his initial contact with the Party, together with an attack on various bourgeois attitudes; in this piece Upward also argued that a writer 'needed' the working classes and could help them if he chose. The second piece that he showed Auden was a journal describing his gradual progress towards Communism. Auden read this during May or June 1932, and at about this time he also saw Upward's short story 'Sunday', in which a young office worker, after contemplating his own neurosis and insecurity, decides that he will 'make a start' by attending a Communist meeting.

Upward and Carritt were by no means alone among Auden's friends in being attracted by Communism. The failure of Ramsay MacDonald's Labour government, and the feeling that his formation of a coalition in 1931 had finally betrayed the Labour cause, was leading many people whose attitudes had previously been only vaguely left-wing to turn towards Communism, on the grounds that it was the only ideology that still offered hope of redressing the vast economic injustices of the Depression, and of combating the Fascist forces which seemed to be gaining strength every day in Europe and Asia. Stephen Spender, observing the Berlin Communists at work (much as Auden had done) was 'impressed by the overwhelming accusation made by Communism against bourgeois society'. Cecil Day-Lewis was working on a sequence of poems, *The Magnetic Mountain,* which was to show that poetry is compatible with revolution – the sequence, incidentally, drew heavily on Auden's style and imagery for its details. Of Auden's close friends, only Christopher Isherwood refused to commit himself to a political standpoint, maintaining what he described as his 'ambiguous position as an outsider, a non-joiner'; though even he was impressed by Edward Upward's views.

It was in August 1932, shortly before he began work at the Downs School, that Auden wrote a poem which was printed the next month in *Twentieth Century* magazine, under the title 'A Communist to others'. These are the first three stanzas:

Comrades, who when the sirens roar
From office, shop and factory pour
  'Neath evening sky;
By cops directed to the fug
Of talkie-houses for a drug
Or down canals to find a hug
  Until you die:

We know, remember, what it is
That keeps you celebrating this
  Sad ceremonial;
We know the terrifying brink
From which in dreams you nightly shrink.
'I shall be sacked without', you think,
  'A testimonial'.

We cannot put on airs with you
The fears that hurt you hurt us too
  Only we say
That like all nightmares these are fake
If you would help us we could make
Our eyes to open, and awake
  Shall find night day.

The poem goes on to address those who have oppressed the workers, albeit unconsciously: the elegant middle-class young man; the person who takes flight from reality into religion; the wise and witty university intellectual. On all these a curse is pronounced:

Let fever sweat them till they tremble,
Cramp rack their limbs till they resemble
  Cartoons by Goya:
Their daughters sterile be in rut,
May cancer rot their herring gut,
The circular madness on them shut,
  Or paranoia.

The poem, in its original version, next turns to the 'Unhappy poet' who has taken refuge in private emotion, and tells him: 'You need us more than you suppose / And you could help us if you chose.' And it concludes by addressing the working classes once again, reassuring them that 'Love outside our own election / Holds us in unseen connection: / O trust that ever.'

    If it were not for the word 'Comrades' in the opening line and the title 'A Communist to others', it would be easy to imagine that the poem was not about Communism at all, but that the speaker was a revolutionary with a Lawrentian rather than a Marxist creed. These doubts are increased by the fact that when Auden reprinted the poem in *Look, Stranger!* four years later he changed 'Comrades' to 'Brothers', and omitted several stanzas which were specifically Communist in tone. He also dropped the title – though this is probably not significant, as most of the poems in *Look, Stranger!* are printed without titles. Moreover the metre and tone of the poem, both reminiscent of Burns's satirical verse, make it seem more like something from *The Orators* than a serious piece of politics. Such political colouring as it does have is largely a direct borrowing from Edward Upward's writings. The factory worker's nightmare that he will be 'sacked without a testimonial' comes from Upward's short story 'Sunday', where the narrator expresses exactly the same fear. (Upward points out that, unlike the office employee in his story, a factory worker would probably not have a testimonial anyway.) And the declaration to the poet that he 'needs' Communism and could help the cause – lines which were dropped from the version in *Look, Stranger!* – is taken from Upward's piece describing his first contact with Marxism. It begins to seem as if Auden's Communism, if it can be called that, was distinctly second-hand.

He borrowed nothing directly from Upward in another poem he wrote on the same theme during the next month, September 1932. This was the 'little ditty to go to the tune of Frankie and Johnny' which he sent to Snodgrass. But again the tone simply does not seem serious:

> I have a handsome profile
> I've been to a great public school
> I've a little money invested
> Then why do I feel such a fool
> As if I owned a world that has had its day?
>
> You certainly have good reason
> For feeling as you do
> No wonder you are anxious
> Because it's perfectly true
> You own a world that has had its day.

In the remaining stanzas the ex-public schoolboy suggests various ways in which he can escape the coming collapse of his world – emigrating, writing a book, becoming religious, taking to vice, even joining the working classes – but the reply is always the same, and the poem ends by telling him 'Go down with your world that has had its day.'

These two poems by themselves – they were not followed by anything in exactly the same vein – would not amount to much evidence of a 'Communist phase' if it were not that, shortly after writing them, Auden began to say much the same thing in prose. On 15 October 1932 the *New Statesman* published his review of Bertrand Russell's *Education and the Social Order,* in which, while largely praising the book, he attacked

Russell for being interested merely in rational enquiry rather than real social change. 'Does Mr Russell', he asked, 'never contemplate the possibility that intellectual curiosity is neurotic, a compensation for those isolated from a social group, sexually starved, or physically weak?' And he concluded: 'The failure of modern education lies. . . in the fact that nobody genuinely believes in our society, for which the children are being trained.'

Seven months later, in May 1933, he wrote in another review: 'We live in an age in which the collapse of all previous standards coincides with the perfection in technique for the centralised distribution of ideas; some kind of revolution is inevitable, and will as inevitably be imposed from above by a minority.' He went on to say that, in order that the majority should have some say in this minority-dominated society, it was important to create more 'highbrows', people who try to organise and influence and explain what is going on around them – which seems, incidentally, to be a contradiction of his criticism of Russell. He concluded this review: 'Mass production, advertising, the divorce between mental and manual labour, magazine stories, the abuse of leisure, all these are symptoms of an invalid society, and can only be finally cured by attending to the cause.'

From these articles alone it would be difficult to be certain whether the revolution he expected, and perhaps hoped for, was to be Communist or Fascist in character. One might suspect, from a casual reading of an article he published in the *Criterion* at this time, that he was still flirting with the Lawrentian Fascism with which he had amused himself in *The Orators;* in this review he talks of a 'dictator of the country', and seems to be concerned not so much to prevent such a dictatorship – he declares dramatically 'liberalism is gone for ever' – as to ensure that the dictator should have 'no personal or class axe to grind'. He concludes this review: 'We must hurry or it will be too late.'

In fact the *Criterion* article was not his manifesto for a benevolent Fascist dictatorship, but an account of what seemed to him the present state of society, in which 'whoever possesses the instruments of know-ledge, the press, the wireless, and the Ministry of Education is the dictator of the country'. And in another article, this time intended for popular readership and published in the *Daily Herald* in April 1933 under the title 'How to be Masters of the Machine', he made it quite clear that the post-revolutionary society that he desired would not be Fascist but Communist: 'If you are to make the theory fact, you must first establish a Socialist State in which everyone can feel secure, and, secondly, have enough self-knowledge and common sense to ensure that machines are employed by your needs, and not your needs by the machinery.'

His support for Marxism was made clear some time later, when he contributed to a symposium on *The Arts To-day*, published in 1935. Here, he argued that Marx and Freud had equal value as diagnosticians of society's illness: 'Both are right. As long as civilisation remains as it is, the number of patients the psychologist can cure are very few, and as soon as socialism attains power, it must learn to direct its own interior energy and will need the psychologist.' Writing at this period, he also maintained that the Church's hostility to Communism was wrong. He said that a Christian must agree with the Communist view that violence is necessary to achieve the ideal society: 'Unless the Christian denies the value of any Government whatsoever, he must admit. . . the necessity for violence, and judge the means by its end. He cannot deny, if he is honest, the reality of the class conflict, and unless he can offer a better method of surpassing it. . . than the Communists, he must accept it.' And he added: 'In fact Communism is the only political theory that really holds the Christian position of absolute equality in value of every individual, and the evil of all State restraint.'

Auden, then, was certainly attracted by Marxism at this time. He later remarked that its great appeal had been 'in its romantic promise that with the triumph of Communism the State shall wither away'. He also realised that the rise of Hitler had shown how easily the values of liberal humanism, in which he had been brought up, could be overthrown. 'The novelty and shock of the Nazis', he wrote, 'was that they made no pretence of believing in justice and liberty for all.' On the other hand he was also aware of the wrongs being perpetrated in the Soviet Union in the name of Communism; but, like Upward and others of his friends who were attracted to the Communist Party, he refused to believe that this was because of a real flaw in the Marxist system. Looking back thirty years later he said: 'English Communism was insular. We knew what was happening in Russia. Purges and so on. But we felt England wasn't like that. We said, "Oh, you know how the Russians are, always violent. Here it will be different."' Most of all, he had for some time been conducting a personal search for an ideology, the stages of which had been marked by his allegiance at various times to the theories of John Layard, D. H. Lawrence and Gerald Heard. Communism provided another possible solution.

He was probably thinking partly of himself when he wrote during 1932 that the 'increasing attraction [of Communism] for the bourgeois lies in its demand for self-surrender for those individuals who, isolated, feel themselves emotionally at sea'. And it seems that during the latter part of 1932 he seriously contemplated becoming a Communist – or even believed that he already was one. In December he wrote to Henry Barnford Parkes on the subject of *The Orators:* 'The book is, as I didn't realise when I was writing it, a stage in my conversion to Communism.'

Yet, even at this time, he seems not to have held Communist views with any seriousness. The two 1932 poems 'A Communist to others' and 'I have a handsome profile' are, as Stephen Spender has put it, no more than dallyings in the subject, an exercise in expressing a point of view that is not really Auden's own; and this seems to have been the case with his later, much more fragmentary use of Marxist ideas in his poetry and his plays. Certainly Auden, unlike Day-Lewis and Spender, never made any attempt to join the British Communist Party itself; and Isherwood believed that his interest in Communism was not at all serious. 'He now outwardly supported Marxism,' Isherwood wrote of Auden as he was in the mid-1930s, 'or at any rate didn't protest when it was preached, but this was halfhearted and largely to humour [myself] and a few other friends.'

Looking back on this period of his life only a few years later, Auden passed a harsh judgement on his interest in Communism. He talked about it as having been a sedentary intellectual's longing to enter the world of action, 'a day-dream of being important', and said there was also an element of 'old-fashioned social climbing' in it, a desire to receive approval from his contemporaries. He elaborated on this in an interview towards the end of his life: 'It was extremely difficult as a writer [during the 1930s] to be quite honest with oneself; because there was always conflict between what one was really interested in, and a mixture of social conscience about what was going on, and also I think sheer conceit and a wish to be important.' Yet he was not especially ashamed of the fact that his poetry at this period preached ideas to which he did not really subscribe. He declared that, though a poet's emotions must be involved in his work, in poetry 'all facts and all beliefs cease to be true or false and become interesting possibilities'.

Even at the time when he was writing poems like 'A Communist to others' and talking of his 'conversion' to Communism, he seems to have been certain that he would remain outside the actual Communist Party. In the autumn of 1932 he concluded a letter to Rupert Doone: 'No. I am a bourgeois. I shall not join the C.P.'

★

Following his two 'Communist' poems, Auden wrote, in the next month, October 1932, a pastiche eighteenth-century ballad 'O what is that sound which so thrills the ear', in which a political rebel leaves his lover to fight for the cause. The poem was first published in *New Verse*, a magazine founded at the beginning of 1933 by an Oxford graduate of Auden's generation, Geoffrey Grigson, who was now working in London as a literary journalist. *New Verse* was created by Grigson in order to print, and criticise, the work of contemporary poets; from now on, many of Auden's poems appeared in it soon after they were written, which was exactly what Grigson had intended. He said some years later: '*New Verse* came into existence because of Auden.' Grigson wrote to Auden to ensure his co-operation before beginning, and Auden replied: 'Why do you want to start a poetry review. Is it really as important as all

that? I'm glad you like poetry but cant we take it a little more lightly.'
But he added: 'If you do start one and want my stuff, of course you can
have it.'

He spent Christmas 1932 in the Lake District, and then went off to
Berlin to stay with Isherwood for ten days. They discussed Auden's
hope, which he still had, of writing something for the Group Theatre.
Isherwood made a few suggestions, but they did not attempt another
collaboration. A few months earlier, in the spring of 1932, they had
planned to write a play set in a preparatory school, but apparently
nothing whatever came of this, though the poem 'O Love, the interest
itself in thoughtless Heaven' which Auden wrote in May 1932 was
intended to be the prologue to a play, perhaps this one.

Back at the Downs School for the start of the 1933 spring term, Auden
presumably turned once again to the long poem 'In the year of my
youth', the first Canto of which had been finished a month or so earlier,
shortly before he left for Berlin. Certainly at some time between now
and the summer he wrote a further 330 lines. But then he abandoned it;
and it is not difficult to see why.

Canto II begins with the dreamer being woken in his hotel room by
Sampson; it is the morning of what is apparently going to be a manhunt
by the ruling classes for those of the proletariat who have abandoned city
life and hidden themselves outlaw-like in the hills. The dreamer washes
himself and dresses, and Auden describes this in a passage which is
apparently meant to be reminiscent both of Dante's ablutions at the
beginning of the *Purgatorio*, from which the second Canto of 'In the year
of my youth' takes its order of events, and of Belinda's *toilette* in *The
Rape of the Lock*. Pope's style is cleverly adapted to describe the modern
implements of the wash-basin ('the sterilized brush. . . a ribbon of swan-
white paste. . . sweet-smelling soap, sad to germs') but all this is rather
pointless fun. The dreamer then goes downstairs and climbs into Sampson's
car. The two of them drive out of the town; and as the car begins to
climb a hill – a parallel to the ascent of Purgatory in Dante's poem –
Sampson again expounds his theory of the disintegration of human
personality in recent centuries, this time using phrases lifted by Auden
directly from Gerald Heard's writing on the subject. He and the dreamer
then arrive at a country house, where they observe the arrival of the
others who are to take part in 'the Chase', as Sampson called it in the first
Canto. Auden launches into a catalogue of 'county' figures, whom he
describes as each one arrives:

> From Puffin Conyers, place for peacocks,
> Came General Gorse of the white moustache,
> Beside him Betty his obedient wife,
> Christopher their son with the shishi walk,
> And Antonelli their Italian chauffeur,

> A family in fortune, rich in Rolls.
> Then driving dangerously in a blue Daimler
> Admiral Hotham with his breakwater chin
> From Honeypot Hall, haunt of doves,
> His wife Faun, frequent in embraces,
> And one-eyed Bert, his faithful A. B.

There are a few more lines of this sort, and then the poem peters out.

Auden seems to have realised that he had nothing to say. Gerald Heard's ideas had been arbitrarily thrown into the poem in an attempt to provide an ideology from which it could grow, but neither they nor the vaguely Marxist tone could provide an adequate foundation for such an ambitious work, while the figure of the dreamer (Auden himself) is too self-absorbed and unresponsive to match up to the Dante-like role assigned to him. Auden might have had fun if he had gone on to describe the manhunt, but it would only have been fun of the calibre of 'The Enemies of a Bishop'. What started as an attempt to emulate *The Divine Comedy* seemed likely to end in mere schoolboy jokes.

Auden did not write any other poetry during the first three months of 1933. He seems to have realised that his admiration for Heard and his flirtation with Communism did not add up to a workable set of ideas, a real dogma of the kind on which he always needed to base his poetry. He was starved of an ideology. Perhaps this is what he meant when he wrote to Nob Snodgrass on 21 February: 'I am living miserably like a hen scratching for food.'

Ironically it was exactly a month later that he began to be hailed as the leader of a new ideological movement in literature. On 21 March *New Country* was published, an anthology of prose and verse edited by the Communist writer and schoolmaster Michael Roberts. The book's contributors included, besides Auden, Spender, Day-Lewis, Isherwood, Upward, and Rex Warner; and people were soon talking about them and the other writers whose work was represented in *New Country* as 'the Auden Group'.

That they should do so was not very surprising. Two of the poets in the book hailed Auden as a leader, much in the terms in which he himself had saluted the infant John Warner in *The Orators*. Charles Madge described how Auden's verse had changed his vision of life, and Day-Lewis in a poem from his sequence *The Magnetic Mountain* used Auden as a figure in his own mythology: 'Look west, Wystan, lone flyer, birdman, my bully boy! . . . / Gain altitude, Auden, then let the base beware!' Auden's own contributions to the volume included 'A Communist to others', which could be regarded as a summing up of the whole book, the tone of which was generally revolutionary and often specifically Communist. An essay by Spender discussed the role of the poet in a revolutionary situation. Upward's short story 'Sunday' concluded with the hero deciding to attend a Communist meeting, and – most of all – Michael Roberts's preface was virtually a call to revolutionary arms. Roberts, who had edited a quieter-toned but similar collection by several of the same people in 1932 under the title *New Signatures*, had joined the Communist Party some years earlier (and had been expelled from it as a Trotskyite); he now wrote in *New Country:* 'It is time that those who would conserve something which is still valuable in England began to see that only a revolution can save their standards.'

It seemed to many that here was an identifiable literary group with a common outlook. Bonamy Dobrée in *The Listener* described them as 'communists with an intense love for England', and F. R. Leavis talked about 'the Communism of the Group'. Young men such as Philip Toynbee began to look to Auden and his friends as providing artistic leadership. 'It was not only', wrote Toynbee many years later, 'that they were conscious of international fascism, and had looked quite hard at some of the less cosy sides of contemporary England. . . They shared my own intimate anxieties and hopes: they knew what it was to be a young, highly self-conscious middle-class Englishman at that particular time in history.'

Yet Geoffrey Grigson, reviewing *New Country* as soon as it was published, scorned the notion that Auden and his friends were a 'Group'. He asked: 'What joins these writers except paper? How, as an artist, is Auden united with Day Lewis, Day Lewis with Spender, Spender with Upward? . . . Spender's article, Auden's poems and Day Lewis's "Magnetic Mountain" prove it stupid to keep in fancy these three as triune.' And Auden himself said thirty years later: 'Even when we seemed to share some common concern – political, let us say – our approaches to it, our sensibilities and techniques were always different.' This is not to deny Auden's influence on several of the contributors to *New Country;* and of course at Oxford he had thought in terms of a Group or Gang of his friends. But by the time those friends did begin to wield some power in the literary world, he himself had lost interest in such a notion and was concerned almost exclusively with his own problems as a poet.[1]

He was clearly still at a loss about what ideological direction to take during April 1933, shortly after *New Country* was published, for in a month he broke his poetic silence to write another dream-poem, a short one this time, in which the subject is the ship 'Wystan Auden Esquire'. This vessel is voyaging in hope of finding an earthly paradise, the Islands of Milk and Honey, 'Where there's neither death nor old age / And the poor have all the money'. The ship is under the command of a female captain who bears a certain resemblance to Auden's mother; the mate,

---

[1] He did, however, believe that he had a common purpose as a writer with Isherwood. This is mentioned by him in several poems, both published and unpublished.

who is henpecked by her, similarly resembles his father – though captain and mate are probably also meant as representatives of aspects of Auden's own psychology. As to the map on which the whole voyage depends, 'There were plenty of notes in the margin / But of land there wasn't a sign'. Auden dreams that he himself is a seagull observing this Hunting-of-the-Snark-like voyage while he hovers above the ship; the poem ends with the captain shooting him, hissing 'Saboteur, spy' as she does so.

He did not publish this poem. But he took up its theme the next month, May, when he wrote a sestina, later titled 'Paysage Moralisé', which begins 'Hearing of harvests rotting in the valleys'. It was an accomplished technical exercise – a sestina is based on a pattern of six words, one of which appears at the end of each line in a different order in each stanza – but was also a serious piece of private argument with himself; for it concludes with the determination to 'rebuild our cities, not dream of islands' – a renunciation, in fact, of the 'Islands of Milk and Honey'. Yet the poem did not say how this renunciation could be achieved. Auden did not yet have an answer. But very shortly he began to find one.

★

Two very important things now happened to him. The first was that he fell in love with someone much younger than himself. This led immediately to the introduction of a whole new element into his poetry. During the summer of 1933 he began to write a series of love-sonnets in a style that was quite new to him. His previous poems about love had been compressed and highly obscure (as in the pieces he wrote at Oxford about frustrated love) or terse and syntactically oblique in the manner of Laura Riding. But suddenly all this changed:

> The fruit in which your parents hid you, boy,
> Their death, is summer perfect: at its core
> You grow already. . .
>
> Turn not towards me lest I turn to you:
> Stretch not your hands towards your harm and me. . .
>
> On the provincial lawn I watch you play,
> To me and to your brothers a success
> Upon whose charm the world has still to lay
> Her suffocating motherly caress.

It was not that Auden ceased to be obscure; the new love-poems were often as 'difficult' as his earlier work. But there was something about them that made them compelling in a way that the earlier poems had not been.

What was this special characteristic? In part it was the dream-like quality of the poems:

> At the far end of the enormous room
> An orchestra is playing to the rich,
> The drumtaps nagging like a nervous twitch,
> The fiddle soaring like a flying dream:
> At tables round me all the winners sit,
> Lean over talking to a lovely prize,
> And I imagine you before my eyes
> Flushed with the wine I order and my wit.

But it was not this alone that was new: the dream was already one of Auden's favourite devices in his poetry. What was different was the combination of the dream–quality with an entirely new willingness on Auden's part to be drawn fully into the experience of love.

Of course, the new sonnets were not really 'about' the loved person but about Auden's own feelings. He himself said of this, many years later: 'The girl whose boy-friend starts writing her love poems should be on her guard. Perhaps he really does love her, but one thing is certain: while he was writing his poems he was not thinking of her but of his own feelings about her, and that is suspicious. Let her remember St Augustine's confession of his feelings after the death of someone he loved very much: "I would rather have been deprived of my friend than of my grief."' But while Augustine's observation could certainly be applied to Auden's undergraduate love-poems, where the young men addressed might as well be figments of his imagination, something had changed in him by the time he came to write the 1933 sonnets.

He had in fact ceased to be self-conscious in the particular intensely introverted way that characterised his undergraduate poems. He himself was, as an undergraduate, fully aware of this self-consciousness, both in love and in writing, and he discussed it in a letter to Bill McElwee written in 1927:

> I have my birthday present for you Katherine Mansfield's Journal which I hope you will appreciate. I have been reading it and shall keep it until we return to Oxford. Her remarks about the relation between art and life are true for the most part. One must be clean in mind. I am so conscious of my failure in this, of one's self-conscious satisfaction with one's work. Writing must be like shitting, one's sole feeling that of a natural function properly performed, and I get excited about it. A commonplace thought this. Perhaps the bugger is always the worst offender.

In part this self-consciousness never left him. It grew out of the fact that he lived through his intellect rather than his emotions. As he himself put it in a 1929 poem, 'Coming out of me living is always thinking'. But in the summer of 1933 he began for the first time to involve himself, in his poetry, in the experience of being in love – in exactly the way he had failed to involve himself in the experiences he presented to himself in 'In the year of my youth'. Many of the new love-sonnets show this involvement:

> Blessing this moon
> Like treasures touching sides, how many lie,
> Successful lovers who were once as I;
> But in your northern house you sleep alone. . .
> And I find nothing sensible to do,
> But, shivering, look towards the north and you.

The cause of his change lay no doubt partly in maturity. He was now twenty-six, and had ceased to treat his love-affairs as if they were public-school gossip. Margaret Gardiner noticed that his earlier love of intrigue 'completely changed as he grew older and his relationships involved real feelings. He became more and more reticent, and only very rarely talked about himself and then usually obliquely.' Partly the new lyricism in his love-poetry was the result of a desire to 'loosen' his poetic style. Looking back on this stylistic change he wrote, in 1937: 'I used to try and concentrate the poem so much that there wasnt a word that wasnt essential. This leads to becoming boring and constipated.' He modelled this new loosened style largely on Yeats, who became, during this period, as important a master to him as Hardy and Eliot had been in earlier phases. The change was the result, too, of another important event in the summer of 1933. If his falling in love at this time was, to use his own term for such things, a 'Vision of Eros', then the other vital experience of this summer was a 'Vision of Agape'.

He was now extremely happy at the Downs School. He had created a role for himself in the school that was part analyst-leader-healer, part clown, part colleague. He loved being a member of a team, together with the other teaching staff, and he made friends very easily among them, especially with Maurice Feild the art master and his wife Alexandra. 'He loved family homes and often frequented ours,' recalled Feild of his friendship with Auden; 'he wrote somewhere that he only loved people who made him laugh. I think this was an exaggeration, but he and my wife laughed a lot and I was happy to be the butt for their laughter: once he got into our son's large purple pram which prank I am told I disapproved of: I thought he might break the springs.'

There was plenty of music at the school, and Auden, besides strumming hymn tunes on the piano in his usual fashion or singing ridiculous words to psalm-chants to amuse the boys, also sang seriously in the school's Bach Choir, even occasionally taking a solo. He was encouraged by

Geoffrey Hoyland the headmaster to invite his friends to the school, and such people as Spender, Nevill Coghill, Day-Lewis, Robert Medley and Rupert Doone came over to see him. He also acquired a car, an old buff-coloured four-seater Morris, in which he took the Feilds and others from the school for drives around the Malverns and through the Herefordshire farmlands on summer evenings. His driving was energetic and erratic. 'He did not worry whether the car was on the road or the grass verge,' recalled Maurice Feild, 'and delighted in bumping together those on the back seat.' And, for much of the summer term, he slept out of doors.

This was a regular custom for boys at the school – if not usually for masters – if the weather allowed it; and June 1933 was particularly hot and dry. 'For a fortnight', recorded the school magazine, 'thirty or more seniors slept out in the orchard under the stars and much enjoyed it. Occasionally there was a shower, but we pulled a tarpaulin over our heads and went to sleep again. Some of us got to know the stars for the first time.' Auden decided he would follow suit, and, with the aid of Maurice Feild and others, manhandled his iron bedstead with its mountain of blankets down the stairs into the garden of the Lodge, the bachelor masters' house. Here he slept for several weeks, putting up an umbrella if it rained. Sometimes a group of geese came to share the shelter of the umbrella.

He had never been happier. It was perhaps this, together with the fact that he was in love,[1] that led him to experience a quite novel sensation one June evening. He published an account of this experience thirty years later, not claiming it explicitly as his own, but saying that it was something 'for the authenticity of which I can vouch':

> One fine summer night in June 1933 I was sitting on a lawn after dinner with three colleagues, two women and one man. We liked each other well enough but we were certainly not intimate friends, nor had any one of us a sexual interest in another. Incidentally, we had not drunk any alcohol. We were talking casually about every-day matters when, quite suddenly and unexpectedly, something happened. I felt myself invaded by a power which, though I consented to it, was irresistible and certainly not mine. For the first time in my life I knew exactly – because, thanks to the power, I was doing it – what it means to love one's neighbour as oneself. I was also certain, though the conversation continued to be perfectly ordinary, that my three colleagues were having the same experience. (In the case of one of them, I was later able to confirm this.) My

[1]This probably played a large part in it. In his account of the 'Vision of Eros', Auden said that the experience of being in love produces a strong feeling of good-will towards other people: 'Even in [the lover's] relations to others, conduct which before he fell in love seemed natural and proper, judged by his new standard of what he feels it should be to be worthy of her, now seems base and ignoble' (*Forewords and Afterwords*, p. 64).

personal feelings towards them were unchanged – they were still colleagues, not intimate friends – but I felt their existence as themselves to be of infinite value and I rejoiced in it.

I recalled with shame the many occasions on which I had been spiteful, snobbish, selfish, but the immediate joy was greater than the shame, for I knew that, so long as I was possessed by this spirit, it would be literally impossible for me deliberately to injure another human being. I also knew that the power would, of course, be withdrawn sooner or later and that, when it did, my greeds and self-regard would return. The experience lasted at its full intensity for about two hours when we said good-night to each other and went to bed. When I awoke the next morning, it was still present, though weaker, and it did not vanish completely for two days or so. The memory of the experience has not prevented me from making use of others, grossly and often, but it has made it much more difficult for me to deceive myself about what I am up to when I do.

The identity of the 'three colleagues' is not known for certain, but according to Maurice Feild they may have been Hilda Woodhams, who taught music, Margaret Sant, who looked after the junior boys in the school, and Ross Coates, a young man who was briefly on the staff.

Following this experience, Auden did not turn to religion. He still thought, as he put it, that 'I had done with Christianity for good', and in an essay published the next year he expressed doubts as to whether there was any future for the Church: whether, as he put it, 'any large-scale organization which professes no political programme, is likely to command wide interest in the near future'. But he did immediately seek an opportunity of putting into print his new understanding of 'Agape', the selfless love of one's neighbour. He asked Eliot if he could review for the *Criterion* Violet Clifton's *The Book of Talbot*, a biography of a Roman Catholic explorer written by his widow. In the review, which was duly printed in that magazine in the autumn, Auden made no pretence of being interested in Mrs Clifton's ostensible subject-matter, her husband's life as an explorer. What struck him was, he said, its author's love for her subject. 'Love', he wrote, 'has allowed Lady Clifton to constellate round Talbot the whole of her experience and make it significant. One cannot conceive of her needing to write another line; one feels that she has put down everything.' He concluded his review by saying that the book 'shows more clearly than anything I have read for a long time that the first criterion of success in any human activity, the necessary pre-liminary, whether to scientific discovery or to artistic vision, is intensity of attention or, less pompously, love.'

He expressed this new understanding in a lyrical poem written during that June. It was a celebration not just of Agape but also of the physical beauty of the schoolboys around him, of his own private experience of being in love, and of the extraordinary yet quite simple sensation of lying in bed under the stars. He dedicated it to the Downs School headmaster, Geoffrey Hoyland.

> Out on the lawn I lie in bed,
> Vega conspicuous overhead
>   In the windless nights of June;
> Forests of green have done complete
> The day's activity; my feet
>   Point to the rising moon.
>
> Lucky, this point in time and space
> Is chosen as my working place;
>   Where the sexy airs of summer,
> The bathing hours and the bare arms,
> The leisured drives through a land of farms,
>   Are good to the newcomer.
>
> Equal with colleagues in a ring
> I sit on each calm evening,
>   Enchanted as the flowers
> The opening light draws out of hiding
> From leaves with all its dove-like pleading
>   Its logic and its powers.
>
> That later we, though parted then
> May still recall these evenings when
>   Fear gave his watch no look;
> The lion griefs loped from the shade
> And on our knees their muzzles laid,
>   And Death put down his book.
>
> Moreover, eyes in which I learn
> That I am glad to look, return
>   My glances every day;
> And when the birds and rising sun
> Waken me, I shall speak with one
>   Who has not gone away.

These opening stanzas of 'Out on the lawn' might suggest that Auden had abandoned the socio-political concerns that he had tried to introduce into his recent poetry, and was allowing himself to relax into a self-satisfied delight with his own circumstances. But this was precisely what he was not doing. The poem goes on to consider this very problem, asking 'what doubtful act allows / Our freedom in this English house, / Our picnics in the sun'. It tries to provide an answer, declaring that soon will come a major upheaval in the form of war or revolution, but that, when this upheaval is over, the lyrical love which the poem celebrates – part Eros, part Agape – will play a part in the re-establishment of civilisation, the 'rebuilding of cities', to use Auden's own phrase. Love, concludes the poem, 'may calm / The pulse of nervous nations'.

This, however, proved to be too glib for Auden's own satisfaction, and throughout the summer of 1933 he continued to be exercised by the question. Several of the love-sonnets that he was writing pose the problem that love seems to be an escape, an evasion of the real issues; or rather, that Eros, the love that is described in these poems, does not have the redeeming power of Agape. In the face of erotic love, the lover becomes a mere dreamer, not yet the 'redeemer' of mankind that he hoped to be.[1] Love offers a 'preposterous guarantee' that 'there are no poor' – it tries to screen lovers from the real state of the world. This was a problem to which Auden could as yet find no solution.

In August he sent five of the love-sonnets to Geoffrey Grigson for publication in *New Verse*. Grigson recalled of Auden's contributions to the magazine: 'They came on half sheets of notepaper, on long sheets of lined foolscap, in that writing an airborne daddy-longlegs might have managed with one dangling leg, sometimes in pencil, sometimes smudged and still less easy to decipher. They had to be typed before they went to the printer, and in the act of typing each poem established itself. It was rather like old-fashioned developing in the dark-room, but more certain, more exciting – there at last on the white page, to be clearer still on the galley, the first entire sight of a new poem joining our literature.'

★

Auden spent part of his 1933 summer holiday staying with the Snodgrass family at Helensburgh, where he displayed his usual characteristics as a guest – 'I wonder', he wrote to 'Mop' Snodgrass after his visit, 'how many pieces of furniture I burned with cigarette ends.' Also during the summer he drove down to Kent in his car and stayed for three nights, from 2 to 5 August, with Harold Nicolson and Vita Sackville-West at Sissinghurst. Nicolson had met Auden when he came to lecture at the Downs School at the end of the summer term. On that occasion, Auden read Nicolson some of his new poems. Nicolson, who apparently knew Auden's published work, commented: 'They show a desire to be more simple.' Now, on his last evening at Sissinghurst, Auden read his hosts part of 'In the year of my youth'.

This seems surprising in view of the fact that he had apparently abandoned work on the poem some months earlier. Perhaps he was now considering taking it up again or reworking it. At all events Nicolson was not unimpressed by it. He wrote in his diary: 'The idea is Gerald Heard as Virgil guiding him through modern life. It is not so much a

[1]Edward Mendelson argues, in *Early Auden,* that for a time Auden perhaps did hope to be a redeemer, both of society and of individuals. Certainly there is a good deal in his early poetry to suggest this.

defence of communism as an attack upon all the ideas of comfort and complacency which will make communism difficult to achieve in this country.' Nicolson felt that he himself was under attack: 'A man like Auden with his fierce repudiation of half-way houses and his gentle integrity makes one feel terribly discontented with one's own smug successfulness. I go to bed feeling terribly Edwardian and back-number, and yet, thank God, delighted that people like Wystan Auden should actually exist.'

Despite the encouragement that Nicolson presumably gave him, Auden did not attempt to continue or reconstruct 'In the year of my youth'. Instead, he turned back to another piece of work that he had abandoned almost a year earlier: the commission to write a text for performance by the Group Theatre. In fact he was probably already at work on this by the time he went to Sissinghurst, for he handed the completed text to Rupert Doone and Robert Medley some time during the summer, and sent it to Faber & Faber at the end of August. It was entitled *The Dance of Death*.

Doone and Medley had provided him with two suggestions; the first of these, the Orpheus choral ballet, having failed, he turned to the second, a *danse macabre*,[1] which he decided to use as the foundation for a piece of writing on a political theme. That he turned once more to politics was apparently due to events in Germany earlier in 1933, when the Reichstag in Berlin was set on fire; the Nazis, who were effectively in power, accused the Communists of being responsible, and made it the excuse for mass arrests and the declaration of a state of emergency; but Auden and most of his friends, including Isherwood, who left Berlin shortly afterwards, were convinced that the whole thing had been planned by the Nazis themselves, and that war would be the eventual outcome of Hitler's ambitions. Auden himself later recorded that he had expected war ever since reading *Mein Kampf*. 'In Hitler's determination to be the master of Europe and Russia', he said, 'there was something profoundly self-destructive.'

It seems that Auden's reaction to events in Germany helped to sharpen the political content of *The Dance of Death*. Robert Medley certainly believed this to be the case. But this does not mean that it was a serious political play. Auden's principal concern was to attempt something new on the stage: not just the 'total theatre' that Doone had envisaged, a fusion of dance, mime, and words both spoken and sung; but also a sweeping-away of the cobwebs that hung about drama at that time.

---

[1]Michael Sidnell, historian of the Group Theatre, suggests that there may have been not two suggestions, an Orpheus choral ballet and a *danse macabre* play, but one mixed-genre work intended to combine both themes. He thinks that Auden's early work on the project in the summer and autumn of 1932, which he then abandoned, was in effect a first draft of *The Dance of Death* and not an independent composition on the Orpheus theme alone. Since Auden's 1932 draft has not survived, it is impossible to be certain of the truth.

Seven years earlier, in 1926, Auden had declared to Isherwood that 'the whole of modern realistic drama since Tchekhov had got to go', and in 'Paid On Both Sides' he had already demonstrated that the country-house charade could be as powerful a vehicle for dramatic writing as the conventional play.[1] Now, in *The Dance of Death*, he made use of all available forms of 'low' theatre – music-hall, pantomime, revue, cabaret – to show that these could be of service to the modern writer. The political theme took second place to this technical experiment. Indeed Auden treated it rather as a joke.

The Dance of Death uses a bare stage with a small jazz orchestra and an Announcer, who explains at the outset that the performance will present 'a picture of the decline of a class' – at which point the chorus in the Group Theatre production interjected: 'Middle Class'. The figure of Death-the-dancer, a role created for Rupert Doone, stands for the death-wish of that class. The action begins with the Middle Class seen as being by nature fun-loving. The chorus prance about in bathing suits. But the intervention of the Dancer, together with the theatre manager, who stands for capitalism, soon has them arrayed in military uniform and singing a militaristic song. The Announcer then declares that war has been outlawed; but the proletariat – represented by actors planted in the audience – clamours for revolution. The Dancer and Announcer respond by converting this into racist nationalism, and they encourage the chorus to beat up the theatre manager on the grounds that he is 'a dirty Jew'. The chorus then forms up in the shape of a ship: 'The ship of England crosses the ocean', they sing, 'Our keel rides on to the Promised Land.' The Audience (proletariat) acts the part of waves, and rocks the ship. The Dancer then collapses in a fit, the point perhaps being that the death-wish itself is weakened as the bourgeoisie now try, for a time, to find some practical way out of their predicament. Their search for a solution is allegorised as follows: first, the chorus declare they will follow a doctrine which is part back-to-nature ('Live on a farm / Well out of harm') and part D. H. Lawrence ('The will of the blood is the only good / We must learn to know it'); the Announcer preaches Lawrence's dogma that 'Man must be the leader whom women must obey.' This is rejected in favour of a plan to fly alone / to the Alone', and the Dancer now becomes a Pilot who is going to make a flight into metaphysics – 'to reach the very heart of Reality'. But the flight fails and the Dancer falls; the bourgeoisie, in other words are incapable of mysticism. Capitalism (the manager) now returns to make a final appeal to solidarity, which he does by means of opening a night-club called 'the Alma Mater', a symbol for nostalgia.

[1]He gave his opinion of one leading figure in modern realistic drama in a letter to David Ayerst, written in 1926: 'I went to see a Noel Coward the other day and could do nothing but say

> "Is it like this
> In Death's other kingdom?"'

This, too, fails, and the Dancer dies. Karl Marx now enters, and is hailed by the chorus: 'O Mr Marx, you've gathered / All the material facts / You know the economic / Reasons for our acts' (these words are sung to the tune of the Wedding March). Marx declares of the Dancer: 'The instruments of production have been too much for him. He is liquidated.' The play ends with the stage direction: 'Exeunt to a Dead March.'

The Dance of Death was probably written very quickly. There is no serious poetry in it, and much of the dialogue makes no pretence to be other than doggerel:

> He's marvellous
> He's Greek
> When I see him
> My legs go weak.
>
> Lend me your comb
> To do my hair
> I must look my best
> When he is here.

There is some skill in the songs, which use a wide range of popular idiom, but they do not parody their models (musical comedy, school song, patriotic ballad, etc.) so much as equal them in triteness:

> Gents from Norway
> Ladies from Sweden
> Don't stand in the doorway
> Come, this is what you've been needing. . .
> Come out into the sun.

Rupert Doone and Robert Medley, when they received the manuscript, were rather taken aback: *The Dance of Death* was not at all what they had been expecting. But after the initial shock they declared themselves to be delighted with it, and they immediately began to make arrangements for a Group Theatre production. Faber & Faber, too, were pleased enough with the play to publish it a few weeks before Christmas 1933. Reviews were not favourable. The *Times Literary Supplement* called it 'thin', and Gavin Ewart in *New Verse* said it lacked the vigour and aliveness of Auden's *Poems* and *The Orators*. F. R. Leavis in *Scrutiny* attacked Auden for writing lines for the proletariat such as: 'E's a bit of olright, ain't 'e Bill?' But Auden remained undismayed by these criticisms. He told Naomi Mitchison: 'The Dance of Death is meant for acting not reading. It depends so much on the music and the dancing to give it body.'

The Group Theatre made their arrangements swiftly, and the play was scheduled for its first performance at the end of February 1934. Meanwhile Auden occupied himself at the Downs School by producing Cocteau's *Orphée* with the boys; he told Naomi Mitchison that it had been 'a great success', and the school magazine's reviewer agreed, though he said it had rather mystified the audience. Auden spent Christmas at Wescoe, his family's Lake District cottage, and then travelled to London to stay with Isherwood, who was trying to make arrangements for his current German boyfriend Heinz to enter England. Auden accompanied Isherwood to Harwich, where Heinz's boat was due to arrive, but the attempt was a failure, because of one of the immigration officers suspected Isherwood's motives. According to Isherwood, Auden remarked of this official that he had understood the whole situation – 'because he's *one of us*'.

The Dance of Death was to be performed for two successive Sunday nights, 25 February and 4 March 1934, before an audience of Group Theatre subscribers at the Westminster Theatre in London. As it was a short play, the rest of the evening was to be taken up with a production of the Noah's Flood play from the medieval Chester cycle, under the title *The Deluge*.[1] Rupert Doone had originally intended to direct *The Dance of Death* on his own, but he found that it was impossible to do this and take the part of the Dancer at the same time, so he enlisted Tyrone Guthrie, with whom he had worked at Cambridge, as co-producer. As to the music, Auden had wanted it to be written by the twenty-eight-year-old composer Michael Tippett, a friend of David Ayerst; but Doone declared he did not want anything so highbrow, and instead chose a young man named Herbert Murrill, who provided adequate musical pastiche of the kind that the text required.[2] During rehearsals, Robert Medley, who was designing the production, observed that Auden was unfailingly co-operative, agreeing to any suggestions for changes, and writing new lines on the spot whenever he was asked for them.

The Group Theatre were well aware that the published text of *The Dance of Death* had been badly received, and that many people's expectations were that the performance would be, as Medley put it, 'Wystan's funeral'. Its success was therefore all the more remarkable. Audiences at both the Sunday evenings were delighted, and gave it an ovation, and those few drama critics who bothered to come wrote in praise of it. The *New Statesman* reviewer called it 'a return to reality and to mystery', and said it had 'absolutely nothing in common with the degenerate theatre of

---

[1] In *W. H. Auden: A Bibliography, 1924-1969* (p. 252) it is stated that Auden adapted *The Deluge* for performance by the Group Theatre. According to Robert Medley, his only contribution was to suggest (with Nevill Coghill) various ways in which the medieval English of the original might be modified to suit the ears of a modern audience.

[2] Sir Michael Tippett says that the suggestion was never discussed with him, though he knew Auden slightly, having met him, at David Ayerst's instigation, at the McElwees' home in Somerset.

the present age'; he admitted it was 'by no means a masterpiece', but concluded: 'It is of greater importance for the future of drama than all the "masterpieces" of Mr Noel Coward, Mr Somerset Maugham, and the pseudo-realistic school.' Similarly, the critic of the *New English Weekly*, while admitting that there were 'surprisingly juvenile patches' in it, continued: 'It is as a whole an original and fertile work *in the theatre*, giving hope that we may again infuse vitality into our decrepit Drama. Mr Auden has sharply opposed the accepted clutter, and the audience rose to demonstrate that something had at last HAPPENED on a London stage.'

★

During the spring term of 1934, while *The Dance of Death* was being given its Sunday performances in London, Auden organised a Downs School production of *The Deluge*, the medieval Flood play that had been performed by the Group Theatre. Nearly the whole school took part. Sheets were stripped from the beds and draped over the junior boys, who rushed up and down to represent waves. Auden, who himself spoke the part of God, hidden in the rafters, was an energetic, enthusiastic, tireless producer, hurrying about giving orders with a cigarette constantly in his hand.

He was at about this time beginning to tackle another 'educational' project which had a similar degree of unconventionality: an anthology of poetry for schools, in which the poems would appear in alphabetical order, with no indication of authorship (except in the index), and which would include not just the usual stuff of school anthologies but also verse by D. H. Lawrence, Vachel Lindsay, T. S. Eliot, and Lewis Carroll, as well as hymns, excerpts from the Bible, and nursery nonsense jingles. This was *The Poet's Tongue,* an attempt to show schoolchildren that 'poetry' could mean all these things – that it was simply, as Auden put it in the introduction to the book, 'memorable speech'. He explained this further: 'We shall do poetry a great disservice if we confine it only to the major experiences of life. . . Poetry is no better and no worse than human nature; it is profound and shallow, sophisticated and naïve, dull and witty, bawdy and chaste in turn.' He worked on *The Poet's Tongue* with, as co-editor, a schoolmaster friend named John Garrett, who had been an undergraduate at Exeter College, Oxford, and had probably been intro-duced to Auden by Nevill Coghill. The anthology was published in June 1935, and was reprinted many times. Critics praised it as a complete break from the usual type of school anthology; Denys Thompson wrote in *Scrutiny*: 'It is bound to let in a good deal of fresh air in places where it is badly needed.'

After the summer term ended, Auden made a car trip through Europe, during August, with two old boys of the Downs School, Michael Yates and Peter Roger. The latter now worked as a gardener at the school, and Auden seems to have been having an affair with him. They took the ferry to Ostend, and drove across Belgium into Germany, staying at Cologne, Eisenach and Dresden. In a diary of the trip written for the Downs School magazine, Auden observed of Nazi–dominated Germany that it was 'being run by a mixture of gangsters and the sort of school prefect who is good at Corps'. And at Eisenach: 'Sat in a café in the market square listening to Hitler shouting from Hamburg. Sounded like a Latin lesson.' They then crossed Czechoslovakia, with the intention of visiting the Carpathians and 'Dracula' country; Auden told Naomi Mitchison that the trip was 'stimulated I believe by childish memories of Dracula'. But Peter Roger was suffering from a bad leg, and they shortened their journey, travelling south to Budapest and then across to Vienna. They came back through the Tyrol and Switzerland – 'Hate Switzerland,' commented Auden; 'cooking rotten and architecture hideous.' The trip did nothing to make him enjoy tourism for its own sake. He resolutely maintained that he disliked natural scenery. 'Personally', he wrote in his account of the tour, 'give me a good hotel and a petrol pump or city streets in a fog.'[1]

Before setting off for this European tour and again after returning, Auden worked at a new play which he had conceived for the Group Theatre. Or rather, he turned back to three previously abandoned or unused pieces of work and incorporated them all into the play. It was called 'The Chase', and the three elements which went into it were 'The Enemies of a Bishop', 'The Fronny', and 'In the year of my youth'. During the summer term of 1934 he told Naomi Mitchison: 'The epic has turned into a dramma [sic], which is coasting along slowly.' It seems to have gone through more than one version, for on 5 August he told Doone and Medley: 'I'm getting on with the play and am completely recasting it in a way which will make it more suitable I think to the Group theatre. My only difficult demand is a good verse speaking chorus which I think you will be able to provide.' By October the play was finished.

'The Chase' begins with a chorus that sets the scene first in general terms – 'The Summer holds: upon its glittering Lake / Lie Europe and the islands' – and then describes the particular landscape in which the action opens. This is lead-mining country, as in 'The Enemies of a Bishop'; but for the Mortmere-like comedy of the earlier play Auden substitutes social comment. Windyacre Mine in the parish of Pressan Ambo is the scene of an industrial dispute, as a result of the owner's

[1]This holiday provides an interesting example of Auden acquiring a phrase for a poem. In a diary entry during their stay in Czechoslovakia, he wrote: 'Went our first and last walk after lunch and inspected the new railway they are building. Very pansy.' The poem 'A Bride in the 30s', written the following autumn, includes the line: 'Lucky to Love the new pansy railway.'

attempt to install automated machinery; and one of the play's sub-plots tells how a strike is called, riots occur, and martial law is declared. Most of this occurs off-stage; the main action is a re-working of the plot of 'The Fronny'. Alan Norman, a young man chosen by lot, goes in search of the missing aristocrat Francis Crewe – whose first name is that of Francis Turville-Petre, the original 'Fronny', and whose second name was perhaps taken from the Lord Crewe Arms at Blanchland, near Hadrian's Wall, where Auden and Gabriel Carritt stayed during their 1930 walking-tour. Alan follows Francis's trail to such places as the Nineveh Hotel, where he meets the film-star Lou Vipond, and a hospital where Francis dies on the operating table. Another sub-plot, taken directly from 'The Enemies of a Bishop', involves Augustus Bicknell the Reformatory principal, and his love for one of the escaped boys who is dressed in women's clothing. The other boy, George, disguises himself in a dogskin, in which he accompanies Alan on his search.

In the first two plays, Auden's poetry had been inserted virtually at random moments, and the action came to a halt while it was recited. In 'The Chase' he made more of an attempt to integrate it with the play. Besides giving a number of poetic speeches to a chorus, he introduced 'The Witnesses', two figures who are recognisably Titt and Tool from 'In the year of my youth', and who appear in various guises to comment on the action in a Fate-like manner.

'The Chase' brims over with events, and swings abruptly between low comedy, as in the passages dealing with the fortunes of the Reformatory boys, and serious psychological comment – the Vicar is given a speech, based on the writings of Gerald Heard and virtually copied from 'In the year of my youth', in which he traces the root of the present social troubles to the fatal division between body and mind in 'economic man'. There is some attempt to break down the barriers of theatrical convention, and Auden uses such devices as audience-participation and the entry of characters through the auditorium. There is also some fine writing in it – for example, a speech beginning 'What was the weather on Eternity's worst day?', which Auden had written in 1933 and published in the journal *Life & Letters* as 'Sermon by an Armament Manufacturer', in which Communism is presented as it appears from the viewpoint of the bourgeoisie, as a new offensive against God by the powers of Hell. The play's ending is entirely serious in tone: Alan Norman, who by implication represents the anti-Fascist outlook, is shot down by the forces of Fascism, and dies in the arms of Francis's sister Iris – whose name Auden probably took from Nob Snodgrass's sister. The chorus concludes with the message: 'If we end to-day with the apparent triumph of reaction or folly: there is an alternative ending. / And the choice is your own.' But the play is still too deeply rooted in its predecessors, 'The Enemies of a Bishop' and 'The Fronny', to be more than, at best, an intriguing amusement, and, at worst, a schoolboy hotchpotch.

A typescript of 'The Chase' reached Faber & Faber in the autumn of 1934, and another copy was sent by Auden to Rupert Doone. In Doone's opinion the play was not up to the standard he expected of Auden; nevertheless he began to organise a Group Theatre production for the following spring. Faber's decided they would publish the play, and announced it for the following March. Auden himself, however, was now beginning to have second thoughts. In November he asked Faber's to return the typescript so that he could improve it. He had already sent a copy to Christopher Isherwood, who was at present living temporarily with his boyfriend Heinz in Copenhagen. Isherwood now began, in several letters to Auden, to make suggestions for improving the play. Auden decided to visit Isherwood so that they could discuss this further, and he persuaded Faber's to advance him enough money to make the trip by air – which greatly impressed Isherwood, who still regarded flying as an act of daring. Auden assumed that, despite Isherwood's help, the play would remain entirely his own work; at the beginning of January 1935, shortly before leaving for Copenhagen, he wrote to Nob Snodgrass's sister Iris: 'Am just finishing a play which is to be done in London in April or thereabouts.' He was only in Copenhagen for four days; but by the time he returned to London on 13 January the play had become a very different piece of work, by two authors.

★

Isherwood's major suggestion was that the story should concentrate entirely on Alan's search for Francis, and that the Reformatory sub-plot should be removed, along with all references to the lead-mine strike. He and Auden also hatched the idea that the person inside the dogskin should be Francis himself, and that this should be the answer to the mystery of his whereabouts; Alan should set off on his quest for Francis with the 'dog' just as before, and should only discover the true nature of his companion towards the end of the play. This simplification of the play's outline would allow freedom to develop individual episodes into revue sketches or cabaret turns. The play would in fact become more like a pantomime, in which a thin and not very important plot could act as a vehicle for a series of virtually independent items. Auden himself, looking back many years later, said that pantomime had been 'the most important single influence' on the new version of the play.

The theme was now different from 'The Chase'. Gone was the attempt to analyse the cause of social unrest. Instead the point was now, as Auden put it, to present a 'tour of contemporary societies with political over-tones'. Alan and the Dog's quest would take them across the Channel, through a country governed by a ruthless monarchy (Ostnia), and into another which was in the hands of Fascists (Westland). Europe was to be presented as being just as rotten as the English village.

Isherwood had already made substantial proposals for new scenes by the time Auden came out to Copenhagen. In a letter dated 23 November he offered what he called 'suggestions towards a scenario'. These included making the newspaper reporters who appear in 'The Chase' into journalists 'of the international type, which ferrets around everywhere behind the scenes'; writing a scene where revolutionary leaders are executed without trial and their wives are then offered champagne and cake as a consolation (an idea taken from the behaviour of the wife of the Austrian chancellor Dollfuss, who allegedly took cakes to the widows of executed socialists); inserting another scene where the followers of a Fascist leader are portrayed as lunatics in an asylum; replacing Miss Lou Vipond, in Alan's scene of love-making with her, with a tailor's dummy (an idea revived from 'The Enemies of a Bishop'); providing a cabaret turn for the Nineveh Hotel where 'a Rembrandt is slashed, amid loud applause'; and concluding the play with Francis jumping out of the dogskin, delivering a speech denouncing the villagers, and leaving with Alan. Further letters from Isherwood to Auden made other suggestions, and in Copenhagen the two planned the reconstruction of the play in detail. Three weeks after Auden returned to England, Isherwood wrote to Spender: 'It has gradually turned into a completely new work, but keeping the best things from the old version.'

He and Auden in fact rewrote it as a collaboration, partly while they were together in Copenhagen and partly by correspondence afterwards. Isherwood provided the prose dialogue for most of the new scenes that he himself suggested,[1] while Auden wrote several new song-lyrics and a number of new scenes: a visit by Alan to the Inferno-like Red Light District of Ostnia; an encounter with a financier on a train; and some dialogue with a poet, two lovers, and a pair of invalids in Paradise Park. Isherwood revised these scenes and was responsible for several details in them. Auden also agreed to cut out the Witnesses and give most of their lines to the Chorus, for whom he also wrote some more verse describing the state of the English landscape and the cities of Europe.[2]

Isherwood finished typing the play early in February 1935. He and

---

[1] Isherwood's contributions were: I.ii (dialogue with the journalists and barman on the boat), most of I.iv (the executions in the Ostnian palace), a good deal of II.i (the Westland lunatic asylum), the cabaret turn by Destructive Desmond (III.ii), and the dialogue of the Feet in II.v (there had been a similar dialogue in *The Chase*, but the idea of making them represent, respectively, Instinct and Reason was Isherwood's).

[2] Edward Mendelson points out, in *Early Auden*, that these lines describing the landscape, which are often praised as some of Auden's most beautiful work, are lifted, detail by detail, from Anthony Collett's *The Changing Face of England* (1926, republished 1932). For example, Auden's lines 'Calm at this moment the Dutch sea so shallow / That sunk St Paul's would ever show its golden cross' are based on Collett's 'Not only is the North Sea so shallow that if St Paul's was planted anywhere between the Dutch and English coasts the golden cross would shine above water. . .'

Auden planned to call it 'Where is Francis?' But Rupert Doone suggested another title, which he probably meant as an allusion to two lines in Eliot's 'Whispers of Immortality': 'Webster was much possessed by death / And saw the skull beneath the skin.' Auden and Isherwood agreed to adopt Doone's title: *The Dog Beneath the Skin.*

Faber's had agreed to defer publication of 'The Chase' until Auden had revised it. Now, he sent them *The Dog Beneath the Skin* with Isherwood's name on the title page as co-author. Eliot was not happy about this, and, though he re-advertised the play under its new title, he credited Auden alone with authorship. Auden, furious, wrote to Eliot describing in detail Isherwood's contribution, and only then did Eliot agree to crediting them both with the work. The play went to press; meanwhile Isherwood proposed a new ending, in which Mildred Luce, a half-mad woman who claims that her two sons were killed by German snipers in the Great War (she had first appeared in 'In the year of my youth'), shoots Francis before he can make his escape with Alan. Doone decided to accept this new version for the Group Theatre production which was scheduled for January 1936 as part of the company's projected London season. But the alteration came too late for the published text, which was issued in May 1935 – to mixed reviews. John Garrett, loyal to his collaborator on *The Poet's Tongue,* called the play good satire; but the *Times Literary Supplement*, while praising the richness of language, said it was 'rather like an undergraduate rag'. I.M. Parsons in the *Spectator* compared it to *Murder in the Cathedral*, which had just been published, and wrote that in contrast '*The Dog Beneath the Skin* is a shoddy affair, a half-baked little satire which gets nowhere. If it had been written by Mr Brown and Mr Smith, instead of by two intelligent young men like Mr Auden and Mr Isherwood, nobody would have bothered to publish it, and nobody would have been the loser.' Auden commented of this very hostile review, in a letter to Nob Snodgrass, who had written praising the play: 'Glad you liked old Dogskin. It got the Spectator on the raw.' Meanwhile he was already thinking about another piece of work for the Group Theatre. In April he wrote to Michael Roberts, who in his spare time was an amateur mountaineer: 'I want to see you soon, to talk about climbing, which is to be the subject of my next play.'

★

At the Downs School at Christmas 1934 Auden organised a stage production not unlike *The Dog Beneath the Skin* in character. He wrote to Nob Snodgrass after it was over: 'Last term was a hectic rush as I was producing a revue including the whole school and staff, a cast of about 113. Music and lyrics by me. Some very hot numbers. I wish you could have seen it.' He dictated the tunes, in the key of C major, to Maurice Feild's wife Alex, who transposed them and provided harmony. When it was all over, the Feilds managed to preserve a few of Auden's songs, of which this is a typical example:

> New boy
> Oh, it's hard to be a new boy
> To be no better than a Jew boy
> Strange terrifying faces
> Come and ask me my name
> Until in a corner
> I hide for shame
> Just a don't-know-what-to-do-boy
> At a public school.

Not all the songs were so innocent; in one number, Auden himself appeared on the stage, in a wig and sequinned gown, and sang a song that he used in *The Dog Beneath the Skin:* 'On the Rhondda / My time I squander / Watching for my miner boy.' No doubt this was intended to amuse those of his friends who had made the journey to Colwall to see the show, including Rupert Doone and Stephen Spender. But the entertainment also pleased the audience for a deeper reason. The school magazine commented that its success 'was largely due to the fact that we were allowed to be ourselves. . . We were persuaded. . . into letting ourselves go'.

This was Auden's third year teaching at the Downs. Writing to Snodgrass, he described himself as being 'a power behind the throne'. But he felt it was time to consider moving. Early in 1934 he thought about going to teach English in Russia, but this came to nothing; in the autumn of that year he made approaches to Bryanston to see if there might be a job for him, this being the public school with the closest association with the Downs; several of Auden's former pupils were there, and the senior English master was Wilfred Cowley, who had shared digs at Oxford with Cecil Day-Lewis and Rex Warner. In October 1934 Auden told a friend: 'Am probably going to Bryanston next year', and by the spring of 1935 he had been officially appointed to the staff. But he was not easy in his mind about the prospect of teaching at a public school; in early April 1935 he told Michael Roberts: 'I'm off to Bryanston in September, full of doubts.' Two weeks later the whole arrangement was cancelled. Geoffrey Hoyland, the Downs School head-master, was due to preach at Bryanston; Auden said in his own account of the incident that he 'wrote a letter to an ex-pupil containing an unfortunate exhortation to put an onion in the chalice.[1] Boy showed

---

[1]The ex-pupil to whom the letter was sent was Michael Paget-Jones. According to Michael Yates, who was then at Bryanston, Auden wrote: 'I hear G. H. is coming to preach next Sunday. Put an onion in the chalice for me.' Auden later alleged that the headmaster of Bryanston, T. F. Coade, 'stole' the letter – see the line in 'Last Will and Testament': 'And T. F. C. may keep the letter that he stole' (*Letters from Iceland*, 2nd ed. (1967), p. 246).

letter in pride to prefect, prefect in shock to headmaster so voila!'

Auden wrote to Michael Roberts: 'I am very much in two minds as to what to do. Whether to go on teaching or not. If I do, I think a secondary day school.[1] Could you give me your advice. . . What I *think* I should really like is a B.B.C. job connected with education.'

This was on 22 April. About six weeks later a request came from Isherwood that Auden should do something that he, Isherwood, did not feel able to, but which he knew needed to be done: marry Thomas Mann's daughter Erika in order to give her a British passport.

Isherwood had known Klaus Mann, the eldest son, for several years, and in May 1935 was introduced to Klaus's sister Erika, who had come to Amsterdam, where Isherwood was now living with Heinz. Erika Mann was aged thirty; she had studied acting under Max Reinhardt, and besides working in the theatre had been a journalist and even on one occasion a rally driver, winning a prize for driving six thousand miles around Europe in ten days while sending in newspaper stories of her own progress. Since 1933 she had run a satirical cabaret, the 'Pfeffermühle' (Peppermill), which performed songs and sketches that were largely anti-Nazi in character, and which were mostly written by Erika herself. Klaus Mann described the Pfeffermühle repertoire as 'at once acid and graceful, not without poetic and nostalgic undertones'. The company included a highly gifted actress, Therese Giehese, by whom Isherwood was greatly struck in a scene where she 'turned the globe of the world on her lap like a sick child and crooned weirdly over it'.

Erika Mann herself was strikingly handsome, slim and dark haired. She had been married – though in fact she was largely lesbian by inclination – but was divorced from her husband, the actor Gustaf Gründgens, once a left-wing sympathiser who had become involved with the Nazis, and was eventually appointed director of the Berlin State Theatre. With the coming to power of Hitler, Erika Mann and her cabaret left Germany and took their revue on tour around Europe; she also managed to smuggle the unfinished manuscript of her father's novel *Joseph and his Brothers* out of Germany and hand it over to him. After travelling for two years with the Pfeffermühle she heard, in the early spring of 1935, that the Berlin authorities planned to take away her German citizenship. Her response was to approach the nearest unattached Englishman, who happened to be Christopher Isherwood, and ask, not without embarrassment, if he would marry her so that she could obtan a passport as a British citizen.

Isherwood felt 'honoured, excited, amused', but he refused, feeling that it would compromise Heinz if he became involved with such a celebrated anti-Nazi, and realising also that he had a deep horror of marriage. He therefore – with Erika Mann's agreement – wrote to

[1] i.e., a secondary school that was part of the state system, not a privately run public school.

Auden, suggesting that he might be able to help. Auden wired back: 'DELIGHTED'. Erika Mann immediately set off for England.

Auden had now given up his room in the masters' bachelor quarters at the Downs School, and was living in a cottage on the edge of a neighbouring estate, which he facetiously named 'Lawrence Villa', apparently in honour of the affair he was having with Peter Roger, the young man who worked in the school gardens. (To one visitor who came to the Downs, the poet Gavin Ewart, it seemed that Auden 'was living in the garden shed, with the gardener'; but this was an exaggeration.) Auden shared Lawrence Villa with another member of the school staff, Austin Wright, who during June 1935 became his confidant over the whole business of the marriage. Here is Wright's account of it:

'Isherwood wrote saying that Erika Mann's life was constantly in danger. She was in political cabaret in Amsterdam. Shots fired in the theatre. She had to change her hotel every night. Would Auden marry her and provide a British passport? This, Wystan said, was a question you decided at once. And he did. But in no time he was full of worries about what his mother would think – staunch Anglo-Catholics. And what about Geoffrey Hoyland? "We shall see the headmaster pacing the lawn."'

Erika Mann promised to send some photographs of herself to her future husband. 'There was a longish delay,' recalls Austin Wright. 'The postbox at the Downs was a thing inside the door with a little glass front so that you could see if anything had come. And so every day there were pokings with a stick when the post arrived – at about 4 p.m. – and FINALLY a large envelope was detected. I was with Auden. We went straight off to Lawrence Villa and it was feverishly torn apart and spilled out on to the floor. "There is my wife!" Theatrical photographs of course – angled this way and that. Eton crop – a sharp swirl over one eye. Black black eyes. (Her mother's daughter.) And in costume.'

The story is usually told that Erika Mann arrived at Malvern only very shortly before the wedding – having, it is said, first got off the train at the wrong station (Malvern Link instead of Great Malvern) and greeted the only man on the platform with the words 'It is so kind of you to marry me!' Another version of the same story has Auden arriving just in time for the train, rushing up to the first woman he sees, throwing his arms around her neck, and exclaiming: 'Darling, how lovely to *meet* you!' – whereupon the woman scampers in terror. Austin Wright's account shows that neither anecdote is true, and that Auden met Erika Mann a few days before the wedding; though the true story is almost as comic as the fictitious versions.

'She was invited over during the summer term,' recalls Wright. 'Again I was taken – playing Pylades to Orestes – and we were to meet her at a village pub some way away. (Wystan drove right over a small central village green, dragging a huge white stone under the car.) And there she

1 (a) Auden in his mother's arms: a photograph given by him to Elizabeth Mayer after his mother's death in 1941.

1 (b) Auden as a small child: a photograph found among the papers of John Layard.

2 (a)   The Auden family on holiday at Rhayader in August 1913. (*Left to right:*) Dr G. A. Auden, Wystan, Bernard, John, Constance Auden.

2 (b)   Wystan leaning over the rail at the water-works, Rhayader, August 1913. 'Those beautiful machines that never talked/But let the small boy worship them ...'

3 (a) The Auden brothers. (*Left to right:*) Bernard, John, Wystan.

3 (b) Wystan Auden during his days at preparatory school.

4 (a) Wystan Auden during his schooldays.

4 (b) (*Left to right:*) Wystan, his father, and his brother John at the Lake District cottage during the 1920s.

5 (a) and (b)   Auden and Christopher   Isherwood, photographed at Oxford in 1928 by Eric Bramall, at the suggestion of Stanley Fisher.

6 (a) and (b) Further photographs from the 1928 session.

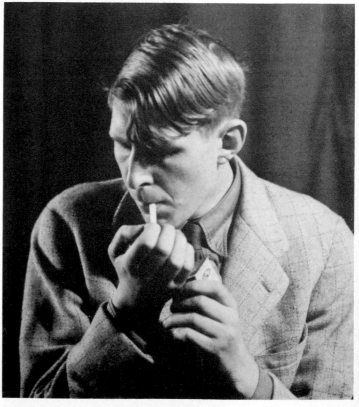

7 (a)   Gabriel Carritt in 1930.

7 (b)   Auden and John Layard in
Germany in 1929, probably photo-
graphed at Rotehütte in the Harz
Mountains.

Wystan.   Stephen   Christopher.

8 (a) Auden, Stephen Spender and Christopher Isherwood at Rügen Island in 1931; a print given to Gabriel Carritt and signed by all three.

8 (b) Auden, Isherwood and Spender photographed by Howard Coster in the early 1930s.

9 Part of the manuscript of 'O Love, the interest itself in thoughtless Heaven', from the poetry notebook that Auden was using at the time. The poem was written in May 1932.

10 The Downs School, Colwall, summer 1933. Auden sits at the right-hand end of the staff row, with Peter Roger next to him. Maurice Feild is third from the left of the staff row, and Geoffrey Hoyland, the headmaster, is the man in spectacles in the middle of the staff row, with a small child on his knee. Michael Yates stands immediately to the left of him in the row behind.

11 (a) Auden and Erika Mann: a photograph taken just after their wedding on 15 June 1935. Peter Roger stands on the left, holding John Feild, whose mother, Alexandra Feild (wife of Maurice Feild, the Downs School art teacher) is on the right.

11 (b) Auden and Isherwood: a photograph probably taken in Portugal during March 1936, when they were writing *The Ascent of F6*. This print was given to E. R. Dodds; on it, Auden has written 'Who towards the really better', a quotation from his poem 'Certainly our city, with the byres of poverty down to . . .'

12 (a) Louis MacNeice, photographed by Auden in Iceland, 1936.

12 (b) Auden and E. M. Forster photographed in Dover by a seafront photographer.

was. She was nine-tenths a man – I mean no pun. But it couldn't have gone better – for the homosexual Wystan, ideal. She insisted on driving us back to Malvern – yes, she had a licence and was an international car-rally driver.'

It was agreed that they should be married at Ledbury, a small town near the school. 'Ledbury registry office was a clever choice,' writes Austin Wright. 'In those days wonderfully warm and sleepy. We [Auden and Wright] went over one afternoon to see the Registrar. A tiny square room of an office; huge musty ledgers piled and leaning against walls and cupboards, and a dear little old man behind glasses. Of course Wystan didn't know any of the answers to the questions – her name? "Well, she has been married and divorced – I don't know." "It doesn't matter, tell me later. Her age? – Never mind." Wystan *was* able to provide some information about himself, and we emerged into the heavy sunshine. "He would have married me to the poker," Wystan said.'

On 14 June, the day before the ceremony, Auden took Erika Mann over to Cheltenham to visit Cecil Day-Lewis and his wife. Before the wedding, he and Erika also signed an agreement to make no financial claims on each other. Auden also made it clear to his friends that he wanted no wedding presents. On 15 June, the marriage took place, with Maurice Feild and Peter Roger as witnesses. They all returned to the Feilds' house, where photographs were taken by Maurice and Alex Feild, but there was no celebration, though Austin Wright recalls that a bunch of flowers and cabbage leaves was tied on to the radiator-knob of Auden's car. Auden then drove Erika to the Abbey Hotel at Malvern, where she was staying, and returned to school to continue his day's teaching. Most people at the Downs knew the purpose of the marriage, and very little was said about it. Auden wrote to Spender: 'I didn't see her till the ceremony and perhaps I shall never see her again. But she is very nice.'

Some days later, a telegram arrived at the Downs: 'MEINE LIEBE DEINE LIEBE ALLE MANSCHEN GLEICH.' (My love, your love, all people the same.) It was unsigned. Austin Wright remembers that Auden 'couldn't understand what was meant by it.

★

It was at about this time, the middle of June 1935, that Auden found a new job. He wrote to Basil Wright, a friend and old schoolfellow of Day-Lewis, whom he had met at Oxford in 1927 and who was now working as a director for the documentary film producer John Grierson at the recently established film unit attached to the General Post Office. Auden asked Wright if there was any chance of a job at the unit, whose work appealed to him – Grierson had a reputation for making documentaries which presented the lives of ordinary working men on the

screen in a way that was regarded as both accurate and exciting. Basil
Wright passed Auden's letter to Grierson, and the result was swift. Not
only was Auden offered a full-time job with the unit starting in September,
which he accepted, even though it would pay only about half his present
salary, but he was also asked to begin work immediately on commentaries for two documentary films. Towards the end of the summer
term he wrote to Nob Snodgrass: 'I'm leaving teaching pro tem at any
rate to work for Grierson at the G.P.O. Film Unit. . . At the moment
I'm writing them choruses for a film about the Night Mail to Scotland.
Have to get in all the Scotch place names I can find.'

The second commentary, part spoken and part sung, was for an
experimental documentary about the lives of North of England miners,
to be called *Coal Face*. Both films were to have specially composed
music, and as the film unit's budget was very small they could only
afford to hire a young and unknown composer for the job. They chose a
young man of twenty-two who had recently finished studying at the
Royal College of Music, Benjamin Britten. On 4 July, Basil Wright
came down to Malvern to see Auden, bringing Britten with him.

The atmosphere at that meeting was, Wright remembered, 'relaxed
and cordial', though he and Auden both found Britten 'extremely
young'. Afterwards, Britten got swiftly to work, and had soon composed
music for Auden's verse for *Night Mail,* the film about the Scottish mail
train, and for his lyric 'O lurcher-loving collier', which was to be
included in *Coal Face*. Auden was very impressed. 'What immediately
struck me,' he later wrote, 'about Britten the composer, was his
extraordinary musical sensitivity in relation to the English language.
One had always been told that English was an impossible tongue to set
or to sing. Since I already knew the songs of the Elizabethan composers
like Dowland, I knew this to be false, but the influence of that very great
composer, Handel, on the setting of English had been unfortunate.
There was Sullivan's setting of Gilbert's light verse to be sure, but then this
music seemed so boring. Here at last was a composer who could set the
language without undue distortion.' As to Britten, on the day of their
first meeting he described Auden in his diary as 'the most amazing man,
a very brilliant & attractive personality'.

A couple of weeks after his first meeting with Britten, Auden said
goodbye to his friends at the Downs School and, at least 'pro tem', gave
up schoolmastering.

7

Traveller

Auden's time at the Downs School had been the happiest period of his life so far. He had lived and worked there in a state of contentment, and his poetry had entered a period of extraordinary fertility. On the other hand he had been in an ideological muddle. His earlier enthusiasm for the Layard–Lane–Lawrence–Groddeck doctrines had faded (though it had not vanished entirely), and he was as yet unable to replace it with any other dogma which he could use as a firm base for his poetry. Neither Gerald Heard's explanation of the ills of society nor the Communism of friends like Edward Upward proved to be more than passing attractions to him. He played with them in his poems, but quickly realised that he should not pose as a propagandist. In his introduction to *The Poet's Tongue*, published during his last term at the Downs, he wrote: 'Poetry is not concerned with telling people what to do, but with extending our knowledge of good and evil, perhaps making the necessity for action more urgent and its nature more clear, but only leading us to the point where it is possible for us to make a rational and moral choice.'

During the summer holiday after leaving the Downs School, he reviewed his own state of mind in a poem that he wrote for Isherwood's birthday in August – 'August for the people and their favourite islands'. The poem recalled his and Isherwood's holiday in the Isle of Wight in 1926, when both their imaginations had been coloured by 'Mortmere': 'Our hopes were set still on the spies' career, / Prizing the glasses and the old felt hat, / And all the secrets we discovered were / Extraordinary and false. . .' Then, five years later in 1931, came the holiday on Rügen Island, and a period in which 'the word is love' – that is, when they believed that all the ills of the world could be cured by love, chiefly sexual – and in which Auden's writings (especially *The Orators*) had the manner of 'private joking in a panelled room'. The poem then rejects these ideas and 'every flabby fancy' of the past years, and declares that Auden and his friends can no longer indulge in this sort of foolery:

'Louder to-day the wireless roars / Its warnings and its lies, and it's impossible / Among the well-shaped cosily to flit.' No longer can they ignore the frightening events in the world around them; and the poem concludes with a call to Isherwood, with his 'strict and adult pen', to expose the squalor and falsity of society and indicate the road to reform – to 'Make action urgent and its nature clear', a phrase repeated from the introduction to *The Poet's Tongue*.

This, then, was Auden's state of mind in August 1935: a rejection of the past and a hope of discovering a course of action which could alleviate the evils of society. On 1 September he began work in films.

★

The G.P.O. Film Unit was the creation of John Grierson, a thirty-seven-year-old Scot who regarded the cinema not principally as an art-form but as a means of influencing public opinion. 'I have no great interest in films as such,' he wrote. 'I look on cinema as a pulpit, and use it as a propagandist.' After studying the cinema and other popular media in America, Grierson came back to Britain in 1927 determined to find an organisation which would allow him to make films that were both educational and persuasive. The Empire Marketing Board agreed to take him on as Films Officer, and for them he made his first film, *Drifters*, which illustrated the work of the North Sea herring fisheries. It aroused immediate interest, coming at a time when British cinema was studio-bound and conventional. Grierson's location-shooting and his imaginative technique – influenced by Eisenstein and Pudovkin – seemed startlingly novel, and the film vindicated his belief that he could 'make a drama from the ordinary' without resorting to the falsifying style of Hollywood. Its interest in the lives of ordinary working men also made it implicitly, if only mildly, left-wing in tone. Grierson admitted that he and those who worked with him were 'a little worried about the way the world was going', and hoped to 'crystallise sentiments in a muddled world and create a will towards civic participation'.

Grierson and the team he built up at the Empire Marketing Board made more than a hundred films in a little over three years, on subjects such as a day in the life of a Border shepherd, the work of the London food markets, and salmon fishing in Scotland. The films were shown to film-club audiences, to schools and colleges, and later as part of the 'supporting programme' in the more highbrow London cinemas. When in 1933 the Empire Marketing Board was dissolved, Grierson managed to arrange for the General Post Office to take over the Film Unit. The G.P.O. did not oblige the film-makers to confine their subject-matter to the work of the Post Office itself, and they were allowed to make films on the wider topic of communications in general. 'We gradually began to see', wrote Grierson, 'the magic of modern communications. We saw the gale warning behind the Central Telegraph Office, the paradox of nationalism and internationalism behind the cable service, the choral beauty of the night mail.' They were also able to deal with quite different subjects, such as the lives of coal miners. It was at this point, just as the Unit's horizons were widening, that Auden joined them.

The Unit was based in London, at 21 Soho Square, where there were offices, a projection theatre, and a cutting-room. There was also a small studio a few miles away at Blackheath. None of the staff was highly paid: the skilled technicians received about six pounds a week and the production staff about a pound less. Auden received three pounds. 'My salary is not princely', he wrote to a friend, 'and I find it very difficult to make ends meet.' He saved money by lodging at first with Basil Wright, the director at the Unit who had arranged for him to have the job.

Auden was by no means the Unit's first recruit who had no experience of making films. Grierson, a good teacher, often took on people who had proved their ability in other fields, such as the young painter William Coldstream, who was currently working with the Unit as an editor and assistant director – Coldstream, who already knew Auden slightly, had joined the Unit about eighteen months earlier, partly because he had a social conscience and felt that painting was not enough, and partly because his pictures were not selling and he wanted steady employment. But Grierson was no longer taking quite such a close interest in his recruits as he had in Empire Marketing Board days. 'I didn't see very much of Grierson,' recalled Auden, adding: 'I worked regularly with Cavalcanti.'

The Brazilian-born Alberto Cavalcanti, then in his late thirties, had already made a reputation as a film-maker in France. He came to London to work for Grierson because he was bored with the French commercial film industry, and he brought with him something that few other members of the Unit then had, experience with 'talkies'. During 1935 he worked on the soundtrack of the Unit's mining documentary *Coal Face,* using Benjamin Britten's music and words largely written by Auden. The musical score was written for only a small group of players, for financial reasons, but was highly imaginative, employing among other things the recording of certain instruments reproduced backwards. A mixed choir also took part, and Auden's madrigal 'O lurcher-loving collier' was sung by women's voices. As to the spoken words, a commentator gave a factual account of the mining process and its products, and described the working conditions. There was also included on the soundtrack – and Auden was probably responsible for writing this – a series of recitations by voices representing the miners themselves. This included a list of the various jobs: 'Hewer, inspector, banksman, driver', etc.; there were also statistics: 'Every year in Great Britain, one in every five miners is injured'; and, as an indication that an accident has happened, the bleak statement: 'Cannot account for two hundred lamps'

– that is, two hundred miners have failed to return to the surface.

Coal Face was completed not long after Auden joined the Film Unit, and was released before the end of 1935. It was intended only as an experiment; even so, it largely failed on its own terms. The words of the Auden–Britten madrigal and many of the recitations by the miners' voices were obscured by the voice of the commentator, who in several places spoke over them, so that (as Auden told Isherwood) 'even the producer himself admitted that they were quite inaudible'. Moreover, despite the efforts of the cameramen and the laboratory, much of the film was, as a member of the Unit put it, 'bloody dark'. In some shots there was very little to be seen. The reviewer in *Sight and Sound* attacked it as 'incoherent in conception and ineffectual in execution'.

Auden's other chief project at the beginning of his time with the Unit was to work on *Night Mail*. This film, an account of the 'Postal Special' train which ran nightly from London to Glasgow, was conceived by Grierson and Basil Wright, and was directed chiefly by Wright and Harry Watt, with a soundtrack supervised by Cavalcanti. The initial scenario was for a straightforward documentary giving a picture of the job of the mail-sorters on board the train as it sped through the night. But in this form the film was felt to lack something. According to Wright, 'We'd seen the rough assembly of the film, Grierson, Cavalcanti and I, and somebody, probably Grierson, said, "There's something missing. . . What we haven't got here is anything about the people who're going to get the letters. We've only had the machinery of getting letters from one point to the other. What about the people who write them and the people who get them?"' So the idea came about that a coda should be added, describing the train's progress in imaginative terms, and turning finally to the letters themselves and their recipients. This was to be done on the soundtrack by a poem commissioned from Auden.

He had written the first draft of the poem during July 1935, while still teaching at the Downs School, but though he told Nob Snodgrass he had been asked to include 'all the Scotch place names I can find' the poem was in fact concerned less with the Scottish scenery than with the rhythm of the train itself:

> This is the night mail crossing the border,
> Bringing the cheque and the postal order,
> Letters for the rich, letters for the poor,
> The shop at the corner and the girl next door.

'We were experimenting', said Auden of *Night Mail*, 'to see whether poetry could be used in films, and I think we showed it could.'

The first draft of the poem included lines which Harry Watt felt could not be matched with adequate images on the screen – lines such as 'Uplands heaped like slaughtered horses', and 'this country, whose scribbled coastline traps the wild Atlantic in a maze of stone'. Watt observed: 'No picture we put on the screen could be as strong at that.' These lines and others like them were cut. Benjamin Britten then provided a musical accompaniment for the poem, again using a small group, which this time included sandpaper and a wind machine. The poem itself was spoken partly by Grierson and partly by Stuart Legg, a member of the Unit's staff who was chosen because he could manage the very fast pace required. Even so, there was no time for him to take breath between phrases. 'So we had to work out a method,' recalled Watt. 'Legg would take an enormous breath and start off: "This is the night mail crossing the border bringing the cheque and the postal order letters for the rich. . ." and so on, until he ran completely out of breath, went "Huh". We had to mark where he went "Huh", and then he had to start again further back.'

When Auden began full-time work at the Unit, some sequences of *Night Mail* were still being filmed, and he went on location with Wright and Watt to watch the shooting and learn the technique of directing. Watt, who 'didn't give a damn' about Auden's reputation as a poet, made no special effort to be pleasant to him. 'He was just an assistant director, as far as I was concerned,' Watt said, 'and that meant humping the gear and walking miles, and he used to turn up late. Of course, he was an extraordinary looking young man. He looked exactly like a half-witted Swedish deckhand: his jacket was far too short in the sleeves, and he had huge, boney, red hands and big, lumpy wrists and dirty old flannel trousers and an old sports jacket and this blond towhead, and then the rather plummy, frightfully good accent, which was very surprising coming out of him. He just got kicked around like any young assistant would have got kicked around, and I don't think he liked it very much.'

Basil Wright was kinder to Auden, whom he quickly decided was 'no fool technically'. Part of a sequence was shot at Broad Street Station in London, which was used to simulate Crewe Junction, and was lent to the Unit by the railway authorities for a weekend. The film crew was under some pressure, and Wright handed over to Auden responsibility for a shot in which a line of platform trolleys brought the mailbags over to the 'Postal Special' from another train which had just arrived. Auden, with a second camera unit, directed this shot unsupervised, and Wright did not see it until the rushes. When *Night Mail* was completed he thought it 'one of the most beautifully organised shots in the film'.[1]

Although other members of the Unit besides Harry Watt may have been initially suspicious of Auden's manner and appearance, the general verdict on him was favourable. Even Watt eventually became impressed

[1] Some of the shooting was done at Crewe itself. According to Auden, 'We got a shot of a guard at Crewe, and he dropped dead about thirty seconds later.' This made a good story, but the truth, according to Wright, is that the man was not a guard but a senior railway official, and it was not until some weeks later that he died.

by Auden's professionalism while he was rewriting the *Night Mail* commentary to fit the specific requirements of the film. The only office-space available for him to work in at 21 Soho Square was a passage that he had to share with the Unit's messenger boys, who, when not running errands, made a great deal of noise. 'There, on that old Post Office table,' recalled Watt, 'he wrote the most beautiful verse. He kept bringing it, and – the cheek of us, in a way – we turned down so much. He'd say, "All right, that's quite all right. Just roll it up and throw it away."'

When *Night Mail* was released early in 1936 it proved to be the Unit's biggest box-office success so far. Auden's verses and Britten's music attracted particular attention. But by this time Auden was far from happy about his job at the Unit.

There had in fact been difficulties from the beginning, if only of a social kind. Out of working hours, Basil Wright found Auden far from easy as a lodger. Wright's flat, which was in a smart 'contemporary' block in Highgate, included a Blüthner baby grand piano among its furnishings, on which Auden would strum hymns before breakfast. He smoked while playing, and was in the habit of resting his cigarette on the end of the keyboard. One day, inevitably, he burnt a groove in the piano – and was entirely unrepentant. 'I don't see what all the fuss is about,' he replied to Wright's remonstrations. 'It doesn't alter the tone.' This was the occasion of his first row with Wright. The second came some weeks later, when Wright complained that Auden had overspent the budget of a film he was helping to produce, *Calendar of the Year*. Auden, in reply, burst into a tirade against the whole Unit and its working methods. As a result of this, he moved out of Wright's flat and began to lodge with William Coldstream and his wife Nancy at their house in Upper Park Road, Hampstead. The Coldstreams were less particular about their furniture than Wright, and they found him a congenial lodger.

Auden's outburst laid bare his disappointment with his job. Part of the trouble was, no doubt, simply that he was unused to being 'junior boy' in an organisation; the role of apprentice can scarcely have appealed to him. Another cause was the fact that he did not have enough to occupy him, or at least enough regular work. Tasks only came his way sporadically: a few days of frantic activity around the clock would be followed by periods of idleness. 'I found it tiring', he said, 'when I was hanging about the office with nothing to do at all. Of course, sometimes I was up all night working. But I like an organised life. I work regular hours.' Yet another reason for his discontent must have been that, after *Coal Face* and *Night Mail*, Grierson did not find another use for his talents that equalled, let alone excelled, the demands of those two films.

In *Calendar of the Year,* an account of the work of the Post Office through the changing seasons, Auden again helped with the direction, as well as acting as production manager, and was struck by the tiresome-ness of the postal officials who were supposed to be helping with the film. 'We had to take some pictures of people in a trunk telephone exchange,' he remembered. 'It was supposed to be New Year's Eve. I found out that these people were very tired and worked in their shirt sleeves. So I got them into shirt sleeves, got the camera man, and when the supervisor came he said: "We can't show government officials in their shirt sleeves."' Auden himself appeared in this film for a few seconds, as Father Christmas in a London department store, asking children what they would like for presents: he appeared to be rather overawed by them, while his accent – which was indeed, to use Harry Watt's word, 'plummy' – seemed a little too upper-crust for the role.

One of the few projects initiated by Grierson which promised to be artistically stimulating on Auden's terms was a film intended to deal with the introduction of African slaves into the West Indies, the subsequent abolition of slavery, and the later development of the islands. Britten was to write the music, Auden the commentary. Auden described the proposed soundtrack as 'a most elaborate affair, beginning with quotations from Aristotle about slavery and including a setting of a poem by Blake'. This is an excerpt from a portion that survives of the shooting (or editing) script:

Fade in to modern map of W[est] I[ndies] and seaboard showing steamship routes	*Bass Recit.* Still at their accustomed hour The cities and oceans swing westward into the segment of eternal shadow Their revolutions unaltered since first to this chain of islands, motionless in the
cut to Long shots of W.I and liners	Caribbean Sea like a resting scorpion The Captains came, eager from Europe, white to the West.
cut to Negro fishermen mix to Negro children in fields mix to negress on barge cut to locomotive mix to machine mix to Tractor	*Female Voice (spoken)* Today nearly all manual work in the West Indies is done by Negroes. Attempts to form settlements of European labourers have been unsuccessful. Physical necessities are few, few clothes, fuel only for cooking, and food at hand to be picked. *Bass Recit.* And still they come, new from those nations to which the study of that which can be weighed and measured is a consuming love.

The film was to be called *Negroes*. But during Auden's time on the staff of the Unit it was not made, because, he said, 'it turned out there were no visuals' – though Basil Wright thinks that the film was to be based on some footage he had shot in the West Indies about three years earlier. Britten did write at least part of the score for the film, and Auden remembered that this contained 'some wonderful music'; the project was revived a few years later and the film was actually made by the Unit in some form, under the title *God's Chillun,* but it was apparently never released.

Auden also probably wrote part of the commentary for a production by Strand Films, on behalf of the British Travel Association, entitled *Beside the Seaside*. He is not named in the credits, but he seems to have been referring to this film when he said, in a lecture to the North London Film Society early in 1936, that he had 'just contributed to a publicity film, "By the Sea-side", in which poetry had been applied. . . as a general emotional commentary'. It was apparently for this film that he wrote the poem 'Look, stranger, on this island now', though it was not used in the soundtrack. He also asked Isherwood to write some dialogue for a proposed film on English middle-class life, but this does not seem to have got further than the initial idea.

The success of *Night Mail* did lead Grierson to plan an ambitious sequel, which was to be called *Air Mail to Australia,* and Auden was apparently chosen to direct it or co-direct it. The idea was to take a camera crew on board the mail plane, filming its journey and the stops along the way. A date in October or November 1935 seems to have been fixed for this, for Isherwood mentioned in a letter to a friend on 10 October that 'Wystan. . . is leaving very soon to film the Australian air-route'. In fact Auden did leave London on about this date, and travelled to Switzerland, having, it seems, decided to use the film project as a means of visiting the family he described as 'my in-laws'.

At the time of his marriage to Erika Mann, he apparently had no intention of regarding the arrangement as more than a formality, but it seems that he had now decided to take the relationship a little more seriously. This, at any rate, is how it seemed to Golo Mann, Erika's brother, when Auden arrived on 12 October at the Mann family home at Küsnacht on Lake Zurich.

Thomas Mann was undoubtedly very grateful to Auden for the help he had given his daughter, and now that he met Auden he was (thought Golo Mann) 'impressed and amused' by him, though he scarcely knew Auden's work as a writer or took any interest in it. Auden's attitude to Mann's work was at the time much the same: he felt no great admiration for him, but was friendly towards him when they met. Later he did sometimes praise Mann's work; in 1938 he called Mann's book *The Coming Victory* 'the best brief statement of what democracy means which I have read'; and two years later he commended him for having 'a profound sense of what Kierkegaard called the Dialectic'. Later still, he became equivocal or critical, and was known to remark to friends: 'Who's the most boring German writer? My father-in-law!'

As to Auden's attitude towards Erika, Golo Mann described it as initially 'nothing but amusement'. But he swiftly came to admire her. The next year, 1936, he dedicated his new book of poems to her, and that autumn he wrote to a friend whom he had not met for some years: 'Since I saw you I've married (for passport reasons) Erika Mann, Thomas' daughter, who is a wonderful person.'

After staying with the Manns for two days, Auden left for Zurich airport; Golo Mann believed he was intending to fly by stages to Australia for the film project. But something seems to have made him change his mind, and instead (after perhaps returning first to London) he paid a visit to Brussels, where Christopher Isherwood had now moved with Heinz. Auden stayed briefly with Isherwood and showed him some of the verse he was writing for the Film Unit, before travelling back to London. There is some evidence that the Italian invasion of Ethiopia had postponed the filming of the air-route. Another factor may have been money: according to Basil Wright, the Unit would have been very hard pressed to finance such a project. At all events, *Air Mail to Australia* was abandoned.

Undoubtedly the frustration of so many fruitless ideas contributed to Auden's unhappiness with his job at the Unit. During the rest of the winter, he and William Coldstream took to slipping out of the office as often as possible, to drink coffee in a Lyons Corner House and grumble about their colleagues and their work, or lack of it. Auden also hated living in London – 'horrible London', he called it, looking back on this winter. Almost the only real reward he found at the Unit was his friendship with Benjamin Britten.

'Benjy', as Auden called him, was more than six years his junior, and was markedly unsure of himself in fields other than music; he admitted in his diary that Auden, with his 'vital brains', gave him an 'appalling inferiority complex'. Auden determined to take Britten under his wing, schoolmaster-fashion, and help him to broaden his knowledge of the world. He encouraged Britten to pay more attention to the other arts, especially English poetry, and he probably also urged him to attend to the current political situation. Certanly he discussed Britten's sexual problems with him, and sorted them out in much the same manner that he had dealt with Isherwood's in 1926, putting on his favourite role of analyst-healer. Britten was amazed by his bluntness and crude language.

Britten's inclinations were homosexual, and Auden made it his task to 'bring him out' – encourage him to throw aside all repression. He may have done this with the assistance of Isherwood; Basil Wright remembers Isherwood making a giggling reference to Britten's sexual education. Isherwood, while not recalling precise details, writes of this: 'No doubt both of us tried to bring him out, if he seemed to us to need it. We were extraordinarily interfering in this respect – as bossy as a pair of self-assured young psychiatrists – he [Auden] wasn't a doctor's son and I wasn't an ex-medical student for nothing!'

Auden cast his advice to Britten on matters of sex in the form of a poem, which Britten later set to music:

> Underneath the abject willow
>   Lover, sulk no more;
> Act from thought should quickly follow:
>   What is thinking for?
> Your unique and moping station
>   Proves you cold;
>   Stand up and fold
> Your map of desolation. . .

He put the same sentiment in slightly cruder terms in another context a few months later:

> For my friend Benjamin Britten, composer, I beg
> That fortune send him soon a passionate affair.

Another poem which Auden dedicated to Britten and which Britten set to music is 'Night covers up the rigid land', written in March 1936. This poem suggests that Auden was in love with Britten, but that Britten had rejected him, perhaps for someone else. It talks of its subject's 'dark caressive head', and declares: 'You love your life and I love you, / So I must lie alone.' Peter Pears, who became Britten's lifelong companion, agrees that Britten may indeed have rejected Auden, and is certain that there was no love-affair. He writes of the two poems 'Underneath the abject willow' and 'Night covers up the rigid land': 'They were not poems, to my eyes, of a received lover, rather of a rejected one. Wystan may have been "in love" with Ben, but there was never an "affair".' Christopher Isherwood writes of this: 'If there was sex between Auden and Britten, I remember nothing of it. My guess would be No. Nothing between Britten and me, either.'

During the winter when he and Auden were working with the Film Unit, Britten was commissioned to write a work for the Norwich & Norfolk Triennial Festival, and he asked Auden to devise a libretto. Auden chose as a theme man's relations to the animals, and selected three poems to illustrate this: a medieval prayer for deliverance from rats, an anonymous dirge for the death of a monkey, and Ravenscroft's 'Hawking for the Partridge'. To these he added a prologue, 'They are our past and our future', and an epilogue whose first line gave the title to the whole work: *Our Hunting Fathers*. Britten scored it for high voice and symphony orchestra, allowing the words full play and taking care that they should be audible. But the work was not a great success at its first hearing, and has not often been performed since then. In 1936 a critic commented on 'so much talent. . . expended on so arid a subject'.

By the time he and Britten were at work on *Our Hunting Fathers,* Auden had given vent to some of his frustration about work at the Film Unit in an article in *The Listener*. This was a review of Paul Rotha's book on documentary film, and Auden used it as an opportunity to attack the whole concept of the documentary. He made four points: first, that film 'is not the best medium for factual information', but is better adapted to creating emotional attitudes; second, that films are made ridiculously quickly because of cost, so that the makers do not get time to understand the subject properly; third, that, though documentaries are supposed to portray 'real life', most film-directors are upper-middle-class themselves and fail to understand the working class; fourth (no doubt remembering the episode of the shirt-sleeves), that sponsorship by government departments or big industry is bound to limit the film-maker's freedom – it was unlikely, said Auden, that such organisations would 'ever willingly pay for an exact picture of the human life within their enormous buildings'.

John Grierson read what Auden had written, and was himself probably responsible for the reply which appeared in *World Film News*. This reply denied that all documentary directors were upper-middle-class, and alleged that they were forced 'to live and learn with workmen under working conditions' while making their films. Not all of Auden's criticisms were answered, and the reply concluded on a personal note: 'As Auden's apprenticeship matures he may feel less despondent.' But Auden was not prepared to follow this advice. In Feburuary 1936 he took leave of absence from the Film Unit in order to concentrate on his writing. A few weeks later, instead of returning to work in Soho Square, he sent in his resignation, having been on the Unit's pay-roll for less than six months.[1]

★

He did not look for another full-time job, and began instead to depend for income upon what he could make from his writing. That he should decide to do so was perhaps partly the result of the success of Group Theatre productions of two of his plays during the autumn and winter he spent with the Film Unit.

At the beginning of October 1935 the Group Theatre opened what was

[1] Much later in his life, Auden wrote two more film commentaries. The first was for the film *Runner,* describing the athlete Bruce Kidd, which was produced in 1962 by the National Film Board of Canada. Auden said of this commentary: 'Unfortunately it required two speakers and only had one; it wasn't very well spoken either. I should have been there to direct it.' In 1968 he wrote a verse narration for the film *US,* shown in the United States pavilion at Hemisfair '68, San Antonio, Texas.

to be a season of several months at the Westminster Theatre in London with a new version of the Doone–Guthrie production of *The Dance of Death,* performed as a double bill with Eliot's *Sweeney Agonistes.* Doone again danced the role of Death in the Auden play, John Allen played the Announcer, and the cabaret songs were sung by Hedli Anderson, a remarkable performer who was later to marry Louis MacNeice. *The Dance of Death* was billed as 'a political musical comedy'.

On the printed page, Auden's play looks slight and even facile compared to Eliot's, but once again it proved itself a highly effective piece of theatre for its time. The greater number of critics greeted it with enthusiasm, preferring it to *Sweeney,* which several of them judged to be pretentious nonsense. Ashley Dukes, in *Theatre Arts Monthly,* wrote of the Auden piece: 'It is pointed, theatrically effective, and sometimes humorous as well as witty. I cannot recall being bored by it for an instant. . . What is important is a correlation of acting, movement and words unlike anything else in today's theatre experience. . . Here is a writer for a future poet's theatre. . . And if this time the result is a blend of some inspiration and much nonsense, that is no fault of the way of going to work.'

This promised well for the new Auden–Isherwood play *The Dog Beneath the Skin,* which was to open at the Westminster Theatre four months later, at the end of January 1936. Auden himself was on hand for rehearsals of the new play – Isherwood did not come to England for the production – and again he impressed the company by his willingness to co-operate and his readiness to alter and adapt the script. As things turned out, a number of alterations were necessary.

It had already been decided by Doone, who was to produce the play single-handed (he was not performing in it himself), that the production should adopt the revised ending written by Auden and Isherwood since the play's published text had gone to press. In this version, Francis, instead of leaving Pressan Ambo to join 'the army of the other side' (which seems to imply Communism), delivers a speech attacking the villagers for their Fascism and their hypocrisy. He reveals that, for example, Mildred Luce, who mourns the death of her sons at the hands of the Germans during the war, never had any sons and was not even married, though she once was engaged to a German officer. Enraged, she shoots him, and the journalists agree to hush up his death, just as in the published play they agree to ignore his treachery to Pressan.

This ending, which does not really provide a better conclusion to the play than the original text, was in fact one of the less radical changes that Doone made when putting the play on stage. A good deal was cut, and unfortunately these cuts included some of the best passages, such as the concluding lines of the opening chorus (from 'Climb up the crane, learn the sailor's words'), the touts' stanzas describing the various forms of prostitution in the Red Light District (presumably cut for reasons of delicacy), many lines in the speech of the Leader of Westland (apparently omitted to reduce his resemblance to Hitler), and the entire sermon by the Vicar in the last scene – the speech beginning 'What was the weather on Eternity's worst day?' Another loss at this stage of the production was the cabaret turn by Destructive Desmond, the Rembrandt-slasher. This was omitted not, as has been suggested, because of censorship – according to Robert Medley the Lord Chamberlain's office demanded no major cuts – but because Desmond Walter-Ellis, to whom the part had been allocated, proved in rehearsal to be unsuited to the grotesque style of comedy required to bring off the performance. Yet another change was, in Alan's love-scene, to have the Dummy's lines spoken not by Alan himself but by an actress.

A few days before the opening night, a further cut had to be made. 'I'm very depressed', Auden wrote to Nob Snodgrass, 'as, owing to the King's death the owner of the theatre has got cold feet about the Ostnia scene and wont have it.' Without this episode of the executions in the Ostnian palace the play was shorn of much of its remaining satire.

The Dog Beneath the Skin opened on the night of 30 January 1936. Gyles Isham and Veronica Turleigh were the chorus, billed as 'The Witnesses', John Allen played Alan Norman, Geoffrey Wincott was the Dog (Francis), Robert Eddison the Poet, and Max Adrian the Curate. Hedli Anderson sang several of the songs, the music was once again by Herbert Murrill, and the designer was, of course, Robert Medley. Though the Group Theatre aimed to be innovatory in its style, Doone's production was rather old-fashioned; the curtain was lowered and incidental music was played between scenes, even though most of the scene-changes were done with lighting effects, and the 'set' was little more than a bare cyclorama. The acting was not of a very high standard: Julian Symons, writing in *Twentieth Century Verse,* compared the performance to the work of a church hall dramatic society.[1] But this did not matter very much to the first-night audience, who were disposed to be uncritical and sympathetic. Most of the professional reviewers were kind, too. *The Times* was cautious, but called the play 'an entertaining revue', while at the other end of the political spectrum the *Daily Worker* judged it 'one of the best plays of the season', and praised its 'striking assaults on the social system'. *The Observer* judged it 'full of fun and charged with both wit and beauty', while the *Sunday Times* declared: 'This play ought to run for five years.' Certainly there were dissenting voices; Cyril Connolly in the *New Statesman* remarked that 'the bareness

[1] Robert Medley points out that Doone had wanted the curtain to remain up throughout each act, but had decided that the stage was too small for scene-changes to be done in these circumstances, and reluctantly decided to lower it between scenes. As to the acting, Medley remarks that, because of the Group Theatre's pioneer status and the unrewarding nature of many of the parts in *The Dog Beneath the Skin,* it was not possible to obtain professional actors of a uniformly high standard.

of the stage reflected the poverty of the lines', while Kenneth Allott in *New Verse* observed: 'Mr Auden is not a dramatist but a poet interested in the theatre.' But the reaction of critics and audience taken as a whole was sufficiently favourable to keep the play running for six weeks, which, if not the five years the *Sunday Times* had predicted, was not bad for an unconventional play at an unfashionable theatre. Performances continued until Saturday 14 March, after which it was replaced, a week later, by the Group Theatre's production of *Fulgens and Lucrece,* the earliest known English secular play.

Auden had a hand in a revival of 'Dogskin', as he and Isherwood nicknamed the play, in New York in 1947. On this occasion he did not have a copy of the revised ending with him, and he wrote a new conclusion in which Francis is stabbed to death by Mildred Luce. But this was no more satisfactory than the other versions, and when he was teaching at Smith College in Massachusetts in 1953 he set a competition in which students were to devise a new closing scene. His own suggestion was that a great white cat should begin the chase all over again.

Auden's mature judgement on the play, nearly forty years later, was that the choruses were a piece of self-indulgence that damage the play as drama. (On the other hand, when the play is read, rather than performed, the choruses seem in many ways superior to the rest.) Despite this censure, Auden confessed to a 'private weakness' for this exuberant, irrepressible play.

★

'Dogskin' was enough of a success for Doone and Medley to ask its authors to create something else for the Group Theatre. Auden and Isherwood were entirely happy to begin another collaboration; as Isherwood put it, 'it had now become a function of their friendship'. Auden, too, liked the stimulus of joint authorship. 'It's exciting,' he said. 'When a collaboration works, the two people concerned become a third person, who is different from either of them in isolation.'

Isherwood and Heinz had been obliged to leave Belgium, because the authorities would not renew Heinz's residence permit. They were now in Portugal, living in a cottage at Sintra, near Lisbon, and on 16 March Auden joined them there for a month, so that he and Isherwood could begin work on the new play. It was the first time for several years that he and Isherwood had been together for more than a few days at a stretch. 'Wystan hasn't changed in the least,' Isherwood wrote in his diary. 'His clothes are still out at the elbows, his stubby nail-bitten fingers still dirty and sticky with nicotine; he still drinks a dozen cups of tea a day, has to have a hot bath every night, piles his bed with blankets, overcoats, carpets and rugs; he still eats ravenously – though not as much as he once did – and nearly sheds tears if the food isn't to his taste; he still smokes like a factory chimney and pockets all the matches in the house. But although I found myself glaring nervously whenever he shovelled food into his mouth while reading at meals; although I was often annoyed by his fussing and the mess he made – still I never for one moment was more than annoyed. I never felt opposed to him in my deepest being – as I sometimes feel opposed to almost everyone I know. We are, after all, of the same sort.'

They quickly got to work on the play, so quickly that some planning must have been done before Auden's visit. Both of them felt they must write something more serious than 'Dogskin', and a year earlier Auden had decided that the subject should be mountaineering. Given, as seems to have been the case, his wish to deal with the theme of heroism, this was not a surprising choice. Climbing was the favourite activity of several people he knew well. His brother John was an accomplished mountaineer, as were also Michael Spender (Stephen's brother) and Michael Roberts and his wife Janet Adam Smith. In his schooldays Auden had attended an illustrated lecture about Everest by G. L. Mallory, who later vanished while climbing that peak. The brother of Geoffrey Hoyland, headmaster of the Downs School, was killed on Mont Blanc in 1934. It is not surprising that Auden became interested in the psychology of mountaineers. 'I wonder', he wrote some years later, 'if the psychologists can explain why it is that mountaineering should so strongly appeal to the intellectual, the book-loving, the introvert.'

The plot of the new play, to which they gave the working title 'The Summit', was sketched out by Isherwood, always the more disciplined playwright of the two, and it reflected his own preoccupations just as much as Auden's. Isherwood saw it as the chance to create a parable expounding an idea which had interested him for many years: that heroes who undertake exploits of daring and bravado are not true heroes at all, but are driven to this behaviour by neurotic flaws in their personalities. Such a hero, declared Isherwood, is a 'Truly Weak Man'; in contrast a 'Truly Strong Man' is someone who does his job without fuss and does not pose as something other than he is. It is the Truly Weak Man who sets himself what Isherwood called 'The Test', a challenge that he must meet in order to prove his strength. So, in the new play, Michael Ransom, a celebrated mountaineer, agrees to climb the notorious peak F6 not because his country requires him to (which it does, for political reasons) but because he is driven to it by his mother, who all through her life has tried (she says) to make him 'the truly strong'.[1]

---

[1] The play was also intended to be a comment on T. E. Lawrence, who had died only a few months earlier. Isherwood described Lawrence as a divided person, an adolescent who had never matured; Auden saw him rather differently, as someone who began by choosing blind action but later realised that such action could not be an escape from rational thought – see *The English Auden*, pp. 320–1. Isherwood's view of Lawrence, rather than Auden's,

Auden and Isherwood wrote separate parts of the play, 'Wystan writing indoors', recalled Isherwood, 'with the curtains drawn; Christopher writing out in the garden, with his shirt off in the sunshine'. Isherwood observed that while his own first drafts were usually very crude, Auden generally achieved at his first attempt something that was very close to the final version.

'Our respective work on this play was fairly sharply defined,' wrote Isherwood in his diary. 'We interfered very little with each other's work. The only scene on which we really collaborated was the last. It was understood, throughout, that Wystan's speciality was to be the "woozy" and mine the "straight" bits.' By 'woozy' Isherwood meant the passages where he and Auden decided a heightening of style was needed. Auden usually employed verse for these, though he also wrote certain sections as 'poetic' prose – Ransom's prologue, his conversation with the Abbot in the mountain monastery, and his soliloquy to the skull of a dead climber. He also provided songs, and passages of verse to be spoken by two characters functioning as a chorus, 'Mr and Mrs A.', an ordinary suburban couple who listen to the news of Ransom's expedition on the wireless.[1]

One afternoon when they were not working, Auden insisted that Isherwood join him on a scramble up the Sintra hills, so as to get themselves into the mood of mountaineers; the result, said Isherwood, was 'laughter, lost footings, slitherings and screams'. Another day Isherwood and Heinz took him to see what they described as 'the horrible old afternoon gamblers' in the casino at Estoril, which prompted Auden to write the poem 'Casino' ('Only the hands are living; to the wheel attracted'). They also met Ernst Toller, the left-wing playwright who had been imprisoned in Germany for his part in the Communist bid for power in Bavaria, and who was now staying briefly at Sintra with his wife. Auden's admiration for Toller is indicated by the fact that later this year he helped to translate the lyrics for Toller's play with music, *Nie Wieder Friede!*, a satire on contemporary political events which was published in English, with music by Herbert Murrill, as *No More Peace!*

prevailed in the play; but Isherwood warned against taking the play too literally as an allegory of Lawrence – see *Christopher and His Kind*, p. 181.

Stephen Spender, in a programme note to a Cambridge Mummers stage version of *The Orators*, suggests that T. E. Lawrence also lies behind the figure of the Airman in that book.

[1] The invention of 'Mr and Mrs A.' may have sprung from T. S. Eliot's objection to the chorus in *The Dog Beneath the Skin*. After attending a performance, Eliot wrote to Rupert Doone to say that he had enjoyed it, though he regretted some of the cuts; he added: 'What did irritate me was the chorus – not that Veronica Turleigh is not very good indeed: but these interruptions of the action become more and more irritating as the play goes on, and one tires of having things explained and being preached at. I do think Auden ought to find a different method in his next play.' (Letter dated 5 March 1936, now in the Berg Collection, New York Public Library; quoted by kind permission of Mrs Valerie Eliot.)

On 17 April, after staying with Isherwood for a month, Auden left Lisbon by train, taking with him the completed manuscript of the new play, which was eventually given the title *The Ascent of F6*, the mountain's name being derived from K2, the second highest peak in the world, which John Auden had mentioned in conversations with his brother. When the play was published, it was dedicated to John.

While writing it, Auden had concerned himself, over and above its main theme, with another more personal topic, the question of what ought to be his own role as a poet in society. In the mountain monastery, Ransom looks into a crystal and sees – or rather, hears – a vision in which crowds call out to him to save, help, lead and heal them. The abbot perceives that Ransom is tempted to take on this messianic role. 'You know your powers and your intelligence,' he tells him. 'You could ask the world to follow you and it would serve you with blind obedience.' But he warns Ransom that the penalty would be self-destruction: 'Woe to the governors, for, by the very operation of their duty, however excellent, they themselves are destroyed.' He offers Ransom another choice: to remain in the monastery and take up the contemplative life. Ransom very nearly accepts. But in the end he is mastered by the desire to reach the peak and perform the public act. The result is that he destroys himself.

Auden's success as a poet had been of a particular kind. He was looked up to by many of his generation as a leader. He himself was by no means averse to this in some ways, for, like Ransom, he had a private vision of himself as analyst-leader-healer, an 'indifferent redeemer', a role that he exercised in his friends' lives whenever the opportunity was offered. But the other kind of leadership was a different matter. 'I knew', he said, looking back thirty years later, 'that a certain kind of success had nothing to do with what I really cared about, and of course one would have to pay for it later.' He seems, in fact, to have meant *The Ascent of F6* to be in part a parable of his own dilemma. '*F6* was the end,' he said in an interview in 1963. 'I knew I must leave [England] when I wrote it. . . I knew it because I knew then that if I stayed, I would inevitably become a member of the British establishment.'

★

Soon after returning from Portugal, Auden paid a visit to Bryanston School to see his friend Wilfred Cowley, the senior English master. While he was there he took his old Downs School pupil Michael Yates out to lunch. 'During lunch', remember Yates, 'he asked me if the family were as usual going to the Isle of Man for the holidays. I said yes, except that I myself with three other boys and a master were going to Iceland. He became excited. . .'

Such was Auden's excitement that he immediately proposed to Faber

& Faber that they should give him a contract for a travel book about Iceland, and should advance him enough money to finance his trip. Faber's agreed. Auden then wrote to Michael Yates to say he would be leaving for Iceland in June, some weeks before the Bryanston party, but hoped that the master in charge of the school expedition would allow him to join them when the boys arrived in Iceland, as he would like to include an account of their travels in his book. Yates raised the matter with the master, who was in fact Geoffrey Hoyland's half-brother W. F. (Bill) Hoyland, who taught biology at Bryanston, and who proved perfectly agreeable to adding Auden to the party.

Auden had several motives for the journey. One was sheer curiosity to see Iceland, which had been, as he put it, 'holy ground' in his imagination since childhood, thanks to his father's enthusiasm for all things Icelandic. But he seems also to have hoped that by distancing himself a little, both geographically and culturally, from his own life and from European society and its crises he might obtain a better view of himself and his environment. There was, too, an element of sheer fun in the project; it was to be a holiday, a temporary escape.

In the middle of May, not long before leaving for Iceland, he attended a rather odd wedding. He felt that other homosexuals ought, in cases where help was needed, to make similar marriages to his own; as he put it, 'What are buggers for?' Erika Mann's friend and fellow actress in the 'Peppermill' cabaret, Therese Giehse, now needed a British passport herself, and Auden managed to find a husband for her. This was a friend of E. M. Forster's, whose real name was John Simpson but who wrote fiction as 'John Hampson'. Simpson/Hampson, a kindly man who worked as a male nurse to the mentally-defective son of a family in a Birmingham suburb, was physically tiny, and of peculiar appearance, not the least because he chose to dress entirely in brown. On 20 May, Therese Giehse was married to him in a Birmingham registry office.

Auden arranged the whole thing, with the help of Louis MacNeice and R. D. Smith, a Birmingham University undergraduate and friend of MacNeice and himself,[1] who were to act as witnesses. Under Auden's instructions, they gathered in a somewhat conspiratorial manner to meet Therese Giehse on the station platform, and were taken aback when she arrived to find that she was heavily built, as broad as she was tall, wearing a very mannish tweed coat and skirt, and carrying a huge bouquet; she entirely dwarfed the tiny bridegroom, who looked as if a puff of wind would carry him away. At the registry office, Auden, dressed in striped trousers with a carnation, helped the bride, whose

[1]Smith, who later became a distinguished BBC radio producer, asked MacNeice and Auden for contributions to an undergraduate revue. Auden supplied the song-lyric 'The chimney sweepers / Wash their faces and forget to wash the neck', later used in *The Ascent of F6*, but told Smith he should not really use it as the revue ought to be written solely by undergraduates. It was not used.

English was poor, to answer the astonished registrar's questions. Afterwards, Auden led them to a pub and bought large brandies for everyone, declaring 'It's on Thomas Mann.' He would have played the pub's piano to add some jollity to the occasion, but the instrument proved to be locked, and when R. D. Smith asked for the key he was told that the pub's landlord had just died and had been laid out on the billiard table in the bar next door.

Some months later, Auden provided a kind of wedding present for Therese Giehse, in the form of a cabaret sketch which he wrote for her during the summer of 1936, entitled 'Alfred'. Her role in it was that of an old woman who, says the stage direction, 'has something about her that reminds us of certain prominent European figures'; she mumbles sentimentally over her pet goose, Alfred, yet brandishes a knife with very obvious intentions towards him.

Auden sailed for Iceland, from Hull, early in June. After toying with the idea of visiting Finland first, he had decided to go straight to Reykjavik. The voyage took about five days, and he was bored and sometimes sea-sick, but he amused himself by reading, apparently for the first time, Byron's *Don Juan*, which he thought 'fine'.

The boat's gradual approach to Iceland delighted him. He described it in a poem:

> And the great plains are for ever where the cold fish is hunted,
> And everywhere; the light birds flicker and flaunt;
> Under a scolding flag the lover
> Of islands may see
>
> Faintly, his limited hope; and he nears the glitter
> Of glaciers, the sterile immature mountains. . .

But when he finally disembarked at Reykjavik he found the Icelandic capital rather drab. 'Most of the town is built of corrugated iron,' he wrote. 'The three chief buildings are the Roman Catholic church, the (unfinished) theatre and the students' hostel, which looks like waiting-rooms of an airport.' It was at this hostel, the Studentagardur, that he took a room.

Here he spent 'a very miserable first week', because everyone to whom he had introductions was away. He sat gloomily in the Borg, the only hotel with a drinks licence, drinking 'at ruinous expense' and listening to the dance-band in the ballroom. He knew no Icelandic, but found that English and German were widely spoken; and gradually he began to meet people and pick up gossip – he was told that homosexuality was rare in Iceland. He began to do some sightseeing, and made a short journey to Thingvellir, 'the stock beauty spot', where he stayed a night or two. While there he made his first attempt at riding, which he knew would be useful, since the Bryanston party were to travel mainly on horseback. On this first try he 'fell right over the horse's neck while getting on in full view of a party of picnickers'. Later he went to Laugvatn, not far from Thingvellir, where, riding again, he 'shocked an English girl by yelling for help'.

Apart from these expeditions, and a journey to Mukalot eastward along the coast, he spent most of his first month in Reykjavik. He soon came to dislike Icelandic food, which he said made him think of 'a little boy who had got loose with Mother's medicine-chest'. The very sweet hot soups particularly disgusted him – he alleged they were made largely with brilliantine – and of the dried fish, a staple food, he wrote: 'It varies in toughness. The tougher kind tastes like toe-nails, and the softer kind like the skin off the soles of one's feet.' But he liked the coffee, which he drank as often as he usually consumed tea. 'I must have drunk about 1,500 cups in three months,' he wrote at the end of the trip.

He realised very well that he was not a professional traveller, the sort of person by whom most travel books are written, 'handsome, sunburnt, reserved, speaking fluent Icelandic'. Nor did he have any idea what kind of book he should write. He said he felt 'like a small boy who knows he's got an exam tomorrow, for which he has done no work whatsoever'. He also thought that most travel books were boring because they simply repeated the same pattern of events – journeys, meals, accommodation, dangers, and so on – or took refuge from this in trying to be essays on life, the kind of thing which he said he was 'neither clever nor sensitive enough to manage'. But he began to learn something about modern Icelandic poetry, and he was struck by the fact that 'any average educated person one meets can turn out competent verse'. He bought records of folk music, and was introduced to Arni Pällson, the Professor of Icelandic History. He also made friends among the Reykjavik students, from whom he learnt songs and proverbs. But he decided that the people of modern Iceland bore little resemblance to their ancestors; he found them 'not nearly so foreign as the Irish or the yokels of Somerset. You can't imagine any of them behaving like the people in the sagas, saying "That was an ill word" and shooting the other man dead. Disappointing, still one needn't travel if one wants to see odd behaviour.'

On 13 July he began a tour around western and northern Iceland which lasted just over two weeks, bringing him back south again in time to meet the Bryanston party, who were coming out from England at the beginning of August. He had as guide and travelling-companion for the first part of his journey a young Icelander, Ragnar Jonasson, and together they left Reykjavik by bus. Auden took with him a set of proofs of his new book of poetry, which had just arrived from Faber's. He had entitled the book 'Poems 1936', but T. S. Eliot wrote to say that the sales manager thought this title would mislead readers into expecting a complete retrospective collection. Eliot added: 'Frank Morley [another director] thought he had found a brilliant suggestion for a title with *Vin*

Audinaire, but the sales manager does not like that either.' (Morley's joke was eventually used in a 1937 Faber advertisement for Auden's books.) Auden wrote back to Eliot: 'Morley's suggestion is certainly brilliant but what would St John Irvine say.' He proposed, for the title of the book, 'It's a Way', the last words of the last poem in it, or, as an alternative, 'The Island', adding: 'On the analogy of *Burnt Norton* I might call it *Piddle-in-the-hole.*'

His bus journey from Reykjavik was not very pleasant. Many of the passengers were sick, which the driver said was common among Icelanders. After travelling northwards, Auden and his friend got off at a farm near Hredvatn, where they stayed for a couple of nights. Auden played the harmonium, an instrument often found in Icelandic farms and cottages, and joined the farmer's family for a game of rummy. He soon discovered that cards were an Icelandic passion, and began to make it his own habitual way of spending the evening during the trip, not least because he could talk and make jokes while playing. He and Ragnar also went boating and riding. Auden now regarded himself as quite a horseman: 'To my great joy I got a really frisky horse who bucked and galloped as hard as one could wish.'

From Hredvatn, they travelled on northwards, sometimes by bus and sometimes by milk cart, staying at farms and inns. Auden inspected a cheese works and a hospital, dined with a doctor, and began to catch a cold. On 20 July he and his companion reached the town of Akureyri on the north coast, and came in touch again with information from the outside world. 'Have just heard for the first time', Auden wrote in his journal, 'of the civil war in Spain.'

He reacted to the news of the Spanish Fascist uprising in a poem he was writing, 'Journey to Iceland', which was an admission that, despite the fun of the trip, he could not turn his back on the rest of the world. 'Europe is absent. This is an island and therefore / Unreal,' he wrote. But, despite this, 'the world is, and the present, and the lie.' Europe, and Spain, could not be escaped.

From Akureyri he and Ragnar went east along the coast, then south through the desert to Grimstadur, then east again. It was in the bus during this journey that Auden, his cold now 'boiling over like a geysir', had an idea for the travel book – a consequence of having read Byron on the voyage from England: 'I suddenly thought I might write him [Byron] a chatty letter in light verse about anything I could think of, Europe, literature, myself. He's the right person I think, because he was a townee, a European, and disliked Wordsworth and all that kind of approach to nature, and I find that very sympathetic. This letter in itself will have very little to do with Iceland, but will be rather a description of an effect of travelling in distant places which is to make one reflect on one's past and one's culture from the outside.' From this came the idea for the whole book. The poem to Byron was to be 'a central thread on which I shall hang other letters to different people more directly about Iceland. Who the people will be I haven't the slightest idea yet, but I must choose them, so that each letter deals with its subject in a different and significant way.' He immediately began work on the first canto of 'Letter to Lord Byron'.

The poem, written in the *Don Juan* stanza form, emerged on the pages as exuberant and witty, and excited Auden as 'a kind of thing I've never tried to do before'. By the end of the month he had drafted the first canto, and had already begun the second. But he could not keep his mind entirely from the news – or lack of it. 'I wish I knew how things were really going in Spain,' he wrote.

He spent the last days of July at Egilsstadur, a large farm in east Iceland, having said goodbye to Ragnar, who was travelling on. Here he rode the farmer's prize horse – 'The moment we got on the road, we set off at full gallop. . . The farmer said, "You've ridden a lot in England, I expect."' On 2 August the farmer drove him into Seðisfjördur, the principal east-coast port, where the only bed he could find was in a 'home for decayed old ladies'. After three days he embarked on the ship *Nova* and sailed back along the north coast, a voyage which he found 'so boring I can hardly remember a thing'. On Sunday 9 August he was back in Reykjavik. Waiting for him there was Louis MacNeice.

At some stage – Auden could not subsequently remember when – he had asked MacNeice to join him in Iceland and collaborate on the travel book, an indication (as Auden himself said) that the two of them had now developed 'a mutual professional respect and a personal rapport without which collaboration is unthinkable'. MacNeice had admired Auden's poetry for many years, and often reviewed it very enthusiastically. Auden in his turn greatly valued what he described as MacNeice's resistance in his own poetry to 'fake feelings'. He now found MacNeice, in the weeks that followed, an ideal travelling companion; he called him 'funny, observant, tolerant and good-tempered', and declared: 'I have very rarely in my life enjoyed myself so much as I did during those weeks when we were constantly together.'

MacNeice's first marriage had just broken up, and he was about to start a new lecturing job at Bedford College in London. Like Auden, he too had come to Iceland hoping (as he put it) to 'get the focus' of ordinary life by standing away from it for a little. He and Auden spent a week together in Reykjavik while Auden made some arrangements for the next part of the trip, for which they were to be joined by the Bryanston boys. The school party, consisting of four boys and Bill Hoyland, the master in charge, arrived on 17 August, and swiftly set out from Reykjavik to begin a journey on horseback around the Langjökull icefield, Auden and MacNeice riding with them.

Auden had arranged the guides and the horses – which he did by leaving another party stranded. He was greatly annoyed to discover that

MacNeice had come from London without any tent or gear, and only reluctantly agreed to share with him – 'Ora pro nobis, please, this evening, won't you?' he apostrophised the shade of Lord Byron; 'We shall be sleeping in a tent to-night. . .' His fears proved justified. The tent, which was missing part of its pole, was far too short for them, and their feet stuck out of the doorway. Auden lay down on a pneumatic mattress – MacNeice said he looked like something out of Breughel when blowing it up – and adopted the foetal position, which left MacNeice almost no room. It began to rain, and the tent, which they had pitched with both skins of the canvas touching, began to subside and close in on them 'like something in Edgar Allan Poe'. The Bryanston boys, who being properly equipped had a dry night, woke the next morning to see no sign of either poet except a flattened tent on the ground. 'Perhaps they had sneaked off to the nearby tin hut for coffee,' wondered Michael Yates. 'Then the tent undulated and two wet cross faces appeared.'

The journey around the icefield now began in earnest. Two guides led them, and there were seventeen horses or ponies in all, which allowed several for spares and baggage-carrying. Auden now regarded himself as an experienced rider, but any impression of competence was entirely offset by his peculiar appearance. He chose to wear an outfit of which the innermost layer was pyjamas, on top of which were two shirts, two jackets, flannel trousers, riding breeches, a coat, and, finally, yellow oilskins. 'When he walks', said MacNeice, 'he moves like something that is more at home in the water.'

The journey around the Langjökull took eight days. They passed through lava-strewn deserts, eventually reaching the icefield itself and examining the glacier at close quarters. Auden took little interest in the landscape, which he compared to 'a party after which no one had tidied up'. He was much more interested in observing Bill Hoyland – 'very large, very red, and bespectacled' – and in noting how the boys reacted to the tough life. He teased them when they complained of the conditions, telling them that since they had come there in order to demonstrate their toughness they should now do so – 'Though heaven knows why you want to!' They in turn found his energy amazing. He rose at six o'clock with the others, acted as an interpreter between Hoyland and the guides, who could speak some German, and in any spare moments leapt about taking photographs. He now held that photography was '*the* democratic art', on the grounds that no technical skill was required, so that anyone could take good pictures. Certainly he himself paid little attention to technicalities and, as Michael Yates put it, 'would stumble about the lava like some amphibious monster taking the most extraordinary art shots: the backside of a horse followed by the guide Ari's bottom, a boot, distant views or half-hidden faces between our legs'. When the travel book was eventually published, it contained some distinctly strange pictures.

After the tent-disaster of the first night, Auden and MacNeice managed fairly satisfactorily, though MacNeice complained that 'everything he touches turns to cigarettes', and the two of them were discovered early one morning lying asleep with their *heads* outside the tent doorway. But they were able to spend most nights in the shelter of rest-huts or farms, and only had to depend on their camping equipment for brewing tea or coffee and cooking food. Even this, however, led to disaster. Auden's stove, an ancient primus which was their only source of heat, eventually fell to pieces, with the result that cold food became the diet. (Auden once made tea with water from a hot spring.) They were, on the whole, glad to get back on 25 August to Reykjavik.

Bill Hoyland and three of the Bryanston boys sailed for England two days later, but Michael Yates and MacNeice stayed on for the third and final part of Auden's trip. After sleeping the night at Reykjavik lunatic asylum as guests of the doctor in charge – who talked to them in Latin – the three left by boat for Borganes, whence they went across land and stayed at the farm near Hredvatn where Auden had been in July. Here they spent a few days, and then returned by road to Reykjavik and sailed again, this time on the *Dettifoss,* for the north-west of Iceland, where they stayed as Isafjördur, not far south of the Arctic Circle. Auden thought this the most beautiful part of Iceland, but there was little to do; he, MacNeice and Yates slept at the Salvation Army hostel, into which they managed to smuggle a bottle of Spanish brandy obtained from the British Vice-Consul. After a three-day trip to Melgraseyri, they returned to Reykjavik, and – again on the *Dettifoss* – left, on about 10 September, for Hull. On the boat and after returning home, Auden completed 'Letter to Lord Byron', which had turned out to have a largely autobiographical content – not least because Isherwood's semi-fictionalised account of his own recent life, *Lions and Shadows,* was about to appear. 'I must be quick', wrote Auden, 'if I'm to get my oar in / Before his revelations bring the law in.'

As a holiday, a piece of fun, the trip had been a huge success. But whether Auden's more ambitious objectives had been achieved was another question. He had absorbed a great amount of sheer information about Iceland, but he was too independent, too self-sufficient, to respond quite freely to what he saw. It was not an experience that changed him. Nor could he distance himself from his own life, and observe it from some way off, as he and MacNeice had hoped to do. The news about Spain had immediately brought him back to the 'real' world again. As he said to himself, 'We are all too deeply involved with Europe to be able, or even to wish to escape.'

★

Now that he had no means of employment other than his writing, Auden lived for much of the time at his parents' home in Birmingham. He had, in a sense, never left home, for during his five years as a schoolmaster it had been to the Birmingham house that he returned for much of the holidays. Difficulties with his parents may have continued, but he could not easily have afforded a house or flat of his own. In fact his mother, whatever her opinion of his poetry and sexual life, gave him some help with his work, answering his business letters on his behalf as best she could whenever he was away. From his point of view, home was as good a place as any in which to work, and he got on with his writing according to a strict routine. Somebody who came to know him well at this time, Brian Howard, one of the Christ Church 'aesthetes' of Auden's undergraduate days, was amazed at his energy. 'He upset me a great deal', wrote Howard, who was himself dissolute and disorganised, 'by saying that he got up every day (he lives in Birmingham) at 8.15, breakfasted and answered letters until ten, worked until lunch, then again from two to four, and then never worked a stroke after that – read, talked. He said that he couldn't allow himself to read after ten or eleven (!) at night, and that unless you had a physical rhythm it was all quite impossible. I said "You talk like my mother!" '

On 24 September, Faber's published the new Auden–Isherwood play, *The Ascent of F6*. Reviews were mixed, with a bias towards the unfavourable. Cecil Day-Lewis thought it an improvement on *The Dog Beneath the Skin,* but regarded the moral message as veering towards Fascism; Janet Adam Smith (Michael Roberts's wife) judged it as a successful piece of satire but thought the psychological theme muddled; Stephen Spender said that neither author had given of his best in it, and called Ransom 'a colossal prig'; E. M. Forster judged that there was a conflict between the psychology and other elements in the play.

The Ascent of F6 was not due to be performed by the Group Theatre until six months later, and Auden and Isherwood decided to revise two sections of it in the light of these criticisms, particularly Spender's and Forster's. They rewrote the end of the monastery scene to show more clearly, as Isherwood explained in a letter to Forster, that it was Ransom's followers who finally forced him to go on up the mountain and turn his back on the contemplative life. They also reconstructed the scene on the summit, in the hope of clarifying the role of Ransom's mother in the destruction of her son; Isherwood told Forster that they were trying to make her seem 'more like a dictator's public; submitting to him and yet preying on him'. Having completed these revisions, they found that there was still time to incorporate them in the American edition of the play, since Auden's literary agent Curtis Brown had forgotten to deliver the manuscript to the New York publishers Random House, who were to issue it in the States. (Random House had already published *The Dog Beneath the Skin* and a one-volume selection of Auden's work, called simply *Poems* and comprising the 1930–33 British *Poems*, *The Orators*, and *The Dance of Death*.) On 6 October Auden wrote to Bennett Cerf at Random House: 'Isherwood and I are now altering it [*F6*] quite considerably. Faber published it early against our will and I shall be very glad if the American edition were to be the definitive one.' And he told Nob Snodgrass: 'Revised edition of F6 due out soon is I hope much better.'

A month after the British publication of the play, Faber's brought out Auden's new book of poems. His letter to them from Iceland suggesting alternative titles had not reached London in time, and Eliot had decided to call the book *Look, Stranger!*, words taken from one of the poems in the volume ('Look, stranger, on this island now'). Auden was cross, but again he was able to remedy the matter in America, as the manuscript destined for Random House had, like that of *F6*, been sitting forgotten in Curtis Brown's office. He now wrote to Bennett Cerf: 'Faber invented a bloody title while I was away without telling me. It sounds like the work of a vegetarian lady novelist. Will you please call the American edition *On this island*.' Random House complied.

The first British printing, of 2,350 copies, sold out in six weeks, and reviews were almost unanimously warm. Edwin Muir praised Auden for the variety and originality of his poetry, and said he had achieved a new clarity in this volume. Stephen Spender called it 'a remarkable development' from the first book of poems, and Cecil Day-Lewis talked of 'a happy marriage of personality and technique'. Louis MacNeice in *The Listener* declared: 'It is Mr Auden who has brought back humanity to English poetry.' Almost the only sour note was struck by F. R. Leavis, who in his magazine *Scrutiny* was now under way with an anti-Auden campaign that was to last for the rest of both their lives. 'He has no organization.' wrote Leavis of *Look, Stranger!* '[He] still makes far too much of his poetry out of private neuroses and memories.'

Auden's income from his books of poetry could not contribute more than minimally to his upkeep, though he did also make small amounts of money by publishing individual poems as they were written, in such magazines as *New Verse*, John Lehmann's *New Writing*, and *The Listener*, whose literary editor J. R. Ackerley (one of E. M. Forster's friends) sometimes also commissioned book reviews from him.[1] But he depended chiefly on sums of money advanced by his publishers, and did not hesitate to scold them if he thought them wayward with their payments. 'As regards the Iceland book I have a bone to pick with you,' he wrote to Bennett Cerf at Random House in October 1936. 'When I saw you in London you said that I should have £50 on signature. The contract arrived after I left, saying £50 on publication, with the result that I had to

[1] Auden's poetry had been published in *The Listener* on many occasions, beginning in 1933, when, at the instigation of Janet Adam Smith, who was the assistant editor, 'The Witnesses' was printed in a poetry supplement to the magazine – and incurred the wrath of John Reith, the BBC's Director General, who could discern no meaning in the poem.

borrow. I expect that this was a misunderstanding, but I *was* cross with you.' He had no respect for publishers. 'They are all animals,' he once said.

Late in 1936, Auden worked again on the soundtrack of a documentary film, this time for Paul Rotha at Strand films. The film, entitled *The Way to the Sea*, described and celebrated the electrification of the London to Portsmouth railway line. It included a section which was obviously modelled on *Night Mail,* the intention again being to relate the subject to ordinary people. But this time the material was simply too mundane and unromantic to justify lines like this, describing the switching on of the electric current: 'The line waits – the train waits – the drivers are waiting – waiting for power!' And Auden's description of London day-trippers sitting on the beach would have been more appropriate to the sunbathers of his days in Weimar Germany: 'For the athletic and beautiful, the fullest opportunities to be active, and to be admired.' The commentary, written in Auden's most detached and hawk-like manner, seemed supercilious towards the common people it described: 'Night. The spectacle fades. The tiny lives depart with their human loves.' Auden's section of the film had music by Benjamin Britten – the two of them worked on the soundtrack during December 1936 – but even this failed to rescue it from a stilted artificiality.[1]

In November and December, Auden and MacNeice got down to the task of putting the Iceland book together, Auden staying for some days in MacNeice's Hampstead flat for the purpose. On 5 November he wrote to Naomi Mitchison: 'Am up to the ears in a sort of travel book about Iceland. I've never enjoyed anything so much before, but I expect that's a bad sign.' Auden had chosen to address his 'letters' to Isherwood, Dick Crossman, William Coldstream, and 'E. M. A.' – a set of initials standing for Erika Mann Auden. MacNeice contributed an absurd and very funny account of their adventures with the Bryanston party, whom he disguised as a group of schoolgirls travelling around the icefield with their school-mistress, 'Miss Greenhalge', a name belonging to one of the staff at Larchfield Academy where Auden had taught; MacNeice also composed a verse-letter to two friends, and an 'Eclogue from Iceland'. On 8 December, Auden wrote to his and MacNeice's friend E. R. Dodds: 'Louis has done a lovely eclogue for the Iceland book and the whole thing is finished except the testament we are going to do together. I think the Byron letter (about 1300 lines) is rather a success. I'll send it to you as soon as it comes back from the typist.' The 'testament' was a Last Will and Testament in verse, in which he and MacNeice made a series of facetious bequests to their friends (and enemies), somewhat on the lines of the will in 'The Fronny'.

[1] It has now been established that *The Way to the Sea* was intended as a parody of the documentary style and a leg-pull of the authorities who commissioned it. See Donald Mitchell, *Britten & Auden in the Thirties* (Faber, 1981), pp. 88-93.

While working on *Letters from Iceland*, Auden thought of going back into full-time employment. 'I'm looking for a W.E.A. [Workers' Educational Association] job in Yorkshire next year,' he told Naomi Mitchison. But a month later he had settled on a different course of action. 'I've decided', he wrote on 8 December to E. R. Dodds, 'to go out in the new year, as soon as the book is finished, to join the International Brigade in Spain.'

★

During this autumn, European Communist parties were beginning to recruit volunteers from their members and others to go to Spain and help fight for the Republican cause against Franco's right-wing nationalists. Large numbers answered this call, many of whom were exiles from Germany, Italy, and other right-wing authoritarian regimes; for they saw the Spanish cause as the long-awaited war against their common enemy, Fascism. In England, too, the struggle in Spain seemed to many to be the apocalyptic battle they had been hoping for. Cecil Day-Lewis declared it to be a conflict of 'light against darkness'; Stephen Spender said it 'offered the twentieth century an 1848'; and Rex Warner wrote: 'Spain has torn the veil of Europe.' The British Government adopted an official policy of non-intervention, but by the end of 1936 there was a steady trickle of British volunteers leaving for Spain. Some were manual workers, but many were intellectuals. John Cornford, the young poet to whom Auden had given advice some years earlier, was among the first, and another early volunteer was a friend of Auden's devotee Michael Davidson, a women painter named Felicia Browne. There were of course casualties – both Cornford and Browne were killed in the first six months of the war – but the International Brigade's recruitment continued, and by December 1936 there were probably more than a thousand volunteers from all over Europe fighting on the left-wing side. For many of them it was a chance to experience what the previous generation had gone through in the First World War, perhaps even to appease the guilt they felt at not having fought during 1914-18; to use a term adopted by Isherwood in *Lions and Shadows*, they were setting themselves a 'Test'. As one of them said, 'We had a greater need of going to Spain than the Spanish Republic had need of us.'

This was exactly Auden's state of mind, the reason why he was now drawn towards Spain. He had been searching for a long time for something that would 'make action urgent and its nature clear', and here now was a cause that did precisely that. In his letter to Dodds announcing that he was going to Spain, he explained: 'I so dislike everyday political activities that I won't do them, but here is something I can do as a citizen and now as a writer, and as I have no dependents, I feel I ought to go.' He added: 'Please don't tell anyone about this. I shan't break it to my parents till after Xmas.'[1] At about the same time, the beginning of December, he also wrote to Isherwood, and to Erika Mann and her family, to announce his decision.[2]

Dodds wrote back, asking Auden for an explanation. Auden replied as follows:

> I am not one of those who believe that poetry need or even should be directly political, but in a critical period such as ours, I do believe that the poet must have direct knowledge of the major political events.
>
> It is possible that in some periods, the poet can absorb and feel all in the ordinary every day life, perhaps the supreme masters always can, but for the second order and particularly to-day, what he can write about is what he has experienced in his own person. Academic knowledge is not enough.
>
> I feel I can speak with authority about la Condition Humaine of only a small class of English intellectuals and professional people and the time has come to gamble on something bigger.
>
> I shall probably be a bloody bad soldier but how can I speak to/for them without becoming one?

There was no mention in any of this of the Spanish cause itself.

He spent Christmas at home in Birmingham, then went with his family to the Lake District, where he told Dodds he intended to walk 'to help me to get into training'. He planned his departure for early January, but was apparently having second thoughts as to what his role might be in Spain. He told Isherwood that it would be 'either ambulance-driving or fighting. I hope the former.' On 4 January he wrote to Frederic Prokosch, an American poet who during the 1930s printed limited editions of several of Auden's poems: 'I'm going to Spain at the end of this week to drive an ambulance. Why not come too?' At about the same time he told Nob Snodgrass: 'I'm off in a week to drive an ambulance in Madrid. Wont it be cold.'

Before leaving, he wrote two poems which were both valedictory in tone, one more explicitly than the other. The first, 'It's farewell to the

---

[1] It is possible, though unlikely, that the timing of his decision to go to Spain may have had something to do with the fact that, in mid-November, he stayed briefly at Cambridge with Louis MacNeice's friend from schooldays Anthony Blunt (then a Fellow of Trinity College), who was an active Marxist. Blunt – who did not know Auden well – may have talked to him about supporting the Spanish cause.

[2] According to Erika and Klaus Mann's book *Escape to Life* (1939) he wrote: 'I am going to Spain. It isn't enough for us to stand up for our Spanish comrades with words. I want to be with them.' But this neither sounds like Auden's style as a letter–writer, nor bears much relation to the reasons he gave to Dodds.

drawing-room's civilised cry', was a piece of self-parody, a send-up of himself as the warrior hero:

> I shall ride the parade in a platinum car,
> My features shall shine, my name shall be Star,
> Day-long and night-long the bells I shall peal,
> And down the long street I shall turn the cartwheel.

The speaker in the poem is, however, on the Fascist rather than the Communist side of the struggle, and the piece, like the Vicar's sermon in *The Dog Beneath the Skin* and 'The Chase', is a view of the ideological war from the other camp. Auden wrote out this poem on the flyleaf of the score of Benjamin Britten's *Sinfonietta* (Opus 1) on 8 January, when he spent much of the morning with Britten at a Lyons Corner House in Tottenham Court Road, drinking coffee and talking. Two days later, Britten wrote in his diary: 'Wystan hasn't gone yet – expects to go tomorrow – because the medical unit he was going with was stopped by the government.'[1]

The second poem that Auden wrote during these days before leaving for Spain became, in the years that followed, the most famous of all his short lyrics: 'Lay your sleeping head, my love, / Human on my faithless arm.' It was in fact the end of a sequence, the last of the love-poems he wrote during the 1930s. All of them, from the first sonnets composed at the Downs School to the 1936 'Dear, though the night is gone' and 'Fish in the unruffled lakes', celebrated a love that was uncertain and transitory. But they transcend the private events that caused them. They are not usually even explicitly homosexual: their subject is the impermanence of all love, whatever sex the loved one may be, and they are summed up in a stanza of the last poem:

> Certainty, fidelity,
> On the stroke of midnight pass
> Like vibrations of a bell,
> And fashionable madmen raise
> Their pedantic boring cry:
> Every farthing of the cost,
> All the dreaded cards foretell,
> Shall be paid, but from this night
> Not a whisper, not a thought,
> Not a kiss nor look be lost.

★

'FAMOUS POET TO DRIVE AMBULANCE IN SPAIN', announced the *Daily Worker* on 12 January 1937, and on that day William Coldstream saw Auden off from Victoria Station on the boat train to Paris. Auden was

[1] See further, on this and other topics, Donald Mitchell, *Britten & Auden in the Thirties* (Faber, 1981), which quotes from a number of entries in Britten's diaries about his friendship with Auden.

going there to meet Isherwood, who had come from Brussels to see him on his way to Spain. In Paris, the two spent a drunken day with Brian Howard, who was living there. Next day, Isherwood accompanied Auden to catch a train bound for the Franco-Spanish frontier. It was, said Isherwood, despite their jokes 'a solemn parting'.

Auden's movements after he left Paris are difficult to trace with certainty. He seems to have written no letters home from Spain; on his return he rarely discussed what had happened to him, and he wrote no connected account of his experiences. Only a few fragments make it possible to reconstruct an outline of what he saw and where he went.

He probably entered Spain at Port Bou, the border town where many International Brigade recruits arrived by rail from France. From there, he apparently went next, probably by train, to Barcelona. Certainly he visited that city at some stage during his time in Spain, and what he saw there remained vivid in his memory.

He could in fact have come to no more appropriate place to learn the character of the civil war on the Republican side, for Barcelona in January 1937 was a microcosm of Republican Spain. At first sight the city appeared – to such Englishmen as George Orwell and Stephen Spender, both of whom visited it during this period – to be what many people had long hoped for, a living example of the socialist society. Private ownership and privilege had almost vanished. Nearly every sizeable building was in the hands of workers, who were also controlling most of the public services. Shops and cafés bore notices saying they had been collectivised. All servile terms of speech had disappeared, and the regular form of address was 'Comrade'. Loudspeakers broadcast revolutionary songs day and night. But there was a food crisis, and, during January 1937, bread queues of three or four hundred people became daily sights – and were sometimes dispersed roughly by assault guards using rifle butts. This crisis was partly the result of the decision by the food minister, a Communist, to abolish the 'bread committees' which were run by anarchists. Wall-posters used the food shortage as an excuse for a battle of slogans: 'More bread! Less committees!' And the arguments between parties continued, for the Republicans, far from being united against the common enemy, were split into factions of every kind, whose struggles against each other were almost as bitter as the fighting against Franco's nationalists.

All this Auden observed. Looking back on his time in Spain he said: 'The politics were particularly unpleasant.' But he was struck even more, during his time in Barcelona, by what had happened to the churches. 'I found', he said, 'as I walked through the city that all the churches were closed and there was not a priest to be seen. To my astonishment, this discovery left me profoundly shocked and disturbed.'

To say that the churches were 'closed' was an understatement. There were fifty-eight of them in the city, and such was the strength of anti-

Catholic feeling that almost all of them had been burned. Some had escaped with serious damage to their structures and their statuary, while remaining standing; others had been completely gutted, and were being demolished by gangs of workmen.

Auden's sense of shock at this puzzled and worried him. 'The feeling was far too intense', he said, 'to be the result of a mere liberal dislike of intolerance, the notion that it is wrong to stop people from doing what they like, even if it is something silly like going to church. I could not escape acknowledging that, however I had consciously ignored and rejected the Church for sixteen years, the existence of churches and what went on in them had all the time been very important to me. If that was the case, what then?'

Auden probably spent several days in Barcelona. At some time before 25 January he travelled on southwards, and reached Valencia, hoping no doubt to remain there only a brief time before being sent to the front with an ambulance unit.

Valencia was now a place of considerable importance in the civil war, for since the previous November the Republican government had been based there, having moved its headquarters from Madrid when the capital began to be threatened by Franco's forces. 'Since the Government moved here', wrote Auden a few days after his arrival, 'the hotels are crammed to bursting with officials, soldiers and journalists. There are porters at the station and a few horse-cabs, but no taxis, in order to save petrol. Food is plentiful, indeed an hotel lunch is heavier than one could wish. There is a bull-fight in aid of the hospitals; there is a variety show where an emaciated-looking tap-dancer does an extremely sinister dance of the machine-guns.'

He managed to get a room at the Hotel Victoria, the journalists' headquarters. 'The foreign correspondents come in for their dinner,' he wrote, 'conspicuous as actresses.' His plan was apparently to enlist with an ambulance unit and leave, probably for Madrid, where Franco's troops were making their third attempt since November to take the city from the Republicans, and where casualities were very heavy. But this was not what happened. Instead, Auden, as he described it later, 'waited around, could find nothing to do'.

He had apparently gone out to Spain with a medical unit organised by the Spanish Medical Aid Committee, the British group that was providing doctors, orderlies and ambulances – which were much needed, because nearly all the Spanish army doctors were serving with Franco's troops. It is not clear why Medical Aid did not now make use of Auden as a driver or stretcher-bearer. Auden had his own explanation: he told an interviewer in the 1960s that by this stage of the war the Communist Party was 'running everything', and that he was given a hard time because he had 'always stopped short of joining'. On another occasion he said: 'They didn't give me anything to do – perhaps because I wasn't a party member.' Certainly the Medical Aid Committee included Communists; however, very many of its volunteers were not Party members, but merely left-wing sympathisers like Auden.[1] The question of why he was not used by them therefore remains unanswered. Administrative muddle, and even overstaffing seem possibilities, while it is also conceivable that Medical Aid was unwilling to employ so erratic a driver; Michael Yates has remarked that Auden's not being given charge of an ambulance was 'a mercy for the wounded'.

Auden's non-membership of the Communist Party does not, in fact, seem to have stigmatised him at all in Spain – at least, not according to an account by Claud Cockburn. His story, told many years later, is that the British Communists who were involved with the civil war planned that Auden should 'go to the front, write some pieces saying hurrah for the Republic. . . Unfortunately, he took the whole thing terribly seriously. . . We got a car laid on for him and everything. We thought we'd whisk him to Madrid and that the whole thing would be a matter of a week before the end-product started firing. But not at all; the bloody man went off and got a donkey and went round Spain with this creature. From Valencia to the Front. He got six miles from Valencia before the mule kicked him or something and only then did he return and get in the car and do his proper job.'

This story sounds a little fantastic and Auden denied at least part of it – he said it had been impossible to get a car because of the 'bureaucratic wall' that surrounded the Republican war effort. (Yet might not the notion of a donkey-journey have appealed to him after his riding experiences in Iceland?) At all events the plan, if there really was one, to make him into a Communist propagandist came to very little, though he does seem to have become involved, at least for a few days, with one of the Valencia broadcasting stations.

Radio broadcasts played an important part in the civil war. On the nationalist side, the voluble General Queipo el Llano harangued his listeners nightly from Seville. The Republicans for their part operated, among other networks, an English-language service from Barcelona which sent out daily news bulletins to English-speaking countries. These bulletins gave emphasis to news of civilian life, so as to persuade overseas listeners that Spanish socialism was proving a success.

Auden, after he had returned to England, told Isherwood that he had worked for a short time in Spain as a propaganda broadcaster. Exactly what he meant by this is not clear. It is possible that he broadcast from the Barcelona English-language station. More probably he contributed to the broadcasts that the Socialist Party were at this time sending out from

---

[1] See Viscount Churchill, *All My Sins Remembered* (1964), pp. 160–66, for an account of the Committee's work in Spain. He describes its founders as 'three well-known medical men, a famous scientist, several trade unionists, and one communist'.

Valencia. Their radio station apparently did use English-speaking broad-
casters, as Stephen Spender, who came out to Spain shortly after Auden,
was encouraged to apply for a job there, though by the time he arrived,
in late February or early March, it had closed down. It seems most likely
that Auden took part briefly in its broadcasts, during late January or
February. He mentioned to Isherwood that he had been disappointed to
discover that the transmitter had only a small range, and this suggests an
organisation such as the one in Valencia.

By the end of January he seems to have achieved little more than
writing and sending to London six paragraphs for the *New Statesman*,
which were printed in the issue of 30 January under the title 'Impressions
of Valencia'. The article described the appearance of the city, with its
illustrated map showing the progress of the war and its wall-posters
caricaturing Franco and his aides, and it went on to talk about the
crowds. 'Everywhere there are the people,' Auden wrote. 'They are here
in corduroy breeches with pistols on their hip, in uniform, in civilian
suits and berets. They are here, sleeping in the hotels, eating in the
restaurants, in the cafés drinking and having their shoes cleaned. They
are here, driving fast cars on business, running the trains and the trams,
keeping the streets clean, doing all those things that the gentry cannot
believe will be properly done unless they are there to keep an eye on
them. This is the bloodthirsty and unshaven Anarchy of the bourgeois
cartoon, the end of civilisation from which Hitler has sworn to deliver
Europe. For a revolution is really taking place, not an odd shuffle or two
in cabinet appointments. In the last six months these people have been
learning what it is to inherit their own country and once a man has tasted
freedom he will not lightly give it up.'

This article, quite apart from its clichés, made no mention of the
ruined churches in Barcelona, nor of Auden's own failure to find a role
for himself in the war. Nor did it describe the unhappy complexities of
Republican politics, which Auden must have seen at even closer quarters
now that he was in the city which housed the government. He would
almost certainly have realised how largely ineffective that government
was, with at its head Manuel Azaña y Diaz, the detached intellectual
who, though he was President, rarely appeared in public and was himself
deeply depressed about much that was happening in the Republic. As to
the Communists within the Republican ranks, it was becoming apparent
to many observers that they were playing a largely anti-revolutionary
and almost right-wing role, doing their best to defer real revolution on
behalf of Soviet Russia, which was anxious in its own interests not to
upset the balance of European power. The U.S.S.R. did provide some
military aid to the Republicans, but only reluctantly, and at a price. The
politics of the war certainly were, as Auden observed, 'unpleasant'.

He would have learnt a good deal about the political situation from the
foreign correspondents at the Hotel Victoria. Among these was Arthur

Koestler, who wrote for the *News Chronicle* and worked on behalf of the Comintern (Third Communist International). Koestler had come to Spain the previous year posing as a nationalist sympathiser, but was recognised and imprisoned by the nationalists as a spy, eventually being released through an exchange of prisoners. Koestler and Auden spent an evening drinking together in the Hotel Victoria, along with what Koestler described as 'a small cosmopolitan crowd of a peculiar kind', which consisted of Basil Murray (the rakish son of the classical scholar Gilbert Murray), a Rumanian pilot with a bad leg, a Norwegian girl journalist, and Michael Kolzov, the Spanish correspondent for *Pravda*, who was in close personal touch with Stalin. 'I only met Auden again twelve years later,' wrote Koestler, 'yet he too still remembered that party, and its strangely oppressive atmosphere. It had originally, I think, been created by the pilot who, when we all got a little drunk, kept repeating that he knew he was going to die, hopped around excitedly on his game leg, and had to be carried to bed.'

This was on 25 January 1937. Auden seems to have remained in Valencia for nearly a month more, for he said he spent his thirtieth birthday, which fell on 21 February, in that city. Perhaps he spent part of this time broadcasting. Almost certainly he was trying to get to the front in some capacity. Probably the government bureaucracy was an obstacle. At any rate for about a month nothing seems to have happened to him.

It was probably now that he met, in Valencia, Cyril Connolly and his wife Jean. Connolly, who was reporting on the war and was accompanied by the socialist peer Lord Antrim, admired Auden's poetry but had never met him; he had been told by Isherwood to look him up in Valencia.[1] 'Auden, who was working for the government radio, seemed overjoyed to meet us,' wrote Connolly, 'and ordered a bottle of Spanish champagne, a detail which delighted Isherwood, who said it would have convinced him that it was the real Auden and not some imposter.' The Connollys subsequently met Auden again in Barcelona, perhaps on Auden's return journey to England, where they had lunch together and went for a walk. 'Auden retired to pee behind a bush', remembered Connolly, 'and was immediately seized by two militia men – or were they military police? They were very indignant at this abuse of public property.'

One other Englishman recorded a glimpse of Auden in Spain. This was the poet Roy Campbell, whose sympathies were pro-Franco and anti-left-wing. In an article written in 1950 Campbell declared of Auden: 'He has always been attracted by safety and the most violent action he ever saw was when he was playing table-tennis at Tossa del Mar on behalf of the Spanish Republicans – apart from the violent exercise he got with his knife and fork.' Tossa is a small resort on the Costa Brava not

---

[1] Connolly's memoir of Auden (in the *Tribute* volume) gives the date of this meeting as May 1937, but by that time Auden had left Spain.

far north of Barcelona. If Campbell's remark is based on any historical truth and is not merely the product of the vendetta he conducted against Auden and other left-wing poets of the 1930s, it suggests that Auden, at some time during his visit to Spain, may have stayed at the Casa Johnstone, a hotel in Tossa owned by a former *News Chronicle* journalist, Archie Johnstone, whom Arthur Koestler would presumably have known. The hotel was a centre for British supporters of the Republican cause, and among the amusements offered there were games of table-tennis.

On 6 February, while Auden was apparently still in Valencia, the fighting intensified around Madrid. Several hundred British volunteers with the International Brigade were involved, and casualties were heavy. Auden may well have become even more impatient to reach the front himself. On the other hand, the longer he remained in Spain the more he seems to have become aware of the impossibility of giving the Republican cause his wholehearted support.

Both nationalists and Republicans were behaving with remarkable cruelty to those of opposing sympathies who happened to be on the wrong side of the battle line. Political prisoners were executed, and anybody remotely suspected of being a traitor was likely to be rounded up by a gang of self-appointed executioners and shot. Atrocities were widespread, and on the Republican side were directed particularly at priests. Parish clergy were tortured and then shot, several bishops were murdered (one was killed in front of two thousand spectators), and monks and nuns were maltreated in large numbers. In all, several thousand clergy and members of religious orders fell victim to Republican persecutors, and this was only a fraction of the total number of people murdered on the Republican side. Members of the government were themselves appalled, and foreign observers reacted with horror. Auden himself said: 'Just seeing what Civil War was like was a shock. Nothing good could come of it. . . One asked oneself, did one want to win?'

At last Auden managed to make an arrangement by which he could get to the front. In a note which he left for Stephen Spender, who was due to arrive in Valencia shortly, he said he was about to leave for Sariñena, 'for I think 1 month at Aragon Front'. The note is undated, but must have been written some time shortly after Auden's birthday on 21 February, which he had spent in Valencia.

Sariñena lies between Saragossa and Barbastro, about two hundred miles to the north-west of Valencia. In February 1937 it was on that part of the front line which ran through the province of Aragon. Auden seems to have reached Sariñena, for he told an interviewer many years later that he went 'to the front near Zaragoza (Saragossa) and Barbastro'.

He recorded nothing of what he saw there, but it is possible to get some idea of what he may have experienced from an account of the Aragon front written by George Orwell, in his book *Homage to Catalonia*.

Orwell, who was at this time serving in the Republican army in Aragon, alongside Spaniards rather than with members of the International Brigade, gives a picture of stalemate trench warfare almost without event, for at this time the Aragon front was very quiet, hostilities being chiefly concentrated around Madrid. 'Between January and late March [1937]', writes Orwell, 'little or nothing happened. . . In the hills around Zaragoza, it was simply the mingled boredom and discomfort of stationary warfare. A life as uneventful as the city clerk's, and almost as regular.'

Orwell was a member of the militia of the P.O.U.M., the anti-Stalinist Marxist party. Like the anarchists, the P.O.U.M. organised their troops on egalitarian principles, with social equality between officers and men. 'When you gave an order', said Orwell, 'you gave it as comrade to comrade and not as superior to inferior.' This system did not survive very long, but in February 1937 Auden would have seen it in action. On the other hand morale was not high. Enthusiasm for the war effort among the men was quickly eroded by boredom, and by what Orwell called 'the futility. . . the inconclusiveness of such a kind of war'.

Auden originally planned to stay in Spain for about four or five months. In mid-January his mother, who was looking after his business correspondence while he was away, wrote to an enquirer: 'If all goes well he does not expect to return until May.' But on about 2 March, only a few days after he had set out from Valencia for the front, he was already on his way home, and on 4 March he was back in London. There had presumably been nothing for him to see on the Aragon front, and his patience – and perhaps his money – had probably run out. The best course must have seemed to give up and go back to England.

'He was unwilling to talk about his experiences,' wrote Isherwood, who saw him immediately on his return, 'but they had obviously been unsatisfactory; he felt that he hadn't been allowed to be really useful.' Stephen Spender recorded much the same thing: 'He returned home after a very short visit of which he never spoke.'

Auden himself said, many years later, of this silence: 'I did not wish to talk about Spain when I returned because I was upset by many things I saw or heard about. Some of them were described better than I could ever have done by George Orwell, in *Homage to Catalonia*. Others were what I learned about the treatment of priests.' He did not speak out against the character and actions of Republican Spain because he still hoped for the defeat of Franco. 'I was shocked and disillusioned,' he said. 'But any disillusion of mine could only be of advantage to Franco. And however I felt, I certainly didn't want Franco to win. It is always a moral problem when to speak. To speak at the wrong time can do great harm. Franco won. What was the use? If the Republic had been victorious, then there would have been reason to speak out about what was wrong with it.'

Orwell echoed these words in *Homage to Catalonia*. He too wanted

Franco to be beaten. 'Since 1930 the Fascists had won all the victories; it was time they got a beating, it hardly mattered from whom.' But he was under no illusion as to the character of the war. 'I suppose', he wrote, 'there is no one who spent more than a few weeks in Spain without being in some degree disillusioned. . . As for the newspaper talk about this being a "war for democracy", it was plain eyewash.'

★

On the night that he returned to London, Auden attended a performance of *The Ascent of F6*. The Group Theatre production, at the Mercury, a small theatre in the Notting Hill district of London, had been in rehearsal during February, with Isherwood at hand to do any rewriting required by Rupert Doone, who was again directing, and had opened on 26 February. Reviews of the production were as mixed as those of the published text. The *News Chronicle* called it 'the most notable thing in our Theatre', but Hugh Gordon Porteus in the *New English Weekly* complained that the incidental music, by Benjamin Britten, was (though good in itself) a distraction, and criticised the performance of William Devlin as Ransom, especially in that part of the play where Auden required him to deliver some lines of almost ludicrous Shakespearian pastiche ('O senseless hurricanes, / That waste yourselves upon the unvexed rock. . .'). 'He delivers his perilous Shakespearian stuff', wrote Porteus, 'like a dying insect precipitating its last eggs. He hurls himself, twice, right off the stage, bawling and cooing his lines in the tragedian tradition (it is really very awful indeed!).' Julian Symons in *Twentieth Century Verse* said that the play was inferior to *The Dog Beneath the Skin* in almost every respect except the character of Ransom – and, like Porteus, he found Devlin's performance as Ransom unacceptable.

Isherwood had been obliged to make a number of minor changes or cuts in the text, and Auden, during the performance he attended on 4 March, remarked on these in a loud whisper: 'My *dear*, what have you *done* to it?' The biggest change was the ending, for it had been decided that the curtain should fall as Ransom collapses before the figure of his mother on the mountain-top, and that the final scene, in which the initiators of Ransom's expedition comment on his death, should be omitted. (This scene was also left out of the second edition of *F6* published by Faber's in March 1937.) A number of people in the audience found this abbreviated ending unsatisfactory. Among these was W. B. Yeats, who admired Auden's work, though he was critical of its obscurity, and who told Doone he thought parts of *F6* were 'magnificent'. Yeats suggested that the play might do better to conclude with the mother revealed as Britannia – an idea which Doone and Medley liked, but which was not adopted.

Despite its mixed reviews, *F6* easily filled the small auditorium of the

Mercury, and after two months there, and three days at the Arts Theatre, Cambridge, was transferred to a West End theatre, the Little, where it was billed as 'The Everest play' and ran for a further five weeks. The next year it was performed twice, in the spring and autumn, by the Birmingham Repertory Theatre; both authors attended one of the autumn performances. In September 1938 a shortened version was broadcast on the BBC's television service, and the following summer the Group Theatre revived it at the Old Vic. Doone again directed, but the part of Ransom was this time taken by Alec Guinness, whose performance was the exact opposite of Devlin's – the *New Statesman* reviewer commented that he 'conveyed the ascetic qualities of a modern saint and man of action with superb quiet'. The ending was changed yet again, and this time the figure of Mrs Ransom was seen merely as a silent apparition. But this effect proved inadequate, and Auden once remarked: 'We never did get that ending right.' In truth *F6*, like *The Dog Beneath the Skin*, was a play entirely incapable of any satisfactory conclusion.

After attending the performance on 4 March, Auden left London and went with Isherwood to the Lake District, where according to a newspaper report the two of them intended to work on a revue for the Group Theatre. If this was true, nothing came of it. Auden spent part of his time reading a book that he was reviewing for *New Verse;* he also wrote a poem about the Spanish Civil War. These two pieces of work proved to be closely interrelated.

The book was *Illusion and Reality: A Study of the Sources of Poetry,* by the young critic Christopher Caudwell, who had just been killed in Spain – he died during the defence of Madrid early in February. Caudwell, whose real name was Christopher St John Sprigg, was a Marxist, if an unorthodox one, and his book used Marx's theory of the relation between economics and society to explain the development of English poetry from the sixteenth century to the present time. In his concluding chapter, on 'The Future of Poetry', Caudwell talked about the radical changes that were being forced on the contemporary world by economic forces. 'These changes', he wrote, 'do not happen "automatically", for history is made by men's actions, although their actions by no means always have the effect they are intended to have. The results of history are by no means willed by any men.' Auden was greatly impressed by Caudwell's book. Writing in *New Verse* he called it 'the most important book on poetry since the books of Dr Richards'. He also used something very much like Caudwell's view of history and its relation to the action of individual men as the framework of his poem about Spain.[1]

The poem begins with one of Auden's hawk-like, Hardyesque views from a great height. This time the view is of history: 'Yesterday all the

[1] The relation between Caudwell's book and Auden's poems was first pointed out by Samuel Hynes in *The Auden Generation.*

past. The language of size / Spreading to China along the trade-routes; the diffusion / Of the counting-frame and the cromlech'. Gradually, stanza by stanza, this telescopic account of past eras moves forward to the present time: 'Yesterday the installation of dynamos and turbines; / The construction of railways. . . / . . . But to-day the struggle.' Now a series of figures appear: first the poet, then the scientific researcher, and finally the whole mass of humanity, all demanding that they shall be shown the real nature of 'History, the operator, the / Organiser'. The voice of History answers them: 'O no, I am not the Mover. . . I am whatever you do. . . I am your choice, your decision: yes, I am Spain.'

Only now, after fourteen stanzas, more than half the poem, does Auden turn to the Spanish war. He describes the arrival in Spain of the volunteers, who 'came to present their lives', and he talks about their reasons for coming. But he does not do this in political terms. Instead, he presents the struggle of socialism against Fascism as the struggle of humanity against its own weaknesses and faults, its fear and greed:

> . . . For the fears which made us respond
> To the medicine ad. and the brochure of winter cruises
>   Have become invading battalions;
> And our faces, the institute-face, the chain-store, the ruin
> Are projecting their greed as the firing squad and the bomb.

Auden explained this more fully in a piece of prose he wrote two years later: 'A war is not produced out of a hat by a few politicians: it is the consequence of an infinite number of private acts of fear, violence and hatred.' In contrast, the poem now declares, it is the good qualities of human nature that lead to resistance, defence, and care of the wounded: 'Our moments of tenderness blossom / As the ambulance and the sandbag; / Our hours of friendship into a people's army.'

Now the poem turns to the future, giving glimpses which half suggest that a brave new world of socialism is on the way once 'the struggle' is over:

> To-morrow the exchanging of tips on the breeding of terriers,
>   The eager election of chairmen
> By a sudden forest of hands. . .

But the fighting continues, and today, in the time of war, there must be 'the inevitable increase in the chances of death', even 'The conscious acceptance of guilt in the necessary murder' – not to mention the tiresomeness of political activity, 'the expending of powers / On the flat ephemeral pamphlet and the boring meeting'. And if the struggle fails, then History cannot be summoned as a *deus ex machina* to set things right, for History is only the sum of men's actions:

The stars are dead; the animals will not look:
We are left alone with our day, and the time is short and
    History to the defeated
May say Alas but cannot help or pardon.

Spain was finished by the end of March. Faber's had agreed to print it in the form of a pamphlet, the royalties from which were to go to the work of Medical Aid in Spain. (It is not clear whether this arrangement was made before Auden began to write the poem.) The printers began typesetting on 1 April, and the poem was published on 20 May in an initial edition of nearly three thousand copies; another two thousand were printed in July. Reviewers without any particular political commitment generally praised it. Geoffrey Grigson in *New Verse,* for example, thought it 'an organic, grave, sensible and moving statement, more reasonable and more free of bigotry than any other political poem written for some years'. But Communist critics pointed out that it was concerned less with Spain than with Auden's own reactions to it. Edgell Rickword called it 'a reflection of the poet's continuing isolation, falsifying the perspective of social development and delaying the re-integration of the poet into the body of society'.

Three years after *Spain* was published, George Orwell, while praising it as 'one of the few decent things that have been written about the Spanish war', criticised Auden for the line 'The conscious acceptance of guilt in the necessary murder', objecting that this could only have been written by someone 'to whom murder is at most a *word*'. Auden himself said of the line: 'I was *not* excusing totalitarian crimes but only trying to say what, surely, every decent person thinks if he finds himself unable to adopt the absolute pacifist position. . . If there is such a thing as a just war, then murder can be necessary for the sake of justice.' However, possibly as a result of Orwell's criticism, he changed the line to 'The conscious acceptance of guilt in the fact of murder'. This was in his collection *Another Time* (1940), and in the text of the poem printed in that volume he also abbreviated into one stanza the original three which presented the war as humanity's fight against its own weaknesses, and entirely omitted the passage about 'the exchanging of tips on the breeding of terriers, / The eager election of chairmen. . .'. In doing so, he reduced the degree to which *Spain* could be identified with the Republican cause – the reference to a 'people's army' was among the passages omitted.

Besides being published by Faber's, *Spain* was printed during the spring of 1937 by Nancy Cunard, granddaughter of the shipping magnate, who was publishing a series of poems in aid of the Spanish Republic. Auden sent her a manuscript of the poem before Faber's had produced their version, and, despite the illegibility of his handwriting, she managed to produce a reasonably accurate version. She also decided to organise a poll of well-known writers, who were asked to express their opinions on

the Spanish war. Auden agreed to be one of twelve signatories to the
initial question which she sent out to her chosen authors: 'Are you for, or
against, the legal Government and the People of Republican Spain? Are
you for, or against, Franco and Fascism?'

Auden duly sent in his own answer, with this covering note: 'I have
my doubts as to the value of such pronouncements, but here mine is for
what its worth.' This is what he wrote:

> I support the Valencia Government in Spain because its defeat by
> the forces of International Fascism would be a major disaster for
> Europe. It would make a European war more probable; and the
> spread of Fascist Ideology and practice to countries as yet com-
> paratively free from them, which would inevitably follow upon a
> Fascist victory in Spain, would create an atmosphere in which the
> creative artist and all who care for justice, liberty and culture would
> find it impossible to work or even exist.

This said nothing about the character of Republican Spain, and was
certainly milder in tone – more lukewarm, indeed – than many of the
answers to the questionnaire. Edgell Rickword, for example, wrote:
'Support for the people of Spain and their legal Republican Government
means the triumph of life over death. . . the birth of a free and happy
world.' But many others, including Spender and MacNeice, were as
cautious as Auden.

On 13 April, Auden went to Paris, apparently so that he could make
enquiries about Isherwood's boyfriend Heinz, who was known to be
there; Isherwood had an infected mouth and was unable to go himself. In
Paris he met, for the first time, two people who were to remain his
friends for the rest of his life, James and Tania Stern.

James Stern, who belonged to a celebrated family of bankers, and was
himself the son of an English cavalry officer and an Irish mother, had
worked for a time in the family's banks in England and Germany, but
hated it, and was now in Paris earning a precarious living as a writer of
short stories and a translator. His wife Tania, the daughter of a German
psychiatrist, made a little money for them both by teaching gymnastic
exercises. They lived on a top floor in the Quai de l'Horloge, where the
view across the Seine was so beautiful that Stern found it almost
impossible to work. He and his wife already knew Isherwood, and now
(probably as a result of an introduction by Cyril Connolly) they made
the acquaintance of Auden.

He sat with them and other friends at a café table, reading a book while
the others talked, and drinking coffee while the others drank wine or
aperitifs. He also, as Stern recalled, 'refused to see any good in the
French'.

Auden's attitude to France was certainly largely hostile. He spoke the language adequately, though in a poor accent, and could read easily in it; indeed, his list of favourite poets included the name of Paul Valéry, of whom he once wrote: 'Whenever I feel myself in danger of becoming *un homme sérieux,* it is on Valéry, *un homme d'esprit* if ever there was one, more often than on any other poet, I believe, that I call for aid.' But Valéry was the exception, and Auden's general rule was 'Frogs don't understand poetry.' He did admire Rimbaud, Proust and Baudelaire, but he qualified this admiration by saying that they would have been much better if they had written in English. There was, of course, an element of deliberate outrageousness in this, but his dislike of France did run deep. 'The French *petit bourgeois*', he once said, 'is the most disgusting specimen of humanity you can think of.'

As to James Stern's short stories, Auden had been introduced to them by Isherwood three years earlier, and he greatly admired them. In a review in 1938 he called Stern 'one of the most moving and original short story writers who has appeared for a long time'; and in a letter to an American publisher he described Stern as 'one of the very few English writers of fiction under forty of permanent importance'. He was to see much of Stern in the following years.

After his Paris trip, Auden returned to England – and to the Downs School, where he had been asked to teach for the summer term. 'Well here I am,' he wrote to Nob Snodgrass from the school, 'but only for the term while the regular man is away.' His view of his pupils had changed in the two years since he had last taught there; in a poem called 'Schoolchildren' which he wrote soon after his return to the Downs, he admitted that the notion expressed in *The Orators* of schoolboys as participants in the war or rebellion against 'the Enemy' needed to be reassessed now that he had seen a real war:

> . . . The improper word
> Scribbled upon the fountain, is that all the rebellion?
> The storm of tears shed in the corner, are these
> The seeds of the new life?

In fact a streak of bitterness and pessimism runs through all the poems that he wrote this spring and summer, after his return from Spain. 'Orpheus' seems to ask whether art can be successful either as entertainment or as philosophy. 'Wrapped in a yielding air' presents man moving through a life marked by 'further griefs and greater'. Both these poems are opaque and difficult to interpret, but others that Auden wrote during these months were very simple in style. Most were in ballad-form. 'Miss Gee', 'James Honeyman' and 'Victor' were exercises in various forms of gruesomeness. The first applied Groddeck's theory of disease to the case of a spinster whose death from cancer of the liver is ascribed to her 'foiled creative fire'. The second was a ballad of chemical warfare, and the third a tale of a wife-murderer – Auden said of it: 'Victor was really somebody by that name, at school where I was; he used to send anonymous letters.' Taken together, these poems produce a distinctly bitter view of the world. It was not until November of this year, in another ballad, the celebrated 'As I walked out one evening, / Walking down Bristol Street', that Auden could redress the balance and declare that 'Life remains a blessing / Although you cannot bless.'

During this summer term at the Downs School, he collaborated again with Benjamin Britten, this time on a radio programme entitled *Up the Garden Path*, their personal selection of bad poetry and bad music, which was broadcast on the BBC Regional Programme one evening in June. Three days later, Britten came to the Downs to give a recital to the boys, together with Hedli Anderson, who performed many of the songs in the Group Theatre productions of the Auden–Isherwood plays. The school magazine recorded of this recital: 'One of Wizz's friends, Miss Hedlie Anderson, sang to us in Library, accompanied by Mr Britain.' Presumably the performance included Britten's *Four Cabaret Songs,* settings of poems by Auden composed by Britten this year but never published, and perhaps also his song-cycle for high voice, *On This Island,* consisting of five poems from *Look, Stranger!* Britten's visit to the school coincided with that of another of Auden's friends, William Coldstream, who had left the G.P.O. Film unit even before Auden had done so, and had returned to full-time painting, largely on Auden's advice. He was at the Downs to paint Auden's portrait. Yet another visitor was Brian Howard, who came to stay for some days. Howard, like Isherwood, was now in a continuous state of distraction about his German boyfriend, who was fleeing from the Nazis. Auden, presumably to encourage him to get down to some work – though dissolute, Howard was an able writer – suggested that they should collaborate on a book: a treatise on the division between intellect and intuition, with examples, to be taken from popular writings, of the dangers induced by this and by authoritarianism in literature. Howard was very enthusiastic, but was by nature incapable of tackling such a long-term project, and the book was never written.

Auden's private feelings about Spain might have been expected to discourage him from ever going back to that country, but in midsummer 1937 he was intending to do exactly that. He was among a group of British writers, including Stephen Spender, who planned to attend an International Writers' Congress in Valencia and Madrid at the beginning of July, which was being held to discuss the attitude of intellectuals to the Spanish war. But on 4 July the London newspapers reported that the Foreign Office had refused visas to the British delegates, including Auden, on the grounds that 'the only categories of persons allowed to go to Spain were commercial people, or those who were doing work for the Duchess of Atholl's Relief Committee'. Auden, therefore, did not make the journey – though Spender got there on a forged passport.

Auden did, however, continue to make plans for further overseas travel. In May 1937 he and Spender planned a joint lecture tour in America, and they agreed with Auden's agent Curtis Brown to write a book on that country, perhaps on the lines of *Letters from Iceland*. The tour was to take place later in 1937; but was first postponed and eventually dropped. Then, a little later in the summer, Auden's American publisher, Bennett Cerf of Random House, persuaded Faber & Faber that he and they should jointly commission Auden and Isherwood to write a travel book, which was to be about the Far East – though the precise choice of itinerary was to be left to the authors, who began to discuss possible journeys.

At the end of the summer term, Auden left the Downs School for the last time, and, a few days later, went to Oxford, perhaps to visit Nevill Coghill, or possibly to call on John Masefield, then Poet Laureate, whom he knew a little; Masefield had been Auden's guest at the Downs School in 1933 to see the boys perform the miracle-play *Deluge;* he remarked to I. A. Richards that he considered Auden 'a man of genius. . . a dynamic person'. While in Oxford, Auden was introduced to a member of the Oxford University Press's editorial staff who was himself a poet and author, and who sometimes visited the Masefields. This was Charles Williams.

Williams, then in his early fifties, commanded adoring attention from a small but devoted circle of readers for his strange novels, best described as theological thrillers, his works on Christianity, his plays, and his poetry, all of which gave expression to his highly idiosyncratic and romantic view of the Christian religion – a view moulded by such diverse influences as Dante and Rosicrucianism. The Oxford University Press employed him in its London office, where he worked on books of general rather than academic interest; and he was therefore open to suggestions such as the one that Auden now made to him.

'I met W. H. Auden for the first time at Oxford on Wednesday,' wrote Williams in an internal memorandum dated 30 July. 'He is an extraordinarily pleasant creature, and we found ourselves in passionate agreement against the more conservative poets, such as Binyon, Richard Church, and even a doubtful Wilfred Gibson. We talked of the *Oxford Book of Modern Verse*, against which he raised the usual objection that it was not of the same authority as the other Oxford Books of verse.[1] He then went on to say that he very much wanted to do an Oxford Book of Light Verse. . . I said I would submit the idea. . . My own inclination, subject to the judgement of the financiers, is that it would be quite a good idea to collect Auden's name. He is still generally regarded as the most important of the young poets at present, and likely to be more

[1]W. B. Yeats edited this book, published in 1936. Auden later called it 'the most deplorable book ever issued under the imprint of that highly respected firm'.

important if he develops. About that of course I can say nothing. He may fail as so many have failed. Even so, however, if the book were desirable and tolerable we should be no worse off, and if he really becomes a figure we should be better off.'

The result of this meeting was a commission from the Press, eight weeks later, for Auden to compile such a book as he had suggested. The meeting with Williams – whom he saw again in London on 20 September – was important to him, not, however, for this reason so much as for quite a different one. 'For the first time in my life', he said of it, '[I] felt myself in the presence of personal sanctity.'

This was a not uncommon experience among people who met Williams for the first time – T. S. Eliot said much the same thing about him. Williams had an extraordinary radiance that made a profound impression; he emanated love. Auden later said of his encounter with Williams, whom he did not identify by name: 'I had met many good people before who made me feel ashamed of my own shortcomings, but in the presence of this man – we never discussed anything but literary business – I did not feel ashamed. I felt transformed into a person who was incapable of doing or thinking anything base or unloving. (I later discovered that he had had a similar effect on many other people.)' Auden's meeting with Williams did not have any immediate effect on his views about religion. But it made him aware of the existence of something that seemed to him to be sanctity.

*

Auden spent early August staying with Stephen Spender, who had recently got married, and who with his wife Inez had rented a house in Kent, near the coast. Spender had just got back from the Writers' Conference in Valencia, and he told Auden that much of the delegates' energy had been expended in criticising André Gide for his recent book attacking the Soviet Union. Some at the conference had declared quite explicitly that the truth about the U.S.S.R. should be suppressed in the interest of the greater cause of Communism. Spender deplored this attitude, and Auden told him: 'You're quite right. Exigence is never an excuse for not telling the truth.' Spender later wrote: 'This conversation remains in my mind as a turning point in our attitudes towards politics during the thirties.'

On 9 August, Auden went with the Spenders to have tea at Sissinghurst. Harold Nicolson wrote in his diary: 'Wystan is grubbier than ever and Stephen is as like Shelley as ever.' It was now some years since Auden had cared at all about his appearance. Tidiness seemed utterly unimportant to him, even objectionable; he hated buying clothes, and would only do so under protest, choosing the first thing that was offered to him in the shop. Inner order, not outward appearance, was what mattered.

At some time during the late spring or early summer, Auden went with Isherwood to a week-end conference at John Piper's country home to discuss the future of the Group Theatre. There, they behaved badly, failing to observe the timetable of events and generally fooling around, Auden strumming on the piano at all hours. They seemed to be impatient with the Group Theatre's aims now, and were certainly increasingly irritated by Rupert Doone. Robert Medley also had the impression that after the comparative commercial success of *F6* they had tasted blood, and he gathered that they were planning for their next play something that would be a hit in the West End rather than cater specially for the Group Theatre's needs. In this, they were encouraged by two of Isherwood's friends, the film director Berthold Viertel and the actress Beatrix Lehmann.

In August, Isherwood wrote to John Lehmann, Beatrix's brother and the editor of *New Writing,* that his and Auden's plans for the future were 'distracted and vague'. They might, he said, come out to Vienna, where Lehmann was living at present, but Auden wanted to stay in England 'to save money'. Isherwood was at a loose end now that Heinz had been obliged to return to Germany. He and Auden had to decide on an itinerary for their travel book for Faber's and Random House. The question was answered for them by events in the Far East.

War had broken out between China and Japan; the first clashes were in early July, and by mid-August the Japanese had taken Peking and were attacking Shanghai. It was the latest in a series of acts of aggression by Japan, whose government was semi-Fascist; China, meanwhile, maintained an uneasy internal alliance between Chiang Kai-shek's nationalist government and the Chinese Communist Party under Mao Tse-tung and Chou En-lai, an alliance which existed solely for the purpose of defeating the Japanese. Despite these complexities, the Sino-Japanese war seemed to many Western observers simply the Eastern front of what would soon become a world war between Fascism and socialism. Auden and Isherwood, whose publishers had specified that the travel book should be about an Asian country or countries, now decided to go to China as observers, hoping that, unlike Spain, it would not (as Isherwood put it) be 'crowded with star literary observers'. For both of them it was in a sense a second chance. Isherwood had by his own admission regretted not going to Spain – he had stayed behind because of Heinz – while Auden, though he had gone there, had failed to achieve anything. China seemed hopeful. As Auden remarked, 'We'll have a war all of our very own'.

They began to make arrangements for the trip. Faber's agreed to advance some money, though Auden commented that it was hardly enough. One encouraging fact was the success of Auden's first travel book, *Letters from Iceland*. The Book Society had adopted it as one of their selections, and by the time it was published on 6 August 1937 a total of 8,000 copies had already been subscribed. Reviews were generally enthusiastic. Some critics thought it rather self-indulgent and were annoyed by the jokiness, but most judged it good entertainment. Auden's income no doubt benefited a little from its success; at any rate he was able to write to a friend a few months later: 'I make enough money to live on.'

As to their immediate plans, Auden and Isherwood decided to spend the remainder of August and the beginning of September in Dover, where they would write their new play and also see something of E. M. Forster, who was staying there. Forster had first come to Dover the previous summer to convalesce from an operation. He liked the town, and several of his homosexual friends had developed a taste for it too, not least because they could pick up soldiers from the local barracks. Isherwood now knew Forster well – he had been introduced to him about six years earlier by Spender's friend William Plomer – and he admired him deeply both as a novelist and as a man, describing him as 'the anti-heroic hero, with his straggly straw moustache, his light gay blue baby-eyes and his elderly stoop. . . his tweed cap (which is too small for him) and the odd-shaped brown paper parcels in which he carries his belongings from country to town and back again'. Auden regarded Forster as both remarkable and important; in a review written in 1934 he talked of Forster's 'sense of the mystery of life', and called him one of the 'examples permanent and alert' of those who believe that the fight to save humanity can be won by mental action. Now that he came to know Forster well, he regarded him with even deeper admiration.

Auden and Isherwood stayed in lodgings at 9 East Cliff, Dover. As usual, Auden passed the time largely indoors, writing, with the blinds drawn. Forster's friend May Buckingham described him 'emerging from his rooms, with white face, blinking like an owl'. Much of his time was spent working on the new play with Isherwood, but he also wrote a poem, 'Dover'.

This poem pictures Dover not just as a seaside town but as a way out of England, a place of departure; while for those who remain, Dover, and perhaps England itself, can only offer makeshift, unreliable happiness:

> And the cry of the gulls at dawn is sad like work:
> The soldier guards the traveller who pays for the soldier;
> Each one prays in the dusk for himself, and neither
> Controls the years. Some are temporary heroes:
>   Some of these people are happy.

It is a poem about a frontier; and the play that Auden now wrote with Isherwood was called *On the Frontier*.

The frontier of the title is the border between Westland and Ostnia, and once again those two fictitious countries, which had featured in 'Dogskin' and *F6*, were used by Auden and Isherwood to exemplify the struggle between Fascism and its opponents. But the form in which they cast their story this time was neither the pantomime-buffoonery of 'Dogskin' nor the quest-narrative of *F6*. Instead, they set it in a style to which they had been encouraged by Beatrix Lehmann and Berthold Viertel, a 'well made play' such as they believed would please a West End audience. The play even began in the style of so many commercial pieces, with a butler taking orders from a secretary: 'Manners, your master will be lunching on the terrace this morning.' The subsequent action, involving an influential industrialist, a Fascist dictator, and a pair of lovers caught 'on the frontier' of the war between Ostnia and Westland, was constructed on an orderly principle very far from the wild abandon of 'Dogskin' and its predecessors, and was confined to two realistic stage-sets. The role of the chorus was restricted to a few 'front-cloth' scenes in which they appeared as workers, soldiers, and the like – passages that were presumably included chiefly to cover scene-changes. And, apart from some mostly undistinguished verse given to the chorus, there was almost no poetry in the play.

Auden had apparently intended this some time in advance. Discussing his theatrical writing with Dilys Powell after she had written a review of *F6*, he said: 'I feel I must soft pedal the poetry a little', giving as his reason a wish to concentrate on simplifying the external significance of the drama into 'a boy's adventure story'. But *On the Frontier* is not like a boy's adventure story; it resembles that genre much less than do its predecessors, and the paucity of poetry in it seems to be the result of its authors' intention to write a commercial success rather than of any deeper artistic motive. It is true that Auden did use verse for the non-realistic scenes where the two lovers cross the frontier in their imagination, and are able to be together; but these 'mystical' scenes, as Louis MacNeice said, make one 'long for a sack to put one's head in'.

Anna and Eric, the lovers, are negligible as characters, as is almost everyone in the play except Valerian, the industrialist; and even he, though he talks well and wittily, does not go deep. According to Robert Medley, the original script made a vivid character out of Lessep, Valerian's secretary, who was in this early version his homosexual lover and a thorough 'bad lot'. But Auden and Isherwood decided that this would be unacceptable to West End taste, and they modified Lessep into the nonentity that he is in the published text.

The poverty of theatrical imagination in the play was not surprising, considering Auden and Isherwood's motives in writing it. More odd is its ideology, which is, to say the least, confused. The chief theme, the folly of worshipping national leaders and the senselessness of war, fails to engage the attention because Ostnia and Westland remain the cardboard countries they were in the earlier plays, and real political issues are not discussed. The point is frequently made that control is in the hands neither of the leaders nor of the populace, but of sinister figures such as Valerian; all political beliefs seem useless beside the power of such as him. Yet this conclusion is not followed through, for Valerian himself dies at the end of the play simply because of one man's personal grudge. As for Auden's experiences in Spain, these seem to be reflected in the implied attacks at various points in the play on Communism and People's Armies, or at least on the foolish hopes that engender them: 'Think what you like, vote for what you like. What difference does it make?' 'Perhaps we were all wrong. War seems so beastly when it actually happens!' 'You poor fish. . . You will imagine that, in a People's Army, it is against your principles to obey orders – and then wonder why it is that, in spite of your superior numbers, you are always beaten.' Yet at the end, Eric, who of all the characters has most reason to reject the ideals which have led the two countries into war – he is a pacifist, and is shot at a barricade – delivers a speech in which he declares that 'we must kill and suffer and know why. . . This struggle was my struggle. Even if I would / I could not stand apart.' If any political conclusion is to be found in *On the Frontier,* it lies in the extraordinarily lame words 'What are we fighting for? I feel so muddled. . . Perhaps "country" and "frontier" are old-fashioned words that don't mean anything now.'

Precisely how Auden and Isherwood divided their writing on the play is not clear. Auden was certainly responsible for at least part of the prose, as well as the verse, and the long speech by Valerian in the opening scene is undoubtedly his. But he and Isherwood no longer made the distinction betwen 'woozy' and 'straight': the style was much more integrated. They worked fast, in fact very fast – which may be one reason for the play's thinness – and on 31 August, Isherwood wrote on a postcard from Dover to Edward Upward: 'Our play nearly ready.' Two weeks later, Auden, who by that time had left Dover and gone to his parents' home in Harborne, told Bennett Cerf at Random House: 'Isherwood and I have just finished a new play *On the Frontier.'*

It was not quite finished. Spender and other friends read the script and made criticisms, in reply to which Auden and Isherwood, working at Isherwood's family home in London, rewrote the lovers' dream scene and the closing of the play. *On the Frontier* was proving as difficult to conclude as its predecessors. On 9 October Auden, back at Harborne, told a potential 'backer' of the play, who had been shown the typescript: 'The last scene has been rewritten, and is, I hope, more satisfactory now. . . I agree that the poetic side of the play is lightweight, but it seemed to turn out that way. At one time we had the whole of the lovers dream scene (Act II scene i) in verse with choral interruptions, but when it was done it seemed all wrong somehow. I hope that the fact that the whole of the interludes [i.e. the chorus scenes] are snug, and, for the last one, will have quite an elaborate musical accompaniment, will give them both length and weight.'

The recipient of this letter was J. M. Keynes, the Cambridge economist and Fellow of King's College, who founded the Arts Theatre at Cambridge

in 1936 – his wife was the dancer and actress Lydia Lopokova – and ran it
virtually as a personal concern, frequently making up losses out of his
own pocket. The performances of *F6* at his theatre during the previous
April had impressed him, though he was not uncritical of the play, and
after reading *On the Frontier* he told its authors that he would very much
like to finance a Group Theatre production at Cambridge.

Early in November 1937, Auden, Isherwood and Rupert Doone
visited Keynes at his home at Firle in Sussex to discuss arrangements.
Keynes agreed to take over the management of the play in full, as the
Group Theatre had no funds. The hope was that after a week's performances at Cambridge the play could be taken on tour around the
provinces, or perhaps to London. Keynes would make up any loss; the
Group Theatre could take any profits. The only snag was that Auden and
Isherwood were now expecting to leave for China at any moment. The
intention had been to produce the play during the spring, but Keynes felt
that the authors' presence would be essential to a satisfactory production.
He therefore wrote to Auden and Isherwood asking them to postpone their
trip, perhaps until April or May. Auden replied on 18 November 1937:
'It is a nuisance about China, but I dont see how Christopher and I can
put it off so long. Britten [who was writing the music] and Spender will
have to keep an eye on things for us, and I hope you will too.' Keynes,
however, still insisted that Auden and Isherwood must be there for the
production, so finally it was decided to put it off until they returned from
China.

No sooner was this arranged than their China visit was postponed.
Auden had accepted an invitation to join a delegation of writers and other
artists that was to go to Spain and demonstrate solidarity with the
Republican government. In an undated letter to the Oxford University
Press, Auden wrote: 'I'm going to Spain next week, for a fortnight.'
Isherwood agreed rather unenthusiastically to come too. But there were
delays and complications over travel permits, and the date of departure
was postponed several times. At length Auden and Isherwood decided
that they could wait no longer, and withdrew their names from the
delegation, making bookings to sail for China in mid-January 1938.

Auden, meanwhile, had been named as the winner of the 1937 King's
Gold Medal for Poetry, an award given to the author of what was judged
to be the best first or second volume of verse published in the previous twelve
months by a poet under thirty-five – in Auden's case *Look, Stranger!* The
choice of Auden as winner was no doubt largely due to John Masefield,
who as Poet Laureate was chairman of the committee which made the
award. Masefield presented Auden to George VI on 23 November 1937
when, wearing a tail-coat borrowed from Cyril Connolly, Auden came
to Buckingham Palace to receive the medal. The award annoyed many of
Auden's supporters, who saw it as something of a betrayal of the Left.
Stephen Spender, while admitting that he was equally alarmed by Day-

Lewis's and his own 'growing respectability' as poets, said that Auden's acceptance of the medal was 'part of a process by which the writer who has a good heart at the age of twenty and is therefore a socialist, develops a good brain at forty and becomes a conservative'. He concluded: 'I wish that Auden had decided against that Medal.' And an editorial in Geoffrey Grigson's *New Verse* commented: 'It may be true that the joke is much more on the medal than it is on Auden. Anyone who knows Auden will realise that, but there is no good reason for taking the Royal Medal, all the same.'

Yet Auden, far from beginning to lose his position as the leader of a literary movement, seemed this autumn to be more revered than ever. *New Verse* published an 'Auden Double Number' dedicated entirely to articles about him, including a series of comments on Auden by other contemporary writers. Among these was Edwin Muir, who wrote: 'It may be that he belongs in too particular a sense to his age, but such direct control of language and boldness of imagination are given only to poets of genius'; Graham Greene, who called Auden 'a long way the finest living poet'; Sir Hugh Walpole – 'I delight in Auden's poetry'; Charles Madge – 'The original, but gawky, style has not developed. . . But there is still so much energy left that his personality, if not his poetry, is certain to have an increasing effect'; and Dylan Thomas – 'I think he is a wide and deep poet. . . and as potentially productive of greatness, as any poet writing in English. . . P. S. – Congratulations on Auden's seventieth birthday.' Geoffrey Grigson summed up the prevailing feeling when, in *New Verse* a few months later, he talked of the Thirties and its poets as 'the Auden Age and the Auden Circle'.[1]

Auden himself did not allow his head to be turned by praise. He was in fact remarkably free from vanity. This is not to say he was humble or did not know his own worth. He had complete confidence in his abilities; and it was this very self-confidence that protected him from flattery. He disliked listening to admirers talking at length about his work – 'Usually', he said, 'they praise you for the wrong reasons' – and preferred, if he showed a poem to a friend, to be told simply 'I like it.' (The exceptions were Isherwood, and, later, Chester Kallman, whose detailed comments and criticisms were welcomed by Auden.) Towards the end of his life he wrote:

[1]Another indication of fame is the mention of Auden's name in a footnote on p. 279 of James Joyce's *Finnegans Wake* (1939): '. . . rite go round, kill kackle, kook kettle and (remember all should I forget to do) bolt the thor. Auden. Wasn't it just divining that dog. . .' etc. Auden subsequently referred in a letter to 'Joyce, whom I can't honestly say I care for much, even if I am immortalised by getting my name into Finnegans Wake'. (To Mrs A. E. Dodds, n.d.) In an article in *Common Sense,* X, 3 (March 1941), pp. 89–90, he expressed a qualified admiration for Joyce's work. In an interview for *Isis* (8 November 1967, p. 14) he said: 'Joyce was an undoubted genius. But a madman. . . He asked you to stand in the same relation to his writing as you must to your life. It is as if he said you must spend your whole life reading me and never give me up or escape.'

Praise? Unimportant,
but jolly to remember
while falling asleep.

As to published reviews of his work, he cultivated an air of detachment, and as he grew older largely ceased to read them – though he did once admit: 'Some of us keep up an air of stoic indifference to reviews. . . but we all care.' On the other hand his success did not altogether stop him from being jealous of other poets. He once admitted that he felt unhappy whenever he heard that a recognised contemporary was bringing out a new book.

During the autumn of 1937, after finishing *On the Frontier,* he worked at two projects. One was the *Oxford Book of Light Verse,* for which he asked, and was given, an advance of £100. The book, as Auden explained to Charles Williams, was to differ from most collections of light verse by ignoring what he called *vers de société,* that is, the work of such people as A. P. Herbert and A. A. Milne. His real interest, he said, was in *popular* verse – he told the Press he would have preferred the volume to be called *The Oxford Book of Light and Popular Verse* – because he believed that popular writing, even more than 'serious' poetry, demonstrates clearly the differences between the sensibilities of different ages of civilisation, since it usually reflects not one man's taste so much as the taste of his audience. 'Light verse can be serious,' Auden wrote in the introduction to the volume, drafted this autumn. 'It has only come to mean *vers de société,* triolets, smoke-room limericks, because, under the social conditions which produced the Romantic Revival, and which have persisted, more or less, ever since, it has only been in trivial matters that poets have felt in sufficient intimacy with their audience to be able to forget themselves and their singing-robes.' During October, November and December he selected poems for the book, chosen from three categories: poetry written for performance (ballads and folk-songs), poetry dealing with the everyday social life of its period (such as the work of Chaucer, Pope and Byron), and such nursery rhymes and nonsense poetry as Auden believed had a general appeal.

His second project this autumn was to write the script of a radio programme commissioned by John Pudney, who was now a producer with the B.B.C. The subject was 'Hadrian's Wall from Caesar to the National Trust', which appealed to Auden not just because the Wall ran through his favourite lead-mining country, but also, as he wrote in the *Radio Times,* because it 'stood as a symbol for a certain imperialistic conception of life, for military discipline and an international order; in opposition to the Celtic and Germanic tribal loyalties which overwhelmed it. . . The front of history now lies elsewhere, but the same issues, of order versus liberty. . . still remain.' Auden's script for the programme included a good deal of verse, some describing the scenery through which the Wall runs, and some presenting the character of the Roman soldiers who manned it – among these was a piece called 'Roman Wall Blues'. This was the programme's conclusion:

> That man is born a savage, there needs no other proof than the Roman Wall. It characterises both nations as robbers and murderers. Our old historians always termed the Scots barbarians. To this I assent. They surprised the innocent, murdered them, laid waste the country and left the place. Julius Caesar, Agricola, Antoninus, Severus, etc., went one step further than the Scots. They surprised, murdered, plundered, and kept possession. Our venerable ancestors too, the Saxons, Danes, and Normans who came over in swarms, butchered, robbed and possessed; although they had no more right than I have to your coat. Whoever deprives an unoffending man of his right, is a barbarian.

'Hadrian's Wall' was broadcast from Newcastle on 25 November, with music written by Benjamin Britten – Auden said he and Britten were 'both rather proud' of the programme. John Pudney, who had had no further sexual involvement with Auden since their encounter in 1932, and who was chiefly heterosexual in his inclinations, became aware that Auden and Britten now (as he put it) both 'belonged to that homosexual world which closed certain doors to strangers'.

Auden and Isherwood were due to leave for China on 19 January 1938. Auden's work on the *Oxford Book of Light Verse* was far from finished, though the Press was expecting him to deliver the manuscript before he left. He solved this problem by handing over the unfinished book to Mrs A. E. Dodds, wife of his Birmingham friend E. R. Dodds, who was now Regius Professor of Greek at Oxford. She had to do her best. 'All Mr Auden's typescript needs checking,' she wrote to the Press. 'He gave me the references from memory and a good many are wrong. Also, some poems are taken from inaccurate versions. . . Even when I find the poem where Mr Auden says it is, I find an entirely different version.' (She also noticed that many of the poems Auden had chosen had already appeared in his anthology *The Poet's Tongue,* while others were taken from Walter de la Mare's *Come Hither.*) In the weeks that followed, she and John Mulgan, the editor at the Press responsible for the book, managed to assemble it between them, in some instances actually making the selection of poems themselves. Dodds later remarked that his wife had been an 'active collaborator' on the project; Auden dedicated the book to Dodds, but Dodds said he thought it was his wife who really deserved the dedication. Auden, meanwhile, was well aware of the inadequacy of his work. He wrote to Mrs Dodds, after leaving for the Far East: 'I keep waking up in the night and thinking of all the mistakes in the light verse text.'

His and Isherwood's departure was marked by a party in London on the night of 18 January, held at a studio in Chiswick under the auspices of the Group Theatre. The guests included E. M. Forster, Rose Macaulay, Geoffrey Grigson, John Hayward, Jean Connolly, Brian Howard, and Benjamin Britten and Hedli Anderson, who performed the Auden–Britten *Four Cabaret Songs*. Next morning, Auden and Isherwood left for China.

*

They were taking the boat-train to Paris, and, even though the Chinese war held none of the glamour of Spain, there were press reporters and cameramen to see them off at Victoria. In one pose for the cameras, Isherwood put his arm round Auden's shoulder and grinned; Auden looked bored and faintly embarrassed.

From Paris they travelled to Marseilles, where they embarked on the *Aramis,* which would call first at Port Said. During their crossing of the Mediterranean, Auden wrote a poem; it took the form of a popular song, with the refrain 'O tell me the truth about love'. This is the last stanza:

> When it comes, will it come without warning
>   Just as I'm picking my nose,
> Will it knock on my door in the morning
>   Or tread in the bus on my toes,
> Will it come like a change in the weather,
>   Will its greeting be courteous or bluff,
> Will it alter my life altogether?
>   O tell me the truth about love.

Auden was in fact asking this question entirely seriously.

He had certainly fallen in love during the 1930s; the series of love-poems concluding with 'Lay your sleeping head' were the product of real feelings. But the love that had prompted these poems apparently now seemed to have no future in it for Auden, and he was in a state of some private unhappiness, even despair. Isherwood recorded, in his diary later in their China trip, an episode of 'Wystan in tears, telling me that no one would ever love him, that he would never have my sexual success'. Isherwood, besides being flattered, was privately sceptical about this, believing, not without justification, that in fact innumerable young men would to to bed willingly with Auden. It also seemed to him – or at least did so in 1979, looking back – that there was a certain amount of self-torture in Auden's behaviour. Recalling a line in Auden's sonnet 'The fruit in which your parents hid you, boy', in which the loved one is described as sending 'the writer howling to his art', Isherwood remarked: 'You've got to have something to howl about.' Yet in 1938 on board ship

he did realise that Auden's poem 'O tell me the truth about love' had a
serious point to it. Auden himself later said of it: 'For me personally it
was a very important poem. Christopher spotted its importance. It's
amazing how prophetic those things can be because it was just after that
that I met the person who did, really, change things for me so completely.'
That meeting was to happen a little more than a year later.

   The *Aramis* reached Port Said after four days. Auden and Isherwood
disembarked and were met by Francis Turville-Petre, 'Fronny' himself,
who was now living in Egypt. He assured them that Port Said, which
they had been told was the sex capital of the world, was in fact deadly
dull, and he took them instead to the Pyramids, which they in turn found
uninteresting, though the Sphinx impressed them with what Auden
called its 'huge hurt face'. Auden sent a postcard to the Dodds: 'The
Pyramids are very disappointing but the Sphinx is alright, but doesnt
believe in Progress or the Classics. Coleridge was wrong. The stars do
not rush out in the tropics.' Next day he and Isherwood rejoined the
Aramis at Suez and headed for Hong Kong. Auden's usual shipboard
gloom was deepened, Isherwood noticed, by the fact that he was now so
far from his beloved chilly North. On 4 February he wrote to Cyril
Connolly: 'The Indian Ocean is crashingly dull.'

   While crossing the Indian Ocean, he wrote a poem, 'The Voyage',
which seems to be questioning his own motives behind all the journeys
he had made and was now making. The poem asks if 'the traveller' will
ever discover, on any of his journeys, the 'Good Place' for which he is
searching:

> No, he discovers nothing: he does not want to arrive.
> The journey is false; the false journey really an illness
> On the false island where the heart cannot act and will not suffer:
> He condones the fever; he is weaker than he thought; his weakness is real.

He and Isherwood arrived in Hong Kong on 16 February, and thought
it hideous. Auden was especially contemptuous of the British residents,
one of whom remarked of the Sino-Japanese war that it was merely a
quarrel between two sets of natives. Auden's poem 'Hongkong' (actually
written some months later, in Brussels) was, however, more subtle in its
condemnation of the city, which it pictures as a smoothly-mannered
society which regards the war as something merely rather unpleasant,
happening off-stage and out of sight. After staying for ten days with the
Vice-Chancellor of the University, Auden and Isherwood left Hong
Kong and sailed up the estuary to Canton, since renamed Kwangchow.
Until this moment a sense of unreality had possessed them both; it
pervades both Auden's poem 'The Voyage' and the travel-diary which
Isherwood was keeping, in which he wrote: 'This whole enormous
voyage [has] the quality of a dream.' They arrived in Canton, were met

by a representative of the British Consulate, and were given tea by the British missionaries who were to be their hosts. As tea was being served, an air-raid began. 'At that moment,' wrote Isherwood, 'suddenly, I arrived in China.'

In the days that followed, they interviewed the mayor of Canton, lunched with the Governor of Kwantung Province, and dined with a Chinese colonel and his wife. 'The Chinese are charming and chaste,' Auden wrote to Mrs Dodds. 'They have two kinds of faces – pretty but insipid flowers, and sympathetic frogs.' The Chinese in their turn were puzzled and amused by their visitors' appearance. Isherwood was dressed in what he considered a manner appropriate to a war-correspondent – a beret, a turtle-neck sweater, and riding boots. Auden went about in a big shapeless tweed overcoat and a woolly cap, often wearing carpet-slippers because he was having trouble with corns. The two of them caused curiosity and laughter in the street. They went shopping, bought camp-beds and mosquito nets, and ordered visiting cards with their names in Chinese characters, spelt phonetically: 'Y Hsiao Wu' and 'Au Dung'.

On 4 March they left Canton by train for Hankow (Wuhan), a journey of three days. To pass the time and prevent constipation, which they soon discovered to be a hazard, they took to swaying to and fro in their seats, singing in falsetto voices and reading aloud from Trollope and Scott. The Chinese guards peered through the compartment window in wonder.

Hankow, they discovered on arrival, was the real capital of wartime China. 'Today', Isherwood wrote in his diary on 8 March, 'Auden and I agreed that we would rather be in Hankow at this moment than anywhere else on earth.' They were allowed to pitch their camp-beds in the British Consulate, where they quickly became friendly with one of the staff, Basil Boothby. They teased him for his 'establishment' manners, while he in turn thought that Auden looked like 'a big, mad, white rabbit'. A servant, Chiang, was found for them, and they attended one of the daily press conferences which were patronised mainly by 'real' journalists, such as they themselves did not claim to be. They hastened to explain to these reporters that they were 'mere trippers, who had come to China to write a book'. They were in fact not at all sure of their role, or of what they were really supposed to be doing. They knew nothing about Far Eastern affairs, and had to take everything that they were told at face value. An American bishop informed them that the future of China lay with the Communists; an adviser to Chiang Kai-shek was sceptical about whether there was in fact any real Communism in China at all; and a German officer assisting the nationalists assured them that China would win the war if only its troops would 'stand up straight and do as they're told'. Then, on 12 March, they were told – by the German contingent itself – that Hitler had invaded Austria. 'The bottom seemed to drop out of the world,' wrote Isherwood. 'By this evening a European war may have broken out. . . Shall we go back? What does China matter to us in comparison with this?'

They did not, of course, go back. Their next meeting was with Agnes Smedley, an English spinster who had made a reputation as a long-time friend of the Communists. Auden described her as 'one of the great melancholy domineering frumps'. She received them ironically – 'Do you always throw your coats on the floor?' – and from her they obtained an introduction to the Hankow office of the Communist Eighth Route Army. Calling there, they were received in friendly fashion, but decided not to visit this celebrated fighting-unit, as so many journalists had already done so. They did, however, meet Madame Chiang Kai-shek, who spoke excellent English, and asked Auden if poets liked cake – 'I thought perhaps they preferred only spiritual food.' They questioned her about the nationalists' willingness to co-operate with the Communists after the war was over. She replied: 'The question is: will the Communists co-operate with us?' As they were leaving, Chiang himself arrived, and agreed to pose with his wife for Auden's camera. Auden later told Mrs Dodds that he 'looks like a country doctor'. He and Isherwood began to come to the conclusion that no working alliance between nationalists and Communists would be possible after the war; but they did not feel that the Communists would take over. 'The greatest probability', they wrote in an article shortly after their China visit, 'would seem to be some form of military dictatorship.' It became apparent to them very quickly that the Chinese-Japanese war was not simply a struggle between socialism and Fascism – any more than Spain had been.

Chinese food amused them. 'A Chinese dinner-table', wrote Auden, 'looks as if it were set, not for eating but for a lesson in water-colour painting, with little dishes of coloured sauces, and chopsticks like brushes and paint rags to wipe the chopsticks on. Many of the dishes, such as birds-nest soups and ancient eggs, I found delicious, but I drew the line at black beetles.' He and Isherwood developed the game of praising to their hosts the dishes that they liked least. 'Delicious!' Auden murmured as he munched what seemed to be a small sponge soaked in glue. Isherwood replied by devouring, with smiles of exquisite pleasure, an orange that seemed to taste of bitter aloes and contained what appeared to be a large weevil. They had, in other words, given up the attempt to understand a strange culture, and had retreated into their usual amusement of private jokes. They were two schoolboys on holiday among a crowd of comic foreigners.

One evening they watched an air raid from the roof of a high building. On such occasions Isherwood admitted, at least privately, to fear; but Auden would declare: 'Nothing is going to happen. I know it won't, nothing like that ever happens to *me*.' A few days after leaving Hankow, they took a room in a bomb-damaged hotel at a time when more raids seemed likely. Isherwood could not get to sleep because of nerves, but observed enviously that Auden 'slept deeply, with the long, calm snores of the truly strong'.

Their plan was to get to the front line. Travelling north by train for several hundred miles, they endured endless delays. Once, their train was halted for more than six hours in the middle of nowhere. Another time their servant told the other passengers, for the sake of passing the time, that his masters were two doctors – 'much to our alarm', wrote Isherwood, for he and Auden expected in consequence to have to perform operations on wounded soldiers returning from the front. Auden, however, said that they would be better than nothing, and might as well try if asked.

Left for so many hours with only each other for company, they took to arguing metaphysics. Isherwood suspected that Auden now had distinct Christian leanings – or rather, that he had never really quite abandoned the religious beliefs of his childhood, whatever he might say to the contrary. Isherwood also thought he detected an element of religious feeling in Auden's contributions to the plays they had written. 'When we collaborate,' Isherwood wrote shortly after they had finished *On the Frontier,* 'I have to keep a sharp eye on him – or down flop the characters on their knees; another constant danger is that of choral interruptions by angel-voices.' (Isherwood was probably thinking especially of the original version of the lovers' dream-scene in *On the Frontier,* which was later abandoned.) Auden did not in fact regard himself as anything like a Christian believer, even though his meetings with Charles Williams had opened his eyes to the existence of personal sanctity. His state of mind at present was probably something like, and was probably influenced by, E. M. Forster's humanist agnosticism – though Auden's form of it was more pessimistic than Forster's. He did, however, delight in mocking Isherwood's present hostility to religion, telling him: 'Careful, careful, my dear – if you go on like that, you'll have *such* a conversion, one of these days!'

Eventually they reached the front, near Sü-chow, travelling the last thirty miles in hired rickshaws. Auden's habit of taking photographs attracted attention as they travelled, as did his Arctic costume of huge overcoat and cap. 'Collectively', remarked Isherwood, 'we most resemble a group of characters in one of Jules Verne's stories about lunatic English explorers.' On arrival, they were taken on a tour of the Chinese defences, riding on ponies; Isherwood noticed that Auden had become a daring if somewhat unorthodox horseman. It was quiet, and they were able to spend the night sleeping in a commandeered house. Next morning they observed a dog gnawing at a half-buried corpse, and were told it was the body of a spy who had been shot – an odd echo of 'Paid on Both Sides'. This day they went into the actual front line, and on their journey, during a pause for refreshments, 'found ourselves discussing the poetry of Robert Bridges'. Once they were in the trenches, Auden began to take photographs, popping his head above the parapet and declaring: 'I don't believe that there are any Japs here at all.' Isherwood noted that his words 'were interrupted by three tremendous detonations'. A little later, they had to lie flat as Japanese planes passed overhead. Isherwood began to worry about their being an exposed target, but Auden photographed him, declaring: 'You look wonderful with your great nose cleaving the summer air.' As Isherwood wrote to Spender, Auden 'knows he won't be killed, because Nanny would never allow it, and It Can't Happen Here. So whenever we get into any danger . . . he sulks and fusses: "Why can't they SHOOT?" or "It's not nearly LOUD enough." '

From the Sü-chow front they travelled by slow and tedious stages to Sian, hoping to reach another part of the front line at Cheng-tu. This proved impossible, so they returned to Hankow, arriving there on 14 April. Auden had written a sonnet on a dead Chinese soldier, and he read it aloud at a tea-party for Chinese intellectuals. A translation was subsequently published in the newspaper *Ta Kung Pao*. The line 'Abandoned by his general and his lice', which was apparently considered unbecoming, was changed by the translator to 'The rich and the poor are combining to fight.' Auden also recited the poem to a gathering at the British Consulate, where he and Isherwood were again staying. Isherwood noted that Auden was getting all the limelight, and would no longer play the role of 'admiring younger brother' to Isherwood himself. William Empson, the poet and critic, who had met them in Hong Kong, was of the same opinion; Auden, he observed, was so much the centre of attention that Isherwood hardly had the chance to make any impression.

The two of them began to arrange to visit the south-eastern front, hoping perhaps even to penetrate the Japanese lines and reach occupied Shanghai. There were many difficulties. Auden wrote to Mrs Dodds on 20 April: 'Looking for the war in China is like a novel by Kafka.' They watched another air-raid, and afterwards visited the slums where many of the bombs had fallen, missing their target, the Arsenal. Here they saw the injured and dying. 'War', Auden wrote afterwards, 'is bombing a disused arsenal, missing it and killing a few old women . . . War is untidy, inefficient, obscure, and largely a matter of chance.'

Eventually they set off for the south-east, staying on the way at an improbable hotel named Journey's End, run by an English proprietor on the lines of a prep school, with house-boys instead of pupils. 'It was all far, far too beautiful to be real,' wrote Isherwood. But Auden was suffering from the after-effects of dysentery, and at Nanchang he was given treatment as an out-patient at the American Mission Hospital. 'After two months', he told Mrs Dodds, 'we are pro Chinese and pro missionary'; though he was moved to fury by an American who asked him if he was 'insured with Jesus'. He was still unwell some days later, and could not eat. Yet when he and Isherwood were warned against a particular brand of cigarettes which was believed to have been poisoned by the Japanese, he immediately bought a packet and began to smoke them.

This time their last few miles to the front, at Meiki, had to be done on foot, in the company of a tiresome Chinese journalist and of Peter Fleming the travel-writer, who was in China to report for *The Times*. They and Fleming were at first a little suspicious of each other, but this suspicion soon evaporated, and Auden, as they walked, fell deep into argument with Fleming about Soviet Russia. He and Isherwood also entertained themselves by reciting passages from an imaginary travel book called 'With Fleming to the Front'. On arrival, they found that the commanding officers were dismayed to see them. Meiki was already in danger from the Japanese, a retreat was imminent, and they were ordered to leave immediately, which they did after a broken night's sleep. By 18 May they were in Kin-hwa, Auden declaring 'We've been on a journey with Fleming in China, and now we're real travellers for ever and ever; we need never go further than Brighton again.' From Kin-hwa they went, via Wenchow and a steamer up the coast, to Shanghai.

Though the city was under Japanese occupation, the international diplomats continued their lives as usual. Auden and Isherwood stayed in comfort as guests of the British Ambassador, Sir Archibald Clark-Kerr, whom they had met in Hankow. They had lunch with four Japanese businessmen, who, when Auden and Isherwood spoke their minds about the Japanese bombing of civilians, merely answered: 'That is certainly a most interesting point of view.' During their stay, they visited the slums and factories, where they were appalled by the conditions; they also made use of a homosexual bath-house where tea was served during massage – they called these sessions 'afternoon holidays from their social conscience'. They decided to return to England by way of the United States, and, after at first failing to get U.S. visas, mentioned that they were staying with the British Ambassador – and were at once given visas allowing them to visit America as often as they liked during the next twelve months. They sailed from Shanghai on 12 June.

Auden had been delighted by China. 'I thought it the nicest country I had ever been in,' he told E. R. Dodds, though he added that it would probably be dangerous to try to live there: 'A European whose virtues and vices are those of a will *opposed* to nature, could not switch round completely, I think, without going to seed.' But neither he nor Isherwood had come away with more than (as Auden put it) a 'tourist's acquaintance' with China. Auden later said of this: 'China was utterly different. Spain was a culture one knew. One could understand what was happening, what things meant. But China was impossible to know. A country which, quite apart from fighting a war, just had no respect towards human life.' He and Isherwood had in a sense left China empty-handed. But there remained America.

Their voyage, on the *Empress of Asia*, took them briefly to Japan, which they crossed by train, spending the night in Tokyo before rejoining their boat. At the end of June they landed at Vancouver, and took a train across the North American continent to New York. Here they were met by George Davis, the fiction editor of *Harper's Bazaar,* who had got to know them both in London the previous year. Davis was acting as their unofficial American agent, and he now handed over a large sum of dollars which he had already earned for them by placing an article about China with *Harper's Bazaar*. Under his guidance, they began to see the New York sights. They were interviewed, photographed, introduced to celebrities, offered pep pills and sleeping pills, which Auden gladly accepted, and were given sexual introductions – Davis was himself homosexual. Isherwood was paired with a beautiful blond boy, and similar arrangements were made for Auden. To both of them, New York seemed immensely exciting, an outlier of Europe vitalised by America. Then, after two weeks, they returned to England.

*

Only a very short time later, Auden went abroad once again, this time to Brussels, where he rented a room at 83 Rue des Confédérés, and began work on the poems that were to be his contribution to *Journey to a War,* the book on China, for which Isherwood was meanwhile writing a prose narrative based on the travel diaries that both of them had kept. 'Am having a nice time here,' Auden wrote from Brussels to John Mulgan at the Oxford University Press, 'bathing and café crawling.' He worked during the mornings, and spent much of the afternoon at a swimming pool where Belgian boys congregated. He told Mrs Dodds that the Brussels working class were '*so* gay and charming', and he soon acquired a temporary boyfriend, whom he referred to as 'Petit Jacques'.

Mrs Dodds was still putting the finishing touches to the *Oxford Book of Light Verse* on his behalf, and she wrote to him with last-minute queries, such as the identity of poets whose names he had not given in full. 'I don't KNOW who Austin was,' he replied to one such enquiry. 'I'm sure it wasnt Alfred. Lets call him Samuel.' In the same letter (31 August) he told her he had been visiting the Brussels art gallery 'and trying to appreciate Rubens. The daring and vitality take one's breath away, but what is it all ABOUT?' And on 5 September, enclosing a set of manuscripts: 'Are the enclosed trash, or not? I am much too close to them to know. . . They are the first part of a sonnet sequence for the China book. Please let me have them back, with comments, as they are the only copies.'

The sonnet sequence was entitled 'In Time of War', and began, just as *Spain* had done, with a survey of human history. But whereas in *Spain* the survey had been dispassionate and drew no moral conclusion, here the moral was clear. We are, declared Auden, 'A race of promise that has never proved its worth'. History (in the sonnets) is seen as a failure to achieve 'The Good Place'. The war in China, to which the second part of the sequence turns, is shown to be a product of this universal human failure; it is simply, as Auden says in the verse Commentary which accompanies the sonnets and gives a more didactic exposition of their ideas, 'the local variant of a struggle in which all. . . are profoundly implicated'.

Although the sonnets and the Commentary may at first sight appear to deal with war only in general terms, they do in fact make use of many details and episodes that Auden and Isherwood observed in China – the air-raids, the generals with their maps, a hospital, a dead soldier, a garden-party of diplomats. But the poems return finally to a consideration of the wider plight of Man, who sighs in vain for 'the warm nude ages of instinctive poise', and is 'hostile to brotherhood and feeling' (a passage taken extensively from 'In the year of my youth'), yet among whom voices of wisdom are always speaking if only he will listen to them. These voices can teach how 'The enemies of life may be more passionately attacked'; and their message has a distinctly Forsterian ring about it: 'Men are not innocent as beasts and never can be. . . Only the free have disposition to be truthful. . . Only the just possess the will-power to be free.' Indeed, Auden, together with Isherwood, dedicated the book on the Chinese war to Forster, with a sonnet paying tribute to his novels. Yet there seems to be another influence at work on Auden, for the survey of history which begins the sequence draws its images largely from the Christian story, and the Commentary ends with a voice that sounds very much as if it were praying: 'O teach me to outgrow my madness. . .'

'Have finished the sonnet sequence,' Auden wrote to Mrs Dodds from Brussels late in September, 'and am in that horrible state, of not feeling ready to start a longish poem on our trip which I am to write' – he was referring to the Commentary – 'and have nothing proper to do except to think about the International Situation, and the foulness of the British and even more the French governments.' Hitler was threatening Czechoslavakia with his demands for the return of the Sudetenland, the French were reacting entirely passively, abandoning their Czech allies, and Britain already seemed to be acquiescing, though some show of resistance had been made, and there was a partial mobilisation of British troops. Auden himself, recalling this period of his life two years later, said that he had listened to the news of the deepening European crisis 'with a happy excitement, secretly hoping there would be a war', not just because he wanted to see Hitler defeated but because of 'the personal problem which in 1938 was still unsolved and which in despair I was looking to world events to solve for me'. From the original context of this remark, it is clear that the personal problem was his despair about failing to find love.

He returned to London on 28 September, having now decided that the crisis was a false alarm, not through his own political acumen but because he had been told so by a fortune-teller in Brussels. 'Well, my dear,' he announced to Isherwood, who met him at Victoria Station, 'there isn't going to be a war, you know!' A few minutes later, they saw the placards announcing the 'Dramatic Peace Move' of Munich.

Auden travelled up to his parents' house in Birmingham, where he settled down to write the verse Commentary for the China book, sending the manuscript to Mrs Dodds when it was finished: 'Please let me have your comments. I am very uncertain whether this kind of thing is possible without becoming a prosy pompous old bore.' He told her that he had to have an operation – possibly for a recurrence of the anal fissure – and had decided to return to Brussels for this in December. What he did not tell her, or, apparently, any of his friends, was that he and Isherwood had decided to emigrate to America.

★

Exactly when they made this decision is not clear, if indeed there ever was a clear and final decision. According to Isherwood, while they were in New York in July on their way back from China, Auden had told him that he wanted to settle permanently in the U.S.A. – or rather, in New York itself. Auden later declared that they had both agreed on it then, but Isherwood's memory was rather that he himself had not strong feelings; he had moved around so much that another change of country would not be so significant for him as it would for Auden, and he left it to Auden to decide, feeling only that if Auden chose to emigrate, he would too.

At the beginning of August 1938, Auden's brother John, who was on leave from his work as a geologist in India, came to stay with him in Brussels. Looking back, John Auden is absolutely certain that the two of them discussed, during this week, Wystan's definite wish not just to return to America for a visit but to stay there and become a U.S. citizen. And it seems that, by early October, Auden had come to a definite agreement with Isherwood that they would both go back to the States some time in the near future, probably on a permanent basis. 'But they were in no hurry,' wrote Isherwood many years later. 'The special visa they had got from the Americans in Shanghai made them feel all the more relaxed. Because of it, they would have no further formalities to go through. They could leave at short notice whenever they decided to.'

So much for the timing of their decision. There remains the question of why they decided to go. There is no clear answer; this seems, in fact, to have been one of those decisions which are made without a set of precise reasons. Certainly in later years Auden and Isherwood both gave various explanations, and many of these explanations are convincing in themselves; yet the fact that they were given with the benefit of hindsight means that they need to be treated carefully. It is best, while looking at them, to examine also Auden's particular circumstances at the time the decision was made.

It was now three years since he had lived a settled life in England. His almost idyllic time at the Downs School had been followed by a period of 'no fixed abode', in which foreign travel played an increasingly important part. Short trips to the nearer European countries had been followed by major expeditions to Iceland, Spain and China; and these journeys were, as he fully realised, attempts to discover an idealogy. He was trying to find the personal ideals for which he had been searching ever since the collapse of his Lane–Layard–Lawrence beliefs; these he had failed to replace either with Gerald Heard's view of personality or with Marxism, with which he had only toyed. Each of his foreign trips had been in its different way an attempt to 'make action urgent and its nature clear'. Iceland, he had hoped, would allow him to distance himself from European culture and view it objectively; the experiment had failed, because he was unable to shake off Europe so easily. Spain was an attempt, as he put it at the time, to 'gamble on something bigger', to widen his experience in the hope that this would enrich his mind. This, too, had failed, because the Spanish war was not the clear-cut set of issues he had hoped to find. As to the China trip, it had done no more than strengthen his growing belief in universal human failure. Was he now to give up, to come back to England and resume the literary life in the hope that this, after all, would show him what he was looking for? He cannot have had much faith in this prospect.

The English literary world had never appealed to him. 'Chuck all this literary business,' he had written to John Pudney in 1932; and in later years, after his departure for America, he maintained that he had found literary life in England peculiarly stultifying because of its 'family' atmosphere. 'The English', he wrote, 'have a greater talent than any other people for creating an agreeable family life; that is why it is such a threat to their artistic and intellectual life. If the atmosphere were not so charming, it would be less of a temptation.' Elsewhere he explained how this had affected his decision to leave England: 'I felt the situation for me in England was becoming impossible. I couldn't grow up. English life is for me a family life, and I love my family but I don't want to live with them.'[1]

His discontent with English society in fact ran deeper than this. Shortly before he made his decision to leave the country he wrote two pieces of prose which showed his uneasiness. The first was his preface to

[1]He was, of course, doing just that – living with his family in Birmingham for much of the time he spent in England. Apart from his parents' house and his lodgings at the schools where he taught, he never had a home of his own in England. Was this, in a small way, a contributory factor to his decision to leave?

the *Oxford Book of Light Verse,* in which he declared that 'the old pre-industrial community and culture' which made successful poetry possible had vanished. In such a culture, he argued, the poet and his audience had been interested in the same things, and poetry consequently had a clearly defined task. But the Industrial Revolution had initiated a society in which the poet became differentiated from the mass of humanity, and could speak only to the limited number of people who had the same intellectual background as his own. The remedy that Auden offered for this malaise was not a return to the old state of affairs, but the creation of 'a democracy in which each citizen is as fully conscious and capable of making a rational choice, as in the past has been possible only for the wealthier few' – this being a context in which the poet could once again be in touch with his audience. When Auden wrote this, late in 1937, he perhaps still thought that such a society could be created in England, or at least in Europe. A year later he had decided that it could not.

This is shown by 'The Sportsmen: A Parable', which was printed in *New Verse* in the autumn of 1938. This pictured the growth of modern society as an increasingly wooded tract of country in which the sports-man (the artist) has been obliged to abandon his original pursuit of duck-shooting (simple art-forms which pleased a primitive society) for more sophisticated sports (the art of recent centuries) until the density of trees (the complexity of society) makes even these difficult. News comes of 'a far country where the inhabitants had cleared the land of timber, so that duck had once more become plentiful and shooting parties were again in fashion' (the utopia of the socialist state). But all attempts to follow this example and chop down the trees are forestalled by various vested interests, and the only result is that the sportsmen decide to make artificial ducks out of clay and old newspapers, in the hope that they can persuade the villagers that these are real duck that they have shot (a reference to the attempt during the 1930s to create proletarian art in Europe).

'The Sportsmen' presents a despairing picture of Europe, at least from the point of view of the artist, and Auden said the same thing more bluntly at about this time to his friend A. H. Campbell; looking out of a window in Birmingham he remarked that he was sure that European society was finished. So he turned to America, not because he had any dream of it as the perfect society, but because he regarded it as a place where the options were still open, and where no set pattern of civilisation had yet been developed. As he put it in July 1939: 'What England can give me, I feel it already has, and that I can never lose it. America is so vast. . .'

The decision to emigrate was, then, partly a result of the discontent Auden had been feeling for several years, and of the belief that he could remedy this by a change in life-style. He expressed this clearly in a letter to Henry Treece written in the autumn of 1937:

You can only write about the things you know and what you know depends on how you live. . . The artist. . . can only tell the truth about things he knows and is interested in, and that depends on where and how he lives. . . If he is not content with his knowledge, he can only change his life, so it can give him the knowledge he would like to have.

Quite apart from his unhappiness about English society in general, he felt, it seems, that he was himself in an increasingly impossible position within that society. His role as what Edward Mendelson has called 'Court Poet of the Left' had its attractions, and at first he had played the part expected of him. But *The Ascent of F6* expressed his fears about the dangers of public success, and by 1938 the role had become intolerable simply because he did not have the political beliefs to sustain it.

He was now taking only a very moderate political line. In 1936, in 'Letter to Lord Byron', he prophesied that he would end up 'A selfish pink old Liberal', and this was roughly what he had now become. His present attitude to society was liberal and unrevolutionary. 'No society can be absolutely good,' he wrote in a 1938 article summarising his beliefs. 'All desire happiness and goodness, but their conceptions of these may and do conflict with one another.' He admitted that 'Liberal Democracy', with its belief in the innate goodness of human nature, was too weak to withstand Fascism, but his only proposal for change was the introduction of what he called 'Social Democracy', which would admit that 'man is not born free or good', and would take steps to curb extremism. But even this modified liberalism did not really reflect his true state of mind. The fact is that he was beginning to lose all interest in politics.

He began to discover this during the autumn of 1938, as a result of having to lecture about 'the anti-fascist struggle' in China. 'I get very depressed running all over the place chatting about China,' he told Mrs Dodds. 'The Cambridge Socialist Club want a China lunch of bread and cheese. Derby Diocesan Training College suggest a tea. . . Does it do any good? Should I be better employed at my own work? If so am I being immoral? Or is this just selfish? VERY TIRED of train journeys.' Looking back a few months later, he remarked, in a letter to Mrs Dodds, that it was the talks on China which first made him realise that his involvement with politics was, and perhaps always had been, a sham.

This, then, was his general state of mind lying behind the decision to emigrate from England – a state of mind that, where politics was concerned, was entirely shared by Isherwood, who realised this autumn that neither of them could any longer swallow 'the Popular Front, the party line, the anti-fascist struggle'. As to patriotism, it was not a concept that Auden was prepared to accept without question. He was of the opinion that 'to regard national statehood as anything more than a technical convenience of social organisation – and few do not – is idolatry'. And some years later he wrote:

> Patriots? Little boys,
> obsessed by Bigness,
> Big Pricks, Big Money, Big Bangs.

There was also, beside all this, one simple reason why he wanted to go to the U.S.A. During their stay in New York in July he and Isherwood realised how much opportunity there would be in America for them to earn money as writers. The large sum of dollars that George Davis handed them made just as much impression as the other delights of American life. In 1946 Auden, looking back on his decision, told a friend: 'I came to America because it's easier to make money here, to live by your wits.'

*

He and Isherwood eventually set the date of their departure for the middle of January 1939, exactly a year after they had left for China. They wanted to wait until the China book was finished and *On the Frontier* staged. J. M. Keynes wrote to them from Cambridge asking if they wanted to change the play in the light of Munich. They decided not to; they had already revised it extensively on their voyage back from China, and privately they had now lost faith in it. 'The subject', Auden admitted in a letter to Spender, 'is too contemporary for a semi-realistic play.'

On the Frontier went into rehearsal at Cambridge with Doone directing. Wyndham Goldie played Valerian, Ernest Milton was the Dictator of Westland, and Keynes's wife Lydia Lopokova played Anna. Benjamin Britten had written a musical score for piano, percussion and two trumpets; he played the piano himself for a fee of £10. The part of the radio announcer was taken by Peter Pears, whom Britten had first met in March 1937, and who also appeared in the play as a dancer, soldier and war correspondent. Robert Medley was again the designer. The play opened for six performances on Monday 14 November. Next morning the *Manchester Guardian* called it 'an indisputable success', and the *New Statesman* reviewer agreed: but Louis MacNeice could only praise it as a 'not entirely successful play on a really important subject', and many who attended the performance at Cambridge agreed with the verdict of Kenneth Allott in *New Verse,* who said that in it Auden and Isherwood had 'not exploited a tenth of their ability', and complained of 'the downright dullness of much of the writing'. Meanwhile prolonged negotiations by Keynes and his staff had failed to arrange a provincial tour for the play, and it was eventually agreed that it should be staged in London for just one night, which it duly was, at the Globe Theatre, on

Sunday 12 February 1939. There had been some hope that this London performance might interest a West End management in the play, but it did not, and *On the Frontier* thereafter (in Isherwood's words) 'passed away painlessly'. Auden, looking back many years later on his theatrical collaborations with Isherwood, remarked that 'none of them will quite do'; and certainly neither author had given of his best in them. Yet they were, in their quirky, patchy way, the unsteady beginning of a real revolution in English drama.

Auden's *Oxford Book of Light Verse* was published in October 1938, and earned reviews as mixed as those of *On the Frontier*. Many critics were irritated by the absence of, as the *Times Literary Supplement* put it, 'what most people mean by light verse'. Yet the book was praised for liveliness and originality, and sold very well, continuing to be reprinted regularly for the rest of Auden's life and after – indeed, up to the present time. The Oxford University Press was not, however, entirely pleased with Auden, who had included in it a piece by Dunbar in which the medieval Scots vocabulary did not disguise indelicacy; it included such lines as 'Yit be his feirris he wald have fukkit'. They arranged that the poem should be removed when the book was reprinted, on the grounds that 'the travellers said it dished the book with the girls' schools'. It was replaced by a more seemly piece of Dunbar. Auden, thirty years later, got the original poem into print again in his anthology *A Certain World*.

It was presumably during the autumn of 1938 that Auden worked, together with T. C. Worsley, on a pamphlet for the Hogarth Press entitled *Education – Today and Tomorrow*. 'I am sorry Nature no more intended me to write about Education than it intended Louis to review,' Auden told Mrs Dodds, 'but livings must be earned.' Worsley wrote most of the sections on 'Fact' and 'Suggestion', Auden providing the central part of the booklet, on 'Theory'. They made it a kind of love-hate poem about the English public schools, in two of which institutions Worsley had taught. Auden remarked to Worsley a year or so later that he supposed the Second World War would 'mean the last of them this time', but he said he hoped there would still be some kind of boarding-schools, 'or what will happen to English romanticism?'.

Journey to a War was finished in December and sent to Faber's. When it was published the following March, Evelyn Waugh in the *Spectator* took the opportunity to call Auden 'a public bore', but most reviews were favourable, and Geoffrey Grigson in *New Verse* judged the sonnets to be triumphantly successful. Meanwhile John Lehmann, who was now running the Hogarth Press, became aware of Auden and Isherwood's intention of returning to America, though not of their plan to settle there; and at the time of Munich he commissioned from them a travel book on the U.S.A., on the same lines as the China volume, to be called *Address Not Known* – a project which would help them finance their journey. Another not dissimilar idea with which the two of them toyed, either now or early in 1939, when they had reached the U.S.A., was a film scenario entitled *The Life of an American* – Auden had been working briefly in films again, having contributed a few lines of commentary to John Grierson's documentary *The Londoners.* The scenario suggested that the central role should be taken by the camera itself, an idea that recalls the phrase in Isherwood's *Goodbye to Berlin,* 'I am a camera'. Nothing came of the idea.

Auden left England for a few weeks at the beginning of December 1938. He went first to Paris, where he gave a lecture in English at the Sorbonne on 'The Outlook for "Poetic Drama" '; the lecture was inconclusive and largely anecdotal in content. In Paris he met the English poet David Gascoyne. 'Even at the age of 40,' Gascoyne wrote of Auden in his diary, 'he will carry the head of an undergraduate on his shoulders. At 31, he still has an air of disguising only with a difficultly acquired social manner the petulance and embarrassment of an adolescent.' By 12 December, Auden was in Brussels, this time staying with Isherwood in a flat at 70 Square Marie-Louise, overlooking an ornamental lake adorned with ducks. 'It would make a very nice Ibsen set,' Auden told Mrs Dodds, 'the more so because I have upset my tummy somehow and sit gloomily in the window, imagining that the house is being watched. I hope the muses are going to be kind and visit me its about time they did.' In fact during the next four weeks he wrote about a dozen poems – 'Musée des Beaux Arts', suggested by the Brussels art gallery, 'Edward Lear', 'Gare du Midi', 'A. E. Housman', and others, many of which were among the best he had done. He also acquired another Belgian boyfriend – 'Pierre is a dream', he wrote to John Lehmann – and on New Year's Eve he gave a party, for which he wrote a set of celebratory verses addressed, perhaps as a kind of farewell, to his friends, both those present and, in this stanza, spread across Europe:

> My next toast most willingly carries
>   Good will to our friends overseas,
> To Brian drinking in Paris,
>   To Fronny drinking in Greece,
> To Bill who might learn to paint faster,
>   To Ben who writes tunes in his sleep,
> To Berthold who looks like a Master,
>   To Rupert who looks like a sheep,
> To the three or four Tonies, and even
>   To Jean who – thank God – isn't here,
> To Morgan and Edward and Stephen,
>   We wish a most happy New Year.[1]

[1] Those addressed are, in order of mention: Brian Howard; Francis Turville-Petre; William Coldstream; Benjamin Britten; Berthold Viertel; Rupert Doone; various friends or friends' boyfriends who were named (or known as) Tony, including Tony Bower, an American friend of the Connollys; Jean, a Belgian boy whom Auden and Isherwood had

Early in January 1939, Auden and Isherwood came back to London. The proposed travel book about America now seemed to both of them to be a non-starter, but Auden badly needed money, so he persuaded John Lehmann, who had intended to publish it, to give him an advance on his next book of poems instead, assuring him quite incorrectly that he was not under contract to Faber's and that the Hogarth Press could certainly publish it. He also told the Oxford University Press: 'I leave for America to-morrow week and am *very* hard up for cash. Do you think O.U.P. could see their way to letting me have a little more on Light Verse? S.O.S. S.O.S.' They sent him £75 on account.

On 18 January he and Isherwood caught a train to Southampton. Their plan was to spend their last night in England on board their ship, the *Champlain,* so as to cut the partings short. They were seen off from London by one of Isherwood's young men, and by E. M. Forster. The boat train pulled out. 'Well,' said Isherwood, 'we're off again.' 'Goody,' said Auden.

met in Brussels on a previous visit, and who had made scenes of various kinds; Morgan (E. M.) Forster; Edward Upward; and Stephen Spender. The poem was circulated in typescript among Auden's friends.

II

America – and Europe

1

'Chester, my chum'

On the morning of 26 January 1939 the snow was falling heavily in New York City. It was the coldest day so far that winter; blocks of ice were seen floating in the Hudson River. About the middle of the day news came that, in Spain, Barcelona had fallen to Franco, and the Spanish Republicans had in effect lost the war. This was the day on which Auden and Isherwood arrived in New York.

'There they stood in the driving snow', recalled Isherwood, remembering how he and Auden looked up at 'the made-in-France Giantess with her liberty torch, which now seemed to threaten, not welcome, the newcomer; and the Red Indian island with its appalling towers. . . You could feel it vibrating with the tension of the nervous New World, aggressively flaunting its rude steel nudity. We're Americans here – and we keep at it, twenty-four hours a day, *being* Americans. . . Don't you come snooting us with your European traditions – we know the mess they've got you into. Do things our way or take the next boat back. . . Are you quitting or staying? It's no skin off *our* nose. We promise nothing. Here, you'll be on your own.'

In fact they were not quite on their own. Erika and Klaus Mann, who now lived largely in the U.S.A., met them on the quarantine launch when they arrived. Isherwood quickly took up again with his New York boyfriend of the previous summer, and he and Auden found a temporary base at the George Washington Hotel on 23rd Street and Lexington Avenue, which offered cheap rooms to long-stay guests. They began to contact acquaintances from their July visit, and through these soon made some new friends, among them Lincoln Kirstein, founder of the New York City Ballet and a friend of Stephen Spender; Auden described Kirstein as 'a little farouche in manner sometimes but really extremely nice'. Through the Manns, Auden also began to get to know a number of refugees from Nazi Germany, such as Wolfgang Köhler, the pioneer of Gestalt psychology, who was teaching in America. Auden called Köhler

'one of the greatest men I've ever met'. But the fact that his friends
included many exiles seems to have made him all the more aware of the
unwelcoming character of New York. 'Say this city has ten million
souls,' he wrote in a poem a few weeks after arriving,

> Some are living in mansions, some are living in holes:
>   Yet there's no place for us, my dear, yet there's no place for us. . .
>
> Dreamed I saw a building with a thousand floors,
> A thousand windows and a thousand doors;
> Not one of them was ours, my dear, not one of them was ours.

The poem was accepted by the *New Yorker,* which printed it in April 1939.

Auden's name was already known in American literary circles; Random
House had published U.S. editions of all his books, and though their
sales were markedly lower than in England there was by now a small cult
following for his poetry in the States, especially among college students.
For example, the young poet William Meredith, who was at Princeton in
the late 1930s, described Auden as '*our* poet, the poet of our generation';
similarly Anthony Hecht, who was at Harvard during this period, called
him 'a "cult" figure whose work we prized the more because it was
Orphic and obscure'. The New York writer Delmore Schwartz, in a
1939 article assessing Auden, declared: 'The fact remains that Auden's
sheer natural gifts are incomparable'; while the poet Richard Eberhart
wrote: 'Auden's coming to America may prove to be as significant as
Eliot's leaving it.' But admiration in literary circles was not in itself
enough to provide Auden with a living, and he was already looking for
other means of support besides his writing.

Soon after arriving he gave an interview to the *New York Times* in
which he said he was hoping to get some work as a teacher. He explained
that he wished to write a book on America – the project which he and
Isherwood had planned the previous autumn – and said he thought the
best way to study the country would be to spend eighteen months
teaching in various schools. 'I cannot expect to get a position as a teacher
in the public or State schools,' he told the reporter, 'but I hope to find a
place in private schools for a short time in different sections of the
country.' Meanwhile he and Isherwood scraped a small temporary
living, chiefly from the liberal magazines. Auden went to the offices of
the *Nation* and asked if he could review books for them, to which they
agreed; and he made a similar arrangement with *New Republic* and
Common Sense. These magazines and several others also began to print
his poems. He sent typescripts of these new poems to Mrs Dodds in
England, asking her to pass them on to London editors. 'Will you sit on
the MSS. you think lousy,' he told her, 'and send the rest, if any, to
suitable periodicals.'

The new poems had, to use a phrase from one of them, an 'extraordinary mildness' about them, a feeling of calm after storm, which had indeed pervaded Auden's poetry ever since his decision the previous autumn that he would leave England. Several of them were, like many of the poems he had written in Brussels during the autumn and winter, concerned with the lives and characters of other writers, and their success or failure in finding a proper role for themselves. Two of the new poems, 'Matthew Arnold' and 'Voltaire at Ferney', were suggested by books on these men which Auden was reading for review, while the finest of them arose from the death in January 1939 of its subject, W. B. Yeats.

Yeats had been an important influence on Auden's poetic style during the 1930s, but Auden did not have an unmitigated admiration for him. An obituary article he wrote at the same time as the poem, which is cast in the form of a trial in a court of law – 'The Public v. the Late Mr William Butler Yeats' – has a prosecuting counsel delivering a number of hostile criticisms which are not altogether rebutted by the case for the defence. Yeats is accused of shutting his mind to the real issues and ideas of his age, and of neglecting 'scientific method' and preferring to interest himself in magic. By contrast the poem was scarcely critical of Yeats; in fact it was not really about him, but about the nature and function of poetry – and thus really about Auden himself.

The opening stanzas describe, in a dramatic account of Yeats's death, how at a poet's dissolution his work continues to live and be changed in the minds of his readers: 'The words of a dead man / Are modified in the guts of the living.' In the first version of the poem, published in the *New Republic* on 8 March 1939, this opening section was immediately followed by the stanzas beginning 'Earth, receive an honoured guest', which concluded the poem. But when the elegy next appeared in print, in the *London Mercury* in April, Auden had added a brief middle section. These new lines were the result of a crucial decision he had made in March.

Soon after he arrived in America, he was invited – just as he had been in England – to give several lectures and speeches of a political nature, and he accepted, despite the doubts he had begun to feel about whether this was his proper role. He travelled to the University of North Carolina and addressed the Human Relations Institute there on the topic of the European crisis, remarking that the U.S.A. was wise to adopt an isolationist foreign policy for the time being, but adding: 'We in England always like to think that we may be able to call on you for help in case we shall need it.' (This at any rate was how the *New York Times* reported the speech, though the phrase 'We in England' seems surprising in the circumstances.) He also spoke at a dinner in New York on 16 March which was held to raise money for refugees from the Spanish war. His speech on this occasion scarcely took a political line; its message was that democracy could be made an effective weapon against Fascism only if 'we personally behave like democrats in our private, as public lives' – in other words, private spiritual health was just as important as fair government. But the ending of the speech was certainly a piece of deliberate rhetoric:

> If we interpret brotherhood as meaning we must do nothing to hurt anybody's feelings, if we use our liberty of speech not to find out how best to do things, but to air our learning and show off our personalities. . . then it will not be long before we suffer a worse fate than that of Spain, worse because it will not be tragic. For it will not be Germany, it will not be Italy, but our own people who will say 'To hell with talk, to hell with truth, to hell with freedom,' will rise up and sweep us away, and by God, ladies and gentlemen, we shall deserve it.

This was too much for his conscience. A few months later he wrote to Mrs Dodds, with whom he was keeping up a regular correspondence, on the subject of what he called 'my change of heart' in the matter of politics: 'The real decision came after making a speech at a dinner in New York to get money for Spanish Refugees when I suddenly found I could really do it, that I could make a fighting demagogic speech and have the audience roaring. I felt just covered with dirt afterwards.' And he told her: 'Never, *never* again will I speak at a political meeting.'

This decision was reflected in the lines that he now added to his poem about Yeats. These lines point out that 'mad Ireland', which was the cause of Yeats becoming a poet, has remained completely unchanged by anything that he wrote: 'Ireland has her madness and her weather still, / For poetry makes nothing happen.' The poet cannot do anything that will change society.

In these lines, all Auden's attempts during the previous ten years to involve his poetry in politics and society were categorically rejected. He reiterated that rejection, in the words of the 'Counsel for the Defence', in his obituary article on Yeats, which was probably written at the same time as the new section of the poem: 'Art', he wrote, 'is a product of history, not a cause. . . so that the question of whether art should or should not be propaganda is unreal. . . If not a poem had been written, not a picture painted, not a bar of music composed, the history of man would be materially unchanged.' Auden was to repeat this, in similar words, again and again for the rest of his life.

This was the end of his involvement in politics. In a questionnaire about his beliefs which he set himself during the summer of 1939 he made it clear that, though his sympathies still remained left-wing, he now regarded conventional political activity as (at least for himself) quite fruitless. 'I believe Socialism to be right,' he wrote, 'but believe the theory and practice of revolution to be wrong in the sense that I do not believe it will conquer Fascism and establish Socialism. . . Of course it matters whether the Chinese win or the Japanese: of course the oppressed can improve their condition by successful revolt: but even if the Chinese lose, or the oppressed are suppressed, it does not mean the end of progress, only that its rate of development is slower. . . If war could have been avoided it would be better still. . . What is required of an individual is that he shall try to increase his knowledge of how to act effectively and try always not to act contrary to his knowledge. Only in that way is it possible to raise the average level of the mass and so to improve political action.'

At the beginning of April 1939, Auden and Isherwood left their hotel and moved to a cheap apartment which they rented on East 81st Street in the Yorkville district of Manhattan. Isherwood's boyfriend moved in with them. 'We're pretty busy,' Auden wrote to Mrs Dodds, 'but have no money.' On 6 April the two of them, together with Louis MacNeice, who was visiting America, gave a talk and poetry-reading to the League of American Writers under the title 'Modern Trends in English Poetry and Prose'. The programme was in fact a hotch-potch, with Auden and MacNeice simply reading their own poems and Isherwood talking mostly about the Chinese war. Auden's untidy appearance and 'Oxford' accent greatly amused some members of the audience, among them the twenty-two-year-old poet Harold Norse, then a student at Brooklyn College. 'The place was overheated,' recalled Norse. 'Somebody offered to open a window, and Auden screamed "Oh, I would LOVE that!" and we all broke up.' Norse and his neighbour, an eighteen-year-old blond-haired boy from the same college, named Chester Kallman, sat in a front row winking and smiling at Auden and Isherwood, who they knew were homosexuals. After the performance Norse and Kallman went on stage and asked if they could interview Auden, whose poetry they much admired, for their college magazine. Auden was offhand, but Isherwood behaved in a more friendly fashion and gave them the address of the Yorkville apartment. Two days later a call was paid, not by Norse but by Kallman. Auden was at first irritated, having apparently expected the visitor to be some other young man who had caught his eye in the poetry-reading – very possibly Norse himself. He muttered to Isherwood something about it being 'the wrong blond'. But during the course of Chester Kallman's visit he changed his mind.

A short time later, Kallman told Harold Norse: 'Wystan is in love with me.'

★

Chester Simon Kallman was fourteen years younger than Auden. He was born in New York on 7 January 1921, the son of Edward Kallman, a Manhattan dentist whose own parents were Latvian Jewish emigrés to the United States. Dr Kallman was quite well educated; besides studying dentistry at Columbia, he had taken literature courses, and he also had a taste for classical music. He encouraged Chester to play records on a wind-up phonograph when he was a small child; Chester cranked the handle so hard that he got blisters. At the age of two, before he could read, Chester knew the various records by sight from the marks on their labels.

Chester's mother Bertha had been brought up in a family that was much involved with Jewish theatre in New York; she had performed on the stage as a child, and had much of the actress in her, though before her marriage she had worked as a nurse. When Chester was four, she became pregnant again, and developed a blood clot. She was kept motionless in bed, but died of a coronary thrombosis. Many years later, Chester described her death in a poem:

> It takes ten days to kill a mother
> On a double bed.
> Only once, he remembers,
> Her one son visited.
>
> Blood, that feeds and drains the soul
> And shakes the wedding band,
> Served her heart with a dead object
> It could not keep in hand.

He idolised her memory for the rest of his life. 'Mothers', Auden once wrote to him, 'have much to do with your queerness and mine.'

His father soon married again, and after the second wife had given birth to a son she grew resentful of Chester and began to ill-treat him. This second marriage eventually broke up and was followed by a third, but again the wife had no affection for Chester. The boy was now spending much of his time with his paternal grandparents, who ran a restaurant in Coney Island. His grandmother, 'Bobby' Kallman, was much admired for her cooking, and Chester himself began as he grew up to learn something of her skill with food. He became very deeply attached to his aunt Sadie, who took the place of a mother for him; but she allowed him to depend too much on her, and he was bitterly pained when, in his eighth year, she got married and left is grandparents' house. 'She promised to marry *me*,' he told his grandmother.

As an adolescent, he was sent to Abraham Lincoln High School in Brooklyn, and then to Brooklyn College, where he majored in English literature. He helped to run the college literary magazine, and when Auden and Isherwood arrived in New York he determined, with his friend Harold Norse, to interview them.

He had been born with red hair, but it later became golden, and at eighteen years old, when he first met Auden, he was, in a friend's words, 'if not a beauty, then an intriguing good looker'. His eyes were violet-coloured, with dark shadows beneath them that seemed strangely dissipated in someone so young. His mouth was full and sensuous, and his face mobile and good at comic expressions. A friend of Auden observed that there was something about him that was both angelic and demonic.

He was remarkably well read and was not ashamed of expressing his own opinions. He annoyed Harold Norse by attacking Whitman, whom Norse admired; his own chosen models were Henry James, Proust and Flaubert. When he called at Auden and Isherwood's Yorkville apartment that day, he surprised Auden by recognising esoteric literary allusions in the conversation, and capping them with others. Largely as a result of this he was asked to call again.

He had certainly had affairs with girls, but also with boys, though he was not yet committed to homosexuality. His erotic interests were characterised by a highly romantic temperament; he liked to weave fantasies around lovers, especially if they were absent; a friend remarked: 'He loved you best if you were far away.' He was 'tarty' in manner, making eyes at likely people. Auden, who cheerfully accepted sex when it came his way, presumably responded readily to these advances. Moreover Chester was sexually 'well hung' which always appealed to Auden. Soon, as Chester told Harold Norse, he was indeed in love with the boy. He gave Chester a copy of Blake, inscribed with two lines from his own poem, written on the Mediterranean in 1938, 'O tell me the truth about love':

> When it comes, will it come without warning
> Just as I'm picking my nose?

That poem also included the quesion: 'Will it [i.e. love] alter my life altogether?' Now, in Chester's copy of *On This Island*, Auden wrote: 'To Chester / who told me the truth / (I was quite right; It did).'

A few weeks after meeting Chester, he wrote to Mrs Dodds in England: 'Of course I know that Love as a fever does not last, but for some years now I've known that the one thing I really needed was marriage, and I think I have enough experience and judgement to know that this relationship is going to be marriage with all its boredoms and rewards.'

Why should he have fallen in love with Chester Kallman? It was partly, as the remark to Mrs Dodds hinted, the unsatisfactory nature of most of the affairs he had had up to this time. There had been many sexual adventures, but, to use a phrase from Auden's later poem 'The Sea and the Mirror', few of these had been more than 'a quick cold clasp now and then in some *louche* hotel'. Certainly he had fallen in love during past years, but it had been – he now felt – with quite the wrong sort of person. At Oxford he had become enamoured of such people as Bill McElwee and Gabriel Carritt, who were physically tough, enjoyed sport, were outward-looking, and differed from him in almost every conceivable way. He was in fact seeking to attach himself to quite another world than his own; and those boys and young men with whom he had fallen in love during his schoolmastering years had mostly belonged to that world too. He wrote of this, in a 1938 article on A. E. Housman, whose predicament he clearly believed had been the same as his own: 'There are two worlds and you cannot belong to them both. If you belong to the second of these worlds [the world of the sensitive intellectual] you will be unhappy because you will always be in love with the first [the world of the athletic non-intellectual], while at the same time you will despise it. The first world on the other hand will not return your love because it is in its nature to love only itself. Socrates will always fall in love with Alcibiades; Alcibiades will only be a little flattered and rather puzzled.'

Auden's meeting with Chester Kallman showed him that this pattern could be broken, that he had been making the wrong choice. 'I've spent years', he told Mrs Dodds, 'believing that I could only love the world of the Alter Ego, but I was very foolish, because the w. of the A.E. doesnt respond. Now I realise that I wanted someone like myself.'

Chester was 'like' Auden in that he possessed an extremely quick mind. 'He is', Auden was sometimes known to remark, 'a far cleverer person than I am.' This was an exaggeration, but certainly Chester was highly able, sure of himself, and not at all hesitant about disagreeing with Auden. 'I think you overestimate *Winter's Tale,'* he wrote to Auden; 'it is certainly inferior to *The Tempest* – and I found most of *Pericles* maddening and vilely versified – especially the first two acts – after which it did, I admit, hit home. Perhaps the pastoral element in "W.T." alienated me, the "wonderful roguish" shepherds leave me a little cold.'

Quite apart from his literary enthusiasms, Chester's conversation was laced with a wit whose sharpness was largely the result of his Brooklyn Jewish background, a background which Auden found fascinating. 'It is in you, a Jew,' he wrote to Chester, 'that I, a Gentile, inheriting an O-so-genteel anti-semitism, have found my happiness.' Though Auden was brought up in a tolerant and liberal home he had certainly inherited the vague suspicion of Jews that was customary among the English middle classes, and his involvement with Chester had an element in it of breaking down old prejudice. A friend of Chester's noticed Auden's determination 'to absorb Chester: his middle class New York Jewish background – its jokes, its charm, its peculiar intolerances, its humorous sayings, even its food and its language. He never could, of course, but this background remained to Wystan a continual source of fascination, of mystery, and of desire.'

Of all these elements it was perhaps the jokes that Auden appreciated most. 'Among those whom I like or admire,' he once wrote, 'I can find no common denominator, but among those whom I love, I can: all of them make me laugh.' Chester was a connoisseur of 'camp' popular songs, and Auden began to learn fragments of them from him. He took to singing in a squeaky Brooklyn accent such lines as

> Take back your minks,
> Take back your poils,
> What makes you think
> I'm just one of dem goils?

His attraction to Chester was not, then, just a sexual one. Indeed it seems as if actual sex played only a small part in it even at the beginning. Their preferences in bed were different, Chester not sharing Auden's fondness for oral sex but being, to use Auden's term for A. E. Housman, an 'anal passive'. Auden's remarks on Oscar Wilde's relations with Lord Alfred Douglas could probably be applied with some accuracy to his own with Chester: 'It is clear that Wilde's infatuation for Bosie was not primarily a sexual one; one surmises that any sexual relations they may have had were infrequent and probably not very satisfactory.' What attracted Auden much more was the possibility of taking up Chester intellectually and moulding him, Pygmalion-fashion. Again, he was probably thinking of his own case when he talked of Shakespeare's relations with the young man in the Sonnets: 'He has selected someone at a stage of possibility. He wants to make an image so that the person will not be a dream but rather someone he knows as he knows his own interest. He wishes the other to have a free will yet his free will is to be the same as [his own].'

In actual fact in the early months of their relationship it was Chester who moulded Auden rather than the other way round, at least in one important respect. He introduced Auden to opera. Auden had been brought up, despite his enthusiasm for music, to be almost totally ignorant of opera – 'to think', as he put it, 'that opera was impossible'. This attitude was typical of his parents' generation in England, which believed, as he said, that 'the great Mozart operas might just do because Mozart was Mozart', but regarded Wagner and Verdi as vulgar and considered Rossini, Bellini and Donizetti to be 'simply beyond the pale'.[1] Auden had scarcely encountered opera before he came to New York. Now, Chester began to play him records of famous performances, and the two of them began to go regularly to the Metropolitan Opera House. Less than a year after meeting Chester, Auden wrote to a friend in England: 'My chief luxury is the opera.'

---

[1]John Auden comments on this: 'Maybe. But my mother and her sisters before their marriage went often to Bayreuth to hear Wagner.' It is also true that Mrs Auden taught Wystan the love-duet from *Tristan*.

He also told another friend: 'I've become a Wagner fan'; and he was soon writing an article describing Wagner as 'the greatest and most typical modern artist'. But he gave equal honours to Verdi and Mozart, calling them 'the top composers'; and he also admired Donizetti and Bellini – he liked to make the latter one of his tests of good taste, declaring: 'No gentleman can fail to admire Bellini.' Some of this may have been the result of real enthusiasm on his part; much of it was certainly a wish to share Chester's tastes – for example, he took over wholesale Chester's prejudice against Brahms. From Chester he also acquired a repertoire of anecdotes about prima donnas. All this had a 'camp' element about it that had been foreign to him up to this time; and he developed other small 'camp' mannerisms. Sometimes he signed notes to friends 'Auntie Whizz', or would sing the refrain of an Australian girls' school song: 'Who are we? Who are we? We are the girls!'

By the late spring of 1939, 'Chester, my chum', as Auden once called him,[1] had become the centre of his life. Chester himself was in turn deeply attached to Auden, not least because of his deep admiration for Auden's poetry – he called him 'the greatest English poet since Milton'. Auden, however, felt, at least at times, uncertain of Chester's feelings towards him. After they had known each other for a few weeks he wrote in a poem:

> . . . what reason have you to love me,
> Who have neither the prettiness and moisture of youth,
> > the appeal of the baby,
> The fencing wit of the old successful life,
> > Nor brutality's fascination? . . .
> Have you really the wish to endure the boredom of healing
> What without you will never get well?

But he was sufficiently certain that the relationship would endure to be telling his friends about it as early as May, only a month after he had met Chester. Already he was referring to it as 'marriage', was wearing a wedding ring, and was talking about going with Chester on a summer holiday that would be 'our honeymoon'. He also began to write a series of love-poems.

It is always dangerous to identify Auden's love-poetry too closely with one lover or set of circumstances, so much did he transmute his personal experiences before making them into verse. But he himself listed, in a letter to a friend in 1947, a number of poems which he said had grown out of what he called 'l'affaire C', his love for Chester. The earliest of these were 'The Prophets' ('Perhaps I alway knew what they were saying') and 'Not as that dream Napoleon', both written in the month after he met Chester. Both show the tremendous faith he had already put in Chester as a source of security:

[1]Cf. 'Derek my chum', a reference to his Helensburgh boyfriend, in *The Orators*.

> For now I have the answer from the face
> That never will go back into a book
> But asks for all my life, and is the Place
> Where all I touch is moved to an embrace,
> And there is no such thing as a vain look.

This is utterly different from Auden's love-poetry of the mid-1930s, where the recurrent note was infidelity and insecurity – 'Lay your sleeping head, my love, / Human on my faithless arm. . . / Certainty, fidelity / On the stroke of midnight pass.' In fact this insecurity had contributed to the poignancy of the earlier love-poems; by contrast, the 1939 love-poetry which Auden addressed to Chester was far less memorable. Nothing as remarkable as 'Lay your sleeping head' emerged from the new love-affair. Yet as an indication of Auden's feelings of trust and faith in Chester, the 1939 poems are revealing. A third poem, written in the autumn of that year, emphasises fidelity in its closing words: 'and we / The life-long day shall part no more.' And when in September 1939 Auden composed an epithalamium for the wedding of Erika Mann's sister Elizabeth, the poem was in fact also privately addressed to himself and Chester:

> May this bed of marriage be
> Symbol now of the rebirth
> Asked of old humanity:
> Let creative limbs explore
> All creation's pleasure then.[1]

And to Chester he wrote, in a verse-letter composed after they had been together for two years: 'You are to me, emotionally a mother, physically a father, and intellectually a son. . . I believe in your creative gift. . . I rely absolutely upon your critical judgement. . . With my body, I worship yours.'[2]

★

Chester did not move into Auden's apartment, but continued to live at home while studying at Brooklyn College; Auden was soon on friendly terms with Chester's father, whom he addressed in a letter as 'Nicest and Best of Dentists', and who raised few objections to his son's new

[1]Auden wrote another poem on the subject of marriage at some time during 1940, entitled 'In Sickness and in Health'. It was printed some years later with a dedication to his friends Maurice and Gwen Mandelbaum at Swarthmore College, but this dedication was made at the request of Mrs Mandelbaum, and post-dates the composition of the poem, which, though not in Auden's list of poems inspired by 'l'affaire C', undoubtedly refers to his and Chester's 'marriage'.

[2]The marriage service in the Church of England includes the words 'With my body I thee worship'.

friendship. Auden was still sharing his apartment with Isherwood, who was on the whole enthusiastic about Auden's new affair, and did what he could to promote it.[1] Nevertheless it was shortly after Auden met Kallman that he and Isherwood parted company.

Isherwood had in fact decided to leave New York with his own boyfriend, and travel across America by bus to California, partly in the hope of finding work in films, but largely because Gerald Heard was now living there. Heard, together with his fellow emigré Aldous Huxley, had begun to preach pacifism, and Isherwood, who wrote to Spender 'I have suddenly realised that I am a pacifist', wanted to be with him. He also had begun to feel privately that he was inadequate in New York, 'that Wystan was the dominant figure who was going to succeed there'. He and Auden collaborated on what was to be their last piece of writing together, an article for *Vogue* on 'Young British Writers On The Way Up'; and then, early in May, he left New York and began his journey west. He and Auden kept in touch and saw each other quite often in the years that followed, but their period of closeness was over. Isherwood's former role in Auden's life now belonged to Chester Kallman. Auden realised this when he dedicated his 1945 *Collected Poetry* jointly to Isherwood and Kallman.

Just as Isherwood was departing for California, Auden himself left New York for four weeks to be a guest teacher at St Mark's School, Southborough, Massachusetts. The poet Richard Eberhart, who was on the staff at the school, had read the *New York Times* interview in which Auden expressed an interest in teaching in private schools, and Eberhart proposed to his headmaster that Auden be invited to St Mark's. The school trustees were cautious, and one of them went to see Auden in New York to talk to him before it was finally decided to invite him to St Mark's for a month.

The result was, for Eberhart and the school, a lively four weeks. Auden visited all the classes and taught English to several of them on a regular basis. 'He employs very modern and obviously sensible methods,' noted Eberhart. 'For instance, instead of asking boys to paraphrase a quatrain of Gray's Elegy, he will excise key words, put in odd or nonsense words in their place, then ask the boys to hit the meaning of the original as nearly as they can by sensibility (they were too young to have known the poem), i.e. put in "right" words.' A pupil at St Mark's recalled that 'the first assignment he gave to our class was to write a story or essay in which every sentence contained a lie'.

[1]It is stated in the American edition of Jonathan Fryer's life of Isherwood that Isherwood disliked Chester Kallman from the outset, and that Auden said that this was because of anti-semitism, the reason he usually gave for any hostility shown to Chester by his friends. In a conversation with the present writer, Isherwood denies this, and says he liked Kallman and was not critical of Auden's choice of lover; though he agrees that in later years he sometimes found Kallman tiresome.

Eberhart was astonished by Auden's energy. 'He would make tea, or come in and grab this typewriter and dash off a poem on it (scandalously punctuated, but he would take advice, change pointing of lines here and there). . . or wolf his food at some faculty wife's dinner, his plate always empty before the maid ever got around the table – dear old Whizz.' Auden also alarmed Eberhart by a habit he had adopted, which itself was partly responsible for this energy. 'In the dining hall,' recalled Eberhart, 'on a Sunday morning, he placed a small, round, white pill at the top of my plate. I rejected it, saying I had no need of drugs. He said they gave him a lift of several hours every morning. It was benzedrine.'

Auden and Isherwood had acquired, during their first visit to New York in July 1938, a taste for benzedrine first thing in the morning, as an 'upper' to give them energy to start the day, and for seconal or some other sleeping-pill last thing at night as a 'downer'. Auden on his return to America had resumed this routine, and was indeed to continue it for the next twenty years or so. He called it 'the chemical life'.

He once argued in a letter to Stephen Spender that the drug routine was necessary to him because he was fundamentally a weak character, and must therefore build up an elaborate system of habits, 'the regime of an *invalid*'. It would probably be nearer the truth to say he liked drugs because they made him efficient – they produced instant activity when awake and instant sleep when in bed – and because, like food and sex, and (later in his life) drink, they were pleasant and might as well be used when available. Both his 'uppers' and his 'downers' were of equal importance to him. In several letters to New York friends written in later years when he was abroad for the summer, he asked for further supplies to be sent: 'S.O.S. repeat S.O.S. I must have left half my store of Bennies [benzedrine] in Paris. At any rate I shall run short. Could you possibly find means to procure a hundred (100) and air-mail them to me.'

Auden was not impressed by St Mark's School. 'It sets out to be the American Eton and no Jews are admitted,' he told Mrs Dodds. 'Some of the boys are so rich that they have to be taken home by a master at the end of term to prevent their being kidnapped. There is and can be no specialisation as the college board entrance exam which is about School Cert standard has to be taken at the end of their school career, and there aren't any scholarships because that would be undemocratic. "I don't want my boy to be top of the form," says the American parent (they really do), "I want him to be average." Result. A wonderful library and gramophone records etc. which no one uses. The boys nice but quite helpless. Two came in the other evening and asked how they were to get to know about poetry. When I said they'd better try reading some, they were quite surprised.' Some months after leaving St Mark's he wrote to T. C. Worsley, with whom he had written the pamphlet *Education Today – and Tomorrow,* that he thought the standard of education in America 'unbelievably low', adding: 'No one does any work or learns *anything.*'

He wrote several poems while at St Mark's. Richard Eberhart was greatly struck by his willingness to alter them as a result of criticism. 'He is very fluent in this way,' noted Eberhart, 'changes, revises, cuts, remakes at will.' One of these poems was an elegy on Ernst Toller, the left-wing German playwright whom Auden had met in Portugal in 1936 and who hanged himself in a New York hotel in mid-May 1939. Another poem, never collected and of a much more private nature, expressed his anxiety about leaving Chester in New York:

> . . . Now, when my work is over, I sit at the window,
> The senses huddled like cattle observing nothing,
> Or run to the lavatory; in the net of the ribs
>   The heart flails like a salmon.
>
> O but I was mad to come here, even for money;
> To put myself at the mercy of the postman and the daydream,
> That incorrigible nightmare in which you lie weeping or ill,
>   Or drowned in the arms of another;
>
> To have left you now, when I know what this warm May weather
> Does to the city: how it brings out the plump little girls and
> Truculent sailors into the parks and sets
>   The bowels of boys on fire. . .
>
>   O never leave me.
> Never. Only the closest attention of your mouth
>   Can make me worthy of loving.

Despite this anxiety, when he got back to New York in June all was well, and Chester was waiting for him. He stayed a few days at the George Washington Hotel (having given up the apartment he had shared with Isherwood), visited Thomas Mann and his family briefly at Princeton, where the Manns were now living, and then on 20 June left New York with Chester for their 'honeymoon', which was to be a journey by stages westward across America. The prospect of a European war now seemed strong, but Auden wrote to Mrs Dodds: 'I will have nothing to do with any of it till there *is* a war, then I shall join an American Red Cross Unit, and if America comes in, a neutral one, and if possible look after wounded Germans. Meanwhile art and the personal life.' As to the prospect of his 'honeymoon' and the life with Chester that seemed to be promised for the future, he wrote to John Lehmann: 'My heart is so full and I am so mad with happiness that I don't know what to do.' He also sent a letter to someone with whom he had not been in touch for a long time – John Layard. 'Dear John,' he wrote, 'Just a line to let you know that at last after all these years, Mr Right – yes it's still a mister, but it doesnt matter – has appeared. And my dear old lame shadow puts its arms round my neck and says "Thank you. You *have* been an old Bore, you know, but lets forget about that. Now I can fly back to Heaven where I belong. So long. Remember me to John Layard. I always liked that man." Love, Wystan. P.S. Given up biting my nails.'

★

He and Chester left New York by Greyhound bus and travelled first southwards, via Washington, Charleston, and Georgia, to New Orleans, where they sent Auden's brother John a postcard with the message 'honeymoon greetings'. Then they went west to New Mexico. 'We had a terrific 50 hour bus ride from New Orleans to Santa Fé,' Auden wrote to Chester's father. From Santa Fé they moved up to Taos and stayed a few days in a hotel. They had made arrangements to rent a house for a few weeks, but the house turned out to be no good – 'It was standing and that was about all,' Auden wrote to Dr Kallman on 5 July. 'The best room was inhabited by hens. However I've found a cabin up the mountains nearly 9000 ft up which is quite heavenly for the rest of July and then we move into one of Frieda Lawrence's [D. H. Lawrence's widow] houses about 2 miles out of town. We move up this afternoon with hams, wine, toilet paper etc. We went to see Frieda yesterday who you *must* meet. She is the original Earth-Mother. C got an attack of nose-bleeding due to the altitude and had to greet her from the ground.' He also wrote to Mrs Dodds: 'Up the road lives Frieda Lawrence who really is all one expected, and a chapel containing the ashes of D. H. which is rather creepy. Cars of women pilgrims go up every day to stand reverently there and wonder what it would have been like to sleep with him.'

Auden and Chester soon settled into their cabin. 'Here we are ensconced in a log cabin,' he told Mrs Dodds on 11 July, 'with the most wonderful view you can imagine over towards the mountains of Colorado, our horizon is about 300 miles long. It's very pioneer and you would laugh to see me rising at six a.m. to chop wood and draw water, and this life certainly brings home to me my lack of muscular co-ordination. Tell me, do you burn yourself much on the stove when you are cooking?'

During their weeks in the cabin, Auden worked at a piece of writing he had begun during the spring. Its form was largely modelled on Pascal's *Pensées,* and it also owed much to Blake. 'It is just a new Marriage of Heaven and Hell that I am doing', he explained to Mrs Dodds, and his title, 'The Prolific and the Devourer', was based on a quotation from Blake's book. The work was in fact a kind of catechism of his beliefs at this time. None of it was published during his life, but a typescript survives, and provides a remarkable picture of his mind at a period when his attitudes were beginning to undergo a very great change – the last, in fact, of many such changes that he experienced in his search for an ideology.

Part I of 'The Prolific and the Devourer' contains a repudiation of the notion that an artist should be involved in politics. The artist and the politician are characterised respectively in Blake's terms as the 'Prolific' who creates and the 'Devourer' who consumes. Auden then turns to his own recent history:

> Few of the artists who round about 1931 began to take up politics as an exciting new subject to write about, had the faintest idea what they were letting themselves in for. They have been carried along on a wave which is travelling too fast to let them think what they are doing or where they are going. But if they are neither to ruin themselves nor harm the political causes in which they believe, they must stop and consider their position again. Their follies of the last eight years will provide them with plenty of food for thought. . . As far as the course of political events is concerned they might just as well have done nothing. As regards their own work, a few have profited, but how few.

And he concludes this section of the book:

> Artists and politicians would get along better in a time of crisis like the present, if the latter would only realise that the political history of the world would have been the same if not a poem had been written, not a picture painted nor a bar of music composed.

Having disposed of politics, Auden turns to a subject which was now beginning to occupy his mind more and more: the question of religious belief.

'Nevertheless,' he begins Part II of his book, 'whoever you are, artist, scientist, or politician, there remains the problem of how you are to live. . . Let us start, like Pascal, with one observation and one assumption: That, on the whole, Man is more often unhappy than happy. That this unhappiness is unnatural: Man not only desires happiness but ought to be happy.' From this assumption, Auden then deduces that he must accept that 'there are laws which govern human life', and that 'for the most part we do not live according to these laws'. He has argued the existence of such laws on purely humanist and non-religious grounds. But he now says: 'Call them for convenience divine laws.'

In fact his argument now takes on a distinctly religious tone and phraseology:

> There are two and only two philosophies of life, the true and the false: all the apparently infinite varieties are varieties of the false. Or rather there is only the True Way and the false philosophies. For the Way cannot be codified as a philosophy: that would be to suppose that perfect knowledge of the whole of reality is possible, indeed that it is already known. The Way is only a way, the method we must adopt if we are to obtain any valid knowledge.

The falseness of these 'false philosophies' lies, he says, in their dualism: they are always based on a division into two parts of what is really a whole. This may be a theological dualism (God and Satan) or a meta-physical one (body and soul, energy and matter) or a political one (State and individual, bourgeoisie and proletariat). Against such dualism Auden asserts: 'That there are not "good" and "evil" existences. . . Everything that is is holy. . . Evil is not an existence but a state of disharmony between existences.'

He now turns to an examination of Christianity. First, he explains some of the principal items of Christian doctrine in humanist terms. 'Forgiveness of sins', he says, means showing the person who was in error the effect of his action. The 'Evil One' does not exist, but it is legitimate to speak of such a being because it describes our own state of mind at certain times. 'Hell' is a state of being which those who are in it could leave at any time and yet do not dare to; and so on. But what of Christianity itself?

All religions, Auden now declares, are attempts to identify and delineate the divine laws. These attempts are made more difficult because the divine laws themselves change as society changes: 'Human laws which were once a reasonably approximate reflection of the divine laws cease to be so.' All 'advanced' religions, as opposed to primitive, are trying to forecast the direction in which society is moving and to deduce what the divine laws will be in the future – in other words they are ahead of social change and are positing an ethic for an ideal society in the future, 'the kingdom of God'. We can judge the various religions, says Auden, by the accuracy of their predictions. And, he continues, 'Jesus convinces me that he was right because what he taught has become consistently more and more the necessary and natural attitude for man as society has developed the way it has, i.e. he forecast our historical evolution correctly. . . Epicureanism is only possible for the rich, Stoicism for the highly educated. Buddhism makes social life impossible: Confucianism is only applicable to village life: Mahommedism [sic] becomes corrupt in cities. . . [But] if we reject the Gospels, then we must reject modern life. Industrialism is only workable if we accept Jesus' view of life, and conversely his view of life is more workable under industrialism.' (He gives no explanation of this last point.)

All this is, of course, an attempt to accept Christianity on entirely secular, humanist, and non-supernatural terms. Indeed Auden declares that 'any religious teaching is, at bottom, prudent advice to the human race about how to be successful in the evolutionary struggle'. As to supernaturalism, he argues that Jesus' teaching was really quite devoid of it: 'Jesus took such care to avoid making any statement for or against survival after death and the existence of a supernatural world that one can only conclude that he considered this belief unimportant.' He explains the miracles of Jesus as being self-healings by the sick and insane combined with imperfections of knowledge in the observers. And his general conclusion is to judge supernaturalism to be, if not necessarily wrong, then at least irrelevant. 'There may or may not be a supernatural world,' he declares, but he says it would be wrong 'to think like Pascal that its existence or non-existence should make any difference to our life here'.

He now turns his attention, in Part III of 'The Prolific and the Devourer', to the Church, and judges it to have been mistaken in making a personal religion of the worship of Jesus – 'a false idol', he calls it. Then, in the fourth and final part of the book, he examines his own specific beliefs at this moment, and sets himself a series of questions.

'Do you believe in God?' he asks himself, and answers: 'If by God you mean a creator who is distinct from and independent of the creation, an omnipotent free-willing immaterial agent, no.' He is, however, prepared to use religious terminology as a convenient label for the various intellectual concepts of existence. 'If anyone chooses to call our knowledge of existence knowledge of God, to call Essence the Father, Form the Son, and Motion the Holy Ghost, I don't mind: nomenclature is purely a matter of convenience. . . But no religious dogma. . . can be anything but poetry. . . As to the supernatural: again, if you mean a world governed by laws which bear no relation to the laws we know, I don't believe in it. I only believe that our knowledge is limited but capable of extension.'

He dismisses both the Catholic and Protestant churches, and then declares that it has always been a weakness of organised Christianity that it has neglected techniques of private meditation. 'In the East there has always been a better tradition of private meditation. . . It is becoming more and more obvious that ordinary medicine, psychology, gymnastics and dietetics, Western Mysticism and Eastern Yoga are partial techniques with a common aim. It is therefore our task to synthesise these various pieces into a common ever-advancing technique.'

And then – quite suddenly – he asks himself if he has become a pacifist. The answer is, in effect, yes:

> Certainly my position forbids me to act as a combatant in any war. But if by pacifism you mean simply the refusal to bear arms, I have very little use for it. Nothing costs one less to do, for no one wants to do it. No social ostracism or imprisonment could possibly be as unpleasant as having to face a bayonet charge: personally I would rather face a firing squad. . . To think that it is enough to refuse to be a soldier and that one can behave as one chooses as a private citizen, is to be quite willing to cause a war but only unwilling to suffer the consequences.

He then asks himself if he is 'going to settle down to the cultivation of your garden and your own soul while the world perishes?', and answers 'no', declaring that 'there are a number of actions which are both non-violent and necessary'. These actions are, he says, those 'in which you unite thought and intention and treat others with love and as equals'. Such actions are 'making history and defeating Hitlers or rather making the world impossible for Hitlers. . . What those [actions] are you must decide for yourself. There will be violence and wars for many many years to come, and they will accomplish something, but you must leave their conduct to those who sincerely believe in them.'

★

At the beginning of August, Auden and Chester Kallman left New Mexico. 'Chester's heart, a legacy of rheumatic fever, didn't like the altitude,' Auden told Mrs Dodds. They travelled westwards by bus, Auden finding Arizona and Nevada 'quite astonishing: the mountains *really* look like those in fairy stories'. He also mentioned, in his letter to Mrs Dodds, his work on 'The Prolific and the Devourer': 'I've been hard at work on my pensées, and so have had no time to write poetry. I realise that if one does take up a pacifist position one has got to go in for spiritual exercises to make oneself genuine and effective, so I suppose I shall have to look for a yogic teacher or someone when I get back to New York. The trouble about Christians was that they separated the contemplative and the active life, so that the active never learnt technique. But, please dont tell a *soul* about this as everyone will giggle and think I've gone crazy.'

By 7 August he and Chester had reached California and were staying at Laguna Beach. 'It's lovely here,' Auden wrote to Chester's father,' full of flowers and palms like the Riviera, and good food though alas, lobsters have gone out of season. . . I've read my first detective story since I came to the States. C is getting quite a tan and I scribble away.'

At the end of the month he and Chester began their journey back to New York. Auden was still at work on 'The Prolific and the Devourer'. 'Done a lot of pensées,' he told Mrs Dodds, 'and a poem on Pascal which I will send you soon if nothing awful happens.' The Pascal poem surveyed its subject's life and concluded with an account of the 'night of fire', a religious experience which had profoundly changed Pascal's life and had preceded his writing of the *Pensées*.

The European crisis was now worsening; Ribbentrop had signed the pact with Stalin which made war virtually certain. 'There is a radio in this coach,' Auden wrote to Mrs Dodds while journeying back east on 29 August, 'so that every hour or so, one has a violent pain in one's stomach as the news comes on. By the time you get this, I suppose, we shall know one way or the other. . . The other day I burst into tears on hearing the news bulletin.' A few months later he recalled these days of crisis: 'Whenever I listened to the radio I started to cry. My attitude had changed [since the Munich crisis of the previous autumn] because the personal problem which in 1938 was still unsolved and which in despair I was looking to world events to solve for me, was solved this year.'

By 31 August he and Chester were back in New York. Auden waited for the expected news of the outbreak of war, and began to consider the implications of his new ideas.

2

Conversion

The Germans invaded Poland on the first day of September. Auden wrote a poem entitled 'September 1, 1939'.

> I sit in one of the dives
> On Fifty-Second Street
> Uncertain and afraid
> As the clever hopes expire
> Of a low dishonest decade:
> Waves of anger and fear
> Circulate over the bright
> And darkened lands of the earth,
> Obsessing our private lives;
> The unmentionable odour of death
> Offends the September night.

The poem was a restatement in verse of 'The Prolific and the Devourer'. It looked beyond the lights and music of the New York bar, beyond the 'blind skyscrapers' of Manhattan, to perceive that the human race was no more than 'Children afraid of the night / Who have never been happy or good'. And it concluded with Auden determining that his own role must be to 'Show an affirming flame ' and proclaim, in the words of 'The Prolific and the Devourer', that humanity can only save itself by performing acts 'in which you unite thought and intention and treat others with love and as equals':

> All I have is a voice
> To undo the folded lie,
> The romantic lie in the brain
> Of the sensual man-in-the-street
> And the lie of Authority
> Whose buildings grope the sky:

> There is no such thing as the State
> And no one exists alone;
> Hunger allows no choice
> To the citizen or the police;
> We must love one another or die.

The poem alluded to Nijinsky's remark in his diary: 'Some politicians are hypocrites like Diaghilev, who does not want universal love, but to be loved alone. I want universal love.' Auden told Mrs Dodds: 'The day war was declared I opened Nijinsky's diary at random (the one he wrote as he was going mad) and read "I want to cry but God orders me to go on writing. He does not want me to be idle." And write I do, hoping that it is not only a deceptive form of idleness.'

The poem's closing words were echoed in a book-review Auden wrote about two weeks later for one of New York magazines – as usual he was using reviews as an opportunity to conduct in public his own internal debate with himself. 'There is one way to the true knowledge and only one,' he wrote, 'a praxis which, if defined in terms of human relations, we should call love.' But there was still no question in his mind of this view becoming anything that could be called religious belief. In another review, published early in September, he suggested that belief in God as a conscious agent outside Man was 'dualist' and therefore wrong, and he again interpreted Christianity in strictly non-supernatural terms:

> Man is aware that his actions do not express his real nature. God is a term for what he imagines that nature to be. Thus man is always making God in his own image. In so far as Jesus was the first person to make the image correspond to the fact, he revealed God to man . . . 'My Father' [in the sayings of Jesus] is the real nature of man; 'I' his conscious awareness of that nature.

Meanwhile he worked some of the ideas from 'The Prolific and the Devourer' into a number of short poems. As to the book itself, he showed the typescript to several friends and sent a copy to Mrs Dodds, but he decided that he probably would not publish it, partly because, as he told Chester Kallman, he was now dissatisfied with its mandarin, superior tone of voice, and also perhaps because he already sensed that the book was not a conclusion to the change of opinion he had been undergoing, but was merely a stage along the way which he would soon leave behind.

★

He was once again staying at the George Washington Hotel. 'How are you? Where are you?' he wrote to Mrs Dodds early in September. 'Do write and tell me if you [are] alright. I understand the censorship in England is frightful now; we are fairly well informed here as to the war, but nobody I know has had any private letters from England, since it began. . . My own plans v. uncertain. . . Read Thucydides every day, and wish you were all here.'

Just as the first war news began to come through, he met an old friend who had recently arrived in New York, Benjamin Britten. Together with Peter Pears, Britten had crossed the Atlantic early in the summer of 1939 for a tour of Canada, after which they both came to New York. They, or at least Pears, intended to return to England at the end of August, but when war broke out they decided to stay at least for the time being. Britten was attracted by the idea of living in America; his music was getting only a mixed reception in England and he was not finding enough work there; he hoped for better things in the States. As to the war, he had strong inclinations towards pacifism. He was also influenced by Auden's decision to come to America, which seemed to him an example he could follow.

He and Pears were now staying with friends on Long Island. Pears had visited America in 1936, and on the boat going over he had met a German refugee, Elizabeth Mayer; she was bringing her children from Munich to join her husband, William Mayer, a Jewish psychiatrist who had already fled the Nazis and found a job in the U.S.A. Now that Pears was back in America he contacted the Mayers, who immediately made him and Britten welcome as long-term guests at Amityville on Long Island, where Dr Mayer worked for a clinic and lived with his family in a tiny cottage in its grounds. There were only two bedrooms, but the children were made to sleep downstairs, and Pears and Britten were given a room to themselves as well as unlimited use of the Bechstein grand piano; for Elizabeth Mayer loved to be surrounded by artists. She had held open house to musicians and painters in her Munich days, and now she gladly put the interests of her talented guests before those of her family. She was delighted when on 4 September Britten's friend Wystan Auden came to visit them.

This visit was the first of many, for Auden and Elizabeth Mayer quickly became the warmest of friends. She was in her fifty-sixth year, and both in appearance and manner she bore a striking resemblance to Auden's own mother – which was noted by Auden's brother John, who met her some time later. Her history was eventful: her own father had been chaplain to the Grand Duke of Mecklenburg, but from an early age she had tried to escape the formal, aristocratic atmosphere of her home, and had studied music at Stuttgart in the hope of becoming a concert pianist. She also distressed her family by calling off her engagement to a suitable young man and marrying Dr Mayer, a Jew, instead. Her marriage and the raising of a family ended her prospect of a musical career, but she transferred her ambitions to her children, who she hoped would become professional musicians. By 1939 it was apparent that this hope would not be fulfilled; so she now began to make Britten and Pears the focus of her hopes and enthusiasm. Her daughter Beata later commented: 'Ben and Peter were in a way the children she had always wanted to have.' Auden, too, was somebody she was glad to nurture. While the two musicians worked in one room he was given another in which to write – which he quickly filled with cigarette smoke – while Elizabeth Mayer brought him endless cups of tea. 'Dearest and Best of Fairy Godmothers', he called her in a letter, and in a poem he praised her 'learned peacefulness'. Not everyone who met her was so impressed; V. S. Yanovsky, who got to know Auden in the late 1940s and was introduced by him to Elizabeth Mayer, remarked that 'despite a certain undeniable charm [she] bored me to death. . . She behaved like a recognized celebrity, a *grande dame,* talked constantly, dropped names. . . I once asked Wystan, "What attracted you so much to her?" After some hesitation he said: "Das Ewig-Weibliche!" (the eternal Womanly).'

She became in fact much the sort of confidant that Mrs Dodds had been to him by letter in recent months; she provided him with the kind of female friendship which seemed to be an aspect of his homosexuality, and in which motherliness played a part. He was not, however, as frank with her about his sexual nature as he had been with Mrs Dodds, sensing perhaps that she would be shocked if he were to refer to it explicitly. She for her part was undoubtedly half aware of his and her musician guests sexual character, but she seems to have pushed it to the back of her mind. Meanwhile Chester Kallman began to accompany Auden on his visits to the Mayer home – the two of them were present at a birthday party for Britten on 22 November 1939 – but was privately not liked much by the Mayers, who found his Brooklyn manner jarring, and always hoped that Auden could arrive without him.

Auden and Britten began to plan another collaboration. The New York office of Britten's publishers Boosey & Hawkes suggested that he might write something for performance by American high schools, and he and Auden decided to start work on an operetta based on the American folk-legend of Paul Bunyan.

This fictitious frontier hero, the lumberjacks' equivalent of Davy Crockett, had been the subject of oral tales in the nineteenth century. These stories had now been collected and reshaped in several books, and Auden went to the New York Public Library and read them.[1] By the end of October 1939 he had begun work on the libretto. He told Mrs Dodds: 'I am hard at work on my Operetta which is rather fun.'

---

[1] Daniel Hoffman, in his book *Paul Bunyan,* shows that Auden's principal sources were books by Esther Shephard and James Stevens, both entitled *Paul Bunyan* and published in 1924 and 1925 repectively.

The hero of the traditional Paul Bunyan stories is a gigantic lumber-jack, vastly tall and with superhuman powers. Such a figure could not easily be put on to a stage, and Auden and Britten decided to make Bunyan an off-stage voice, speaking rather than singing, an invisible presence who would dominate the action of the operetta. Bunyan in fact becomes in Auden's hands the spirit or presiding genius of pioneer America, and the Bunyan legends are reconstructed, as Auden put it, into a parable of 'the development of the continent from a virgin forest. . . to settlement and cultivation'. The libretto was also concerned with Auden's own feelings about the prospect that life in America offered him.

The story is narrated by a ballad-singer, who describes in simple couplets the birth and childhood of Bunyan. The first act of the operetta, set in a clearing in the virgin forest, begins with Bunyan's voice declaring that this 'is America, but not yet'. He summons all 'disturbers of the public order. . . energetic madmen' to come and join him, and the pioneers duly arrive. Among them is Slim, a young man who falls in love with Paul Bunyan's daughter, Tiny, who is of normal size. In the second act, there is unrest among the men, and eventually the time comes for the pioneers to depart and give way to a more sophisticated society – 'the clerk. . . with his well-washed face. . . the architect with his sober plan'. *Paul Bunyan* concludes with a Christmas party at which it is announced that Slim, who will marry Tiny, has been appointed manager of 'a very large Hotel in Mid Manhattan'. Hel Helson will go to Washington to join the Administration 'As a leading man / In the Federal Plan / Of Public works for the nation', while Paul Bunyan's clerk Johnny Inkslinger is summoned by telegram to Hollywood to be 'Technical Adviser. . . for an all-star lumber picture'. Last of all Paul himself describes the new challenge of industrialised America, in words which reflect Auden's own reasons for choosing to live in the U.S.A.:

> The pattern is already clear
> That machinery imposes
> On you as the frontier closes,
> Gone the natural disciplines
> And the life of choice begins. . .
> America's destroyed and recreated, America is what you do,
> America is you and I, America is what you choose to make it.

The libretto of *Paul Bunyan* is as exuberant and undisciplined as were Auden's early attempts at writing plays. Like them it sets doggerel alongside fine lyric poetry, so that its style ranges from lines like 'It's all right, Hel, you're not dead, / You are lying in your bed' to this lyric, sung in celebration of Tiny's betrothal to Slim:

Carry her over the water,
  And set her down under the tree,
Where the culvers white all day and night,
  And the winds from every quarter,
Sing agreeably, agreeably, agreeably of love.

Auden himself remarked some years later that at the time he was writing
Paul Bunyan he 'knew nothing. . .[of] what is required of a librettist'; and
certainly his new enthusiasm for going to the opera with Chester
Kallman had not yet taught him the discipline demanded by the medium.
But Britten was delighted with the libretto. 'What a breath of fresh air
that stuff of Wystan's seems', he wrote to Elizabeth Mayer while he was
briefly away from her home and was working on the score. The music
that he composed for it reflected the stylistic mixture of the libretto: it
ranged from grand-opera choruses accompanied by full symphony
orchestra to 'Country and Western' settings for the ballad-singer, using a
small group with guitar.

A great deal of the opera had been written by February 1940, but Britten
was by then ill with a recurrent streptococcal infection. Auden characteristically suggested that this might be psychosomatic, the result of the
indecision Britten was now feeling about staying permanently in the
U.S.A. 'I do hope, Ben dear,' he wrote to him, 'that you are recovering
and that your illness was the pangs of rebirth and not simply an outraged
cry of homesickness.' By this time Columbia University's music department had agreed to stage the première of the opera, but were complaining
that it was too difficult. Britten, however, continued to be unwell and
apparently stopped working on the score for several months, so that no
date for a production was yet arranged.

About three weeks after returning from his 'honeymoon' with Chester,
Auden left his hotel and moved once again into an apartment, this time in
Brooklyn Heights, where he rented an upper floor of 1 Montague
Terrace, a house with a view straight across the East River to Manhattan.
'This house', he told Mrs Dodds on 27 October, 'has the most beautiful
view in New York: looking out over water at the towers of Manhattan.
The skyscrapers with the exception of Radio City which is one of the
architectural wonders of the world, are ugly close to but lovely from a
distance.' He was short of money – he wrote to the Oxford University
Press asking for a further sum on account for the *Oxford Book of Light
Verse* – but he continued to make small amounts from reviewing.
Meanwhile Random House accepted a new book of his poems, to be
published in the spring of 1940. 'I've just done the proofs,' he told Mrs
Dodds on 26 November 1939, 'and *How* I wished you were here to do
them for me. I haven't sent Faber the manuscript yet. Do you think I
ought to give my English royalties to the Red Cross for the duration? At
the moment there dont seem to be many wounded, but one never knows

when it will start.' He lent some money to William Empson, who was returning to England from the Far East via the U.S.A. and had been robbed, so that he could not pay his fare home. Empson recalled of Auden's kindness: 'When you consider that all money from England was frozen, and he was certain that I could not repay him, his behaviour should be recognized as noble.' (Empson did in fact manage to repay Auden before leaving.) Auden was also beginning to lend money to Chester Kallman – in effect to give it, for Chester was extravagant and was perfectly happy to make use of anything that came his way. Auden some-times lectured him on his carelessness with money, but to little effect.

Chester was now back at Brooklyn College, but he came to Auden's apartment every afternoon when he had finished classes, and spent much of his weekends with Auden too. 'It is a lovely cold Sunday afternoon,' Auden wrote to Mrs Dodds late in November 1939. 'Chester is reading *Measure for Measure*; the radio is playing the St Matthew Passion, and the tugs go backwards and forwards in the bay.'

On weekdays Auden observed a strict routine. 'I rise at six thirty and work more or less till four,' he told T. C. Worsley. He took his lunch in a cafeteria, where he also liked to sit writing for an hour or two during the morning if there was no music playing on the juke box; for the rest of the time he worked in his apartment, generally with the curtains drawn. He was in fact beginning to become obsessive about his timetable. Certain hours were fixed for writing, certain hours for reading, certain points of the day for eating, and certain times for receiving his friends or going out. Interruptions of this schedule were treated with ill-concealed irritation, and friends quickly learnt not to bother him except at the permitted hours. The clock governed him, rather than his natural appetites; once when a joker set its hands back two hours he worked through his lunch-time without being at all aware of hunger. As to the notion of working, like some writers, far into the small hours, he dismissed it with more than contempt: 'Only the Hitlers of the world work at night; no honest artist does.'

He described himself as an example of 'Punctual Man', the type who defends himself against the onslaught of the modern world by strict attention to the clock – a type who, he said, is in effect a modern Stoic, for such a person realises that 'the surest way to discipline passion is to discipline time: decide what you want or ought to do during the day, then always do it at exactly the same moment every day, and passion will give you no trouble'. Elsewhere he wrote: 'To achieve anything today, an artist has to develop a conscious strictness in respect of time which in former ages might have seemed neurotic and selfish, for he must never forget that he is living in a state of siege.' He himself was immensely well organized – 'too much so', suggested one of his friends, 'as if afraid of losing direction'. Yet his insistence on routine apparently helped him to sustain his huge output of work over the years.

By the end of 1939 he was having a regular flow of new poems published in American periodicals. His friend George Davis, who had welcomed him and Isherwood to New York in 1938, accepted a Christmas ode for *Harper's Bazaar* ('Around the three actors in any blessed event') and the *Kenyon Review* printed his elegy on Sigmund Freud, who had just died. This elegy was in syllabic metre – that is, the length of each line was determined by a given number of syllables rather than by feet. Auden learnt this technique from Marianne Moore, whose poetry he had known for some years but which he was only now coming to admire. Miss Moore herself, who lived in New York and whom Auden soon got to know, was described by him as 'one of the nicest people I have ever met. She looks the perfect maiden aunt.'

Besides writing, he was also undertaking more teaching, having been asked to conduct an evening class in poetry for the League of American Writers during their fall term. The class, held by this left-wing organisation at 381 Fourth Avenue on Monday evenings, proved a success, with twenty-six people signing on, the largest attendance the League had ever known. Auden told Mrs Dodds he was enjoying it, but added that there were too many pupils for comfort – 'Compared with children, they need so much more coaxing to get anything out of them. I never realised before how shy and nervy adults are.' The class helped for the time being to provide him with an answer to the question of what his own work, other than writing, ought to be. 'It isnt that I think one shouldnt do any "social" work,' he wrote to Mrs Dodds, 'but one must do something that is in one's nature to do, and for me that means "teaching".'

By undertaking paid work he was violating the terms of his entry visa into the U.S.A., and indeed he had already done so by teaching at St Mark's School the previous spring. On his return to New York from his 'honeymoon' he found a letter from the immigration authorities ordering him out of the country because of this violation. The letter had not been forwarded to him, and the date by which he was supposed to leave had already passed. His New York publishers Random House, when they learnt of this, put him in touch with a Federal official named Walter Louchheim, whose wife Katie was a poet; and during September, Auden flew to Washington to stay with the Louchheims and be coached by them for a private and unofficial interview with James Houghteling, Commissioner of Immigration and a cousin of Roosevelt, whom he duly saw. No record of the interview with Houghteling survives, but it seems that Auden did as he was advised by the Louchheims, telling Houghteling that he had not been paid for teaching at St Mark's, and had merely received room and board. Auden afterwards wrote a poem for the Louchheims with the refrain 'The truth is not the proper thing to tell.' It appears that Houghteling managed to delay any official action about the violation and the order to leave the U.S.A., on the understanding that Auden would go to Canada and then return across the border as part of the regular quota of British immigrants. This Auden did, on 24 November 1939, re-entering the U.S.A. from Montreal 'as a British immigrant under a non-preference quota No. 4201'.

'Just got back from Canada', he wrote to Mrs Dodds on 26 November, 'where I had to go in order to start becoming American. . . In the course of my medical examination I had to take down my trousers to show that I hadn't any sociable disease: the doctor was very surprised because I dont wear underclothes and the following dialogue took place: Doc: What's your job? Me: I'm an author. Doc: O I see: nudist, eh?' Although he was now allowed to take paid employment in America he was still not a United States citizen. If asked his nationality during this period he would answer: 'I am a New Yorker.'

His letters to Mrs Dodds suggest that he was now uncertain what attitude to take about the war. 'We are very isolationist,' he wrote to her late in 1939, describing the American attitude to its progress, 'and some think it a shame that so few people have been killed yet and say its not a proper war at all. But for me it is a great relief every morning to find that Hitler hasnt started trying that day.' He told her he was hoping to get his German exile friends to produce 'some material which we might distribute' – presumably anti-Hitler propaganda designed to encourage America to enter the war, or at least to sympathise with the British cause – 'but it is a difficult job,' he added. 'The efforts I have seen so far are either so statistical that no one would read them or so bitter that they would only have the opposite effect from what they intend.'

Meanwhile, and somewhat contradictorily, he carried out his resolve from the previous summer to undergo some sort of 'spiritual exercises' which might help him 'take up a pacifist position'. Or rather, he decided first to join the gymnastic classes which were being given in an apartment on East 68th Street by a friend of his, Tania Stern, whom he had first met with her husband James in Paris in 1937. The Sterns had left France shortly before the war and come to New York, where they were scraping a living, he from his short stories and she from her classes. She taught relaxation and breathing-exercises with the intention of making her pupils more aware of their bodies. 'I haven't started Yogi yet', Auden told Mrs Dodds, 'but am doing a preparatory course of physical exercises with a German girl; *most* painful, but illuminating.'

Tania Stern soon found that Auden, though a keen pupil, was too clumsy and impatient to benefit from what she had to teach; she felt that he was dismissing his body as quite unimportant to him. She also observed that he seemed to have no tactile sense whatever: his fingers were stubby and unfeeling – he was still biting his nails, despite what he had told John Layard – and his feet were flat-footed and clumsy – a cause of his corns, which now often pained him badly, with the result that he wore slippers more and more whenever he had the opportunity. But he continued to attend the classes, bringing Chester Kallman with him, and was always attentive, treating the proceedings with great seriousness; he became very fond of Tania Stern, and was perhaps for a time almost in love with her.

He was now thoroughly settled in New York. It was not that he had any delusions about the country he had chosen to live in; he remarked of the American climate with its extremes of heat and cold: 'Nature never intended human beings to live here.' And in an article written a few years after arriving in America he noted, among features of the American scene, 'the unspeakable juke-boxes. . . the insane salads. . . the anonymous countryside littered with heterogeneous *dreck* and the synonymous cities besotted with electric signs'. He sometimes admitted to being homesick for the English landscape. As to American literature, he told a friend he thought it 'not very good', and he noted that 'the first feature that strikes a European about characters in American fiction. . . is their extreme loneliness'. Yet he was entirely happy.

He wrote to Margaret Gardiner: 'I never wish to see England again. All I want is, when this is over, for all of you to come over here.' And he told her: 'For the first time I am leading a life which remotely approximates to the way I think I ought to live.'

Two months after the outbreak of war, in November 1939, he went to a cinema in Yorkville, the district of Manhattan where he and Isherwood had lived for a few weeks in the spring. It was largely a German-speaking area, and the film he saw was *Sieg im Poland,* an account by the Nazis of their conquest of Poland. When Poles appeared on the screen he was startled to hear a number of people in the audience scream 'Kill them!' He later said of this: 'I wondered then, why I reacted as I did against this denial of every humanistic value. The answer brought me back to the church.'

★

He had been through many changes of heart since reaching adulthood, but all the dogmas he had adopted or played with – post-Freudian psychology, Marxism, and the liberal-socialist-democratic outlook that had been his final political stance before leaving England – had one thing in common: they were all based on a belief in the natural goodness of man. They all claimed that if one specific evil were removed, be it sexual repression, the domination of the proletariat by the bourgeoisie, or Fascism, then humanity would be happy and unrest would cease. Even the viewpoint which Auden had reached in the summer of 1939 during his 'honeymoon', a viewpoint (expressed in 'The Prolific and the Devourer') which might be called liberal humanism with religious and pacifist overtones, was still based on a belief in man's natural goodness. Its message was, in the words of the poem which summed it up, 'We must love one another or die': that is, only the exercise of love between

human beings would save humanity from self-destruction. The implication was that if humanity followed this precept and so obeyed a 'divine
law' it *could* save itself, being fundamentally good. Auden's experience in
the Yorkville cinema in November 1939 radically shook this belief. He
now became convinced that human nature was not and never could be
good. The behaviour of those members of the audience who shouted
'Kill them!' was indeed, as he said, 'a denial of every humanistic value'.

In the weeks that followed this experience he considered its implications. It was not just a question of shattered optimism: the whole
ground of his outlook had shifted beneath his feet. If humanity were not
innately good, then on what basis could he legitimately object to the
murderous shouts of the Germans in that cinema audience, or indeed to
the behaviour of Hitler himself? Were not the Nazis merely being true to
their own nature, to all our natures? What reason could he give for his
strong, instinctive, ineradicable hatred of the Nazis and all that they
stood for? He had to find some new objective ground from which to
argue against Hitler. 'There had', as he put it, 'to be some reason why
[Hitler] was utterly wrong.'

Auden began to remark to his friends on this desperate need for
objective criteria from which to oppose Hitler: 'The English intellectuals
who now cry to Heaven against the evil incarnated in Hitler have no
Heaven to cry to,' he told Erika Mann's brother Golo; 'they have
nothing to offer and their prospects echo in empty space.' It seemed
utterly clear to him now that liberalism had a fatal flaw in it.

'The whole trend of liberal thought', he wrote during 1940, 'has been
to undermine faith in the absolute. . . It has tried to make reason the
judge. . . But since life is a changing process. . . the attempt to find a
humanistic basis for keeping a promise, works logically with the conclusion, "I can break it whenever I feel it convenient." ' He was now
certain that he must renew that 'faith in the absolute' which appeared to
him to be the only possible ground for moral judgement. As he put it in a
poem written a short time after visiting the Yorkville cinema:

> Either we serve the Unconditional
> Or some Hitlerian monster will supply
> An iron convention to do evil by.

So it was that he now began a search for, in the words of this same
poem, 'the vision that objectifies'. He began to read some books of
theology.

★

It seems that the first theological work that he studied was *The Descent of
the Dove,* the latest book by Charles Williams. Auden had not been in

contact again with Williams since their two brief meetings in the summer of 1937 during the negotiations about the *Oxford Book of Light Verse,* nor had he previously read anything by him; but he was deeply impressed by the new book.

Williams was, both as a man and a writer, utterly different from Auden: highly romantic, not easily sympathetic to modern poetry, fond of ritual, ornate in his style, and with a taste not unlike Yeats's for magic and neo-magical practices. Yet he resembled Auden in certain important respects. Like Auden his intellectual life was largely a search for synthesis and order, an attempt to find the formulas which would express and interpret the whole of human existence. And like Auden he rejected nothing in his search for this synthesis; all facets of human life were of equal value and importance to him. Auden therefore found in *The Descent of the Dove* a mind which, though it often expressed itself with ritualistic richness, was in some ways remarkably similar to his own.

Williams's book was subtitled 'A Short History of the Holy Spirit in the Church'; it was in fact a historical account of Christendom from its beginning to the present age. Its argument was based on a view which Auden himself had reached the previous summer: that, in Auden's own words in 'The Prolific and the Devourer', 'There are not "good" and "evil" existences. . . [but] everything that is is holy'; that 'no existence is without relation to and influence upon all other existences'. This was exactly Williams's view; he gave to it a name of his own devising, 'co-inherence'.

> All mankind [Williams wrote] is held together by its web of existence. . . The co-inherence reaches back to the beginning as it stretches on to the end. . . Whatever ages of time lay between us and Adam, yet we were in him and we were he.

Williams saw the whole of history as an interrelated web of cause and effect, and his book argued that all events, whether they seemed good or evil at the time, were in fact the working of God:

> The history of Christendom is the history of an operation. It is the operation of the Holy Ghost. . . Our causes are concealed, and mankind becomes to us a mass of contending unrelated effects. It is the effort to relate the effects conveniently without touching, without (often) understanding, the causes that makes life difficult. The Church is . . . the exhibition and correction of all causes.

In other words the Church reveals the divine purpose behind history. And, said Williams, the Incarnation of Christ 'reconciled the natural world with the world of the kingdom of heaven' – that is, reconciled humanity with the divine purpose itself.

Early in 1940 Auden wrote a letter to Williams. 'He said', Williams told his wife, 'he just wanted to tell me how moved he was by the *Dove* (and he no Christian) and he was sending me his new book [his new selection of poems, *Another Time*] "as a poor return". He adds that he was reminded once again "of a curious fact that though I've only met you twice, in times of difficulty and doubt recalling you has been of great help to me" '. Auden wrote again to Williams a few months later, this time telling him that 'one day the *Dove* will be honoured for the great book it is'.

Six pages of *The Descent of the Dove* are taken up with an acount of the ideas of a Christian thinker whose works Auden had apparently not yet read, but which he now quickly began to study, very probably as a result of the passage about them in Williams's book. This was Søren Kierkegaard. On 11 March 1940 Auden wrote to E. R. Dodds: 'Am reading Kierkegaard's Journal at the moment which is fascinating. ' Soon he had studied the greater part of Kierkegaard's writings, and, as he later put it to a friend, they 'knocked the conceit' out of him. He was, he said, 'bowled over by their originality. . . and by the sharpness of their insights'.

Again, as with Williams's book, he must in a sense have recognised himself in Kierkegaard's writings, for Kierkegaard's early intellectual development bore a marked resemblance to his own. Kierkegaard had, like Auden, been brought up in the Church by one parent especially, in his case his father; and like Auden he had a very ambiguous attitude towards that parent. He felt that his childhood had been responsible for his neurosis, and compared himself to a ship that had sustained damage at its launching. He also believed that there could be no such thing as 'inherited' Christianity; each individual must rediscover his religious beliefs for himself. And he argued that this was likely to happen in three stages or categories of experience – stages which exactly corresponded to those that Auden had been through in the past fifteen years.

Kierkegaard's first stage of experience was the 'aesthetic', in which the individual lives merely for the joys of the present moment – much as Auden had done in his largely amoral days as an undergraduate. This, said Kierkegaard, would soon prove inadequate and would offer the individual the choice of moving into a higher, 'ethical' stage. If he took that choice, this 'ethical' stage would be one in which he made moral judgements and abided by them – much as Auden had tried to do during the years in which he interested himself in politics and the crises of society. But, declared Kierkegaard, this 'ethical' state would soon in its turn prove inadequate, because it made no claims on any transcendent notion of eternity, and because its foundation, a belief in the individual's (or humanity's) basic righteousness would soon prove false – which was precisely what Auden had just realised. In consequence, Kierkegaard argued, a new decision becomes necessary. The individual must either abandon himself to despair, or must throw himself entirely on the mercy of God.

If he accepts the latter choice, he enters at last a 'religious' state in which he is 'alone with his guilt before God' – though in doing so he 'finally chooses *himself* and his relation to the Origin of his self'. This final step can be made not by logical reasoning, but only by faith. Indeed it is not a step at all, but a leap – 'a leap into the void, a total surrender to God in which Man abandons any foothold and in an ultimate choice realizes his freedom'. Nor can this choice, once made, be shaken: 'By a leap, faith takes man beyond all rational thought into a new world.'

While Auden was reading Williams and Kierkegaard, late in 1939 and early in 1940, he was beginning, for the first time since adolescence, to go now and then to church, though only (as he put it) 'in a tentative and experimental sort of way'. He was also starting a long poem which was to give expression to the ideas now occupying his mind.

★

He spent part of Christmas 1939 with the Mayers on Long Island, and on New Year's Day 1940 he wrote a note to Elizabeth Mayer:

1.1.40
                          1 Montague Terrace, Brooklyn Heights, NYC
Dear Elizabeth,
   The breakfast symphony hour is on, a Haydn to-day, Manhattan is defying the new year, and I want to wish you a very rich 1940.
   1939 was a very decisive year for me and one of its most important events was meeting you. I'm not going to say you cant imagine what peace and joy you give to me every time, because you know it very well; how you would have delighted Goethe and shocked Baudelaire who expected La Femme to be 'naturally c'est-à-dire abominable'. . .
   I must stop now and do a dreary chore of a review, when I want to start my poem to you.
                          Much love, my dear
                          Wystan.

The poem was soon under way. It was addressed to Elizabeth Mayer, and was entitled 'New Year Letter'.

   It consisted largely of a reworking of the ideas Auden had expressed in 'The Prolific and the Devourer'. But those ideas were now enriched and extended by his recent reading – he said that *The Descent of the Dove* was 'the source of many ideas in the poem' – and the conclusion he reached in it was markedly different from that in the prose work.

   Part I of 'New Year Letter' is chiefly concerned, like the first section of 'The Prolific and the Devourer', with the artist's role in society. Auden declares bluntly: 'No words men write can stop the war.' Art must not try to be 'a midwife to society'. Yet, though he is to avoid direct involvement in social issues, the artist is nevertheless called upon to 'set in order', to organise our perceptions of the world; and as such the artist's is 'the greatest of vocations', a calling which lays its practitioners constantly open to the judgement not just of their contemporaries but of the whole tradition of artists who have preceded them. Auden here pictures a tribunal of his chosen masters: Blake, Voltaire, Hardy, Rilke and others, including Dryden, upon whose style the poem is largely modelled. Then in Part II he turns to the present crisis, a world war which has ended a 'scrambling decade'; and he considers, just as he had in the second and subsequent parts of 'The Prolific and the Devourer', the question of how humanity is to discover the eternal truths or 'divine laws' which govern existence.

He does this chiefly through a consideration of untruths, which he personifies as 'the Prince of lies', the Devil who lures us from our proper path – and who in doing so actually shows us what that proper path is. Auden probably took this idea from Charles Williams, who was always emphasising that 'the Devil' is merely the working-out of God's purpose in an oblique fashion. Now, Auden considers the various untruths to which his generation has subscribed, among them the dogma of D. H. Lawrence with its call to men to 'throw away intelligence'; and also the Marxist teaching on account of which 'we waited for the day / The State would wither clean away, / Expecting the Millennium / That theory promised us would come'. These and other half-truths to which he and his contemporaries had listened only demonstrate (he says) that all human law is imperfect, and the eternal truth constantly eludes humanity's grasp. Yet these half-truths are not entirely lies, and we can draw something of value out of them if we employ 'the gift of double focus'.

This last image, which concludes Part II of 'New Year Letter', is not adequately explained by Auden in its context. But he did expound the idea clearly, in a review of biography of Abraham Lincoln, written while he was at work on the poem. 'The one infallible symptom of greatness', he wrote, 'is the capacity for double focus. [Great men] know that all absolutes are heretical[1] but that one can only act in a given circumstance by assuming one. . . They are sceptical about human nature but not despairing; they know that they are weak but not helpless: perfection is impossible but one can be or do better or worse.'

Having reached a note of cautious optimism, Auden brings his poem back to the New Year theme. Part III opens with the view of the New Year festivities seen from his window in Brooklyn Heights:

---

[1]Auden means, of course, all *human* absolutes, rather than the divine Absolute for which he was searching during this period.

> Across East River in the night
> Manhattan is ablaze with light.
> No shadow dares to criticize
> The popular festivities,
> Hard liquor causes everywhere
> A general *détente,* and Care
> For this state function of Good Will
> Is diplomatically ill:
> The Old Year dies a noisy death.

He then recalls the hours he spent at Christmas in the Mayer household on Long Island – 'Our privileged community', he calls it, membership of which has given him an experience of perfection, harmony and love. Such an experience happens every day to someone, but it cannot be permanent, and our natural state (says Auden) is the perpetual purgatory-like struggle of living, in which we must try to 'serve mankind's *imperium*'. But how is this to be done? 'How', Auden asks, 'to be the patriots of the Now?'

He reached this part of 'New Year Letter' by the end of February 1940. 'Your poem creeps along', he wrote to Elizabeth Mayer, 'but versified metaphysical argument is very difficult.' And he told Mrs Dodds that he was 'writing a longish philosophical poem in octosyllabic couplets. So far I've done about 1100 lines. Will send as soon as finished. At the moment it seems quite good but I dont know if anyone will have the patience to read it.' Meanwhile he entered into a correspondence with E. R. Dodds on the subject with which the closing passage of the poem was chiefly concerned: his own reasons for deciding to remain in America.

When Auden and Isherwood sailed from England in January 1939, such newspapers as took note of their departure reported that they were going to America to lecture, and to see about the possibility of staging *On the Frontier* there – the implication being that the visit was only temporary. But a year later, when the war was four months old, it became plain to Auden's friends that he had no plans to return. E. R. Dodds discussed the matter with Auden's parents, and apparently remarked that he thought it a pity that Wystan had made his decision, for Dr Auden replied: 'We both fully agree about Wystan and U.S.A. You may remember how at first he felt that U.S.A. stood for a negation of all his convictions.' Dodds also raised the subject, by correspondence, with Auden himself, and on 16 January 1940 Auden wrote Dodds a long letter about it.

'For the past ten years', he told Dodds, 'we have all been talking about the isolation of the artist from the community, the dangers of ivory-towerism, the importance of roots. I am now quite certain that 90% of what we said was bosh'. He told Dodds he now realised that everyone was isolated: the Machine Age had destroyed all sense of community; the village had been replaced by the factory. The old notion of people having 'roots', of their belonging to one place, no longer meant anything:

> You may speak of England as roots, but after all what is my England? My childhood and my English friends. The England of 13 Court Oak Rd Harborne [the house in which his parents now lived] is a completely foreign country to the England of 12 Court Oak Rd and vice versa. The ice-cream soda jerker is every bit as isolated as the highbrow artist.

This fact, he argued, had not yet been perceived in Europe. Society in European countries was in fact rootless and community-less, but people had not faced up to this fact and were still pretending that the old way of life existed. On the other hand America did not make any such pretence. 'Here', he told Dodds, 'it is impossible to deceive oneself.' And this was the reason why he wanted to stay in America:

> Its a terrifying place and I daresay I'm no tougher than the rest, but to attempt the more difficult seems to me the only thing worth while. At least I know what I am trying to do, which most American writers don't, which is to live deliberately without roots. I would put it like this. America may break one completely, but the best of which one is capable is more likely to be drawn out of one here than anywhere else.

He echoed these words in the closing passage of 'New Year Letter', arguing that America's virtue is its honesty in admitting that 'Aloneness is man's real condition':

> More even than in Europe, here
> The choice of patterns is made clear
> Which the machine imposes, what
> Is possible and what is not.
> To what conditions we must bow
> In building the Just City now.

Some time later, he said the same thing more bluntly in a letter to Naomi Mitchison: 'I like it here just because it is the Great Void where you have to balance without handholds.'

Dodds received Auden's letter in February 1940. He was sceptical, and suggested that Auden might be deceiving himself. He told Auden he thought village life did still exist, despite an industrialised society. Auden replied early in March by sending Dodds a questionnaire he had set himself about is reasons for remaining in America. While not contradicting his earlier argument, this letter-questionnaire was much more candid. Auden in fact now admitted that his chief reason for wanting to stay in America was Chester Kallman:

> *War or no war, do you want to stay in America?*
> Yes.
> *Why?*
> First and foremost because, for the first time, I have a happy personal life. Secondly or because of the firstly, I can write here.
> *But you have no guarantee that this state of things will continue.*
> No.
> *If it wasn't for your private life, would you go back to England?*
> I don't know. Judging by my past behaviour I probably should. Trouble is attractive when one is not tied.
> *Do you feel perfectly happy about staying here?*
> No.
> *Why?*
> Because Dodds thinks I should go back, and because I am embarrassed at being so happy when many of my greatest friends are having an unpleasant time.
> *Do you care what happens to England?*
> Given England, not in the least. To me England is bits of the country like the Pennine Moors and my English friends. If they were all safely out of the country, I should feel about the English as I feel about the Spanish or the Chinese or the Germans. It matters what happens to them as it matters what happens to all members of the human race, but my concern is as a fellow human being not as a fellow countryman. . .
> *On what conditions would you come back to England?*
> If anyone can convince me that there is something that has to be done, by a writer with my kind of gifts that can only be done in England and is so important that it justifies smashing his private life (which also has certain responsibilities). I am neither a politician nor a novelist, reportage is not my business. If I come back, as far as I can see the chances are I should have much the same life as I do here, i.e. reading, writing and teaching. I came here with the intention of settling here. I am sceptical about the value of writers to a belligerent country, but of course I may be deceiving myself. I am afraid as I suppose most people are of what may happen.

After receiving this letter from Auden, Dodds did not continue the discussion.

Just as Auden was explaining himself to Dodds, Cyril Connolly in his new magazine *Horizon* was calling Auden and Isherwood's emigration to America 'the most important literary event since the outbreak of the Spanish War' because it was a rejection of the involvement of literature with politics during the 1930s. It was far from clear whether or not Connolly approved of his friends' action – he called them 'ambitious young men with a strong instinct of self-preservation, and an eye on the main chance.' Auden commented of Connolly's article: 'I think it meant to be friendly.' But most of the remarks on this topic which were now beginning to be published were openly hostile.

Harold Nicolson's earlier friendship with Auden did not stop him writing in the *Spectator* that he thought Auden's continuing presence in America – and the presence of Isherwood, Gerald Heard and Aldous Huxley – might dissuade Americans from believing in the rightness of the anti-Hitler cause, since 'four of our most liberated intelligences refuse to identify themselves. . . with those who fight'. The *Spectator* also printed an epigram, said to be by the Dean of St Paul's:

> 'This Europe stinks', you cried – swift to desert
> Your stricken country in her sore distress.
> You may not care, but still I will assert
> Since you have left us, here the stink is less.

A writer in the *Daily Mail,* echoing Nicolson, asked 'why Americans should be invited to risk a single drop of blood when young Englishmen remain in America instead of coming here to help our war effort', and called Auden 'a disgrace to poetry'. The *Daily Mirror* columnist 'Cassandra' amended Auden's dedicatory verse to *The Orators* ('Private faces in public places / Are wiser and nicer / Than public faces in private places') to read:

> Poetical faces in distant places
> Are safer and sounder
> Than poetical faces in homeland places.

And in his new novel *Put Out More Flags* Evelyn Waugh introduced the characters of two left-wing literary collaborators named 'Parsnip and Pimpernell', who disconcerted their acolytes by decamping to the U.S.A. when war broke out.

Even Parliament took notice. On 13 June 1940 in the House of Commons, Sir Jocelyn Lucas M.P. asked the Parliamentary Secretary to the Ministry of Labour 'whether British citizens of military age, such as Mr W. H. Auden and Mr Christopher Isherwood, who have gone to the United States and expressed their determination not to return to this country until war is over,[1] will be summoned back for registration and calling up, in view of the fact that they are seeking refuge abroad?' The minister in his reply confused Auden with H. W. ('Bunny') Austin,

---

[1] Auden and Isherwood had, of course, expressed no such determination.

a lawn tennis player who had gone to America in December 1939 as a representative of the Oxford Group; the minister said that 'Mr Austin gave an undertaking. . . that he would return if called upon to do so.' Sir Jocelyn Lucas pointed out the mistake, and asked if Auden and Isherwood ought not to lose their British citizenship unless they registered as conscientious objectors. But there was no official reply to this, and as far as Parliament was concerned the matter rested there.

The next year, 1941, there was a faint suggestion that some official action might be taken when C. K. (later Sir Charles) Webster, head of the British Information Services in New York, who was concerned with encouraging American support for the war effort, remarked in a conversation with Isaiah Berlin, who was then working for him, that the spectacle of young Britons such as Auden knocking about in the United States without apparent concern for the war did the British cause no good; but Webster seems to have done nothing about it. A contrary view was expressed by the poet Katharine Biddle, who was married to the U.S. Attorney General, and who remarked to Isaiah Berlin that the death of English poets in the First World War was a melancholy story, and ought not to be allowed to happen again; she said she hoped that Auden would be saved from such a fate.

In Britain, some of those left-wing intellectuals who had supported and admired Auden during the 1930s were beginning to be shocked by his decision to remain in America. But at least some of his friends defended him publicly. E. M. Forster wrote to the *Spectator* (5 July 1940) suggesting that the attacks on Auden and other emigrés were really motivated by jealousy of the life they were leading in America. Some months later, Louis MacNeice argued in *Horizon* (February 1941) that what mattered was whether Auden and the others could profit as writers from their decision to live in America – which he thought they could. But Auden himself kept silent.

When Golo Mann showed him a hostile article in an English paper and suggested that Auden ought to reply to it, he said abruptly: 'There is no point.' Meanwhile at some time in the late spring or early summer of 1940, shortly before the fall of France, he decided to contact the British authorities. 'I went to the British Embassy', he told Mrs Dodds in mid-June, 'to see if they had any suggestions and was told that only technically qualified people are wanted back.'

After this, he rarely again discussed his reasons for remaining in America while war continued. An exception was a letter he wrote in March 1941 to Stephen Spender, who had recently published an article in the *New Statesman* (16 November 1940) which was implicitly critical of Auden for not returning to England. Auden told Spender:

If I thought I should be a competent soldier or air-warden I should come back to-morrow. It is impossible for me to know whether it is reason or just cowardice that makes me think I shouldnt be of much military effectiveness. All I can do, therefore, is to be willing to do anything when and if the Government ask me (which I told the Embassy here). As a writer and a pedagogue the problem is different, for the intellectual warfare goes on always & everywhere, & no one has a right to say that this place or that time is where all intellectuals ought to be. I believe that personally America is the best, but of course the only proof lies in what one produces.

What is one to make of Auden's reasons for not going back to England? The first and most important point to note is that he was in a muddle – or at least that he gave different reasons on different occasions, with no apparent consistency. He was probably being entirely honest when he told Dodds his chief reason for wanting to stay in America was Chester Kallman; and there can also be little doubt that he genuinely felt that America had more to offer him as a writer. Yet he does not seem to have faced the question whether he had a moral duty to help, however trivially, in the fight against Hitler. Perhaps he felt, as a result of his deliberations during the previous summer, that such a duty did not exist for him, was not one of those 'actions. . . in which you unite thought and intention and treat others with love'. But if that was the case, why did he go to the British Embassy and, in effect, offer his services should they want him for the war effort? Was it really true that, as he told Spender, he was not coming back to England because he thought he would be no use as a soldier or even an air-raid warden?

Most probably he did not know his own mind. His decision to emigrate to America had been taken quite casually, and he was only now, a year or more later, beginning to face up to the implications of that decision. Meanwhile many people in England assumed he was not returning simply because of cowardice, and imagined he was unwilling to face the austerity and danger of war. To believe this would be to misjudge Auden's character. He never showed the slightest sign of cowardice – as he said to Dodds, his usual inclination was to seek out trouble rather than flee from it. His decision to remain in America in the face of criticism, though it seems to have been the result of a whole series of conflicting feelings rather than of a closely-reasoned argument, itself required no small amount of nerve.

He finished 'New Year Letter' in April 1940. The poem concluded with a declaration, reminiscent of that in 'September 1, 1939', that 'We need to love all since we are / Each a unique particular.' But Auden was not prepared to go beyond this general assertion of Agape; and 'New Year Letter' finishes with an invocation that borrows many images and phrases from *The Descent of the Dove:*

O Unicorn among the cedars,
To whom no magic charm can lead us. . .
O Dove of science and of light,
Upon the branches of the night,
O Icthus playful in the deep
Sea-lodges that forever keep
Their secret of excitement hidden,
O sudden Wind that blows unbidden,
Parting the quiet reeds, O Voice
Within the labyrinth of choice
Only the passive listener hears,
O Clock and Keeper of the years,
O Source of equity and rest. . .
Disturb our negligence and chill,
Convict our pride of its offence. . .
Send strength sufficient for our day,
And point our knowledge on its way,
O da quod jubes, Domine.

The poem had worked its way to a position that was very nearly
Christian.

★

'I've finished my long poem (1700 lines),' Auden told Mrs Dodds on 21
April 1940, 'and will send it you as soon as I have a rough typed copy.
Will you and the Master [Dodds] go through it very carefully for
intellectual errors.' Meanwhile his new book of poetry, *Another Time,*
was published in America in 1940; Faber issued a British edition five
months later. The book included poems from Auden's last two years in
England as well as more recent work, so that alongside poems from 1939
reflecting his change of views was a whole range of earlier pieces,
including 'Spain' and 'Lay your sleeping head'. The book was on the
whole well reviewed, and a moderately large number of copies were sold
on both sides of the Atlantic, while *Some Poems,* a selection from all
Auden's work up to this time published by Faber in 1940, achieved sales
of nearly twelve thousand copies during the next five years. The controversy over Auden's residence in America had not diminished his popularity
as a poet in England.

During these months he continued his chosen form of 'social work' –
teaching. He had broken off his association with the League of American
Writers, for whom he had taught the poetry class in the autumn of 1939;
the League was a Communist organisation, and objected to his publishing
an article, 'The Public v. the Late Mr William Butler Yeats', in the
Partisan Review, which it regarded as a 'Trotskyite' journal. Auden
therefore left the League, and instead began to teach once a week at the

New School for Social Research, a New York institution offering a university education to adult students. Its faculty included a number of distinguished European exiles; Auden described it as 'quite a good place but O so German of 1925 – and they seem to have learned nothing since'. His lectures at the New School were on 'Poetry and Culture'. Meanwhile he also earned some money by writing for the radio. The Columbia Broadcasting System commissioned a play from him, and he gave them an expanded version, lasting half an hour, of 'Alfred', the monologue he had written in 1936 for Therese Giehse, about the old woman and her goose. It was broadcast in June 1940 with May Whitty speaking the part. Auden allegedly gave it the title 'The Psychological Experiences and Sensations of the Woman who Killed the Goose That Laid the Golden Egg'; C.B.S. re-titled it *The Dark Valley*. It was an unremarkable piece of work, an overstretching of the original idea, but Benjamin Britten wrote some music for it which Auden called 'lovely'. Further commissions were forthcoming from C.B.S.. Auden collaborated with James Stern on a radio adaptation of D. H. Lawrence's short story 'The Rocking-Horse Winner', again with music by Britten; Stern was co-opted because of his knowledge of horse-racing. Auden also undertook the 'hack' job of making a thirty-minute radio version of *Pride and Prejudice*, but his script for this had to be entirely rewritten by the producer before it was broadcast. He had no great aptitude for, or interest in, radio as a medium.

He had now decided that 'New Year Letter' should form the central part of a book with the title *The Double Man*, a phrase suggested by some words of Montaigne quoted by Charles Williams in *The Descent of the Dove*: 'We are, I know not how, double in ourselves, so that we believe what we disbelieve, and cannot rid ourselves of what we condemn.' This aphorism, besides being applicable to the remark about 'double focus' at the end of Part II of 'New Year Letter', may have seemed to Auden to be a pertinent comment on his own state of mind during the previous decade, a period during which he had toyed, half believingly and half disbelievingly, with so many different ideologies and philosophies. Besides 'New Year Letter', *The Double Man* was to include a set of 'Notes' to the central poem, and a sequence of sonnets that would express its theme in different terms. Auden tackled these parts of the book during his 1940 summer holiday.

He spent part of this holiday staying for a few days with the Mann family, who had now moved from Princeton to California, where they had taken a house in Pacific Palisades. 'Am staying with the wife and in-laws', Auden wrote to a friend on 6 August. 'Nice house but O God I hate California. To tell the honest truth, I dont like desert to live in. I prefer Wordsworth and New England.' He was now quite attached to Erika Mann; according to her brother Golo 'they liked each other decidedly', and the relationship had matured into what Golo called 'serious friendship with even – believe it or not – a slight erotical touch'.

While in California, Auden also saw Isherwood, who was living near Hollywood and was working at film scripts for M.G.M. Isherwood was also deeply involved with the study of the Hindu philosophy Vedanta, under the guidance of Gerald Heard and a Hindu monk, Swami Prabhavananda; Auden did not take this very seriously, though he was impressed by Isherwood's account of the Swami's personality.

He spent most of the rest of the summer of 1940, both before and after his Californian trip, at Williamsburg in Massachusetts, first of all staying on a farm, probably with Chester Kallman. He was there in June when Britain seemed threatened by an imminent German invasion across the Channel from occupied France. 'I keep thinking of you all,' he told Mrs Dodds, 'and wishing you were here and wondering who that I know has been killed, and what will happen anyway.' He asked her to let him know if he could help find homes for British children in the States, and told her that if she knew of cases of hardship she should get in touch with his mother, whom he had requested 'to use any cash there may be in my English bank for relief'. Meanwhile he reported that he was 'getting on with my book [*The Double Man*], doing the notes to the long poem (partly verse, partly prose), then a sonnet sequence'.

The Notes to 'New Year Letter' eventually occupied about eighty pages of print, more than the poem itself. They consisted of short verses or epigrams serving as amplifications of the 'Letter', and also a large number of quotations from books that Auden admired. The range of these books indicates the scope of his interests and his eclecticism in his search for ideas – they include a study of the biological process of induction in embryos, Thucydides' *History of the Peloponnesian War*, and Margaret Mead on South Sea Island culture, as well as Kierkegaard, Charles Williams, and Groddeck (whom Auden still admired). But the quotations and the verse-notes do not illuminate the main poem so much as raise subsidiary issues, and Auden later dropped them when he reprinted 'New Year Letter', though he did eventually republish some of the verse-notes as separate pieces. The sonnet sequence was called 'The Quest', and it used the quest-motif, which Auden had already employed in his plays, as a framework for an account of a spiritual journey which was by implication Christian. At about the time he was working on the sonnets, on 14 July 1940, Auden wrote to Charles Williams: 'I am trying to learn a little about the Practice of the Presence, but O dear, the Spirit and the Flesh are as unwilling as they are weak.'

After his return from California to the east coast he stayed with Mina Curtiss, sister of his New York friend Lincoln Kirstein, in her house at Williamsburg. She helped him with his typing; earlier in the summer she had also arranged for him to give an address at nearby Smith College, where she taught in the English department. He used the occasion – the Commencement Address on graduation day, 17 June – to discuss the attitude of America to the war, and told his audience that no decision about intervention or isolation, or indeed about anything, could be reached without 'making some absolute presuppositions, or acts of faith'.

Towards the end of the summer Benjamin Britten and Peter Pears joined him for some days at Mina Curtiss's house, and he and Britten worked once more on *Paul Bunyan,* as well as discussing a 'Hymn to St Cecilia' which Auden had written and Britten was to set. Then, in early September, Auden returned to New York, planning to find a new and larger apartment where Chester could live with him. The search was at first fruitless, and he decided to stay on at Montague Terrace. But then later in September he was offered a room in a house some streets away, and he accepted.

The invitation came from George Davis, who had been his host in New York during the first visit with Isherwood, and who had now rented a large house in Middagh Street, Brooklyn Heights, to share with a number of his friends. Auden moved into 7 Middagh Street early in October 1940, and among those who joined him there as residents of the house was Golo Mann.

Mann noticed that a small change was taking place in Auden's pattern of life. 'On Sundays', he recorded of Auden, 'he began to disappear for a couple of hours and returned with a look of happiness on his face. After a few weeks he confided in me the object of these mysterious excursions: the Episcopalian Church.'

*

So, in about October 1940, Auden resumed the religious beliefs and practices of his childhood. From now on he attended Holy Communion early on Sunday mornings – avoiding later services so that he did not have to hear sermons – and regularly said private prayers. As he expressed it in a poem written not long afterwards:

> O here and now our endless journey stops.
> We never left the place where we were born.

The last stage of his conversion had simply been a quiet and gradual decision to accept Christianity as a true premise. The experience had been undramatic, even rather dry. Certainly there was, to use Kierkegaard's term, a 'leap of faith'; but Auden had come to the conclusion that such leaps are made in all spheres of life, and that, as he put it, 'when the ground crumbles under their feet, [people] *have* to leap even into uncertainty if they are to avoid certain destruction'.

He remained fully aware that there was no rational proof of the truth of Christian doctrine; he once remarked that all attempts to argue or disprove the existence of God are 'returned unopened to the sender', and he commented in a poem: 'The Real is what will strike you as really absurd.' His attitude to faith was exactly expressed by a maxim of Anselm that he quoted in 'New Year Letter': '*Credo ut intelligam*', 'I believe in order that I may understand.' Faith might itself be irrational, but it was the door to a system of thought which could explain the whole of human existence; and it was for such a system that he had been searching throughout his adult life.

Auden's conversion had apparently been an exclusively intellectual process rather than a spiritual experience; and this remained characteristic of his religion in the years that followed it.[1] 'I am not mystical,' he told a friend. 'One must beware of calling moods of euphoria mystical encounters.' Certainly he did come to believe later in life that he had once or twice 'heard' God, and he did regard prayer as a process not just of speaking but of listening. 'The serious part of prayer,' he wrote, 'begins when we have got our begging over with and listen for the Voice of what I would call the Holy Spirit.' But he said that his dominant religious experience was of 'distance from God', and that he was prone to what he called 'a Barthian exaggeration of God's transcendence'. On the other hand, with the sort of contradiction that was typical of him in all spheres of his life, he came to accept the actual existence of the Devil – to an interviewer's question in 1972, 'Do you believe in the Devil?', he answered simply 'Yes'; and though he said he regarded theosophy and spiritualism as 'a joke', he was inclined to believe in black magic, graphology, and the telepathic power of cats. This was the same attitude of mind that had led him in 1938 to say that he believed a Brussels fortune-teller's prediction that there would be no war.

He continued to keep abreast of modern theology, and studied the work of Rudolf Bultmann and other New Testament critics, remarking of the Resurrection: 'It does make a difference if it really happened, doesn't it?' Possibly, as one of his friends suspected, he did not entirely believe in it himself. On the other hand he had long accepted the

---

[1]The dry, almost agnostic, character of Auden's faith is shown by a passage in a sermon he gave in Westminster Abbey on 16 October 1966: 'Those of us who have the nerve to call ourselves Christians will do well to be extremely reticent on the subject. Indeed, it is almost the definition of a Christian that he is somebody who *knows* he isn't one, either in faith or morals. Where faith is concerned, very few of us have the right to say more than – to vary a saying of Simone Weil's – "I believe in a God who is like the True God in everything except that he does not exist, for I have not yet reached the point where God exists." As for loving and forgiving our enemies, the less we say about that the better. Our lack of faith and love are facts we have to acknowledge, but we shall not improve either by a morbid and essentially narcissistic moaning over our deficiencies. Let us rather ask, with caution and humour – given our time and place and talents, what, if our faith and love were perfect, would we be glad to find it obvious to do?' (Text of the sermon lent to the author by Janet Carleton.)

Christian doctrine of the Fall as, in his eyes, a representation of a fact of human psychology: he saw it, he said, as a symbol of the point in history where Man developed self-consciousness and became aware of the possibility of freedom and autonomy. As to the great theological problem of the existence of suffering and evil in the world, it did not much occupy his mind; in a later poem he remarked that it 'seems idle to discuss' whether it might be God's anger or merely his compassion which leaves humanity to do as it wishes, even if the result is largely evil. And though he often stressed the significance of sin and guilt and, like Kierkegaard, claimed to regard Man as standing alone with his sins before God, his own personal sense of sin sometimes seemed (as Stephen Spender noticed) to be 'curiously theoretical' and not deeply felt.

This was reflected in the attitude he took to his sexuality after his conversion – or rather, his lack of attitude. Christopher Isherwood observed of Auden's view of homosexual behaviour: 'His religion condemned it and he agreed that it was sinful, though he fully intended to go on sinning.' This is a simplification, but is in essence true; in a poem written a few years after his conversion, Auden quoted with evident if half-joking approval Augustine's celebrated phrase, 'Make me chaste, Lord, but not yet.' There seem to have been three reasons why he did not feel that this attitude was in conflict with his religion.

The first was his belief that, of all human functions, sex is the least controllable by the personality. In 1940 he wrote a short poem, one of the Notes to 'New Year Letter', describing how a baby, as he grows, begins to gain some control over his physique, but has to struggle against other forces in his body, of which his penis is one:

> Never will his prick[1] belong
> To his world of right and wrong,
> Nor its values comprehend
> Who is foe and who is friend.

This may appear to be a claim that sex has nothing to do with morality. But the passage in 'The Prolific and the Devourer' on which the poem is based shows otherwise:

At first the baby sees his limbs as belonging to the outside world. When he has learnt to control them, he accepts them as parts of himself. What we call the 'I', in fact, is the area over which our will is immediately operative. Thus, if we have a toothache, we seem to be two people, the suffering 'I' and the hostile outer world of the tooth. His penis never fully belongs to a man.

[1]Early editions have 'sex'.

Auden's second reason for tolerating his own homosexuality after his conversion seems to have been that he expected a very high level of sinfulness in himself. To a friend he described his theological position as 'Augustinian, not Thomist', and like Augustine he put tremendous emphasis on the grace of God as the saving power, rather than on any natural goodness or good works in Man. G. S. Fraser has remarked of Auden: 'To avoid despair he has to put most of his money on Grace since he knows he is going to fall down on Works. The trouble about such a type of Christianity is that to the outside observer it might appear to make no practical difference.' Fraser exaggerated: Auden did try not to 'fall down on Works', and privately performed many acts of generosity and kindness. Nevertheless where sex was concerned he did regard himself as largely unregenerate.

His third reason was more positive. He considered Eros (sexual-romantic love) to be an approach towards Agape, the selfless love of God – a view frequently expounded in the writings of Charles Williams. Auden wrote of this: 'Agape is the fulfilment and correction of eros, not its contradiction.' He argued that to undervalue sexual love was actually heretical: it denied the goodness of the physical bodies created by God. And in an unpublished verse-letter to Chester Kallman he showed that he regarded his love for Chester largely as a Vision of Agape: 'It is through you', he wrote, 'that God has chosen to show me my beatitude.'[1]

Those close to Auden were, of course, aware of his conversion. Elizabeth Mayer had, after her Lutheran upbringing, drifted away from religious belief; she now seemed pleased that one of the effects of her friendship with Auden was to encourage him to return to Christianity, but she did not go back to it herself. As to Chester Kallman, he had been brought up by his father without religion, yet despite this and his strong consciousness of being Jewish he was sympathetic to Christianity. Auden seems to have had hopes of encouraging Chester to join the Church; two poems from the period immediately after his conversion, 'Time will say nothing but I told you so' and 'Leap Before You Look', were privately listed by him among those addressed to or concerned with Chester, and they reflect his hope of communicating to Chester the implications of the conversion. The second poem concludes:

> Although I love you, you will have to leap;
> Our dream of safety has to disappear.

[1] It is possible – though there is no evidence for this – that the timing of Auden's conversion was the result of his relationship with Chester, and that until he had settled down to a steady homosexual 'marriage' he could not have contemplated returning to Christianity. His undergraduate friend V. M. Allom writes of Auden's Oxford days: 'I think now that the true obstacle to his calling himself a Christian at this time. . . was an acute consciousness that no homosexual can live without sinning unless he is prepared to live as a eunuch.'

Chester, however, did not follow Auden into the Church.

Several of Auden's friends wondered why, after his conversion, it was the Episcopalian Church that he joined, or rather, re-joined, and not the Roman Catholic. The conversion had been motivated by a wish to find and accept an absolute and unconditional dogma, and it might have been expected that someone conducting such a search should end up as a Catholic rather than a Protestant. Auden was indeed largely drawn towards Rome. He held the Catholic view that the priest's function is to administer the sacraments – which he believed could be done effectively whatever the individual priest's moral character – and he had little patience with the Protestant emphasis on the importance of preaching. On the other hand his theological outlook was, as he said himself, 'Neo-Calvinist (i.e. Barthian)' – he was inclined to accept the Calvinist doctrine of predestination of the grounds that God must know what is to be the fate of individuals – and he declared that 'Truth is catholic, but the search for it is protestant.'

To put it more simply, he returned in almost every detail to the religion of his childhood. He had been brought up a member of the Church of England, of which the Episcopalian Church in America is the exact equivalent – they are both members of the Anglican Communion, which means they are in effect the same church. Within that church, his childhood taste had been for Anglo-Catholic (high church) ritual, and now in 1940 this again became his preference: he described himself as 'Anglo-Catholic though not too spiky' – that is, not too extreme in high church practices.

Auden's search for an ideology did not quite come to an end with his conversion. During the next thirty years his religious beliefs continued, subtly but definitely, to develop. Gradually his Barthian, neo-Calvinist phase of the 1940s relaxed, and by the mid-1950s he was giving expression to the notion of Christianity as a universal dance – an idea he perhaps took from Charles Williams; in his poem 'Compline' Auden talked of 'the dance. . . about the abiding tree' (the Cross transfigured as the Tree of Life). Later still, he liked to emphasise the importance of what he called 'the spirit of carnival' in religion. This was quite a far cry from the severity of his beliefs in the early 1940s.

His sense of humour had always been, and continued to be, very Anglican, with his fondness for strumming tunes from the *English Hymnal* on the piano and bellowing favourite lines from unintentionally funny hymns. He also invented a parlour-game called 'Purgatory Mates', in which players had to choose two persons of such different character that they would naturally hate each other, but who were to be condemned to live together in Purgatory until they had reached a state of mutual love; examples of such pairs were T. S. Eliot and Walt Whitman, and Tolstoy and Oscar Wilde. Auden also continued to fancy himself, in more hilarious moments, as a lunatic clergyman of the Church of England.

'Wouldn't it be nice to be a minor canon?' he remarked to a friend. Among his impersonations was that of a bishop preaching at a public school. 'I like to think', he once said, apparently in all seriousness, 'that if I hadn't been a poet, I might have become an Anglican bishop – politically liberal, I hope; theologically and liturgically conservative, I know.'

3

Crisis

Auden finished *The Double Man*, the book consisting of 'New Year Letter', the Notes, and the sonnet sequence 'The Quest', in October 1940, just as he began to go regularly again to church. He had promised the English edition not to Faber & Faber but to John Lehmann at the Hogarth Press, in replacement for the travel book on America which Lehmann had commissioned in 1938 but which had never been written; and early in 1939 Auden had received a sum of money from Lehmann as an advance on royalties. Lehmann now advertised *The Double Man* in Hogarth announcements – whereupon T. S. Eliot told him that Auden was in fact contracted to Faber's, and had no right to offer the book to another publisher. Lehmann, distressed and angry with Auden, wrote to him for an explanation. In reply there came neither apologies nor excuses but a telegram from New York: 'I am incapable of dealing with this.'

Eliot settled the matter by reimbursing Lehmann for the advance he had paid to Auden and taking over *The Double Man* for Faber's. But he did not want to advertise a book that had appeared in another firm's announcements, so, without asking Auden, he changed the book's title to *New Year Letter*. He also noticed that the words 'the double man' appeared in a verse prologue to the volume, so, again without asking Auden, who he hoped would not notice, he changed this phrase to 'the invisible twin'. Meanwhile Auden had given his American publishers Random House a manuscript of the book that differed – in the Notes to 'New Year Letter' – from the English version. When the book was published the following spring it therefore had two titles and two texts.

The company that Auden was now keeping contrasted oddly with the inner intellectual and spiritual life he had chosen. The house into which he moved early in October 1940, 7 Middagh Street, Brooklyn Heights, quickly became known for the bohemian character of its inhabitants. George Davis had acquired the house, a brownstone building in a quiet side-street under the shadow of Brooklyn Bridge, with the intention of sharing it with some of the artistic friends he had made through his work as a New York literary editor; and these quickly moved in. Auden was among the first; he paid Davis $25 a month for a sitting-room and bedroom on the top floor. Another early resident was Carson McCullers, who had recently made a reputation with her novel *The Heart is a Lonely Hunter*; her marriage had foundered, and she was now falling in love with a succession of women, including Erika Mann. Soon after she and Auden had arrived in the Middagh Street house, Benjamin Britten and Peter Pears, who were beginning to find Elizabeth Mayer's hospitality suffocating, left her Long Island home and moved in too, renting a room from George Davis; Britten also installed a Steinway grand piano in the communal sitting-room. Golo Mann joined the household too, as did Paul Bowles, musician and writer, with his wife Jane (also a writer), and Oliver Smith the theatre designer. Louis MacNeice came for a short visit. Another resident – or more probably a regular visitor – was a friend of George Davis, whose book *The G-String Murders* he was ghost-writing, the striptease artist Gypsy Rose Lee.

Auden called the house 'our menagerie', and indeed for some weeks the residents included a trained chimpanzee with its keeper; while another inmate specialised in the parlour-trick of inserting a cigarette into his anus and puffing out smoke. When George Davis, giving an interview about the house to the *New Yorker,* said 'It's a boarding house'; the reporter understandably thought he had said 'bawdy house'. Britten and Pears found the establishment altogether too raffish for their taste – Pears later called it 'sordid beyond belief' – but Auden was perfectly happy there, and had soon assumed the role of father to the household; or rather, mother.

He insisted that meals, which were prepared and served by a negro cook and maid, should begin punctually. He himself sat at the head of the table. 'He would preface a meal', recalled Paul Bowles, 'by announcing: "We've got a roast and two veg, salad and savoury, and there will be no political discussion." ' He instituted and organised a system of individual prices for each meal, and as Golo Mann remembered 'it was a serious question how many meals anyone had missed, after due notification in advance'. Once a week he would go round from room to room collecting the money. If a party was held in the sitting-room he would announce that guests must leave by one a.m.; and sharply at that hour would insist that they did, often to the disgruntlement of his fellow hosts. With this blend of the maternal and the schoolmasterly he kept the household running smoothly.

Those of Auden's friends who visited him at Middagh Street noticed this marked contrast between the rest of the household and his own manner. James Stern recalled 'George naked at the piano with a cigarette in his mouth, Carson on the ground with half a gallon of sherry, and then Wystan bursting in like a headmaster, announcing: "Now then, dinner!" '

In certain matters Auden was becoming more and more punctilious. He disliked people leaving food on their plates, or using more than a sliver of lavatory paper. And, though generous in almost every other respect, he was always angry if someone helped themselves to his cigarettes, even if they were old friends. 'You must buy your own,' he would say severely.[1] He also had very rigid rules on what women might or might not do in public: 'There are two things I don't like – to see women drinking hard liquor and to see them standing at bars without escorts.'

On the other hand his punctiliousness did not extend to his own appearance. He called himself 'one of those persons who generally look like an unmade bed', and he seemed on the whole rather proud of this. 'The way he dresses', he wrote later in a verse-profile of himself, 'reveals an angry baby, / howling to be dressed.' In the 1920s and early 1930s he had been perfectly willing to turn out neatly for smart occasions, but now when he and Chester Kallman appeared at the Metropolitan Opera his tuxedo, which had been made for him in his last year at Oxford, had grease-spots all over it, and he usually wore sneakers or slippers to accompany it. Chester called him 'the most dishevelled child of all disciplinarians'.

How is this apparent contrast, between his orderly running of the Middagh Street household and his disorderly appearance to be explained? The answer seems to be that he regarded the two things as of quite different value. Clothes and appearance did not matter; the way he dressed did not interfere with his work. An orderly timetable, on the other hand, was essential to his life; it was only by imposing it on himself that he could get his work done, and he consequently believed in the value of imposing it on others. There was also in his adopting the role of house-mother at Middagh Street an element of recreating the strict

---

[1]The most extreme example of this was an occasion in the 1950s when Stephen Spender came to stay with him on Ischia. Spender recalls: 'In the course of the afternoon which I spent with him, I happened to take one of his cigarettes. He said, "Why don't you have cigarettes of your own?" And I said, "As a matter of fact, I would have bought some but I don't have any Italian money – I have just English money with me." "Well," he said, "I'd be happy to change some for you. Give me a pound." Then he looked up the rate of exchange in the *Herald Tribune*, and he said, "Well my dear, I'm afraid the pound's doing very badly. I can only give you a hundred lira, but now you can go downstairs and buy some cigarettes."' ('The Art of Poetry, xxv' [interview with Peter Stiff], *Paris Review*, 77 (Winter-Spring 1980), pp. 127–8.) Spender believes that this anecdote demonstrates what he calls Auden's 'odd quirk of meanness'. But Auden's attitude was so extreme as to seem like deliberate outrageousness, a parody of the mean host. Spender himself, in the same interview, continues: 'A few months later, Auden was staying with us in the country, in England. Our daughter at that time was always talking about having a horse. But we couldn't quite afford it, so Auden said: "Well look, Stephen, what Lizzie wants most in this world is a horse. Here's fifty pounds towards buying her one." This was the same person.'

Edwardian upbringing of his childhood. He had a deep nostalgic affection for the manners and rules of that childhood, and, as his years as an exile in America went by, he began more and more to model his domestic life (at least in matters of routine) according to a pattern of nursery strictness.

He was, then, prepared to tolerate and even enjoy the Middagh Street household's raffishness, provided it did not interfere with the self-discipline out of which his work as a poet grew. He also enjoyed playing the schoolmaster to his fellow-inmates. And in no circumstances was he prepared to follow the stereotype of 'poetic' behaviour. His comment on this subject was: 'Sorry, my dear, one mustn't be bohemian!'

At about the time he moved to Middagh Street he was beginning to drink alcohol in larger quantities than before: almost always wine, usually a cheap Italian or Californian red, scarcely ever at this period hard liquor. He treated wine in the same manner as he treated food, as something to be consumed briskly in large quantities at the correct hour of the day, which in this case was the evening; he never drank while he was working.

He could drink a lot without becoming either bellicose or maudlin. But wine did make him, as he said himself, 'prone to hold forth'. On many evenings, with a bottle or more inside him, his conversation ceased to take account of his listeners and became a monologue about whatever was occupying his mind, a series of pronouncements which were, as Golo Mann remarked, 'always *ex cathedra*. . . not subject to discussion'.

By the late autumn of 1940 he was thoroughly settled into Middagh Street. The household now included two cats, one of which slept on his bed, which, as he was a cat-lover, delighted him. He was, as usual, rising soon after six a.m. to work, and he asked Paul Bowles's wife Jane to get up at this hour too and help him with his typing. To her husband's astonishment, she accepted, and the two of them would work for three hours or so before breakfast. Meanwhile Auden continued to lecture on poetry once a week at the New School for Social Research, and in his spare time read a lot of philosophy, history and theology, including the writings of Paul Tillich, which he found 'exciting'. He told Mrs Dodds: 'My life is very uneventful.'

At about this time he began to get to know the theologian Reinhold Niebuhr. He reviewed Niebuhr's *Christianity and Power Politics* in the *Nation*; Niebuhr and his English-born wife Ursula, herself a theologian, were intrigued by the review, and wrote to Auden arranging to meet. It was the beginning of a long friendship.

Niebuhr, who was then in his late forties, taught at Union Theological Seminary in New York, and he and his wife began to invite Auden regularly to their apartment, or to visit him in the strange household at Middagh Street. The friendship had a frivolous side: Auden and Ursula Niebuhr swapped Anglican jokes and played gramophone records of English trains and church bells; moreover the Niebuhrs noticed that

Auden seemed to need, at least now and then, a dose of family life – for example at Christmas, when he enjoyed eating dinner with them. On a more serious level, he and the Niebuhrs discussed many points of theology.

They had much in common: Reinhold Niebuhr's book *An Interpretation of Christian Ethics*, published in America in 1936, exactly echoed Auden's belief that modern liberalism had collapsed, with the result that it was now impossible for liberals to challenge Hitler or pass judgement on the Nazis. Niebuhr branded the whole of modern secular liberal culture as 'a devitalized and secularized religion in which the presuppositions of a Christian tradition have been rationalized and read into the processes of history and nature, supposedly discovered by objective science'; and he called for a return to Christianity itself as providing 'a transcendent perspective upon the issues at stake'. Auden, of course, agreed fervently with this. He greatly admired Reinhold Niebuhr's mind and character – he called him 'a benevolent eagle' – and when early in 1941 Niebuhr published the first volume of his book *The Nature and Destiny of Man*, Auden praised it in a review as 'the most lucid and balanced statement of orthodox Protestantism that we are likely to see for a long time'. He did not, however, comment publicly on what many people regarded as the most distinctive aspect of Niebuhr's thought: his demand that Christians should involve themselves in political affairs and, specifically, that America should intervene in the war.

Niebuhr had become known during the 1930s for his left-wing views; he founded a 'Fellowship of Socialist Christians' and ran for office on a socialist ticket, though eventually he broke with socialism because of its non-interventionist foreign policy and became a Democrat. He had also once been a pacifist (in reaction to the First World War) but he now believed that it was utterly wrong to suppose that there were universally applicable non-violent solutions to political problems. He was doing his best to persuade Christians who were influenced by pacifism that they ought to support the war against Hitler. His book *Christianity and Power Politics* was strongly critical of the pacifist outlook. Auden's review of it in the *Nation* discussed its theology, but made no comment at all on the book's anti-pacifist line and its demand that America should enter the war.

Ursula Niebuhr supposed that this was because, as a new arrival in the States and not yet an American citizen, Auden may have wished not to interfere in matters of foreign policy. She had the impression that he was sympathetic to her husband's anti-pacifist views. Certainly Auden does not seem, after his return to the Church in the autumn of 1940, to have continued to contemplate taking up a 'pacifist position'; his moves towards pacifism during the summer and autumn of 1939 were apparently a blind alley out of which he retreated. Nor did he take up Yoga, as he had once contemplated. Yet to Erika Mann, who saw quite a lot of him during 1940 and 1941 when he came to her parents' house, it seemed that he was extraordinarily detached from the war and unwilling to commit himself to the anti-Hitler cause. This infuriated her. When she visited England in the summer of 1942 she talked about it to newspaper reporters, who were eager for news of Auden. 'Erika Mann does not attempt to defend or condone him,' reported the *Evening Standard*. 'She just cannot understand his "pseudo-detachment". Even the entry of Russia failed to move him. But though Auden tries to pretend he is uninterested in the war, she told me he jumped for joy when the *Bismarck* was sunk.'

Auden was no doubt partly reacting against the sheer strength of the anti-Nazi cry raised by Erika and some other members of her family, who were virulent on the subject of Hitler and the war. Their almost hysterical tone no doubt encouraged him to adopt a more neutral manner when discussing the subject with them. Yet his attitude to the war does seem to have remained largely one of detachment.

In the first draft of 'New Year Letter', written in the spring of 1940, he included a passage which makes this clear. The lines follow the section in Part III where he asks to which of the many present-day causes he should give his allegiance:

> Louder than all the others roar
> The governments that run the war
> [word illegible] claiming each to be
> The *patrios* of civility
> For which no man will question why
> It's sweet and decorous to die.
> I hear them; no, it is not they
> Whom all but traitors will obey.
> 'England', 'La France', 'Das Reich', their words
> Are like the names of extinct birds
> Or peasant-women's quaint old charms
> For bringing lovers to their arms,
> Which would be only pretty, save
> That they bring thousands to their grave.
> For maudlin stupid Mr Chips
> Owns several heavy battleships,
> Ridiculous young Lohengrin
> Has camps to put his audience in.
> Cher Monsieur Prudhomme aime la gloire
> Et l'amour-propre et le pouvoir
> And the plain proletarian lie
> Is held up in position by
> Noble police and the ornate
> Grandezza of the Russian State.

These lines were considerably modified in the published text so that they no longer referred to particular nations, though the sentiments behind the published version remain much the same.

This feeling of detachment from the war is evident too in a review Auden wrote in July 1940 of Rilke's *Wartime Letters*, in which he showed himself sympathetic to the negative attitude taken by Rilke to the First World War. Rilke had written: 'Not to understand: yes, that was my entire occupation in these years.' Of this Auden said:

> To call this an ivory-tower attitude would be a cheap and wicked lie. To resist compensating for the sense of guilt that every non-combatant feels at not sharing the physical sufferings of those at the front, by indulging in an orgy of patriotic hatred all the more violent because it is ineffective; to be conscious but to refuse to understand, is a positive act that calls for courage of a high order [though] to distinguish it from selfish or cowardly indifference may at the time be difficult for the outsider.

One might suppose from this that Rilke's attitude was one that he entirely shared. Yet in actual fact this sense of detachment from the war seems only to have come upon him in certain moods or contexts; for on other occasions he was quite prepared to commit himself. In January 1941 he wrote in *Decision*, a magazine started by Klaus Mann, that 'the defeat of Hitler is an immediate necessity about which there can be no discussion'. He told Stephen Spender that 'in spite of everything' he supported the Allies; and in another letter to Spender he grew quite belligerent:

> What has to be done to defend Civilisation? In order of immediate importance: (1) To kill Germans and destroy German property. (2) to prevent as many English lives and as much English property as possible from being killed and destroyed. (3) to create things from houses to poems that are worth preserving. (4) to educate people to understand what civilisation really means and involves. . . I have absolutely no patience with Pacifism as a political movement, as if one could do all the things in one's personal life that create wars and then pretend that to refuse to fight is a sacrifice and not a luxury.

His attitude to the war, then, was as complicated and even contradictory as were his various arguments for remaining in America during it. Again it would probably be true to say that he did not know his own mind, or at least that he had a whole set of attitudes and reasons which did not always agree with each other and which tended to change depending on his audience. He was as uncertain in these matters as he had been when half-involving himself in politics during the 1930s. He had now, of course, abandoned all attempts to advocate a political creed in his poetry.

But this did not prevent him from taking an interest in the American presidential election of 1940, in which, though he had no vote, he supported Roosevelt, whose policy was anti-isolationist and in favour of the intervention of America in the war. Auden wrote to a friend just before the election: 'I hope our side will win: I am worried.'

The Double Man was published by Random House in March 1941; Auden gave Chester Kallman a copy inscribed: 'To Chester who knows both halves.' Faber & Faber published their edition, *New Year Letter*, two months later. Reviewers on both sides of the Atlantic were more impressed by the book's poetic style than by its argument; several of them felt, along with Edwin Muir in *Horizon*, that it was an argumentative journey 'towards something which is never reached', though George Every in *Theology* observed that the goal of Auden's quest was in fact Christianity, and Charles Williams, whose own writings had inspired so much of the book, wrote in the *Dublin Review*: 'It is, after its own manner, a pattern of the Way.' As to the book's allusion to Auden's reasons for remaining in America, among those convinced, or at least impressed, by this was his own father, who wrote in 1941 that he 'rejoiced at his [Wystan's] determination to remain in America with its greater possibilities for real development of thought and philosophy' – a change of heart from his earlier opinion on the subject.

In May 1941, Auden and Britten's operetta *Paul Bunyan*, now complete, received its première at Columbia University in New York, where the University's Theater Associates presented it for a week's performances in the Brander Matthews Hall. The performers were members of the Music Department, augmented by a chorus from the New York Schola Cantorum. Hugh Ross conducted, and the stage director was Milton Smith.

The operetta was, as Auden put it bluntly, 'a failure'. The New York critics treated it severely. *Time* called it an 'anaemic operetta put up by two British expatriates' and said it was 'as bewildering and irritating a treatment of the outsize lumberman as any two Englishmen could have devised'. The *New Yorker* said it 'didn't jell'. The music was received slightly better than the libretto, and the *New York Times* commended Britten for his ability to set a text. But generally the critics, as Britten himself put it, 'damned it unmercifully' – though he added: 'The public seemed to find something enjoyable in the performance.'

Britten, whose self-confidence was not nearly as great as Auden's, was in fact deeply hurt by the reviews, and after the première he made no further attempt to have *Paul Bunyan* performed again; indeed for a long time he discouraged any suggestion that it might be revived. Not until 1976 did he reluctantly agree to its being given another production, in a revised version, at the Aldeburgh Festival. On this occasion it proved a great success, partly, of course, because the audience was keen to discover what this full-length and virtually unknown Auden-Britten collaboration was like. It was subsequently broadcast on the radio, a medium to which it is well suited, and which brings out its charm and vivacity while making less obtrusive some of the absurdities of the plot.

★

Auden was now beginning to be in demand as a speaker and lecturer. In January 1941 he gave a lecture at the University of Michigan at Ann Arbor; in February he taught for a week at Pennsylvania State College; and the next month he spoke at a dinner at Yale University. But his finances were still shaky. In 1940 he was grateful to be taken up by a wealthy patron of the arts, Caroline Newton, the middle-aged and unmarried daughter of A. E. Newton, bibliophile and expert on Samuel Johnson. She took Auden to the theatre, gave him a wristwatch which he admired, and became infatuated with him. Eventually she offered him financial help; he wrote to her: 'I have thought and thought about your offer, and all I can say is, yes, I will take the money.' He explained that this was because he was now bearing much of the cost of Chester Kallman's college fees, Chester's father being unwilling or unable to pay them; and he concluded his letter: 'The only proof of gratitude I can give is what I succeed in writing.'

By the summer of 1941 President Roosevelt, elected for a third term of office, had introduced conscription, and Auden, though not an American citizen, faced the prospect of being drafted for military service. He told Caroline Newton that he minded this only because he was worried about Chester's future if he himself joined the forces. But for the time being he heard nothing from the authorities; and during the summer, probably some time during the first two and a half weeks of July, a crisis occurred which overshadowed this concern. Auden discovered that Chester had taken another lover.

Auden went completely to pieces. 'I was forced to know', he afterwards wrote of the days that followed his discovery of Chester's unfaithfulness, 'what it is like to feel oneself the prey of demonic powers, in both the Greek and the Christian sense, stripped of self-control and self-respect, behaving like a ham actor in a Strindberg play.'

Chester's new lover was a young Englishman serving in the navy, who visited Middagh Street, and whom Chester had known for some time before having an affair with him. Auden, in a state bordering on insanity, seriously contemplated murdering the young man. 'On account of you,' he afterwards told Chester, 'I have been, in intention and almost in act, a murderer.' Some years later he remarked to a friend: 'It's frightening how easy it is to commit murder in America. Just a drink too much – I can see myself doing it. In England one feels all the social restraints held one back. But here anything can happen.' And in a poem addressed to Chester at the time of the crisis he wrote:

O my love, O my love,
In the night of fire and snow
Save me from evil.

Chester, meanwhile, told Auden that, though they could continue as friends, he would never go to bed with him again.

Chester's behaviour was only to be expected. He had never loved Auden with the same intensity as he was loved by him. He was still only twenty years old, and Auden, fourteen years his senior, had in his eyes the role of patron and protector rather than lover. Even this had its difficulties, for Chester sometimes resented Auden's patronage. Moreover Auden tended to treat him as a schoolmaster treats a clever pupil, showing him off to friends when it was convenient and pleasant to do so, but brushing him aside or leaving him in the background when there was serious conversation to be had. Tania Stern and other friends began to point out that this was not necessary, and said to Auden that if he was serious about Chester he should not exclude him; but the damage was already done, and Chester's unfaithfulness was no doubt partly in revenge for this. It was also the result of his temperament; he could not be satisfied, as Auden could, by a steady relationship with one person. Auden, in the years before meeting Chester, had certainly taken sex where he could find it, but he had always been searching for a permanent love-affair; he called himself 'by nature monandrous'. Chester by contrast was someone who wanted a succession of sexual and romantic thrills. Undoubtedly the relationship with Auden soon began to lack sexual excitement for him.

On 19 July 1941, apparently shortly after he had learnt of Chester's new love-affair, Auden had to leave New York and spend a week at Olivet College in Michigan, teaching at a summer school. From Olivet he wrote to Ursula Niebuhr that 'for a combination of reasons, personal, artistic and climatic, I have felt very lonely and low here'. He had intended that on his return to New York at the end of July he and Chester should go together to the summer home of Caroline Newton at Jamestown, Rhode Island. Despite the crisis between them, the two went there as planned, and Auden spent the following weeks trying to come to terms with what had happened, and with the prospect that his future life now offered him.

In his eyes Chester's behaviour was not simply a betrayal of a love-affair but a breaking of what Auden regarded as marriage-vows. He had used the term 'marriage' to describe his bond with Chester ever since the relationship began, and possibly the two of them had sworn actual vows. Auden's poem 'In Sickness and in Health', arising from his love for Chester, implies this when it talks of 'This round O of faithfulness we swear'.

Auden wrote no poetry during his month at Jamestown; but some lines that he composed a few months later describe his state of mind at this time. The speaker in the poem is St Joseph, confronted by Mary's apparent sexual infidelity when she has conceived Jesus; but Auden privately admitted that the poem was also about his own betrayal by Chester. 'Joseph', he told a friend, 'is me.'

> Where are you, Father, where?
> Caught in the jealous trap
> Of an empty house I hear
> As I sit alone in the dark
> Everything, everything,
> The drip of the bathroom tap,
> The creak of the sofa spring,
> The wind in the air-shaft, all
> Making the same remark
> Stupidly, stupidly,
> Over and over again.
> Father, what have I done?. . .
> How then am I to know,
> Father, that you are just?. . .
> All I ask is one
> Important and elegant proof
> That what my Love had done
> Was really at your will
> And that your will is Love.

The Christian faith to which he had returned less than a year earlier was being put to the severest test.

Then, about three weeks after he had arrived at Jamestown, Auden heard from England that his mother, aged seventy-two, had died in her sleep. The news came in a telegram which was read over the telephone to Caroline Newton. That evening, she, Chester Kallman and Auden were due to dine with an Admiral King at Newport, Rhode Island. Caroline Newton gave the news to Chester, asking him to break it to Auden. Chester came into the room, and said: 'We're not going to King's.' Auden remarked: 'Goody, goody.' Chester continued: 'The reason is your mother has died.' Auden sat in silence for a long while. Then he said: 'How like her that her last act on earth should be to get me out of a social engagement that I didn't want.' Then he burst into tears.

Afterwards he wrote to a friend: 'I was surprised at the violence of my feelings, though I had known it was likely. When mother dies, one is, for the first time, really alone in the world, and that is hard.'

Because of the war, mail from England was often delayed, and a letter to him from his mother arrived after she had died. He told his brother John that he could not bring himself to open it. Her death seemed to him an immense watershed. Afterwards he told several people that it had been a primary reason for his return to religion; though in fact his conversion had been completed almost a year before she died.

At the beginning of September 1941 he left Jamestown and returned to New York. He wrote to Caroline Newton: 'I only want to tell you that my month at Jamestown was, quite apart from its pleasure, a greater help to me than you will ever know. For a number of reasons, this summer has been a very difficult time for me, and without the rest and friendship which you gave me, I don't know how I should ever have got through it.'

He had already managed to find someone who could partly take over his mother's role in his life. Elizabeth Mayer had been a mother-figure to him ever since they had met, and now he gave her a photograph of himself as a baby in his mother's arms, inscribed: 'Elizabeth. I know my mother would be (and is) very happy to see who has taken her place.'

No such substitute could be found for Chester, nor did Auden seek for one. He had decided to accept Chester's demand that they should remain as friends but not lovers, with Chester seeking sexual relationships elsewhere.[1] Meanwhile the question of Auden's immediate future was solved by an invitation to be Associate Professor of English at the University of Michigan at Ann Arbor, where he had lectured briefly in January. The appointment was for a period of one year; Auden accepted it with the proviso that he might be drafted into the army at any moment. At the end of September 1941 he moved to Ann Arbor.

Chester remained in New York. He had now graduated from Brooklyn College, and began to take a course in shorthand and typing. He and Auden kept in touch by letter; or rather, Auden wrote frequently, but received only occasional replies from Chester which did not always match the warmth of his own letters. His always began 'Dearest Chester' and ended 'All my love', but Chester sometimes started his replies merely with 'Dear Wystan' and signed them simply 'Love'. Auden accepted this wryly. 'If equal affection cannot be,' he wrote in a poem some years later, 'Let the more loving one be me.'

He had come to terms quite quickly with the facts of the situation. 'Chester is in New York where there is an English sailor,' he wrote to Caroline Newton from Ann Arbor in January 1942. 'They are both very happy, which makes me so.' The trouble was that Chester was not content to remain with the same lover, but soon embarked on a series of promiscuous adventures. Auden was made profoundly unhappy by this. 'Promiscuity is so much harder to take', he told Caroline Newton,

---

[1]Christopher Isherwood, in a conversation with the present writer, recalls visiting Auden and Chester Kallman at Jamestown during the summer of 1941 in order to try to help sort out the crisis. He went for walks with Chester, and listened to Chester's declarations that he would never sleep with Auden again. Isherwood says he carefully avoided taking sides in the issue. He was at Jamestown briefly from about 24 August, having come east from California to make arrangements about his work in a Quaker hostel later that year.

'because it fills one with jealousy and anxiety for his spiritual welfare while a genuine love fills one with jealousy and respect.'

Chester sometimes wrote to Auden to describe the progress of his sexual affairs. For example: 'Still no word from Willy. If only I had some inkling where or how he was.' Auden in his turn encouraged Chester to confide in him: 'You must tell me more about Willy later. I'm sorry for your sake that you have fallen deeper than you once thought you had, because I suspect Willy of being as great a heart-menace as you are.' A friend observed that Chester's histrionic behaviour in love-affairs resembled, and indeed was perhaps modelled on, that of his favourite operatic heroines. Auden for his own part once admitted that he imagined himself in the role of the ageing Marschallin in *Rosenkavalier,* sadly agreeing to resign her lover into the arms of a young rival. Eventually he even came to accept Chester's promiscuity, with the difficulties that it produced. 'The triple situation,' he wrote in 1947, 'of being sexually jealous, like a wife, anxious like a momma, and competitive like a brother, is not easy for my kind of temperament. Still, it is my bed and I must lie on it.'

The remark about being 'competitive like a brother' refers to the fact that Auden, too, was now seeking sexual gratification elsewhere. He returned, in fact, to his old pattern, taking sex where he could find it, yet not going too much out of his way to get it. He described himself as 'too timid to cruise' – that is, to search for sex, as Chester did, in public lavatories and the like. Instead, he usually found his sexual partners by meeting them socially or getting to know them through his work as a teacher and lecturer. They tended to be college students or other young men of some intelligence but not great ability. Sometimes he gave Chester particulars of them. 'For my companion at L'Elisir d'Amore see my last letter,' he wrote on one occasion. 'Further details. Age 21: Height 6': size 7½-8". Condition uncircumcised but sympathetic. Occupation: Wall-Street Clerk (Insurance). Hobby. Playing the 'cello. Disposition sweet. Intelligence β –.' With young men such as this he would have affairs lasting a few weeks or even months, but rarely longer. When such people were not available he would sometimes resort to male prostitutes. But he still loved only Chester. 'Though —— is in the highest degree my dish,' he wrote to Chester when describing one young man, 'this girl is invulnerable to all but one, you old Brunhilde.'

He continued to be as protective towards Chester as ever, and to defend him against all criticisms. 'I hope I know Chester's faults as well as I know yours and mine,' he wrote to a friend who had been critical of Chester, 'but I also know that he is one of the three or four people who have had a profound and direct influence on my intellectual life.' He broke off his friendship with Mina Curtiss, who had been host to him during the summer of 1940, because she was rude about Chester; and others who were unenthusiastic towards Chester received similar treatment. Cyril Connolly once asked Chester, whom he regarded as a parasite on Auden: 'How does it feel to be Alice B. Toklas to Gertrude Stein?' Auden was furious. 'I shan't rest until Cyril Connolly is either dead or in a lunatic asylum,' he remarked to a friend. 'It's on account of Chester.' He even claimed that as a result of Connolly's rudeness he had taken steps which brought the eventual demise of Connolly's magazine *Horizon* – though by the mid 1950s he and Connolly were on good terms again.

His loyalty to Chester meant that very few friends were aware that there had been a change in the relationship between the two of them. Indeed, Auden was always happier and more affable when Chester was present. Only occasionally did his deeper feelings become apparent. Stephen Spender was once sitting at an open-air café table with the two of them when Chester got up, crossed the street, and began to make advances to a young man. Spender saw that though Auden went on talking, there were tears running down his cheeks.

When the blow of Chester's unfaithfulness fell on him in July 1941, Auden had tried to understand how such a thing could be consonant with the will of a loving God. Gradually during the following months he came to think of what had happened to him almost as a trial that God had imposed. The poem 'Canzone', which he wrote in September 1942, talks of a 'conscious trial' set by 'our God of Love'; and Auden expressed much the same idea in more frivolous fashion in a letter to a friend: 'Miss God appears to have decided that I am to be a writer, but have no other fun, and no talent for making others as happy as I would like them to be.'

Certainly he suffered much loneliness as a result of what had happened. In the months that immediately followed the crisis, Chester's behaviour to him was often thoughtless and cruel; Chester would ask for money, which he then wasted on his boyfriends, and he would disappear for weeks at a time without sending any news. Auden guessed that Chester was in fact testing his love, to reassure himself that it would not fail – the result, he said, of being underloved in childhood. He also typically explained Chester's promiscuity as growing from a wish to compensate for a curvature of the spine from which Chester suffered; the curvature was slight at first but much more apparent later. Meanwhile Auden's dream of a 'married' state was now entirely shattered. In February 1943 he wrote to Elizabeth Mayer: 'There are days when the knowledge that there will never be a place which I can call home, that there will never be a person with whom I shall be one flesh, seems more than I can bear, and if it wasnt for you, and a few – how few – like you, I dont think I could.' Yet in a way he also welcomed this loneliness and, in the years that immediately followed the crisis, made it the centre of his artistic life.

In a lecture on Shakespeare's sonnets in 1946 he remarked that the artist is not likely to be content with a relationship in which his love is returned with equal force; he wants instead to undergo the experience of unrequited love, in order to test his personality and strengthen it. Ultimately, Auden declared, the artist *is* strong, and can benefit from this situation. As he put it on another occasion: 'Poets are tough and can profit from the most dreadful experiences.' That he himself did so is suggested by the fact that, in the five years after the crisis, he wrote three long poems which were the most ambitious and sustained work he had yet tackled, and which to some extent all grew out of what had happened between him and Chester. He in fact needed the crisis: it provided a vital stimulus to his emotions and imagination. As he himself said of Chester: 'He makes me suffer and commit follies, without which I should soon become like the later Tennyson.' The truth was that his finest and greatest love was not for Chester but for his art. Everything else could be, and was, absorbed into it.

After his initially violent reaction to Chester's unfaithfulness had abated, Auden did not allow the crisis to make him mentally unstable, nor did he let it induce suicidal feelings in himself. He had a bourgeois distaste for insanity, and for suicide. Reviewing a book on suicide in 1972, he wrote: 'At no time in my life have I felt the slightest temptation to commit it, any more than I can imagine myself going off my head. . . Of course, like everybody else, I have my "good" and "bad" days, but I have always felt that to be walking this earth is a miracle I must do my best to deserve.'

Meanwhile, in 1941, the crisis remained largely unresolved for many months. In January 1942, Auden wrote to Spender, whose own first marriage had broken up a short time before: 'I have been having a great personal crisis, like you before me, of which I have reason to suspect that you have an inkling. Things are going to work out alright, I think, but it takes more faith and patience than is natural to me.' And to Chester he wrote from Ann Arbor late in December 1941: 'My thoughts are with you night and day.'

4

Teacher again

At Ann Arbor in the autumn of 1941 Auden found himself in a large co-educational Middle Western state university. For his first semester he lived in a house on Pontiac Street which belonged to an absent member of the faculty; he was also given a small, stark office on the campus. At the beginning he missed New York dreadfully, and felt 'lonelier and more lost than I have since I went to a boarding school'. But he was cheered up when Caroline Newton insisted on giving him the money to buy a car – he chose a 1939 Pontiac – and when he recognised an acquaintance from the previous year among the Ann Arbor students. This was Charles Miller, whom Auden had met briefly at Ann Arbor earlier in the year and to whom he had given a top grade in a University of Michigan poetry contest which he was invited to judge. He now asked Miller if he would share the house on Pontiac Street, and cope with such cooking as might be necessary; Miller was not homosexual, and Auden assured him he would be safe from his attentions. Miller accepted the arrangement, which proved a success.

During Auden's first semester at Ann Arbor, he lectured on 'Fate and the Individual in European Literature', rejecting any suggestion that he should teach either 'creative writing' or modern poetry – he believed that poets who taught for their living should keep as far as possible from their own field of work; he also held that modern literature did not require the assistance of a lecturer to introduce it to undergraduates. His students soon discovered that they were in for something remarkable. The syllabus which he announced included thirty-two set books, ranging from Aeschylus to opera libretti; he also recommended eighteen books of criticism. He arrived to teach his first class in blue jeans, a plaid shirt and a pair of bedroom slippers. He walked up and down as he spoke, often pausing to stare out of the window. The students found it hard at first to understand what he was saying; his English accent was made more incomprehensible by his rapid and indistinct diction. 'Very soon, though,' recalled one of his students, Robert Chapman, 'the power and strangeness of his discourse, and our craning efforts to hear it, began to make his

speech natural and comprehensible. After the initial shock most of us
were as elated as we were puzzled.'

Auden ignored many of the conventions of university teaching. He
forbade his class to take notes because, he said, 'one person cannot really
communicate anything specific to another person and therefore there is
nothing about which to take notes'. He astonished the students by asking
them to translate poems from German, French or Latin, picking for each
of them a language that he or she had not learnt, and explaining that this
must be done solely with the aid of a dictionary and their own wits. Most
of them managed quite well, though they would never have dared try it
before. He also insisted thay they memorise long stretches of poetry,
such as the whole of 'Lycidas'. Some of them rebelled at this; to these, he
simply said that they should try it first before complaining. Again, most
of them found that they liked it.

He put considerable intellectual pressure on them, and while his
demands were too much for some of them, others found it an exhilarating
experience. 'It was such a shock to know in my senior year', recalled one
of them, 'that my education in arts and ideas was totally shallow. That
class turned me around and directed me to a new (post-formal education)
search.' Another student wrote: 'He gave me a sense of the relatedness
and inter-relevance of all human effort and understanding. . . Since I
became afterwards a medievalist within literary studies, I can attribute
my first interest directly to Auden.'

Auden himself did not enjoy teaching undergraduates so much as
schoolboys; there was not the same opportunity to help to form their
minds, and he said: 'By that time, one feels the undergraduates should be
teaching themselves.' But he was agreeably surprised by the standard
that some of his students achieved by the end of the first semester, and he
also enjoyed getting to know them socially. He gave 'At Homes' to them
in his house, playing opera records, encouraging them to talk freely, and
providing plenty of cheap wine for them to drink – not realising that
many of them had scarcely touched alcohol before, with the result that
there were one or two minor incidents of drunkenness. He himself was
puzzled by some of the features of American university life. 'I went to a
dinner earlier in the week at a fraternity,' he told Caroline Newton.
'What an anthropological curiosity. I'd rather be dead than live in one.'

He made friends among faculty members, particularly with James
Rettger of the English department, and with Albert Stevens and his wife
Angelyn, herself a graduate student who was attending Auden's classes
on an informal basis. He spent much time at the Stevens's home,
gravitating as he so often did towards family life; and he began to seem to
them an almost charismatic figure. By talking to Angelyn Stevens, he
helped her (she believed) to overcome allergies from which she was
suffering. As a result of this, she felt able to have another child, for
whose birth Auden wrote the poem 'Mundus et Infans'; the child was

given the Christian names Wystan Auden. The consequence was that Auden began to be in demand from 'a front row of married women who keep ringing me up to cure some friend of cancer or haemmorhoids [sic]. And the really dreadful thing is that in my heart of hearts I believe that I can, if I really give my energy to it.' Later in the 1940s he again involved himself in the personal problems of married couples, not always with such happy results. He was at this period of his life deeply interested in the institution of marriage, and he would keep asking questions about how marriages worked – possibly because he wanted to learn anything that might help to keep his own 'marriage' to Chester going. What he did not realise was that the will-power of others was not as strong as his own, and that, if the marriage he was scrutinising was already unstable, his intensive questioning might expose latent difficulties and perhaps exacerbate them. The result was sometimes disastrous. 'Why do all the women I meet go mad?' he asked James Stern.

He had soon organised his life at Ann Arbor into the strict routine that he always demanded of himself. On weekdays he rose at six and worked until nine, telling his class: 'No telephone calls before 9 a.m.' By October, not long after beginning his new job, he had started to write a long poem whose working title was 'A Christmas Oratorio'.

'For the Time Being', as it was eventually called, had three purposes. The first was that it should be a memorial to his mother, to whom it was dedicated. That he should choose a religious subject for this purpose was natural, so closely did he associate her with his religious beliefs. It was, in fact, the only occasion on which he used Christianity as a direct poetic subject; and he was wary of doing it. He said he believed that all art was secular, and was not therefore really a fit vehicle for Christian belief. 'Culture', he said, 'is one of Caesar's things.' His second purpose in writing the oratorio was entirely secular: to construct a major work which Benjamin Britten could set to music. On 27 November 1941 Britten, together with Peter Pears and Elizabeth Mayer, came to stay with Auden at Ann Arbor, and Britten and Auden discussed the project. The third and more private purpose in writing 'For the Time Being' was to come to terms, through his Christian beliefs, with the crisis in his relationship with Chester. It was with this in mind that he composed the section entitled 'The Temptation of St Joseph'.

Just as his first semester at Ann Arbor came to an end, the Japanese attacked Pearl Harbour and America committed itself to the war. Auden, who was still awaiting his army draft, helped Angelyn Stevens with rationing arrangements for the neighbourhood, volunteering to deal specially with sugar restrictions because he hated the stuff so much himself. At Christmas he was joined by Chester, and the two of them travelled to California, eating their Christmas dinner with Christopher Isherwood. Auden was still unimpressed by Isherwood's Vedanta, calling it 'exotic' and dismissing Gerald Heard's espousal of it as 'heretical'. He declared to Isherwood: 'My dear, it's simply *not* a gentleman's religion.' He also claimed to deplore Isherwood's involvement with films, on the grounds that 'I consider the two most evil technical inventions so far to have been the internal combustion engine and the camera' – but this was 'lunatic clergyman' stuff, a dogmatic pronouncement made for the sheer outrageousness of it; it was also a contradiction of his 1936 praise of photography as 'the only democratic art'.

Auden and Chester also visited the Manns in California, but things were not easy now between them and Auden. They disliked Chester – Auden of course complained that this was because of anti-semitism – and they made sharp remarks about his having accepted money from Caroline Newton; they also seemed, he thought, to be jealous of his success as a writer. Moreover they were offended by his criticisms of Klaus Mann, whom he considered to be wasting his life in New York, pretending too much and achieving too little. As a result of these differences, Auden's previously warm feelings towards Erika Mann faded into merely social relations. Indeed he told a friend that he did not want to see the family again, except Thomas Mann, whom he still liked and admired; and there is no record of any further meetings between him and Erika; though when she died in 1969 she left him a small sum of money in gratitude for what he had done for her; and at Auden's own death, there was found among the few private papers he had brought to Christ Church, Oxford, a photostat of the marriage certificate, carefully preserved.

After Christmas 1941, Chester returned to New York, where in January 1942 he celebrated his twenty-first birthday – which gave rise to the poem 'Many Happy Returns'; though this was actually cast in the form of a birthday ode for the seven-year-old son of his Ann Arbor friends the Rettgers. Chester had now decided to take up his education again, and Auden, at his own expense, arranged for him to begin studying in graduate school at Ann Arbor, so that the two of them could live there together. Chester arrived in February. 'It won't be altogether easy,' Auden remarked to Caroline Newton.

In fact the arrangement did not work at all badly. There were difficulties between the two of them in the months that followed – Auden later referred to having let 'le faux-Chester. . . shit on my face' during this period. But domestically all went well. The two of them occupied an apartment at 1504 Brooklyn Avenue, and Auden found that Chester was 'a real genius at cooking'. They played records of opera at all hours of the day, and their home soon became a centre for the homosexual element on the Ann Arbor campus. After Auden had left Ann Arbor, he wrote a bawdy masque for this group; they performed it in January 1943. The manuscript has apparently now disappeared,[1] but the

---

[1]Auden could not find it when he wanted to show it to a friend at his New York apartment one day in 1946; he remarked: 'I do hope the F.B.I. hasn't been prying up here.'

title page read as follows: 'The Queen's Masque, by Bojo the Homo, played by Kallman's Klever Kompanions'. The characters were 'Mabel, Lizzie, 1st Echo, 2nd Echo, Queen of Dullness'. Auden remarked of it to a friend: 'It's *really* obscene. You must never let anybody see it.'

His homosexuality was now known to the university authorities, who were reputedly a little concerned about having brought a 'deviate' to the campus; indeed his whole reputation was poor with them, on account of such things as his giving the students a free hand with the wine bottles at his 'At Homes'. But no action was taken or apparently contemplated. Indeed the university made special efforts to arrange with the military Draft Board that Auden should not be called up for war service until he had finished his year of teaching. The Draft Board agreed to this. 'Meanwhile', Auden told Spender, 'I go on with my writing – an enormous oratorio.'

'For the Time Being', if not enormous in length, is certainly ambitious in scope. The first part, 'Advent', presents Man in the moral dilemma that Auden himself had faced in 1939: the collapse of his ethics in the face of humanity's evil. The following sections, 'The Annunciation', 'The Temptation of St Joseph', 'The Summons', 'At the Manger' and 'The Meditation of Simeon', retrace the intellectual and emotional experiences through which Auden had passed on his quest for the Absolute; while in 'The Massacre of the Innocents' Herod is presented as a rational liberal humanist – someone holding the views that Auden had found unworkable – who cannot bring himself to believe without proof and is therefore unhappily obliged to order the massacre: 'O dear, why couldn't this wretched infant be born somewhere else? Why can't people be sensible?' The oratorio concludes with 'The Flight into Egypt', in which the desert becomes a symbol of modern decadence; and with a speech by the narrator, reminding us that we are still in the modern world, with the memory of Christmas fading behind us; we are in 'the Time Being' which is 'in a sense, the most trying time of all'.

At about the beginning of February 1942 Auden sent Britten some of the text, hoping to hear what he thought of it. Britten was apparently encouraging,[1] and urged Auden to go on with it. Auden worked at it during the spring and early summer of 1942, hoping to finish it before he was drafted; on the strength of it, he applied for, and was awarded, a Guggenheim fellowship worth about two thousand dollars. 'For the Time Being' was finished by about August 1942. But meanwhile Britten and Pears had left America and sailed back to England. They had decided that they could not remain in the U.S.A. for the very reason that Auden felt he could: they lacked roots there.[2] Once they had arrived in England, Britten was busy for many months, and in January 1943 he had still not

[1] Auden scarcely ever kept letters that he received, usually throwing them away as soon as they were read. None of Britten's letters to him survives.

[2] See Auden's letter to Britten on the subject of Britten's development as an artist written

begun work on the oratorio, though Auden was hoping he would do so soon. Yet in the event he never did.

Or rather, he set only two sections to music, for performance in a BBC radio programme in 1944: the chorale 'Our Father, whose creative Will', and the 'Shepherds' Carol' which was originally part of the text, but which Auden removed before publication. This carol has the refrain 'O lift your little pinkie and touch the winter sky./ Love's all over the mountains where the beautiful go to die'. 'Pinkie', as Auden often explained, is slang for 'finger', and not for penis, as some have faintly suspected. He told Angelyn Stevens, who saw the carol in manuscript, that he had in mind the fingers of chubby angels that decorate baroque churches.

According to Sir Peter Pears, Britten's reason for not setting the oratorio was simply its immense length. Pears writes: 'Ben had expected [it] as a text for music, but it turned out to be a major opus, quite unsuitable without *vast* cuts for an oratorio libretto. My memory (very bad) tells me that Ben realised then that he could not take Wystan seriously as a librettist and/or Wystan could not take him (Ben) seriously as a composer. He, Ben, was hurt and bored by this. I *do* remember the receipt of "For the Time Being" and how Ben was bitterly disappointed with, for instance, the Fugue (a few syllables are enough for a fugue) –Wystan wrote 7 stanzas of 10 lines each [the section 'Great is Caesar: He has conquered Seven Kingdoms', which is headed 'Fugal-Chorus']. Actually in 1941, we had been on the West Coast for the whole of the summer, and hadn't seen Wystan since May and *Paul Bunyan*. Ben hadn't had a chance to work with him on the Oratorio. . . And one of the things Ben had learnt from *Paul Bunyan* was that in creating new large-scale musical works it was of the *utmost importance* that the poet and composer should work together from the outset. When a large section of the work arrived, Ben was desperate at how far Wystan had gone ahead without him, and as he was much more confident of himself as a composer now, he abandoned the whole idea.

'We had, too, decided to come back to England, which Wystan highly disapproved of, and so came the cooling. Ben was on a different track now, and he was no longer prepared to be dominated – bullied – by Wystan, whose musical feeling he was very well aware of. Anyway Ben was thinking about *Peter Grimes* [his next opera, based on a poem by Crabbe, which he had first read in America] and perhaps he may be said to have said goodbye to working with Wystan with his marvellous setting of the Hymn to St Cecilia, which he wrote crossing the Atlantic on the way home.'

Auden's feelings about Britten's decision not to set 'For the Time Being' are not recorded, but he was presumably disappointed. He was also a little upset by Britten's comparative coolness towards Elizabeth Mayer,

just before Britten left for England: in Donald Mitchell, *Britten & Auden in the Thirties*, Faber, 1981, pp. 161-2.

to whom Britten did not seem to be expressing adequate gratitude for all she had done. Yet for the moment there was no suggestion that his friendship with Britten had come to an end.

After the 1942 spring semester had finished, Auden left Ann Arbor, selling his car because it would be useless in New York; Chester remained at Ann Arbor to continue his graduate studies. For part of the summer, Auden stayed with Caroline Newton at a new house she had taken in Pennsylvania; he wrote a poem to read at the house-warming party, 'In War Time', which suggests that he was still partly doubtful about the validity of the war. Meanwhile he told a friend that he was contemplating for his next work 'a sort of modern Vita Nuova'.

Caroline Newton was a difficult and neurotic hostess. James and Tania Stern were also her guests for much of the summer, and, especially for two or three weeks while James Stern was away attending a writers' conference in Colorado, Auden and Tania Stern became close confidants, amusing themselves with private jokes against her. When the visit to Pennsylvania was over, Auden stayed in the Sterns' New York apartment for a few days; and it was while he was there that, at last, he was summoned to a military draft board.

'They rejected me yesterday,' he wrote to Caroline Newton on 2 September, ' "They" in this case being the psychiatrist who was both unpleasant and grotesquely ignorant. So that is that.'

The ground for his rejection was his homosexuality, about which he had been quite candid to the board. He told the Sterns: 'I was asked if I had any girl-friends. "Oh yes," I said, "I have lots of friends who are girls!"' When Chester Kallman's turn for the draft came, he was rejected for the same reason.

A friend reported that Auden was 'very much sunk' by the rejection. But he quickly made new plans. He was offered a job as a lecturer in English at Swarthmore College, not far from Caroline Newton's Pennsylvania home – he had presumably made himself known to the college while staying there. On 9 September 1942 he wrote to the college saying that he would like to accept.

★

In the autumn of 1942 when Auden arrived at Swarthmore, the college, a private liberal arts foundation with Quaker associations – like the Downs School where Auden had taught in the 1930s – numbered only five hundred students, but, as Auden said, it was 'considered to have one of the highest academic rankings in the country'. He found most of the faculty 'extremely nice' – he already knew Wolfgang Köhler, the Gestalt psychologist, who held a professorship there – but at first he thought the students 'a little dull'. Later he was to remark that 'the institutions of Higher Learning in America cannot decide whether they are to be Liberal Arts Colleges for the exceptional few or vocational schools for the average many, and so fail to do their duty by either'.

For his first year he was given a room in 'Sunnybank', an eighteenth-century farmhouse a mile from the campus. At first he was unhappy. 'I can't say I like it yet,' he wrote to Caroline Newton. 'Everyone is very nice but not very lively. Am in fact extremely homesick for Ann Arbor where by the time I left I knew all the outrageous people; also of course when Chester isnt around, I feel as if I had a leg or something missing.' He complained that the town of Swarthmore was 'a dump without either a bar or a movie house', and he was depressed to find that there was only a poor train service into Philadelphia, the nearest city. His restlessness was perhaps one reason why, this autumn, he was asking friends for advice about how to get into the Merchant Marine for the duration of the war. But nothing came of this idea, and he had soon settled himself at Swarthmore, with his usual facility for making himself at home any-where. His room quickly became littered with wine-bottles, opera records, cigarette packs and books; and he continued to work to his regular routine of early rising so that he could write before breakfast. Already he had begun another long poem.

Nothing had come of his intention to compose a *Vita Nuova*. (If it had, it may be that Chester Kallman or some figure based on him would have taken the role of Beatrice in Dante's poem, and that the equivalent of the death of Beatrice would have been Chester's unfaithfulness.) Instead, Auden was writing an epilogue to *The Tempest,* a play whose conclusion he though inadequate for its themes; he said: 'Both the repentance of the guilty and the pardon of the injured [in Shakespeare's last scene] seem more formal than real.' On a deeper level, 'The Sea and the Mirror' as he called his new poem was, he said, 'really about the Christian conception of Art'. Shakespeare described art as 'a mirror held up to nature', and Auden's preface and his first section, 'Prospero to Ariel', tackle the dilemma that the artist can merely reflect human nature, not change it; only the religious sense can transcend it with its 'smiling secret'. On another level, 'The Sea and the Mirror', like its predecessor, 'For the Time Being', was concerned with Auden's personal crisis. The section 'Prospero to Ariel' was listed by him as among those poems alluding to his relationship with Chester Kallman; and Prospero's lines certainly express personal pain, mixed with the certainty that the right decision has been made:

> Stay with me, Ariel, while I pack, and with your first free act
> Delight my leaving. . .
> I am glad I have freed you,
> So at last I can really believe I shall die.
> For under your influence death is inconceivable. . .
> O Ariel, Ariel,
> How I shall miss you. Enjoy your element. Good-bye.

Similarly in the next section, where the characters of the play review the manner in which events have changed them, Sebastian's relief at not having committed the murder he contemplated recalls Auden's own murderous thoughts towards Chester's lover during his crisis.

Auden was able to devote a lot of time to 'The Sea and the Mirror' during his first year at Swarthmore, for his appointment at the college involved only part-time lecturing, the rest of his income deriving from the Guggenheim award. His students, like those at Ann Arbor, were soon encountering the oddity of his teaching methods. He would hand them mimeographed copies of poems that were unknown to them, in which he had left blanks for certain words, and would ask them to fill these in – the device he had used while teaching at St Mark's, Southborough, in 1939. Some of the blanks were designed to test their grasp of the rhyme scheme, but many were in the middle of lines and were intended to make them think carefully about the use of language. As at Ann Arbor, he also demanded that they get to know the texts really well, and would often ask them to write down quotations from memory. In contrast, he would often swing away from the immediate subject to some hugely general topic. Setting an examination in Elizabethan literature he asked: 'Explain why the devil is (a) sad and (b) honest.'

Again as at Ann Arbor, he kept his own poetry entirely out of his teaching, and did not give readings. But he made himself readily available to the college for lectures on all kinds of subjects; his topics on these occasions included 'Vocation and Society' and 'Education in a Democratic Society'; later he also taught a course at Swarthmore on 'The History of Ideas, 1660–1760'. He proved himself, in fact, willing to take part in all kinds of Swarthmore activities. He served on committees to judge student poetry, spoke at formal functions, and reviewed productions of plays for the campus newspaper. In these reviews he was often sharp about the choice of play; he dismissed *The Taming of the Shrew* as 'Shakespeare's worst play' (an opinion he often repeated), and called *Night Must Fall,* written by his Christ Church contemporary Emlyn Williams, merely 'an excuse for carrying on charmingly in public'. But he always took care to give detailed and sympathetic critiques of the cast, in which he often displayed a marked admiration for the good looks of some of the male actors.

Swarthmore students were amused and puzzled by him. One of them said he 'looked like a thatched cottage', though he was observed to be more tidily dressed for public lectures. They noticed that when he came back from trips to Philadelphia he brought with him a suitcase full of wine bottles, Swarthmore College and town being 'dry'; that he walked about outdoors in bedroom slippers; that he wore no underclothes and often no socks; and that he often entertained visitors in his bathrobe. He for his part paid little attention to Swarthmore's social habits. 'My seminar on Romanticism starts tomorrow,' he wrote to Ursula Niebuhr. 'Quakers or no Quakers, I shall serve bread and cheese and beer at four o'clock.' In fact he positively urged students towards nonconformity and individualism, telling them that their college years were not to be wasted in being sensible and co-operative. 'Fellow Irresponsibles,' he concluded an article in the campus newspaper, 'follow me.'

He was soon an accepted and popular member of the college; yet in December 1942, a few months after arriving, he wrote to Chester: 'I'm still very lonely here, though some of the faculty are very nice. No sex, not even a piece of trade[1] in N.Y., for Les has moved somewhere.' He occasionally visited Chester at Ann Arbor or met him for a weekend in New York; and sometimes Chester came down for a few days to Swarthmore. In February 1943 Chester finished his studies at Ann Arbor, and stayed on there for a time writing music reviews for a campus newspaper. Auden reported proudly that Chester's critiques were causing a furore because of their outspokenness; to Chester he wrote: 'The Tchaikovsky piece is excellent, though I must go over your English with you.' Eventually Chester returned to New York, where for some time he worked as an official censor of mail to Europe. This was not much to his taste. 'I've worked all day protecting my country,' he wrote to Auden, 'and I'm just about ready to let the enemy have all the secrets it damn pleases.'

He and Auden began to talk about a literary collaboration. In March 1943 Chester wrote to Auden: 'There is a modern verse play in the "ice-maiden", – the woman who could not love *enough*, a destructive force, – she has her tears though, since she did try,[2] this is perhaps our collaboration – and I so much want to write with you. . . You, of course, do not like the theatre – still perhaps I can persuade you to "do it again".' Auden encouraged him to begin work on this idea, but nothing happened.

Auden meanwhile reported that 'The Sea and the Mirror' was 'going quite nicely so far'. By early January 1943 he had finished much of the second section. During the spring semester he was occupied with his seminar at Swarthmore on 'Romanticism from Rousseau to Hitler', which, as one of the students commented, was really an excuse to study the heterogeneous collection of artists who happened to interest him at that moment – they included Kierkegaard, Kafka, Rilke, Pascal, Herman Melville, Berlioz and Isadora Duncan. His aim, now as always, was to produce from such disparate sources a complete scheme or synthesis of ideas – to make intellectual order out of the whole field of human experience. In the hope of persuading his class that this was possible he showed them a chart he had drawn, in which human life was represented as a progress from the Fall towards the final state of Paradise (the City of

[1] i.e. a male prostitute.

[2] Was Chester thinking of his own personality?

God), and which showed the various forms of Hell into which error could lead along the way. He gave no further explanation of the chart; but one of the students, Kenneth Lewars, had 'an uneasy feeling that if one accepted this or that that Auden said, one was on the way to Christian beliefs like Auden's'.[1]

In the late spring of 1943 Auden came to a temporary halt on 'The Sea and the Mirror', being unable to find the right form for the final section, and began several months of what he called 'fruitless prospecting'. In June he stayed with Wolfgang Stolper, who taught economics at Swarthmore, and his wife in New Hampshire; while there he read through the whole of Shakespeare chronologically, which he found 'fun'. Then he went on by himself to Magnolia, a seaside resort near Boston, for July and August. Chester did not write to him, and he began to be tired of 'days of speaking to *no one*'. But he reported that he had at last 'struck oil' on the final section of 'The Sea and the Mirror'.

He hit on the idea of writing a long speech in which Caliban addresses the audience in an ornately literary manner. As Auden explained it: 'The whole point about the verbal style is that, since Caliban is inarticulate, he has to borrow, from Ariel, the most artificial style possible, i.e. that of Henry James.' Auden knew James's work intimately, and liked in later years to tell the story of how, when he was having a telephone installed and was asked by the operator to say something to test the apparatus, he recited from memory a long passage of *The American Scene*. Now, as he resumed work on 'The Sea and the Mirror', James's style came naturally to him, and the result was a brilliant pastiche in which Caliban, representing the animal nature of Man as opposed to Ariel, the spiritual nature, delivers an oration on one of the central concerns of Auden's poetry: the role of the artist in society. The speech emphasises the gap between what men want to be like and what they really are; and its conclusion is that only God, the ultimate Artist, can create 'the perfected Work' of which art itself is only a 'feebly figurative sign'. Auden called Caliban's speech 'by far the most important' in 'The Sea and the Mirror'. Some years later he told a radio producer who had suggested cutting it in a broadcast performance: 'If *I* were to be faced with the problem of cutting, I would cut out everything except this section.' Near the end of his life he named 'Caliban to the Audience', though it is in prose, as the poem of which he was most proud.

When he returned to Swarthmore at the end of the summer of 1943 his Guggenheim Fellowship had come to an end, and he was given a full-time teaching appointment, with the status of Associate Professor. The college was now filled largely with naval cadets, and Auden took twenty of these for English composition, which he found a rather depressing

---

[1]The chart is reproduced in Richard Kostelanetz, ed., *Essaying Essays,* New York: Out of London Press, 1975, facing p. 48. A facsimile also appears in the catalogue of the Auden exhibition at the Berg Collection, New York Public Library (1981).

experience: 'Seeing that they have been at school for twelve years, their ignorance is incredible, and their lack of wish to know anything sad.' He taught them with his mixture of eccentricity and discipline, setting them such tasks as describing the previous day's events *backwards*. He also acted as an instructor in spoken English for a group of Chinese naval officers who were for some reason spending a few weeks at Swarthmore before going to engineering schools; he found them 'very nice to teach', though one of his colleagues wondered how much they and Auden really managed to understand each other. Besides all this he also taught a course one evening each week at Bryn Mawr, the women's college, near Swarthmore. In his spare time he began editing a selection of Tennyson's poetry for a New York publisher; in his introduction to the volume he wrote of Tennyson: 'He had the finest ear, perhaps, of any English poet; he was also undoubtedly the stupidest.' This earned the comment from T. S. Eliot that if Auden had been a better scholar he would have known many stupider.

He was now living on the top floor of a house near the campus, 16 Oberlin Avenue, the home of Maurice Mandelbaum, who taught philosophy at the college, and his wife and children. Auden described his own apartment as 'lovely', and proudly announced that his bed had once belonged to the inventor of a syphilis cure. To visitors he showed off a basket of wax flowers under a glass dome, which he had bought cheaply and described as 'heavenly' (he did not usually indulge in such 'camp' enthusiasms). He spent much time downstairs in the company of the Mandelbaums, who filled the role in his life that the Stevens family had played at Ann Arbor. He rarely ate at home, usually taking his lunch in a drug-store a few blocks away, which was the handiest place for food but had a juke-box that annoyed him – 'I thought I'd go out of my mind if I heard "I'm Dreaming Of A White Christmas" once more', he recalled of these months. His habit of writing while sitting in the drug-store was noticed by a waitress, who one day asked if he was a poet. 'I said "Yes", and she said, "Well, there's a sailor here who'd like to talk to you." He came over and said, "Oh, I'm making a chest for my girl-friend, and I want some verses for it." So I said, "Well, give me the details and it'll cost you two cigars." And I wrote the poem, and got the cigars.' He was very proud of this 'commission'.

'The Sea and the Mirror' was not completed until the middle of February 1944. On finishing it, Auden judged it 'the best I've done so far'. By this time he was involved in another project, the assembling and editing of a retrospective collection of his own poetry. He had proposed this to Random House about a year earlier. At first they were doubtful; he wrote again, pointing out that all his books of poems were now out of print except the American edition of his 1930-33 *Poems,* which included much he would now prefer to be forgotten. 'I hate to behave with the traditional petulant vanity of the author,' he told them, 'but I *should* like people to be able to get hold of my work.' The publishers finally agreed, and he began preparing the volume during the latter part of 1943.

He did not own copies of all his books, and he had to borrow *On This Island* from the Swarthmore college library to mark certain revisions in it for the printer ('Most improperly', said a member of the college staff). There were in fact many textual changes. He accepted Valéry's dictum 'A poem is never finished, only abandoned', to which he added his own comment 'It must not be abandoned too soon.' He had often changed his poems, if only slightly, between their first appearance in magazines and their later collection into book form. The revisions that he now made to his earlier work were a continuation of that process. Some were merely small alterations of language or punctuation. But others were more radical, reflecting the profound changes he had undergone since all but his most recent poetry was published. In May 1942, when he was already contemplating these revisions, he wrote to his friend the poet and critic Louise Bogan: 'Now and then I look through my books and is my face red. One of the troubles of our time is that we are all, I think, precocious as personalities and backward as characters. Looking at old work I keep finding ideas which one had no business to see already at that age, and a style of treatment which one ought to have outgrown years before.'

When he began work on the revisions he decided to omit one entire early work, *The Dance of Death,* from the new collection. Two others, 'Paid on Both Sides' and *The Orators,* were dismembered, and only a few fragments from them were allowed to appear; in the introduction to the volume, Auden dismissed *The Orators* as a 'fair notion fatally injured'. Those pieces from his first book, *Poems,* which were included (many were dropped) were largely left unaltered, perhaps because they were now too remote from him to have any relation to his present mode of thought; but much of the later work underwent major revisions. Private jokes and obscure references were cut out – for example, the line 'Wystan, Stephen, Christopher, all of you' in one of the *Orators* odes was changed to 'Subjects, Objects, all of you'; and 'loony Layard' became 'the suave archdeacon'. As to Auden's period of Communist sympathy, or at least his interest in Communism as an idea for poetry, he omitted 'A Communist to Others' from his new collection, and alongside the text of it in the Swarthmore copy he scribbled: 'O God what rubbish'.

Two poems from his period of liberal humanism tinged with Christian sympathies underwent major changes. He altered the conclusion of the Commentary to his Chinese sonnets, which had formerly been humanist in tone, so that it now had a specifically Christian stamp; and from the poem 'September 1, 1939' he excised the stanza containing the line 'We must love one another or die'. E. M. Forster said of this line that because Auden had written it 'he can command me to follow him'; but Auden now thought the line 'a damned lie', on the grounds that we must die in any case, and decided that the whole passage must be scrapped.[1] Several other poems from the 1930s were also dismissed by him as 'trash'.

He decided to arrange the poems not chronologically but in alphabetical order by first line, a system deliberately intended to obscure the history of his own development. He told Stephen Spender: 'My reason for doing that was not to pretend that I have gone through no historical change, but because there are so very few readers who can be trusted to approach one's poems without a preconceived notion of what that development has been. I wanted to test the reader who believes that my earliest poems are the best; e.g. make him read a poem and then guess its date.' He also added titles to many poems which had not previously had them. Some of these titles were illuminating, but many were ironic or flippant. The mysterious 'Just as his dream foretold, he met them all' was now titled 'Nobody Understands Me'; 'Our hunting fathers told the story' became 'In Father's Footsteps'; and 'Now from my window-sill I watch the night' was headed 'Not All The Candidates Pass'. It was as if Auden were trying to distance himself from the emotions expressed in the poems.

He delivered the revised texts of his collected poetry to Random House just before Christmas 1943, hoping that they would publish the book quickly so that there would be a reasonable interval between it and his next book, which was to consist of 'For the Time Being' and 'The Sea and the Mirror'. But Random House were slow to do anything, and then came a wartime paper shortage, so that eventually, to Auden's annoyance, it was decided to postpone publication until after the other book had been issued. In the event *The Collected Poetry of W. H. Auden,* a title that Auden himself disliked because he said it implied finality, was expanded to include both 'For the Time Being' and 'The Sea and the Mirror'.

Having finished his second year at Swarthmore, Auden spent much of the summer of 1944 in New York, living in the Sterns' apartment on East 52nd Street, which he soon reduced to chaos – Stern could scarcely recognise the place when he came back. Auden found the heat of the city almost unbearable, and took to working in air-conditioned cafeterias. During these weeks he began to write what he originally intended to be a one-page poem, making use of a particular metrical pattern. It turned out to be another major work.

'For the Time Being' had examined the human condition in terms of religion; 'The Sea and the Mirror' did the same in terms of art and its relation to life. Auden's new work tackled the same questions in terms of inner consciousness. Like its predecessors it was in dramatic form. There were four characters, a group of unattached contemporary North

---

[1]When the editor of a 1955 anthology pleaded with Auden to let him include the entire text of the poem, Auden agreed, provided that the reading 'We must love one another and die' was used. Some commentators have taken it to be a misprint.

Americans meeting as strangers in a wartime New York bar, where, in
language as rich as, and often reminiscent of, *The Orators,* and in an
alliterative verse-form close to that of 'In the year of my youth', they
explore their memories and their most private hopes and fears. The four
characters, Malin, Rosetta, Quant and Emble, in fact represent the four
faculties of the personality as characterised by Jung: Thinking, Feeling,
Intuition and Sensation. Auden gave to the poem the title *The Age of
Anxiety.*

'The basic human problem', he wrote in a review published this year
(1944), 'is man's anxiety in time; e.g. his present anxiety over himself in
relation to his past and his parents (Freud), his present anxiety over
himself in relation to his future and his neighbours (Marx), his present
anxiety over himself in relation to eternity and God (Kierkegaard).' *The
Age of Anxiety* was also, like the other major poems of this period of
Auden's life, intended to be an exploration of an aspect of his private
predicament, in this case his loneliness, which he now regarded as a
universal condition. 'As everybody knows,' he wrote, 'we live today in
one world; but not everyone realizes that to live in one world is to live
in a lonely world. . . All the old charms and cosiness have vanished
forever. . . Each must go his way alone, every step of it.'

At the end of the summer of 1944, just before he returned to Swarthmore for a third year, his new book *For the Time Being,* consisting of the
title poem and 'The Sea and the Mirror', was published by Random
House; Faber's followed with a British edition six months later. Most
critics were enthusiastic, and though not everybody thought the oratorio
a success, several agreed with Auden's judgement of 'The Sea and the
Mirror' as his best work yet. The following spring the *Collected Poetry*
was issued in America – Faber's did not yet produce a British version –
and again reviewers had much to say in Auden's praise. There was
some criticism of the exclusion of so many poems, and of the titles he
had given to some of those which were retained, but the book sold
exceptionally well. Nearly fifteen thousand copies were printed during
the first year alone, eleven hundred of these (Auden proudly announced
to his friends) being bought by the U.S. Navy. In the following twenty-
two years the book was reprinted again and again, eventually reaching a
total of some 52,000 copies, an extraordinary achievement for poetry.

Late in 1944 Auden broke off his friendship with Caroline Newton, his
rich patron. She had not bothered to offer any payment to Tania Stern
for gymnastic classes she had attended, on the grounds that Tania was a
friend of hers, and in the subsequent argument she made it clear that she
would only remain friends with Auden if he took her side. He of course
refused to do so, and severed relations with her. He had given Caroline
Newton a number of manuscript poetry notebooks as a partial return for
her gifts of money, and it may be that he was afterwards somewhat
ashamed of these transactions; for in later years he always insisted on

giving manuscripts to friends purely as a token of friendship, and would not in any circumstances sell them.

Auden intended to continue teaching at Swarthmore at least until the summer of 1945; but early that year his plans changed. In March he called on James Stern in New York and said he had been put in touch with someone in the Pentagon who was organising an overseas mission that would last between six months and a year, in which certain civilians would be given military uniform and rank and would undertake some kind of task in Germany once the Nazis had been finally defeated. Auden did not know exactly what this task would be, but he hoped and expected to be chosen because of his knowledge of Germany and its language. Stern noticed that 'his calm was forced, he was highly excited'. He encouraged Stern to contact the organiser of the mission and try to join it. Stern did so, and was successful. In a matter of weeks it was arranged that both men should take part in the 'United States Strategic Bombing Survey' in Germany, whose job would be to discover from the civilian population what had been the effects of the Allied bombing. Auden quickly wound up his affairs at Swarthmore – one of his last actions being to take part in a college production of *The Ascent of F6,* in which he played the part of the silent, cowled monk who holds the crystal for Ransom to look into. Then, late in April 1945, he left for Europe by air, wearing the uniform of a U. S. Army major. His friends observed that he was very proud to be dressed in it.

*

He landed in England, where he was able to spend a few days, remarking to friends: 'My dear, I'm the first major poet to fly the Atlantic.' He went up to the Lake District to see his father, who was now living there, having sold the Harborne house. He also called on a number of his London friends. 'I saw Eliot who is a tower of strength,' he reported to Elizabeth Mayer, 'and I saw Ben and Peter just before they went off to Sadlers Wells for rehearsals. Ben looked older but pretty well and Peter was blooming.' He visited Stephen Spender and John Lehmann, neither of whom had seen him since his emigration. They noticed that his accent had changed, and that he now spoke with an American flattened 'a'. Auden himself, when challenged with this, sometimes claimed it was not American at all, but the result of his Midland upbringing, which was not true; it was a habit he had developed since going to the States in 1939. In fact apart from this one vowel-change his accent had not become American, nor was it to do so in the years that followed. If anything, he grew, with his hasty pronunciation and poor diction, to sound more and more like an Oxford don. His American friends were unanimous in pronouncing his speech entirely English.

In London, John Lehmann was taken aback to find himself being harangued by Auden. 'He launched into a long lecture,' recalled Lehmann, 'quoting detailed statistics. . . on the world power position after the war. Great Britain, her Dominions and Empire had apparently been liquidated, while the two giants, the U.S.A. and the U.S.S.R., towered over the world. Britain, in fact, was lucky to have survived the war at all. There was no word from Uncle Sam Auden about what we had endured. . . On the contrary, the second part of the lecture consisted of an exposé of the superiority of American culture, and a sharp calling to order of myself when, as a kind of desperate gesture of defence, I made some mild criticisms of recent American fiction.' Spender, too, had a row with Auden about a similar lecture, while many of Auden's other English friends had to listen to him making a ferocious attack on their way of life: 'This room is very cold: can't think how you stand it without central heating. No, I won't stay and eat: I simply can't stand British food.' He also told them that 'London hadn't really been bombed.' Meeting Stephen Spender's second wife Natasha for the first time, he surveyed the newly lit-up streets of London and told her expansively: 'I do *love* New York.' His aggression certainly forestalled any criticism of his own absence from Britain during the war – which may have been what it was unconsciously intended to do.[1]

Auden arrived in Germany on about 5 May, while the war was still officially in progress, to begin work as a Bombing Research Analyst in the Morale Division of the U.S. Strategic Bombing Survey, his task being to interview the civilian population and obtain as much information as possible about the effect on 'morale' of the wartime bombing. 'This *Morale* title', he remarked to a friend, 'is illiterate and absurd. How can one learn anything about morals, when one's actions are beyond any kind of morality? *Morale* with an "e" at the end is psycho–sociological nonsense. What they want to say, but don't say, is how many people we killed and how many buildings we destroyed by that wicked bombing.'

By V.E. Day he was in Darmstadt, to the south of Frankfurt, and was billeted in a house belonging to a Nazi couple who had gone into hiding, leaving their children with the grandparents. 'When the couple came home,' Auden recalled, 'I was the one who had to tell them that the grandparents had killed themselves – and had taken it upon themselves to kill their grandchildren, too.' Darmstadt had been devastated in an air-raid the previous autumn. 'The town', Auden wrote to Tania Stern, 'was ninety-two per cent destroyed in thirty minutes. You can't imagine what that looks like unless you see it with your own eyes.' And to a friend he said: 'I cannot help but ask myself, "Was there no other way?" ' He began to interview civilians and find out what he could about their experiences. 'I keep wishing you were here with us to help,' he wrote to

---

[1]Auden did, however, remain deeply fond of much of the landscape of Britain, and at one time after the war contemplated writing one of the Shell guides to English counties.

Elizabeth Mayer, 'and then I think perhaps not, for as I write this sentence I find myself crying.'

James Stern, meanwhile, had travelled to Germany separately and was at Bad Nauheim, not far from Frankfurt, facing the gloomy prospect of joining a team that had to track down and translate hundreds of documents. Auden managed to contact him by telephone, and told him he must come over and join the Darmstadt team as an interviewer. Somehow this transfer was arranged, and Stern was soon working alongside Auden.

He found that Auden had already adapted his military uniform to his own liking, removing the helmet-liner and donning carpet-slippers instead of shoes. He had also managed to find a supply of Rhine wine, which he consumed in large quantities each evening, generally taking at least one full bottle to bed with him. He had, as another friend who met him in Germany observed, the knack of 'attaching to his person the exact support required to make him comfortable'.

The team's work at Darmstadt included several days of 'briefing'. Auden found this very irritating; he described it as 'mid-witted folk talking mid-witted trash in bogus socio-political jargon'. On 29 May he and his colleagues left Darmstadt and set out on a tour of Bavaria. Auden was the team's civilian leader – he dubbed himself 'Research Chief' – and he usually insisted on driving one of the two jeeps they had at their disposal. Stern, sitting beside him, found this alarming, so reckless was he at the wheel.

They travelled first to Munich. Auden described the appearance of the city in a letter to Elizabeth Mayer, who had lived there before the war: 'The city as a whole is gone. The towers of the Frauenkirche remain and half the nave, but why go on.' The team was billeted in a *Schloss* near the Starnberger See, twenty miles outside the town; they rose at six each morning and drove into Munich to begin the day's interviews with civilians, which were conducted in one of the few undamaged houses.

Auden's German was just about up to the task of interviewing, though he spoke without any great care for pronunciation or accuracy. The procedure was for each member of the team to sit alone in a room with a German civilian, who had been selected at random, and ask questions about the bombing. 'The work is very interesting but I'm crying sometimes,' Auden reported to Tania Stern. 'The people. . . are sad beyond belief.' Afterwards he commented of these interviews: 'We asked them if they minded being bombed. We went to a city which lay in ruins and asked if it had been hit. We got no answers that we didn't expect.'

Typically, Auden did not limit himself to the official brief of his team. On his own initiative he made an investigation into the attempt the previous summer to assassinate Hitler. From a friend of Elizabeth Mayer, Dr Else Jaffe (sister of D. H. Lawrence's wife Frieda), he acquired an account of the events leading up to the plot, and of its aftermath, written for him by a leading anti-Nazi, Professor Emil Henk. He also met and had tea with the father of a young man who was one of the four beheaded for their part in the Munich students' uprising of January 1943. Also while he was at Munich he visited a hospital where Jews from concentration camps had been brought. 'I was prepared for their appearance', he told Elizabeth Mayer, 'but not for their voices: they whisper like gnomes.' He asked Tania Stern to cable a hundred dollars of his own money from New York to help a woman who had been in Dachau.

The team moved on from Munich to Kempten, Auden calling on his New York friend Lincoln Kirstein, who was serving at Third U.S. Army Headquarters not far away. Kirstein found that Auden had now acquired the services of a German ex-prisoner of war as driver and a young blond Munich chef named Hans as cook. His jeep, moreover, was laden with all kinds of comforts: cooking pot, mattress, a box of books, a standard lamp, a phonograph with records, a crate of wine, and even a plaque of Wagner's profile.

The team only spent a short time at Kempten, having now been told that they must complete their work not in six months, as originally expected, but in a mere matter of weeks. Next they moved to Nürnberg, where the bomb damage was as bad as at Darmstadt, and where Auden met and entertained a celebrated local pianist who played Beethoven to the research team after dinner – Stern noted that Auden got to know more Germans than anyone else in the team. During their final week at Nürnberg they commuted daily to Erlangen to conduct interviews there. Then, at about the beginning of July, they returned to the Frankfurt area for 'debriefing', Auden staying at a hotel at Bad Homburg. Here he found Nicolas Nabokov, a Russian-born musician and composer and a first cousin of the novelist, who lived in America and whom he had first met eighteen months earlier. Nabokov too was serving with the Bombing Survey, and he and Auden spent much of their time trying to avoid their colleagues. 'Most of them', Auden said, 'are crashing bores, my dear. They have *no*, or *wrong*, ideas about everything.'

Auden's team filed its reports, and returned home, Auden journeying back to New York in mid-August, once again via England. He again visited his father briefly, and called on London friends. Stephen Spender met him again and asked whether he thought the Allied occupation of Germany might achieve any good purpose. 'Something might have been done,' Auden answered, 'but it's too late.'

He was not totally depressed by what he had experienced: he told E. R. Dodds that he hoped it might be possible for him to go and teach in Germany in a year or two. But he said almost nothing to friends of what he had seen and heard while he was there, just as he had said almost nothing on his return from Spain. Before leaving New York in April he had agreed, at least informally, to write a book with James Stern on their

13 (a) Auden and Isher-wood leaving for China in January 1938.

13 (b) Auden in the front line of the Chinese-Japanese war, 1938.

14 (a)   Auden and Isherwood in Central Park, New York; probably taken during their first visit to the city, in July 1938.

14 (b)   Auden and Benjamin Britten in New York during rehearsals for *Paul Bunyan*, 1941.

15 (a) The first photograph to be taken of Auden with Chester Kallman. Chester's father, Edward Kallman, is standing on the left, next to Auden. Chester stands on the right, in the foreground, just behind the fence. The picture was taken in New Jersey in 1939.

15 (b) Chester Kallman on Fire Island in 1946.

16 (a) Elizabeth Mayer in the garden of her home at Amityville, Long Island.

16 (b) Auden and James Stern in Germany with the United States Strategic Bombing Survey (USSBS), 1945.

17   Auden in uniform, 1945.

18   Auden reading Tolkien's *The Hobbit* in the 1940s.

19 (a) Chester Kallman, Rhoda Jaffe and Auden on Fire Island.

19 (b) Auden and Chester Kallman with Maurice Feild and his son John, during their visit to England after their first summer in Ischia, 1948.

20 Auden in 1947: a photograph given to Rhoda Jaffe.

21 (a)   Auden looks on while Chester Kallman talks to an unidentified person, probably early 1960s.

21 (b)   Yannis Boras and Chester Kallman at Kirchstetten in the mid 1960s.

22 (a) Auden at the wedding of his niece Rita, London, April 1965.

22 (b) Auden at Christ Church, Oxford, in the late 1960s.

23   Auden in the late 1960s.

24 (a) (b) (c) (d) Four drawings of Auden made on the last night of
his life by the Austrian artist Anton Schumich, at the poetry reading in the
Palais Palffy, Vienna, 28 September 1973.

experiences in Germany; but on his return he showed no sign of wanting to do it, and the project was never discussed again; Stern instead wrote the book by himself, under the title *The Hidden Damage*. The only direct result that Auden's experiences in Germany had for his writing was the poem 'Memorial for the City', which he composed in 1949 in memory of Charles Williams, who died at the end of the war, but which was also a record of what he had seen in Darmstadt, Munich and Nürnberg:

> Across the square,
> Between the burnt-out Law Courts and Police Headquarters,
> Past the Cathedral far too damaged to repair,
> Around the Grand Hotel patched up to hold reporters,
>> Near huts of some Emergency Committee,
>> The barbed wire runs through the abolished City.

★

On his return to America from Germany at the end of the summer of 1945, Auden again made his home in New York, and did not take any further full-time teaching appointments. His period of professional university teaching was now over, and though in the years that followed he often took short-term teaching appointments or acted as a visiting lecturer, he never again sought or accepted a staff post. Instead, just as he had done during his latter years in England, he earned the greater part of his income from literary work.

He was never short of work. Besides continuing to earn money from magazines which printed new poems by him, he soon became much in demand by publishers who wanted him to edit and write introductions to anthologies and the work of other writers. During the period immediately following his return from Germany he put together a new edition of James's *The American Scene* for Scribner's, and made a selection, with an introduction, of John Betjeman's verse, for Doubleday.[1] Soon afterwards the Yale University Press appointed him editor of their Younger Poets series, a task he carried out for twelve years, during which he selected for inclusion a remarkable number of poets who later went on to establish significant reputations – poets such as W. S. Merwin, Daniel Hoffman, John Ashbery, James Wright, John Hollander and Adrienne Cecile Rich. At about the same time as he began this work he proposed to the Viking Press that he edit a 'Portable Reader of Translations from Greek and Latin Verse', an idea which was eventually modified into *The*

---

[1]Auden's proposed title for the book was *Betjeman's Bust*. To his irritation, the publishers changed it to *Slick but not Streamlined*.

Portable Greek Reader, which was published in 1948 and became a best-seller.[1]

During the period before and after his trip to Germany, Auden was involved with adapting *The Duchess of Malfi* for the Broadway stage. Elizabeth Bergner wanted to play the title-role, and she and her husband, the producer Paul Czinner, asked Bertolt Brecht to make a new version of Webster's play; in the spring of 1943, Brecht began work on this, collaborating with H. R. Hays, who had translated Brecht's own writings into English. Late in 1943, Brecht, without consulting Hays, enlisted Auden as an additional collaborator, whereupon Hays walked out. During the next three years, work on the script continued at intervals, and Brecht met Auden on a number of occasions to discuss it. It seems that they already knew each other, having perhaps met for the first time when Brecht was in England in 1936. Each admired the other's work, or at least much of it, but they did not get on well personally. Brecht was irritated by Auden's untidiness, while Auden eventually came to develop a deep antipathy to Brecht's character which was presumably the result of his experiences during their collaboration. Towards the end of his life he told James K. Lyon, whose *Bertolt Brecht in America* (1980) discusses the complicated history of the collaboration on *The Duchess,* that he had found Brecht 'an odious person'. (He could not supply details of his meetings with Brecht, saying that memories of the collaboration 'are now nonexistent'.) The collaboration was, as it turned out, quite fruitless. George Rylands, who had produced *The Duchess* with great success in London, was flown to America to direct, and refused to use the Brecht-Auden text which he found waiting for him. The version which was tried out before the production reached New York still named Brecht and Auden as adapters, but it was so different from the text Brecht had worked on that he withdrew his name; and when *The Duchess* eventually reached Broadway in October 1946 it was Auden alone who was credited with the adaptation. This final text included fewer alterations of Webster's original play than had been planned at earlier stages, but there was still some tampering with the original. Auden had provided a soliloquy in which Ferdinand revealed his incestuous passion for his sister, the events of the last act were rearranged, and – though this was not Auden's doing – the part of Bosola was played by the negro actor Canada Lee, wearing pink make-up. Despite incidental music by Benjamin Britten, the production proved a complete failure. Auden himself had not had his heart in it; he called it 'terrible', and told a friend: 'I only did it for the money'.

[1]It is likely that the idea for this Portable Reader grew out of an earlier project, around the winter of 1944, when it was suggested that Auden edit a 'Portable Reader of World Poetry in Translation'. Auden said of this to E. R. Dodds that it was 'a plainly absurd task, but I must do the best I can'. He wrote to a number of poets and literary experts asking for contributions and suggestions, but the project seems to have been dropped in this form during 1945.

At about this time another producer commissioned an English translation of Brecht's *Caucasian Chalk Circle* for Broadway. It was agreed
that Auden should be responsible for it, together with James and Tania
Stern. The translation was completed, with Auden providing what were
in effect entirely fresh song-lyrics which recreated the originals in his
own terms. But he took no part in the prose translation, and Brecht
complained that there was 'too much Stern and too little Auden'. The
proposed production never took place, though the Stern-Auden text,
somewhat revised, was eventually published, and became the standard
English version of the play.

On 20 May 1946 Auden officially became, at last, a citizen of the
United States – after he had submitted to thorough questioning. 'I was
asked whether I'd read Karl Marx,' he told Alan Ansen. 'I answered yes.
. . . He asked me if my wife was charging me with infidelity. . . The
questions are simply in case somebody makes an enquiry in Congress.'

During these months Auden made a series of very temporary homes in
various New York apartments. In the late summer and autumn of 1945
he lived in one room with a bath, but no kitchen, in the basement of 52
Jane Street in Greenwich Village. A few months later he was in a larger
apartment at 421 West 57th Street, not very far from Central Park.
During this period he began to be sought out by undergraduate poets
from the city's universities, who wanted his advice and criticism. One of
these, John Hollander, who was then studying at Columbia, described
him as 'an unofficial teacher, as well as the resident poet of our city'.
Besides Hollander himself, those young poets who valued Auden's
teaching at this time included Allen Ginsberg, Louis Simpson, Daniel
Hoffman, and Richard Howard. To these and to others he communicated
a set of very precise views on the writing of poetry, views which showed
that, despite the innovations he had made and was continuing to make, he
was in matters of poetic technique far more conservative than many
modern poets.

He had now come to believe that all poetry should involve a technical
challenge for the poet. 'My own feeling', he said in 1945, 'is that every
new work one writes should, among other (and of course more important) things, attempt to solve one new technical problem for oneself,
of metric, diction, genre, etc.' He argued that a poem's intellectual or
emotional content could not really be separated from decisions about the
form it was to take; in other words, the choice of form could radically
affect the content. 'Forms', he wrote, 'are chosen by poets because the
most important part of what they have to say seems to go better with
that form than any other;. . . and then, in its turn, the form develops and
shapes the poet's imagination so that he says things which he did not
know he was capable of saying, and at the same time those parts of his
imagination which once had other things to say, dry up from lack of
use.' He was also fond of citing, as a description of the interaction in a

poet's mind between form and imagination, some words that E. M. Forster attributed to an old lady: 'How can I tell what I think until I see what I say?'

It was for this reason that he now so rarely wrote free verse, but almost always chose a formal scheme of prosody for his poems – and was critical of free verse in most other poets' work except that of T. S. Eliot. Of this, he wrote to Stephen Spender:

> My objection to most free verse is that I cannot feel any necessity behind it. . . In Eliot's verse, even if I cant finally analyse it, I feel there is a principle behind what appear to my eyes as arbitrary distortions. The trouble to-day with so many would-be artists is that they see, quite correctly, that many of the greatest works. . . are so extraordinarily free and easy. . . and think that they can start off writing like that. But that sort of grace is the end point of a long process, first of learning technique (every technique is a convention and therefore dangerous) and then unlearning. It is much easier to learn than to unlearn, and most of us will not get further than the learning, but there is no other route to greatness, even if we get stuck half-way.

Towards the end of his life he expressed in verse his belief in the importance of technique:

> Blessed be all metrical rules that forbid automatic responses,
> force us to have second thoughts, free from the fetters of Self.

So it was that young poets who came to him for advice were, first and foremost, told to pay particular attention to technique. He was also not averse to making broad statements to them about the nature of art in general and poetry in particular. Here again, these took a markedly un-modernist line. 'All good art', he often declared, 'is in the nature of a letter written to amuse a sick friend. Too much art, particularly in our time, is only a letter written to oneself.' Elsewhere he wrote more fully of this:

> Try to think of each poem as a letter written to an intimate friend, not always the same friend. But the letter is going to be opened by the postal authorities, and if they do not understand anything, or find it difficult to wade through, then the poem fails.

As to poetry's relation to the emotions, he once suggested that there were two theories about this. According to the first, poetry is a means of inducing desirable emotions and repelling undesirable ones; according to the second, it is, as he put it, 'a game of knowledge, a bringing to consciousness, by naming them, of emotions and their hidden relation-ships'. It was undoubtedly the second theory which he himself held.

His actual method of writing poetry remained much the same through-out his life. He usually worked in a large notebook with a stiff cover, in which he would begin by writing out, on the right-hand page, a first draft of the poem, either in pencil or pen. Sometimes he would make use of a phrase, or a list of words, or a table of rhymes, which he had already jotted down in the notebook; but often the new poem would be begun without any apparent sign of preparation. After writing a first version, he would then insert revisions of some passages on the opposite page, which was otherwise left blank. Next would come a fair copy, which by this time of his life was usually typed – he was an adequate two-fingered typist, and usually wrote his reviews and articles directly on to the machine. After the typing of the fair copy, the poem would usually undergo further changes before it was printed. When, as sometimes happened, a poem failed to turn out satisfactorily, he would simply abandon it, leaving it unfinished in the notebook.

Once one of his poems was completed, he would quickly lose interest in it – or at least did not seem to want to discuss it. It existed, and that was that. Nor did he like to answer questions about a poem's meaning. He said of this: 'When people ask you what a poem means, that you've written, I would suggest, "Well, your guess is as good as mine.". . . What I think it means has nothing to do with "What does it mean." '

As to the question of his audience, he claimed he wrote chiefly for other poets: 'The ideal audience the poet imagines consists of the beautiful who go to bed with him, the powerful who invite him to dinner and tell him secrets of state, and his fellow-poets. The actual audience he gets consists of myopic schoolmasters, pimply young men who eat in cafeterias, and his fellow-poets. This means that, in fact, he writes for his fellow-poets.' Actually he wrote largely for his friends, whether or not they were poets – later in his life, during the 1960s, he developed the habit of sending a copy of a new poem to whichever friends he happened to be corresponding with. Their enthusiasm, if they expressed it, always pleased him more than that of the professional critics.[1]

It was at this period of his life, the later 1940s, that he began to be regularly in demand to give public readings of his poetry. One such occasion was in 1946, when he visited Harvard to recite 'Under Which Lyre', a poem commissioned from him by the university's chapter of Phi Beta Kappa, and in which he argued, much as he had done at Swarthmore, that the young should not conform: 'Thou shalt not do as the dean pleases, / Thou shalt not write thy doctor's thesis / On education.' He greatly liked accepting such invitations to write a piece to order, just as he had enjoyed the request from the Swarthmore sailor to write the poem for the chest. He claimed that all works of art are in a sense

---

[1]During the 1940s he often showed his work in manuscript to Professor Theodore Spencer of Harvard University, whom, at Spencer's death, he described as a 'trusted and not easily replaceable literary confessor' (*New York Times*, 6 February 1949, book review section, p. 14).

'commissions', in that the artist is obliged to create when the idea comes to him; and he suggested that in fact there have probably been more failures among self-commissioned works of art than among those undertaken at the request of a patron.[1] As to public readings, he was for many years a poor performer, speaking his poetry indistinctly and often stumbling over words. He could, however, impress an audience by his ability to recite whole poems from memory, and gradually over the years he developed a more polished technique. Or rather, he learnt to make the most of his lack of polish, deliberately flaunting his unkempt appearance and careless manner of behaviour – he would often arrive on stage untidily dressed and with an old shopping bag full of books – and frequently managing to charm audiences simply by being himself. He happily confessed to friends that in this respect he had become a 'ham'.

★

Not long after his return from Germany his emotional life took another surprising turn. Despite his profoundly unhappy experience in his relationship with Chester Kallman, he still gave the impression of being unhesitatingly committed to having emotional and physical affairs only with members of his own sex. He spent much of his time in the company of other homosexuals – he did not deliberately seek them out as his friends, but he had in many ways an inevitable affinity with people of the same sexual preferences – and he had become quite militant about homosexuality. In 1946 he annoyed Edmund Wilson by alleging that Eisenhower was a homosexual, and that Tristan and Isolde must really have been a pair of lesbians, 'because a man making love to a woman couldn't really get into that rapturous state'. This was no doubt meant to be outrageous, and was not to be taken seriously; on the other hand he did seem really to believe that any unmarried person who was a major artist must be homosexual. He was convinced, for example, not just of Shakespeare's homosexuality but of Beethoven's. He also continued to disapprove of homosexuals who married in order to hide their real nature, and to obtain the benefits of a home and family. What now happened to him therefore seems all the more surprising.

In 1944 he got to know a young woman named Rhoda Jaffe. She was the wife of Milton Klonsky, a friend of Chester Kallman's who later became known as a poet and critic. Milton and Rhoda had both been classmates of Chester's at Brooklyn College; Milton was now studying for a Master's degree at Columbia (and writing radio scripts with Chester, two of which were accepted for broadcasting) while Rhoda

---

[1] One example of Auden accepting an informal commission is his poem 'The Fall of Rome', written in 1947 as a result of Cyril Connolly asking for 'a poem that would make me cry'. Connolly judged the finished poem, which was dedicated to him, to be 'moving though careless' (*Sunday Times*, 2 March 1952, p. 3).

worked as employment director for a New York chain of restaurants. After some time, Auden began to have an affair with her.

Rhoda Jaffe, who was physically very attractive, had been brought up in an orphanage in Patchogue, Long Island, her mother having died when she was still a child, and her father (who had once been quite wealthy, the owner of a Harlem department store) having become bankrupt, therefore being unable or unwilling to support her and her sisters. Another friend of Chester Kallman's, Dorothy Farnan, has written of her: 'Rhoda was a large-boned blonde, with high cheek bones, slanting hazel eyes, and full peasant hips. In her dark sweater and drab skirt she was not unlike some of the ladies of the evening drawn by Toulouse-Lautrec.' While Milton Klonsky and Chester worked on their radio scripts, spending many afternoons grumbling about the idiotic restrictions and rules of the broadcasting companies, 'Rhoda, sombre of face, talked about her problems and her psychiatrist. Life to her was a bit more serious.'

By 1946 she and Milton Klonsky had begun a series of trial separations, and were contemplating ending their marriage; Rhoda was having several brief affairs, and it was at this period that she became, for a time, Auden's mistress.

In the spring of 1946 Auden taught for a semester at Bennington, a distinguished liberal arts college (then for women) in Vermont. While at Bennington he wrote a series of letters to Rhoda Jaffe which give some account of the progress of the affair, which had begun before he left New York. They were addressed to 'Dearest Rhoda'. Auden told her: 'I miss you very much.' They made an assignation for Easter weekend 1946, when Auden planned to visit New York. 'Can I stay at your place?' he asked her. 'If not, could you book a room at a hotel for Mr and Mrs —, Sayville, L[ong] I[sland], and in that case bring a little bag with you.' The assignation presumably took place, for after Auden's return to Bennington he wrote to her: 'The weather is lovely here but the bed is lonely and I wish you were in it. Aren't men *BEASTS*. No finer feelings.'

It is possible that he embarked on the affair because he had now despaired of forming any permanent and satisfactory homosexual relationship, or at least because his relations with Chester were continuing to be very difficult – the fact that they had agreed not to have sex together did not prevent Auden being jealous of Chester's love-affairs. Certainly it seemed to Dorothy Farnan that Rhoda Jaffe had become, for Auden, something of a substitute for Chester: 'Chester disclosed to us one evening that "Wystan is having an affair with a woman." He told us who. It was unbelievable; yet we decided that in some mad way she must have reminded him of Chester. At least she had been in Brooklyn College at the same time, and she was blonde and she was Jewish.'

The psychology of the affair was a subject for speculation with Chester, too, and with Rhoda herself. Milton Klonsky writes: 'When-

ever I met Chester and Rhoda, either together or separately, Auden's
spectacular sexual conversion was sure to be discussed and debated and
alembicated down to a Freudian vapour, with Chester reciting Shakespeare's "Phoenix and the Turtle" and Rhoda claiming that Wystan had
undergone a complete and irrevocable metamorphosis. My own relationship with Wystan deteriorated. . . He must have felt guilty, I suppose,
about having come between Rhoda and me, though our marriage ties
were already quite frayed. (Marianne Moore, who had been an invited
guest at our wedding, and whom Wystan admired and respected,
expressed her strong disapproval to him when she learned of the affair.)
Nevertheless, our relations were still friendly.'

During the spring of 1946 Rhoda was still undecided about whether
she and Milton should get divorced. Auden wrote to her: 'Obviously I
can't say much about you and Milton, being not a disinterested party.'
And in another letter: 'Re Milton. For the present, you must just keep at
a safe distance from each other. Much much love.'

Dorothy Farnan observed that Rhoda seemed to be enjoying the affair
with Auden: 'She got a new black silk dress and wanted Mary [Valentine,
a friend] and me to bleach her hair lighter, because "Wystan wants it to
be blonde". We did. The hair, a straw-like white when we finished,
pleased Wystan, but not Rhoda, for it began to fall off. The next time we
saw her it had been dyed a nice, conservative, dirty blonde again.'
Chester Kallman, meanwhile, made much fun of these goings-on.
Dorothy Farnan remembers that 'he kept us amused for hours with his
incomparable imitations of the couple. It was cruel, I know. But the
concept was ravishingly funny, and Chester made it even funnier.'
Milton Klonsky suspected that Chester was in fact jealous. To Klonsky
himself, the affair did not seem absurd. He writes: 'Wystan must have
found Rhoda's decency and freedom from either literary posturing or
homosexual backbiting a relief. In her relations with people she was
frank and open-hearted, sometimes perhaps naively so, but one could
feel sure that what she said, or was told, in private would not be
contradicted by her or exploited afterwards in public.'

Auden, despite the affair, continued to be as closely concerned about
Chester's well-being as ever. Chester had now been out of work for
some time, and Auden often gave him money. He encouraged him to get
a job; Chester eventually found a clerical post at the United Nations, in
the press review bureau, but he was sacked from this in March 1947 and
did not take another job. He was living in Auden's apartment, at least
intermittently, and when T. S. Eliot came to New York in June 1946 the
two of them gave him dinner, having fussed for days beforehand about
the elaborate menu that Chester was to cook. (Eliot, after this meeting,
wrote to Ursula Niebuhr about Auden's poetry: 'I think his spiritual
development has outstripped his technical development, while his technique is such that it is able almost to deceive us (and himself) into

thinking that it is adequate.'[1]) Auden's strange double emotional life, in which he was involved domestically with Chester and sexually with Rhoda Jaffe, continued for some months. During this period he was at work again on *The Age of Anxiety,* which he had begun before leaving for Germany in 1945; and it seems certain that the character of Rosetta, the Jewish girl who is one of the four speakers in the poem, owes at least something to Rhoda Jaffe.

Auden spent much of the summer of 1946 out of New York, finding the heat of the city unbearable, and having discovered a retreat which entirely suited him. This was a beach house, covered with tarpaper and really little more than a shack, at Cherry Grove on Fire Island, a long narrow strip of sand off the Atlantic coast of Long Island, with a view straight out to sea. The shack, which could be reached by a train journey from Manhattan and then a ferry crossing from Sayville, had been rented in 1943 and 1944 by James and Tania Stern, and was then bought jointly and quite cheaply by the Sterns and Auden. Having done so, they facetiously named it 'Bective Poplars' after James Stern's family home in Ireland, at Bective in County Meath, and Auden's paternal grandmother's house at Horninglow near Repton, 'The Poplars'.

The shack was in a sparsely populated part of Fire Island, several of the other beach houses having been swept away or severely damaged in a storm just before the war. A short distance away, connected by a plank-walk, stood the Fire Island Hotel, whose bar was patronised nightly by the homosexuals who made up a large proportion of the small community's residents – it was stage by stage becoming a 'queens' paradise'.

Auden was delighted by it. 'The beach is wonderful,' he wrote, 'and the climate cool.' Chester liked it too, largely because he could make sexual pick-ups there; and he often joined Auden on the island. There was room in 'Bective Poplars' for guests, if they did not mind roughing it; Stephen Spender (who was visiting America) and Christopher Isherwood with his current lover Bill Caskey stayed there with Auden during the summer of 1947. Auden's poem 'Pleasure Island' describes the setting and the atmosphere:

> . . . a huddle of huts related
> By planks, a dock, a state
> Of undress and improvised abandon
> Upon shadowless sand. . .
> . . . this outpost where nothing is wicked
> But to be sorry or sick.

[1]G. S. Fraser, reviewing *The Age of Anxiety,* came to exactly the opposite opinion: '[Auden's] enormous technical development seems, for the time being, to have outrun his development as a person; he is a skilled craftsman . . . but a less sensitive and alert observer . . . than he was in the 1930s . . . As a kind of ruthless and obstinate exercise in pure technical skill, *The Age of Anxiety* is a striking poem. What it lacks is an alertness to living idioms and current urgencies.' (Review in an unidentified newspaper cutting.)

Early in August 1946 Auden went up briefly from Fire Island to Tanglewood, Massachusetts, to see the American première of Benjamin Britten's new opera *Peter Grimes,* for which Britten himself had returned briefly to the States. He reported that it had been 'fine' to see Britten again; that the performance was 'terrible'; but that 'the work made an impression just the same'. Returning to Fire Island, he arranged for Rhoda Jaffe to join him there for a few nights. 'I'm so looking forward to your coming,' he wrote to her. 'The bar [i.e. the homosexual drinkers at the hotel] IS going to be surprised.' He told her that Chester would be present when she arrived, in order to show her how the cooking-stove in the shack worked; and he ended his letter 'Much much love'. When she did arrive, all three of them posed for a photograph, she standing in the middle, Auden and Chester each with an arm around her.

At the end of the summer of 1946 he returned to New York. The apartment building in which he had lived the previous winter had been sold, and he now found new accommodation, renting an apartment on the fourth floor of 7 Cornelia Street in Greenwich Village, a new building with an elevator. He told Rhoda Jaffe that the apartment was 'too expensive, too small, and in the village which I dislike but it is a new building and quite nice'. It was indeed very cramped, consisting of merely a bed-sitting room and a small kitchen; and there was no space for Chester. The apartment soon degenerated into Auden's usual chaos; Tennessee Williams, who once called there, described it as 'fantastically sordid. . . with beer cans and newspapers all about the floor'; Nicolas Nabokov complained of 'a permanent stink of cat piss' (Auden was now keeping his own cat); and when Stephen Spender tried to let in some daylight the curtains fell down – 'You idiot!' said Auden; 'in any case there's no daylight in New York.' On the other hand visitors did notice that Auden was on friendly terms with the people who served in the grocery, the restaurant, and the liquor store on his street corner. It was as if he wanted to create a feeling of community around him – to put down roots. (Did he really want to be rootless after all?)

Just at this time he began to conduct another evening class, a series of lectures on Shakespeare at the New School for Social Research. His syllabus was simply to discuss all the plays in chronological order, not stinting his criticism. He told the class that *The Taming of the Shrew* was 'a complete failure', and that the musical *Kiss Me Kate* was a much better version of the same story; and when he was scheduled to lecture on *The Merry Wives of Windsor* he declared it to be 'very dull', its only merit being that it had inspired Verdi's *Falstaff* – records of which he then played to the class.

The classes at the New School proved enormously popular – enrolment was so high that one of the staff remarked that it was almost as if Shakespeare were giving lectures on Auden. Much of the force of the lectures came from the fact that Auden did not treat Shakespeare's work simply as literature, but related it to life, and spoke very personally about love, sex, and other relationships, revealing much about himself as he did so.

As a lecturer, Auden was much better when speaking impromptu than when reading from a script. He read woodenly, often misplacing his emphases or making mistakes, and his diction was far from clear. In the spring of 1947 when he gave a series of lectures on 'The Quest in Modern Literature' at Barnard College in New York,[1] at the invitation of Ursula Niebuhr, who was on the faculty there, he was often interrupted by students asking him to spell out on the blackboard the details of what he had just said. On the other hand when talking off the cuff, as he did with his Shakespeare course at the New School, or when answering questions after a lecture, he could be, and almost always was, an exciting and excellent speaker.

His work as a lecturer added, of course, to his income; and when Cyril Connolly visited him in New York late in 1946 he proudly announced that he had made ten thousand dollars during the previous twelve months. He did not in fact seek to earn large sums – he asked Barnard College for only a very modest fee for his lectures there – but he always liked to be remunerated promptly, and would hold out his hand quite without embarrassment at the end of a lecture, asking for his fee. He paid his own bills with similar punctuality, and would never in any circumstances get into debt. He was generous with what he had, often lending or giving money spontaneously. When Geoffrey Grigson called on him in New York while lecturing for the State Department, and admitted to Auden that he was not being well paid, he found dollar bills being showered through his taxi window by Auden as he departed. Similarly when an admirer offered to be Auden's unpaid secretary, Auden accepted the secretarial help but insisted on paying the young man, Howard Griffin, a proper fee for his services.

Auden had worked at his long poem *The Age of Anxiety* since his return from Germany. In its final stages he was helped by Alan Ansen, a young man who was attending his Shakespeare classes, and whom he asked to go through the draft and point out errors in the syllabification of the verse. He later gave Ansen a copy of the poem inscribed: 'To Alan, my conscience, from careless Wystan'. The poem was at last finished in mid-February 1947. Having handed the manuscript to Random House, Auden took a close interest in the appearance of the printed book. He chose a small, elegant, Victorian typeface, and devised a layout which emphasised the poem's declared 'baroque' character. *The Age of Anxiety*, which Auden dedicated to John Betjeman, was published by Random House in July 1947; the first printing sold out quickly and a number of reprints followed. The book was awarded a Pulitzer Prize in 1948; it was

[1]He lectured at Barnard College again at the beginning of 1956.

also Auden's first original volume to have a greater sale in America than in Britain, the Faber edition (published in September 1948) being only a modest success.

Several dramatic performances of *The Age of Anxiety* were later staged by various American groups, and the poem also became the inspiration for the Second Symphony of Leonard Bernstein, a great admirer of Auden. (Auden, however, disliked the Symphony and despised the 1950 Jerome Robbins ballet *The Age of Anxiety* which used it as the score.) The poem itself, however, was not a great success with the critics. Delmore Schwartz thought it the most self-indulgent thing Auden had written, and Randall Jarrell judged it his worst piece of work since *The Dance of Death,* while in England, Patric Dickinson branded it 'persistently boring'. Only some time later did prevailing critical opinion change a little, so that the poem earned the praise it deserved for the richness of its language and its accuracy as a reflection of the spirit of the forties.

It was Auden's last long poem. This was partly because he had now journeyed through all the stages of emigration, conversion, and sexual crisis which marked his progress to maturity, and which had formed the subject of the long poems. From now on when he wanted to write a poetic work on a larger scale he chose to construct not a single long poem but a sequence of shorter pieces linked by one theme. Another reason was that his energy for creating longer works was to be diverted, in the next phase of his life, into another medium, the opera.

By the time that *The Age of Anxiety* was published, Auden was still seeing Rhoda Jaffe, and was still attracted to her. During the summer of 1947 he ended a letter to her: 'Lots and lots of love, darling. You are *so* good, and I'm a neurotic middle aged butterball.' With this letter he sent the poem 'Serenade' ('On and on and on'), telling her: 'I enclose an impersonal (honest) love poem which I defy you to say is obviously written by a queer.' These are the poem's last four lines:

> So my embodied love
> Which, like most feeling, is
> Half humbug and half true,
> Asks neighbourhood of you.

But at the same time he continued to be deeply concerned with Chester, whose love-affairs he described and discussed, in his letters to Rhoda Jaffe, with a maternal solicitude. He also mentioned, in another letter to her from Fire Island, his own admiration for a young man whom he described as '*the* beauty of the island'. Gradually these homosexual concerns reasserted themselves, and his declarations of love for Rhoda Jaffe faded from their correspondence.

None of his friends was clear why the affair had terminated, but it appeared that Rhoda Jaffe bore him no ill-will; she later told Chester's father, of whom she was a dental patient, that 'Wystan was a real man in bed'. They remained friends, and for a time she acted as his secretary, but he had no further sexual involvement with her. She studied for a time at Columbia, eventually receiving a doctorate in sociology. After being divorced from her first husband she was married for a second time, to Al Ordover, and had two children. But this marriage broke up, and she became seriously ill. Eventually she committed suicide.

After his involvement with her, Auden had no more heterosexual affairs, though he did continue, as before, to be on friendly, close, and entirely sexless terms with many women, especially those who could fill something of the role of a mother to him. Looking back on his involvement with Rhoda Jaffe, he told a friend: 'I tried to have an affair with a woman, but it was a great mistake. It was a sin.' And to another friend he said: 'It did not affect me at all. I only felt I was cheating.'

Auden was now forty. He had come to terms with the fact that he would neither have a full homosexual 'marriage' with Chester, nor a real marriage with someone such as Rhoda Jaffe. 'I don't think I am over-anxious about the future,' he wrote to Ursula Niebuhr during 1947, 'though I do quail a bit sometimes before the probability that it will be lonely. When I see you surrounded by family and its problems, I alternate between self-congratulation and bitter envy. I shall probably die in a hotel to the great annoyance of the management, but I suppose when it comes to the point, one won't care so much.'

★

In September 1947, Auden returned to New York from a summer spent largely on Fire Island, where he had attended a carnival at the hotel dressed as Cardinal Pirelli from Firbank's *Valmouth,* with Chester in attendance as an acolyte. He found a message from Ralph Hawkes of the music publishers Boosey & Hawkes that Igor Stravinsky wanted to write an opera based on Hogarth's 'Rake's Progress' engravings. Aldous Huxley, who was a neighbour of Stravinsky's in Hollywood, had suggested Auden as librettist. On 30 September, Hawkes met Auden to talk about the idea, and afterwards reported to Stravinsky that Auden was 'intensely interested and is free to go to work immediately'.

Stravinsky's suggestion could not have been better timed, coming just as Auden had completed and published *The Age of Anxiety* and must have been considering what new major work he could begin. He was also, of course, excited at the prospect of working in a medium to which he was now devoted, and in which he had as yet only fooled around – the libretto of *Paul Bunyan* having really been no more than a piece of fun. Opera now attracted him much more than poetic drama, and it seemed to him, looking back, that the 'heightened' passages in his own plays really belonged to opera. He later said of this: 'I think the opera is the proper place for lyric theatre, rather than the spoken drama. And what I see about some of those early plays is that they now seem to me to be libretti *manqué.'* On top of this, he admired Stravinsky's music very much; he had bought the *Easy Piano Duets* when he was sixteen, and in 1928 he owned records of *Petrouchka.* In 1945, talking to Nicolas Nabokov, he praised Stravinsky's more recent work, saying he preferred it to the composer's 'Russian' period.

After meeting Hawkes, Auden sent a letter to Stravinsky, who had already suggested some preliminary ideas for the libretto. 'I need hardly say', he told the composer, 'that the chance of working with you is the greatest honour of my life.' Stravinsky, who had discovered that Auden could not easily afford the air fair to Hollywood where he lived, replied by offering to pay for Auden's journey there so that they could discuss the project. Auden cabled in answer: 'Generous offer shamefacedly accepted.' On 11 November he set off for eight days with the Stravinskys, having anxiously consulted Nicolas Nabokov as to whether he should take a dinner-jacket, and if he ought to kiss hands with his Russian hosts.

The Stravinskys found him a delightful if slightly odd guest – their maid reported at the end of his stay that the soap and the towels she had put out for him each day remained untouched, and that she had never found even a drop of moisture in his shower or washbasin. He was given a makeshift bed on a studio couch, and, early on the first morning, he and Stravinsky began work, 'primed', as Stravinsky said, 'by coffee and whisky'.

Stravinsky had previously written only one work that could be strictly described as an opera, *The Nightingale,* which he had completed in 1914. Over the following thirty years he composed a number of pieces for the theatre which involved singers – *Les Noces, Oedipus Rex* and *Persephone –* but none of these was exactly an opera; the nearest approach he had made to the medium was *Mavra* (1922), a short piece in the *opera buffa* style intended as a counterblast against Wagner. Since arriving in America in 1939 he had wanted to compose an opera in English, and when in 1947 he visited the Chicago Art Institute and saw Hogarth's 'Rake's Progress' engravings, which were then on exhibition there, he found that they 'immediately suggested a series of operatic scenes to me'. His intention was again to write an anti-Wagnerian piece, reviving the form of the eighteenth-century 'number' opera, in which the action is contained in a series of separate pieces – arias, duets, ensembles, recitatives, and so on – rather than in Wagnerian continuous composition. The particular musical style he had in mind was neo-classical, with much debt to Mozart; he had already sent Auden the scores of four Mozart operas as an indication of what he contemplated, and now, while Auden was staying with him, they both attended a two-piano performance of *Cosí Fan Tutte* in a local hall.

Hogarth's series of eight pictures suggested only the outline of a story.

In the first, the young man Rakewell, who has inherited a sizeable sum from his miserly father, is seen being measured for a suit, and being visited by a mother and her daughter, Sarah Young, whom he has seduced and is now trying to buy off. The second picture shows him at his *levée,* surrounded by dancing-teachers, prize-fighters, landscape gardeners, and others on whom he is wasting his money; the third portrays him at an orgy in a London tavern, where he becomes incapably drunk and is robbed of his cash. He has now spent all his fortune, and the fourth picture shows him being rescued from arrest for debt by Sarah, who gives him her slender savings; in the fifth, he marries a one-eyed rich old woman while Sarah, who has given birth to his child, tries to stop the service. The three concluding pictures show him losing his second fortune in a gaming house, then being thrown into the Fleet prison, and, finally, languishing in Bedlam madhouse, where he is visited by the still loyal Sarah.

Stravinsky's initial suggestions for the opera were only fragmentary. He told Auden he contemplated a finale in the madhouse in which Rakewell should play the fiddle, but this seems to have been the extent of his ideas for the plot.[1] Auden for his part believed that Hogarth's story needed to be changed in one major respect. In its original form it was, he said, 'a bourgeois parable' in which 'wine, women, song, cards, are not so much wrong in themselves as wrong because they waste money'. A modern audience, he said, would require a better moral to the story. There was also the problem that the character of Rakewell in Hogarth's pictures was almost entirely passive, and, said Auden, 'you cannot really have a passive character in an opera'. Thirdly, it seemed to him that of all Hogarth's scenes only two, the orgy and the madhouse, were really operatic in character.

He and Stravinsky began their work by deciding to split Rakewell into two people, so as to make external action out of his moral conflict. These two characters they described, in their outline of the opera, as simply 'Hero' and 'Villain'. The Villain's precise nature was not specified by them, but his role was clearly to be Mephistophelian. Summoned by the Hero's yawn of boredom, he would bring him the news that he had inherited a fortune, and, in the orgy scene that followed, would literally turn the clock back, by supernatural means, so that the night's delights were prolonged. Yet, though half diabolical in character, he was also to be the Hero's *alter ego,* his role in the story being very close to that of the Spectre in Auden and Isherwood's early play 'The Enemies of a Bishop'.

Stravinsky and Auden gradually reconstructed Hogarth's plot. The original character of Sarah Young, named by them in their outline simply as 'Girl', was developed into an active protagonist, desperately

---

[1] According to Auden, this suggestion arose from the figure of a blind beggar in the Bedlam engraving, who is playing a one-stringed fiddle; and it was this figure that actually set Stravinsky's mind to thinking about the opera (*Secondary Worlds,* p. 98).

seeking the Hero when he disappears into the low life of London. His second loss of fortune was to be the result of having poured all his money into manufacturing a machine, shown to him by the Villain, to turn sea-water into gold. Once he had been ruined by this speculation, all his goods were to be publicly auctioned in a chorus-scene. Then would follow a scene in a cemetery, reminiscent of the second act of *Don Giovanni,* in which Villain and Hero were to play dice on a grave; the Villain, losing, was to sink into Hell, but as he disappeared the hero would become insane – hence the concluding scene in the madhouse. There was also to be an Epilogue in which, again as in *Don Giovanni,* the principal characters would point the moral: 'The Devil finds work for idle hands to do.'[1]

Auden and Stravinsky wrote their synopsis in a mixture of English and French; Stravinsky was more at home in French, and it gradually predominated as the work proceeded. They drafted many fragments of dialogue, and made a provisional plan of musical pieces within the scenes. After ten days their work was completed.

Stravinsky, who had previously known nothing of Auden except his commentary to *Night Mail,* quickly became fascinated and delighted by his collaborator. 'When we were not working', he recalled, 'he would explain verse form to me, and almost as quickly as he could write, compose examples.' Auden did not hesitate to make pronouncements in his usual fashion to the composer and his wife: 'Angels are pure intellect. . . Tristan and Isolde were unloved only children. . . The sign of a man's loss of power is when he ceases to care about punctuality.' Stravinsky was amused by him, but also impressed, and after Auden's departure he began to buy books that Auden had mentioned. He also said of him, some time later: 'He is one of the few moralists whose tone I can bear.' Auden for his part had been 'scared stiff', having heard that Stravinsky and his librettist André Gide had quarrelled during the writing of *Perse-phone,* and that Stravinsky had said more than once that, in setting words to music, not the words but only the number of syllables mattered; he was also anxious because Stravinsky had set virtually no English before, and might distort the language to the point of unintelligibility. He quickly found, however, that the composer had a great respect for the libretto and the language in which it was to be written, and also that he was no *prima donna* but, as Auden put it, 'a professional artist, concerned not for his personal glory, but solely for the thing-to-be-made'. He said that Stravinsky was one of the few people he was able both to love and to revere. 'I can't tell you', he wrote to Stravinsky after his visit, 'what a pleasure it is to collaborate with you.'

Auden returned to New York and, before beginning work on the libretto, told Chester Kallman about the plot that he and Stravinsky had

---

[1]The opera thus becomes a parable about idleness, a cardinal sin against Auden's strong work-ethic.

devised. Chester made some slight criticisms. He said he thought that the Villain was not sufficiently explained as a character, and he felt that the yawn which summoned him would be mistaken for a soundless note. Auden was at first irritated. 'Don't just point out little flaws if you have no idea what to put in their place,' he told Chester. Gradually, Chester was impelled into making more constructive suggestions, and, in the days that followed, began to find that 'stray lines for possible arias came into my mind unsummoned'. As a result, Auden decided that Chester should collaborate with him on the writing of the libretto.

They had been hoping for some time to write a dramatic work together. To Auden, such a collaboration would have a particular meaning, for to be united with Chester artistically would be a kind of enactment of marriage, as well as providing a substitute for physical relations. Besides this, the opera's subject-matter was peculiarly appropriate for their collaboration. Chester had more than a touch of the Rake about him, while Auden's devotion to him mirrored the loyalty of Hogarth's heroine to her faithless lover. Stravinsky's friend and assistant Robert Craft later observed that 'Wystan Auden's devotion to Chester Kallman was. . . the real subject of the libretto (the fidelity of true love).'

Even so, Auden was mercilessly critical of Chester's work. He trimmed Chester's first contribution, the announcement of the inheritance by the Villain, now named Nick Shadow, to a fragment of its original length; and when Chester wrote a long dialogue in couplets, Auden said: 'I think you can manage to do it in four lines.' Chester was angry at first; but after these initial arguments they soon 'breezed along', as Chester put it, agreeing in advance who would write which section, and meeting at lunch each day to exchange ideas and to chant what they had written in impromptu French, German and Italian operatic 'translationese'. Each would criticise the other's work and make suggestions, until a final text was arrived at which represented their joint intentions. Auden later said of this: 'Two librettists are not two people but a composite personality.'

The original synopsis was modified by them in several ways. They decided to introduce the device of three wishes, which are given by Nick Shadow to the Hero (whom they named Tom Rakewell), in order, in Chester's words, 'to suggest that he [Tom] had a little will of his own, and to accentuate the sinister quality that the subject seemed to call for'. They also determined to give Tom a manic-depressive personality, so that, as Auden explained, his role would have some musical variety – 'at one moment [he is] up in the clouds, at the next down in the dumps'. This conformed with Auden's belief about opera that 'in order to sing, all characters have to be a little mad'.

The division of labour in Act One of *The Rake's Progress*[1] was so

---

[1]Auden's account of who wrote which sections of the libretto is printed in Vera Stravinsky and Robert Craft, *Stravinsky in Pictures & Documents,* Hutchinson, 1979, p. 650.

arranged that Chester wrote the section of Act One in which the heroine, whom he and Auden named Anne Truelove, bade farewell to Tom, and also the entire third scene of that act in which she determines to go in search of him even though he has been faithless:

> Love cannot falter,
> Cannot desert;
> Though it be shunned
> Or be forgotten,
> Though it be hurt
> If love be love
> It will not alter.

Indeed throughout the opera Chester wrote most of Anne's lines, while Auden composed most of Tom's – an exact, and possibly deliberate, reversal of their roles in real life. Chester later said he had found writing Anne's words 'a task approaching penance' because of 'the sheer invariable goodness of her simple soul'.

As to the verbal style of the libretto, Auden now appreciated, as he had not when writing *Paul Bunyan*, that the words must be entirely subservient to the music, and that restrictions must therefore be imposed upon the language. 'The question of diction', he said, 'is important: you cannot use elaborate metaphors, for example, because [the audience] probably won't hear them. . . The words must be completely at the composer's disposal.' The particular poetic style required for *The Rake's Progress* was, because of Stravinsky's musical intentions, largely eighteenth-century pastiche, here seen in one of Auden's arias for Tom:

> Love, too frequently betrayed
> For some plausible desire
> Or the world's enchanted fire,
> Still thy traitor in his sleep
> Renews the vow he did not keep,
>   Weeping, weeping,
> He kneels before thy wounded shade.

Auden himself said of this aria: 'I would never dream of including it in a volume of poems. A reader, coming across it in isolation, could justifiably complain, among other things, that the style is pastiche and the repetition of the word "weeping" redundant.' But he added: 'Since the music for it which Stravinsky wrote is very beautiful, I must conclude that it is successful.'

The libretto of Act One was sent to Stravinsky on 16 January 1948. Auden told the composer: 'As you will see, I have taken a collaborator, an old friend of mine in whose talents I have the greatest confidence.' Up to this moment, Stravinsky had been told nothing of the co-opting of

Chester into the project, and when he learnt of it he was not pleased, wanting Auden alone as librettist. But he said nothing, largely, no doubt, because of the excellence of what he had been sent. He told Auden he was 'delighted' with Act One, and was anxious only about its length. Auden replied that it could be 'cut ad lib'.

Twelve day later the librettists sent Stravinsky Act Two. Here again they had made some modifications of the original scenario. The machine to turn sea-water into gold was modified into a contraption that could supposedly transform stones into bread; Auden explained that this was a symbol of Man's desire to become God. (On the stage, however, it looks like a piece of pantomime, reminiscent of one of the early Auden–Isherwood plays.) Another alteration was to develop Tom's rich old wife into a more exotic figure. Auden wanted Tom's marriage to symbolise not, as in Hogarth, the temptation to riches, but the sin of abandoning both Reason and Appetite, a meaningless *acte gratuite* which disobeys the laws of both God and Man. Hence he and Chester devised the notion that Tom should marry 'Baba the Turk' – a bearded lady.

'We thought this', they later said, 'a theatrical way of highlighting Tom's motiveless motives.' On the day that she was thought of and named, the two of them 'laughed until we could no longer stand upright'. Yet Baba, arguably the richest single invention in the libretto, has great dignity. 'In her own eyes,' wrote Auden, 'Baba is as much a grande dame as the Marschallin in *Rosenkavalier*.'

The writing of the Third Act was not without its difficulties. Auden was suffering (for three weeks) from trigeminal neuralgia; he told T. S. Eliot it was 'a *most* unpleasant complaint. . . about which, apparently, the doctors know nothing but can only try to reduce the pain by giving one the sort of drug they give to lunatics which gives me the indolent calm of a phoney buddha'. Chester undertook the auctioneer's scene, and his first version was thrown out after some days of work. His final text, however, proved to be a perfect piece of nonsense-writing for the context. Sellem the auctioneer is holding up the various objects for sale:

> Who hears me, knows me; knows me
> A man with value; look at this – *(holding up the stuffed auk)*
> What is it? – Wit
> And Profit: no one, no one
> Could fail to conquer, fail to charm,
> Who had it by to watch. And who could not be
> A nimble planner, having this *(holding up a mounted fish)*
> Before him? Bid
> To get them, get them, hurry!

Again in this act, the librettists modified the original scenario, recasting the graveyard scene so that Tom and Shadow should play cards to decide

Tom's fate, and so that Shadow, having lost and begun his descent into the grave, should lay a curse of madness on Tom, thus preparing for Tom's subsequent insanity. This, in fact, is a little unsatisfactory, there being no obvious reason why such a curse should be pronounced. Moreover the final scene, in Bedlam, may be thought to lack a proper ending. Anne visits Tom, but eventually leaves him to go home with her father, and it is her departure that causes him to break his heart and die. The witty Epilogue (the work of Kallman) points the moral, but as Stravinsky himself remarked many years later this is 'a little too "nifty" '. Like the Auden–Isherwood plays of the 1930s, *The Rake's Progress* seems incapable of an entirely satisfactory ending.

Act Three was finished by the librettists by 9 February 1948, when Auden sent it to Stravinsky. He also arranged to meet the composer in Washington, where Stravinsky was to conduct a concert, on 31 March, so that they could discuss alterations that Stravinsky thought he would require. This occasion was also the first meeting between Stravinsky and Robert Craft, then aged twenty-four. Craft knew Auden slightly, having been introduced to him by a Barnard College student a year earlier after one of Auden's lectures there. He had studied music in New York and had corresponded with Stravinsky for some years, but had never joined him. Soon after being introduced to him by Auden, he was asked to join the composer's household as secretary-cum-musical assistant.

At some stage before the opera was produced, the libretto was shown to T. S. Eliot, whose comments were invited. Many years later, Eliot told Stravinsky he thought it did not succeed in combining the two very different subjects of Hogarth's story and the traditional pact with the Devil; but when he was first shown the libretto he merely pencilled in a few suggested corrections, marking, for example, a split infinitive and a verbal anachronism.

Auden took the opportunity of his March 1948 meeting with Stravinsky to reassure the composer, who was still a little upset by having Chester Kallman's collaboration presented to him as a *fait accompli,* that 'Mr Kallman is a better librettist than I am', that 'the scenes which Mr Kallman wrote are at least as good as mine', and that 'Mr Kallman's talents have not been more widely recognized only because of his friendship with me'. (Auden always referred publicly to 'Mr Kallman' in the context of their collaboration, and never used Chester's first name.) A few days later, in New York, Stravinsky was introduced by Auden to Kallman, and was quickly won over by his sharp mind and sense of humour. He also found Kallman easier to understand than Auden, whose imprecise diction and habit (in Stravinsky's company) of lacing his conversation with bits of French and German, oddly pronounced, did not make for easy comprehension. (A few months later these difficulties were increased when Chester's dentist father fitted Auden with a set of false teeth.) Stravinsky now told both librettists that he was very pleased with 'their' work; and he returned to Hollywood to begin composing the first scene of the opera. He wrote to Ralph Hawkes: 'This work affords me great joy and freshness.'

The two librettists, meanwhile, set off for a holiday in Europe.

★

They took a boat across the Atlantic and arrived in England early in April 1948. Chester had never before seen Britain. Auden took him to Oxford, where he arranged for E. R. Dodds to give them both dinner on high table at Christ Church, and then they both went up to the Lake District to visit Auden's father. This was not a great success. Dr Auden had hoped to have Wystan's company for a longer period than the few days he could spare, and he was also upset by the constant presence of Chester, while Auden for his part was hurt by his father making several anti-semitic remarks, which he took as a deliberate insult to Chester.

Early in May, Auden and Chester went to Paris, where Chester accidentally ran across Christopher Isherwood, who was in Europe with Bill Caskey, and arranged for him to hide in Auden's hotel wardrobe and suddenly reveal himself – with the result, according to Caskey, that 'Wystan nearly had a heart attack'. Then they travelled on to Italy, staying for about two weeks in Florence, and visiting Rome, where they attended the opera.

Auden wrote to Elizabeth Mayer: 'I hadn't realised till I came how like Italy is to my "Mutterland", the Pennines. Am in fact starting on a poem, "In Praise of Limestone", the theme of which is that that rock creates the only truly human landscape.' By this he meant that limestone, with its 'inconstancy' – it dissolves in water – and its habit of forming secret systems of underground caverns and pools (such as the Blue John Mine in Derbyshire which Auden had visited as a child), produces a landscape which is as inconsistent and secret as the human personality. The poem, completed during May 1948, had a relaxed tone that was quite foreign to Auden's pre-war or even wartime poetry, a tone that would appear again in much that he wrote during the following years.

Late in May, he and Chester journeyed down to Naples and took a ferry across to Ischia, the larger of the two islands in the bay, where they had decided to spend several weeks. 'Here we are', Auden wrote to Rhoda Jaffe on 30 May from the Pensione Nettuna in Forio, 'in one of the loveliest spots on earth. Forio itself is the least visited town on the island. Everyone very poor and with nothing to do but religious processions and fishing. . . All prices are expected to be arrived at by a long session of bargaining and we are too Northern to do that well.' Ischia was well-known among homosexuals as a place where sex could easily be had for money, but at first Auden found that there were difficulties. 'Sex has been almost non-existent,' he told Rhoda Jaffe,

'chiefly because you can't do a thing without the whole town knowing –
they wouldn't care, but I am not yet so shameless. Kids of 5 years old
appear on the beach and shove their arses at you giggling.'

The first part of the Ischian holiday was spent in the company of Brian
Howard and his current boyfriend, an Irishman named Sammy, who
stayed with Auden and Chester in their *pensione*. Howard, always
unstable, had become even more dissolute and difficult since Auden
had last spent time with him, in 1937. 'We had one or two dreadful
evenings to begin with,' Auden reported, 'with B.H. going on a drunk
when he becomes paranoiac, but that is over now and I am, anyway,
devoted to him.' Chester meanwhile was enjoying himself sexually
without suffering any of Auden's scruples. 'I make silly little scenes
occasionally,' admitted Auden, 'but otherwise life is harmonious.'

Auden spent most mornings working, chiefly at his poetry. 'It's such a
relief not to have to think for a few months about hack work,' he told
Rhoda Jaffe. He accepted a challenge from Brian Howard, who taunted
him with having no visual sense, and wrote for Howard the poem
'Ischia', in which he made an obvious effort to respond to the island's
landscape with its extinct volcano, Epomeo:

> . . . What design could have washed
> With such delicate yellows
> And pinks and greens your fishing ports
>
> That lean against ample Epomeo, holding on
> To the rigid folds of her skirts?

In fact he fully admitted his lack of visual sense. Writing to Howard at a
later date he called the criticism 'just', but added: 'At the same time, as a
poet, one of the most important lessons one has to learn is to recognise
and accept one's limitations and, if possible, turn them into advantages.'

Later this summer – in fact during August – he wrote a poem which
was deliberately pornographic. His views on the subject of pornography
were that, as a genre, it could have no literary value simply because its
aim was non-literary – to excite the reader sexually. But he admitted that
he himself was highly susceptible to it. 'Words so affect me', he wrote,
'that a pornographic story, for example, excites me sexually more than a
living person can do.'

The poem, unlikely as it may seem, was written by Auden in order to
show Norman Holmes Pearson of Yale University, with whom he was
beginning work on an anthology, *Poets of the English Language,* exactly
what sort of person he himself was. Its title was 'The Platonic Blow'; all
other titles which have been given to it in various publications are the
inventions of the publishers. 'Blow' is slang for *fellatio;* 'Platonic' is used
in the sense of 'ideal'. The poem consists, in the most reliable texts, of
thirty-four stanzas in a style modelled on Charles Williams's poetic cycle

Taliessin through Logres – a style which, as Williams himself had realised, is particularly suited to describing human physique. These are the opening stanzas:

> It was a Spring day, a day for a lay, when the air
> Smelled like a locker-room, a day to blow or get blown;
> Returning from lunch I turned my corner and there
> On a near-by stoop I saw him standing alone.
>
> I glanced as I advanced. The clean white T-shirt outlined
> A forceful torso; the light blue denims divulged
> Much. I observed the snug curves where they hugged the behind,
> I watched the crotch where the cloth intriguingly bulged.
>
> Our eyes met. I felt sick. My knees turned weak.
> I couldn't move. I didn't know what to say.
> In a blur I heard words, myself like a stranger speak
> 'Will you come to my room?' Then a husky voice 'O.K.'

The narrator gives the boy a beer, and learns that he is a mechanic from Illinois. He starts to make advances to the boy, who responds:

> We aligned mouths. We entwined. All act was clutch,
> All fact, contact, the attack and the interlock
> Of tongues, the charms of arms. I shook at the touch
> Of his fresh flesh, I rocked at the shock of his cock.

The poem describes the boy's sexual physique in much detail, and concludes with the narrator performing *fellatio* on him.

As poetry, 'The Platonic Blow' is negligible; as pornography, it has been much admired by readers with similar sexual preferences to Auden's. He never meant it to be published, and only gave copies to a few friends who he knew would like it. While tolerating and indeed welcoming such things in private, he never felt happy about public displays of sexuality. When he attended a performance of the musical *Pal Joey* in 1953 he declared himself outraged by a number in which the chorus-girls turned their bottoms to the audience, revealing bouquets of violets fixed in the cleft; Auden was so upset by this that he dashed from the theatre and did not return. Similarly during the last years of his life he was upset, on his visits to London, by advertisements in the Underground which showed half-naked women.

Because of these feelings about the privacy of sex, he was shocked and upset when, in about 1965, 'The Platonic Blow' began to get into print in various 'underground' magazines and pamphlets, with himself named as author. When questioned about the poem by journalists, he usually refused to admit authorship, though he did once say in an interview that he had written 'a piece of pornography' which was published by somebody who 'didn't have the grace even to pay me'. This was not true; the magazine *Avant-Garde* sent him a cheque for $100 in payment for the poem, but he returned it with an indignant note.

On the island of Ischia in the summer of 1948, Auden gradually managed to accustom himself to the sexual climate. 'The sex situation in Forio is from my point of view exactly what it ought to be,' he wrote to Rhoda Jaffe after spending five weeks there. 'Very few of the men and boys are queer. . . but all of them like a "divertimento" now and then, for which it is considered polite to give 35 cents or a package of cigarettes as a friendly gesture. It is so nice to be with people who are never shocked or psychologically insecure, though half of them don't get enough to eat.' He also began to enjoy swimming in the afternoons, and soon came to appreciate what he described as 'a Catholic bread-and-wine culture where the saints get fireworks on their birthdays and at Corpus Christi God is marched about the street by the same local band that plays for football matches'. Two years earlier he had told Alan Ansen that, if he had enough money, he would have preferred not to live any longer in America, whose climate he largely disliked, but in southern Europe. Now he set about making this dream a reality. 'I have just done something absolutely *crazy,* my dear,' he wrote to Rhoda Jaffe on 6 July 1948. 'I have rented a house here for a year.'

The house, in the Via Santa Lucia at Forio, a little way outside the centre of the town, consisted of three big bedrooms, a couple of sitting rooms, a huge kitchen, a lavatory, two rooms that had lost their roofs in an earthquake, and a hot spring which provided unlimited water. There was also a big garden with fruit, vines and vegetables. The rent, Auden reported, was to be only $230 a year – 'i.e. less than three months rent of my Greenwich Village closet. I feel so giddy and excited.' He did not plan to remain in Ischia for the whole year, for it would be necessary to return to New York for the autumn, winter and early spring in order to earn his living, but he found two friends, Bill Aalto and James Schuyler, who were prepared to live in the house during the winter to keep it habitable.

With these arrangements made, he and Chester concluded their first Ischian visit. At the end of the first week in July they left the island; after revisiting Florence and going to Venice they travelled to Salzburg; then, in August, they went back to England for some weeks.[1] During this time, already thinking about his return to America, Auden wrote a poem, 'A Walk After Dark', which showed his awareness that he was once again at a point of change in his life:

[1]Anne Valery, in her book *The Edge of a Smile* (Peter Owen, 1977, p. 203), gives a glimpse of Auden and Kallman in London during this visit in late summer 1948. They lived in part of a house lent to them by a friend in Paulton's Square, Chelsea. Chester 'made lots of friends' at Chelsea Barracks, and brought home 'a tall guardsman called Morris'. Auden gave a poetry reading which, to judge from Anne Valery's description, was apparently held in the Players' Theatre at Charing Cross.

Now, unready to die
But already at the stage
Where one starts to dislike the young,
I am glad those points in the sky
May also be counted among
The creatures of middle-age. . .

But the stars burn on overhead,
Unconscious of final ends,
As I walk home to bed,
Asking what judgement waits
My person, all my friends,
And these United States.

A critic later called the poem 'a fitting farewell to his American period'.

5

Ischia

By the beginning of February 1949, Stravinsky had finished the music for the first act of *The Rake's Progress;* Auden met him to hear it played over on the piano. Afterwards he told a friend he was 'much impressed' with it, not least because Stravinsky had taken immense trouble to give the words their proper musical value, and to ensure that they would be audible.

Auden's chief work during these months was to write and deliver, in mid-March 1949, a series of lectures for the University of Virginia; he chose as his subject 'The Romantic Iconography of the Sea'. The lectures were afterwards published as *The Enchafèd Flood.* Auden's aim in them was to explain the nature of Romanticism by examining its treatment of a single theme, the sea. The lectures seem to have been chiefly addressed to academics – though Auden's audience at Virginia was puzzled, not least because they could scarcely understand his accent. Yet, as E. M. Forster commented when reviewing the published text in the *Listener,* Auden's study of the romantic mind was 'in itself a poem. Though its tone is critical, it is not constructed like a lecture-course or a thesis.' *The Enchafèd Flood* is so closely-argued and condensed that it is not an easy book to read, but it is the most sustained of, and therefore one of the most interesting, critical writings by Auden. Many later critics have observed that it was Auden who, in the second of the three lectures, 'The Stone and the Shell', first pointed out the importance of the dream in Book V of Wordsworth's *Prelude,* where the dreamer sees a figure who is to guide him through the desert, and who carries a stone and a shell; Auden showed that the stone represents precise knowledge and the shell the gift of poetry or prophesy. Both, Auden remarked, are needed for 'the city', the communal life of mankind, the life of civilisation. Yet at the end of the lectures he concluded that the Romantic mind, 'the nomad wanderer. . . over the ocean', had less to say to the modern world than did 'the less exciting figure of the builder, who renews the ruined walls of the city'. He did not define his meaning, nor explain what form of 'rebuilding' he had in mind. Indeed he seemed as concerned as ever to stand completely aside from involvement in public or political affairs. Ironically this in itself involved him in what threatened to become a political issue.

In 1949 the Bollingen Foundation announced that its first annual poetry prize would be awarded to Ezra Pound for his *Pisan Cantos*. There were many objections raised, because of Pound's open anti-semitism and Fascism. Auden was among the judges who made the award.[1] He had already defended Pound's work in 1946 against a threat by his own publishers Random House to exclude it from a poetry anthology because they objected to Pound's views; Auden told them he would cut all ties with them should they do so. The result of this and similar objections by other writers was that they changed their minds. Auden now went into print, in the *Partisan Review,* to say that, though he thought the *Pisan Cantos* should not be read by anyone who was immature intellectually and likely to be influenced by their sentiments, he still regarded the book as deserving the prize. Afterwards he told Rhoda Jaffe: 'The whole Pound business has turned very ugly. I was misquoted in Congress and half expected to be subpoenaed by a committee.' But nothing further happened, and at the beginning of April 1949, after taking lessons in Italian at a New York evening class, he left for Italy, via England, Chester having already gone to Ischia some months earlier.

'Arrived after a *very* boring voyage', Auden wrote to Stravinsky from Ischia, giving the composer a description of the island's Easter procession – 'the Madonna ran down the street to meet her son, to the sound of explosions' – and invoking the blessing of the local patron saint, Santa Restituta, on *The Rake's Progress*. He soon settled in, and was, he reported, 'writing busily'. He added: 'Chester has turned into a keen gardener watching tenderly over the vegetables. . . Forio thinks us crazy because we eat potatoes, which are to them a mark of abject poverty.'

The garden at the Forio house occupied much of their time, and Auden himself soon began to get 'bitten with the joy of growing vegetables'. He and Chester did not bother much about furnishing the house, equipping the living-room with little more than deck chairs and a few boxes for tables. They engaged a handsome local boy known as Giocondo (though as Robert Craft later observed this was a scarcely believable name) to look after the house, and possibly also to provide sexual services. The boy kept the rooms tidy and laid the table for meals, though visitors noticed that he did not seem to understand much of Auden's Italian. Sometimes when Chester was away from Ischia and visiting the mainland

[1]He was himself awarded a Bollingen Prize in 1954.

in search of sex or opera performances, Giocondo would take over the cooking. Auden reported of this: 'He does his best but. . .'

Auden soon evolved a routine for his Ischian life. He worked all morning, either writing poetry – something he began to confine more and more to the summer months, when there were few distractions – or reading, perhaps a book for review, or simply for interest. His taste at this period was especially for large-scale historical works; in letters to Elizabeth Mayer, E. R. Dodds, and others who took an interest in such things, he mentioned at various times that he was reading Dean Stanley's *History of the Eastern Church,* Toynbee's *A Study of History,* and a three-volume account of the later Roman Empire. He liked detective stories, adored the novels of Ronald Firbank, and was addicted to the 'Lucia' stories of E. F. Benson; but on the whole he rarely bothered with serious fiction – though in one letter written during the 1940s he reported: 'Have just re-read *To The Lighthouse* after many years. Its a masterpiece, I think.'

At midday during his Ischian summers he would stop for one or two moderate drinks, then eat lunch, after which he would go for a walk to a nearby beach to bathe. More work or reading might follow, and in the evening he would go down to Maria's café in the central piazza, where at a round table out of doors he would hold court. Chester and one or two other resident expatriates were usually present, augmented by temporary visitors or by some young English or American student who had heard that Auden could be found there and had come to seek him out. Among those present on these evenings was Michael Davidson, who during Auden's schooldays had encouraged him with his poetry, and who now sometimes visited Ischia because of the attraction of the local boys. 'Many evenings,' wrote Davidson, 'in an Italian summer, I've been one of the few who, emptying flagons of wine, have listened with awe and only a little understanding to Wystan's intellectually spatial orations. There was a highly "intellectual" American who tried to turn discourse into discussion; but one cannot argue with Auden – really, one can only listen. . . Then, towards ten o'clock, he would abruptly stand up almost in the middle of a sentence. "I like people to go to bed early," he'd say with severity; and set off a little lopsidedly for his house at the top of the village.'

Auden was entirely at home on Ischia, yet no one would have mistaken him for an Italian. Robert Craft, who visited him there, described him as 'outstandingly non-aboriginal. . . His hair is sun-hennaed, and his skin raw with sunburn. Nor is his once-white Panama suit any help as a disguise. A gang of gamins single him out and pursue him as we walk, but though he shouts *"Basta"* at them, the foreign ring of the word only increases his plight.'

The new pattern of his life was reflected in the poetry he was writing. He was no longer concerned chiefly with his personal development or private crises, but now looked out on the world with a mind that was entirely settled. Yet this settled tone was largely a tone of resignation; for he had come to believe – or at least liked to suggest – that he was living in a civilisation that was in decline, much as the Roman Empire had declined; and this comparison between the present day and the Fall of Rome became the subject-matter of, or was implicit in, many of his poems at this period:

> The piers are pummelled by the waves;
> In a lonely field the rain
> Lashes an abandoned train;
> Outlaws fill the mountain caves. . .
>
> Cerebrotonic Cato may
> Extol the Ancient Disciplines,
> But the muscle-bound Marines
> Mutiny for food and pay.

The Latin poet he himself most admired was from an earlier period of Roman history: Horace, 'adroitest of makers' (as Auden called him), on whose calm civilised style he had now begun to model his poetry. This change was largely the result of his personal development, but it also reflected the alteration in the world around him. As he expressed it in a poem, the 'old grand manner' which proceeded from 'a resonant heart' – the manner of his own poetry in the 1930s – could not survive unmolested in post-war society:

> All words like Peace and Love,
> All sane affirmative speech,
> Had been soiled, profaned, debased
> To a horrid mechanical screech.

In such a world, he declared, the proper tone of voice was 'the wry, the sotto-voce, / Ironic and monochrome'. Sometimes he gave another reason for his change of voice: poetry, he suggested, was largely magical in character, and it seemed to him therefore that 'a Christian ought to write in prose'. Yet another, and perhaps deeper, cause of the change was his desire not to be self-imitative, not to continue writing the sort of thing that he knew was expected of him. 'Having spent twenty years learning to be himself,' he wrote, '[the poet] finds that he must now start learning not to be himself.'

★

In March 1950, Faber published his *Collected Shorter Poems,* a slightly revised version of the Random House 1945 *Collected Poetry*. In it, Auden restored a few pieces which had been omitted from the 1945 volume, including the entire text of 'Paid on Both Sides'. He also substituted more serious titles for some of those in the 1945 collection which had been especially flippant. The new volume was enthusiastically reviewed in Britain. Geoffrey Grigson wrote: 'He is the lucky possessor of more of the qualities of a great and enduring poet than are given to anyone else writing in English.' Even Auden's old adversary Roy Campbell admitted that 'of all those who are selling the fort today, Auden keeps the most grace, charm and skill.'

A year after the *Collected Shorter Poems* was published in Britain, Random House in New York issued a book of Auden's new poetry, which he called *Nones,* taking the title from one of the poems in it, part of a still uncompleted sequence based on the Offices of the Church. *Nones,* which appeared in a British edition a year later, received mixed reviews: many critics praised Auden's 'confident ease', but also suspected that there was now 'a fundamental undue complacency' in his work (these phrases come from a review by G. S. Fraser). Only Stephen Spender, writing in *Poetry,* judged all to be completely well with Auden. He agreed that the volume had defects, but said these were only 'scratches on the surface of achievements which are often impeccable'. He declared 'In Praise of Limestone', which was in the book, to be 'one of the great poems of this century'.

Auden, meanwhile, had established a regular yearly cycle to his life. The lease on the house of Forio was extended, and was now looked on by him as a permanent arrangement. He spent the late spring and summer of each year there, returning to America, usually via England, in the early autumn. From the autumn of 1949 onwards he made the transatlantic journey by air. On the whole he enjoyed air travel: his poem 'Ode to Gaea', written in 1954, takes advantage of the view from the plane to look down on the earth in his old hawk-like manner – though the poem 'In Transit' (1950) shows that he hated airports.

There were occasional variations in his yearly pattern. In September 1949 he went briefly to Venice, Chester accompanying him, for a P.E.N. conference attended also by Stephen Spender and Cecil Day-Lewis; this was, they decided, the first time all three of them had been together in the same room.[1] In March 1951 he was persuaded by Nicolas Nabokov to go to India and speak at an assembly of the Congress for Cultural Freedom, of which Nabokov was then Secretary General. Besides addressing the Congress, Auden also visited his brother John and family in Calcutta – John had now worked for many years as a geologist employed by the Indian Government – and met for the first time John's daughters, Anita and Rita, then aged nine and eight respectively. Despite this, he did not enjoy India. At the house of Prime Minister Nehru in New Delhi his manners failed him. 'We had to sit on the floor, my dear, and were given

[1]In fact they had all been together for a radio broadcast; 'The Modern Muse', on the BBC National Programme, 18 October 1938.

lukewarm tea,' he grumbled to Nicolas Nabokov. 'A female in costume, with donkey-bells around her ankles danced, jerking and jiggling her head, making eyes at everyone and fanning out her fingers. Preposterous nonsense! I got up and told the Prince that it "wasn't my cup of tea" and that I'd like to go back to my hotel. His daughter, a glum-looking young lady, took me to the door and sent me packing.' The daughter was Mrs Indira Gandhi, then acting as hostess for her father.

Nabokov subsequently tried to persuade Auden to go to Japan on a lecture-tour for the Congress for Cultural Freedom, but he adamantly refused – 'Let Stephen go, he likes that sort of thing.' Yet when in 1964 Spender told him that a group of writers in Budapest had said that his presence at a P.E.N. conference there would impress the authorities and might make their own lives a little easier, he immediately agreed to go, and enjoyed the experience. He told Elizabeth Mayer: 'The meetings themselves were as boring as such meetings always are, but the personal contacts were interesting. All of them, even those from East Germany, were really willing to enter into a dialogue – none turned on the phonograph record.'

At Forio in the early 1950s he settled back happily each spring into a domestic existence. 'Our broad beans and peas were the best on the island this year,' he told E. R. Dodds in May 1950. He and Chester acquired a dog, whom they named Mosé, 'because he arrived after obvious attempts had been made to drown him'. Soon afterwards came a white kitten, Lucina, who proved to the the first of a line of household cats, mostly named after operatic characters. Auden felt a deep affection towards these pets. When one of the cats, Pamina, developed glanders and could not be cured even by an expensive course of injections, he buried her remains at sea, 'near the cemetery'; while the original Lucina eventually received an epitaph in verse: 'At peace under this mandarin, sleep, Lucina, / Blue-eyed Queen of white cats: for you the Ischian wave shall weep. . .'

Auden's autumns and winters in New York were largely occupied with book-reviewing and editorial work. Beginning in the winter of 1948, he collaborated with Norman Holmes Pearson on *Poets of the English Language,* a five-volume anthology for the Viking Press of British and American verse from 1400 to 1914. Pearson made the initial selection, which he then discussed with Auden, who wrote the introductions to each volume. It was Auden's practice when preparing anthologies to cut any pieces of poetry or prose that he wanted to include out of his own copies of books, thus permanently damaging several first editions.

During his autumns and winters in America he would also often undertake short-term teaching commitments. From September 1950 to January 1951 he taught at Mount Holyoke, a women's college at South Hadley, Massachusetts. He reported of this: 'It's been quite fun. Officially I'm a prima donna with a very light teaching schedule; but then people come along and ask me to give a talk on this or that and I daren't refuse. I've lectured, e.g. on Classical Education in England, Sidney Smith, Paul Valéry, and The Concept of Revelation.' While he was there he worked on a translation of Jean Cocteau's Arthurian play *Chevaliers de la Table Ronde,* which was to be performed on the BBC Third Programme and in a stage production at the Edinburgh Festival by the Group Theatre, which had been revived after the war by Rupert Doone. Auden's text, entitled *The Knights of the Round Table,* had alternative passages for radio and stage. The Edinburgh production never took place, but the stage version was eventually performed by a repertory company – not the Group Theatre – at the Salisbury Playhouse in May 1954, and the radio version was broadcast by the BBC on 22 May 1951. The translation was published in a collection of Cocteau's plays in 1964. When he had finished making the translation, Auden was asked by Rupert Doone if he would write, or had perhaps already written, something original that could be performed by the Group Theatre. He replied: 'I'm afraid, alas, I have no plays nor am likely to have in any near future [sic]. . . In the dramatic line I am interested at the moment in opera libretti.'

By this time Stravinsky had completed the score of *The Rake's Progress,* having met Auden on several occasions to discuss minor revisions of the libretto. Plans were made for the première. Stravinsky wanted it to take place in New York, but this proved impossible, largely because he would not play the score to any non-musician – which excluded most potential backers. Eventually Nicolas Nabokov managed to arrange with the Italian cultural authorities that the first performances should take place in Venice, during the biennial festival in the early autumn of 1951. Stravinsky signed a contract, and Auden, hearing that the composer was to receive twenty thousand dollars (a sum that in fact included a fee for conducting the first performance himself), complained to Robert Craft and to Boosey & Hawkes, who were publishing the opera, that no financial arrangements had been made for himself and Chester. These and other difficulties were eventually sorted out, and it was arranged that the librettists should attend rehearsals in Italy with their expenses paid in full. Once this was fixed, Auden set off early in May 1951 for his usual Italian summer, travelling via England.

While in England he stayed, as he often did, with Stephen Spender and his family in London. On the night of 24 May, Spender's wife Natasha received a telephone call from someone asking to speak to Auden. This was Guy Burgess, a Foreign Office official whom Auden had known for some years, and whom he had last met a couple of months earlier while Burgess was working at the British Embassy in Washington. Burgess told Natasha Spender that he wanted to speak to Auden '*very* urgently'. Auden was not in; Natasha Spender asked him to leave a message or a telephone number, but he said 'No, I'll ring back.' Next morning Burgess telephoned once more, but Auden was again not there, and this time Stephen Spender took the call. 'It was a strange call,' Spender said afterwards. 'He praised my book which tells of my divorce from Communism.' (Spender's autobiography *World Within World,* which discussed his disenchantment with the Communist Party during the late 1930s, had just been published.) Burgess did not telephone again, and Auden, who had been told of the first call, thought nothing of it: 'I was busy and thought as one often does in such cases: "O, bother!. . . If it's important, he'll call again." ' He also remarked to Natasha Spender: 'Do I *have* to ring him back? He's always drunk.'

A week later, the Foreign Office announced that Burgess had gone missing on the day of the second call, 25 May, and that with him had vanished another diplomat, Donald Maclean. The rumour quickly spread that both had been Soviet spies, and that Burgess, who had sent his mother a telegram 'Am embarking on long Mediterranean holiday', might be trying to seek sanctuary at Auden's house on Ischia.

Auden had by this time reached the island. 'Well!' he wrote to Spender on 14 June. 'The combination of that phone call and some lady who thought she saw la B in the train on his way to Ischia, has turned this place into a madhouse. The house watched night and day by plain-clothes men, etc. etc.[1] The climax has been the interview with me published in the Daily Express which I dare say you've seen.' This interview, printed on 13 June, stated that Auden had been an under-graduate at Cambridge (sic) with Burgess, and was at school with Maclean; in fact Maclean had been at Gresham's School, but did not arrive there until after Auden had left. Auden was also reported as telling the *Express* that Burgess had been 'an open Communist in the late 1930s', and that Burgess had recently talked to him about the spies Fuchs and Nunn May. Another newspaper, the *Manchester Guardian,* quoted Auden as saying it was 'absolutely fantastic', however, to suggest that Burgess might have decided to go to Russia.

The general impression created by the press during these weeks was that Auden, though professedly now out of sympathy with the Com-munist cause, had nevertheless been intimate with Burgess – who, it was later revealed, was homosexual – and had been privy to whatever plans Burgess had made. Auden was in fact not close to Burgess at all – he almost certainly never had any sexual involvement with him – and he knew nothing about the events behind the disappearance, believing that the two diplomats had been kidnapped. 'The whole business makes me feel sick to my stomach,' he told Spender on 14 June. 'I still believe Guy to be a victim, but the horrible thing about our age is that one cannot be

[1] Peter Roger, with whom Auden had apparently had an affair at the Downs School in the 1930s, and with whom he had remained friends, was on his way to stay with Auden on Ischia when the Burgess-Maclean disappearance became public. He was arrested on the quayside at Naples on the suspicion that he was Burgess, but was allowed to go after police interrogation.

certain.' Six days later, by which time suspicions were growing that Burgess and Maclean had indeed been spies betraying their country to the Russians, he wrote to Spender: 'I feel exactly as you do about the B–M business. Whatever the real facts are, they are unintelligible; even the word betrayed has become meaningless.'

Five years later, Burgess met Tom Driberg in Moscow and gave him an account of his defection to Russia. This included an explanation of the telephone call to the Spenders: 'I'd still got a faint idea,' Burgess said, 'that I might first go to Italy for a holiday. . . I'd been trying to get hold of Wystan Auden. . . If I'd been able to get him and made a definite date to go and stay with him in Ischia, I'd probably have gone straight on there after dropping Donald in Prague.'

When this account was published, Auden denied a report, emanating from Spender, that he would have refused to have Burgess to stay with him had the request been made: 'Had Mr Burgess really proposed visiting me in Ischia, I should have invited him,' he said. And of his present feelings about Burgess he wrote: 'It would be dishonourable of me to deny a friendship because the party in question has become publicly notorious.'

★

Rehearsals for *The Rake's Progress* were held at the end of August 1951 in Milan, for the Venice première was being staged under the auspices of La Scala. Auden and Chester arrived for rehearsals, but they had neglected to make hotel reservations, and alleged to Stravinsky that they were having to put up in a brothel, where (they said) 'the girls were very understanding but the rooms could be rented only by the hour and so were terribly expensive'. At rehearsals, Auden was highly critical of the production, which was being directed by Carl Ebert, who had discussed the staging in detail with Stravinsky but had not consulted the librettists. There were other problems. Auden wrote to Elizabeth Mayer: 'Am exhausted with rehearsals: the music is really wonderful, cast and orchestra excellent. BUT Stravy insists on conducting and (1) he cant conduct. (2) He doesnt know the score. (3) He is deaf. Leitner (from Stuttgart) who prepared the piece is excellent, but the singers are now in despair. Worst of all, my dear, KARL EBURT [sic]. For vanity, insolence, and incompetence I have never met his equal. Just because Chester & I won't let him do his Max Reinhart tricks, he either unconsciously or wilfully rejects every suggestion we make.' Auden's own task was to coach the chorus, no syllable of whose pronunciation sounded English. Meanwhile he delighted in telling everyone that Benjamin Britten, who had seen the score, liked the opera very much – 'everything but the music'. Stravinsky did not find this very funny.

Early in September the *Rake* company transferred itself to Venice.

Auden found that the room booked for him in the Bauer Hotel had neither bath nor view; he fled to the Stravinskys' suite and (reported Robert Craft) 'burst into tears'. The Stravinskys arranged for a better room to be found for him, but they and Craft remained a little shaken by the tears.

The Rake's Progress was premièred on the evening of 11 September 1951, at the Theatro La Fenice, with Auden, according to Stravinsky, 'nervous as an expectant aunt'. Before the performance, he and Chester fortified themselves with a large number of strong dry martinis, this now being a favourite drink with Auden. In Auden's party in the audience were Stephen Spender and Louis MacNeice. The part of Anne was sung by Elizabeth Schwarzkopf, Robert Rounseville was Tom, and Otakar Kraus played Shadow. The performance was peppered with small mistakes, the result of inadequate rehearsals; but, according to Robert Craft, 'by the end of the second act there was an excitement and enthusiasm in the air appropriate to the first performance of a great opera'. Stravinsky, who conducted firmly and with much intensity, was given an ovation, and Auden and Kallman took their bows on stage with him. Afterwards they and Stravinsky stayed up most of the night to celebrate.

At the second performance (conducted by Ferdinand Leitner) Chester Kallman was not present. Robert Craft noticed that Auden slipped out of the theatre early so as not to have to take a bow alone, and receive the share of credit due to his collaborator.

Reviews were generally enthusiastic, though critical of Ebert's production, and in some cases also of the amount of pastiche in Stravinsky's music. Meanwhile many other European opera houses were preparing their own performances. Only a few weeks after the Venice première, productions were mounted at Hamburg, Düsseldorf, Stuttgart, Rome and Zurich. By the spring of 1953 *The Rake's Progress* had been performed more than two hundred times, and it quickly became apparent that it would be one of the very few modern operas to become a permanent addition to the repertoire.

Auden and Kallman had been thinking for some time about another collaboration with Stravinsky. In July 1949, Auden had written to Stravinsky from Ischia: 'Mr Kallman and I are writing a comic libretto about the Muse and her relation with Berlioz, Mendelssohn and Rossini.' This was 'On the Way', a three-act *opéra comique* which they wrote in the form of a detailed synopsis. Its intricate plot – as elaborate as that of 'The Enemies of a Bishop' – gives a central rôle to the Muse, who appears in a different character to each of the three composers (their names in the opera are Mousson, Schöngeist and Pollicini), and involves them in a number of escapades. Shortly after the première of *The Rake's Progress,* Auden and Kallman discussed 'On the Way' with Stravinsky, describing the protagonists as 'Rossini (the man of heart), Berlioz (the man of intellect), and Mendelssohn (the man of sensibility)'. Stravinsky probably found the plot too elaborate and pantomimic; certainly nothing came of the project. But another Auden–Kallman plan for an opera appealed to him much more.

This was 'Delia, or, A Masque of Night', a libretto in one act with a prologue, which Auden and Kallman completed early in 1952 and showed to Stravinsky in the spring of that year. 'Delia' is loosely based on the sixteenth-century play by George Peele, *The Old Wives' Tale,* but – as Joseph Kerman has pointed out – Auden and Kallman reconstructed Peele's plot so that it came to resemble *The Magic Flute.* In Peele's play the maiden Delia, bewitched by the magician Sacrapant, is sought by a whole succession of suitors; but in the libretto only one suitor, the knight Orlando, comes in search of her, and he gains her only after undergoing a series of ordeals reminiscent of the trials of Mozart's Tamino. Similarly Peele's character of Erestus, half man and half bear, is developed by Auden and Kallman into a comic figure, Bungay, temporarily enchanted into a bear, whose function in the story is much like that of Papageno. 'Delia' is written in a sixteenth-century style that reads as effortlessly as does the eighteenth-century pastiche of *The Rake's Progress,* and it is as well constructed as the Hogarth libretto. Auden and Kallman had every reason to hope that Stravinsky would agree to set it.

Stravinsky at first intended to do so; a letter from him to Boosey & Hawkes on 8 January 1952 mentions the project (then in its initial stages) with enthusiasm. Three months later he received the completed libretto, and Auden, who was then in Ischia, wrote to Alan Ansen: 'Am still waiting anxiously to hear what Stravy's reactions to "Delia" are.' Ansen wrote back to say that Stravinsky had said 'no'.

According to Robert Craft, Stravinsky's immediate reason for not setting 'Delia' to music was an offer to compose incidental music for a film of the *Odyssey* to be made by Michael Powell, with Dylan Thomas writing the script. 'Two years were wasted in futile negotiations,' writes Craft, 'by which time Stravinsky had moved too far away from the world of *Delia* to think of taking it up again.' Craft is referring to Stravinsky's growing enthusiasm during the years following *The Rake's Progress* for serialism in his music – a form that he began to adopt largely because of the influence of Craft himself. By coincidence Auden, too, was involved at this period with a projected film of the *Odyssey;* in the spring of 1950 he was summoned from Ischia to Naples by G. W. Pabst, best known for his pre-war film of *The Threepenny Opera,* who wanted Auden to make an English translation of a German script based on Homer, for a film in which Ingrid Bergman was to star. 'To my relief my agent asked too much money,' said Auden.

When Stravinsky did begin to think about writing another opera, he chose Dylan Thomas as his librettist. In May 1953 the two of them discussed a story about the rediscovery of a planet after an atomic disaster, and the re-creation of language, Thomas remarking to Stravinsky:

'Auden is the most skilful of all of us, of course, but I am not at all like him.' Auden made no secret of his resentment at being displaced. He told James Stern he had laid a curse on Thomas – who was in fact already in poor health from heavy drinking, and died the following November leaving the opera unwritten. But Auden's hostility towards Thomas did not run deep; he sat with Thomas in hospital, when he was in an oxygen tent, and, following his death, was a signatory to a public letter appealing for funds to pay the funeral expenses and medical bills, and keep Thomas's family from poverty.

Though Stravinsky's rejection of 'Delia' proved to be final, the libretto was eventually published in the periodical *Botteghe Oscure* in the autumn of 1953. It has never yet been set to music, and still awaits the composer it deserves.

Now that Chester Kallman's name had got into the public eye with *The Rake's Progress*, Auden quickly built on this. He wrote to Stephen Spender, who was in charge of *Encounter,* encouraging him to publish several poems which Chester had submitted. Some time later he put some of Chester's work into the *Faber Book of Modern American Verse,* which he was editing. Meanwhile Chester wrote, by himself, an original libretto, entitled *Panfilo and Lauretta,* which was set to music by the Mexican composer Carlos Chávez and performed, under the title *The Tuscan Players,* in New York in 1957. He also translated Donizetti's *Anne Boleyn* for the New Mexico Opera Association in 1958, and made English versions of *Falstaff* and Mozart's *Seraglio.* Two volumes of poetry were published by him in 1956 and 1963, and when a third book, *The Sense of Occasion,* came out in 1972, Auden himself decided to review it. Many years earlier, he had told Spender: 'I will never write a review of a friend's work. . . It is hard enough to be objective about strangers; it is quite impossible with those whom one knows well and, I hope, loves.' But now he offered a review of Chester's poems to the *New York Times* book review section, and when they refused it he passed it to *Harper's Magazine,* who printed it. In it, he wrote: 'One's feelings about a writer as a person and one's aesthetic judgement of his work affect each other very little, if at all'; and he judged 'The African Ambassador', the final section of Chester's book, to be 'a very remarkable achievement indeed'.

★

A few weeks after the Venetian première of *The Rake's Progress,* Auden changed his New York apartment for a larger one, apparently so that Chester could live with him again. They moved into the fifth floor of a warehouse building at 235 Seventh Avenue. It was a bleak, bare apartment with no hot water and a front door that would not shut properly. The furniture, remarked Robert Craft, looked 'as if it had been purchased with Green Stamps'. It was also very dirty; Craft described chairs covered with dust, cigarette ends in drinks glasses, and, in the bathroom, 'a mirror in which it would be impossible even to *recognize* oneself, a towel that would oblige the user to start over again'. Auden diverted his guests with stories about a mouse that shared the premises: 'There are usually enough scraps lying about for the poor dear to eat.' The Stravinskys, with whom Auden (despite his disappointment over 'Delia') was still on warm terms, sometimes called, especially on or around 7 January, which Chester and Vera Stravinsky shared as a birthday. They found Chester an excellent cook – though, as Robert Craft observed, he was capable of leaving a large quantity of sand in the spinach. One evening Vera Stravinsky went to wash her hands and found a basin full of dirty fluid in the bathroom. She unthinkingly emptied it down the sink and refilled it with clean water – only to learn at dessert time, with mixed emotions, that she had flushed away Chester's chocolate pudding.

Auden seems to have become aware that, in the long run, his domestic situation would not do, for in the summer of 1952 he made an offer of marriage to a woman friend. This was Thekla Pelletti. Highly attractive and in her twenties, she was American by birth, had married an Italian, and was now divorced; she spent the summers of 1951 and 1952 on Ischia, and got to know Auden well. There was no love-affair or any sexual involvement, but he made it plain to her that he would welcome the idea of their marrying, his previous objections to homosexuals' marriages of convenience having apparently now vanished. She was fond of him, but she realised how absurd was the notion of becoming his wife when he remarked to her that, if they were to have a son, 'we must call him Chester'. Though the idea of marriage faded from the picture, she and Auden remained great friends, and when she did eventually become married again — to an American named John Clark — she and her husband were among those whose company he most enjoyed.

Auden's routine of Ischian summers and American winters continued. Later in 1952 he undertook a lecture tour around the U.S.A., under the management of an agency which advertised the various topics on which he was to speak. Several of these were general literary subjects such as 'The Nature of Comedy' and 'The Hero in Modern Poetry', but he also prepared to talk on his own poetry, his methods of writing it, and the ideas and influences that had shaped his career. 'It is a sad fact about our culture', he later remarked, 'that a poet can earn much more money writing or talking about his art than he can by practising it.' He found the tour exhausting – 'I feel like a presidential candidate', he remarked towards the end. Soon after it was over, in the early spring of 1953, he spent a couple of months at Smith College in Massachusetts, with no scheduled teaching duties, though he did give several lectures; he received a fee of five thousand dollars for his services, and was privately glad of the presence on the staff of a young man whom he described as 'charming, bright and lascivious'.

While he was at Smith, the Metropolitan Opera presented a New York production of *The Rake's Progress,* conducted by Fritz Reiner and staged by George Balanchine. This proved a great disappointment – a reviewer complained of 'unimaginative direction, the usual hideous sets and the Met's peculiar acoustics' – and Auden and Kallman were much annoyed. They began, in fact, to build up a list of grievances against the Met and its supremo, Rudolf Bing, which eventually grew so lengthy that they decided to attend no further productions there – though it is doubtful whether Bing noticed their absence.

After Stravinsky's refusal to set 'Delia' to music, it is just conceivable that Auden considered another collaboration with Benjamin Britten. Certainly he did his best to keep in touch with Britten, and usually attempted to see him when he was in England. But he did not meet with a very warm response. Once when in London he called on Britten at a prearranged time, to have tea, and was upset to find that Britten was not there and had left no message of apology. In 1953 Auden went from Ischia to England in mid-June, and attended Britten's new opera *Gloriana,* being performed at Covent Garden as part of the Coronation cele- brations; afterwards he wrote to Elizabeth Mayer: 'It has some of the best operatic music in it, I think, that Ben has done yet, and the Piper sets were superb. Didnt care for the libretto [by William Plomer] and neither Joan Cross nor Peter should sing any more on the stage.' (Joan Cross sang the part of Elizabeth I, and Pears that of Essex.) Auden then went to the Aldeburgh Festival, where, he told Elizabeth Mayer, 'I hope, though faintly, that I shall be able to have a real talk with Sir Benjamin.' After the trip he reported: 'Everyone was charming, but I was never allowed to see Ben alone – I feared as much, still, I was a bit sad.'

Auden made no further serious attempt to renew the friendship, though he did present the Aldeburgh Festival (which Chester insisted on pronouncing as 'Addleborough') with one of his manuscript poetry notebooks to be auctioned for fund-raising; and he would refer sadly, now and then, to what had happened, though without identifying Britten by name: 'If I am loyal to my friends it is only because nobody I know has been as lucky as I have in the friends he has made. Only from one (he is famous and you can probably guess his name) have I been estranged, and that is a constant grief to me.'

He stayed on late at Ischia in 1953, remaining on the island after a summer partly spent teaching Chester and Giocondo how to drive a second-hand car he had bought – '*not* an easy task', he said, and he totally failed where Chester was concerned. In the late autumn he wrote to Elizabeth Mayer from Forio: 'It is the loveliest time of all, wonderful clear lights and white-clouded skies.' Returning to New York, he once again moved dwellings, the apartment building on Seventh Avenue having been sold. This time he rented an upper floor at 77 St Mark's Place, on the Lower East Side.

The neighbourhood was an Italian–Polish–Ukrainian district, quiet if rather grubby, with small shops selling the food of these nationalities. St Mark's Place itself took its name from the church of St Mark-in-the-Bouwerie, a few blocks away, which Auden began to attend for the early Communion on Sunday mornings. Auden's apartment building had once been lived in by Trotsky, while the last tenant of the apartment itself had been (Auden proudly announced) an abortionist who was now in jail. 'Occasionally', said Auden 'nervous people come knocking at the door, asking for the doctor.'

He and Chester moved in during February 1954, Auden grumbling about the expense of the carpenters and painters who had made it habitable. There was a bedroom for each of them (Chester regularly used his for sleeping with young men he had picked up, usually 'rough trade' – tough young homosexuals who would take the active role) and also a spare room in which for a time Auden installed a lodger, a young man who spent most of his time avoiding Auden and Chester and watching television in his room. The main living area consisted of three rooms connected by open arches; Auden set up a big plywood work-top in the front of the three, which overlooked the street, and he used this as his desk. On the mantelpiece he placed a graph barometer which had belonged to his father.[1] Among the pictures that he and Chester hung on the walls was an original Blake watercolour, 'The Act of Creation', which had been a gift from Caroline Newton, and – a little later – two drawings by Don Bachardy, the artist with whom Christopher Isherwood was now living; one was of E. M. Forster and the other of Elizabeth Mayer. There were also several line drawings of male nudes.

Auden soon settled in. He liked the apartment more than anywhere he had lived in New York since the war; he called it 'my N. Y. nest'.

He and Chester combined their house-warming party with a celebration of Auden's forty-seventh birthday, which fell in February 1954. He had previously given birthday-parties every year, considering it essential to mark the event, but they had been small and unremarkable. Now they began to be more elaborate affairs, announced each February by a printed card whose wording, from 1955 onwards, scarcely varied from year to year:

Mr W. H. Auden
requests the honor of the company of

—————————

at a birthday party
on Monday, February twenty-first at nine p.m.
Carriages at one a.m.   R.S.V.P.

[1] When he left the St Mark's Place apartment in 1972, on of his friends noticed that the barometer had – perhaps symbolically – run out of ink.

In his daily life, Auden tended to keep his friends in separate compartments, so that those of one set did not usually get to know those belonging to the others. The birthday-parties were conducted on a similar basis: the opera-literary-homosexual friends would congregate in one room and the academic-theological set in another, while on the sofa between the two sat the elderly ladies, Elizabeth Mayer and Marianne Moore. No food was offered; Californian champagne was served in large quantities in what appeared to be tooth-mugs, while Auden flitted from group to group. Opinions varied as to whether these parties were really enjoyable. One regular guest, V. S. Yanovsky, a Russian emigré writer and doctor of medicine whom Auden came to know through a theological discussion group, The Third Hour, thought them 'an intellectual feast', but there were others who found them awkward affairs. Sometimes there were embarrassing incidents. Yanovsky recorded that at the 1962 party 'a Jewish girl (I never saw her before or after) opened the door to Wystan's bedroom (a sad sight), and Wystan literally threw a fit. He screamed in anger and outrage. . . Chester very expertly calmed him down.' On other occasions at the parties, Auden could be notably kind. Beata Sauerlander, Elizabeth Mayer's daughter, brought her own teenage daughter to one of the parties, and Auden spent a full half-hour talking to her, putting her at her ease and entirely ignoring other guests, because he had discovered that she shared his enthusiasm for the stories of J. R. R. Tolkien.

The birthday-party was only one part of the St Mark's Place ritual. Another was 'teatime', the point in the day at which Auden held open house to those who wished to consult him on literary or academic matters. 'Tea' was in fact a metaphorical term, for callers were just as likely to be given coffee (with powdered milk), and in any case soon after five o'clock martinis were served. Some of those who called at this hour were students seeking help with dissertations on Auden's poetry. To these, he would be polite but brief almost to the point of curtness, giving nothing but the bare essentials of information, sometimes merely in a single word.

On 16 March 1954, just after he had moved into St Mark's Place, Auden had dinner with the Stravinskys. Robert Craft, who as usual was present, recorded that Auden drank 'five martinis and two decanters of wine. God rest his liver!. . . He is becoming more moral by the hour, too ("It is profoundly wicked not to pay one's bills by return mail"), and at this rate will soon be sounding like Moses. . . His face now has the craquelure of an Old Master.' In fact Craft noticed that Auden 'suddenly seems to have aged'.

★

After a 'nice quiet industrious summer' on Ischia in 1954, during which he was visited by his brother John and family, and a 'very busy winter earning dollars' on another American lecture tour, Auden published, in February 1955, a book of new poems, *The Shield of Achilles*. The title was taken from a poem which many critics considered to be a remarkably successful juxtaposition of classical mythology and the desolation that Auden saw in post-war society. The book also included the sequence 'Horae Canonicae', now completed, in which he used the Offices of the Church and the events of Good Friday as the basis for a meditation on the individual's acceptance of guilt in society. Despite the achievement of this sequence, which (especially in 'Nones') included some of Auden's finest poetry, the volume was as a whole severely criticised. A large part of it was occupied with 'Bucolics', a set of poems about the different elements of landscape, partly suggested by Auden's Italian summers but also owing something to his visits to England – 'Streams' grew out of a trip he made to Swaledale in Yorkshire during July 1953. 'Bucolics' had as its subject the whole range of natural scenery, but was domestic and cosy in character. As if to emphasise this, each of the poems was dedicated to one of Auden's friends, often without asking their permission.[1] The tone of the sequence was summed up in the last stanza of 'Lakes':

> It is unlikely I shall ever keep a swan
>   Or build a tower on any small tombolo,
> But that's not going to stop me wondering what sort
>   Of lake I would decide on if I should.
> Moraine, pot, oxbow, glint, sink, crater, piedmont, dimple. . .?
>   Just reeling off their names is ever so comfy.

Undoubtedly Auden meant these last three words to be taken ironically: the implication is that to dream of owning such a retreat from the world is a dangerously complacent activity. But most critics failed to see this, and even those who perceived the irony tended to regard 'Bucolics' as an indication that Auden was declining into a 'comfy' middle age. Randall Jarrell summed up most reviewers' opinions when he wrote: 'Auden has become the most professional poet in the world. . . But to be the most professional poet in the world is not necessarily to be the best. . . Auden is using extraordinary skill in managing a sadly reduced income.' Jarrell had written a number of articles attacking Auden, who was puzzled by this persistence, and – characteristically – ascribed it to a neurotic motive, remarking to Spender: 'I think Jarrell must be in love with me.' But in general he paid no more attention to the critics than he had done for the last twenty years, and went on writing poems in much the same style.

[1]On one occasion he asked J. R. R. Tolkien if he might dedicate a poem to him. But when the poem, 'Homage to Clio', was published there was no such dedication.

He annoyed some of his critics again shortly afterwards by giving a great deal of support to a book which many people thought had no literary value, J. R. R. Tolkien's *The Lord of the Rings*. Auden had read Tolkien's first published story, *The Hobbit,* some years earlier, and he now devoured the new book avidly, obtaining a set of galley proofs of the third volume from Tolkien so that he had plenty of time to read it before writing a review for the *New York Times* - he had already reviewed the first volume in that newspaper and in *Encounter*. He also began a correspondence with Tolkien, whom he had not seen since attending his lectures at Oxford as an undergraduate; he told Tolkien that *The Lord of the Rings* 'is one of the very few books which I shall keep re-reading all my life'. His reviews praised it as one of the great examples of the quest-story, and in a broadcast in the BBC Third Programme he declared: 'If someone dislikes it, I shall never trust their literary judgement about anything again' – a remark that much annoyed Tolkien, who dis-approved of such tests of literary taste. Auden was still as capable of making dogmatic pronouncements as in undergraduate days.[1]

He was also still capable of radically changing his mind. In 1952 he wrote in an article on opera: 'I am violently hostile to the performances of opera in translation.' Yet in the summer of 1955 he and Chester began work on a commission to make a new English translation of *The Magic Flute* for performance on American television.

They were rather shamefaced about this. 'We are inclined to agree with those who believe that operas should always be given in their native tongue,' they wrote in the preface to the translation. 'However, if audiences demand them in their own, they must accept the consequences.' In fact the two of them found that, once they had begun their work, they were completely fascinated by the task.

Their 'translation' was really a radical re-writing of the original libretto. One of their alterations was to substitute, for a literal rendering into English, such words as they thought would be more suitable for singing. They also wrote rhymed verse for the spoken dialogue rather

---

[1] In December 1965, together with Peter Salus (with whom he collaborated on translations from Old Icelandic), Auden attended a meeting of the Tolkien Society in New York, and gave an impromptu talk describing his own meeting with Tolkien in Oxford (which probably took place around 1957). He was critical of Tolkien's house and its decorations, calling them 'hideous'. These remarks were subsequently reported in the New York and London newspapers. Tolkien read them, and wrote to Auden asking if he had really said such a thing. Auden replied, but made no reference to his remarks, and, despite a further letter from Tolkien on the subject, never explained himself or apologised. Tolkien decided to let the matter drop, and soon afterwards wrote a poem in Anglo-Saxon for Auden's 1967 *Festschrift* in the journal *Shenandoah*. Auden was delighted. 'Wasn't it nice of Tolkien to write something in Anglo Saxon?' he wrote to E. R. Dodds. 'I was terribly flattered.'

In 1965 Auden contracted, together with Peter Salus, to write a short book on Tolkien for a series called *Christian Perspectives*. He asked Tolkien for his blessing on the project, but Tolkien expressed strong disapproval, and as a result Auden and Salus did not write the book.

than merely translate the indifferent prose of the original. Most radically, they reorganised the order of events, especially in the second act, so as to develop Schekender and Giesecke's original fairytale-plus-freemasonry story into a quest-tale which was also an allegory of the marriage between Instinct and Reason. Their work earned much praise for this ingenious reconstruction, but one critic pointed out that they had upset the carefully arranged order of Mozart's music, and they were also attacked for their partial failure, despite all Auden's declarations of intent on this subject, to eliminate 'operese' from the language of the libretto. (For example, in Act One, where an earlier translator had written 'Ha! is that a man coming?' they wrote: 'What uncouth shepherd now the path descends?') Their translation was performed with much success on NBC Opera Theatre in January 1956, and was also published; but, perhaps chiefly because of its radical treatment of the story, it has not since been much used for performances of the opera. In the late 1950s there was a serious proposal to translate the Auden–Kallman version back into German for a production, but nothing came of this.

It was at about this time that Auden's old friend Margaret Gardiner wrote to him and arranged to visit him in Ischia. She had not seen him for some time, and she was struck, when she arrived, by the change in his face. Stravinsky had already commented on the wrinkles that were now beginning to cover it: 'Soon we will have to smooth him out to see who it is.' Now, Margaret Gardiner found that 'it took me some time to rediscover the young face I had known beneath this new mask'.

*

Since 1951, Cecil Day-Lewis had been Professor of Poetry at Oxford. According to the terms of the chair, he was now obliged to retire, and the University was preparing to elect his successor; this election is unique at Oxford in that all graduates are entitled to vote, provided they have taken their Master of Arts degree and are present to cast their votes in person. The election had until the 1950s aroused comparatively little interest outside Oxford, but it had now become something of a *cause célèbre*, with the University split between those who thought the chair should be occupied by a literary critic who would deliver good lectures and those who thought that only practising poets should be appointed. A leader of the latter faction was Enid Starkie, the University's independent-minded Reader in French. On 5 August 1955 Auden received a letter from her in which she asked him if he would be a candidate.

At first he refused. He told her he was 'honoured and grateful' to be asked, but said he simply could not afford to accept the professorship, since it only paid a salary of three hundred pounds per annum – it was not a full-time appointment. Moreover the holder was required to be in England during the autumn, spring and summer terms so as to deliver the termly lecture required by the University statutes; and this seemed out of the question to Auden. 'The winter months', Auden wrote to Enid Starkie from Ischia, 'are those in which I earn enough dollars to allow me to live here in the summer and devote myself to the unprofitable occupation of writing poetry. I do not see any way in which I could earn the equivalent if I had to reside in England during that period.' He also thought that his American citizenship might debar him from candidature, and that, even if it did not, it would probably be 'a fatal handicap' in the election.

Enid Starkie was not so easily deterred. She wrote to Auden again, and made it clear to him that she expected a good deal of support for him in the election. Answering her, he was again hesitant, saying that he still could not see how he would manage economically, and suggesting she consider Robert Graves as an alternative candidate – he called Graves 'a fit person for the Chair'. Again, Enid Starkie was firm in her reply, and Auden finally capitulated.

'Please vote for me', he wrote to E. R. Dodds in November; but for the most part he left the canvassing in the capable hands of Enid Starkie, who was being assisted by Nevill Coghill and Lord David Cecil. The newspapers were soon reporting that the two other candidates were to be Harold Nicolson (sponsored by Maurice Bowra of Wadham and John Sparrow of All Souls, neither of whom had any great affection or admiration for Auden) and the distinguished Shakespearian critic G. Wilson Knight. 'There is keen excitement about the election,' wrote Evelyn Waugh in his diary; 'Auden and Nicolson, both homosexual socialists, and an unknown scholar named Knight. I wish I had taken my degree so that I might vote for Knight.'

Auden wrote to a friend: 'My future now hangs on Feb 6th when Convocation meets in Oxford to elect the Professor of Poetry. If I get in, I shall be over in Europe for that time [the five years' term of office], though how I am to earn my living (the professorship hardly pays anything as one only gives three lectures a year) I dont know but Der Gott will provide, I suppose.'

Excitement mounted; the newspapers reported that Oxford under-graduates, though they were not entitled to vote, were mostly supporting Auden. Several of them, including the presidents of the two university dramatic societies and the English Club, wrote to the *Sunday Times* saying that it would be 'most fitting' for him to be elected, and calling him 'one of the greatest living poets'. The words 'AUDEN FOR PROFF' [*sic*] were daubed on the wall of All Souls', and an editorial in the undergraduate magazine *Isis* brought into the open the issue that lay in most people's minds:

It is certainly true that during the last war Mr Auden was in America, while Sir Harold Nicolson was in England, hard at work in the Information Service. And if this were an election to some British Government post, this fact might carry some weight. As it is, nothing can be more irrelevant to an appointment which must combine creative skill and enthusiasm with academic impartiality than the 'war records' of the two candidates.

On Thursday 9 February 1956, the result was announced. Auden had been elected with 216 votes, Nicolson polling 192 and Wilson Knight 91. Enid Starkie sent Auden a telegram with the news. 'How on earth did you manage it?' he wrote back to her. 'I had completely resigned myself to losing. . . *Entre nous,* I'm surprised that the anti-Americans didn't have the political sense to put up a really distinguished scholar, for, if they had, I should immediately have withdrawn. . . I can only hope that I prove worthy of what you have done for me.'

He was still worried about his income during the period of the professorship. 'How am I to live?' he wrote to Spender on 16 February. Yet only a few days later he handed over a cheque to the Catholic social worker Dorothy Day, who needed money to pay a court fine imposed because a hostel for derelicts she was running had transgressed New York fire regulations. Auden went up to her as she came out of court, looking so scruffy that she mistook him for a derelict himself, and muttered 'Here's two–fifty.' Miss Day assumed that he meant $2.50, and thanked him briefly. After he had gone, she discovered that the cheque was for the full amount of the fine, $250.

Early in June 1956, Auden arrived in Oxford to deliver his inaugural lecture. He was given a room in his old college, Christ Church, and when a reporter asked him how he felt he answered: 'Just like a new boy at a public school.' The inaugural was delivered at five o'clock on an uncomfortably hot afternoon, 11 June, in the Sheldonian Theatre, which was full to overflowing, Auden wearing an M.A. gown and an academic cap which tilted more and more over his eyes as the lecture progressed. The lecture was entitled 'Making, Knowing and Judging', and was carefully self-effacing in tone. 'You have chosen for your new Professor', Auden told his audience, 'someone who has no more right to the learned garb he is wearing than he would have to a clerical collar.' He took for his subject an examination of the poet's attitude to literature, as opposed to that of the academic critic. Afterwards he wrote to Chester: 'Never in my life have I been so terrified, but thanks to Santa Restituta, I had a triumph and won over my enemies.'

A few days later he had to take part in Encaenia, the annual ceremony for the awarding of honorary degrees, at which he was obliged to undertake another of the Professor of Poetry's statutory duties, the Creweian Oration. This speech, a review of the events of the past year in Oxford, has to be delivered in Latin; Auden was greatly alarmed by the prospect, and tried to postpone it by suggesting that, the University's

Public Orator (who delivers the speech in alternate years) should swap with him. But in the event he went through with it, having first had his English text rendered into Latin by J. G. Griffith, the classical tutor at Jesus College. The speech was a witty survey of the year's happenings; it mentioned the visit to Oxford of the Soviet leaders Bulganin and Khrushchev, paid tribute to various celebrated Oxonians who had died, and even took sides on a current Oxford controversy, the question of whether a road should be built through Christ Church Meadow. Auden declared himself opposed to the road, and said he was 'willing to die for a tunnel' – this being one of the alternative plans.

From Oxford he went back to Ischia, where he had to move house, his landlord in Forio having become involved in a family squabble about the ownership of Auden's present villa. Auden found another house nearer to the centre of Forio, in the Quarto San Giovanni. He intended to make this his base for the winter as well as the summer during the next five years, while he was Professor of Poetry at Oxford. In fact early in October the University changed its rules, and agreed to allow him to give all three of each year's lectures during a single visit in the summer term, so that he could return to America each winter as usual. But he had already sub-let his New York apartment for the winter of 1956-57, so he remained on Ischia during it. Chester was there with him for part of the time, but often disappeared for long stretches, and did not write. '*Please* drop me a line,' Auden asked him. 'Are you coming for my birthday? What is going on?' To Elizabeth Mayer he wrote: 'It is a bit lonesome here.' But he added: 'I am well and busy.'

In February 1957 he went by plane for a few days to Edinburgh, where he preached at a university service. After another spell in Italy, he was back in England in May to deliver his first set of three lectures at Oxford. He was, in fact, just in time to pay a final visit to his father; for Dr Auden, who had lived for the last few years at Repton, where he had been at school and near where he was born, died at the beginning of May. 'No pain at all, thank God,' Auden wrote to a friend. 'I got to see him two days before the end and he still recognised me.'[1]

[1] Auden's final meeting with his father has been the subject of misunderstanding. In an interview in the *New York Times Magazine* (8 August 1971) Auden was reported as saying: 'He was on his deathbed, writhing in pain and plucking at the bedsheets. I said, "You know, father, you're dying," and he said, "I know I am", and went off into his final coma.' But Richard Hoggart, to whom Auden told the same story, points out that Auden's remarks to his father were neither harsh nor callous, as this account makes them sound, but were a series of grave questions about Dr Auden's state of mind. See the *Listener*, 6 March 1980, p. 315. Richard Hoggart also records, in this article, that in about 1967 he took Auden to visit his old home in Harborne. He says that Auden was 'greatly moved' by seeing it again. The house was demolished in 1979.

John Auden adds: 'Our father . . . did not die writhing in pain and plucking at the bedstead . . . He was visited daily by my cousin Humphrey . . . and his son Derek, and neither has ever mentioned a painful death . . . Wystan would never for effect have given a

At Oxford in May 1957 Auden lectured on the poetry of D. H. Lawrence and Robert Frost, and for his third lecture discussed the use of music in Shakespeare's plays. Shakespeare featured in many of the later lectures he gave during his professorship, as did music – his 1959 list of subjects included 'Translating Opera Libretti'. He also talked on Dickens, Byron, his friend Marianne Moore, and such general topics as 'The Quest Hero' and 'The Hero in Modern Poetry' – a lecture re-used from his American tours. The lectures were lively and aphoristic, and were usually attended by large and enthusiastic audiences. In 1961 *Isis* summed them up as 'by far the most entertaining and provoking' of those currently being given at Oxford on English literature.

Auden did not regard his duties as Professor as ending with the lectures, but made it clear that he would be available for informal conversation each morning in the Cadena Café in Cornmarket Street. Here he would sit, rapidly draining cups of coffee, while undergraduates would come and go, some bringing their own poetry to show him, others wanting to discuss literary topics. He was also sought out by several young men who were making a name for themselves as writers and critics, among them John Wain and Bernard Bergonzi. They found that Auden really preferred talking to listening, and liked to hold forth; but, said one observer in the Cadena, 'if one asked him a serious question, he would answer it'.

While at Oxford, where he usually spent about four weeks each summer term, he generally slept and took his meals in Christ Church, where once again he was soon making his mark on the college. He warmly approved of the formal after-dinner ceremony of dessert each evening, at which members of the Senior Common Room ate their fruit and drank port in an oak-panelled inner sanctum, with the decanters circulating around the table; but he was disconcerted to find that, before dinner, no ice could be produced to chill the dry martinis that he now consumed in large quantities every evening. Before his professorship had come to an end he presented the Common Room with a blank cheque to buy a refrigerator. He also took the opportunity of writing two pieces of occasional verse for the college: an ode for the eightieth birthday of its most venerable resident, Canon Claude Jenkins, and a toast for the college gaudy in 1960. In college, as in the Cadena Café, he encouraged undergraduates to come and talk to him, making them welcome in his rooms, even though this sometimes proved a nuisance. On one occasion one of them, very drunk, was sick all over his work-table. 'Without a comment,' remembered another who was there, 'Auden swept everything into an enamel slop-bucket.' Afterwards 'he said only that it must have been so embarrassing for the undergraduate'.

He made several new friends, soon being on warm terms with

story like that to the *New York Times Magazine,* and the false embellishment must have been due to bad reporting.'

Cuthbert Simpson, the Dean of Christ Church, an American who, said Auden, was the only person in England who could mix a dry martini properly; and with David Luke, the college tutor in German. He also re-met two old friends, Gabriel Carritt and Naomi Mitchison, who both thought him a little reserved on the subject of the changes he had gone through since the 1930s.

Another friend from undergraduate days, A. H. Campbell, invited him to dinner at All Souls, and was surprised to find Auden removing his shoes at the earliest possible opportunity – he now suffered badly from corns and often wore carpet-slippers to ease his feet. The shoes were not put on again, and at the end of the evening Auden walked out of All Souls in his stockinged feet, 'not overly sober'. After trying to get into a big black car at the college gate under the impression that it was a taxi – in fact it belonged to a distinguished guest whose chauffeur was collecting him – he crossed the High Street, still in his stockings and carrying his shoes, and tried to get into Christ Church by the Canterbury Gate. This was locked, and Auden mistakenly assumed that the entire college was shut for the night (there was in fact a porter on duty at Tom Gate). He therefore turned round and, still without putting on his shoes, walked about two thirds of a mile through the town to Walton Street where a friend, John Webster, had a house. He rang Webster's doorbell and asked for a bed for the night, which he was given.[1]

His regular visits to England meant that he became a frequent guest at Stephen Spender's household in London, where his arrivals were always welcomed, not least by the children, Matthew and Lizzie, to whom he seemed rather like an Edwardian bachelor uncle. Spender's wife Natasha always respected the hours of the day when Auden liked to work, and would leave him undisturbed. One morning she went as quietly as possible into his room with an eleven o'clock cup of coffee and was astonished to hear him say: 'I want half a pound of rice, and be sure to bring me the change.' Squashed into the space in the middle of the knee-hole desk was Lizzie; she and Auden were playing at shops, she as shopkeeper, he as customer.

★

At the beginning of June 1957, just as Auden was finishing his first series of lectures at Oxford, it was announced that he had been awarded an

---

[1]This story is concluded by the composer Bryan Kelly, who was in the house at the time: 'All the beds were already occupied so he took two armchairs and slept in them. He had gone by the time we got up the next day — he had been hungry and had eaten a Ryvita biscuit and some raw bacon; the rinds had been dropped on the kitchen floor. He was seen at early morning service still wearing evening dress.' (From 'W. H. Auden, a musical guest', *Royal College of Music Magazine*, Vol. 76, no. 1, Spring term 1980, pp. 15–19.) Auden stayed in a flat occupied by Kelly for one of his visits to Oxford as Professor of Poetry.

Italian literary prize as a recognition of his international reputation as a poet. 'I have just won a prize of *twenty million* lire,' Auden wrote to a friend, 'i.e. over $33,000. I am thinking of using it to buy a house near Vienna.'[1]

His first thought had been to purchase the villa he was renting in Forio, but his landlord got wind of the prize and asked an unreasonable sum for it. There were other reasons, too, for leaving Ischia and finding another summer residence. Auden and Chester had visited Austria the previous autumn, going to the opera at Salzburg and Vienna, and staying at Kitzbühel with Hedwig Petzold, who had given Auden his first heterosexual experience in the 1920s, and with whom he now had a warm but entirely sexless friendship. The idea of living within reach of the Austrian opera houses appealed to them both, and Auden also relished the prospect of being part of a German-speaking community. Austria was a wine-drinking country – a not unimportant factor for him – and he would not, he decided, be sorry to turn his back on the Italian sunshine, which had never really suited either his temperament or his physique. His skin still burnt very easily, and his several years' endurance of this on Ischia may have contributed to the premature and eventually extraordinary wrinkling of his face. A more northern setting would appeal to him. 'I don't like sunshine,' he told a friend. 'I would like Mediterranean life in a northern climate.'

There were also more personal reasons. Ischia was now celebrated as a summer haunt of English-speaking homosexuals, whose increasing presence on the island irritated rather than pleased Auden; even so, Chester's remorselessly promiscuous behaviour caused some scandal, and on at least one occasion Auden reported that there was 'a spot of bother with the local parish priest over one of Chester's visitors'. Meanwhile Auden himself had become involved in a public quarrel with his house-boy Giocondo. His habit had been to send Giocondo a cheque from America each winter to cover housekeeping and wages. This was usually for 60,000 lire, but on one occasion Auden absent-mindedly added an extra nought to the figure. The mistake was discovered, and Auden sent another cheque for the correct sum. But Giocondo kept the first cheque. He seems to have harboured some resentment against Auden, largely no doubt because his duties and role in the household were never clearly defined. He would sometimes be taken to parties as Auden's friend, and Auden also encouraged him to practise painting, at which he had some talent. Yet he was also expected to rise at six in the morning to make Auden's coffee, and was obliged to cope with a perpetual and squalid litter of dirty glasses and cups, full ashtrays, scattered books and papers, grubby clothes, and kitchen mess left by Chester. Eventually Giocondo had a row with Auden, and left his employment; whereupon he presented

[1] *The Times* reported that the prize was worth £1,143 in sterling, but this was an error, the true figure being about £8,300.

the cheque for 600,000 lire to the bank, whose manager, realising that there was not enough money to cover it in the account, informed Auden. The resulting row between Auden and the boy grew to be the chief topic of conversation in Forio, with Giocondo's family and their supporters on one side and Auden's friends on the other; Giocondo himself maintained that he had been given a cheque for such a large sum as a gesture of gratitude for 'favours' rendered. The argument, which went on during the late summer of 1956, no doubt contributed to Auden's wish to change his summer home.

During the summer of 1957 he wrote to Hedwig Petzold's daughter, who lived in Vienna, asking her to help him find a house for the summer months 'and perhaps a home for my old age'. He told her it should ideally be within forty kilometres of Vienna, as he intended to drive regularly into the city to shop and attend the opera. Some weeks later he found an advertisement for a house in the village of Kirchstetten, not far from St Pölten, due west of Vienna and about half an hour's drive from the capital. He and Chester went there, as Auden afterwards recalled in a poem, 'on a pouring wet October day', and decided that they liked the house. They managed to outbid a theatre director who was also keen to buy it, and on 4 October 1957 Auden wrote to Hedwig Petzold: 'On Saturday we bought the Kirchstetten house.' The price was 120,000 schillings, some £3,000 sterling or $12,000 in American money. Auden also bought the existing furniture and fittings, for which he paid another 25,000 schillings.

The cottage – for it was really no more than that – dated from the eighteenth century, and stood in a road called Hinterholz. It had once been a farmhouse, and was built of yellow clay. There was an old pump still standing in the garden, but on the whole the house was plain, almost nondescript. A small upper room, set apart from the rest of the house and reached by an outside staircase, had a dormer window poking out of the pantiled roof. The garden was large, with an orchard and vegetable patch, and a terrace where a table could be set for tea or drinks. Behind, the land sloping up into pine woods, the beginning, indeed of the Wienerwald or Vienna Woods themselves. Opposite the front gate lay fields sown with sugar-beet, beyond which ran the Vienna–Linz auto-bahn, whose heavy traffic was often audible from the house. A lane – really just a cart-track – connected the house with the village of Kirch-stetten and its onion-steepled church.

After buying the house, and spending the autumn in Ischia, Auden crossed the Atlantic for his usual New York winter. During this he gave six lectures at Princeton and also helped with a production of a medieval musical drama, *The Play of Daniel*. This was staged by the New York Pro Musica under the direction of Noah Greenberg, with whom Auden and Chester Kallman had previously edited *An Elizabethan Song Book*. For *The Play of Daniel*, Auden wrote sections of narration in alliterative verse, which, at a number of performances in America and later in England, he himself recited, dressed in the costume of a monk.

After his 1958 summer visit to Oxford to give his lectures, he was back in Kirchstetten at the beginning of July, making arrangements for moving in. He found the house and garden 'even more beautiful than I realised'. He and Chester had arranged to take over from the previous owner the services of an elderly couple, Frau Emma Eiermann and her brother Josef, who were Sudeten-German refugees from Czechoslovakia, and who acted as housekeeper and gardener. Auden decided to pay them one thousand schillings a month, even though Frau Emma herself and Auden's Austrian lawyer both said this was too much. 'They are so nice, and so poor,' he explained, 'that I am happy to overpay them.' A little later he installed running hot and cold water at his own expense in their house.

As the Kirchstetten house would not be ready until September, he and Chester spent the rest of the summer in Ischia, during which they disposed of the lease of the Forio house. 'Never never will I go back there again,' Auden told Hedwig Petzold after this final visit. He marked his farewell to the island and to the southern way of life with a poem, 'Goodbye to the Mezzogiorno', dedicating it to Carlo Izzo, who had translated some of his works into Italian. The poem asserted Auden's own northernness, and concluded that for such a person to attempt to 'go southern' could be self-destructive; yet it ended with a declaration of gratitude to the South for what it had given him:

> . . . though one cannot always
> Remember exactly why one has been happy
> There is no forgetting that one was.

6

'A minor
Atlantic Goethe'

'I am enchanted and so is Chester with our Austrian house,' Auden told a friend. 'It's just like Beatrix Potter.' He and Chester brought one cat, Leonora, from Italy and another, Rhadames, from New York; soon Auden reported that their ménage at Kirchstetten consisted of '3 cats, 2 goats, one pig, 2 hens, and 173 goldfish'. Workmen installed what Auden described as 'a 100% American kitchen', with every kind of gadgetry for Chester, including an infra-red grill. The two of them gave a small housewarming party for the workmen, and on his first Sunday in residence Auden attended the local church. 'To my great surprise,' he reported, 'considering how tiny Kirchstetten is, the singing was quite good.' The church was Catholic, but as there was no Protestant place of worship in the village he continued to attend it, being given a seat in the gallery (as a non-Catholic and as a distinguished resident) from where he bellowed the hymns with much pleasure.

His first period of residence at Kirchstetten, in the autumn of 1958, was soon over, but, after another winter and early spring in New York and his usual visit to Oxford in May 1959, he was back there the following July. He and Chester began to keep a visitors' book,[1] and soon a regular stream of guests were arriving to enjoy the idiosyncratic Auden–Kallman hospitality. Many of these were old friends, such as Margaret Gardiner, Stephen Spender and his family, and Michael Yates, who had been Auden's pupil at the Downs School and had travelled with him around

---

[1] In September 1968 Auden's godson Philip Spender (nephew of Stephen) was at Kirchstetten, and at the end of his visit wrote in the guest book: 'Thank God for boozy godfathers, thank Chester for marvellous tastes.' The first part of this was used by Auden in the opening lines of his poem 'Epistle to a Godson'.

Iceland, and who from the mid-1960s became a regular summer visitor to Kirchstetten with his wife Marny.

Those guests who came by train would usually find Auden waiting for them on the platform, checking the train's arrival-time on his watch and nodding with approval if it was punctual; he was always absurdly early for trains or planes, and had a recurrent nightmare about missing them. 'We have to hurry,' he would say, 'because lunch is in fifteen minutes.' On the short drive in his cream-coloured Volkswagen he would usually explain his delicate social position in the village, pointing out that the only people with whom he was expected to associate were the schoolmaster and his wife, the doctor and his wife, and the priest. 'I'm on very good terms with the local *Bürgermeister,* but I've never invited him over to dinner. For all his qualifications, he doesn't have a degree, and one does know he'd be embarrassed.'

Arriving in the village, he would indicate a neighbouring house to his own, in a square named 'Weinheberplatz' after the house's former owner, Josef Weinheber, a poet who collaborated with the Nazis and killed himself when Austria was liberated. (In 1965 Auden wrote a poem about Weinheber, and read it, in a German translation by Elizabeth Mayer, at a service in the village commemorating the twentieth anniversary of Weinheber's death.) Turning off from the village, he would park the car just where the lane petered out into a mere path running into the wood, and lead his guests up the steep ascent to the house. Drinks would be poured, and then Chester – now a plump, balding man in his early forties – would serve lunch.

The meal would be eaten in the big square living room, which had two tables, one for food and the other for working; though both were usually littered with books, ashtrays and papers, this confusion sometimes giving rise to moments of frenzy between Auden and Chester: 'What's happened to that telegram?' 'It's there.' 'It isn't!' 'It must be. I saw it there yesterday.' The food was invariably excellent, Chester now being a master of all styles of cooking, both European and Asian – though anyone who ventured into the kitchen might be disconcerted by the litter of greasy pans and other detritus.

It was a businesslike house, with few concessions to comfort. There were no carpets, but merely rugs on bare boards, and only three pictures of note: drawings of Stravinsky and Richard Strauss, and an Augustus John etching of Yeats. In the living room stood a large radiogram littered with records. The guest bedroom contained just two plain iron bedsteads and a large crucifix on the wall; while Auden's workroom – the upper room, reached by the outside staircase, and always shown proudly to visitors – was similarly bare, with piles of books (no bookcases), a desk on a raised platform by the window, and a portable typewriter on which Auden composed his book-reviews and articles and made fair copies of his poems. The most prominent object in the workroom was a set of the

Oxford English Dictionary, missing one volume, which was downstairs, Auden invariably using it as a cushion to sit on when at table – as if (a friend observed) he was a child not quite big enough for the nursery furniture.

Guests would be expected to conform to, and would be absorbed into, Auden's daily routine. No formal breakfast would be served, though coffee and local bread could be produced for anyone who asked for it. Auden himself would already have risen and begun work in his upstairs room at about half-past six or seven, and would not appear downstairs for more than a moment or two until mid-morning, when he would announce that it was time to do the shopping. He would take his guests down the lane to the village shop, or into St Pölten by car. Then would follow a beer and a sandwich, at about eleven o'clock, in the local *gasthaus,* where Auden – always greeted warmly by the landlord and customers as 'Herr Professor' – might also take the chance to make an international telephone call, there being no phone in the house. Then back home again, and soon it would be time for the pre-lunch drinks, which in Auden's case would be two glasses of dry vermouth, usually accompanied (during lulls in the conversation) by a crossword puzzle, which he would fill in swiftly and in ink, occasionally arguing over a clue with Chester. This, like all other activities during the day, was strictly controlled by his timetable. 'He checks his watch over and over again,' noted one guest. 'Eating, drinking, writing, shopping, crossword puzzles, even the mailman's arrival – all are timed to the minute and with accompanying routines.'

After lunch Chester would take a siesta, while Auden, who firmly disapproved of sleeping during the day, went on working. Then there might be a walk, or, if it was raining (which was often the case) a drive. But if the weather was fine there might be tea in the garden, where Chester had been sunbathing; and then, at precisely six-thirty, martinis.

'Martini-time,' Auden wrote in a poem describing his view of life at Kirchstetten, 'time to draw the curtains and / choose a composer we should like to hear from.' The radiogram would be switched on and the records of Bellini or Donizetti or Richard Strauss played and argued over, while Auden supervised the mixing of what one guest described as 'the strongest martinis I ever drank'. There were strict rules for this: at mid-day the vodka and the glasses themselves were put into the refrigerator, the vermouth (Noilly Prat) being added at a ratio of about one measure to three of vodka an hour before serving. (Auden had originally made his martinis with gin, but Chester found that vodka had a better effect on him and Auden eventually decided to switch to it.) The result was described by one of Auden's friends as 'lethal'.

Dinner would be accompanied by plenty of wine, usually a Valpolicella, and afterwards there would be more wine and more records. Then, quite early, perhaps at half past nine, Auden would look at his watch and, abruptly announcing his bedtime, would disappear to his own room, where the bedclothes were piled so thickly on his bed that (as Michael Yates remarked) it looked like a blanket store. Here he would smoke a few more cigarettes and drink some wine while reading, before dropping off to sleep.

Guests noticed how Auden and Chester spoke to each other like a long-married couple, each completing the other's anecdotes and reminiscences, capping witticisms, and arguing over dates and literary judgements. One visitor, a journalist, recorded fragments of their conversation:

Mr Auden poured tea. 'Poetry is the only art people haven't learned yet how to consume,' he said, 'like soup. They hang copies of great paintings, they pipe music, and as for novels –'

'They abridge them,' said Mr Kallman, already bent over his crossword puzzle.

Mr Auden offered the chocolate biscuits around and lit a cigarette. Elbows on the table, he held it in front of his mouth as he talked so that his face was like a smoky mask. 'One likes to think that poetry can help in certain ways. Some people write irresponsibly about despair. If they really gave up, they would commit suicide.'

'Or eat too much,' said Mr Kallman, without looking up.

'One of the great things about English for writing poetry is that it is a mongrel language with such a rich vocabulary. Of course it is maddening that the third person singular demands an "s" on the verb and the plural of nouns takes an "s". Let me try and show you what I mean.' He gazed out of the window a moment. 'Take sheep,' he began.

'Sheep is the worst possible example,' said Mr Kallman.

'Well, the lion leaps but the lions leap,' said Mr Auden. He puts his head back and closed his eyes, then recited: 'Dies *in the singular / Common we define / But is plural cases / Are always masculine.* We used to say that at school. I'm sorry, I know I'm hard to understand – that limey accent –'

'Not limey accent, just mumbling', said Mr Kallman.

Of one thing no visitor was in doubt: Auden's deep happiness with his way of life at Kirchstetten. He had small complaints, chiefly about the weather which so often settled in – 'It *never* stops raining,' he wrote to Elizabeth Mayer. But his chief emotion was delight that

> what I dared not hope or fight for
> is, in my fifties, mine.

He told Stephen Spender that sometimes he stood in the garden with tears of gratitude and surprise that he possessed a home of his own; and he looked forward with increasing eagerness each year to the moment when he could leave New York and return to 'my beloved Kirchstetten'.

*

Just as Auden's summers in Ischia had been reflected by what might be called an Italian element in his poetry, so his new home in Austria had an effect on his work too. Robert Craft, meeting him just at the time of the move to Kirchstetten, observed: 'Auden is in a German period.'

Several of his literary projects in the next few months were indeed German in character, though sometimes this was just by chance. In the spring of 1959 it was suggested that he and Chester might collaborate with Christopher Isherwood on the book and lyrics of a musical based on Isherwood's *Goodbye to Berlin,* with, according to one report, Marilyn Monroe as Sally Bowles; but though the three of them met for a preliminary talk, nothing came of it, nor of a renewed attempt to arrange something the next year; and when the musical was eventually written under the title *Cabaret,* neither Auden nor Kallman was involved with it.

They did, however, work during the summer of 1958 on a translation of Brecht and Weill's ballet-with-songs, *The Seven Deadly Sins,* commissioned for a performance in New York with Lotte Lenya singing the role of Annie and George Balanchine as choreographer. Auden, despite his friendship with Lincoln Kirstein, founder of the New York City Ballet, continued to regard ballet as a 'very, very minor art', but he admired Balanchine, and reported that this production was 'a great success'.

During 1960 he and Kallman collaborated on a translation of another Brecht–Weill play, *The Rise and Fall of the City of Mahagonny.* This was made for an American première in which Lotte Lenya was again to take part, but in the event the production was cancelled. The translation was eventually published, though not until after Auden's death. He and Kallman produced a vigorous version which fits the music marvellously, and renders Brecht's songs with great vigour:

> Off to Mahagonny
> Where all the winds refresh
> Where gin and whisky rivers flow
> Past horse- and woman-flesh!
> Green and lovely
> Moon of Alabama
> Shine for us!

These theatrical projects were all to a greater or lesser extent commercial undertakings. Something of more artistic interest to him was the making of an English text of Goethe's *Italienische Reise* ('Italian Journey') to be published in a lavishly-illustrated edition by Pantheon Books of

New York and Collins of London. Originally, a number of translators were to be involved, but in the event the work was done entirely by Auden and Elizabeth Mayer. The method was for her to make a literal translation, which he then polished. He had nurtured this project for many years, having as early as 1945 expressed his hope of one day making 'a *pertinent* and *palatable* translation' of the book, which he regarded as being – even more than most travel books – something of a quest-story. 'It will be great fun to work on,' he wrote to Elizabeth Mayer before they began. 'I wish the old Boy, though, wouldn't talk *quite* so much about Art. He's much better on geology.' The translation took many months to complete, and Auden, despite occasional irritations, became more and more fond of the book's author as he progressed. 'Sometimes', he wrote, 'one feels that he is a pompous old bore, sometimes that he is a dishonest old hypocrite. . . Yet, grumble as one may, one is forced in the end to admit that he was a great poet and a great man.' Auden liked, he said, to think of Goethe not as 'Great Mr G' but as 'Dear Mr G'; and Goethe came, too, to be an image of what he hoped to achieve himself in this period of his life. 'I should like', he wrote in a poem, 'to become, if possible, / a minor atlantic Goethe.'

His interest in Goethe was reflected in two poems he wrote. The first, 'A Change of Air', was composed soon after he had finished the translation of *Italian Journey,* and it deals with the way in which a physical journey may relate to a spiritual quest. Auden told Elizabeth Mayer: 'Though Mr G is not the subject, he prompted it.' The second poem – or 'unwritten poem' as Auden called it, though it is really a collection of prose aphorisms – took its title directly from Goethe's autobiography, *Dichtung und Wahrheit* ('Poetry and Truth'), and set itself the challenge of trying to be an exactly true representation of what is meant by the words 'I love you'. At the end of 'Dichtung und Wahrheit', Auden declares this to be impossible: 'I cannot know exactly what I mean. . . Words cannot verify themselves. So this poem will remain unwritten.' It was, in other words, an intellectual exercise. Yet it was about love, and it was the first poem that Auden had written on that subject since the 1940s. That he should now turn back – if only intellectually – to love-poetry was an indication that there had been certain changes in his life.

As he and Chester grew older, the pain and difficulty of their relationship eased. For a time, in 1949, it seemed to Auden that happiness might be achieved by their both practising sexual abstinence; in May of that year he wrote to Rhoda Jaffe from Ischia: 'To my great delight (Praise be to S[anta] R[estituta]) I find myself completely untroubled by sex; Chester, too, is quite changed, and in consequence our relationship is, for the first time, a really happy one.'[1] This, however, did not last, and Chester soon

---

[1] In a 1934 article, Auden had suggested that, during the 'convalescence' of society from

returned to his passionate love-affairs. But as Auden, and eventually Chester, grew middle-aged, the question of sex between them ceased to matter. Instead, they began to work together as equals on libretti and translations – a productive and entirely happy partnership. Auden celebrated the maturity of their relationship in a poem ostensibly describing their living-room at Kirchstetten, called 'The Common Life':

> . . . that, after twenty-four years,
> we should sit here in Austria
>
> as cater-cousins, under the glassy look
>   of a Naples Bambino,
> the portrayed regards of Strauss and Stravinsky,
>   doing British crossword puzzles,
> is very odd indeed.

Odd it was, but also comforting; and, with release from most of the old tensions associated with Chester, Auden was able to turn his poetry again – if only briefly – to the subject of love.

He was thinking of no single lover in mind while writing 'Dichtung und Wahrheit'. It is an amalgam of different people, just as it is an accumulation of experience and reflection. But three figures do seem to be discernible behind it. One is Chester, glimpsed at such moments as

'The One I worship has more soul than other folks. . .' (*Much funnier*, I should like to say.)

A different person seems to be implied elsewhere in 'Dichtung und Wahrheit', for example in the opening section:

Expecting your arrival tomorrow, I find myself thinking *I love You:* then comes the thought – *I should like to write a poem which would express exactly what I mean when I think these words.*

If Auden had anyone particularly in mind here, it was possibly a young man named Orlan Fox, an undergraduate at Columbia University, whom he met at a New York party in the spring of 1959, the year in which 'Dichtung und Wahrheit' was written. Auden was attracted to Fox partly because he was good-looking, but also because he was well-read and could appeciate what Auden had to say about literature. Fox became his lover for a few years, and for the rest of Auden's life remained a close friend and confidant. From the beginning, their relationship had a master–student element in it, as Fox himself has observed: 'He advised

its neurotic ills, sexual relations might be damaging: 'It is quite possible that the way back to real intimacy is through a kind of asceticism.' (*The English Auden*, p. 321.)

what books I should read. At dinner parties, as the youngest, I opened the wine and served the table as he carved. . . He could also be mother scolding the son over thirty years his junior: "Don't slouch in your seat. Gentlemen sit upright." ' In retrospect, Orlan Fox thinks that Auden was addressing 'Dichtung und Wahrheit' partly to him, not just as someone he loved but also as a representative of a younger generation to whom he wished to impart his insights on the weighty subject of love-poetry and truth.

A third figure can perhaps be discerned behind 'Dichtung und Wahrheit', that of a young Viennese named Hugerl, whom Auden met in a bar at about the time he moved to Kirchstetten, and who now visited him regularly when he was in Austria. (Hugerl's journey from Vienna was usually made by train, and in the closing passage of the piece there is a reference to greeting 'You' at the station.) Their relationship began on purely business terms: 'You were in need of money,' Auden wrote in a poem addressed to Hugerl, 'And I wanted sex.' Though 'Hugie', as Auden called him, was willing to earn cash as a call-boy, he had a girlfriend whom he eventually married, and who once actually appeared at Kirchstetten – an event witnessed by Margaret Gardiner, who was staying there at the time:

> There was a great tidying-up of the sitting-room. . . Some friends were coming out from Vienna for tea. They were, Wystan explained, a young, working-class man, a friend of them both, and his newly-wed bride, whom he was bringing to introduce to them. 'A very delicate situation,' Wystan said, with something of his old, con-spiratorial air. The young couple arrived, the man stiff in his Sunday clothes and the girl, also in her best, a pretty creature but too shy to speak. Wystan and Chester bustled round, handing tea and cakes, making conversation, urbane and attentive hosts, trying – but failing – to put their guests at ease. When at last they left, the constraint fell away like a shed skin. And anyway, it was martini time. 'But she seems nice,' said Wystan. 'Yes,' agreed Chester.

Auden afterwards wrote, in his poem to Hugerl:

> And how much I like Christa
> Who loves you but knows,
> Good girl, when not to be there.

He did not publish this poem in his lifetime, but gave copies to friends who were homosexual. It was a celebration of the betwixt-and-between, though not unpleasing, nature of his relationship with 'Hugie':

Hugerl, for a decade now
My bed-visitor,
An unexpected blessing
In a lucky life,
For how much and how often
You have made me glad. . .

How is it now between us?
Love? Love is far too
Tattered a word. A romance
In full fig it ain't.
Nor a naked letch either:
Let me say we fadge.

★

In April 1960, Auden published his third collection of new poems since the end of the war. Its title, *Homage to Clio,* reflected the volume's concern with aspects of Time and History. The title poem itself addressed Clio, 'Muse of the unique / Historical fact. . . / Muse of Time,' and puzzled over her importance in human action, the theme of the poem being that it is the awareness of these concepts, Time and History, that separates humanity from the purely instinctive life of the animal world.[1] Other poems in the book, too, considered aspects of man's relation to Time, and there was much ingenious thinking behind them; but the critics were united in finding the volume (which also included 'Dichtung und Wahrheit') a disappointment, differing only in their explanation for this. Some simply thought there had been a progressive deterioration in Auden's poetry since the 1930s. On the other hand Thom Gunn argued that much of his recent work had been excellent, and that the failure of *Homage to Clio* was an exception to the pattern of his post-war work. Dom Moraes suggested that the book was 'just the product of another of Mr Auden's masks', the mask this time being that of the academic – the Professor of Poetry at Oxford. As for Auden's own views on the present state of his poetry, he prefaced *Homage to Clio* with a stanza showing he was well aware that the book was the product of a 'dry' season:

Bullroarers cannot keep up the annual rain,
The water-table of a once green champaign
Sinks, will keep on sinking: but why complain? – Against odds
Methods of dry farming may still produce grain.

Whatever the merits and faults of his poetry during these years – and

---

[1] The poem had another layer of meaning. Auden wrote to J. R. R. Tolkien on 14 June 1955, enclosing a typescript of it: '[It] is really, as you will see, a hymn to Our Lady.'

there were, and are, many people who find it more attractive and accessible than his pre-war, more gnomic writing – it certainly did not play the central and vital part in his life that it had during the 1920s and 1930s. In that period, the poetry is the key to understanding his mind, character, and emotions. It throws far more light on his personality than do his letters. In later years this changed, and his poetry from the 1950s and 1960s seems more like a series of footnotes to his life. At this later period he revealed himself more fully in his letters and his prose writings. After his long period of spiritual development and change had reached a climax in the 1940s, his poetry, having recorded and even inspired that development and change, slipped a little into the background. During the later years its former place in his life came to be taken more and more by the form of writing that now excited him most, his opera libretti.

In 1959 he and Chester Kallman made a new translation of Lorenzo da Ponte's libretto of Mozart's *Don Giovanni,* a work which had long fascinated Auden for its portrayal of a hero for whom seduction is a vocation – he called Don Giovanni 'the defiant counter-image of the ascetic saint'. The translation that he and Chester produced made no radical alterations of the plot, of the kind that they had made with *The Magic Flute,* but it still treated the arias with a very free hand, often changing the substance so as to provide words that would really fit the music. The style they chose was lively, and at times very near that of W. S. Gilbert or twentieth-century songwriters. Their translation was used for an NBC Opera Theatre television broadcast in April 1960, and again a year later by the Metropolitan Opera; it was also published. Meanwhile they had begun an original libretto of their own.

The seeds of this were sown in 1954, when Auden met the young German composer Hans Werner Henze, who was holidaying on Ischia. At this time Henze, though only twenty-eight, was already writing his second full-length opera, *König Hirsch;* he showed the score to Auden, who declared himself 'very impressed'. Henze and Auden remained in touch, and when in the late autumn of 1958 Henze was commissioned by South German Radio to write a chamber opera – that is, one with a small cast and no chorus – he asked Auden and Kallman to provide a libretto.

The two men willingly agreed, and Henze came to stay with them at Kirchstetten at the beginning of August 1959 to discuss the opera. 'Our original idea', recalled Auden, 'was that we would have four or five characters, each of whom was mad in a different way' – an idea that followed naturally from his belief that in an opera 'in order to sing, all characters have to be a little mad'. Various forms of insanity seemed possible: there might, they suggested, be one character who lived in the past – a figure who, when the opera was written, became Hilda Mack, a middle-aged widow who believes she is still living in the year when her husband died. Various other characters – a ladies' maid masquerading as a person of importance, a young man of good family who falls in love with her, and an elderly actor (his rival) who believes he is Byron's Manfred – were dreamt up, and then abandoned as not quite right. But a setting in which madness and posturing would not seem out of place soon materialised in the form of an Austrian *gasthaus* high in the Alps at the period just before the First World War; and the original notion of the eccentric actor gradually metamorphosed into a figure around whom (it was now clear) the entire opera would revolve: a great poet. They gave him the name Gregor Mittenhofer.

Mittenhofer bears certain superficial resemblances to Auden. When the opera begins, he is in his fifties, as was Auden when the libretto was written. As a young man he was discovered by a rich patron, Carolina Grafin von Kirchstetten, whose name, besides referring to Auden's summer home, suggests Auden's patron of the early 1940s, Caroline Newton. Since then Carolina has acted as Mittenhofer's secretary and patron. Besides depending heavily on her, he is also supported by another admirer, a physician named Dr Reichmann who keeps him in good health with daily doses of medicine and hormone injections; Auden was still dependent on his daily benzedrine and sleeping pills, supplied by a faithful friend who was his New York doctor. But the opera is not an essay in autobiography. Its subject is not Auden but the kind of poet he desired *not* to be.

Chester would sometimes jokingly refer to Auden as 'the Master', or 'Miss Master'. It was an epithet which greatly annoyed Auden. He did not want to be admired and lionised, as Mittenhofer is in the opera – and as W. B. Yeats was in his lifetime. It was, in fact, Yeats whom Auden and Kallman largely had in mind while they were writing the libretto. The detail of Mittenhofer using the visions of Hilda Mack, the deranged widow, as the raw material of his poetry was taken (said Auden) from Yeats's use of his wife's gifts as a medium, while the medicines and hormone injections refer to Yeats's attempts to rejuvenate himself by means of an operation. In a programme note to the opera, Auden and Kallman explained that its theme was summed up in Yeats's own words: 'The intellect of man is forced to choose / Perfection of the life or of the work.' Mittenhofer chooses the latter, and sacrifices the happiness of others in order to produce great art. All through the opera he is writing a poem. To complete it successfully he in effect murders a pair of lovers and breaks the spirit of the others who surround him. At the end of the opera he 'recites' the poem — it is in fact represented wordlessly in the orchestral score by the interwoven themes of the other characters – and the poem itself provides the title of the opera: *Elegy for Young Lovers*.

The character of Mittenhofer seems to have had another model besides

Yeats, for after the opera was finished Auden wrote to Elizabeth Mayer: 'Though neither Chester nor I realised it at the time, we seem, in *Elegy for Young Lovers,* to have done a rather good portrait of Goethe.'

The text of *Elegy for Young Lovers* was written during the autumn and winter of 1959, largely by Chester Kallman; Auden, when asked for information on the division of work, wrote: 'About 75% is by Mr Kallman.' When it was complete, Auden and Kallman dedicated it to the memory of the librettist they most admired, and on whose work they had largely modelled *Elegy:* Richard Strauss's collaborator Hugo von Hofmannsthal. '*Elegy* was our version of *Arabella,*' Auden told Robert Craft.

Hans Werner Henze visited Kirchstetten again during the summer of 1960, and played tapes of part of the score, which Auden found 'exciting', though he remarked: 'The orchestra is going to be *very* odd.' (It included much percussion, a guitar, a mandoline, a marimba, and a number of electronic and tape-recorded effects.) It was arranged that the première should take place only a few months later, at the Schwetzingen Festival in May 1961, with the text sung in a German version made by Prince Ludwig of Hesse, whom Auden and Kallman knew from his visits to Ischia.

During the months that intervened between the completion of his part in the opera and its first performance, Auden returned to Oxford in October 1960 to give his last two lectures before his Professorship of Poetry came to an end. As to the question of his successor, he gave his implied support (in an article in *The Observer*) to the candidature of Robert Graves, who was duly elected – though Auden remarked in a letter to Spender: 'I do hope that, now he is in fashion, les jeunes wont swallow his literary opinions whole.' For many years, Graves had adopted a hostile attitude to Auden in print, but Auden had not responded in kind; he always praised Graves's work in public, and privately said nothing worse than 'Graves [boasts] he's the oldest poet still fucking.' He and Graves met in New York in 1958, and, though they were rather nervous of each other when alone, got on very well when Graves joined the mêlée of Auden's birthday party.

After his Professorship had finished, Auden continued to visit Oxford for several days each year when travelling between Austria and America. In 1962 Christ Church elected him to an Honorary Studentship, the equivalent of a Fellowship at other colleges, and he declared himself to be 'touched and flattered' by this, though he added: 'I hope it does not mean, either that the establishment is doomed, or that I am doomed to be established.'

He spent much of the winter of 1960 preparing, with Louis Kronenberger, a *Book of Aphorisms* for the Viking Press. The work was much to his taste, for as he grew older he was becoming more and more attracted to the aphorism in his own conversation and writing. Much of his prose writing, from his 1929 journal entries through 'The Prolific and the Devourer' to many of the chapters in his later work *The Dyer's Hand* was aphoristic in character, while his conversation, as he grew older, came to consist almost solely of short statements unsupported by argument. He himself said of the aphorism that it is 'an aristocratic genre. The aphorist does not argue or explain: he asserts. . . It is for the reader to decide. . . whether an aphorism be true or false.'

Elegy for Young Lovers (or, as a legal document concerned with the opera misprinted it, *Allergy*) went into rehearsal in Munich in the spring of 1961, with Chester in attendance to keep an eye on the production. The première at Schwetzingen on 20 May proved on the whole a success, largely because Dietrich Fischer-Dieskau had been cast as Mittenhofer. 'Our opera went well in Germany, I think,' Chester wrote to friends in New York. 'Fischer-Dieskau was fabulous, the sets were God-awful left-over faggot chic by a German heterosexual, and absolutely unpractical for the action. Oh well.'

From Schwetzingen, Auden set off together with Chester 'to realise a life-long day-dream and visit Hammerfest in Norway', this being the most northerly town in the world. They had arrived by 31 May, when Auden wrote to Hedwig Petzold: 'Have always longed to see this place and now I have. Beautiful landscape, no architecture and too much Salvation Army.'

A few weeks later, *Elegy for Young Lovers* went into rehearsal at Glyndebourne for its English première, this time with Carlos Alexander as Mittenhofer. Both librettists and the composer were present at rehearsals, but the atmosphere became more and more uncomfortable, and it began to appear that the opera was dramatically very unsatisfactory. It was decided that the scene on the mountain, when the lovers are caught in a snowstorm, would have to be cut to make the opera a manageable length. During rehearsals, John Christie, the founder of Glyndebourne, encountered Auden without knowing who he was. The story is told that when Auden explained to Christie that he had written the libretto, Christie remarked: 'You shouldn't have.'

Afterwards, Auden reported that the Glyndebourne production 'could have been worse'. Further performances were scheduled for Munich in the autumn, with Fischer-Dieskau again in the cast, and the librettists and composer made some alterations in the opera so that the running-time could be cut without having to remove the mountain scene in its entirety. But it was now too late to save much of *Elegy's* reputation. Andrew Porter, writing some months earlier in the *Musical Times*, had judged the libretto (purely on a reading) to be 'masterly'; but after seeing the opera on stage four times at Glyndebourne and Munich he wrote:

Whatever I may have written in these pages earlier, the Auden–
Kallman libretto is a concoction whose only merit is that it provides
a framework for the music. . . One cannot for a moment believe in
Mittenhofer as a great poet: so the central theme is lost. . . [Yet]
Henze has accepted [the libretto] as if it held a poetic truth; so
despite the disturbing break between the 'sincerity' of the music and
the arbitrary postulates of the text, the work is a success. One feels
no interest in the characters or their fate; one is constantly interested
in the development of the musical complexes associated with them.

   Porter was a little hard on the libretto. It is witty and ingenious,
though the final scenes are a disappointment; as with the Auden–
Isherwood plays and *The Rake's Progress,* there seems to be no way of
ending it satisfactorily. It is, moreover, an undisciplined piece of work
throughout, very different in character from the *Rake* libretto. Henze,
though he certainly had Auden's affection, did not command the same
artistic respect from him as had Stravinsky, and the result was in the end
an extravagant and slightly second-rate piece of work.
   Auden himself became dissatisfied with it, or at least with the problem-
atic mountain scene, which he himself had written. He said after the 1961
productions of *Elegy* that this scene 'will not do at all, and must some day
be completely rewritten'. But the rewriting was never done, and though
the opera was performed in Berlin in 1962 it has never become a popular
repertoire piece.

                                  ★

After four summers at Kirchstetten, Auden was still excited by the
novelty of possessing his own home. In August 1962 he wrote a poem,
'Thanksgiving for a Habitat', celebrating the fact that

                    I, a transplant
              from overseas, at last am dominant
                    over three acres.

He made this poem part of a sequence that considered in turn each room
of the house, in relation to the lives of its occupants. The sequence was
almost completed in July 1964, when he wrote to Elizabeth Mayer:
'Now there's only the Toilet left – rather a ticklish subject.' He dedicated
the poem describing his upstairs workroom, 'The Cave of Making', to
the memory of Louis MacNeice, who had died in 1963. Auden gave an
address at MacNeice's memorial service in London. 'While he was alive,'
he said, 'I cared a great deal what Louis MacNeice thought of what I
wrote; now it will be impossible for me to write anything without
feeling that he is looking over my shoulder.'

Life at Kirchstetten, despite Auden's happiness there, did have its difficulties. In the spring of 1962, before he left New York for Austria, he heard that Hugerl, his Viennese boyfriend, had been arrested for taking part in a series of burglaries in which Auden's Volkswagen, which he had lent to the young man, had been used as a getaway car, and had been damaged. Auden's own house was amongst those burgled by the gang. Auden reacted by doing his best to help Hugerl; he found a lawyer to defend him, and wrote to his friend Hedwig Petzold: 'I hope very much that they will not keep Hugo [sic] in prison too long. . . I don't believe – a view shared by those of his friends I have spoken to – that he is *ganz verdorben* [entirely gone to the bad]. I estimate his chances of leading an honest life at 50/50, and I must do what I can to improve that chance.' When the young man had finished his prison sentence, Auden welcomed him back into his house, and bed, as before. It was suggested by Chester that Hugerl had turned to burglary in order to draw attention to himself as being a real person and not just a sex-object; and the crime, and its aftermath, did make Auden treat him more seriously in their subsequent relations. 'When you stole', he wrote in the poem addressed to Hugerl, 'And were caught and put inside: / Both learned a lesson.'

A few months later the Kirchstetten household began to be augmented, for at least some weeks of each year, by another young man. Chester had begun to make trips to Greece, slipping off from Kirchstetten each July for what he called his 'island holiday': two weeks in the Cyclades followed by another two weeks in Athens, where he found the sexual climate ideal. Auden regretted Chester's absence – 'I am all by myself and, what is worse, obliged to cook for myself, an art for which I have no talent whatsoever,' he told a friend – but he learnt to accept it. Chester meanwhile began to bring Greek boys back to the Kirchstetten house at the end of his holiday. The second of these, and the most notable, was a young man named Yannis Boras, who came from a village near Olympia and was, according to a friend of Auden's and Chester's, 'kind and decent and intelligent', though he and Chester occasionally had high-pitched arguments. Yannis could speak German and so was able to talk to Auden; he could also drive, which was a help, since Auden's attempts to teach Chester had failed. Auden accepted him willingly enough, while Yannis (according to Chester) 'worshipped' Auden. There were, however, occasional difficulties. After Hugerl was released from prison, Auden decided to make him a present of the car, which had never been satisfactorily repaired since the theft. Chester was furious, and, when drunk one evening, told Auden he should have given the car to Yannis. This made Auden equally cross, but the matter soon blew over, and the household returned to a relatively peaceful existence. Hugerl kept the car, and Auden bought another, which was sometimes lent to Yannis.

During the winter of 1961 Auden began to assemble a collection of his essays and lectures, at the request of Random House, which he decided to call *The Dyer's Hand* – a quotation from Shakespeare's Sonnet CXI ('My nature is subdu'd / To what it works in, like the dyer's hand') which Auden had already used as the title of a series of three B.B.C. Third Programme talks on poetry in 1955. The new volume was chiefly based on his lectures at Oxford during the Professorship of Poetry, and on articles he had previously published in journals. He had not kept copies of most of these articles, and his only record of what he had published was a list compiled by his friend and former secretary Alan Ansen. Auden gave the list to Orlan Fox, who was now doing some secretarial work for him in New York, and sent him off to the Public Library to look up various items on it. He instructed Fox to copy out these articles by hand, since he knew no other method of obtaining them. Fox actually wrote out one complete essay before he discovered that he could get photostats.

Auden told Spender that the subject of *The Dyer's Hand* was Christianity and Art: 'That is what the *whole* book is really about, the theme which dictated my selection of pieces and their order.' Certainly his approach to literature in the book was often specifically Christian, in that he used Christian concepts as a means of describing the intellectual-spiritual processes he found at work in literature: for example, he saw the Servant–Master relationship of Sancho Panza and Don Quixote, and also of Jeeves and Bertie Wooster, as a type of Agape. But more apparent to a reader than this theme of Christianity and art is the book's largely aphoristic character – many of the sections are not essays but collections of aphorisms – and the degree of repetition in it. A number of Auden's favourite remarks and literary illustrations appear three or even four times during the course of *The Dyer's Hand;* he did not trouble when putting it together to avoid repeating himself – just as he began to do, a few years later, in his conversation.

Despite this, *The Dyer's Hand* emerged as a vigorous testimony to Auden as a critic – if 'critic' is the right word for someone so positive in his approach to everything he discussed. An appropriate comment on the book would be that made a decade later by Clive James, reviewing Auden's second collection of essays, *Forewords and Afterwords:* 'The range of interest, and none of it mechanical! All of it professional in the best sense, amateur in the best sense, free of bluff, full of life.' *The Dyer's Hand* was published by Random House in November 1962 and by Faber's a few months later. It was well received by the critics, and Auden was especially delighted when *The Dyer,* the journal of that trade, wrote to the publishers asking for a review copy.

While he was assembling *The Dyer's Hand,* Auden began to make plans for another work of translation. Some time earlier he had been introduced by Lincoln Kirstein to Dag Hammarskjöld, Secretary - General of the United Nations, whose knowledge and understanding of poetry Auden found 'remarkable'. He only saw Hammarskjöld a few times, but felt his death in a plane crash in the autumn of 1961 to be 'a personal loss', and described Hammarskjöld as 'one of the two most selfless people I have met in my life'. (He did not say who the other was.) After Hammarskjöld died, the manuscript of *Vagmärken* ('Waymarks'), a diary of his private thoughts, was found in his New York home, and was published in Sweden. Auden was asked to make an English translation of the text. He knew no Swedish, and had to look for a collaborator, finding, by what he called 'a fantastic stroke of good luck', Leif Sjöberg, who taught Scandinavian languages and literature at the State University of New York at Stony Brook. The two began work, Sjöberg providing Auden with a literal translation, and indicating cases where words had alternative meanings. Auden then produced his own, freer version, which he called *Markings*.

He was much in sympathy with Hammarskjöld's book, which was not so much a diary as a collection of *pensées* or aphorisms, and made no reference to Hammarskjöld's public life. He also believed Hammarskjöld to have experienced something of the temptations to a messianic role which he himself had undergone in the 1930s. Auden told Lincoln Kirstein that he found something objectionable in Hammarskjöld's belief that he was the bearer of divine truth; he implied this in his introduction to the translation, which suggested that somebody of Hammarskjöld's character is 'always in great danger of imagining that he *is* God'.

This introduction, which also referred to Hammarskjöld's 'exceptionally aggressive super-ego', was shown in typescript to Hammarskjöld's friend Leif Belfrage, who was then Swedish Permanent Under-Secretary for Foreign Affairs, and a member of the Swedish Academy, which awards the Nobel Prizes. This was in 1964; it was known that Auden had been Hammarskjöld's candidate for the Nobel Prize for Literature, and his chances of receiving it were, up to this time, thought to be good. But it was made clear to Auden that his remarks about Hammarskjöld in the introduction to *Markings* were not acceptable, and would have to be changed if he did not want to fall from favour with the Swedish Academy. Auden, however, was adamant. He printed the introduction without changing anything, remarking philosophically and without bitterness: 'Well, there goes the Nobel Prize.'

The Prize did indeed go elsewhere, both in 1964, when it was offered to Jean-Paul Sartre, and in subsequent years. Towards the end of his life, Auden began to be preoccupied with not having won it, declaring that he would have liked it not for the honour but for the money – he said he would have used it to buy a new organ for the Kirchstetten church. Eventually it became an obsession with him. There seems, however, to be no truth in the story, sometimes told, that he actively lobbied for it.

After *Markings* was finished, Auden continued to collaborate with Leif Sjöberg, and together they translated a number of poems by Gunnar Ekelöf, a Swedish contemporary of Auden's; their edition of his *Selected*

Poems was published in 1971.. Auden also made English versions of
poems by the Russian poet Andrei Voznesensky, for which he was
provided with literal translations by Max Hayward. He came to believe
that tasks like this were an important part of his work. 'Translation is
fruitful in two ways,' he said, 'First, it introduces new kinds of sensibility
and rhetoric. . . and fresh literary forms. . . Second, and perhaps even
more important, the problem of finding an equivalent meaning in a
language with a very different structure from the original develops the
syntax and vocabulary of the former.' Auden's translations often departed
quite radically from the originals, but he was prepared to justify this: 'It
does not particularly matter if the translators have understood their
originals correctly; often, indeed, misunderstanding is, from the point of
view of the native writer, more profitable.' He also argued that 'the only
political duty [for a writer]. . . in all countries and at all times. . . is a duty
to translate the fiction and poetry of other countries so as to make them
available to readers in his own'. (As Stephen Spender had remarked,
'One of Auden's characteristics is to make a cult of whatever he happens
to be doing, which becomes to him what the poet must do.')

During 1962 Auden and Chester Kallman amused themselves briefly
with the translation of another libretto, this time that written by Goldoni
for Dittersdorf's opera *Arcifanfano, King of Fools*. Their version was
performed at New York Town Hall in the autumn of 1965, but was not
published. They also proposed to Hans Werner Henze that they should
write another opera with him.

The idea had occurred to them that the *Bacchae* of Euripides was, as
Auden put it, 'excellent potential material for a grand opera libretto', not
least because it was a myth that seemed remarkably relevant to the
present day. 'Today', said Auden, 'we know only too well that it is as
possible for whole communities to become demonically possessed as it is
for individuals to go off their heads.' They decided that they must make a
number of changes to Euripides' story before it could be fitted to the
operatic stage. They did not want to produce what Chester called 'any
species of that Glucky Greekiness which permits itself to be staged by
combining the Modern Dance with the side-views of a Grecian Urn'.
They also realised that in a modern opera the characters would have to be
given some psychological motivation, an element that was largely
lacking in Euripides. They decided to suggest this motivation by making
each character take a different attitude to religion, and thus to Dionysus
and his rites. Pentheus was to be, in Chester's words, a 'medieval
ascetic', and his mother Agave 'a French Second Empire sensual sceptic',
while Tiresias was to be dressed (according to the directions in the
libretto) as 'an Anglican Archdeacon'. They also made a major addition
to the story in the form of a comic intermezzo, which enacts, in the
manner of *opera buffa*, Pentheus' private imaginings of what is going on
among the followers of Dionysus.

Auden and Kallman substituted for 'Bacchae' or 'Bacchantes' the term 'Bassarids', of which Auden wrote: 'The word *Bassarids* or *Bassariden* really does exist, though to my astonishment it is not in the O.E.D. It means followers of Dionysus of both sexes.' The librettists worked on *The Bassarids* during the summer of 1963; when it was finished, Auden wrote to E. R. Dodds, whom, as the editor of a fine edition of *The Bacchae,* he had asked to look through it and point out errors: 'More than half the credit. . . goes to Chester, who wrote more than half of it.' The libretto was immensely detailed, giving minute directions about costume and movement, and even music; it was also very long, and when Henze set it he was obliged to make major cuts. The première was scheduled for Salzburg in August 1966.

When it took place, the opera proved far more of a success than *Elegy for Young Lovers.* Auden reported to Elizabeth Mayer: 'Paskalis, a young Greek baritone, was superb as Pentheus, ditto ditto Kersten Nayer as Agave. . . I am convinced that Hans has written a masterpiece.' The critics were equally enthusiastic. Andrew Porter, who had been so harsh on the *Elegy* libretto, wrote: '*The Bassarids* is a fine opera. . . a major addition to the repertory.' The opera was performed again by the same company in Berlin a short time afterwards, but a proposed British production by Sadlers Wells was abandoned through lack of funds; and though *The Bassarids* was eventually performed in London after Auden's death, and continues to be regarded as one of Henze's best works, it has not in fact entered the operatic repertoire to anything like the extent that *The Rake's Progress* has done.

In the autumn of 1963, a few months after the *Bassarids* libretto was finished, Auden and Kallman were asked to write the lyrics for a Broadway musical to be based on *Don Quixote,* and to be called *Man of La Mancha.* Auden was doubtful at first, remarking that the script he had been shown 'will have to be rewritten', but eventually he and Chester signed a contract. Auden was devoted to Cervantes' book and its two central characters, and often cited it in his critical writings, though he once alleged jokingly in a lecture that he had never read it right through. He and Chester, working independently, began to write some lyrics for the musical; two of Auden's were later published in a collection of his poems. But it soon transpired that Auden's view of Quixote, as a gifted man who went mad, was not compatible with the intention of the producers, who saw him as a romantic hero, a dreamer of 'the impossible dream'. Auden and Kallman were paid off, and *Man of La Mancha* went ahead without them – with inferior results, as far as the songs were concerned.

The Auden–Kallman collaborations usually took place in the summer months, when both of them were at Kirchstetten; and it was at this time, in 1963, that Chester ceased to return to New York with Auden for the winter. Instead, he would go to Greece, arriving in Athens at about the end of October and remaining there until early April. In Athens he led a largely disorderly life, living in a series of furnished flats with Yannis Boras or some other boyfriend, and, from mid-morning onwards, drinking large quantities of ouzo – though he also invariably cooked a good evening meal for himself and Alan Ansen, Auden's friend and former secretary, who was now living in Athens.

Chester's decision not to live with Auden in New York was partly due to the attractions of life in Athens, but friends had little doubt that he also wanted to assert his independence from Auden. Stephen Spender observed that Chester had begun to 'feel that to some degree Auden had destroyed his personality. . . that insofar as he was a writer himself, Auden acted as his patron. Kallman wrote a poem about this, and those who saw it were startled by the deep resentment in it.'[1]

Chester, however, still depended on Auden for most of his income. He told Bill Caskey, who was also now living in Athens: 'I get it all from Wystan. The boys think I have royalties from the libretti, but you know I don't receive that much. It all comes from dear, sweet Wystan.' If anybody suggested that he was being replaced in Auden's affections by Orlan Fox or some new disciple or lover in New York, he would (remembered Caskey) 'quiver with jealousy'.

The jealousy was unnecessary: nobody took Chester's place in Auden's affections. Chester's refusal to come back to New York profoundly saddened him – though he accepted it stoically. 'Chester is spending the winter in Athens,' he wrote to a friend in December 1965, 'so I am all on my lonesome; but too busy, thank God, to feel sorry for myself.' To Stephen Spender he wrote: 'I cook doggedly and even manage to eat what I make.' His cooking became, as a result of practice, quite passable, and some visitors (if not all) were impressed by his competence. But he was distressed by Chester's frequent failure to write and send him any news for months at a time. 'I should like a letter or at least a p.c. to know your address,' he wrote to Chester in a letter that is typical of many, and which ends: 'All my love, Wystan'.

With Chester absent from New York, the St Mark's Place apartment, which had never been tidy, became more and more of a mess. The maid who came in from an agency once a week in order to clean it up could do little with the chaos made by Auden. 'The kitchen', recalled V. S. Yanovsky, 'became a complete mess and so did the bathroom. "You pee in the toilet?' Auden asked with dignified surprise, after having heard me

---

[1] The poem, which neither the present writer nor Edward Mendelson has seen, was never published by Kallman, nor is it among those of his papers which are now in the University of Texas. Stephen Spender write of it: 'Louis MacNeice told me that Chester had shown him this poem when he (Louis) was in New York during the war. He was very struck by it and said it had considerable point.'

flush (the door did not close any more). . . . "Everybody I know does it in the sink. 'It's a male's privilege." "[1]

Without Chester, Auden seemed not to want to hold the February birthday-party, and it stopped. At about this period he asked Orlan Fox if he would like to start coming to dinner every Friday night, so that they could eat and talk; Fox was to buy the food, Auden the wine. The invitation was put shyly – 'Wystan was shy, deeply shy,' commented Fox – and was accepted, Fox imagining that it must be part of a routine which included similar dinners with other and older friends on other evenings. Some time later he realised that this was not so. Friday nights were Auden's only regular social event.

Some of Auden's younger friends were going through a phase of being interested in drugs, especially L.S.D., and they encouraged Auden to experiment with it. He was perfectly willing, though he would only do so under the professional eye of his New York physician, David Protetch, whom he had known since Protetch was a student at Ann Arbor, and who was tolerant and sympathetic towards Auden's way of life. Protetch came to St Mark's Place early one morning and administered L.S.D. 'All I felt', said Auden afterwards, 'was a slight schizoid dislocation of my body – as though my body didn't quite belong to me, but to somebody else.' On another occasion he took mescaline, but again the effect was unremarkable. 'I think', he concluded, 'we had better stick to wine. It tastes nicer and it has even been known to improve the conversation.'

He followed this advice unstintingly, drinking not just wine but anything else that was at hand. 'Auden for dinner,' Robert Craft wrote in his diary in January 1964. 'He drinks a jug of Gibsons before, a bottle of champagne during, a bottle (sic) of Cherry Heering (did he think it was Chianti?) after dinner. . . Despite this liquid menu, he not only is unblurred, but also performs mental pirouettes for us. . . Not a trip to the "loo" all evening. Labial difficulties occur, to be sure, but they are overcome by a sort of isometric exercise, a screwing up of the rugosities of that nobly corrugated face, and by bursts of music, including some very melodious singing of bits of Rossini's *Petite Messe Solennelle*. Otherwise the only sign of tipsiness is an initial lurch at departure, after which a gyroscope seems to take over.' The gyroscope was, however, not always in evidence. At several poetry readings in the early 1960s Auden was observed by members of his audience to be distinctly the worse for drink.

★

[1] John Auden stayed a night with his brother in New York and was soundly ticked off for flushing the lavatory, 'because I should most certainly have know that the Catskill Mountain reservoirs were almost empty'. He noticed that 'the basin stank horribly'.

In 1964 he made return visits to two places that had been important to him earlier in his life: Iceland and Berlin. The Iceland trip was made at the invitation of that country's government, and of Basil Boothby, whom Auden had met in China in 1938 and who was now British Ambassador in Reykjavik. He arrived there early in April and remained for about two weeks, staying at the British Embassy, attending an official lunch and meeting the President and Prime Minister. Modern Iceland on the whole pleased him; he found much of it changed beyond recognition, Reykjavik in particular now being a city of concrete, steel and glass; but he still felt that the country was 'holy ground' to him. During his time there he went to Hredvatn, the farm where he and Louis MacNeice and Michael Yates had stayed for a few nights in 1936 – and where he was sad to find that the ponies (which he had hoped to ride) had now been replaced by a landrover.

> Twenty-eight years ago
> Three slept well here.
> Now one is married, one dead.
>
> Where the harmonium stood
> A radio: –
> Have the Fittest survived?

These lines were part of a poem in which he described his trip – or rather, not so much a poem as a series of fragments. The form that Auden used in it was the Japanese *haiku*, a three-line stanza which adds up to seventeen syllables, and which was used by Dag Hammarskjöld in *Markings*. The *haiku* was particularly well adapted to the aphoristic character of Auden's thought during this period of his life, and he began to use it often.

From Iceland he went to Sweden, and spent a few days in Stockholm learning what he could from Hammarskjöld's friends about some of the allusions in *Markings*, his translation of which was about to go to press. He found this a very odd experience: 'I felt as if I were in a detective story. Each one I spoke to invariably warned me against believing a word the others said.' By the end of April he was back in Kirchstetten, where he spent much of the summer finishing a new book of poems – 'always a depressing experience,' he wrote to a friend, 'as one wonders what on earth one will be able to write in the future'. The book consisted largely of the sequence about Kirchstetten itself, 'Thanksgiving for a Habitat'; Auden decided to call the book *About the House*. Largely because of the 'Habitat' poems, it was uncharacteristically personal in tone. Auden wrote of this to a friend: 'For the first time I felt old enough to speak in the First Person.'

In the autumn of 1964 he went to West Berlin. It was not his first return visit to Berlin since the 1930s: he had been there three times (for a few days) during the last ten years, and he was saddened by the fact that 'the city of my youth has now gone – the juke box and rock-and-roll have ruined it'. On one of these visits he met a former Berlin boyfriend, an ex-sailor, whom he said had given him 'sleepless nights' in 1929, and whom he was shocked to find was now grossly fat: 'He hadn't just put on weight — he was *grotesque* like someone in a circus.' Now, in September 1964, he arrived to begin six months in Berlin as a membe of an artists-in-residence programme financed by the Ford Foundation.

In prospect this seemed to him the ideal job: 'The Ford Foundation will pay me a handsome salary, the City will provide a free apartment.' Nor were there to be any obligatory lecturing duties. But in practice, once he had settled in, he found that it was not quite so pleasant. He felt he ought not to turn down any requests for lectures and poetry readings, and was soon reporting: 'Have addressed all kinds of gatherings, including G.I.'s and wives of British officers. . . Last week I gave a lecture in German, if you please: it was awfully hard work but I managed to get through it.' On the other hand he found it was difficult to become really involved in Berlin life, or to make friends. He attended a weekly Literary Colloquium at the Technische Hochschule, conducted by Professor Walter Höllerer, in the hope that he might get to know some of the students and invite them to call regularly on him for 'open house'. But his name and his poetry meant little or nothing to them, and the attempt was a failure. He also asked one or two people to dinner, including Günter Grass; but none of this led to real friendship, largely because the Berlin writers and artists rather resented the highly-paid visitors. In January, Auden wrote to Elizabeth Mayer: 'If it weren't for Peter Heyworth, the music critic for the *Observer* who is writing a book on music under the Weimar Republic, I should be very lonely.'

Heyworth had met Auden briefly once or twice before, but had not expected more than a casual acquaintance with him during the Ford Foundation programme, of which he too was a member. He was surprised by the warmth with which Auden now sought his friendship. They began to dine together each Tuesday and Thursday evening, often in Auden's modern and rather dreary flat in Hubertusbaderstrasse, Auden doing the cooking. Heyworth found Auden full of intellectual energy in their conversations, even if he was unwilling to have his opinions challenged; should Heyworth venture to disagree, Auden would reproved him with the reply: 'You old mother's done a lot of thinking.'[1]

Heyworth was a little alarmed one day to learn that Auden had been charged with drunken driving. The precise circumstances are not clear, but it appears that someone reported him for driving in an odd manner

[1]This role of 'your old mother' increasingly appealed to Auden. He liked to substitute these or similar words for the personal pronoun in inappropriate contexts, such as Spender's poem 'I think continually of those who are truly great', which he liked to recite as: 'Your mother thinks continually of those who are truly great'. He was even known to do this with the Bible: 'Your mother is the resurrection and the life.'

one evening. The cause seems not to have been drink, but Auden's difficulty in finding his way through Berlin on a dark rainy night – he said he was peering out of the windscreen in order to see street-signs. However, when the police took him in they did find alcohol on his breath, and he was ordered to appear in court. Heyworth, who accompanied him, saw he had dressed himself like a schoolboy attending Prize Day: his hair was brushed, and he wore a tie and a clean suit. In court he held everyone spellbound by his forthrightness; when asked if he drank alcohol, he replied: 'I've been drinking every night of my adult life.' He was let off – possibly there was a wish not to cause embarrassment in official circles – and as he left the court he remarked to Heyworth: 'Judge was rather a dish, my dear, didn't you think?'

Heyworth formed the impression that sex was no longer very important to Auden. But he did gather that Auden had taken the trouble to acquire the services of a Berlin call-boy, Manfred. Auden complained one day that Manfred had failed to turn up for his regular appointment, which was on a certain day of the week, at teatime, the hour Auden considered appropriate for such things. When Auden complained of the boy's non-appearance, Heyworth inquired whether perhaps he had not been paying him enough. 'Oh, I don't *pay* him,' answered Auden. 'I give him English lessons.' Heyworth suggested that the youth might prefer a few Deutschmarks, but Auden seemed offended: 'Certainly not: I'm a very good teacher!'

While he was in Berlin, Auden worked on two commissions. One was an anthem for Christ Church, Oxford, to be set to music by Sir William Walton, who had once been a chorister of the college and who often met Auden on Ischia, where he had a house. The other was to translate the lyrics from Bertolt Brecht's *Mother Courage* for a production at the National Theatre in London. 'Between ourselves,' Auden wrote to a friend while at work on this, 'I've got a bit bored with old B.B. A great poet but he couldn't think.'

During this winter of 1964-65, T. S. Eliot, who was in his seventy-seventh year, became seriously ill. Early in December the B.B.C. arranged with Auden that he should tape-record a radio obituary which would be used when the time came. Auden found this 'a ghoulish business', and afterwards told Eliot's wife Valerie that he was very uneasy at having done it – she was greatly touched by the care he took to explain and apologise. After Christmas he flew down to Athens for a few days to celebrate Chester's birthday; and it was just then that Eliot died. Auden was pursued to Greece by a television film-crew and was again obliged to deliver a piece about Eliot ('I don't like mass communications,' he said). He declared of Eliot that 'no future changes and fluctuations in taste will consign his work to oblivion'. As to comparisons between himself and Eliot, he once wrote to Louise Bogan, who invariably reviewed Auden's work favourably and who had made a slighting remark about Eliot: 'I shall never be as great and good a man if I live to be a hundred.'

None the less, now that Eliot was dead, Auden's friends had little doubt that he regarded himself as the best living poet of the English language. Yet his last three books of poems, *Nones, The Shield of Achilles* and *Homage to Clio,* had been harshly treated by the critics, and when his new collection *About the House* was published during 1965 it was attacked with the same severity. Most reviewers admired Auden's continuing technical skill, but objected to the cosy tone of many poems (especially the sequences about the Kirchstetten house) which they felt amounted to smugness. More than one critic suggest that Auden was turning his back on the world's real problems. 'What offends, and will go on offending many readers of the later Auden poems,' wrote *The Times,* 'is that what is offered in them as a religious outlook should so often sound so complacent, so indifferent to the world's suffering.'

Auden was in fact, as a private individual, far from indifferent to the world's suffering. In the early 1950s, at a time when he had little money to spare, he provided help for a Finnish child whose family were in difficulties. At about the same time he heard, through a friend, of two Austrian boys in their early teens, who would have to leave school early because there was no money to pay for their continuing education. Auden, though he had no knowledge of or connection with the family, and had not met the boys, sent word that he would undertake the payment of the fees, with the result that the boys were able to continue their education. He did not meet them until some time later, when he became friendly with them and their family. Early in 1957 he offered, and apparently gave, shelter at his house on Ischia to a Hungarian refugee couple. Yet only occasionally would he allow such issues to enter his poetry. When Russia invaded Czechoslovakia in 1968 he published eight bitter lines ('The Ogre does what ogres can, / Deeds quite impossible for Man. . .'); but this was exceptional. He remained convinced of the utter uselessness of trying to change the world through poetry, and when questioned about this would usually reply: 'I know that all the verse I wrote, all the positions I took in the thirties, didn't save a single Jew. These attitudes, these writings, only help oneself. They merely make people who think like one, admire and like one – which is rather embarrassing.' On the particular issue of the Third World, he wrote:

> It's heartless to forget about
>   the underdeveloped countries,
>   but a starving ear is as deaf as a suburban optimist's.

And in *The Dyer's Hand* he concluded that, as a result of the growth of the Machine Age, one of the few remaining jobs for an artist in society is to remind his contemporaries – particularly those in authority – that people have a right to be themselves, and to be frivolous: that human beings 'are people with faces, not anonymous numbers, that *Homo Laborans* is also *Homo Ludens'*.

He tried, just as he had in the 1940s, to avoid giving his opinion about controversial public matters; yet for a time he did admit, even to newspaper reporters, that he supported American military involvement in Vietnam. He did this partly out of sheer cussedness, claiming that he was the only New York intellectual who took such a line, and adding that if he lived in Britain he would now be a Conservative. But he also gave more serious reasons. 'I am not convinced', he wrote to a friend in the mid 1960s, 'that the immediate withdrawal of American troops from S[outh] V[ietnam] is the right solution, though I agree that it could possibly be. . . It goes without saying that war is an atrocious and corrupting business on both sides.'[1] Eventually, however, he did come to believe that a negotiated peace, rather than continued U.S. military action, was an urgent necessity, and at his friend Margaret Gardiner's request he added his signature to a statement urging an immediate end to American procrastination over the peace agreement.

His claim to be Conservative in sympathy was not entirely a piece of posing. 'Can you understand all this Student Revolt business?' he wrote to E. R. Dodds in 1968. 'I can follow when they are making political protests against Vietnam or Germ Warfare, but when it comes to University matters. . . I am bewildered. I can't remember as an undergraduate ever feeling that the regulations prevented me from doing anything I liked.' He was also critical of the boredom expressed by many young people – 'When I was young, we were never bored' – and when in the company of those friends who had remained left-wing he took an almost blimpish line. 'You and your commie friends,' he would say to Margaret Gardiner, 'you and your *New Statesman*. . . You and your Kingsley Martin [its editor]. . . I'd gladly string him up with my own hands.' But his true political position (insofar as he had one) was really still that of a liberal. In 1956 he wrote: 'Unattractive and shallow as one may feel so many liberals to be, how rarely on any concrete social issues does one find the liberal position to be the wrong one.' He disapproved of capital punishment, and thought that prison sentences should not be imposed for crimes of theft – 'The only sensible treatment of thieves', he said, 'is to get them working as soon as possible and deduct a certain amount from their pay every week.' He had remained, as he prophesied in 1936 that he would, a 'pink old Liberal to the last'.

---

[1]He wrote in similar terms in *Authors Take Sides on Vietnam*, a symposium published in 1967: 'I believe a negotiated peace, to which the Viet Cong will ave to be a party, to be possible, but not yet, and that therefore, American troops, alas, must stay in Vietnam until it is. But it would be absurd to call this answer *mine*. It simply means that I am an American citizen who reads the *New York Times*.'

He often liked to suggest that politicians should be done away with, and that national leaders should be chosen quite at random by lottery, with major issues decided by a referendum. As to the question which had so long vexed him, that of the artist's role in society, he began to come to the conclusion that the chief 'political' duty of a writer in the 1960s was to defend the language against the inroads of the modern world, arguing that if the language was allowed to decay then the consequences would be disastrous for everyone. 'To-day', he wrote in 1967, 'nine-tenths of the population use twice as many words as they understand. . . So befuddled, how can the man-in-the-street be expected to resist the black magic of the propagandists, commercial and political?' He liked to quote what seemed to him appalling examples of corrupt language: a reviewer calling a spy-thriller 'enervating' when he meant that it caused a nervous thrill; a person feeling sick who said 'I am nauseous'; and a radio commercial which described an American investment agency as 'integrity-ridden'. Again and again, he cited a dictum of Karl Kraus: 'Speech is the mother, not the handmaid of thought.'

There was in this attitude, as in so many that he took, more than a small element of deliberate nonconformity with fashion. He was still taking the role of the revolutionary, just as he had in his youth, except that now his opponent was not the existing social order but the present-day revolutionaries themselves. As he put it in a 1969 poem:

> At Twenty I tried to
> vex my elders, past Sixty it's the young whom
> I hope to bother.

★

In the summer of 1965, soon after Auden had finished his six months in Berlin, Faber & Faber suggested that he prepare a new edition of his *Collected Shorter Poems,* bringing the book more up to date – the earlier volume had stopped at 1944. He agreed, and used this as an opportunity for a wholesale revision of his work. 'I have been going through everything,' he told Elizabeth Mayer in September 1965, 'revising and gnashing my teeth at my clumsiness in the old days. To-day, at least, I think I know my craft.'

While preparing his 1945 *Collected Poetry* for Random House – the book on which the 1950 Faber *Collected Shorter Poems* was based – he had rejected some poems and rewritten others. Now, in 1965, this process was repeated. Several poems which he had judged acceptable in 1945 were rejected, the most notable being 'Sir, no man's enemy', 'Spain', and 'September 1, 1939'.[1] His objection to the first of these was that its last

---

[1] Auden had also omitted these three poems from a selection of his poetry published in 1958 by Penguin Books, reprinted the next year in America by The Modern Library; since

line, which commends 'New styles of architecture, a change of heart', was a lie. 'I have never like modern architecture,' he said. 'I prefer *old* styles, and one must be honest even about one's prejudices.' This was a wilful misunderstanding of the poem, which is not concerned with actual architecture but with spiritual change; Auden's real objection to 'Sir, no man's enemy' may have been that it addresses somebody who may or may not be God, an ambiguity not suited to his outlook in later life. His overt objection to 'Spain' was along much the same lines. Here again he cited the poem's closing words – 'History to the defeated / may say alas, but cannot help nor pardon' – of which he now remarked: 'To say this is to equate goodness with success. It would have been bad enough if I had ever held this wicked doctrine, but that I should have stated it simply because it sounded to me rhetorically effective is quite inexcusable.' Again there seems to be a deliberate misinterpretation: the lines do not 'equate goodness with success'. Probably Auden's real reason for omitting 'Spain' from his new collection was more subtle; he may well have felt uneasy at contemplating a poem which grew out of his unhappy involvement with the Spanish war. At to 'September 1, 1939', he had, in the 1945 collection, already excised the stanzas containing the words 'We must love one another or die', and now he omitted the entire poem. When a friend objected to his excluding it, Auden replied: 'The reason (artistic) I left England and went to the U.S. was precisely to *stop* me writing poems like "Sept 1st 1939", the most dishonest poem I have ever written. A hang-over from the U.K. It takes time to cure oneself.'

In rejecting the rhetoric of 'September 1, 1939', Auden was rejecting the influence of Yeats, which had been strong over him during the 1930s, and which he now felt had been responsible for his saying many things that he had only half believed. In about 1964 he wrote to Stephen Spender: 'I am incapable of saying a word about W. B. Yeats because, through no fault of his, he has become for me a symbol of my own devil of unauthenticity, of everything which I must try to eliminate from my own poetry, false emotions, inflated rhetoric, empty sonorities. . . His [poems] make me whore after lies.' Elsewhere he said that Yeats, together with Rilke, had made him write 'poems which were false to my personal and poetic nature'.

Auden omitted a few other poems from the volume, all of which were written before 1945. He wanted to reject one of his most celebrated poems from his earlier period, 'Lay your sleeping head, my love', but

this volume contained a great eal of his work up to 1939, their omission is significant, and suggests that he had already rejected them from the canon of his poetry. This 1958 selection also had a number of textual changes. The revisions in the 1966 collection were therefore not all made at the same time (the summer of 1965) and had in some cases been planned several years earlier. Auden had also for some time been marking changes in friends' copies of his poetry.

Chester Kallman persuaded him to leave it in. He made detailed revisions of many poems that he did retain, especially those from the 1930s – his later work he only subjected to minor verbal tinkering. Sometimes his concern was merely to improve the punctuation, which had been inadequate in his earliest work, but often there were major changes. Here, for example, in the left hand column, is part of the original text of 'Dover', written in 1937, and on the right the new version published by Auden in the 1966 *Collected Shorter Poems:*

And filled with the tears of the beaten or calm with fame,	Red after years of failure or bright with fame,
The eyes of the returning thank the historical cliffs:	The eyes of homecomers thank these historical cliffs:
'The heart has at last ceased to lie, and the clock to accuse;	'The mirror can no longer lie nor the clock reproach;
In the shadow under the yew, at the children's party Everything will be explained.'	In the shadow under the yew, at the children's party, Everything must be explained.'
And the old town with its keep and its Georgian houses	The Old Town with its Keep and Georgian houses
Has built its routine upon these unusual moments;	Has built its routine upon such unusual moments;
The vows, the tears, the slight emotional signals	Vows, tears, emotional farewell gestures,
Are here eternal and unremarkable gestures Like ploughing or soldiers' songs.	Are common here, unremarkable actions Like ploughing or a tipsy song.

Auden claimed that such revisions were made to correct 'slovenly verbal habits', and certainly in some instances his new texts were more coherent than the originals. But it is often difficult to see that he has made any real improvement. Many of the changes appear to have been initiated for change's sake. and much of the subtlety of the original is lost without any great improvement in clarity.

He decided that the new collection should be arranged not alphabetically by first line, like its predecessors, but roughly in chronological order of composition. 'To-day,' he wrote of this, 'I believe that I know myself and my poetic intentions better and, if anybody wants to look at my writings from an historical perspective, I have no objection.' He brought the book to a close with poems written in 1957, and included no later work, explaining that this date – the year in which he moved his summer house from Ischia to Kirchstetten – marked the beginning of 'a new chapter in my life which is not yet finished'.

Collected Shorter Poems 1927-1957 was published by Faber's late in

1966, and an American edition appeared a few months later.[1] Critics had already been alerted to Auden's fondness for revision by a book by Joseph Warren Beach, *The Making of the Auden Canon* (1957), which analysed the changes made for the earlier *Collected Poetry*. Forewarned, reviewers now pounced on the new changes. 'I seem almost always to prefer the original versions,' wrote Anthony Hecht in the *Hudson Review*, and Graham Martin in *The Listener* judged that Auden had shown 'a remarkable insensitivity' to the original feeling of many poems. A. Alvarez, writing in *The Observer*, felt that many of the excisions were a mistake, but said that in the end it hardly mattered: 'Some of the axed poems have already become part of the language and literature, whether Auden accepts them or not.'

Alvarez was severely critical of Auden's recent work: 'His later poems strike me as shallow and prolix in a way that is utterly foreign to his early work.' Auden paid no attention to this or to any of the reviews. When asked if he read criticisms of his poetry he replied: 'Of course not. Obviously these things are not meant for me.' But he was sensitive to his friends' opinion. During 1967 the journal *Shenandoah* published a *Festschrift* to mark his sixtieth birthday; among the contributors was Naomi Mitchison, who criticised Auden's omission of what she called 'essential' poems from his collections of his work. Auden drafted a reply, though he did not send it: he told her that he considered himself to be the only judge of what was essential, and added: 'I expect personal friends like you, my dear, to respect my judgement on poetry, which is a professional judgement, rather than yours.' And, of her accusation that he no longer wrote 'memorable' poems: 'If, by memorability, you mean a poem like "Sept 1st 1939", I pray to God that I shall never be memorable again.'

A criticism of a rather different kind was made by Stephen Spender, who remarked in a symposium on one of the poems in *About the House* ('A Change of Air', the piece suggested by Goethe's *Italian Journey*) that it was very flat in tone, could be written out as prose, and expressed only prosaic sentiments. Auden replied at some length:

> In so much 'serious' poetry I find an element of 'theatre', of exaggerated gesture and fuss, of indifference to the naked truth, which, as I get older, increasingly revolts me. This element is mercifully absent from what is conventionally called good prose. in reading the latter, one is only conscious of the truth of what is being

[1]Auden's *Collected Longer Poems* were published by Faber's in 1968 and by Random House the next year. 'Paid on Both Sides' was included in full, but *The Orators* was again omitted. However, a new edition of this, with revisions and excisions, was published by Faber's in 1966 and Random House in 1967. In the *Collected Longer Poems*, 'Paid on Both Sides' was left untouched, but 'Letter to Lord Byron' had cuts and revisions, as in the second edition of *Letters from Iceland* (1967).

said, and it is this consciousness which I would like what I write to
arouse in a reader *first*. Before he is aware of any other qualities it
may have, I want his reaction to be: 'That's true', or, better still,
'That's true: now, why didn't I think of it for myself?' To secure
this effect I am prepared to sacrifice a great many poetic pleasures
and excitements. At the same time, I want what I write to be poetry
as Robert Frost defines it, namely, untranslateable speech. The ideal
at which I aim is a style which shall combine the drab sober
truthfulness of prose with a poetic uniqueness of expression.

He might have added that he often found this hard to achieve. In 1962,
when sending a typescript of the poem 'Thanksgiving for a Habitat' to
Elizabeth Mayer, he remarked: 'To keep the diction and prosody within
a hairsbreadth of being prose without becoming it is a task I find very
difficult.'

In his reply to Spender's criticism, Auden also explained the ideology
of the poems he was now writing:

Whatever else it may or may not be, I want every poem I write to be
a hymn in praise of the English language: hence my fascination with
certain speech-rhythms which can only occur in an uninflected
language rich in monosyllables, my fondness for peculiar words
with no equivalents in other tongues, and my deliberate avoidance
of that kind of visual imagery which has no basis in verbal experience.

Language itself, in other words, now held the place in his poetry that
had once been occupied by the dogmas of Layard, Lawrence, Groddeck,
Marx and Gerald Heard; and the chief ideological work on which he
based his poems was now the thirteen–volume *Oxford English Dictionary*,
his own copy of which was, by 1972, so worn that he was contemplating
buying another. Scattered throughout his current poetry, even more
than in his undergraduate verse, were words such as 'dapatical',[1] 'osse',
'nemorivagant', all used for the sheer delight of it. These words were, he
declared, 'miracles' wrought by 'Dame Philology'.

If the *O.E.D.* was now the Bible to his poetry, his prayer-book was
George Saintsbury's study of English prosody. Auden liked to boast that
he had now written a poem in every known metre; and he was always
searching for new forms.[2] In 1964 he sent a friend a copy of the poem (for

---

[1] Auden was no better at proof-reading in the 1960s than he had been in the 1930s. One of
the many misprints which he allowed to get into the published texts of his poems was
'depatical', in the poem 'Tonight at Seven-thirty' in *About the House*. No such word exists
and Edward Mendelson, when editing the 1976 *Collected Poems*, asked the advice of a
number of Auden's friends and others as to what Auden may have meant. A. H. Campbell
eventually pointed out that the correct reading was undoubtedly 'dapatical', meaning
'sumptuous'.

[2] He told friends he was only able to write triolets if they were pornographic.

the 'Habitat' sequence) describing the guest-room at Kirchstetten, explaining of its form: 'I was reading a book on Chinese poetry, in which I discovered that though Chinese is mostly monosyllabic, it is not entirely so, and Chinese poetry is organised not by syllable but by word count. Since the theme seemed rather "Confucian", I thought it might be fun to write in English on the same principle. As you will see, the counting is in 7s and 5s (standard Chinese practice).'

Form continued to interest him as much as content. When in 1968 Stravinsky contemplated composing an elegy for John F. Kennedy, Auden seized eagerly at the suggestion. (It is interesting to note how many of his poems were now occasional pieces or commissions.) The Kennedy elegy appealed to him largely because of the challenge it offered him as a technician. 'I'm an old hand at this sort of thing,' he told Stravinsky; and he had soon produced the piece. Stravinsky commented: 'Wystan is wholly indifferent to J.F.K.; what he cares about is the form.' This was an exaggeration; but he certainly liked to regard himself as first and foremost a craftsman.

*

The publication of the 1966 *Collected Shorter Poems* served to confirm in the minds of many critics (especially British) the suspicion that Auden had been in a steady and discernible decline as a poet ever since he went to America. This gradually became the accepted or even standard view of Auden, and it has largely remained so, despite the fact that it does not fit the evidence. For a start, it takes no account of his achievement in the long poems of the 1940s, which not only contain lyrical passages as fine as anything he wrote in the 1930s, but which are demonstrations of his constant need to develop and mature, not just intellectually and spiritually but in his poetic technique as well. Nor does the belief in the 'declining Auden' stand up in the face of the sequence 'Horae Canonicae', which he would have been incapable of writing in the 1930s and probably in the 1940s too. Indeed he began work on the sequence in the summer of 1947, when he was asking Ursula Niebuhr questions about the offices of the Church, their exact texts, and their history; but the first poem, 'Prime', was not completed until 1949, and Auden did not finish the sequence until 1954, by which time it had become something of a record of his spiritual development during these years – a development from a drily existential Christian outlook which had characterised him in the 1940s to one in which he could write, at the end of the sequence:

> God bless the Realm, God bless the People;
> God bless this green world temporal:
> *In solitude, for company.*

Perhaps most important of all, the 'declining Auden' view does not bother to understand what Auden was trying to do from the 1950s onwards. Never for one moment content to stand still as a poet and repeat mechanically the kind of performance his readers expected from him, he set out during this period of his life to refine and pare down, to cut away what now seemed to him to have been a large element of falsehood in his pre-war poetry. He did this most obviously in the 1966 *Collected Shorter Poems,* where he consistently rejected rhetoric if it appeared to him empty or dishonest in its intentions. He had to do this for his own satisfaction, and in doing so he shed much light on his own development since the 1930s. Whether his readers benefited from the revisions is another matter; the new versions of his earlier poems may be more 'honest', but they are rarely more attractive as poetry. On the other hand the new poems that he wrote during his later years show the process of refining and paring down at its best.

What was going on in Auden's poetry at this period was perceived by a few critics, who challenged the accepted view of Auden's 'decline', and argued instead that the dry manner of the later Auden was an inevitable, and proper, result of the development and maturing of the earlier poet. Among these critics was Clive James, who, writing in 1973, suggested that Auden, from the very beginning of his poetry, had been, in a sense, struggling against his poetic gift, simply because that gift was so overwhelming. 'It was a Shakespearean gift,' James wrote, 'not just in its magnitude but in its unsettling – and unsettling especially in its possessor – characteristic of making anything sound truer than true.' James observed that Auden, even as an undergraduate writing the poems that went into the 1928 Spender booklet, had 'the artistic equivalent of a Midas touch', and guessed that Auden had actually feared the consequences of this and tried to discipline it from very early. The achievement of the early poetry was, suggested James, the result of a tension between Auden's lyric gift and his attempts to keep that gift under control. As Auden grew older, he became determined to chasten his poetry still more in the interests of truth, and as a consequence the lyricism gradually departed from it. The result, said James, was late poetry that was 'flat champagne, but it's still champagne'. Another critic who did not subscribe to the belief in Auden's decline was John Bayley, who described the process as Auden becoming 'more and more evidently himself in what he wrote' – that is, in cutting away poetic falsehood and making his poetry absolutely true to his own beliefs.

There can be little doubt that Auden would have agreed with everything James and Bayley said. Indeed James was echoing Auden's own words when he said that, in the interests of truth, he was 'prepared to sacrifice a great many poetic pleasures and excitements'. One's view of his later poetry must therefore be moulded not by whether one thinks it more or less attractive than the earlier, but whether one considers truth or excitement the more important quality in a poem.

★

By the mid-1960s Auden's income was at least thirty-five thousand dollars a year. His recent books of poems had only sold moderately well, but both Random House and Faber's were now paying him an exceptionally high royalty of fifteen per cent on everything of his that they published. Large numbers of translations of his books now existed, and produced further income.[1] He also received quite substantial sums for book reviews, and for articles and editorial work. On top of this he often undertook lecture tours around America.

In 1963 he made his first tour for some years, and found it a gruelling experience, crossing and recrossing the continent, sleeping in a different city almost every night. He told an interviewer that he had no idea how to keep his shirts clean on these trips; he supposed the only answer was to let them get dirtier day by day. He carried a bottle of gin or vodka with him everywhere in his suitcase as a precaution against arriving in a 'dry' community. This 'bottle in the bag' and the perils of lecturing were described by him, after the 1963 tour was over, in a poem, 'On the Circuit', which nevertheless ended on a note of gratitude: 'God Bless the U.S.A., so large, / So friendly, and so rich.' Two years later, he was touring again, simply because he believed he needed the money – something that his friends could not understand, for they knew how much he earned from his literary work. Was it, they wondered, because he wanted to leave Chester well provided for? Yet Auden had already insured his life in Chester's favour for seventy-five thousand dollars, often announcing this proudly in the presence of the beneficiary. The answer seems to be that, having been anxious (or at least watchful) about money during most of his adult life, he could not now believe he had achieved financial security. He tended, in fact, to panic more and more in money matters as each year went by, trying to save a little by smoking a pipe instead of cigarettes (this did not last), and telling friends he needed the Nobel Prize not for the honour but for the money it would bring. In fact he was often given literary prizes: in 1967 the U.S.A. National Book Committee awarded him its annual medal, together with five thousand dollars, while in the autumn of 1966 he won the Austrian State Prize for European Literature, which he liked to tell friends was 'presented to me by a Mr Piffl, in *cash!*'[2] And, while he was often anxious about money, he would also admit to being overpaid as a lecturer, the rate for one of his

---

[1]There were German versions of *The Age of Anxiety, For the Time Being,* and *The Dyer's Hand,* as well as of the libretti. The same three books were available in Italian, as well as a translation by Carlo Izzo of ninety poems; and there were lesser quantities in many other languages. A notable exception was French, in which none of Auden's major works was available apart from *The Rake's Progress.*

[2]He was also given a number of honorary doctorates by British and American universities in the 1960s, including (in Britain) Durham, Birmingham, Kent and London, and (in America) Swarthmore Lafayette Colleges.

lectures or readings now being as much as two thousand dollars. 'It's too much,' he would say.[1]

He had little idea how to handle money, and for a long time made no attempt to invest any, keeping it all in the bank and saying 'You never know when you might need it.' His chief concern was to pay his bills by return mail. 'The homes I warm to', he wrote in a poem, 'always convey a feeling / of bills being promptly settled with checks that don't bounce.' One of the few luxuries in which he indulged was first-class travel on overseas plane flights, enjoying the comfort and the chance of meeting someone interesting – such as Boris Karloff, whom he was once delighted to encounter – though he would never disclose his own identity to other travellers, stifling their questions by saying he was 'a medieval historian'. Not until the late 1960s could he be persuaded to look after his money by investing it, and even then he was not very happy about the idea; when his accountant instructed him, for tax reasons, to put some capital into oil wells he said he was 'scared stiff'.

He could be both parsimonious and generous. If people wrote asking for autographs or posing some question about his poetry, and did not enclose a stamped addressed envelope, he usually refused to reply – 'Why should I pay? I do think it's only elementary manners to send money if you want something.' On the other hand he continued with his generosity to his Austrian protégé, and to others whom he helped without making the fact known; and when his brother John's daughters, Rita and Anita, to whom he was greatly attached, became undergraduates at Oxford, he opened accounts for them at Blackwell's bookshop.

During February 1967, the month in which he celebrated his sixtieth birthday, Auden stayed briefly with Christopher Isherwood in California. Isherwood was struck by the fact that Auden had grown 'monumentally' old. 'His face', said Isherwood, 'really belongs in the British Museum.' Auden's friends were indeed beginning to compete with each other for ways of describing his face's extraordinary creases and deep wrinkles. The poet James Merrill called it 'runneled and seamed'; the philosopher Hannah Arendt, a New York friend of Auden's, said it was as though 'life itself had delineated a kind of face-scape to make manifest the "heart's invisible furies" '; and Stephen Spender wrote that it was 'a face upon which experience and thoughts had hammered. . . a face at once armoured and receptive'. But the most graphic description came from Auden himself. 'Your cameraman might enjoy himself,' he remarked to a reporter, 'because my face looks like a wedding-cake left out in the rain.'

His clothes were now almost as remarkable as his face. For some years he had carried his carpet-slippers about with him, changing into them

[1]Besides lecturing, he also occasionally preached sermons, in New York, Oxford Edinburgh, and on one occasion Westminster Abbey. He said of this last sermon: 'How surprised and pleased my mamma would be.'

when he arrived at his destination. 'But suddenly', noticed V. S. Yanovsky, 'he took to walking in them through the streets, in rain and snow, to parties and conferences, shirt buttons missing.' The slippers were worn ostensibly because of corns, but Auden admitted to Orlan Fox that he enjoyed eccentricity: 'At my age, I'm allowed to seem a little dotty.' He also took to wearing for much of the time, for no apparent reason and even in the winter, a pair of very dark glasses, which (as Robert Craft said) made him look like a blind beggar or a jazz musician. His shirts were usually of a dark colour, probably so as to hide their dirtiness. When Yanovsky and his wife gave him a brown turtleneck sweater for a birthday 'he put it on and never – or so it seemed – took it off again. . . For this reason, and also from hygienic considerations, we gave him a dark green one the next year. We never saw him wear it.'

He was drinking as much as ever in the evenings, according to his usual routine of several strong vodka martinis before dinner and much wine with, and after, the meal. Spender thought he drank so heavily 'in order to achieve a certain degree of oblivion', but Chester Kallman disagreed with this, and said it was merely 'a symbol of conviviality'. In fact Auden did not become more convivial as the evening wore on. He would lapse into monologue or a series of aphorisms, so that, as Robert Craft put it, conversation became 'more and more of a one-way street'.

His habit of going to bed early had now become an obsession. The ritual hour for bed gradually crept forwards, until by the late 1960s he would get up from the table promptly at nine o'clock. 'If he was visiting somewhere,' recalled V. S. Yanovsky, 'he would run out in his pantoufles as if rushing to a meaningful rendezvous.' If friends came to dinner at Auden's St Mark's Place apartment, the same rule applied, and they were told to leave promptly at nine.

Having retired to bed at this very early hour, Auden would read for a few minutes while he finished a bottle of wine and smoked more cigarettes – he was still a very heavy smoker, and more than once nearly set fire to himself in bed. Because he had drunk so much, he would rarely sleep through the night, and usually got up in the small hours to empty his bladder. He then needed something to get him back to sleep, having now given up sleeping-pills because of the difficulty of procuring them when away from New York. As a result, he took to putting a glass of vodka by his bed, which he would swallow as a soporific after his trip to the lavatory. He was sleeping later in the mornings now, and could no longer manage to get up in time to work before breakfast. 'I am ashamed of myself', he wrote to Chester in 1968, 'for how long I now sleep – often till 8.45.' Until the mid-1960s he continued to take a 'speed' pill – for many years benzedrine, and later a substitute – on waking in the morning. Sometimes he would swallow another dose later in the day, to counteract tiredness and help him work on without interruption. If a friend suggested he might take a nap instead, he would reply: 'No, no, Mother wouldn't approve.' When he did finally give up these pills, it was only because he found they were no longer having any effect.

He had always tended to repeat himself, making the same remark or telling the same anecdote on any occasion that seemed suitable. Now he would say the same thing to the same people within a short space of time. 'He would call up lateish (for him),' recalled V. S. Yanovsky, 'to tell us the same funny story for the second or third time. "She was asking information about a famous opera. Something like *Christian and His Soldiers*. Turned out she wanted to know about *Tristan and Isolde!*" ' There were also longer set-pieces. A young Christ Church don, Bernard Richards, was present one evening in the early 1960s when Auden, who was visiting Oxford, told his anecdote about the telephone operator asking him to test the apparatus, to which he had responded by reciting a long passage of James's *The American Scene* – a recitation that he proceeded to demonstrate to his Christ Church listeners. 'It was amusing, it was impressive,' said Richards, 'but it was less amusing and less impressive when he did it again, and I heard him do it at least three times on one occasion or another.'

On some evenings his conversation might be nothing more than a string of familiar pieces, produced without much semblance of connected thought: 'Political social history would be no different if Dante, Michelangelo, Byron had never lived. Nothing I wrote against Hitler prevented one Jew from being killed. . . In the end, art is small beer. The really serious things in life are earning one's living so as not to be a parasite, and loving one's neighbour. . . As a poet, my only duty is to defend the language from corruption. . . I left England in 1939 because the cultural life there was a family life. . . Brecht was a horrid man. Yeats and Robert Frost were horrid[1] . . . A lot of trouble could be saved at obscenity trials if the book were given to the jury and the male members were asked to stand up. If they really had erections, it would be safe to assume that the book would be likely to deprave and corrupt. . . Art is our chief means of breaking bread with the dead – you can still enjoy the *Iliad*. . . I like to fancy that, had I taken Anglican Holy Orders, I might now be a bishop. . .'

He liked to make out that he had now given up sex. 'One isn't bothered with sex any more,' he told Margaret Gardiner. 'One's finished with all that.' To other friends he would say: 'Well, at my age, I've put on the widow's cap.' But this was not true. In New York he often made use of the services of a call-boy, who was summoned to appear at tea-time. He wrote a short poem about it, addressing it presumably to Chester:

[1]Richard Hoggart records that Auden explained to him that this criticism of Brecht, Yeats and Frost (the latter of whom Auden met when he came to Oxford for an honorary degree in 1957) was based on a feeling that 'all three were ungenerous towards others, especially the young and the vulnerable'.

When one is lonely (and You,
My Dearest, know why,
as I know why it must be),
steps can be taken, even
a call-boy can help.

To-night, for instance, now that
Bert has been here, I
listen to the piercing screams
of palliardising cats
without self-pity.

According to Stephen Spender, he was not really claiming to have given up physical sex, but was trying to say that he was too old for love-affairs. Spender told him that this was nonsense, and that plenty of people would still willingly go to bed with him; but he would not listen.

The ageing, the repetitions, the eccentricities, saddened Auden's friends. But they did not diminish him in their eyes. 'There was in him', wrote V. S. Yanovsky, 'some inner communion with the great human reality, as there was in Tolstoy – a trait characteristic of all geniuses, despite their fantasies.' This was partly the result of the hugeness of his knowledge. 'It was wonderful to behold the wide range of his accumulated knowledge,' remarked Yanovsky, 'seemingly not related to literature or prosody: theology, physics, biology, psychiatry, music, all interrelated and inte-grated by him in the most creative form.' Another friend who got to know him during the 1960s, Oliver Sacks, was equally struck by this, and especially by the harmony of Auden's world-view: 'Everything, for him stood in mutual awareness, knowing its place, and that of all others: every body, every organ, every atom, every star, the whole grand prosody of nature itself.' So it was that, even during the years of his physical decline (indeed perhaps especially at this time), Auden's friends looked to him as a judge, an arbiter. 'I feel, in many ways, that Wystan understood me better than I understood myself,' wrote Oliver Sacks after Auden's death. 'He became a living mirror for me – someone who could detect and encourage the perception of new vistas, images, and trains-of-thought long before I myself was conscious of them. And if he did this with me, he did it with a hundred others. He showed us ourselves, he drew us into greater possibilities of being – "self-actualiza-tion", to use the current, trendy word – by being himself, wise and tolerant and affectionate as Socrates, completely devoid of censoriousness and moralizing, yet deeply, purely and passionately ethical.'

★

By the mid-1960s Auden had, he said, begun to believe that he would die, simply because he now noticed that most of the people he passed in the street were younger than himself. But he prophesied many more years of life. 'I shall live to be eighty-three,' he told James Stern, remarking that he would probably die of blood poisoning. 'Not of heart-failure?' asked Stern. 'Heart? Strong as a horse. . . My dear, I'm as tough as an old tree.'

There was no sign whatever of any mental deterioration in his work, either poetry or prose, though perhaps he was not quite as energetic as he had once been. In the autumn of 1967 he gave the first T. S. Eliot Memorial Lectures at the University of Kent, at Canterbury, and seemed to have put comparatively little into them; one of the four lectures, 'The World of Opera', consisted of little more than a résumé of the libretti he had written, with a few comments added. On the other hand he proved a great success at 'Poetry International', a new London festival held for the first time in July 1967 and repeated during the following summers, in which Auden regularly took part. 'His control of the audience is phenom-enal' wrote the *Financial Times;* 'no rounds of applause within his allotted fifteen minutes; no encores, no poems written before 1960. He reads intricately constructed later works with a disciplined but pedantic respect for their metre.' Charles Osborne, one of the festival's organisers, wrote in his diary: 'He doesn't read, he knows the poems, seeming to pluck the words from an invisible tele-prompter high in the back of the hall. "Wystan," I ask, "do you know *all* of your poems by heart?" "Heavens, no, I learn the ones I'm going to perform. If I decide to do them again in a few month's time, I'll have to learn them all over again." '

The inauguration of Poetry International brought a slight addition to Auden's yearly routine in the form of a July visit to London, so that he could take part in it; he usually stayed with the Spenders during this visit. Apart from this, the pattern of his life was unchanged, except that in the late autumn of 1967 his Austrian housekeeper, the beloved Frau Emma, died of a heart attack. Auden managed to find an adequate replacement, Frau Strobl, but he was greatly saddened by the loss. *'Liebe Frau Emma,'* he wrote in an elegy, 'oh, how could you go and die. . .?' A few months later his Austrian life was further complicated when he drove his car into a telegraph pole while trying to stop some eggs falling off the passenger seat, and broke his right shoulder, which took many weeks to mend. The following winter a third disaster struck when Chester's boyfriend Yannis Boras was killed in a road accident, driving Auden's car back from Greece to Kirchstetten. 'Chester is desperate,' recorded V. S. Yanovsky, 'Wystan profoundly shocked by it all.' Chester soon acquired another lover, a boy named Kosta, but Yannis's death caused him great distress, and he began to drink more heavily, often starting on the ouzo at breakfast.

Chester was now supposed to be taking part with Auden in a third collaboration with Hans Werner Henze. This was to be a cantata for schools, based on three of Aesop's fables, entitled *Moralities*. But in the event Auden completed the text without Chester's help, Chester having become irritated with Henze's new Communist politics. After this, Henze decided he did not want to compose another opera for the time being; and it was indeed exactly ten years after the première of *The Bassarids* that Henze's next opera, *We Come to the River,* with a libretto by Edward Bond, had its first performance, in 1976.

In about 1968 Auden began to look round for another composer with whom to write an opera; afterwards, he told Michael Yates that he had done this not for his own sake but because he wanted something that would occupy Chester. His first thought was Michael Tippett, whom he had known slightly since the early 1930s, and whose *Midsummer Marriage* he had liked when Peter Heyworth played him a recording in Berlin. He now asked Heyworth to approach Tippett. But Tippett was uneasy at the prospect of working with such a domineering librettist, and preferred to write his own texts. Next, Auden tried Harrison Birtwhistle, by whose music he said he was 'intrigued'. Heyworth arranged a lunch for them both, but during the meal Auden lectured Birtwhistle on the subject of opera and libretti, and again nothing came of it.[1] The ideal collaboration would of course have been with Britten, but that was now impossible. Partly as a result of Britten's coolness towards him, Auden had begun to disparage his old friend's work. 'We saw B. B.'s *Midsummer Night's Dream* the other day,' he wrote to Spender. 'It's dreadful! Pure Kensington.' However, in conversation with Spender, he did say that Britten had 'enormous talent'.

Meanwhile in February 1969 Lincoln Kirstein suggested to Nicolas Nabokov that he should write an opera with Auden and Kallman. Nabokov had made a small but firm reputation in America as a composer. Auden liked his music, which was unfashionably melodic, but alleged that Nabokov had failed to do real justice to his talents because he was too sociable a person – 'He cannot bear to be long enough alone,' said Auden. Nabokov was delighted at Kirstein's suggestion, especially when Kirstein told him that he knew Auden and Kallman had already thought about making an opera of *Love's Labour's Lost.* Kirstein approached the librettists, and soon they and Nabokov had set to work.

Auden was interested in this play simply because it was, he felt, one of the few Shakespearian works that could be turned into an English-language opera without too great a sacrifice of the poetry. He said that it might even prove more effective when set to music. He and Kallman now reduced the original cast to a manageable size, cutting the characters

[1] Peter Heyworth also introduced Auden to David Hockney, and suggested that Hockney might make some drawings of him. This duly happened, but the sitting was not a great success. Hockney brought two other people with him — Ron Kitaj and Peter Schlesinger — and this annoyed Auden, who behaved in a grumpy fashion. 'He gave me the impression', said Hockney, 'of being rather like the headmaster of an English school.' (*Hockney by Hockney,* Thames & Hudson, 1977, p. 194.) The sitting was in Peter Heyworth's London flat.

of Sir Nathaniel, Holofernes, Dull, Costard and Mercede, and reducing the four aristocratic romantic couples to three. They also enlarged the role of Moth (an idea of Kallman's), making him a mischievous Cupid whose machinations are responsible for much of the action. They chose a plain, unremarkable style for the libretto, avoiding Shakespearian pastiche. By the autumn of 1969 they had finished their work, and handed the text to Nabokov.

During this period, Auden undertook a major task of translation, making a modern English text of the *Elder Edda*, the most ancient work of Icelandic mythology. He had two collaborators. The first, Paul B. Taylor, who made the literal translations from which Auden produced his polished versions, had been introduced to Auden by Basil Boothby when Taylor was teaching at the University of Iceland in 1964 and Auden visited that country. The other was Peter H. Salus, who first got to know Auden (again through Boothby) when teaching at a college in New York; his role was to provide notes to the translation. Auden found the work very hard, not least because the original poets assumed that their audience already knew the details of the myths, and left much unexplained. While making the translation he wrote to Peter Salus: 'I am in despair about the more skaldic poems. Even if, which at the moment I doubt, I find it possible to versify them, I don't see how any reader to-day is going to make head or tail of them. The truth is that the whole "skaldic" movement was a poetic blunder.' But he carried on, and when the Auden-Taylor-Salus translation of a selection from the *Elder Edda* was published in 1969 it earned praise for its sturdiness and competence. Auden and Taylor subsequently went on to translate the remaining Old Icelandic traditional poems, though no further volume was published in Auden's lifetime. [1]

Meanwhile Auden was finishing a new book of poems, *City Without Walls,* which was published in September 1969 to much more enthusiastic reviews than he had received for some time. The 'cosiness' of his recent volumes was much less apparent in the new selection, and – perhaps just as important – critics had now come to accept him for what he was, and had ceased to lament the passing of the pre-war Auden. 'The wit in some of the new pieces is little short of magnificent,' John Fletcher wrote in the *Spectator,* adding: 'This latest collection reveals an Auden of classical simplicity and directness.'

Auden was also compiling a 'commonplace book', *A Certain World,* in which he included quotations from almost all his favourite authors. Not surprisingly it turned out in the first draft to be 'an *enormous* tome'. He told his publishers that it was 'a sort of autobiography, the only kind I shall ever write'.

★

[1]Another project of translation, which came to nothing, was a 'Goethe Reader'. This idea was put by Charles Osborne to Faber & Faber, who agreed to publish it provided Auden could be persuaded to collaborate. But Auden died before the work could begin.

By the end of 1969 the district around St Mark's Place, where Auden had his New York apartment, had become (in the words of one journalist) 'crumbling and crime-ridden'. The area formerly known as the Lower East Side, was now largely occupied by hippies and other social drop-outs, who rechristened it 'The East Village', a name that Auden refused to recognise. The streets had grown filthy and dangerous, and when a hired car was sent to take Auden to dinner at the Stravinskys the driver could scarcely be persuaded that anyone respectable lived in such a place. Meanwhile Auden's apartment itself had grown, in Margaret Gardiner's words, 'darker and dustier than ever'. It was becoming too much even for Auden. He wrote to E. R. Dodds: 'My kitchen roof leaks. A blind is broken. Cockroaches abound. O New York!'

Feeling that he could not continue to live there indefinitely by himself, he approached Orlan Fox to ask, shyly, if Fox would consider sharing the apartment with him. But Fox knew how difficult this would be. During those months of 1964-65 when Auden was in Berlin, Fox had rented the apartment from him, and when Auden returned to New York had remained there for a few weeks as his lodger; he soon discovered that Auden wanted him out of the house by nine in the morning, but would get cross if he came home even a few minutes late in the evening. So now, when the invitation to share was made, Fox politely declined – to the regret of several friends of Auden, who had hoped that Fox might have become a replacement for Chester.

Auden also resorted once again to a proposal of marriage, simply in the hope of domestic security. This time the proposal was made to somebody one year older than himself, the political philosopher Hannah Arendt, who had taught for many years at the New School for Social Research and whom Auden had known since 1958. She had been widowed, and she showed much kindness to Auden, concerning herself about the state of his clothes and giving him a handsome sports jacket that had belonged to her husband – 'I'm wearing a dead man's coat,' Auden would say delightedly, pleased that a good thing was not being wasted. But though he and Hannah Arendt became good friends they were never intimate, and she was embarrassed and disconcerted when he suggested marriage. She told him she could not consider it.[1]

Auden had a third plan. During the summer of 1969 he gave an interview at Kirchstetten to a journalist named Jon Bradshaw, who printed an article about him in *Esquire* a few months later which included this passage:

---

[1]Auden made this proposal in 1970, soon after Hannah Arendt's husband died.

Over tea at four p.m., Auden talks of his 'declining days'. . . He wants to retire to Christ Church, Oxford. 'After all, Cambridge did as much for Forster. Next time I'm there, I think I'll broach it to them.'

Even before the *Esquire* interview was published in January 1970, word got around about this, and several reporters visited Auden in New York. Under the headline 'LONELY AUDEN: WILL OXFORD GIVE HIM REFUGE?' the London *Evening Standard* reported (on 10 December 1969) that Auden was engaged in 'delicate negotiations' to return to England, and was 'putting out feelers' to Christ Church in the hope of finding the sort of accommodation that had been provided for E. M. Forster at King's College, Cambridge. 'I have often thought', Auden was quoted as saying, 'that I could have a coronary in my apartment and it would be days before I was found.' The reporter added: 'If Oxford turns him down he may decide to spend half the year in Iceland, a country whose harsh and sunless climate appeals to him.'[1]

This was the first that Christ Church had heard of any such wish. Auden's friend Cuthbert Simpson, who had been Dean, had died the previous summer, and the new Dean, Henry Chadwick, told reporters as tactfully as possible that he knew nothing of Auden's intentions, and that the matter lay with the college's Governing Body. Auden was by now very embarrassed at what had happened. 'I was not suggesting anything of the sort,' he told the *Daily Telegraph*. 'It might be rather nice to live there, of course, but I was not talking about any present situation, and what I said about that was not meant to be published. . . I am not even thinking of returning to England at the present time.'

He had, of course, been thinking perfectly seriously about Christ Church, but he realised that after the press 'leak' it would be inopportune for him to make any proposal to the college yet. For the moment he let the matter rest, though he did admit privately to his friend David Luke, the college tutor in German, that he would be interested should such a thing ever become possible.

For the time being he carried on with the same way of life in New York. Elizabeth Mayer was now in an old people's home – she was in her eighties and had suffered a stroke – and Auden visited her regularly, much to her delight and the gratitude of her family, making the tiresome journey by subway and bus (the home was some way out in the Bronx). He wrote a poem, 'Old People's Home', describing the inmates ('All are limitory, but each has her own / nuance of damage'). V. S. Yanovsky, who once met him there by chance, saw that 'he could not stand the place. . . [He] suffered visibly and after half an hour or so rushed out,

---

[1]Another plan that was half-mooted was that Auden should live in a cottage (a converted outbuilding) in the grounds of his friends Thekla and John Clark's home near Florence.

heaving a sigh of relief.' When Elizabeth Mayer died some months later, Auden read at her funeral the lines he had written for her eightieth birthday, in which he gave thanks for many of years of friendship with her.

He himself now sometimes seemed, said Margaret Gardiner, 'a very old man', even though he was only sixty-two. Stephen Spender remarked to Chester Kallman: 'Wystan has lost all spontaneity'; and Chester agreed emphatically. Perhaps, Spender suggested, this was the price Auden had paid for achieving 'the isolation out of which he wrote his later work'. Whatever the cause, Auden had (wrote Robert Craft early in 1970) 'become almost impossibly touchy. . .as well as tyrannical and quixotic in his opinions, tending to speak almost exclusively in absolutes: "This is right, that is wrong, one must, one mustn't." ' This was not really a new characteristic, but a return to the manner of his undergraduate days. Now, just as then, he would entirely change his mind from day to day, condemning what he had just praised and praising what he had just condemned. V. S. Yanovsky noticed this: ' "I don't like it," he would say of a story or a title. And the next time: "Oh, it's very good." '

His clothes grew worse and worse. He wore the same suit month after month until it was not only covered with grease spots but had entirely worn out, so that one day his trousers would suddenly split themselves. Hannah Arendt tried to convince him that he needed at least two suits, so that one could go to the cleaners or be repaired. But he refused to agree, and this became the subject of endless argument between them. he continued to drink in large quantities, and to chain-smoke Lucky Strikes. He liked to boast that he had never yet had a hangover, and when James Stern pointed out that he was working his way through about fifteen thousand cigarettes a year, he answered: 'Ah, but I don't inhale!'

One or two of his friends noticed that his breathing was becoming slightly laborious, and that he was rather blue about the lips. They encouraged him to see a doctor. But Auden's own New York physician, David Protetch, whom he had known and trusted since the 1940s, had died in May 1969 of cancer of the pituitary. Auden had no idea how to find someone to replace him, fearing (not without justification) that New York doctors consisted chiefly of 'the sadist, the nod-crafty, / and the fee-conscious' – words from a poem he wrote in memory of Protetch. His Kirchstetten doctor retired soon afterwards and from 1970 onwards he had no regular medical attention or check-ups. Meanwhile his friends, even those of them who were medically trained, dared not interfere with his way of life. 'He must know what he is doing,' V. S. Yanovsky (a doctor by profession) would reassure himself. 'He is content this way and nothing interferes with his work.'

Despite the brush with the press over Christ Church, Auden was now talking more and more freely to reporters, both in New York and Austria. Friends thought this odd in someone who had recently written that a writer's private life 'should be of no concern to anybody except himself'. In some respects he gave away little to journalists, merely reciting to them from his store of aphorisms, so that published interviews with him consisted largely of his familiar *dicta,* arranged in varying orders. But in other ways he could be more candid, and he was now half willing to allow journalists to mention his homosexuality. He actually praised (when taking to the Stravinskys) an interview in *Life* which stated: 'To visit Auden in Austria. . . is to be enveloped in the homosexual routine he has created there. . . Auden and Kallman have known each other since 1939. . . Their relationship suggests love that transcends the physical.' On the other hand he had little to say in favour of the new Gay Liberation movement which was bringing homosexuality out into the open. He remarked of this to Robert Craft: 'I'm no advocate of the purely Uranian society myself. I mean, *I* certainly don't want to live *only* with queers.' He was bewildered when he was asked to contribute to the sex-revue *Oh! Calcutta,* and was greatly distressed when the magazine *Avant Garde* published his pornographic poem 'The Platonic Blow': 'I don't want to talk about it! I don't want to talk about it!' he told Yanovsky; and to Stephen Spender's daughter Lizzie, then in her late teens, he said: 'Promise me, my dear, that you will *never* read it.'

In the late 1960s his local church in New York, St Mark-in-the-Bouwerie, abandoned the traditional *Book of Common Prayer* and adopted a modern liturgy. Auden seems at first to have tried to tolerate this, for he spent an afternoon helping the Rector of St Mark's, the Rev. Michael Allan, with the wording of the new service, helping to polish various phrases. But he soon came to hate the change, and began to declare adamantly that the church should instead go back to Latin for its language. He himself ceased going to St Mark's, and began to attend services at a Greek Orthodox church a few blocks away, so as to hear the Mass in a language that was timeless. When he sat on a committee to draft a new text of the psalter that was published in 1970 and 1971, he took a line that he described as arch-conservative.

He continued to punctuate his Austrian months with a midsummer trip to London for 'Poetry International', staying at the Spenders' house in St John's Wood. They found him an exhausting guest. He would expect them to devote themselves entirely to him, complaining if Stephen Spender had to go out unexpectedly at lunch – 'But you can't! Tell them you can't go because *I'm* here.' Dinner parties were difficult because of his insistence on shuffling off to bed at nine, though on other occasions, quite unpredictably, he would sit up so late that the other guests had to struggle to get away before midnight. Spender found that he increasingly disliked seeing anyone else, even old friends or those he much admired. When Spender told him that David Jones was dying, and suggested a visit, he refused. He even said 'no' at first to calling on Cecil Day-Lewis, who was also seriously ill, though when Spender persisted he finally agreed, and the visit was a success – though Day–Lewis privately thought that Auden had 'a very limited stock of jokes and conversational gambits'.[1]

Auden's brother John had now retired from his career as a geologist, first in India and then with the Food and Agriculture Organisation; he and his wife Sheila were now living in London. Wystan began to stay with them on some of his visits there. John sometimes tried to persuade him to come down with him to Gloucestershire to visit Bernard, their elder brother, who had returned from Canada in 1936 and had worked for many years at the Royal Agricultural College in Cirencester. Wystan had kept in touch with Bernard, his wife Betty, and their three children, Jane, Mary and Giles; he often exchanged letters with them, and invited Jane and Giles to visit him for a holiday in Ischia during the 1950s, which each of them did. But he told John he did not really want to see Bernard any more; he did go down to visit him with John in 1968, but felt (he said) that he had nothing in common with Bernard nowadays; and the visit was not repeated.

His life was governed by the ritual of the clock, not merely in his own home but even when he was a guest. When staying with the Spenders, or with James and Tania Stern, who now owned a manor house in Wiltshire, he would insist on absolute punctuality. 'Wystan, are you hungry?' Tania Stern would ask. 'Well, my dear, it's four minutes to one. You are surely not suggesting that lunch is going to be *late?*' Yet he felt no compunction at disrupting others' lives. One day in London he had an appointment to see Peter du Sautoy, who was now Chairman of Faber & Faber; but he failed to turn up. Next day he arrived with no other apology or excuse than a curt 'Sorry I stood you up yesterday.'

Despite his habits as a guest, his hosts liked his visits. 'His departures', wrote James Stern, 'were a sadness, and his arrivals more eagerly anticipated, more welcomed, I think, than those of any other man we have known.' The obsessive punctuality, the inconsiderate habits, the frequent tedium of his monologues and well-worn anecdotes did not obscure the deeper level of kindness, even gentleness, which his old friends had known for so many years. He could also be unexpectedly thoughtful. When he stayed with Richard Hoggart and his family and was invited to do the crossword, he carefully copied it from the newspaper on to a piece of tracing-paper, explaining that he did not want to spoil it for his hosts should they want to complete it themselves. And he always wrote a 'bread-and-butter' letter after leaving – like this one to the Spenders: 'How good you were to me! I do hope my bachelor eccentricities were not *too* tiresome.'

[1] Auden had little contact with Day-Lewis after 1930, but said he was 'proud to believe' that certain characteristics of the detective Nigel Strangeways in Day-Lewis's 'Nicholas Blake' thrillers, especially the early ones, were taken from himself (*Sunday Times*, 4 June 1972).

In April 1970 he and Chester, together with Alan Ansen, made a short visit to Jerusalem, inspired by Chester's Jewish origins. Auden found it 'fascinating' but '*very* expensive'. Ten months later, at the beginning of 1971, he began another American lecture tour, celebrating his sixty-fourth birthday in St Louis, and twice visiting Toronto where he stayed with Peter Salus and his family. At the beginning of this year, in January, he also made a three-day trip to Yale University to speak to a number of student and faculty groups. This trip was organised by Edward Mendelson, a twenty-four-year-old member of the English department, who had written a doctoral thesis on Auden's poetry and was now finishing work, together with a British collaborator, Barry Bloomfield, on the second edition of a highly detailed bibliography of Auden's writings, which Bloomfield had first issued in 1964. Mendelson already knew Auden a little, having called on him a few times while at work on his thesis. Now, Auden told Mendelson that he had decided, some time earlier, to compile a retrospective collection of his book reviews and other essays, but was having difficulty in tracing recent articles, since he really had no idea what he had written. Mendelson replied that he had copies of all Auden's articles, and offered Auden the use of them in compiling the book. Auden examined this collection. About a year later he wrote to Mendelson saying that it might be more sensible if he, Mendelson, were to make the selection for the volume. Mendelson agreed, and began work on the new selection, which was to be called *Forewords and Afterwords*. He soon found Auden wanted some say in the choice of articles for the book, and a certain amount of discussion took place before the two agreed on a final selection.

Just as he was finishing work on *Forewords and Afterwords,* Mendelson received a letter from Auden asking him (in a postscript) to be his literary executor. Auden had in fact already appointed two executors, the poet William Meredith and the literary critic Monroe Spears, both old friends of his – Spears had published a book on Auden's poetry which was full of information obtained from Auden himself. But he now apparently wanted someone younger to be responsible for his literary estate after his death. Mendelson accepted, and during 1972 was instructed by Auden that on his death he must place a notice in the British and American press 'requesting any friends who have letters from me to burn them when they're done with them and on no account to show them to anyone else'. Auden did not include this request in his will, but he mentioned it to many of his friends. Several of them told him they would not pay any attention to it; when this happened, he simply remained silent and raised no objection. T. S. Eliot's widow Valerie pointed out to him, from her own experience since her husband's death, that his attempt to prevent a biography would cause his executors a lot of difficulty. Auden answered, with an impish grin, 'That's their problem!'

When Auden returned to New York from his lecture tour early in

1971, V. S. Yanovsky was disturbed by what he saw and heard. 'Wysṭan back from tour,' he wrote in his diary. 'Unpleasant, in marasmus [wasting away of the body]. Spoke about peeing in the bathtub, farting – could imagine a couple communicating in this way – picking one's nose, eating snot ("delicious"). Something is falling apart in this huge clay body.' The same state of mind was evident in April, when Auden wrote a poem called 'Talking to Myself'. Edward Mendelson later observed of this that, just as he had done in his poems during the late 1920s, Auden was again writing of a doomed landscape – but this time it was 'not an external one, but the microcosmos of his own ageing body':

> Time, we both know, will decay You, and already
> I'm scared of our divorce: I've seen some horrid ones.
> Remember: when *Le Bon Dieu* says to You *Leave him!*',
> please, please, for His sake and mine, pay no attention
> to my piteous *Don'ts*, but bugger off quickly.

*

At about this time Auden was worried by a financial problem. He had thought himself not subject to Austrian taxes, on the grounds that he only lived at Kirchstetten for some months of the year. But the Austrian tax authorities thought differently, and began to make a series of claims against him, basing these, extraordinary as it may seem, partly on the fact that he referred so often to Kirchstetten and to Austrian and German literature in his poems. Eventually the demand reached 930,000 schillings – some £25,000 or $90,000. After negotiations at high level, this was reduced by about half, and Auden settled the claim; but the affair worried him deeply, and it seemed to Michael Yates that this worry was a cause of his decline in physical health.

During the spring of 1971 he worked on a book of clerihews which Faber's were to publish the next Christmas under the title *Academic Graffiti*, with drawings by Filippo Sanjust, who had designed the production of *The Bassarids* and whom Auden called 'the best comic draughtsman since Max Beerbohm'. Some of these clerihews were written in 1952, and had already been published in *Homage to Clio*; they were thought by most reviewers to be rather poor, perhaps even to be a symptom of Auden's dotage. In fact they were the sort of thing he had been writing in his notebooks since undergraduate days.

In the summer of 1971 he paid his usual visit to England for Poetry International, and also went to Oxford where he was given an Honorary D. Litt. He had expected to be in Edinburgh for the première of the new opera he and Chester had written with Nicolas Nabokov, *Love's Labour's Lost,* but the proposed production at the Festival was cancelled, having, according to Auden, been 'talked to death in a jungle of committees'; it was arranged instead for the opera to be performed the next year in Berlin – though this too was cancelled in its turn, and the première did not actually take place until 1973. During this year, Auden also wrote a hymn for the United Nations, commissioned by Dag Hammarskjöld's successor U Thant, and set to music by the cellist Pablo Casals, then aged ninety-four. It was performed in October at a U. N. anniversary concert. Back in New York for the autumn, Auden conducted four seminars at Columbia University for young poets, whom he found 'very bewildering'. Yet he went on holding 'open house' for anybody who wanted to come and ask his advice on poetic technique; and a number of young New York poets did take up this invitation, finding him dogmatic but always exciting as a teacher.

He continued to keep his telephone number in the Manhattan directory, and would agree to see almost anyone who called him up for an appointment. But the telephone had drawbacks. He told his friends that one night it rang and a voice said: 'We are going to castrate you and then kill you.' Auden was proud of his quick reply: 'I think you have the wrong number.' But he no longer enjoyed the atmosphere of the city around him. During 1971 he wrote to Chester, who as usual was in Athens: 'New York is hell.'

Two years had now passed since the publication of his remarks about wanting to retire to Christ Church, and, at the college, David Luke felt that the time was now right to put the matter to his colleagues on the Governing Body. He mentioned it at a meeting early in December 1971, simply in the capacity of a friend of Auden's who knew what his wishes were. Shortly afterwards, Auden, almost for the first time in his life, was taken ill.

Late in December he suffered an attack of vertigo, which frightened him enough to stop him working for a day. Fortunately he had become friends with somebody who, though not a general physician, could give him informal medical advice.

This was Oliver Sacks, who had been born and educated in England and worked in New York as a neurologist. Auden had first met him about six years earlier, and enjoyed his company largely because Sacks was a member of a small group he particularly admired – medical experts who could discuss the philosophy of their science. Sacks was at work on a book, entitled *Awakenings,* about the drug L-Dopa and its effects on sufferers from sleeping-sickness; after reading it in manuscript, Auden called it a masterpiece.

Sacks greatly admired Auden, and – unlike many of Auden's friends – felt he was still spontaneous, still capable of reacting to the world around him. He also admired and was amused by Auden's fondness for the notion of 'cosiness'. 'The first time I had tea with him,' Sacks recalled, 'I found the teapot in a tea-cosy, and my egg in an egg-cosy; and this was in no sense mere eccentricity or oddity – Wystan put them in cosies because he

cared for them personally. . . Once we saw a bird fly to its nest atop a
sooty lamp-post in St Mark's Place: "Look!" exclaimed Wystan. "It's
gone home to its nest. Think how cosy it must be." '

Sacks saw Auden the day after his attack of vertigo, and 'found him
apparently recovered, but shocked in a fundamental, unprecedented
way'. He gave Auden a check-up, and, finding nothing seriously wrong,
guessed that the attack had been caused by an influenza virus. But he and
Auden's other medical friend, V. S. Yanovsky, both felt that there
should be a proper examination in hospital; and this was arranged. 'The
check up did not show much,' reported Yanovsky. 'A slight hyper-
tension, a touch of emphysema, a hint of myocardial ischemia, a little of
this and a little of that – nothing special, a false sense of security.' The
only advice the hospital gave Auden was: 'Cut down on the smoking.'

That Christmas, Chester Kallman returned to New York for the first
time for many years, to attend his father's eightieth birthday celebrations,
Auden having mailed him a cheque to cover the air fare from Athens.
Yanovsky observed the two of them together in St Mark's Place:
'Chester is here, had a book of poetry published. Wants to show us the
book; Wystan has taken off the dust jacket. "Why did you do that?"
"You know perfectly well I always do!" (Real tension.) Chester: middle-
aged, with a belly, hunched over.'

During his visit, Chester brought two youths back to the apartment.
While he was engaged with one in the bedroom, the other rummaged
through Auden's papers and stole his engagement book. Auden was
furious. Later, with Robert Craft and Stravinsky's widow Vera – Stravinsky
himself had died a few months earlier – 'Conversation is like old times. . .
When Wystan announces that his bedtime hour has struck, Chester
admonishes him saying that *he* is not ready to leave, whereupon the
reproved one becomes petulant.'

Chester remained in New York until about the second week in
January. Just over a month later, on 21 February, Auden celebrated his
sixty-fifth birthday. His publishers Random House marked this with a
small *Festschrift* edited by Peter Salus and Paul Taylor, with which Auden
was very pleased. There was also a party, held not at St Mark's Place as
in the old days, but in the Coffee House club, which Random House
had hired for the occasion. By the evening of the party it became
apparent that the celebration would also serve as a farewell; for it had
been announced in the press that Auden was going to leave New York
and live in Oxford, at Christ Church.

The college Governing Body had met again on 26 January 1972 to
consider a proposal to offer him the tenancy of the Brewhouse, a small
cottage standing within the college grounds, which had recently become
vacant. There was a good deal of debate, but at the end of the meeting the
vote was unanimously in favour. Auden was notified, and delightedly
accepted the offer. At the beginning of February the newspapers announced

this, quoting him as saying: 'I'm getting rather old to live alone in the winter and I would rather live in a community. Supposing I had a coronary. It might be weeks before I was found. . . In Oxford I should be missed if I failed to turn up for meals. . . I want to dispel any feeling that I am disgruntled with America or aggravated by life in New York. . . I am going back to England solely because of my age.'

Robert Craft and V. S. Yanovsky were among those at the birthday-party in New York, and both wrote their accounts of it. This is Craft's:

February 21, 1972. We go to Auden's birthday party and combination farewell dinner and last supper, at the Coffee House on West Forty-Fifth Street. It is a mob scene during cocktails, but at the actual cenacle the host is seated at a table that is slightly elevated and, no less appropriately, Arthurianly round. Glasses are tapped for silence, telegrams are read in a not-very-pious hush, and a toast is proposed. But no sooner has the speaker begun with 'I don't know what genius is. . .' than he is interrupted by an indignant 'Well who does?' from, of all people, Auden himself.

And this is Yanovsky's:

2/21/72. Auden's 65th birthday celebration, given by Random House in the private rooms of a restaurant. Wystan not really drunk but dead (first dead and then, to disguise it, drunk). A foreign bulging body planted onto a sofa or moving around. Champagne, toasts, a eulogy. I even throw a glass against the wall, break it skilfully (with a good musical tone). Nothing could overcome this deadly frost around him. He is going away (and not simply to Oxford).

On 18 March the *New York Times* printed an article by Auden that was a valediction to his fellow New Yorkers. 'Let me take this opportunity', he wrote, 'to thank in particular Abe and his coworkers in the liquor store'; On Lok my laundryman; Joseph, Bernard and Maurice in the grocery store at Ninth and Second Avenue; Harold the druggist; John, my mailman; Francy from whom I buy my newspaper, and Charles from whom I buy seeds for my Austrian garden. God bless you all!'

Beginning to consider the problems of packing, he telephoned a Greenwich Village bookseller whom he knew, Robert Wilson, to ask if he would be interested in buying that part of his library that he did not intend to take to England. Wilson came to the apartment and found it in a terrible shambles. To separate the books he wanted to keep from those he was offering for sale, Auden had gone to the shelves, taken out those he was keeping, and literally thrown them on the floor. Wilson told him it would take weeks to go through what was left and estimate the right price to offer. Auden replied that he did not want an estimate: he wanted the shelves cleared immediately, and Wilson could work out a price when he got the books back to the shop.

Wilson and his assistant got to work, and were soon finding books they were sure Auden really meant to keep. But when they showed them to Auden, he brushed them aside: 'When I said take everything, I meant *everything.*' Similarly when Orlan Fox and Oliver Sacks came round to help him pack, he waved his hands at a pile of books and said 'Take a book, some books, anything you want.' To Fox he also gave all the gramophone records that he had kept in New York. Sacks felt that these were not the actions of someone merely moving his home.

On 15 April 1972, Auden left New York by plane for Austria. Fox and Sacks drove him to the airport, arriving about three hours early because of Auden's horror of missing planes or trains. Just before the flight was called, a stranger came up to them and stammered: 'You look like – you *are* Mr Auden. We have been honoured to have you in our country, Sir. . . Good-bye, Mr Auden, God bless you for everything.' Auden and the stranger shook hands, Sacks observing that Auden was greatly moved.

It was not quite his farewell to America. He spent most of the summer in Kirchstetten as usual, making his regular visit to London for Poetry International – during which he was questioned on his feelings about the Poet Laureateship, which had become vacant at the death a short time earlier of Cecil Day-Lewis. Auden answered that if he were offered the post he would not accept it if, as had been suggested, it would mean giving up his American citizenship. He also told *The Times* that to regard him as a candidate was 'a load of bosh. . . I do not covet the post; I have no desire for it' – though he admitted he quite liked the idea of writing occasional poems to order. Soon afterwards the appointment of John Betjeman to be Laureate was announced. Then, on 19 September, Auden flew back to New York for a final packing-up.

This took only a few days, and on 30 September V. S. Yanovsky, with his wife and (again) Orlan Fox, drove him once more to the airport. Yanovsky wrote this account in his diary:

'Auden shabbily dressed, nervous. . . We entered the hell of Departures. He advanced, stooped, with knees bent (giant dwarf), hardly looking around. We had a couple of drinks in the bar (Fox took care of that) and reached the cafeteria. . . I escorted Wystan to the self-service buffet; I expected him to pay, but he did not even make the gesture. . . We came to the first-class lounge. . . "The best age to die (the right age) is at seventy," he declared quietly at a certain moment. "Of course, I know that I'll live much longer, but that's when I should like to go.". . . Suddenly he declared: "Now you must go." So we left him, after kissing or pretending to kiss his huge grey clay cheek. On our way back, the three of us felt as if we were returning from a funeral.'

7

Return to England

Auden arrived in London and stayed for two weeks at his brother John's flat in South Kensington, making a television appearance on the Michael Parkinson 'chat' programme ('I'm quite prepared to go on television and perform,' he said, 'if they pay me') and giving a number of interviews to the press: 'I smoke a little less than 50 cigarettes a day. . . . All that worries me about the smoking is the expense. . . My heart is perfectly sound but what I'm frightened of is a lingering illness. . . . The nicest way I think would be a heart attack. It's cheap and it's quick.'

His latest book of poems, *Epistle to a Godson* (the title poem was addressed to his godson Philip Spender) was published at the beginning of October. Critics were sympathetic: Dannie Abse in the *Sunday Times* remarked that the book 'contains an extraordinary number of successes', and Robert Nye wrote in *The Times:* 'Cosy? Domestic? Of course. But. . . technically there are poems here. . . as skilfully turned as any he has ever written.'

On 16 October 1972, Auden took a train to Oxford, so as to arrive punctually for the start of the Michaelmas Term. But he had already been told by Christ Church that the redecoration of the cottage in which he was to live was not yet complete, so that for the time being he would have to find accommodation elsewhere. Greatly upset by this, he had written to his friend Charles Monteith of Faber & Faber, who was a Fellow of All Souls, asking if that college might have room for him for a few weeks, and this was duly arranged.

Monteith met him at Oxford station and carried his bag to a waiting car, while Auden told a reporter from the *Oxford Mail* how pleased he was to be there, and how he wanted to be 'accessible' to undergraduates. Monteith saw he was in a state of euphoria.

A few days later the *Sunday Times* interviewed him at All Souls:

When we saw him in a cluttered temporary room last week he was still shaking the dust out of his suitcases after the journey from America, while a Sargasso sea of papers, review books and packets of Players spilled out over the floor. . . 'I'm hoping to meet the

students in the local coffee bar at, say, four in the afternoon but, for
the rest of the time, I shall be working.'. . . Auden's voice, like his
poetry, is bright and brittle. But his sentences often tail off at the
ends unfinished. There is a long pause. He looks bored. He throws
in a few 'ums' and 'ahs' as if about to stoke up steam again but no.
There is a total silence and he waits for the next question as he
wheezes over yet another cigarette.

Two evenings after Auden had arrived in All Souls, a young man
named Tilley, later described in the newspapers as a labourer, turned up
at his rooms with a hard-luck story, asking for money for urgent repairs
to his house – he had seen the *Oxford Mail* report that Auden wanted to
be 'accessible'. Auden was in a benevolent mood, the result of his
euphoria at arriving in Oxford, and also of several martinis (this was at
about seven o'clock in the evening). His remaining caution was dispelled
when he asked Tilley why he had come to him in particular, and Tilley
replied: 'God sent me.' Auden wrote Tilley a cheque for fifty pounds,
receiving in return an I.O.U. promising weekly repayments. Late that
night, Auden woke to hear somebody moving about in his sitting room,
and, getting out of bed, discovered it to be Tilley, who explained his
presence by saying he wanted to talk to Auden again. Auden sent him
away, telling him to come back in the morning. Auden then discovered
that his wallet, which contained fifty pounds in cash, was missing, as was
the I.O.U. He decided to go to the bank when it opened in the morning
and stop the cheque he had given Tilley, as well as reporting the theft of the
cash to the police; he assumed that Tilley would not reappear. But in the
morning Tilley did return, entirely denying that he was the thief and
giving Auden a fresh I.O.U. As to the cheque, Auden was unaware that
British banks now opened not at ten o'clock, as they used to, but at half-
past nine, and by the time he got there Tilley had already cashed the
cheque. Auden informed the police, and Tilley was arrested, eventually
appearing at Oxford Crown Court at the beginning of January. Auden
was in court ('unshaven and wearing carpet slippers', said the newspapers) to tell his story, but the fact that Tilley had returned the next
morning must have been taken as casting doubt on whether he was the
thief, and it was also pointed out that Auden's rooms were open to
anyone who cared to walk into the college. Tilley was acquitted. Auden
told the newspapers: 'Ironically enough, I had to leave New York and
come to Oxford in order to get robbed.'[1] The experience could scarcely

[1]This, of course, was not strictly true, as his engagement-book had been stolen from St
Mark's Place by one of Chester's young men about ten months earlier. There had also been
a burglary at St Mark's Place some years before, when a typewriter and other items were
stolen; and another time Auden had forestalled an attemped break-in when he discovered
some youths forcing the skylight above the back bedroom. In London, staying with the
Spenders, Auden one greatly embarrassed his hosts by alleging that another of their guests
had stolen his wallet, which he had in fact probably lost somewhere else in London.

have got his Oxford stay off to a worse start; besides upsetting him greatly, it also, quite unjustifiably, blackened his character; for it was erroneously assumed in University circles that there had been some homosexual intrigue behind the event.

Christ Church had told him that the cottage would be ready at the end of October; but it was not. '*Still* not yet in my cottage,' he wrote to Chester on 1 November. 'Compared with New York, Oxford is far more crowded and the traffic far noisier.' He repeated this complaint to everyone: 'I don't like Oxford as a town. It seems to be six times more crowded, four times as noisy as New York. . . And the shops all seem to be such vast emporia! Even in New York I had little shops at the end of the street I lived in.'

At the beginning of November, Orlan Fox, who was visiting England, came to stay for two nights. He found that Auden had already begun to carry out his plan of going to a coffee-shop at four o'clock every afternoon, so that undergraduates could come and talk to him just as they had done in the Cadena Café during his Professorship of Poetry. But the Cadena no longer existed, and Auden had chosen as its replacement the St Aldate's Coffee House, just across the road from the main gate of Christ Church. This was not in such a central position as the Cadena, and was not especially frequented by undergraduates, partly perhaps because it was attached to an evangelical bookshop. Fox sat there with Auden for an hour or so, and saw several people nudging each other and pointing Auden out, but nobody came up to introduce themselves.

Nevertheless Auden persisted, and after a week or two word got around, and a few people did begin to attend regularly at the Coffee House to talk to him. Not everyone came for what Auden considered the right reasons: some wanted to peer at him out of idle curiosity; some were postgraduates (often from overseas) seeking thesis material; some wanted to show him their experiments in avant-garde verse, about which he was usually rude. But there were also a few whose poetry he liked, and who were prepared to listen to what he had to say: 'Go away and write a sestina! At your age what matters is not what you say in your writing but how you say it. Have you ever tried writing a *cywydd*? It's the classical Welsh medieval metre. . .'

Meanwhile he worked as hard as ever, undertaking book-reviews and editing a selection of George Herbert's poetry for Penguin Books. He wrote no poetry, but that was not unusual for the winter months. He arranged to have a check-up with an Oxford doctor, and was pronounced fit. He attended a party given by the University's English Faculty, and gave a poetry reading in the hall of Balliol College, which, to the organisers' surprise, was packed out, about four hundred people attending and a further two hundred having to be turned away. (He charged no fee for this, nor for any other readings in Oxford.) Then, at last, on 16 November, he moved into his cottage at Christ Church.

It stood to the south of the college, tucked away behind Tom Quadrangle, and was an oddly-shaped sixteenth-century building that had once been used for brewing the college's own beer. It now contained a couple of bedrooms, a sitting room, a bathroom, and a small kitchen, all of which smelt of new paint. 'All well here,' Auden reported to Chester just after moving in. 'The cottage is nice and I have a very nice cleaning woman.' He began to join in college life.

The arrangement with Christ Church was simply that he should be the college's tenant, paying a modest rent (though rather more than the three pounds a week reported in the press) and having no teaching duties or other obligations. As a member of Common Room by virtue of the Honorary Studentship the college had granted him some years earlier, he was entitled to eat all meals on high table in the dining hall free of charge, paying only for the drinks he consumed. Nevertheless it was hoped that he would take an active part in Christ Church affairs. When his residence in Oxford was first announced, *The Times* reported: 'He is expected to perform the sort of function that the late E. M. Forster did as a writer in residence at Cambridge, as a provider of counsel and inspiration, and a source of creativity. Dr Chadwick [the Dean] said: "We expect that he will have as much contact with the undergraduates as with the Senior Common Room. Everybody here is delighted about it." '

By the time Auden finally moved into the Brewhouse, the Michaelmas Term was more than half over. He began to take his meals in hall, and to drink his pre-dinner martinis in the Senior Common Room; but he was rather shocked by what he found. It was now many years since he had spent more than a night or two at Christ Church, and his expectations of college life were really still modelled on his memories of convivial evenings in the 1950s when he was Professor of Poetry. Since that time, Christ Church had changed greatly. The number of senior members had much increased, and, even if he had wanted to, Auden could scarcely have got to know everyone with whom he found himself dining. 'What a lot of us there are!' he would mutter to David Luke at dinner. On the other hand, the ceremony of dessert had largely been abandoned after dinner, and now took place only during formal Guest Nights; on other evenings there might be only two or three people lingering in Common Room after the meal and glancing at a newspaper for a few moments before hurrying off to some other engagement. Auden's hopes of finding pleasant company every night of the week – of living in a community – were disappointed. Some time later, Chester Kallman remarked that what had caused Auden most distress during these months 'was that the institution of Common Room at Christ Church seemed to have all but vanished. What he missed was not his drink but the conviviality.'

Just over a month after moving into his cottage, Auden left Oxford to spend Christmas 1972 with James and Tania Stern at the house near Salisbury where they had lived since leaving America in the 1950s. Their other guest was an old friend of Auden's, Sonia Orwell, widow of George Orwell, who arrived (like Auden) on 24 December and left three days later. The Sterns expected that Auden would do the same, but he stayed on; and they began to realise, without ever discussing it with him, that he was not looking forward to going back to Oxford.

It was not a happy time. Auden sat in front of the fire all day, doing crosswords and reading a book by Hannah Arendt that he had found in his bedroom. The Sterns also noticed that he kept going to the shelves and looking at copies of his own books. They found it impossible to engage him in real conversation. He spurned the freshly-ground coffee that they had bought specially for him, insisting on the instant variety; he also made them order for him the *Daily Telegraph* rather than their usual *Times,* explaining: 'One gets more right-wing as one gets older.' And, though James Stern dropped hints about the price of drink, he made it clear that he wanted plenty of vodka to be provided for him (he did not offer to pay). He took the vodka upstairs with him at night, and by the morning had often consumed the greater part of a bottle. He would not go further than the front door – 'A *walk?* What on earth *for?*' – and when a planned visit by car to the writer Christopher Sykes, who lived forty miles away, had to be cancelled because a blanket of fog had come down, he was visibly pleased, returning delightedly to the fire and his crossword. A few months later he wrote a poem about this:

> Grown used to New York weather,
> all too familiar with Smog,
> You, Her unsullied Sister,
> I'd quite forgotten and what
> You bring to British winters:
> now native knowledge returns. . .
> Thank You, Thank You, Thank You, Fog.

At the beginning of January he went back to Oxford and resumed his Christ Church life. On Sunday mornings he would attend the eight o'clock Holy Communion in Christ Church Cathedral, arriving in his carpet-slippers exactly as the service began, and shuffling out before the final prayers. For most of the day he would be invisible, but he always appeared in Common Room before dinner to swallow his martinis before going up to hall to eat, and, even though he might be the only person doing so, would return there ('rather pathetically', said David Luke) to drink a couple of glasses of port, perhaps with a few large brandies too, after the meal was over. Orlan Fox, on his visit to Oxford, had noticed that Auden had added brandy to his nightly habits, and was altogether drinking more than usual.

Those members of Common Room at Christ Church who already knew him well – especially David Luke and J. I. M. Stewart – did their best to make conversation with him at dinner, but it was not easy. They found that, as Auden's New York friends already knew very well, his talk had largely dwindled into the recitation of the same set of ideas, not always well adapted to his audience. 'Of course, everyone pees in his bath,' he might remark to a distinguished visitor. He would also interrupt, or refuse to listen to, other people. 'No, no,' he would say if, for example, someone wanted to talk about dreams, 'we don't want to hear about that. The subconscious is inherently boring.' If the Christ Church organist Simon Preston was dining in hall, Auden would enjoy arguing with him about music (or at least lecturing him about it); and he was glad to listen to a couple of the younger research dons whose 'shop' interested him. But David Luke and J. I. M. Stewart were largely distressed by what they saw. 'I can't have been the only person', wrote Stewart, 'greatly and sadly struck by how very much he had aged. . . It was a little difficult to hold his attention to anything one could think of as possibly interesting to him. In fact he gave me perhaps my first strong impression of what can be the extreme loneliness of old age.'

His Christ Church friends saw him mostly in the evenings, when the drink was having its effect. By day he was a little better. Isaiah Berlin, who had known him since they had first met in America in the 1940s, talked to him a few times and found his mind still unimpaired and vigorous. Peter Walker, then a suffragan bishop in the diocese of Oxford and living in Christ Church, called on him sometimes in the daytime, being a great admirer of his poetry, and thought that he was very tired but otherwise unaffected. Auden was always pleased when Walker was celebrant at the Cathedral eight o'clock Sunday communion – 'I can't bear expression being put into the Mass,' he would tell him – and said to David Luke that the friendship with Walker was one of the things that had made his coming to Oxford worthwhile.

One of the few other people to break through the barrier of self-defensive repetition and anecdote was Andrew Motion, an undergraduate who had begun to show Auden his poetry. Motion became a regular visitor at the Brewhouse, learning that it was necessary to arrive exactly on time to avoid Auden's displeasure. He found no sign of mental decay in Auden; he was much encouraged when Auden praised his poems and talked about them in some detail, rather than fobbing him off with the usual general technical advice that he handed out in the St Aldate's Coffee House. Once, Motion suspected that Auden was making 'bedroom eyes' at him, opening the bedroom door and asking pointedly 'What would you like?' Motion decided to interpret this as the offer of a drink, and no further sexual suggestion was made.

Though Walker and Motion discovered that Auden was willing to engage in friendship, they were the exceptions. He took no trouble to make new acquaintances in Oxford – if he was invited to speak to local groups, he would deliver a cursory talk for a few minutes and then rush home to bed – and even old friends found it difficult to get through the shell. Naomi Mitchison called on him at Christ Church and thought he had 'dried up'. And when Margaret Gardiner came to visit him, she felt he did not really fit into his surroundings:

'You're late,' was his greeting. 'I had given you up.'

'I'm sorry,' I said. 'I couldn't get a taxi. But I'm only a little late – it's twenty to five.'

'Tea', said Wystan severely, 'is at four o'clock.'. . .

He complained that he was eating too much as a result of taking so many meals in college. And the new, clean, packaged flat was really not at all his style.

'All the same, it's pleasant, isn't it – and surely very convenient?' I said as I was leaving.

'It's all right,' he answered grudgingly and then, with an impish smile: 'But the sink is the wrong height for me to pee into.'

At the end of January 1973 Auden went up to London to record a television interview with his old friend Richard Crossman. They did not have much to say to each other, either on or off camera. Auden thought Crossman had become 'coarse'; Crossman was irritated by Auden's rejection of his own earlier, younger self. 'The Auden I talked to', he later wrote, 'had been re-shaped to a respectable mould. . . Looking at him I couldn't help thinking of an old tortoise peering at me out of his shell.'[1]

A few days later, Auden went to Brussels for the première of his new opera, *Love's Labour's Lost*. The performance, by the Deutsche Oper of West Belin, was a mild success, though Nabokov's score contained too much pastiche to make a big impression. It was performed again by the same company during the next two years, but has not been revived since. In Brussels, Nabokov observed that Auden was 'getting older, crankier, lonelier, cracking the same jokes. . . "Had I chosen the orders I would now be a bishop": five times in two days. . .'

Auden returned to Oxford, where there were now (as David Luke put it) 'signs of adjustment on both sides'. The Christ Church English tutors persuaded him to go to a party for graduates in that subject, and to sit in on a seminar; it was also planned that he would take part in another seminar, on Shakespeare, in the autumn. He also attended an undergraduate production of *The Dog Beneath the Skin* at the Playhouse, for which he approved a few textual changes; he congratulated the cast and the director, Mark Morris, on a 'swell job'. The role of the Poet in

---

[1]Stephen Spender writes: 'Crossman asked me (in the early 70s) to ask Auden to dine with him and our respective wives at the Garrick Club. In the course of the evening, I heard Crossman say to Auden: "Don't you remember when we were undergraduates how we went for walks and I showed you my poems?" Auden said: "You never wrote poetry. You were never interested in anything but politics." '

the play had been adapted to make him an ageing figure with a heavily-lined face. 'Do you think this is supposed to be me?' Auden asked with relish.

If things were improving in some ways, in other respects they seem to have got slightly worse. Some of Auden's fellow members of Common Room at Christ Church began to suggest that a word should be dropped in his ear to the effect that his conversation was repetitive and not always pleasing to those who dined with him. Exactly what happened is not clear. Representations were made to David Luke, but he would not agree to raise the matter with Auden. Roy Harrod, who had briefly tutored Auden in economics in 1926 and who sometimes visited the college during his retirement, told Charles Monteith that something had been said to Auden on the subject, apparently by Harrod himself; he said that Auden had taken the criticism very much to heart, and answered bluntly 'Oh, you mean I bore them.' The result, said Harrod, was to make Auden unwilling to talk at dinner at all during the rest of the term.[1]

Auden left Oxford in April, went briefly to Yorkshire to read his poems at the Ilkley Literature Festival, stayed for a few days with his brother John in London, and then set off for Kirchstetten. The arrangement with Christ Church was that he should live in Oxford only during the autumn and spring terms, and should spend his summers in Austria as usual, not returning to Oxford until October.

At Kirchstetten, the lane in which his house stood had now been renamed 'Audenstrasse'. Auden had forestalled an earlier attempt by the village to do this, declaring that it sounded posthumous. He now said that he was embarrassed by the change of name, and refused to use it on his letterhead, still giving his address as 'Hinterholz 6'. Privately, though, he sometimes admitted that he was pleased.

On arriving at Kirchstetten he settled down to writing his first poems since the previous summer. He would have done this in any case, always insisting that one should write poetry with regularity, whether or not anything issued from the effort. But there was probably also a sense of release at getting back to Austria – and getting away from Oxford. Among the poems he now composed was 'A Thanksgiving', a verse catalogue of some of those who had influenced him so much over the years: Hardy, Yeats, Charles Williams, Kierkegaard, Horace, Goethe, and others. The poem took up the theme of another he had composed the previous year, 'A Lullaby', in which he wrote:

---

[1]David Luke says that if Harrod made any such representations to Auden, it must have been a self-appointed task; Harrod was ot a one-man deputation from his fellow members of Common Room. Nor does he agree that Auden fell largely silent for the rest of the term, though he accepts that he would have been hurt and annoyed by anything that was said to him about his conversation.

Let your last thinks all be thanks:
praise your parents who gave you
a Super-Ego of strength
that saves you so much bother. . .

Now for oblivion: let
the belly-mind take over. . .
Should dreams haunt you, heed them not,
for all, both sweet and horrid,
are jokes in dubious taste,
too jejune to have truck with.
Sleep, Big Baby, sleep your fill.

There were as usual a lot of visitors at Kirchstetten, mostly old friends. Auden also had plenty of work to do. He and Leif Sjöberg had decided to translate a book of poems by the Nobel Prizewinner Pär Lagerkvist, and this occupied Auden for much of the summer. In mid-June he flew to London for Poetry International, staying with the Spenders as usual; Chester accompanied him to read some of his own poems during the festival, Auden having asked Charles Osborne if he would agree to this. Osborne thought that Auden was if anything 'in sprightlier health than he had been for some time'. But two months later, back at Kirchstetten, Auden gave rather a different account of himself to E. R. Dodds:

August 31st.
Dear Dodds:
    Hope life is not being too difficult for you. Here it has not been easy. First Chester had some kind of physical breakdown – liver trouble, arthritis in the neck, trembling hands etc. – and had to spend two weeks in hospital. He is much better now, but has to take many kinds of pills. For my part, I'm beginning to feel my age. My mind seems to function all right, but my body gets very easily fatigued. The doctor diagnoses a weak heart, whatever that means, and I, too, have to take pills.
    Did you happen to see my review of your book in the New York Review of Books? If so, I hope you found it O.K.
    Hope the poem overleaf ['Archaeology'] will entertain you.
                    Yours ever
                    Wystan

Towards the end of September, he and Chester closed the Kirchstetten house for the winter and went off to Vienna for a weekend, Auden having been engaged to give a poetry recital there before he returned to Oxford for the start of the 1973 autumn term. He had many longer-term plans: a new edition of his *Collected Shorter Poems* (he had begun to make further revisions to his poetry almost as soon as the 1966 collection was published); a revised *Oxford Book of Light Verse* which had been commissioned by the Oxford University Press, and which he planned to edit with Edward Mendelson; and a lecture tour around America in February 1974 – he had written to his New York agent about this, asking to be put up in faculty homes rather than hotels, so that somebody could keep an eye on him all the time. Meanwhile he and Chester, before leaving Kirchstetten, had written a short libretto for the composer John Gardiner, an antimasque entitled *The Entertainment of the Senses,* to be performed in London the following February, as an interpolation to James Shirley's seventeenth-century masque *Cupid and Death.* The libretto, largely the work of Chester, presented each of the senses in turn in a set of satirical songs, which treated sensual indulgence as absurd but worth pursuing in view of the ever-present shadow of mortality: 'Life is short, so enjoy / Whatever contact your flesh / May at the moment crave: / There's no sex-life in the grave.'

On the Friday evening, 28 September 1973, Auden went to the Palais Palffy in Josefplatz to give his poetry-reading, to the Austrian Society of Literature. Afterwards he was offered supper, but he declined, saying that he was tired, and asked to be driven back to his hotel, the Altenburgerhof in Walfischgasse, in 'a *nice* car'. Next morning, Saturday, Chester knocked on his door at nine o'clock, but could get no answer. He tried the door and found it locked, which puzzled him. He called the management, and the door was forced open. Auden was lying in bed; Chester could see at once that he was dead. 'He was lying on the wrong side. He never lay on his left side. He thought it was bad for his heart. He was cold when I touched him.'

During his last summer at Kirchstetten, Auden had written a haiku, which Chester told friends had actually been the last poem that he had composed:

> He still loves life
> But O O O O how he wishes
> The good Lord would take him.[1]

★

A limited autopsy was performed, and it confirmed what was already assumed, that Auden had died of a heart attack. It appeared that there had also been a number of previous small attacks, and some bronchial irregularities.[2]

[1]No manuscript of the haiku has been found. Chester Kallman repeated it from memory to Edward Mendelson, and told him that Auden had shown it to him, but he (Chester), superstitious over the stated wish for death, told him to cross it out, which Auden did, and perhaps discarded it entirely. There are 19 syllables, as opposed to the 17 of the haiku-form, but Chester explained that Auden's practice was to elide two adjacent vowels, so that O O O O would count as two syllables and not four.

[2]The death certificate give the cause of death as: 'Arteriosclerosis, hypertrophy of the

News of Auden's death was given to Christopher Isherwood by a telephone call from Reuter's news agency, who wanted a comment; but Isherwood was too distressed to say anything. Chester Kallman later recorded some of his own feelings in a poem:

> Wystan is gone; a gift of fertile years
> And now of emptiness: I found him dead
> Turning icy-blue on a hotel bed. . .
> I shared his work and life as best I could
> For both of us, often impatiently.
> So it was; let it be.

Chester went back to Kirchstetten, and John Auden and Thekla Clark came to collect Wystan's belongings from the American Consulate in Vienna. Arrangements were made for the funeral to be held the following Thursday, 4 October, in Kirchstetten, where he had wished to be buried. Meanwhile on the Wednesday night, in New York, a memorial service for him was held in the Cathedral of St John the Divine, in which a number of his American friends took part.[1]

During the days before the funeral, those people who were close to Auden and could manage the journey to Austria began to arrive by air or train in Vienna, and to make their way to Kirchstetten. Among these were Stephen Spender, John Auden's daughter Rita and her husband Peter Mudford, Michael and Marny Yates, Alan Ansen, Sonia Orwell, David Luke, Charles Monteith, and Edward Mendelson, who flew from America. Hugerl and his wife Christa were there, looking very formal and stiff and saying little to anyone. Charles Osborne came from London as the representative of the Arts Council. On the morning of the funeral they were joined at the church by representatives of the Austrian Poetry Society and the American and British consulates, and by a large number of local people who had come to see the 'Herr Professor' to his grave. Michael Yates provides this account of the funeral:

'It had all been arranged with calm care following Wystan's wishes. In addition, the village had decided they wanted the funeral to be theirs as much as that of Wystan's friends, and had therefore arranged a band and a formal procession. At the house, the large coffin was in what had been Wystan's bedroom, which had been cleaned and emptied of its customary jumble, including his bed; the coffin was raised up at an angle surrounded

heart, endocarditis'. The time of death is given as 9.30 a.m., but this was possibly the time at which the body was examined by the doctor signing the certificate. Chester Kallman maintained (though he could not know it) that Auden had died before midnight.

[1]There was also a memorial service in Christ Church, Oxford, on 27 October, at which Stephen Spender gave an address.

by wreaths and flowers. In the garden there were a few T.V. film men, press and photographers; fortunately the place was not swarming with them.

'There was wine in the living-cum-dining-room where the personal mourners were gathering. Chester came in as the last people were arriving from Vienna; he was naturally in a distressed state. Whilst those who wished to talk, and could, were doing so, the coffin was carried past the window. Chester then stood up, saying with some vehemence: "I want all film people with their microphones, photographers, and the press to leave the garden, also any other person not invited to be in the house to go." Then he said: "There is something I have to do. Wystan said that before his funeral he wanted Siegfried's Funeral March to be played, so will you stand?"[1] The correct gramophone record had already been selected, and the needle was now set down in the right groove. The effect of that music could be read in most faces.

'When it finished, Chester led everyone out into the sunshine to where the procession with its band, local officials, and other mourners was waiting. It was quite still and silent except for the endless "autobahn". Chester then said: "I want John [Auden] on my left and Michael [Yates] on my right. Will the rest please take your places behind us."

'It was about half a mile from the house to the small onion-domed church. The band was not too funereal, so the procession moved without that deadening effect which Wystan would not have liked. At first, Chester contained his emotion by characteristically talking about Maria Callas and opera; but soon he withdrew into a private stunned silence.

'Although Wystan had asked to be buried at Kirchstetten, special dispensation had to be obtained. As he was an Anglican but nevertheless a regular worshipper at the local Catholic church, it had been agreed[2] that he be buried jointly by an Anglican priest and the local Catholic priest, the words being spoken alternately in English and German. After a short service in the church the coffin was carried to the chosen position.

'And so he was buried, simply,·without high ceremony, calmly but sadly. For those closest to him, the final moment was one of unbearable parting.

'When all was complete, about forty people went to the "Gasthaus" below the church for lunch. Afterwards, the personal friends who remained with Chester walked slowly in the afternoon sunshine back to

---

[1]In 1962, dining with the Stravinskys, Auden declared: 'When my time is up I'll want Siegfried's Funeral Music and not a dry eye in the house.'

[2]This had been arranged after John Auden and Chester Kallman had discussed the matter with the Kirchstetten Catholic priest. The Anglican priest was the chaplain from the British Embassy in Vienna.

the house. Charles Osborne had already arranged a dinner in Vienna that evening, with those who were staying in the city, and now felt he should invite Chester too. Chester was pleased, but said he would like everybody to be there. It is probable that such a wish was part of the intense Jewish and family side to his nature. So the private dinner became general, in support of Chester. That evening in Vienna, the sad exhaustion of the long day was gradually succeeded by an increasingly merry party which did not end until train time for those returning to Kirchstetten was near. Wystan would surely have approved of such enjoyment – except for the fact that it went on long past his bed-time.'

★

Auden's will left everything to 'Chester Simon Kallman', unless Chester should predecease him, in which case the estate would have passed to his nieces Rita and Anita, John Auden's daughters. Chester returned to Athens for the winter of 1973, and came back to Kirchstetten the following spring. But he was now in very poor health, and, more than this, seemed to have no purpose to his life. He told Alan Ansen: 'I've lost my criterion.' In the autumn of 1974 he attended a ceremony at Westminster Abbey in London when John Betjeman, as Poet Laureate, unveiled a memorial stone to Auden in Poet's Corner; but Chester looked so bowed and bent now that many of Auden's friends failed to recognise him. The following January he died in Athens, apparently of heart-failure – there was no autopsy. He was fifty-four.

His will left everything to Auden, and was therefore invalid. As a result, his estate and that of Auden passed to his closest surviving relative, his father, Dr Edward Kallman, by then in his mid-eighties. Dr Kallman shortly afterwards married Dorothy Farnan, who had known Chester and his family since the 1940s. In 1979 she and her husband sued the New York Public Library for the return of those of Auden's papers – including his 1929 Berlin journal – which had been in Auden's possession at the time of his death, and had therefore passed to Chester, who had gathered them together and directed Edward Mendelson to deliver them to the Library. Chester had died before making any deed of gift to the Library, and the Kallmans argued that he had not really made a gift, but had only left the papers in storage at the Library. A number of Auden's and Chester's friends gave evidence for the other side, testifying that Chester had indeed wanted the papers to be a gift to the Library, in accordance with Auden's wish, often stated, that manuscripts should be donated rather than sold. ('Shameless envious Age!', Auden wrote, 'when the Public will shell out more cash for / note-books and sketches that were never intended for them / than for perfected works.') It was also stated in court that Chester had meant to make a new will leaving Auden's copyrights and royalties to Auden's nieces Anita and Rita, as

Auden had wished him to do. The Kallmans lost the case; they retained the copyrights and royalties, but the papers remain with the Library.

Before his death, Chester had sold the Kirchstetten house to the housekeeper, Frau Strobl, on condition that he could continue to live there in the summer. The house was later, with the aid of the Austrian Society of Literature and the Lower Austrian provincial government, designated a memorial to Auden. On Sunday 20 February 1977, the population of Kirchstetten paraded to the graveyard with band, choir and wreaths, to mark Auden's seventieth birthday, which would have fallen the next day.

His last book of poems, *Thank You, Fog,* was published in September 1974, with a note explaining that he had not completed it at the time of his death. Soon afterwards came a new edition of the *Collected Poems,* incorporating his latest (and last) revisions, and *The English Auden,* in which Edward Mendelson put into print once again the original texts of the poems written between 1927 and 1939, many of which Auden had later changed or rejected.

Among the innumerable obituaries, that in *The Times* declared: 'W. H. Auden, for long the *enfant terrible* of English poetry. . . emerges finally as its undisputed master. . . It was Auden above all who showed how the full range of traditional forms could be revived in the service of the kind of moral and social realism that a world in crisis demanded. In this way he was in the vanguard of a versatile and publicly accessible art.' Not everyone agreed with this judgement; Edward Upward, who had not seen Auden since the 1930s, wrote in a memoir of him: 'He seemed to have deliberately chosen not to become the truly great poet that I was sure he could have become. I had never doubted that he would have a permanent place among the English poets, but I had come to think – and I still think – that it will not be as high a place as it could have been.'

A judgement of the whole of Auden's achievement depends, of course, on how his later poetry is viewed – whether as a 'decline,' or (as Auden himself saw it, and as the more perceptive critics have realised) an attempt to purge his poetry of false rhetoric and to make it serve the interests of truth, at whatever cost. But whatever one's views, it is impossible to dissent from the comment of John Lehmann when he put it that, among poets, 'none, I believe, has shown such an extraordinary capacity to speak through poetry, with a poet's vision, about the whole of life'. Geoffrey Grigson, in the *Tribute* to Auden which was published in 1975, wrote much the same thing: 'If we follow him round, as he celebrates, investigates, discards, adds, re-attempts, we find in him explicit recipes for being human.' And a re-reading of Auden's poetry, through all its decades and in all its many versions, shows us how right Lincoln Kirstein is to place him 'with Picasso in painting, Stravinsky in music: a master of the uses of our whole past, projected into the present and prophesying a future.'

Auden himself said his had been a happy life. 'I have a marvellous censor that refuses to let me remember, if it's any way back, anything unpleasant,' he remarked not long before his death; and in 1965 he wrote of his as 'a life which has, so far, been unusually happy'. And, some years earlier: 'I'm really a sanguine person. I've always found existence enjoyable. Even when one is hurt and has to bellow, still one is always fundamentally happy to be able to.'

On his memorial stone at Westminster Abbey are carved two lines from his elegy on Yeats: 'In the prison of his days / Teach the free man how to praise.' Auden was aware of the danger of poets writing their own epitaphs; he remarked of Yeats's 'Horseman, pass by!' that the passer-by who visited the grave was more likely to be a motorist. But one might choose for him the final stanza of his poem 'At the Grave of Henry James':

> All will be judged. Master of nuance and scruple,
> Pray for me and for all writers, living or dead:
>   Because there are many whose works
> Are in better taste than their lives, because there is no end
> To the vanity of our calling, make intercession
>   For the treason of all clerks.

Appendices

APPENDIX A

Bibliography

The abbreviations in **bold type** are those used in the notes (Appendix B) which give the sources of quotations.

1. THE PUBLISHED WRITINGS OF W. H. AUDEN

For a comprehensive list of these, the reader is referred to B. C. Bloomfield and Edward Mendelson, *W. H. Auden, A Bibliography, 1924-1969,* University Press of Virginia, second edition, 1972. This volume, of which a third edition is in preparation, is indispensable to any serious student of Auden's work. What follows is merely a handlist of Auden's principal books, with only minimal details of publication.

Poems, privately printed by Stephen Spender, 1928
Poems, Faber & Faber, 1930; second edition, 1933
The Orators: An English Study, Faber & Faber, 1932; second edition, 1934; third
    edition, 1966; first separate American edition, 1967
The Dance of Death, Faber & Faber, 1933
Poems, Random House (New York), 1934 (containing all the poems in the 1933
    Faber edition of *Poems,* together with *The Orators* (first edition text) and *The
    Dance of Death*)
The Dog Beneath the Skin (with Christopher Isherwood), Faber & Faber, 1935;
    Random House, 1935 [**DBS**][1]
The Ascent of F6, Faber & Faber, 1936; Random House (revised text), 1937 [**F6**][2]
Look, Stranger!, Faber & Faber, 1936; published by Random House in 1937 as *On
    This Island*
Spain, Faber & Faber, 1937
Letters from Iceland (with Louis MacNeice), Faber & Faber, 1937; Random House,
    1937; second English edition, 1967; second American edition, 1969 [**LFI**][3]
On the Frontier (with Christopher Isherwood), Faber & Faber, 1938; Random
    House, 1939 [**OTF**][2]
Education Today and Tomorrow (with T. C. Worsley), Hogarth Press, 1939

---

[1]The edition referred to in the notes in this book is that issued as a Faber paperback in 1968.
[2]The edition of *The Ascent of F6* and *On the Frontier* referred to in the notes in this book is the volume containing both plays issued as a Faber paperback in 1958.
[3]The notes in this book refer to the second English edition.

Journey to a War (with Christopher Isherwood), Faber & Faber, 1939; Random House, 1939; second English edition, 1973 [**JTAW**]

Another Time, Random House, 1940; Faber & Faber, 1940 [**AT**]

The Double Man, Random House, 1941; published by Faber & Faber in 1940 as *New Year Letter* (there are certain textual differences between these two volumes)

For the Time Being, Random House, 1944; Faber & Faber, 1945

The Collected Poetry, Random House, 1945 [**CP45**]

The Age of Anxiety, Random House, 1947; Faber & Faber, 1948

Collected Shorter Poems, 1930 -1944, Faber & Faber, 1950

The Enchafèd Flood, Random House, 1950; Faber & Faber, 1951

Nones, Random House, 1951; Faber & Faber, 1952 [**Nones**]

The Rake's Progress (libretto, with Chester Kallman), Boosey & Hawkes, 1951; second edition, 1966; edition accompanying boxed record set Columbia M3S 710 (CBS BRG 72278-80), 1964 (includes notes by Igor Stravinsky, Vera Stravinsky and Chester Kallman) [**RP**][1]

The Shield of Achilles, Random House, 1955; Faber & Faber, 1955

The Magic Flute (libretto translated by Auden and Chester Kallman), Random House, 1956; Faber & Faber, 1957

W. H. Auden: a selection by the author, Penguin Books, 1958; published by The Modern Library in 1958 as *Selected Poetry*

Homage to Clio, Random House, 1960; Faber & Faber, 1960 [**HC**]

Elegy for Young Lovers (libretto, with Chester Kallman), Schott, 1961

The Dyer's Hand, Random House, 1962; Faber & Faber, 1963 [**DH**]

About the House, Random House, 1965; Faber & Faber, 1966

The Bassarids (libretto, with Chester Kallman), Schott, 1966

Collected Shorter Poems, 1927-1957, Faber & Faber, 1966; Random House, 1967 [**CSP66**]

Collected Longer Poems, Faber & Faber, 1968; Random House, 1969

Secondary Worlds, Faber & Faber, 1969; Random House, 1969 [**SW**]

City Without Walls, Faber & Faber, 1969; Random House, 1970

A Certain World, Random House, 1970; Faber & Faber, 1971 [**ACW**]

Academic Graffiti, Faber & Faber, 1971; Random House, 1972

Epistle to a Godson, Random House, 1972; Faber & Faber, 1972

Love's Labour's Lost (libretto, with Chester Kallman), published in vocal score by Bote & Bock, 1972

Forewords and Afterwords, Random House, 1973; Faber & Faber, 1973 [**FA**]

Thank You, Fog, Faber & Faber, 1974; Random House, 1974 [**TYF**]

Collected Poems, edited by Edward Mendelson, Faber & Faber, 1976; Random House, 1976 [**CP**]

The English Auden, edited by Edward Mendelson, Faber & Faber, 1977; Random House, 1978 [**EA**]

Selected Poems, new edition, edited by Edward Mendelson, Vintage Books, 1979; Faber & Faber, 1979 [**SP**][2]

[1]The edition referred to in the notes is that accompanying this boxed record set.

[2]Earlier volumes entitled *Selected Poems* were published in 1938 and 1968.

2. LETTERS AND OTHER MANUSCRIPTS BY W. H. AUDEN

Many of the letters and other manuscripts cited in this book are held in these institutions:

The Henry W. and Albert A. Berg Collection, the New York Public Library,
    Astor, Lenox and Tilden Foundations [**Berg**][1]
The Department of Western Manuscripts, Bodleian Library,
    Oxford [**Bodleian**]
The British Library (British Museum), London [**BM**]
The Butler Library, Columbia University, New York [**Butler**][1]
The Humanities Research Center, University of Texas at Austin [**HRC**][1]

The following is a list of the most substantial groups of letters and other manuscripts cited in this book, together with a note of their location, if they are in a public institution. Where no location is specified, the material is still in private hands:

Dodds collection (MSS. of Auden's juvenilia, given by his mother to E. R. Dodds):
    Bodleian [**Dodds collection**]
Fisher collection (MSS. of Auden's juvenilia and undergraduate poems, collected
    by A. S. T. Fisher) [**Fisher collection**]
Letters to E. R. and Mrs A. E. Dodds: Bodleian [**to ERD / AED**]
Letters to Rhoda Jaffe: Berg [**to RJ**]
Letters to Chester Kallman: several locations; see specific notes for location of
    particular letters [**to CK**]
Letters to Elizabeth Mayer: Berg [**to EM**]
Letters to Hedwig Petzold: Berg [**to HP**]
Letters to Arnold ('Nob') Snodgrass: Berg [**to AS**]
Letters to Stephen Spender [**to SS**]

Where other letters and manuscripts are cited, an indication of their location is given in the notes.

3. BOOKS AND ARTICLES CONTAINING BIOGRAPHICAL REFERENCES TO W. H. AUDEN

Few literary biographies, autobiographies or memoirs covering the period of Auden's life do not contain at least some passing reference to him. The following is merely a list of those works which have been cited most frequently in this book.

Ansen, Alan, (unpublished) notes on conversations with Auden in New York
    during 1946 (Berg Collection: see above, section 2) [**Ansen**]
Bloomfield, B. C. and Mendelson, Edward, *W. H. Auden, A Bibliography, 1924–
    1969*, University Press of Virginia, second edition, 1972 [**Bibliography**]

---

[1] I am very grateful to these libraries for their permission to quote from manuscripts in their keeping.

Craft, Robert, *Stravinsky: Chronicle of a Friendship*, Victor Gollancz, 1972 [**Chronicle**]

Davidson, Michael, *The World, the Flesh and Myself*, Arthur Barker, 1962 [**Davidson**]

Day Lewis, C., *The Buried Day*, Chatto & Windus, 1960 [**Buried Day**]

Dodds, E. R., *Missing Persons: an autobiography*, Oxford, Clarendon Press, 1977 [**Missing Persons**]

Finney, Brian, *Christopher Isherwood: a critical biography*, Faber & Faber, 1979 [**Finney**]

Fisher, A. S. T., 'Up at Oxford with Poets' (unpublished memoir of Auden and other poets with whom Fisher was an undergraduate; typescript kindly lent by the author) [**Fisher**]

Gardiner, Margaret, 'Auden: a memoir', *New Review*, III, 28 (July 1976), 9–19 [**Gardiner**]

Harvard Advocate, CVIII, 2 & 3: special issue, 'W. H. Auden, 1907–1973' [**HA**]

Isherwood, Christopher, *Christopher and his Kind*, Eyre Methuen, 1977 [**CAHK**]

Isherwood, Christopher, *Lions and Shadows: an education in the twenties*, Hogarth Press, 1938 [**L & S**]

MacNeice, Louis, *The Strings are False: an unfinished autobiography*, Faber & Faber, 1965 [**Strings**]

Mitchison, Naomi, *You May Well Ask: a memoir, 1920–1940*, Victor Gollancz, 1979 [**You May Well Ask**]

Pike, J. A., ed., *Modern Canterbury Pilgrims*, A. R. Mowbray, 1956 [**Modern Canterbury Pilgrims**]

Plimpton, George, ed., *Writers at Work: the Paris Review interviews*, 4th series, Secker & Warburg, 1977 [**Paris Review**]

Pudney, John, *Home and Away*, Michael Joseph, 1960 [**Pudney (Home)**]

Pudney, John, *Thank Goodness for Cake*, Michael Joseph, 1978 [**Pudney (Cake)**]

Scobie, W. I., 'W. H. Auden, In Faithless Arms, In Faithful Love', *Advocate* (San Mateo, California), 14 June 1978, Book Section, 24–27 [**Advocate**]

Spears, Monroe K. (ed.), *Auden: a Collection of Critical Essays*, (Twentieth Century Views), New Jersey: Prentice-Hall, 1964 [**TCVA**]

Spears, Monroe K., *The Poetry of W. H. Auden: the Disenchanted Island*, New York: Oxford University Press, 1963 [**Spears**]

Spender, Stephen, *World Within World*, Readers Union edition, 1953 [**WWW**]

Spender, Stephen, ed., *W.H. Auden, a tribute* Weidenfeld & Nicolson, 1975 [**TR**]

Stravinsky, Igor and Craft, Robert, *Memories and Commentaries*, Faber & Faber, 1960 [**Memories & Commentaries**]

Stravinsky, Vera and Craft, Robert, *Stravinsky in Pictures and Documents*, Hutchinson, 1979 [**Strav./Craft**]

Sussex, Elizabeth, *The Rise and Fall of British Film Documentary*, University of California Press, 1976 [**Sussex**]

Upward, Edward, 'Remembering the earlier Auden', *Adam International Review*, 1973–4, 17–22 [**Upward**]

Yanovsky, V. S., 'W.H. Auden', *Antaeus*, 1 ̣ ̣.̣ ̣.̣utumn 1975), 107–135 [**Yanovsky**]

APPENDIX B

Sources of quotations

The quotations used in the text are identified in this list by the number of the page on which they appear, and by the first few words quoted. When two or more quotations from the same source follow each other in a brief space, I have generally used only the first few words of the first quotation for identification. Abbreviations refer to the Bibliography (Appendix A) where the full title of the work or source is given.

page

xv   'Biographies of writers', ACW vii. 'gossip-writers and voyeurs', *For W.H Auden, February 21, 1972*, ed. P.H. Salus and P.B. Taylor, Random House, 1972, 34. 'to make a biography impossible', to Edward Mendelson, 9 May 1972.

xvi 'flexible enough', Edward Mendelson, 'Authorised Biography and its Discontents', *Harvard English Studies* (1978), 10. 'No poet should', *Buried Day* 25. 'The biography of an artist', FA 89f. 'I do believe', ibid. 247.

3   'I, after all', EA 208. 'a conscious spiritual', EA 334. 'the lifelong conviction', FA 503.

4   'a rather Hamlet-like', ACW 331. 'furious', to J.R.R. Tolkien, 28 July 1955 (Estate of J.R.R. Tolkien). 'Why shun a', ACW 17. 'Hug a shady', TR 179. 'Litotes', HA 18. 'Marry him if', *Paris Review* 264.

5   'one of those persons', FA 515. 'Those at the gasworks', EA 191. 'numinous', CP 623.

6   'Clearer than Scafell', EA 175. 'a childhood full', CP 581. 'There are certain', FA 486. 'No gentler father', EA 191. 'Too gentle, I', FA 500f. 'Ma should have', *Observer Magazine,* 7 November 1971, 41f. 'loved us and', FA 499.

7   'My first religious', *Modern Canterbury Pilgrims* 33.

8   'pure Nordic', FA 496. 'In my childhood', LFI 8. 'In my father's', FA 497. 'My father's library', EA 397.

9   'the only English', TR 90. 'When I was', foreword to Angus Stewart, *Sense and Inconsequence,* Michael deHartington, 1972. 'care more for', ACW 156. 'Healing is not a', CP 627.

10   'phlegmatic, earnest', FA 499. 'quick, short-tempered', ibid. 'most of the adults', *Observer Magazine,* 7 November 1971, 41f.

11   'illness could be', CP 602. 'a precocious', FA 508. 'very odd indeed', FA 501. 'Tommy did as', British Library Add. MS. 52430, fol. 8.

12   'I think we', EA 359. 'understand the mechanism', ibid. 335. 'No one thinks', EA 198. 'The so-called traumatic', *New Republic,* 10 February 1941, 185f. 'a world still', *Southern Review,* Summer 1940, 81. *'Sat 9th Aug.',* holiday diary in the possession of Dr John Auden.

13   'Those beautiful machines', CP 203.

14   'thought myself', EA 191. 'I spent a', FA 502. 'sole autocrat', *Southern Review,* Summer 1940, 78. 'A word like', DH 34. 'I doubt if', EA 398.

16   'I am certain', FA 505. 'a primitive tribe', EA 398.

17   'Anybody who has', ACW 146. 'Minus times Minus', ibid. 92. 'hairy monsters with', EA 398. 'it did not surprise', ibid. 'Assistant masters', FA 505. 'all at sea', EA 192. 'earliest visions', ibid. 'Auden, I see', FA 505.

18   'No. 1 machine-gun', *St Edmund's School Chronicle,* June 1917, 53–5. 'The Great War', EA 192.

19   'I like to see', ibid. 'talking for effect', TR 35. 'a rabbit at', EA 322. 'I think I can', FA 508. 'grubby and inferior', *Southern Review,* Summer 1940, 78. 'doomed to a life', ibid.

20   'a not unimportant', *Common Sense,* January 1940, 23. 'Left Haslemere', holiday diary in the possession of Dr John Auden. 'To some degree', FA 500.

21   'never really came', ibid. 'Father at the wars', CP 602. 'really something', Ansen. 'To several', L & S 181f. 'I see him frowning', ibid. 182. 'a small boy', *New Statesman,* 9 June 1956, 656.

22 'I think God', *Paris Review* 249. 'They ought to be', L & S 182.
23 'In Rookhope', CP 182. 'The defenestration', *Times Literary Supplement*, 5 November 1971, 1390.
24 'We all have', TR 33. 'of showing us', EA 323. 'From listening to', ibid.
25 'I believe no more' and 'But if you deny', EA 325. 'It meant that', ibid.
26 'A really good prefect', EA 324. 'period of ecclesiastical', FA 517. 'nothing but vague', EA 326. 'quite straightforward', *Modern Canterbury Pilgrims* 34. 'that people only' and 'liable to evoke', ibid. 35. 'life is ruled', EA 397.
28 'a grand time', EA 322. 'An argument, TR 40. 'Kicking a little', EA 194.
29 'and in the quiet', B.C. Bloomfield, *W.H. Auden: A Bibliography*, 1st ed., University Press of Virginia, 1964, ix. 'The twinkling lamps', Dodds collection. A MS. of this poem owned by A.S.T. Fisher and published by him in *Notes and Queries*, October 1974, 371, has several textual differences.
30 'Far into the vast', *The Gresham*, 16 December 1922, 23. A MS. of the poem is in the Dodds collection, and has several textual differences. 'Never again will', DH 36. 'without finding what', *Southern Review*, Summer 1940, 78. 'red wrists', TR 39.
31 'It reflected', ibid. 'the most unlikely', ibid. 42. 'You shouldn't waste', EA 323. 'Feeling responsible', TR 39f. 'only the two', EA 322.
32 'On the cold waterfall' and 'Autumn is come', Dodds collection. 'probably a retreat', *Observer Magazine*, 7 November 1971, 36. 'To me Art's', EA 185.
33 'O Scarlet Beauty', Dodds collection. 'that he himself', TR 39. 'Who deafened our ears', Fisher collection.
34 'that poetry does', DH 36. The poems cited in the second paragraph on this page are all in the Dodds collection. 'sheaves of poems', TR 40. 'I wonder what' and 'So sorry I', Dodds collection. 'Yes, always now', Dodds collection.
35 'The dangers of', *Southern Review*, Summer 1940, 81. 'For more than', ibid. 'that broad unpampered', ibid. 'What are we men', Fisher collection. The iron wheel hangs', Dodds collection.
36 'The smelting-mill stack', TR 75. 'What I valued', *Southern Review*, Summer 1940, 83. 'In Zoology I', Dodds collection. 'Section these dwellings', DBS 117. 'I have a little', Dodds collection.
37 'This is the', Davidson 1. 'Auden, as I', ibid. 127. 'bewitched', 'The maturity of', and 'that I had', ibid. 'not on moral', FA 509. 'He once told', Davidson 129. 'he was kind', ibid. 'I owe him', FA 509.
38 'palace revolution', *Southern Review*, summer 1940, 80. 'When we were', L & S 187. 'here and there', Fisher collection. 'To my generation', FA 332. 'Wake and be merry', Fisher collection. 'It was quiet in there', Dodds collection; printed in L & S 186 with slightly different punctuation.
39 'It is a', *Public School Verse 1923-24*, Heinemann, 1924. 18. 'The wagtails splutter', Fisher collection.
40 'went for long', FA 508. 'The pelvis', *Paris Review* 249. 'He fell in love', Pudney, *Cake*, 71. 'He would climb', Pudney, *Home*, 46. 'lectured me about', Pudney, *Cake*, 51. 'Wystan did not', Pudney, *Home*, 45. 'Wystan declared', ibid. 47.
41 'had made up', Davidson 128. 'Wystan perceived', TR 41. 'a confirmed anarchist', *Common Sense*, January 1940, 23. 'The Motor Bike', Fisher collection. 'a convenient hotel', WWW 34.
42 'hard upon a' and subsequent reminiscences by A.S.T. Fisher are from his unpubished memoir of Auden; see Appendix A. 'loud, confident', *Buried Day* 185.
43 'loosely put together', TR 46. 'volcano-like' and 'insufficient weaning', L & S 193. 'memorable speech' and 'no poetry', EA 327. 'he nearly always', Gardiner 15.
44 'We draw our squares', *Oxford Poetry 1926*, Blackwell, 1926, 6.
45 'the digestion', to CK [December 1941] (HRC). 'Boiled ham!' TR 245. 'his large, white', L & S 193. 'I just wanted', TR 113.
46 'True, he had', L & S 183. 'they were neither', 'efficient, imitative', and 'an essentially slapdash', ibid. 185.
47 'the sharpness and power', David Ayerst to the author, 14 April 1980. 'Either the print', EA 326. 'There were three', FA 511. 'that debauched', EA 195. 'I discovered', 'This left me', and 'the master decadents', *Strings* 103.
48 'As surely as', EA 437. 'Self-knowledge', WWW 46.
49 'You know what', Fisher. 'the pathetic thrill' and 'That is the right', to W.L. McElwee [*c*. August 1927] (British Library). 'There still lingers', to V.M. Allom [July 1927].
50 'Look here', Fisher collection. 'Genius is always' and 'You gauge Wystan', Fisher collection.
52 'out of sheer', FA 514. 'It happened that', ibid. 'Inflation in Germany', ibid. 511. 'I was not cut', FA 498.
53 'When I am', *Encounter*. April 1954, 3-4. 'I had no', FA 513. 'far too snooty', ibid. 'One morning', *For W.H. Auden, February 21, 1972*, ed. P.H. Salus and P.B. Taylor, Random House, 1972, 35. 'He was not', FA 513.
54 'Wanting to plan', *For W.H. Auden* (see note to p. 53), 35. 'a most bleak', EA 183. 'no use', unidentified newspaper interview dated November 1937, in the possession of Giles Auden. 'At his best', *From Anne to Victoria*, ed. B. Dobrée, Cassell, 1937, 105. 'pre-eminent in', *A Choice of Dryden's Verse*, ed. W.H. Auden, Faber, 1973, 9.

55 'really admired', TR 44. 'it was my', ACW 22. 'Wrenn was so much', unpublished interview with Robert H. Boyer, 11 January 1972. 'I do not remember', DH 41f. 'Anglo-Saxon and', ibid. 'In general the', to John Pudney [April 1931] (Berg). 'more intuitive', EA 182. 'My own recommendation', to ERD, 21 June [1968].

56 'If it is', *Observer*, 5 February 1961, 21. 'In addition to', ibid. 'curious and suggestive', L & S 191. 'guilty at being', FA 513. 'I knew very well', ibid. 'At nineteen', ibid. 514.

57 'chaste' and 'read it, at first', Tom Driberg, *Ruling Passions*, Cape, 1977, 58. 'Whatever its character', *Southern Review*, summer 1940, 83. 'I have torn up', *T.S. Eliot: A symposium*, ed. R. March and Tambimuttu, Editions Poetry, 1948, 82. 'Under such pines', *Oxford University Review*, 18 November 1926, 177. 'Love mutual has', *Oxford Poetry 1926*, Blackwell, 1926, 1-3.

58 'poetry is not', T.S. Eliot, *Selected Prose*, Penguin, 1953, 30. 'The poet must', *Buried Day* 157. 'dull canal . . . round', T.S. ELiot, *Collected Poems 1909-1962*. Faber, 1963, 70. 'Wystan's favourite', *Buried Day* 177. 'As likely as', ibid. 'Like Tennyson', to A.S.T. Fisher [1972].

59 'Six feet from', *Oxford Outlook*, June 1926, 180. 'one of the very', Spears 67. 'Hopkins ought to', John Lehmann, *The Whispering Gallery*, Longmans, 1955, 329. 'which one could', *Southern Review*, summer 1940, 85f. 'the greatest long poem', to P.H. Salus, 8 July [1965] (Berg). 'We groin with', *Oxford Poetry 1925*, Blackwell, 1925, 4.

60 'Themes for a', *Oxford Outlook*, May 1926, 120. 'The lips so apt', *Cherwell*, 22 May 1926, 130. 'Fine evenings always', *Oxford Magazine*, 19 June 1926, 8. 'We have endeavoured', *Oxford Poetry 1926*, Blackwell 1926, preface.

61 'My mother is', to David Ayerst [probably early September 1926]. 'Laughter is the', L & S 189. 'Of course, intellect's, ibid. 'merely experimenting', ibid. 190. 'he really wanted', ibid. '[Wystan], who was', ibid. 190f.

62 'they couldn't be', CAHK 42. 'yearningly romantic', ibid. 10.

63 'He intruded', L & S 194. 'fairly took', ibid. 195. 'found his shameless', ibid. 'unromantically, but', CAHK 197. 'stumpy immature', L & S 183. 'squat spruce body', EA 156. 'whenever an opportunity', CAHK 197. 'Their friendship', ibid.

64 'The value of', Christopher Isherwood to the author, 23 September 1979. 'I can never', John Betjeman, *Slick but not Streamlined*, Doubleday, 1948, 9.

65 'He was always', *Shenandoah*, Winter 1967, 47. 'I was not "in" ', *New York Review of Books*. 16 October 1967. 12. 'at an age when', ibid. 'If at Oxford', FA 512.

66 'Rex who looked', verse-letter to C. Day-Lewis [1929] (HRC). 'exceptional intelligence' and 'It was his', *Buried Day* 176. absolutely the *only*', L & S 214. 'the saga world', ibid. 215. 'I did not understand', TR 46. 'tripe', *Partisan Review*, November 1948, 1207. 'impressed themselves', TCVA 27.

67 'When he did', TR 125. 'who bans from recall', CP 668. 'one of Auden's', TCVA 31. 'manifestations of', DH 9f. 'If an undergraduate', DH 40. 'By nature I', transcript of radio discussion on 19 March 1941, in files of magazine *Decision* (Yale University Library). 'Always remember', to Caroline Newton [21 January 1943] (Berg). 'I am really', to SS [autumn 1940].

68 'really very kind', *Partisan Review*, November 1948, 1207. 'had what madmen', *Missing Persons* 123. 'perhaps best taken', *Buried Day* 177. 'knew its own', ibid. 178. 'learned a good deal' and 'Yeats as an', *Kenyon Review*, spring 1948, 187. 'my own verse', *Buried Day* 178. 'this tall dark', *Encounter*, November 1963, 48. 'You came away', *Strings* 114. 'You here?', British Library Add. MS. 59618.

69 'I had a', to David Ayerst [? January 1927]. 'Dearest Tante Hedwig': Auden's letters to Hedwig Petzold are in the Berg Collection. 'Of my stay', to W.L. McElwee [Easter 1927] (British Library).

70 'I had dinner', to Christopher Isherwood [probably June 1927]. 'I am very slow', EA xiii. 'On the whole', ibid. 'Here all is', to W.L. McElwee [summer 1927] (British Library). 'That day the', *Oxford Poetry 1927*, Blackwell, 1927. 'the formation', ibid. 5. 'Emotion is no', ibid. vi.

71 'I chose this lean country', EA 439f.

73 'I once went', *Badger* (Downs School magazine), autumn 1934, 22. 'On the frontier', EA 440. 'should be its', *Shenandoah*, Winter 1967. 47. 'Who stands, the crux', EA 22.

74 'Suppose they met', ibid. 'Nor was that final', ibid. 24. 'I am depressed', to W.L. McElwee [Easter 1927] (British Library). 'His sayings were', *For W.H. Auden* (see note to p. 53), 38. 'Calling on Auden', WWW 43f.

75 'towering angel', *Strings* 113. 'a group of', WWW 44. 'After I had', ibid. 44f. 'like an amateur', ibid. 88.

76 'mildly tormenting', ibid. 42. 'Because sap fell', EA 441. 'The snub-nosed', British Library Add. MS. 52430, fol. 65. 'Your peculiar', to Gabriel Carritt, 31 October [1931].

77 'Re the poem', ibid. 'I realise that', to Gabriel Carritt, 6 October 1930.'Auden, despite his', WWW 46.

78 'Mrs Carritt', TR 57. 'Auden's belief' and 'Never mind', TR 47. 'Dick. . . whose mind', verse-letter to C. Day-Lewis [1929] (HRC).

79 'Taller to-day', EA 26. 'seemed to be', to Monroe K. Spears, 21 July 1962.

80 'I am just', to W.L. McElwee [Good Friday, 1928] (British Library). 'Schools are becoming', to W.L. McElwee [probably Easter vacation, 1928] (British Library). 'a figure we', J.I.M. Stewart to the author, 27 July 1979.

81 'I didn't do', BBC television interview broadcast on 28 November 1965. 'It is hardly', DH 41, 43. 'Surprise has', unpublished memoir of Auden by V.M. Allom. 'My dear David', to David Ayerst [summer 1928].

82 'in Spa for', to David Ayerst [summer 1928]. 'They refuse to', EA xiii.

83 'Logical punctuation', LFI 109. 'I found many', *Missing Persons* 121. 'a game to', WWW 46. 'an intellectual', ibid. 52. 'a conceptualizer', TR 150. 'As you know', to SS [autumn 1940].

84 'my fiancée', to C. Day-Lewis, quoted in Sean Day-Lewis's biography of his father (1980). 'I knew no', FA 521. I am going', to David Ayerst [August 1928].

85 'wonderful German', *Oxford German Studies* I (1966), 166. 'revelling in', to EM, 1 March 1943.

86 'horrified at his' and other quotations from Layard's (at present unpublished) autobiography were made available through the kindness of James Greene. 'human nature is', Homer Lane, *Talks to Parents and Teachers*, Allen & Unwin, 1928, 130. ' "Be good and" ', EA 300.

87 'It is the impulse', D.H. Lawrence, *Fantasia of the Unconscious*, Penguin, 1971, 68, 83. 'It was his', DH 278. 'to grow straight', André Gide, *Fruits of the Earth*, Secker & Warburg, 1949, 151f.

88 'We are lived', CP 199. 'the It's attempts', Georg Groddeck, *The Unknown Self*, C.W. Daniel, 1929, 81. 'If the It', ibid. 'The way of sickness', ibid. 83. 'the suppression of rage', J.W. Layard, 'Malekula; Flying Tricksters. . .', *Journal of the Royal Anthropological Institute*, 1930, 521n. 'lack of spirituality', John Layard, *The Lady of the Hare*, Faber, 1944, 64.

89 'deceit of instinct', EA 21. 'the immense', EA 66. 'To those brought up', *Oxford and the Groups*, ed. R.H.S. Crossman, Blackwell, 1934, 97. 'fell for him' and other Layard quotations, see note to p. 86.

90 'During my first' and other quotations from the journal: Auden's Berlin journal is in the Berg Collection. 'I like sex', Layard's autobiography (see note to p. 86). 'The German' and 'Berlin is the', to Patience McElwee [December 1928] (British Library, filed with letters to W.L. McElwee). 'the most elemental', to C. Day-Lewis; see note to p. 84.

91 'I am having', to W.L. McElwee, 31 December 1928 (British Library). 'foiled creative fire', EA 215. 'this annoying' and 'The pure-in-heart', L & S 303f. 'I am perfectly', to Patience McElwee [December 1928] (British Library).

92 'Who'd have thought', recalled by Stephen Spender in conversation with the author, June 1979. The rhymes on psychosomatic illness are in a verse notebook now in the British Library (Add. MS. 52430). 'writing a text book', to Naomi Mitchison [April 1930] (Berg). The chart and 'Glossary' are in the notebook described above.

95 'goes to Eliot', to W.L. McElwee, 31 December 1928 (British Library). 'quite a brilliant' and 'This fellow', Bibliography 3. 'Damn this laziness', see note to p. 90. 'Should poets marry?', verse letter to C. Day-Lewis [1929] (HRC).

96 'I have moved', to W.L. McElwee, 31 December 1928 (British Library). 'From scars where', EA 28. 'We made all', EA 26. 'Christophers visit' and 'Pimping for someone', see note to p. 90. 'Before this loved one', EA 31.

97 'the only living', quoted in Laura Riding, *Collected Poems*, Cassell/Random House, 1938, xxii. 'X—ray eyes', CAHK 13. 'Boys had', see note to p. 90. 'Love by ambition', EA 30. 'It was Easter', EA 37.

98 'I have often thought', see note to p. 90. 'Give me ten', see note to p. 90. 'Do I want poetry', EA 301. 'What I cant', see note to p. 90.

99 'J — "You know" ', see note to p. 90. 'If he wants', Gardiner 11. 'I like the way', see note to p. 90.

100 'Does your friend', see note to p. 90. 'April 2nd', ibid. 'Ostensibly Wystan', see note to p. 86. 'I arrived', ibid.

101 'April 3rd', see note to p. 90. 'an exceedingly dirty', L & S 299.

102 'Walking home', EA 38. 'All this time', ibid. 'One suddenly realised', BBC television interview, broadcast on 28 November 1965.

103 'assumed vaguely', Gardiner 11. 'Upon this line' and 'Sentries against', EA 32, 33. 'His room was', CAHK 14.

104 'Read about us', ibid. 16. 'I loved my', to W.L. McElwee [summer 1929] (British Library). 'homesick for Germany', to John Layard [July 1929]. 'I know so', to EM [March 1943]. 'It is not', see note to p. 90. 'I am probably', to John Layard [29 July 1929]. 'As you know', to W.L. McElwee [summer 1929] (British Library).

105 'Many homosexuals' and 'I don't believe', *You May Well Ask* 122. 'Homosexuality is', ibid. 'The mere fact', *Criterion*, January 1933, 288f. A carbon typescript of 'The Enemies of a Bishop' is in the Berg Collection.

107 'very funny', to W.L. McElwee [summer 1929] (British Library). 'no more than' and 'The bishop is', TR 77. 'I manage to', to W.L. McElwee [summer 1929] (British Library).

108 'Being alone', EA 39. 'The unemployed', *Oxford and the Groups*, ed. R.H.S. Crossman, Blackwell, 1934, 94. 'I have sixpence', to John Layard [July 1929].

109 'Will you wheel', EA 35. 'Do you by', *You May Well Ask* 188. 'the stigmata', to John Layard [1930]. 'the thing turned', to John Layard [26 February 1930].

110 'to help me', ibid. 'I found', FA 517.

111 'Schoolmastering suits', to John Auden [summer 1930] (Berg). 'Now I'm up here', verse-letter to Gabriel Carritt [1930]. There is a MS. in Carritt's possession, and a version is in a verse notebook in the British Library (Add. MS. 53430). 'Twelve year old', Ansen.

112 'Born in Helensburgh', unpublished memoir of Auden at Larchfield by Norman Wright. 'He told me', Gardiner 14. 'to cut my', recalled by Gabriel Carritt in conversation with the author, summer 1979. 'this Wimbledon', *Buried Day* 190. 'the wicked city', Upward 14. 'I don't think', *You May Well Ask* 122. 'Compton Mackenzie', EA 106.

113 'Get there if', EA 48.
114 'Consider this', EA 46. 'So long as', *Listener*, 7 January 1965, 5.'The reason is', EA 302. 'must quote with', *Criterion*, April 1934, 497. 'I have never', *Listener*, 7 January 1965, 5. 'keep silent', DH 10. 'Make it a', to Anita Money [1965]. 'an unbook', *New York Review of Books*, 5 August 1965, 12. 'The one thing', DH 9.
115 'I had a', to John Auden [summer 1930] (Berg). 'I am much', to Naomi Mitchison [summer 1930] (Berg). 'Father Parker's', to John Auden [summer 1930] (Berg). 'Some suggestions', quoted in *Twentieth Century Literature*, December 1976, 278. 'I am writing', to John Auden [summer 1930] (Berg). 'I have nearly', *You May Well Ask* 119.
116 'Between attention', 'Doom is dark', and 'What's in your', EA 53, 55, 56. 'is so often', *Times Literary Supplement*, 19 march 1931, 221. 'As for Mr Auden', *Listener*, 29 October 1930, 711. 'Am I really', *You May Well Ask* 119. 'I find it', to ERD, 27 September [1968].
117 'Mr Auden's poetry', *Adelphi*, December 1930, 251f. 'Mr Auden's attempt', *Oxford Outlook*, March 1931, 59-61. 'The poems of the', *Week-end Review*, 25 October 1930, 592, 594. 'made a greater', Pudney, *Cake*, 52. 'how that pale', *Shenandoah*, Winter 1967, 43. 'There waited', *New Country*, ed. Michael Roberts, Hogarth Press, 1933, 232.
118 Dylan Thomas's copy of *Poems* is in the Humanities Research Center, University of Texas at Austin. 'Whatever its', P. Stansky & W. Abrahams, *Journey to the Frontier*, Constable, 1966, 164. 'It was Eliot', *T.S. Eliot, A study of his writings by several hands*, ed. B. Rajan, Dobson, 1947, 109. 'You might do', Stansky & Abrahams (see above), 174. 'Never write', to John Pudney [April 1931] (Berg). 'I shall never', to Edward Upward, 6 October 1930.
119 'When on my', Upward 20. 'I was walking' and 'put on a', ibid. 19. 'Having abdicated', EA 45.
120 The text of *The Orators* has been reprinted in EA.
121 'seems to me', quoted in Valerie Eliot to the author, 8 May 1980. 'Relieved of the', D.H. Lawrence, *Fantasia of the Unconscious*, Penguin, 1971, 88. 'One is clever', R.K. Gordon, *Anglo-Saxon Poetry*, Everyman, 1926, 349. 'Keep the girls', Lawrence (see above) 87.
122 'In a sense' and 'Formally I am', *You May Well Ask* 120f. 'The central theme', EX xxv.
123 'If it is not', *You May Well Ask* 122. 'I am now writing', ibid. 121. 'the situation seen', ibid.
124 'The genesis of', to 'Mrs Kuratt', 16 August [1932] (Lockwood Memorial Library, State University of New York, Buffalo). 'like a June', *Chronicle* 287.
126 'War breaks out!' General Ludendorff, *The Coming War*, Faber, 1931, 98.
128 'I shall be here', Upward 22.
129 'On the whole', to John Pudney [April 1931] (Berg). 'It is meant', EA xv.
130 'My name on' and 'My guess', introduction to 3rd ed. of *The Orators*, Faber, 1967. 'I have been', to Gabriel Carritt, 31 October [1931]. 'in sweat and blood', programme note by Spender to Cambridge Mummers' production of *The Orators*, 4 & 6 September [n.y.]. 'The second part', quoted in Valerie Eliot to the author, 8 May 1980. 'The school gathers', to Gabriel Carritt, 31 October [1931]. 'The house with', *You May Well Ask* 122f.
131 'The English', to Mrs Snodgrass [? 1933] (Berg). 'It's pleasant', EA 196. 'Those [homosexuals]', FA 451. 'My Helensburgh', to Gabriel Carritt, 31 October [1931]. 'Who goes with', EA 113. 'Please introduce', *You May Well Ask* 121.
132 'He had a', recalled by Arnold Snodgrass in conversation with the author, April 1979. 'Don't worry', ibid.
133 'I agree with', to Naomi Mitchison, 18 October 1932 (Berg). 'I've had a', EA xv. The first part of the poem 'A Happy New Year' is printed in EA 444-51.
134 'It's awfully important', HA 35. 'Lords of Limit' and other quotations from the second part of 'A Happy New Year', EA 115f. 'put a limit', D.H. Lawrence, *Apocalypse*, Martin Secker, 1932, 148.
135 'I have finished', *You May Well Ask* 123. 'Heard was reputed', P.N. Furbank, *E.M. Forster: A Life*, Vol. II, Secker & Warburg, 1978, 136. 'abstruse scientific', CAHK 83.
136 'noble amateur' and 'towards the really', *Times Literary Supplement*, 16 January 1976, 53. 'I didn't take', EA xv. 'Mr Auden is', *Criterion*, October 1932, 131-4. 'The subject of', *Oxford Magazine*, 10 November 1932, 158-9.
137 'He experiences', *Adelphi*, August 1932, 793-6. 'Eliot was warm', HA 38. 'I chiefly worry', T.S. Eliot to Herbert Read, 11 December 1930 (quoted by kind permission of Mrs Valerie Eliot). 'O, my magnet', EA 116f. 'friendly but' and 'I really want', *You May Well Ask* 118. 'uninteresting poetry' and 'bore', quoted in John Pearson, *Facades*, Macmillan, 1978, 299, 306. 'She's just like', to Arnold Snodgrass, 23 July 1932 (Berg).
138 'self-sufficient and', etc., *Theatre Newsletter*, 29 September 1951, 5.
139 'Rupert sometimes', 'an art only', and 'Rupert blanched', recalled by Robert Medley in conversation with the author, June 1980. 'Auden, Robert Medley', *Theatre Newsletter*, 29 September 1951, 5. 'a sort of', to AS, 28 July 1932 (Berg). 'I'm getting on', to Rupert Doone, 20 July 1932 (Berg). 'Have you a', to AS, 23 July 1932 (Berg). 'I have just', to AS [late July 1932] (Berg).
140 'As to jobs', to John Pudney, 28 July 1932 (Berg). 'Do come if', to AS, 28 July 1932 (Berg). 'Your subject is', to John Pudney, 27 July 1932 (Berg). 'wanted to see', Pudney, *Cake* 52. 'I know those', to John Pudney, 28 July 1932 (Berg). 'There were no', Pudney, *Cake* 42.
141 'My dear John', to John Pudney, 18 September 1932 (Berg). 'Here on the', EA 141.

468   W. H. Auden: A Biography

142 'Our money comes', *You May Well Ask* 123. 'This place is', to Iris and Alan Sinkinson, 4 October 1932 (Berg). 'It's funny to', ibid. 'once thought of', Ansen. 'frightfully busy', to Rupert Doone [autumn 1932] (Berg). 'fantastic', 'the reaction', and 'e.g. if they', EA 318. 'By all means', *Criterion*, July 1934, 705.

143 'To us his arrival', *Badger* (Downs School Magazine), Autumn 1974, 34. 'Auden's fists', *Chronicle* 71. 'His classes', *Badger* (as above).

144 'This place is', to Gabriel Carritt [autumn 1932]. 'Off to Oxford', to AS [autumn 1932] (Berg). 'I've written a', to Rupert Doone, 19 October 1932 (Berg). 'I'm getting to', to John Hayward, 28 July 1932 (King's College, Cambridge, Hayward Papers). The MS of 'In the year of my youth' is in the library of Swarthmore College, Pennsylvania. The poem has been published, with notes and commentary by Lucy McDiarmid, in *Review of English Studies*, n.s. XXIX, 115 (1978).

147 'I am very', *You May Well Ask* 123. 'I peg away', to AS [autumn 1932] (Berg). 'I have a handsome', EA 123. 'It is later than', ibid. 47.

148 'impressed by the', WWW 116. 'ambiguous position', CAHK 81. 'Comrades, who when', EA 120ff; the poem's textual variations are discussed in an appendix to EA.

150 'I have a handsome', EA 123.

151 'Does Mr Russell', EA 315. 'We live in', ibid. 317. 'dictator of' and 'liberalism is', *Criterion*, January 1933, 289. 'whoever possesses', ibid. 'If you are to', EA 317.

152 'Both are right', EA 341. 'Unless the Christian', ibid. 353. 'in its romantic', ibid. 405. 'The novelty and', *Modern Canterbury Pilgrims* 40. 'English Communism', unpublished interview for *Time* magazine by T.G. Foote, 1963. 'increasing attraction', EA 14. 'The book is', *Colby Library Quarterly*, December 1977, 276.

153 'He now outwardly', CAHK 181. 'a day-dream', transcript of radio discussion, March 1941, in files of magazine *Decision* (Yale University Library). 'old-fashioned social', EA 405. 'It was extremely', BBC television interview, broadcast on 28 November 1965. 'all facts and', DH 19. 'No. I am', to Rupert Doone [autumn 1932] (Berg). '*New Verse* came', *New Verse*, May 1939, 49. 'Why do you', to Geoffrey Grigson, 11 October 1932 (HRC).

155 'I am living', to AS, 21 February 1933 (Berg). 'the Auden Group', e.g. Julian Symons, *The Thirties*, Faber, 1975, 32. 'Look west, Wystan', *New Country*, ed. Michael Roberts, Hogarth, 1933, 223f.

156 'It is time', ibid. 11. 'communists with an', *Listener*, 14 June 1933, 958. 'the Communism of', *Scrutiny*, June 1933, 74. 'It was not', *Observer Magazine*, 20 June 1976, 17. 'What joins these', *New Verse*, March 1933, 15-17. 'Even when we', *Encounter*, November 1963, 48. 'Where there's neither', EA 133.

157 rebuild our cities', EA 136. 'The fruit in', EA 148. 'Turn not towards', ibid. 146.

158 'At the far end', EA 147. 'The girl whose', *Poets at Work*, introduced by Charles D. Abbott, Harcourt Brace, 1948, 175. 'I have my', to W.L. McElwee [summer 1927] (British Library).

159 'Coming out of', EA 37. 'Blessing this moon', ibid. 147. 'completely changed', Gardiner 14. 'I used to', to an unidentified correspondent, 8 November 1937 (HRC). 'He loved family', unpublished memoir of Auden by Maurice Feild.

160 'He did not worry', *Badger* (Downs School magazine), autumn 1974, 33. 'For a fortnight', ibid., autumn 1934, 4. 'for the authenticity' and 'One fine summer', FA 69f.

161 'I had done', FA 70. 'any large-scale', *Oxford and the Groups*, ed. R.H.S. Crossman, Blackwell, 1934, 100. 'Love has allowed', EA 319.

162 'Out on the lawn', EA 136ff.

163 'redeemer', EA 148. 'there are no poor', ibid. 146. 'They came on', TR 14. 'I wonder', to Mrs Snodgrass [? 1933] (Berg). 'They show a', MS. of Harold Nicolson's diary, entry for 18 July 1933 (Balliol College Library, Oxford; quoted by kind permission of Nigel Nicolson and Messrs Collins). 'The idea is', Harold Nicolson, *Diaries and Letters, 1930-1939*, Collins, 1966, 153.

164 'In Hitler's', *New York Review of Books*, 31 August 1972, 6.

165 'the whole of modern', L & S 215.

166 'thin', *Times Literary Supplement*, 15 March 1934, 190. 'The Dance of', *You May Well Ask* 125.

167 'a great success', *You May Well Ask* 125. 'because he's', CAHK 125. 'Wystan's funeral', conversation with the author, June 1979. 'a return to', *New Statesman*, 3 March 1934, 303.

168 'surprisingly juvenile', *New English Weekly*, 12 April 1934, 617. 'memorable speech', EA 327. 'We shall do', ibid. 328. 'It is bound', *Scrutiny*, September 1935, 306-8.

169 'being run by', *Badger*, autumn 1934, 22. 'stimulated I believe', *You May Well Ask* 124. 'Hate Switzerland', *Badger*, spring 1935, 18. 'Personally give me', ibid., autumn 1934, 22. 'The epic has', *You May Well Ask* 124. 'I'm getting on', to Rupert Doone & Robert Medley, 5 August 1934 (Berg). All quotations from 'The Chase' are taken from the carbon typescript which is in the library of Exeter College, Oxford (MS. 198).

171 'Am just finishing', to Alan and Iris Sinkinson [January 1935] (Berg). 'the most important', *Oxford German Studies* I (1966), 169. 'tour of contemporary', ibid. 170.

172 'suggestions towards', *Huntington Library Quarterly*, August 1968, 378. 'It has gradually', Finney 108.

173 'rather like a', *Times Literary Supplement*, 11 July 1935, 108. '*The Dog Beneath*', *Spectator*, 28 June 1935, 1112. 'Glad you liked', to AS [July 1935] (Berg). 'I want to', to Michael Roberts [5 April 1935] (Berg). 'Last term was', to AS [December 1934] (Berg).

174 'New boy', MS. in the possession of Maurice and Alexandra Feild. 'was largely due', *Badger,* spring 1935, 19. 'a power behind', to Alan and Iris Sinkinson [January 1935] (Berg). 'Am probably going', ibid. 'I'm off to', to Michael Roberts [5 April 1935] (Berg). 'wrote a letter', to Michael Roberts [22 April 1935] (Berg).

175 'I am very', ibid. 'at once acid', Klaus Mann, *The Turning Point,* Gollancz, 1944, 216. 'turned the globe', CAHK 156. 'honoured, excited', ibid. 157.

176 'was living in', Gavin Ewart, speech at PEN International, London, 21 May 1980. 'Isherwood wrote', and other quotations from Austin Wright: these are taken from Austin Wright to Maurice Feild, 12 May 1977, subsequently revised by Mr Wright in correspondence with the author, 1980. 'It is so kind', *New Review,* March 1977, 42. 'Darling, how lovely', anecdote told to the author by James Stern.

177 'I didn't see', Finney, 120.

178 'I'm leaving teaching', to AS [July 1935] (Berg). 'relaxed and', *Musical Times,* November 1963, 779. 'What immediately', MS. by Auden on Britten and the GPO film unit, in possession of Stephen Spender. 'the most amazing', Charles Osborne, *W.H. Auden, the Life of a Poet,* Eyre Methuen, 1980, 109.

179 'Poetry is not', EA 329. 'Our hopes were', 'the word is', 'private joking' and 'every flabby', ibid. 156.

180 'Louder to-day' and 'Make action', EA 156f. 'I have no great', *Grierson on Documentary,* ed. Forsyth Hardy, Collins, 1946, 12. 'make a drama', 'a little worried' and 'crystallise sentiments', ibid. 15. 'We gradually', ibid. 12.

181 'My salary is', to ERD [autumn 1935]. 'I didn't see', Sussex 66. 'Hewer, inspector', transcribed from soundtrack of *Coal Face* (print in National Film Archive, British Film Institute, London).

182 'even the producer', John Lehmann, *Thrown to the Woolfs,* Weidenfeld & Nicolson, 1978, 52. 'bloody dark', Sussex 76. 'incoherent in', *Sight and Sound,* Winter 1935-6, 177. 'We'd seen the rough', Sussex 70. 'all the Scotch', to AS [July 1935]. 'This is the night mail' and 'Uplands heaped', EA 290.

183 'No picture', Sussex 7. 'So we had', ibid. 73.'didn't give a' and 'He was just', ibid. 67. 'no fool', Basil Wright in conversation with the author, March 1979. 'one of the most', ibid.

184 'There, on that', Sussex 71. 'I don't see', Basil Wright in conversation with the author, March 1979. 'I found it', Sussex 72.

185 'We had to', *France-Grande Bretagne,* July-August 1939, 229. The fragment of the script from the film *Negroes* is at the Humanities Research Center, University of Texas at Austin. 'a most elaborate', manuscript in possession of Stephen Spender.

186 'it turned out', ibid. 'some wonderful', ibid. 'just contributed', *Janus,* May 1936, 12. 'Wystan . . . is leaving', Isherwood to John Lehmann, 10 October 1935 (HRC). 'impressed and amused', Golo Mann to the author, 10 May 1979. 'the best brief', *Town Crier* (Birmingham), 14 October 1938, 2. 'a profound sense', *Saturday Review of Literature,* 8 June 1940, 14.

187 'Who's the most', information from Edward Mendelson, who obtained it from Chester Kallman. 'nothing but', Golo Mann to the author, 10 May 1979. 'Since I saw you', to HP [January 1938]. 'horrible London', LFI 217. 'vital brains' and 'appalling inferiority', *Times Literary Supplement,* 15 February 1980, 180. 'No doubt', Isherwood to the author, 17 April 1980.

188 'Underneath the', EA 160. 'For my friend', LFI 238. 'dark caressive', EA 162. 'They were not', Sir Peter Pears to the author, 24 April 1980. 'If there was', Isherwood to the author, 17 April 1980.

189 'so much talent', E.W. White, *Benjamin Britten,* Boosey & Hawkes, 1954, 23. 'is not the', EA 356. 'to live' and 'As Auden's', *World Film News,* April 1936.

190 'a political', pamphlet in Group Theatre archive (Berg). 'It is pointed', *Theatre Arts Monthly,* December 1935, 906f. The production script of *The Dog Beneath the Skin* is in the Berg Collection, New York Public Library.

191 'I'm very depressed', to AS [January 1936]. 'an entertaining', *Times,* 31 January 1936. 'one of the', *Daily Worker,* 7 February 1936. Remarks from the *Observer* and the *Sunday Times* were quoted in advertisements for the play in *The Times* during February 1936. 'the bareness', *New Statesman,* 8 February 1936, 188.

192 'Mr Auden is', *New Verse,* February-March 1936, 15. 'private weakness', *Paris Review* 260. 'it had now', CAHK 179. 'It's exciting', *Paris Review* 260. Wystan hasn't', CAHK 180.

193 'I wonder if', FA 480. 'the truly strong', F6 37.

194 'Wystan writing', CAHK 179. 'Our respective', ibid. 180. laughter, lost', ibid. 179. 'the horrible old', ibid.

195 'You know your', F6 58. 'I knew that', interview for BBC television, broadcast on 28 November 1965. 'During lunch', TR 60.

196 'holy ground', LFI 8. 'What are buggers', P.N. Furbank, *E.M. Forster: A Life,* Vol. II, Secker & Warburg, 1978, 213.

197 'It's on Thomas', ibid. 'has something about', *New Writing,* Autumn 1936, 201. 'fine', EA 169. 'And the great', ibid. 203. 'Most of the', LFI 25. 'a very miserable', ibid. 106. 'at ruinous', ibid. 'the stock', ibid. 108.

198 'fell right over', LFI 142. 'shocked an', ibid. 'a little boy', ibid. 181. 'It varies', ibid. 40. 'I must have', ibid. 'handsome, sunburnt', ibid. 136. 'like a small', ibid. 106. 'neither clever', ibid. 140.

'any average', ibid. 110. 'not nearly so', ibid. 184. 'Frank Morley', quotation kindly supplied by Mrs Valerie Eliot.

199 'Morley's suggestion', ibid. 'On the analogy', EA xviii. 'To my great', LFI 113. 'Have just heard', ibid. 121. 'Europe is absent', EA 203. 'boiling over', LFI 137. 'I suddenly', LFI 139f.

200 'a kind of', LFI 144. 'I wish I', ibid. 145. 'The moment we', ibid. 142. 'home for', ibid. 145. 'so boring', ibid. 146. 'a mutual', *Encounter*, November 1963, 49. 'fake feelings', *Listener*, 24 October 1963, 646. 'funny, observant' and 'I have very', *Encounter* (as above). 'get the focus', LFI 31.

201 'Ora pro nobis', EA 188. 'Like something', LFI 161. 'Perhaps they', TR 61. 'he moves', TR 62. 'a party after', ibid. 'very large', LFI 159. 'Though heaven', TR 63. '*the* democratic', LFI 135. 'would stumble', TR 63.

202 'everything he touches', LFI 166. 'I must be', EA 190. 'We are all', LFI 28.

203 'He upset', Marie-Jaqueline Lancaster (ed.), *Brian Howard: Portrait of a Failure*, Anthony Blond, 1968, 373. 'a colossal', *Left Review*, November 1936, 779–82. 'more like a', Finney 163.

204 'Isherwood and', to Bennett Cerf, 6 October 1936 (Butler). 'Revised edition', to AS [Christmas 1936]. 'Faber invented', to Bennett Cerf [*c.* November 1936] (Butler). 'a remarkable development', *Left Review* (see note to p. 203). 'It is Mr Auden', *Listener*, 30 December 1936, 1257. 'He has no', *Scrutiny*, December 1936, 323–7. 'As regards the', to Bennett Cerf, 6 October 1936 (Butler).

205 'They are all', TR 101. Auden's commentary for *The Way to the Sea* has been transcribed (with different punctuation) and published in Donald Mitchell, *Britten & Auden in the Thirties*, Faber, 1981, 90–93. 'Am up to', *You May Well Ask* 124. 'Louis has done', to ERD, 8 December 1936.

206 'I'm looking for', to Naomi Mitchison [autumn 1936] (Berg). 'I've decided', to ERD [December 1936]. Quotations from Day-Lewis, Spender and Warner are taken from Hugh Thomas, *The Spanish Civil War*, Pelican, 3rd ed., 1977, 347. 'We had a', ibid., 453. 'I so dislike', to ERD [December 1936].

207 'I am not one', to ERD, 8 December 1936. 'to help me', ibid. 'either ambulance-driving', CAHK 195, 'I'm going to', to Frederic Prokosch [January 1937] (Berg). 'I'm off in', to AS [Christmas 1936].

208 'I shall ride the', EA 209. 'Wystan hasn't', Donald Mitchell, *Britten and Auden in the Thirties*, Faber, 1981, 141. 'Certainty, fidelity', EA 207. 'Famous poet, Samuel Hynes, *The Auden Generation*, Bodley Head, 1976, 251.

209 'a solemn', CAHK 197. 'The politics', unpublished interview for *Time* by T.G. Foote, 1963. 'I found', *Modern Canterbury Pilgrims* 41.

210 'The feeling was', ibid. 'Since the Government', EA 361. 'The foreign', ibid. 'waited around' *Time* interview (see note to p. 209). 'running everything' and 'always stopped', ibid. 'They didn't give me', *New York Times Magazine*, 8 August 1971, 101ff.

211 'a mercy for', Michael Yates to the author, 4 February 1979. 'go to the front', *Oxford Review*, 11–12 (n.d.), 51. 'bureaucratic wall', *Albion* (Elmira, New York), IV, 1 (1972), 7.

212 'Everywhere there', EA 361.

213 'a small' and 'I only met', Arthur Koestler, *The Invisible Writing*, Collins, 1954, 336f. 'Auden, who', TR 69. 'Auden retired', TR 70. 'He has always', *Nine*, Autumn 1950, 344–6.

214 'Just seeing what', *Time* interview (see note to p. 209). 'for I think', to SS [February 1937]. 'to the front', *Time* interview (see note to p. 209).

215 'Between January', George Orwell, *Homage to Catalonia*, Penguin, 1966, 25. 'When you gave', ibid. 19. 'the futility', ibid. 26. 'If all goes', Constance Orwell to P.E.N., 20 January 1937 (HRC). 'He was unwilling', CAHK 201. 'He returned', WWW 213. 'I did not wish', Hugh D. Ford, *A Poet's War*, University of Pennsylvania Press, 1965, 288. 'I was shocked', *Time* interview (see note to p. 209).

216 'Since 1930', Orwell, op. cit. (see note to p. 215), 174. 'I suppose', ibid. 173. 'the most notable', quoted in newspaper advertisements for *The Ascent of F6*. 'He delivers his', *New English Weekly*, 11 March 1937, 433. 'My *dear*', CAHK 201. 'magnificent', W.B. Yeats to Rupert Doone, 18 March [1937] (Berg).

217 'conveyed the ascetic', *New Statesman*, 1 July 1929, 13. 'We never did', *Bibliography* 21. 'These changes', Christopher Caudwell, *Illusion and Reality*, 2nd ed., Lawrence & Wishart, 1946, 271. 'the most important', *New Verse*, May 1937, 22. The original text of *Spain* is in SP 51–55.

218 'A war is', 'The Prolific and the Devourer', MS at HRC.

219 'An organic', *New Verse*, May 1937, 22. 'a reflection', ibid., November 1937, 22. 'to whom murder', George Orwell, *Inside the Whale*, Gollancz, 1940, 169. (Orwell's essay was previously published separately, and may have been read by Auden before he revised the poem; see Bernard Crick's biography of Orwell.) 'I was *not*', Spears 157.

220 'I have my', to Nancy Cunard [summer 1937] (HRC). 'I support the', *Authors Take Sides on the Spanish War*, Left Review, 1937, 6. 'Support for the', ibid. 'refused to see', TR 125.

221 'Whenever I feel', introduction to Paul Valéry, *Analects*, transl. S. Gilbert, Princeton University Press, 1970, xvii. 'Frogs don't', TR 96. 'The French', Ansen. 'one of the', to Alfred A. Knopf, 15 December 1939 (HRC). 'Well here I', to AS [summer 1937]. 'The improper', EA 217.

222 'Victor was', Ansen. 'Life remains', EA 228. 'the only categories', *Morning Post*, 5 July 1937.

223 'a man of', Constance Babington Smith, *John Masefield: A Life*, Oxford University Press, 1978, 202. 'I met W.H. Auden', internal memorandum, 30 July 1937, in files of the Oxford University Press; quoted by kind permission of the Delegates.

224 'For the first', *Modern Canterbury Pilgrims* 41. 'I had met', ibid. 'You're quite right' and 'This conversation', Stephen Spender, *The Thirties and After,* Fontana, 1978, 31. 'Wystan is grubbier', Harold Nicolson, *Diaries and Letters,* Collins, 1966, 310.

225 'distracted and' and 'to save money', John Lehmann, *Thrown to the Woolfs,* Weidenfeld & Nicolson, 1978, 55. 'crowded with', CAHK 215. 'we'll have a', ibid.

226 'I make enough', to HP [January 1938]. 'the anti-heroic', Christopher Isherwood, *Down There on a Visit,* Methuen, 1962, 177. 'examples permanent', *Scrutiny,* December 1934, 303-6. 'emerging from', Furbank (see note to p. 196), 211n. 'And the cry', EA 223.

227 'I feel I', to Dilys Powell [1936] (HRC). 'long for a', *Spectator,* 18 November 1938, 858.

228 'Our play nearly', reproduced in facsimile in Upward. 'Isherwood and I', *Bibliography* 35. 'The last scene', to J.M. Keynes, 9 October 1937 (King's College, Cambridge).

229 'It is a nuisance', to J.M. Keynes, 18 November 1937 (King's College, Cambridge). 'I'm going to', to John Mulgan [autumn 1937] (Oxford University Press).

230 'growing respectability' and 'I rather wish', *New Verse,* autumn 1938, 14f. The quotations from 'Sixteen Comments on Auden', *New Verse,* November 1937, 23-9. 'the Auden Age', ibid., March 1938, 19. 'Usually they praise', Yanovsky 115.

231 'Praise? Unimportant', CP 582. 'Some of us', FA 413.

232 'That man is', script of 'Hadrian's Wall' in BBC Written Archives. 'both rather', MS in possession of Stephen Spender. 'belonged to that', Pudney, *Cake* 53. 'All Mr Auden's', Mrs. A.E. Dodds to John Mulgan, 5 February 1938 and 31 March 1938 (Oxford University Press). 'I keep waking up', to AED, 20 April [1938].

233 'When it comes', EA 231. 'Wystan in tears ', CAHK 227. 'the writer howling', EA 148. 'You've got to', telephone conversation with the author, September 1979.

234 'For me personally', Ansen. 'huge hurt', EA 232. 'The Pyramids', to AED [January 1937]. 'The Indian', TR 72. 'No, he discovers', EA 231. 'This whole enormous', JTAW 18.

235 'At that moment', JTAW 22. 'The Chinese', to AED, 20 April [1938]. 'Today, Auden and', JTAW 39. 'a big, mad', TR 94. 'mere trippers', JTAW 43. 'stand up straight', ibid. 48. 'The bottom seemed', ibid. 9.

236 'By this evening', ibid. 'one of the', to AED, 20 April [1938]. 'Do you always', JTAW 51. 'I thought perhaps', ibid. 55. 'looks like a', to AED, 20 April [1938]. 'The greatest probability', *New Republic,* 1 June 1938, 97. 'A Chinese', *Listener,* 2 February 1939, 247. 'Nothing is going', CAHK 225.

237 'slept deeply', JTAW 65. 'much to our', ibid. 86. 'I have to keep', TR 74. 'Careful, careful', CAHK 228. 'Collectively we most', JTAW 94. 'found ourselves', ibid. 104.

238 'were interrupted', ibid. 'You look', ibid. 105. 'knows he won't', Finney 139. 'The rich and', JTAW 151. 'admiring younger', CAHK 226. 'Looking for the', to AED, 20 April [1938]. 'War is', *Listener* (see note to p. 236). 'It was all', JTAW 169. 'After two', to AED, 20 April [1938]. 'insured with', CAHK 180.

239 'We've been on', JTAW 222. 'That is certainly', ibid. 235. 'afternoon holidays', CAHK 229. 'I thought it', to ERD, 1 February 1944. 'a tourist's', *New Republic,* 6 December 1939, 208f. 'China was utterly', *Time* interview (see note to p. 209).

240 'Am having a', to John Mulgan [August 1938] (Oxford University Press). 'so gay and', to AED, 29 August 1938. 'I don't', to AED, 31 August 1938. 'Are the enclosed', to AED, 5 September 1938.

241 'A race of', EA 256. 'the local', ibid. 164. 'Men are', ibid. 268. 'O teach', ibid. 169. 'Have finished', to AED [September 1938]. 'with a happy', *Common Sense,* January 1940, 23f.

242 'Well, my', CAHK 240. 'Please let me', to AED [autumn 1938]. 'But they were', CAHK 241.

243 'Chuck all this', to John Pudney, 18 September 1932 (Berg). 'The English have', FA 382. 'I felt the', interview for BBC television, broadcast on 28 November 1965.

244 'the old pre-industrial', EA 368. 'a democracy in', ibid. 'What England can', to AED [July 1939].

245 'You can only', to Henry Treece [autumn 1937]. 'A selfish pink', EA 190. 'All desire', EA 177. 'man is not', *New Era in Home and School,* January 1939, 7. 'I get very', to AED [autumn 1938]. 'the Popular Front', CAHK 248. 'to regard', *Nation,* 23 September 1944, 355.

246 'Patriots? Little boys', CP 592. 'I came to', Ansen. 'The subject is', Finney 139. 'an indisputable', *Manchester Guardian,* 16 November 1938. 'not entirely', *Spectator,* 18 November 1938, 858. 'not exploited', *New Verse,* January 1939, 24f.

247 'passed away', CAHK 244. 'none of them', *Paris Review* 260. 'what most people', *Times Literary Supplement,* 5 November 1938, 712. 'the travellers', ibid., 14 July 1978, 798. 'I am sorry', to AED [autumn 1938]. 'mean the last', to T.C. Worsley [*c.* 1940] (Butler). 'a public', *Spectator,* 24 March 1939, 498.

248 'Even at the', David Gascoyne, *Paris Journal, 1937-1939,* Enitharmon Press, 1978, 104. 'It would make', to AED, 15 December 1938. 'Pierre is a', to John Lehmann, 30 December 1938. 'My next toast', typescript in the possession of John Lehmann.

249 'I leave for', to John Mulgan [January 1939] (Oxford University Press). 'Well, we're off', CAHK 247.

253 'There they stood', CAHK 251f. 'a little farouche', to ERD, 21 August [n.y., 1950s].

254 'one of the', to AED, n.d. 'Say this city', CP 210. 'our poet', HA 10. 'a "cult" figure', ibid. 48. 'The fact remains', *Kenyon Review,* winter 1939, 45. 'Auden's coming', *We Moderns: Gotham Book*

Mart 1920–40, catalogue no. 42, 12. 'I cannot expect', *New York Times,* 12 March 1939, 24 (not in final edition). 'Will you sit', to AED [1939].

255 'The words of a', EA 242. 'We in England', *New York Times,* 5 April 1939, 10. 'we personally behave', *Bookseller's Quarterly,* May 1939, 8.

256 'If we interpret', ibid. 'my change' and 'The real decision', to AED [11 July 1939]. 'Never, *never*', to AED [May 1939]. 'Art is a product', EA 393. 'I believe Socialism', 'The Prolific and the Devourer', MS at HRC.

257 'We're pretty', to ERD, 17 March 1939. 'The place was', Jonathan Fryer, *Isherwood,* New English Library, 1977, 191. 'the wrong blond', ibid. 'Wystan is', *Advoate* 24.

258 'It takes ten days', Chester Kallman, *Absent and Present,* Wesleyan University Press, 1963, 49. 'Mothers have much', verse-letter to Chester Kallman, Christmas Day 1941 (HRC). 'She promised', recalled in Dorothy Kallman to the author, 13 May 1980. 'if not a', David Jackson to the author, 5 May 1979.

259 'He loved you', Dorothy Kallman to the author, 13 May 1980. 'Of course I know', to AED [11 July 1939]. 'a quick cold', CP 334.

260 'There are two', EA 362. 'I've spent years', to AED [11 July 1939]. 'He is a far', *Advocate* 25. 'I think you', Chester Kallman to Auden, 9–10 March [1943 ?]. 'It is in', verse-letter to Chester Kallman, Christmas Day 1941 (HRC). 'to absorb Chester', Dorothy Kallman to the author, 7 July 1979. 'Among those whom', DH 372.

261 'Take back your', TR 177. 'anal passive', FA 327. 'It is clear', FA 310. 'He has selected', *Partisan Review,* January/February 1953, 84. 'to think that', BBC radio interview with Auden, Kallman and Hans Werner Henze, recorded on 17 July 1961. 'the great Mozart', *Opera,* January 1961, 12. 'My chief', to AED, 28 February 1940.

262 'I've become a', to T.C. Worsley [*c.*1940] (Butler). 'the greatest and', *English Institute Annual,* 1940, 5. 'the top composers', notes by Alan Ansen on a lecture by Auden at the New School for Social Research (Berg). 'No gentleman', TR 178. 'Auntie Whizz', to Alan Ansen, n.d. (Berg). 'Who are we?', Ansen. 'Chester, my chum', CP 650. 'the greatest', James Merrill to the author, May 1979. 'what reason have you', *Hika* (Kenyon College), June 1939, 9. 'marriage', to AED [11 July 1939]. 'our honeymoon', to AED [29 May 1939]. 'l'affaire C', to Alan Ansen, 27 August [1947] (Berg).

263 'For now I have'. CP 203. 'and we / The life-long', AT 61. 'May this bed', EA 454. 'You are to me', verse-letter to Chester Kallman, Christmas Day 1941 (HRC). 'Nicest and best', to Edward Kallman, 7 August 1939 (HRC).

264 'I have suddenly', Finney 173. 'He employs', Joel Roache, *Richard Eberhart,* Oxford University Press (New York) 1971, 104.

265 'He would make', ibid. 104f. 'In the dining hall', HA 30. 'the chemical life', CAHK 234. 'the regime of', to SS, 12 April 1942 (King's College, Cambridge). 'S.O.S. repeat', to Alan Ansen, n.d. (Berg). 'It sets out', to AED [May 1939]. 'unbelievably low', to T.C. Worsley [*c.*1940] (Butler).

266 'He is very', Roache, op. cit. (see note to p. 264), 105. 'Now when my', *Hika* (see note to p. 262), 9. 'I will have', to AED [May 1939]. 'My heart is', to John Lehmanns, 9 June 1939 (HRC). 'Dear John', to John Layard [1939].

267 'honeymoon greetings', to John Auden [1939] (Berg). 'We had a terrific', to Edward Kallman, 5 July 1939 (HRC). 'It was standing', ibid. 'Up the road', to AED [11 July 1939]. 'Here we are', ibid. 'It is just', to AED [May 1939].

268 'Few of the' and 'Artists and politicians', EA 403. Quotations from the unpublished portions of 'The Prolific and the Devourer' are taken from the MS at HRC.

271 'Chester's heart', to AED, 7 August 1939. 'I've been hard', ibid. 'It's lovely', to Edward Kallman, 7 August 1949 (HRC). 'Done a lot', to AED [29 August 1939]. 'There is a radio', ibid.

272 'Whenever I', *Common Sense,* January 1940, 24.

273 'I sit in', EA 245.

274 'Some politicians', quoted in John Fuller, *A Reader's Guide to W.H. Auden,* Thames and Hudson, 1970, 259. 'The day war', to AED [1939]. 'There is one way', *Nation,* 7 October 1939, 386. 'Man is aware', ibid., 9 September 1939, 273. 'How are you?', to AED, 26 November 1939.

276 'Ben and Peter', unpublished account of Britten and Pears in America by Caroline Seebohm. 'Dearest and best', to EM (n.d.). 'learned peacefulness', CP 193. 'despite a certain', Yanovsky 123. 'I am hard', to AED, 26 November 1939.

277 'the development of', *Paul Bunyan,* Faber Music, 1978, ix. The quotations from the libretto of *Paul Bunyan* are taken from the vocal score (Faber, 1978).

278 'knew nothing', MS in possession of Stephen Spender. 'What a breath', Seebohm (see note to p. 276). 'I do hope', to EM and others, 22 February 1940 (Berg). 'This house has', to AED, 27 October 1939. 'I've just done', to AED, 26 November 1939.

279 'When you consider', HA 31. 'It is a', to AED, 26 November 1939. 'I rise at', to T.C. Worsley [*c.*1940] (Butler). 'Only the Hitlers', TR 173. 'the surest way', DH 41. 'To achieve anything', *New York Times Book Review,* 4 February 1951, 3. 'too much so', Yanovsky 108.

280 'one of the nicest', to ERD 21 August [n.y., 1950s]. 'Compared with children', to AED, 26 November 1939. 'It isn't that', to AED [1940]. 'The truth is not', *Washington Post,* 5 November

1978, magazine section, 20ff.
281 'as a British', information from Auden's correspondence with Random House (Butler). 'Just got back', to AED, 26 November 1939. 'I am a', TR 104. 'We are very' and 'some material which', to AED, 27 October 1939. 'I haven't started', to AED, 26 November 1939.
282 'Nature never intended', DH 317. 'the unspeakable', ibid. 323. 'not very good', to T.C. Worsley [c.1940] (Butler). 'the first feature', *Common Sense,* January 1940, 23f. 'I never wish' and 'For the first', EA xx. 'I wondered', *New York Times Magazine,* 8 August 1971, 10ff.
283 'There had to be', TR 89. 'The English', ibid. 102. 'The whole trend' *Decision,* January 1941, 50. 'Either we serve', EA 460.
284 'All mankind', Charles Williams, *The Descent of the Dove,* Eerdmans, 1964, 69. 'The history of', ibid. 1. 'reconciled the', ibid. 235.
285 'He said he just', Charles Williams to Michal Williams, 12 March 1940 (Wade Collection, Wheaton College, Illinois). 'one day the *Dove*', Charles Williams to Michal Williams, 16 October 1940 (Wade Collection). 'Am reading Kierkegaard's', to ERD, 11 March 1940. 'knocked the conceit', recalled by Oliver Sacks in conversation with the author, New York, May 1979. 'bowled over', FA 183.
286 'alone with his' and 'he finally chooses', Louis Dupré, *Kierkegaard as Theologian,* Sheed & Ward, 1963, 48. 'a leap into', ibid. 101. 'in a tentative', *Modern Canterbury Pilgrims* 41. 'Dear Elizabeth', to EM, 1 January 1940.
287 'The one infallible', *Common Sense,* March 1940, 25.
288 'Your poem creeps', to EM, 22 February 1940. 'writing a longish', to AED, 28 February 1940. 'We both fully', G.A. Auden to ERD, 28 December 1939 (Bodleian). 'For the past', to ERD, 16 January 1940.
289 'You may speak', ibid. 'I like it here', *You May Well Ask* 26.
290 'War or no war', to ERD [1940]. 'the most important', *Horizon,* February 1940, 68-9.
291 'I think it meant', to AED, 28 February 1940. 'four of our', Furbank (see note to p. 196), 238. 'This Europe', ibid. 'why Americans should', *Daily Mail,* 27 May 1941. 'Poetical faces', *Daily Mirror,* 15 August 1940. 'whether British citizens', Furbank (see above), 329f.
292 'There is no', TR 101. 'I went to', to AED [1940]. 'If I thought', to SS, 13 March 1941.
294 'I've finished', to AED, 21 April 1940.
295 'quite a good', to AED [1940]. 'lovely', to EM [1940]. 'We are, I know', Williams, op. cit. (see note to p. 284), 192. 'Nice house but', to Mina Curtiss [1940] (Berg). 'they liked each', Golo Mann to the author, 10 May 1979.
296 'serious friendship', ibid. 'I keep thinking', to AED [summer 1940]. 'to use any', ibid. 'getting on with', ibid. 'I am trying', to Charles Williams, 14 July 1940 (Wade Collection, Wheaton College, Illinois).
297 'making some absolute', TR 105. 'On Sundays', ibid. 102. 'O here and now', CP 294. 'when the grounds', FA 179.
298 'The Real is', CP 274. *'Credo ut',* CP 169. 'I am not', TR 90f. 'heard', CP 583. 'The serious part', FA 470. 'Do you believe', *Paris Review* 168. 'a joke', *New Yorker,* 19 March 1955, 130. 'It does make', TR 108.
299 'seems idle', CP 509. 'curiously theoretical', WWW 258. 'His religion', CAHK 249.' 'Make me chaste', CP 466. 'Never will his', CP 232. (The text in *The Double Man* (1941) has: 'Never will his sex belong / To his world of right and wrong, / Its libido comprehend / Who is foe and who is friend.') 'At first the', EA 394.
300 'Augustinian, not', TR 106. 'To avoid despair', *New Statesman,* 1 March 1952, 249. 'Agape is the, *Theology,* November 1950, 412. 'It is through', verse-letter to Chester Kallman, Christmas Day 1941 (HRC). 'Although I love', CP 244.
301 'Neo-Calvinist', to 'Bill', 13 November 1943 (HRC), 'Truth is catholic', TR 99. 'Anglo-Catholic though', TR 106. 'the dance', CP 485. 'the spirit of carnival', *New York Times,* 2 February 1971, 37.
302 'Wouldn't it', TR 116. 'I like to think', ibid.
303 'I am incapable', John Lehmann, *Thrown to the Woolfs,* Weidenfeld & Nicolson, 1978, 77.
304 'our menagerie', *Encounter,* November 1963. 49. 'It's a boarding', Virginia Spencer Carr, *The Lonely Hunter,* Doubleday, 1975, 123. 'sordid beyond belief', Seebohm (see note to p. 276). 'He would preface', Paul Bowles, *Without Stopping,* Putnam, 1972, 233. 'George naked', recalled by James Stern in conversation with the author, London, August 1979.
305 'There are two', Ansen. 'one of those', FA 374. 'The way he', CP 581. 'the most dishevelled', *For W.H. Auden* (see note to p. xv), 49.
306 'Sorry, my', *Paris Review* 254. 'prone to', CP 581. 'always *ex*', TR 99. 'exciting', ibid. 106. 'My life is', to AED [1941].
307 'a devitalized' and 'a transcendent', Reinhold Niebuhr, *An Interpretation of Christian Ethics,* Meridian Books (New York), 1960, 117, 119. 'a benevolent', TR 112. 'the most lucid', *New Republic,* 2 June 1941, 765-6.
308 'Erika Mann does', *Evening Standard,* 9 July 1941. 'Louder than all', MS of 'New Year Letter' in Humanities Research Center, University of Texas at Austin.
309 'To call this', *New Republic,* 8 July 1940, 59. 'the defeat', *Decision,* January 1941, 52. 'in spite of',

to SS (n.d.). 'What has to be', to SS, 13 March 1941.

310   'I hope our side', to Caroline Newton [2 November 1940] (Berg). 'To Chester', copy in possession of Robert Wilson. 'towards something', *Horizon,* August 1941, 139-43. 'It is, after', *Dublin Review,* July 1941, 99-101. 'rejoiced at his', G.A. Auden to Caroline Newton, 7 October 1941 (Berg). 'a failure', MS in possession of Stephen Spender. Quotes from reviews of *Paul Bunyan* are taken from E.W. White, *Benjamin Britten,* 3rd ed., Booesy & Hawkes, 1970, 98. 'The public seemed', ibid. 33.

311   'I have thought' and 'The only', to Caroline Newton [April 1941] (Berg). 'I was forced', *Modern Canterbury Pilgrims* 41. 'On account of', verse-letter to Chester Kallman, Christmas Day 1941 (HRC). 'It's frightening', Ansen.

312   'O my love', CP 214. 'by nature', CP 583. 'for a combination', TR 109. 'This round O', CP 249.

313   'Joseph is me', Ansen. 'Where are you', CP 281-2. 'We're not going', told by Chester Kallman to Edward Mendelson. 'I was surprised', to Alan Ansen [October 1947](Berg).

314   'I only want', to Caroline Newton, 6 September 1941 (Berg). 'Elizabeth. I know', photograph in possession of Beata Sauerlander. 'If equal affection', CP 445. 'Chester is in', to Caroline Newton, 19 January 1942 (Berg). 'Promiscuity is so', ibid.

315   'Still no word', Chester Kallman to Auden, 9-10 March (? 1943). 'You must tell me', to CK [December 1942]. 'The triple situation', to RJ, 14 July 1947. 'too timid', CP 581. 'For my companion', to CK (n.d.). 'Though — ', to CK [December 1942]. 'I hope I know', to Mina Curtiss, 14 January [1942] (Berg).

316   'How does it', recalled by Sheila Auden in conversation with the author, London, spring 1979. 'I shan't rest', Ansen. 'conscious trial' and 'our God of love', CP 157. 'Miss God appears', to RJ [June 1947]. 'There are days', to EM [February 1943].

317   'Poets are tough', FA 106. 'He makes me', to Caroline Newton, 10 January 1942 (Berg). 'At no time', *New York Review of Books,* 20 April 1972, 3. 'I have been', to SS, 16 January 1942. 'My thoughts are', to CK [December 1941] (HRC).

318   'lonelier and more', to Caroline Newton [autumn 1941] (Berg). 'Very soon', *Michigan Quarterly Review,* Fall 1978, 508.

319   'one person cannot', ibid. 509. 'It was such a', ibid. 513. 'He gave me', ibid. 514. 'By that time', *Time* interview (see note to p. 209). 'I went to', to Caroline Newton [October 1941] (Berg).

320   'a front row', to Louise Bogan [28 May 1942], Amherst College Library. 'Why do all', TR 123. 'No telephone', unpublished memoir of Auden by Albert & Angelyn Stevens. 'Culture is one of', DH 458. 'exotic' and 'heretical', Ansen.

321   'My dear', William Caskey to the author, 24 June 1979. 'I consider the', *New York Review of Books,* 27 January 1972, 19. 'It won't be', to Caroline Newton, 10 January 1942 (Berg). 'le faux-Chester', to C.K., n.d. 'a real genius', to EM [February 1942].

322   The title page of *The Queen's Masque* and Auden's comments: Ansen. 'Meanwhile I go', to SS, 16 January 1942.

323   'The Shepherds' Carol' is published in Britten's setting by Boosey & Hawkes. 'Ben had expected', Sir Peter Pears to the author, 18 April 1980.

324   'a sort of modern', to EM [April 1942]. 'They rejected', to Caroline Newton, 2 September 1942 (Berg). 'I was asked', James Stern to the author, 27 May 1980. 'very much sunk', Edmund Wilson, *Letters on Literature and Politics,* Routledge, 1977, 432. 'considered to have', to ERD, 1 February 1944. 'a little dull', ibid. 'the institutions', DH 320.

325   'I can't say', to EM (n.d.). 'Both the repentance', DH 128. 'really about the', TR 111. 'Stay with me', CP 316.

326   'Explain why the', *Swarthmore College Bulletin,* March 1962, 4. 'Shakespeare's worst play, *Phoenix* (Swarthmore College), 19 December 1944, 3. 'an excuse for', ibid., 13 April 1943, 6. 'looked like a', *Connecticut Review,* April 1968, 45. 'My seminar', TR 112.

327   'Fellow Irresponsibles, *Swarthmore College Bulletin,* March 1962, 3. 'I'm still very', to CK [December 1942]. 'The Tchaikovsky', ibid. 'I've worked', Chester Kallman to Auden, 30 November (n.y.). 'There is a', Chester Kallman to Auden, 9-10 March [1943 ?]. 'going quite nicely', to EM, 9 January 1943.

328   'an uneasy feeling', *Connecticut Review,* April 1968, 45. 'fruitless prospecting', to EM, 17 July 1943. 'fun', ibid. 'days of speaking', to CK, 2 August 1943. 'struck oil', to EM, 17 July 1943. 'The whole point', to Frederick Bradnum, 16 January 1960 (BBC Written Archives). 'feebly figurative sign', CP 340. 'by far the most', and 'If *I* were', to Frederick Bradnum (as above).

329   'Seeing that they', to ERD, 1 February 1944. 'very nice', ibid. 'He had the', FA 222. 'lovely' and heavenly', to EM [autumn 1943]. 'I thought I'd', Ansen. 'I said "Yes" ', BBC radio interview with Peter Porter, broadcast on 29 April 1966. 'the best I've', to EM [March 1944]. 'I hate to', to Saxe Commins, 16 January 1942 (Butler).

330   'It must not', B.C. Bloomfield, *W.H. Auden: A Bibliography,* University of Virginia Press, 1964, vii-ix. 'Now and then', to Louise Bogan [18 May 1942] (Amherst College Library). 'fair notion', preface to CP 45. 'Subjects, Objects', CP 45 153. 'the suave archdeacon', ibid. 155. 'O God, what', *Swathmore College Bulletin,* March 1962, 6. 'he can command', *Listener,* 16 April 1951, 673. 'a damned lie', Bloomfield (see above), viii.

331   'trash', John Fuller, *A Reader's Guide to W.H. Auden,* Thames & Hudson, 1970, 251. 'My reason

for', to SS, 10 June 1951.
332 'The basic human', *New Republic*, 15 May 1944, 683ff. 'As everybody knows', *Harper's Magazine*, July 1948, 40.
333 'his calm was', James Stern, *The Hidden Damage,* Harcourt Brace, 1947, 4. 'My dear, I'm', *Times Literary Supplement,* 28 March 1975, 827. 'I saw Eliot', to EM, 9 May 1945.
334 'He launched into', John Lehmann, *I Am My Brother,* Longmans, 1960, 290. 'This room is very', recalled by Sir Isaiah Berlin in conversation with the author, Oxford, May 1979. 'London hadn't really', Edmund Wilson, *Letters on Literature and Politics,* Routledge, 1977, 429. 'I do *love*', recalled by Natasha Spender in conversation with the author, London, June 1980. 'This *Morale*', TR 136. 'When the couple', *New York Times Magazine,* 8 August 1971, 10ff. 'The town was', TR 126. 'I cannot help', ibid. 145. 'I keep wishing', to EM, 9 May 1945 (Berg).
335 'attaching to his', TR 131. 'mid-witted folk', ibid. 136. 'The city as a', to EM, 4 June 1945 (Berg). 'The work is', TR 126. 'We asked them', *Time* interview (see note to p. 209).
336 'I was prepared', to EM, 4 June 1945. 'Most of them', TR 136. 'Something might', TCVA 33.
337 'Across the square', CP 452.
338 'terrible', to EM [October 1946]. 'I only did', Ansen.
339 'I was asked', ibid. 'an unofficial', TR 196. 'My own feeling', to ERD, 20 January 1945. 'Forms are chosen', Bonamy Dobrée (ed.), *From Anne to Victoria,* Cassell, 1937, 100. 'How can I', HA 32.
340 'My objection', to SS, 20 June 1951. 'Blessed be all', CP 642. 'All good art', to Henry Treece [autumn 1937] (HRC). 'Try to think', to an unknown correspondent, 8 November 1937 (Berg). a game of', *Poets at Work,* introduced by Charles D. Abbott, Harcourt Brace, 1948, 173.
341 'When people ask', HA 32-3. 'The ideal audience', *Poets at Work* (see note to p. 340), 176. 'Thou shalt not', CP 262.
342 'because a man', *Times Literary Supplement,* 1 April 1977, 401.
343 'Rhoda was a' and other quotations from Dorothy Farnan, Dorothy Kallman to the author, 14 June 1980. 'I miss you', to RJ [*c.* 1946]. 'Can I stay', to RJ, 14 April 1946. 'The weather is', to RJ, 2 May 1946. 'Whenever I met', Milton Klonsky to the author, 16 July 1980.
344 'Obviously I can't', to RJ, 2 May 1946. 'Wystan must have', Milton Klonsky to the author, 16 July 1980. 'I think his spiritual', TR 114.
345 'The beach is', to ERD, 30 March 1947. 'a huddle of', *Nones* 28.
346 'fine', 'terrible', and 'the work made', to RJ, 9 August 1946. 'I'm so looking', to RJ, 15 August 1946. 'too expensive', to RJ, 27 August 1946. 'fantastically sordid', HA 59. 'a permanent', TR 147. 'You idiot!', WWW 257. 'a complete failure', notes on the lecture by Alan Ansen (Berg). 'very dull', ibid.
347 'To Alan', copy in Berg Collection, New York Public Library.
348 'persistently boring', *Horizon,* May 1949, 377-8. 'Lots and lots', to RJ, 17 June 1947. 'So my embodied', CP 215. '*the* beauty', to RJ [1947].
349 'Wystan was', Dorothy Kallman to the author, 14 June 1980. 'I tried to', Gardiner 16. 'It did not', Yanovsky 123. 'I don't think', TR 118. 'intensely interested', Strav./Craft 396. 'I think the opera', interview with Peter Porter for BBC Radio, broadcast 29 April 1966.
350 'I need hardly', *Memories and Commentaries* 155. 'Generous offer', ibid. 156. 'primed by coffee', ibid. 'immediately suggested', ibid. 154.
351 'a bourgeois parable', unscripted talk for BBC Third Programme, 18 August 1953 (BBC Written Archives). 'you cannot really', ibid.
352 Stravinsky and Auden's working synopsis for *The Rake's Progress* is printed as an appendix to *Memories & Commentaries.* 'When we were', *Memories and Commentaries* 157. 'Angels are pure', ibid. 'He is one', ibid. 158. 'scared stiff', Strav./Craft 397. 'a professional', ibid. 'I can't tell', *Memories and Commentaries* 160.
353 'Don't just point', RP 33. 'stray lines', ibid. 'Wystan Auden's devotion', TR 153. 'I think you can', RP 33. 'breezed along', ibid. 'Two librettists', Strav./Craft 650. 'to suggest that', RP 33. 'at one moment', SW 99. 'in order to', radio discussion between Auden, Kallman and Hans Werner Henze, recorded by BBC on 17 July 1961 (BBC Written Archives).
354 'a task approaching', RP 33. 'The question of', unscripted talk (see note to p. 351). 'I would never', *Opera,* January 1952, 35. 'As you will', *Memories and Commentaries* 160.
355 'delighted' and 'cut ad lib', ibid. 161. 'We thought this', RP 34. 'laughed until', ibid. 33. 'In her own', SW 101.
356 'a little too', RP 6. 'Mr Kallman is' and 'the scenes which', TR 149f.
357 'This work affords', Strav./Craft 401. 'Wystan nearly', William Caskey to the author, 24 June 1979. 'I hadn't realised', to EM, 8 May [1948]. 'Here we are', to RJ, 30 May 1948. 'Sex has been', ibid.
358 'We had one', ibid. 'I make silly', ibid. 'It's such a', ibid. 'What design could', *Nones* 26. 'At the same', Marie-Jacqueline Lancaster (ed.), *Brian Howard: Portrait of a Failure,* Blond, 1968, 493. 'Words so affect', EA 397.
359 'It was a Spring', *The Platonic Blow,* Fuck You Press, 1965 (copy in Bodleian Library). 'a piece of', *Daily Telegraph Magazine,* 9 August 1968.
360 'The sex situation', to RJ, 6 July 1948. 'a Catholic', to J. R. R. Tolkein, 14 June 1955. 'I have just', to RJ, 6 July 1948.

361 'Now, unready to', *Nones* 80f. 'A fitting farewell', John Fuller, *A Reader's Guide to W. H. Auden*, Thames & Hudson, 1970, 187.

362 'much impressed', to John Hayward, 25 October [1948] (King's College, Cambridge). 'in itself a', *Listener*, 26 April 1951, 673. 'the nomad wanderer', *The Enchaféd Flood*. Faber, 1950, 125.

363 'The whole Pound', to RJ, 16 August 1949. 'Arrived after', *Memories and Commentaries* 163. 'writing busily' and 'Chester has turned', to EM, 30 May [1949]. 'bitten with', to ERD, 27 May 1949.

364 'He does his', to EM, 6 June [1950]. 'Have just re-read', to EM [July 1942]. 'Many evenings', Davidson 129–30. 'outstanding non-aboriginal', *Chronicle* 25.

365 'The piers are pummelled', CP 445. 'adroitest of', ibid. 671. 'All words like', ibid. 472. 'a Christian ought', ibid. 17. 'Having spent', DH 52.

366 'He is the', *World Review*, November 1950, 30. 'Of all those', *Nine*, autumn 1950, 345. 'confident ease' and 'a fundamental', *New Statesman*, 1 March 1952, 249. 'scratches on the', *Poetry*, September 1951, 352–6. 'We had to sit', TR 148.

367 'Let Stephen', ibid. 'The meetings', to EM [October 1964]. 'Our broad beans', to ERD, 26 May [1950]. 'because he arrived', ibid. 'near the cemetery', to CK, 26 January [n.y.] (Berg). 'At peace under', CP 435. 'It's been quiet', to Howard Griffin, 27 January [1951] (Berg).

368 'I'm afraid', to Rupert Doone, 7 March [1951] (Berg). 'very urgently', 'No, I'll ring', and 'It was a strange', *Daily Express*, 16 June 1951.

369 'I was busy', letter from Auden printed in *Sunday Times*, 20 January 1957. 'Do I have', *Times Literary Supplement*, 14 March 1980, 294. 'Am embarking on', Tom Driberg, *Guy Burgess: a portrait with background*, Weidenfield, 1956, 99. 'Well! The combination', to SS, 14 June 1951. 'an open Communist', *Daily Express*, 13 June 1951. 'absolutely fantastic', *Manchester Guardian*, 11 June 1951. 'The whole business', to SS, 14 June 1951.

370 'I feel exactly', to SS, 20 June 1951. 'I'd still got', Driberg (see note to p. 369) 99. 'Had Mr Burgess', *Sunday Times* (see note to p. 369). 'It would be dishonourable', ibid. 'the girls were', TR 153. 'Am exhausted', to EM [September 1951]. 'everything but', *Chronicle* 26.

371 'burst into tears', ibid. 28. 'nervous as an', ibid. 29. 'by the end', E. W. White, *Stravinsky*, Faber, 1966, 427. 'Rossini (the man of heart)', Strav./Craft 415. The synopsis of 'On the Way' is at the Humanities Research Center, University of Texas at Austin. 'Mr Kallman and I', to Igor Stravinsky, 2 July 1949.

372 'Am still waiting', to Alan Ansen, 17 April [1952] (Berg). 'Two years were', Robert Craft to the author, 18 April 1980. 'To my relief', to ERD, 26 May [1950].

373 'Auden is the', *Chronicle* 43. 'I will never', to SS, 13 March 1941. 'One's feelings', FA 427. 'as if it had', *Chronicle* 40.

374 'a mirror in' and 'There are usually', ibid. 'we must call him', recalled by Thekla Clark in conversation with the author, London, February 1980. 'It is a sad', DH xi. 'I feel like', to Alan Ansen [November 1952] (Berg). 'charming, bright', to Howard Griffin, 22 April [1953] (Berg).

375 'unimaginative direction', Strav./Craft 418. 'It has some', to EM, 16 July [1953]. 'I hope, though', to EM [June 1953]. 'Everyone was', to EM, 16 July [1953]. 'If I am', HA 10. 'not an easy', to Alan Ansen, 16 July [1953]. 'It is the loveliest', to EM, 8 November [1953].

376 'Occasionally nervous', to HP, 17 February [1954]. 'my N.Y. nest', to Alan Collins, 23 February [1967] (Butler).

377 'an intellectual', Yanovsky 127. 'A Jewish', ibid. 'five martinis', Strav./Craft 416.

378 'nice quiet', to EM, 1 July [1954]. 'very busy', to HP, 14 May [1955]. 'It is unlikely', CP 431. 'Auden has become', *Yale Review*, June 1955, 607. 'I think Jarrell', MS notes by Stephen Spender on first draft of the present book.

379 'is one of the very', to J. R. R. Tolkien [April 1955]. 'If someone dislikes', *Times Literary Supplement*, 8 December 1955. 'I am violently', *Partisan Review*, January–February 1952, 18. 'We are inclined', Auden & Kallman (transl.), *The Magic Flute*, Random House, 1956, xiv.

380 'it took me some', Gardiner 15. 'honoured and grateful', Joanna Richardson, *Enid Starkie*, Oxford University Press, 1973, 196f.

381 'The winter months', ibid. ' a fit person', ibid. 197. 'Please vote', to ERD, 7 November [1955]. 'There is keen', *The Diaries of Evelyn Waugh*, Weidenfeld, 1973, 753. 'My future now', to HP, 13 January [1956]. 'most fitting' and 'one of the greatest', *Sunday Times*, 5 February 1956. 'It is certainly', *Isis*, 8 February 1956.

382 'How on earth', Richardson (see note to p. 380), 198. 'How am I', to SS, 16 February 1956. 'Here's two-fifty', TR 214. 'Just like a', *Evening Standard*, 11 June 1956. 'You have chosen', DH 32. 'Never in my', to CK, 25 June [1956].

383 'willing to die', *Oratio Creweiana MDCCCCLVI* (University of Oxford). 'Please drop me', to CK, 25 June 1956. 'Are you coming', to CK, 26 January [n.y.] (Berg). 'It is a bit', to EM, 19 December [1956]. 'No pain', to HP [June 1957].

384 'by far the most', quoted in *Observer*, 5 February 1961. 'if one asked', *Adam International Review*, 1973–4, 24ff. 'Without a comment', *Daily Telegraph Magazine*, 9 August 1968, 20.

385 'I want half a', recalled by Natasha Spender in conversation with the author, London, June 1980.

386 'I have just', to HP, [June 1957]. 'I don't like', Charles Osborne, *W. H. Auden: the Life of a Poet*, Eyre Methuen, 1980, 246. 'a spot of bother', to Alan Ansen, 8 July [n.y.] (Berg).

387 'and perhaps a', to Christa Esders, 15 July 1957 (Berg). 'a pouring wet', CP 569. 'On Saturday', to HP, 4 October [1957].

388 'even more beautiful', to HP, 3 July [1958]. 'They are so', to HP, 11 October [1958]. 'Never never will', ibid. 'though one cannot', CP 488.

389 'I am enchanted', to Howard Griffin, 28 September [1958] (Berg). '3 cats', to Geoffrey Grigson, n.d. (Butler). 'a 100% American', to Howard Griffin, 28 September [1958] (Berg). 'To my great', to HP, 3 July [July 1958]. The visitor's book is now in the Humanities Research Center, University of Texas at Austin.

390 'We have to hurry' and 'I'm on very', *New York Times Magazine*, 8 August 1971, 10ff. 'What's happened to', Gardiner 18.

391 'He checks his', *Life*, 30 January 1970, 52ff. 'Martini–time', CP 633. 'the strongest', TR 92.

392 'Mr Auden poured', *American Scholar*, Spring 1967, 267-9. 'It *never*', to EM, 8 August [1960]. 'what I dared', CP 520.

393 'my beloved', to HP, 1 April [1960]. 'Auden is in', *Chronicle* 70. 'very, very minor', TR 145. 'a great success', to HP [December 1958].

394 'a *pertinent*', TR 145. 'I wish the', to EM, 7 July [1960]. 'Sometimes one feels', FA 150. 'Great Mr G', 'Dear Mr G', ibid. 'I should like', CP 522. 'Though Mr G', to EM, 18 September [1961]. 'I cannot know', CP 499. 'To my great', to RJ, 17 May 1949.

395 'that, after' CP 538. 'The One I', ibid. 499. 'Expecting your', ibid. 491. 'He advised', TR 175f.

396 'You were in', CP 561. 'There was a great', Gardiner 18. 'And how much', CP 561.

397 'Hugerl, for a', ibid. 'Muse of the', CP 465. 'just the product', *Time & Tide*, 9 July 1960, 803. 'Bullroarers cannot', HC dedication.

398 'the defiant', DH 192. 'very impressed', to EM, 1 July [1954]. 'Our original', BBC radio discussion between Auden, Kallman and Henze, recorded 17 July 1961 (BBC Written Archives). 'in order to', ibid.

399 'The intellect', quoted by Auden in his note to the Glyndebourne programme of *Elegy*. 'Though neither Chester', to EM, 16 March [1965].

400 'About 75%', Spears 341. '*Elegy* was our', *Chronicle* 211. 'exciting' and 'The orchestra', to EM, 8 August [1960]. 'I do hope', to SS, 13 May 1961. 'Graves [boasts]', *Chronicle* 159. 'touched and', to HP, 21 August [1962]. 'I hope it', to J. R. R. Tolkien, 18 January 1963.

401 'an aristocratic', Malcolm de Chazal, *Plastic Sense*, Herder & Herfer, 1971, 7. 'Our opera', Chester Kallman to Toni & Noah Greenberg, 31 May 1961. 'to realise a', to HP, 25 April [1961]. 'Have always', to HP [May 1961]. 'You shouldn't have', Anthony Gishford (ed.), *Grand Opera*, Weidenfeld, 1972, 190. 'Could have been', to EM, 8 August [1961]. 'masterly', *Musical Times*, CII (1961), 418-9.

402 'Whatever I may', ibid. 639-40. 'will not do', SW 108. 'I, a transplant', CP 520. 'Now there's', to EM, 10 July [1964]. 'While he was', MS of address at memorial service, in possession of Stephen Spender.

403 'I hope very', to HP, 14 April [1962]. 'When you stole', CP 561. 'I am all', to HP [July 1959]. 'kind and', James Merrill to the author, May 1979. 'worshipped', TR 227.

404 'That is what', to SS, n.d. 'The range of', *Times Literary Supplement*, 12 October 1973, 212: reprinted in Clive James, *At the Pillars of Hercules*, Faber, 1979.

405 'a personal', Dag Hammarskjöld, *Markings*, Knopf, 1964, 14. 'one of the', ibid. 4. 'a fantastic', ibid. 25. 'always in great', ibid. 18. 'exceptionally aggressive', ibid. 16. 'Well, there goes', information from Edward Mendelson.

406 'Translation is', Auden & Pearson (ed.), *Poets of the English Language*, Vol. II, Viking, 1978, xv. 'It does not particularly', ibid. 'the only political', I. Duczynska (ed.), *The Plough and the Pen*, Peter Owen, 1963, 10. 'One of Auden's', TCVA 31. 'excellent potential', SW 109. 'Today we know', ibid. 'any species of', MS note on the libretto of *The Bassarids* by Chester Kallman (HRC).

407 'The word *Bassarids*', to EM, 18 July (1966). 'More than half', to ERD, 8 October [n.y.]. 'Paskalis, a young', to EM, 9 August [1966]. '*The Bassarids* is', *Musical Times*, October 1966, 887. 'will have to', *Evening Standard*, 18 September, 1963.

408 'feel that to', *Advocate* 26. 'I get it', ibid. 'quiver with', ibid. 'Chester is spending', to Howard Griffin, 31 December [1965] (Berg). 'I cook', to SS, 12 November [n.y.]. 'I should like', to CK, 1 January [1968] (HRC). 'The kitchen became', Yanovsky 120.

409 'Wystan was shy', TR 173. 'All I felt', *New York Times Magazine*, 8 August 1971, 10ff. 'we had better', *Mid-Century*, January 1962, 3-7. 'Auden for dinner', *Chronicle* 156.

410 'holy ground', LFI 8. 'Twenty–eight years', CP 546. 'I felt as', to Peter Salus, 15 June [1964] (Berg). 'always a depressing', 11 August [1964] (Berg). 'For the first', to Howard Griffin, 31 December [1965] (Berg). 'the city of', to EM, 7 July [1960].

411 'sleepless nights' and 'He hadn't', to HP, 14 May [1955]. 'The Ford', to EM, 11 June [1963]. 'Have addressed', to Peter Salus, 10 April [1965] (Berg). 'If it weren't', to EM, 13 January [1965]. 'Your old', recalled by Peter Heyworth in conversation with the author, London, spring 1979.

412 'I've been' and 'Judge was', ibid. 'Oh, I don't *pay*', ibid. 'Between ourselves', to HP, 12 January [1965]. 'a ghoulish', to EM, 13 January [1965]. 'I don't like', ibid. 'no future', *Listener*, 7 January 1965, 5.

413 'I shall never', to Louise Bogan, 13 April 1945 (Amherst College Library). 'What offends', *Times*, 3 February 1966. 'The Ogre does', CP 604. 'I know that all', TR 89. 'It's heartless', CP 522.
414 'are people with', DH 88. 'I am not convinced', to Peter Salus, 26 August [n.y.] (Berg). 'Can you understand', to ERD, 21 June [1968]. 'When I was', *Times*, 11 July 1969. 'You and your', Gardiner 15f. 'Unattractive and shallow', FA 166. 'The only sensible', to HP, 14 April [1962]. 'pink old', EA 190.
415 'To-day, nine', Owen Barfield, *History in English Words*, Eerdmans, 1967, 9. 'Speech is the', SW 122. 'At Twenty', CP 540. 'I have been', to EM [September 1965].
416 'I have never', CSP66 15. 'To say this', ibid. 'The reason', draft to Naomi Mitchison, 1 April 1967 (Berg). 'I am incapable', to SS, 20 May [n.y.]. 'poems which were', Anthony Ostroff (ed.), *The Contemporary Poet as Artist and Critic*, Little Brown, 1964. 185.
417 'slovenly verbal', CSP66 16. 'To-day, I believe', ibid. 15. 'a new chapter', ibid. 16.
418 'I seem almost', *Hudson Review*, spring 1968, 207. 'a remarkable', *Listener*, 22 February 1967, 267. 'Some of the axed', *Observer*, 27 November 1966. 'His later', ibid. 'Of course not', *Paris Review* 245. 'I expect personal', draft to Naomi Mitchison, 1 April 1967 (Berg). 'In so much', Ostroff (see note to p. 416) 185f.
419 'To keep the', to EM, 8 September [1962]. 'Whatever else', Ostroff (see note to p. 416) 185f.
420 'I was reading', to Peter Salus, 9 July [1964] (Berg). 'I'm an old' and 'Wystan is wholly', *Chronicle* 257. 'God bless the', CP 486.
421 'It was a', *Times Literary Supplement*, 12 January 1973, 15f; reprinted in Clive James, *At the Pillars of Hercules*, Faber, 1979. 'more and more', *Times Literary Supplement*, 4 October 1974, 1076.
422 'God bless the', CP 549. 'presented to me', to Jacques Barzun, 14 November 1966 (Butler).
423 'It's too much', Yanovksy 119. 'You never know', TR 180. 'The homes I', CP 537. 'a medieval', *Newsweek*, 29 January 1968, 54. 'scared stiff', to CK, 10 December [n.y.] (HRC). 'Why should I', *Daily Mail*, 14 October 1972. 'monumentally' and 'His face', Finney 269. 'runneled and seamed', James Merrill, *Mirabell*, Atheneum 1978, 70. 'life itself', TR 182. 'a face upon', ibid. 245. 'Your cameraman', interview by Christopher Burstall, 1965.
424 'But suddenly', Yanovksy 117. 'At my age', TR 179. 'he put it', Yanovksy 117. 'in order to', *Observer*, 6 October 1974. 'a symbol', draft letter to the *Observer* by Chester Kallman, 23 October 1974 (HRC). 'more and more', *Chronicle* 260. 'If he was', Yanovsky 121. 'I am ashamed', to CK, 1 January [1968] (HRC).
425 'No, no, Mother', Yanovsky 121. 'He would call', ibid. 'It was amusing', unpublished memoir of Auden by Bernard Richards. 'One isn't bothered', Gardiner 19. 'Well, at my age', TR 175.
426 'When one is', CP 562. 'There was in', Yanovsky 108. 'Everything for him', TR 190f.
427 'I shall live', TR 124. 'His control', *Financial Times*, 12 July 1971. 'He doesn't read', Charles Osborne, *W. H. Auden, the life of a poet*, Eyre Methuen, 1980, 322f. *'Liebe Frau'*, CP 575. 'Chester is desperate', Yanovsky 129.
428 'intrigued', BBC radio interview with Hans Keller, recorded 10 July 1971. 'We saw B.B.'s', to SS [n.d.]. 'enormous talent', MS note by Stephen Spender on first draft of the present book. 'He cannot bear', *Chronicle* 258.
429 'I am in', to Peter Salus, 29 August 1968 (Berg). 'The wit in some', *Spectator*, 13 December 1969, 827-8. 'an *enormous*', to Jason Epstein, 21 July 1968 (Butler). 'a sort of', ibid.
430 'darker and dustier', Gardiner 18. 'My kitchen', to ERD, 2 January 1966. 'I'm wearing a', Yanovsky 116.
431 'Over tea', *Esquire*, January 1970, 139. 'I was not', *Daily Telegraph*, 13 January 1970. 'he could not', Yanovsky 122.
432 'a very old', Gardiner 19. 'Wystan has lost', recalled by Stephen Spender in conversation with the author, London, June 1979. 'the isolation', TR 8. 'become almost', *Chronicle* 374. '"I don't like"', Yanovsky 121. 'Ah, but I', TR 124. 'the sadist', CP 627. 'He must know', Yanovsky 117.
433 'should be of', ACW vii. 'To visit', *Life*, 30 January 1970, 52ff. 'I'm no advocate', *Chronicle* 395. '*I* don't want', Yanovsky 116. 'Promise me', recalled by Natasha Spender in conversation with the author, London, June 1980. 'But you can't!', recalled by Stephen Spender in conversation with the author, London, June 1979.
434 'a very limited', Sean Day-Lewis, *C. Day-Lewis*, Weidenfeld, 1980, 297. 'Wystan, are you', TR 125. 'Sorry I stood', recalled by Peter du Sautoy in conversation with the author, London, July 1979. 'His departures', TR 124. 'How good you', to Stephen and Natasha Spender, 5 November [n.y.].
435 'fascinating' and *'very* expensive', to Robert Lederer, 25 April 1970 (Berg). 'requesting any friends', HA 10. 'That's their problem', recalled by Valerie Eliot in conversation with the author, March 1980.
436 'Wystan back', Yanovsky 131. 'not an external', SP xvii. 'Time, we both', CP 654. 'the best comic', to Geoffrey Grigson, 5 April [1971] (Berg). 'talked to death', *Evening Standard*, 1 August 1971.
437 '*very* bewildering', to Jacques Barzun, 23 November 1971 (Butler). 'We are going', *Evening Standard*, 18 August 1971. 'New York is', to CK, 1 November [1972] (HRC). 'The first time', TR 189.
438 'found him apparently', TR 192. 'The check-up', Yanovsky 118. 'Chester is here', ibid. 131.

'Conversation is like', TR 155. 'I'm getting rather', *Evening Standard*, 7 February 1972.
439   'In Oxford', *Daily Telegraph*, 8 February 1972. 'We go to', TR 155. 'Auden's 65th', Yanovsky 131. 'Let me take', *New York Times*, 18 March 1972, 31.
440   'When I said', Robert Wilson, *Auden's Library* (privately printed). 'You look like', TR 188. 'a load of', *Times,* 22 June 1972. 'Auden shabbily', Yanovsky 132f.
441   'I'm quite prepared', *Daily Mail*, 14 October 1972. 'I smoke', ibid. 'an extraordinary', *Sunday Times*, 8 October 1972. 'Cosy?' *Times*, 12 October 1972. 'When we saw', *Sunday Times,* 29 October 1972.
442   'unshaven and', *Sun*, 5 January 1973. 'Ironically enough', Daily Telegraph, 30 January 1973.
443   '*Still* not', to CK, 1 November 1972 (HRC). 'I don't like', *Radio Times*, 27 January 1973. 'Go away and', recalled by Andrew Motion in conversation with the author, June 1979; see also TR 207.
444   'All well', to CK, 19 December [1972] (HRC). 'He is expected', *Times*, 8 February 1972. 'What a lot', TR 204. 'was that the', draft letter by Chester Kallman to the *Observer*, 23 October 1974 (HRC).
445   'One gets more', recalled by James and Tania Stern in conversation with the author, Wiltshire, August 1979. 'A *walk?*', TR 125. 'Grown used to', CP 657f. 'rather pathetically', TR 205.
446   'Of course', TR 180. 'No, no, we don't, unpublished memoir of Auden by Bernard Richards. 'I can't have been', J. I. M. Stewart to the author, 27 July 1979. 'I can't bear', *Theology*, November 1977, 430. 'What would you', recalled by Andrew Motion in conversation with the author, summer 1979.
447   'dried up', recalled by Naomi Mitchison in conversation with the author, Oxford, January 1979. 'You're late', Gardiner 19. 'coarse', recalled by Sir Isaiah Berlin in conversation with the author, Oxford, May 1979. 'The Auden I', *Times*, 14 November 1973. 'getting older', TR 148. 'signs of adjustment', TR 208. 'swell job', ibid.
448   'Do you think' ibid. 'Oh, you mean', information from Charles Monteith.
449   'Let your last', CP 672f. 'in sprightlier', HA 62. 'Dear Dodds', to ERD, 31 August [1973].
450   'Life is short', TYF 49. 'in a *nice*', TR 30. 'He was lying', Charles Osborne, *W. H. Auden, the life of a poet*, Eyre Methuen, 1980, 306. 'He still loves', TYF 13.
451   'Wystan is gone', TR 227. Michael Yates's account of the funeral was specially written for this book in April 1980.
453   'I've lost my', Alan Ansen to the author, 30 May 1979. 'Shameless envious', CP 643.
454   'W. H. Auden, for long', *Times*, 1 October 1973. 'He seemed to', Upward 22. 'none, I believe', John Lehmann, *The Whispering Gallery,* Longmans, 1955, 255. 'If we follow', TR 25. 'with Picasso', Lincoln Kirstein to the author, 10 August 1980.
455   'I have a', *Listener*, 22 February 1973, 240. 'a life which', LFI 9. 'I'm really a', Ansen. 'All will be judged', CP 243.

APPENDIX C

Acknowledgements

As I stated at the outset, this is not an 'authorised' or 'official' biography of Auden, and it was undertaken on my own initiative rather than under the auspices of his Estate. Nevertheless I have had such a great degree of support from Auden's literary executor, Professor Edward Mendelson, that it is difficult for me to make an adequate acknowledgement to him. Besides giving me *carte blanche* to quote from Auden's letters and other unpublished manuscripts (in which connection I must also thank Curtis Brown Academic Ltd, the Henry W. and Albert A. Berg Collection of the New York Public Library (Astor, Lenox and Tilden Foundations), the Humanities Research Center of the University of Texas at Austin, and other libraries holding Auden manuscripts) he supplied me with a mass of information to which I would not otherwise have had access, and allowed me to read the typescript of his book *Early Auden,* which contains much unique material. Perhaps most valuably of all, he read my own book in type-script at its various stages, and in proof, and spent many hours making suggestions and corrections. To echo the words of E. R. Dodds on the subject of his wife's contribution to Auden's *Oxford Book of Light Verse,* I feel that Edward Mendelson has been an 'active collaborator' in this biography, and should really receive an equal share of any credit. All errors, on the other hand, should be blamed entirely on me.

From the outset of my work I approached Auden's friends and family in the hope that they would talk to me, or write to me, about their memories of him. Every one of these approaches bore fruit: some people were hesitant at first, bearing in mind Auden's own views on his biography, but as time passed everyone began to help me, often very generously. I was lent letters, photographs, and manuscripts of poems; my questions were answered very thoroughly I was also given much hospitality. Later, the draft text of my book was read by a number of those listed here, and corrections and suggestions for improvement were made. In alphabetical order, those I wish to thank are as follows – and any omission in this or subsequent lists is purely accidental and will, I hope, be forgiven: V. M. Allom, Alan Ansen, Giles Auden, Dr John B. Auden, his wife Sheila and his daughters Anita Money and Rita Mudford, David Ayerst, Sir Isaiah Berlin, Professor A. H. Campbell, Janet Carleton (Janet Adam Smith), Gabriel Carritt, Thekla Clark, the late Professor Nevill Coghill, Sir William Coldstream, Robert Craft, the late Professor E. R. Dodds, Valerie Eliot, Maurice and Alexandra Feild, the Rev. A. S. T. Fisher, Orlan Fox, Margaret Gardiner, Dr T. O. Garland, Geoffrey Grigson, Hans Werner Henze, Peter

Heyworth, Christopher Isherwood, Lincoln Kirstein, Milton Klonsky, John Lehmann, Dr David Luke, Hedli MacNeice (Hedli Anderson), Maurice Mandelbaum, Golo Mann, Robert Medley, James Merrill, Charles Miller, Lady Mitchison (Naomi Mitchison), Charles Monteith, Ursula Niebuhr, Sir Peter Pears, Dr Oliver Sacks, Peter H. Salus, Beata Sauerlander, Elisabeth Sifton, Iris Sinkinson, Arnold Snodgrass, Stephen and Natasha Spender, James and Tania Stern, Albert and Angelyn Stevens, J. I. M. Stewart, Paul B. Taylor, Edward Upward, Rex Warner, Austin Wright, Basil Wright, and Michale and Marny Yates.

I was greatly helped in my researches into Chester Kallman's life and relationship with Auden by his father, Dr Edward Kallman, and especially by Dr Kallman's wife Dorothy (Dorothy Farnan), who answered all my questions patiently and in great detail, as well as lending me photographs.

Many other people helped me generously in my work, and I owe many thanks to the following for information, advice, the loan of letters and other documents, recollections of Auden, and every kind of assistance: Derek Auden, Don Bachardy, Frank Beecroft, Anthony Blunt, Brenda Boughton, Professor Robert H. Boyer, Keith Brace, John Byrne, William Caskey, Professor Henry Chadwick, Wayne Cogswell, Valentine Cunningham, the Rev. M. A. David, Jill Day-Lewis (Jill Balcon), Sean Day-Lewis, Ursula Dronke, Peter du Sautoy, John Ezard, Baroness Faithfull, Brian Finney, Dr Michael Fordham, Jonathan Fryer, Livia Gollancz, Roger Green, Mrs Toni Greenberg, James Greene, Lady Harrod, Andrew Harvey, David Jackson, Francis King, Richard Layard, Professor Hugh Lloyd-Jones, Donald Mitchell, Andrew Motion, John Bernard Myers, Frederic Prokosch, Mrs H. W. Purvis, Bernard Richards, the Rt. Rev. P. C. Rodger, Mary Sandbach, Winifred Sandford, Caroline Seebohm, Professor Tom Shippey, Michael Sidnell, Sir Sacheverell Sitwell, Matthew Spender, Christopher Tolkien, Philip Toynbee, Joan Turville-Petre, Mark Vessey, J. William Vinson, John Willett, Robert Wilson and Norman Wright.

Without John Fuller's *Reader's Guide to W. H. Auden* (Thames & Hudson, 1970) I would have been hard pressed to interpret many of Auden's poems. John Fuller himself has also given advice and encouragement. I must also acknowledge Samuel Hynes's *The Auden Generation* (Bodley Head, 1976), from which I have taken several leads. But the most essential book for any biographer of Auden must be Barry Bloomfield and Edward Mendelson's massive *Bibliography* fully described elsewhere (Appendix A), a rock of research on which all subsequent studies must rest.

A large number of libraries and other institutions have helped me during my research, and I am grateful to the following organisations and members of their staff: the Library of Balliol College, Oxford; BBC Sound Archives; BBC Written Archives; the Berg Collection, New York Public Library; Birmingham Public Library; the Bodleian Library Oxford; Bristol Public Library; the Britten Estate; Butler Library Columbia University; the Library of Christ Church, Oxford; the Downs School, Colwall (especially D. C. Boyd and John Knights); the Library of Exeter College, Oxford; Faber Music Ltd. (especially Patrick Carnegy); the Library of Gresham's School, Holt; the Houghton Library, Harvard University; the Humanities Research Center, University of Texas at Austin; the Library of King's College, Cambridge (especially M. A. Halls); Lomond School, Helensburgh (formerly Larchfield Academy); the Marx Memorial Library,

London (Nan Green); the National Film Archive; the National Portrait Gallery; Oxford University Press (Hugo Brunner); Sotheby & Co. (R. L. Davids); the Library of Swarthmore College; Viking Press (Edwin Kennebeck and Alan Williams); the Wade Collection, Wheaton College; and Yale University Library and the Beinecke Library at Yale. Mrs Jean Dodds searched through the papers of the late John Layard and unearthed many items relating to Auden.

Permission to quote from Auden's published works was kindly granted by Faber & Faber Ltd, and by Random House, Inc., to whom I am most grateful. The publishers of other writers' works quoted in the book are acknowledged in the notes.

Genealogical research was undertaken by John S. Griffiths; and I owe a special debt of thanks to Douglas Anderson for tracing and supplying me with copies of many of Auden'a articles in American periodicals not obtainable with ease in England. Douglas Anderson also helped me with my research in New York. I must also thank Henary Hardy and Mary Jane Mowat for reading the book carefully in typescript and making invaluable suggestions for its improvement. Christine Kelly shared with me the compiling of the index, and my father and Roger Green made up for my inadequacy as a proof-reader. My final thanks, however, should be to Auden himself for living a life that has been such a pleasure to write about.

INDEX OF TITLES AND FIRST LINES
of individual poems by Auden

GENERAL INDEX